Table B-1 Critical Values of the *t*-Distribution

Degrees of Freedom	One-Sided: 10% Two-Sided: 20%	5% 10%	2.5% 5%	1% 2%	0.5% 1%
	Level of Significance				
1	3.078	6.314	12.706	31.821	63.657
2	1.886	2.920	4.303	6.965	9.925
3	1.638	2.353	3.182	4.541	5.841
4	1.533	2.132	2.776	3.747	4.604
5	1.476	2.015	2.571	3.365	4.032
6	1.440	1.943	2.447	3.143	3.707
7	1.415	1.895	2.365	2.998	3.499
8	1.397	1.860	2.306	2.896	3.355
9	1.383	1.833	2.262	2.821	3.250
10	1.372	1.812	2.228	2.764	3.169
11	1.363	1.796	2.201	2.718	3.106
12	1.356	1.782	2.179	2.681	3.055
13	1.350	1.771	2.160	2.650	3.012
14	1.345	1.761	2.145	2.624	2.977
15	1.341	1.753	2.131	2.602	2.947
16	1.337	1.746	2.120	2.583	2.921
17	1.333	1.740	2.110	2.567	2.898
18	1.330	1.734	2.101	2.552	2.878
19	1.328	1.729	2.093	2.539	2.861
20	1.325	1.725	2.086	2.528	2.845
21	1.323	1.721	2.080	2.518	2.831
22	1.321	1.717	2.074	2.508	2.819
23	1.319	1.714	2.069	2.500	2.807
24	1.318	1.711	2.064	2.492	2.797
25	1.316	1.708	2.060	2.485	2.787
26	1.315	1.706	2.056	2.479	2.779
27	1.314	1.703	2.052	2.473	2.771
28	1.313	1.701	2.048	2.467	2.763
29	1.311	1.699	2.045	2.462	2.756
30	1.310	1.697	2.042	2.457	2.750
40	1.303	1.684	2.021	2.423	2.704
60	1.296	1.671	2.000	2.390	2.660
120	1.289	1.658	1.980	2.358	2.617
(Normal) ∞	1.282	1.645	1.960	2.326	2.576

Source: Reprinted from Table IV in Sir Ronald A. Fisher, *Statistical Methods for Research Workers*, 14th ed. (copyright © 1970, University of Adelaide) with permission of Hafner, a division of the Macmillan Publishing Company, Inc.

USING
ECONOMETRICS

SIXTH EDITION

USING ECONOMETRICS
A Practical Guide

A. H. Studenmund
Occidental College

Boston   Columbus   Indianapolis   New York   San Francisco   Upper Saddle River
Amsterdam   Cape Town   Dubai   London   Madrid   Milan   Munich   Paris   Montreal   Toronto
Delhi   Mexico City   Sao Paulo   Sydney   Hong Kong   Seoul   Singapore   Taipei   Tokyo

Editor in Chief: Donna Battista
Senior Acquisitions Editor: Adrienne D'Ambrosio
Editorial Assistant: Laura A. Murphy
Senior Marketing Manager: Elizabeth Averbeck
Marketing Assistant: Ian Gold
Managing Editor: Nancy H. Fenton
Senior Production Project Manager: Kathryn Dinovo
Senior Manufacturing Buyer: Carol Melville
Cover Designer: Jodi Notowitz
Text Permissions Project Supervisor: Michael Joyce
Media Project Manager: Lisa Rinaldi
Media Producer: Angela Lee
Supplements Production Coordinator: Alison Eusden
Full-Service Project Management: Nesbitt Graphics, Inc.
Printer/Binder: Edwards Brothers
Cover Printer: Lehigh Phoenix

1 2 3 4 5 6 7 8 9 10—<EB>—13 12 11 10 09

ISBN-13: 978-0-13-137998-5
ISBN-10:   0-13-137998-4

Dedicated to

Sally Newhall

Barbara Studenmund

David Studenmund

The Pearson Series in Economics

Abel/Bernanke/Croushore
Macroeconomics*

Bade/Parkin
Foundations of Economics*

Bierman/Fernandez
*Game Theory with
Economic Applications*

Blanchard
Macroeconomics

Blau/Ferber/Winkler
*The Economics of Women,
Men and Work*

**Boardman/Greenberg /
Vining/Weimer**
Cost-Benefit Analysis

Boyer
*Principles of Transportation
Economics*

Branson
*Macroeconomic Theory and
Policy*

Brock/Adams
*The Structure of American
Industry*

Bruce
*Public Finance and the
American Economy*

Carlton/Perloff
*Modern Industrial
Organization*

Case/Fair/Oster
Principles of Economics*

Caves/Frankel/Jones
*World Trade and Payments:
An Introduction*

Chapman
*Environmental Economics:
Theory, Application, and Policy*

Cooter/Ulen
Law & Economics

Downs
*An Economic Theory
of Democracy*

Ehrenberg/Smith
Modern Labor Economics

Ekelund/Ressler/Tollison
Economics*

Farnham
Economics for Managers

Folland/Goodman/Stano
*The Economics of Health
and Health Care*

Fort
Sports Economics

Froyen
Macroeconomics

Fusfeld
The Age of the Economist

Gerber
International Economics

Gordon
Macroeconomics

Greene
Econometric Analysis

Gregory
Essentials of Economics

Gregory/Stuart
*Russian and Soviet
Economic Performance
and Structure*

Hartwick/Olewiler
*The Economics of Natural
Resource Use*

Heilbroner/Milberg
*The Making of the Economic
Society*

Heyne/Boettke/Prychitko
The Economic Way of Thinking

Hoffman/Averett
*Women and the Economy:
Family, Work, and Pay*

Holt
*Markets, Games and Strategic
Behavior*

Hubbard
*Money, the Financial System,
and the Economy*

Hubbard/OBrien
Economics*

Hughes/Cain
American Economic History

Husted/Melvin
International Economics

Jehle/Reny
*Advanced Microeconomic
Theory*

Johnson-Lans
A Health Economics Primer

Keat/Young
Managerial Economics

Klein
*Mathematical Methods
for Economics*

Krugman/Obstfeld
*International Economics:
Theory & Policy**

Laidler
The Demand for Money

Leeds/von Allmen
The Economics of Sports

Leeds/von Allmen/Schiming
Economics*

Lipsey/Ragan/Storer
Economics*

Lynn
*Economic Development:
Theory and Practice for
a Divided World*

Melvin
International Money and Finance

Miller
Economics Today*

Understanding Modern Economics

Miller/Benjamin
The Economics of Macro Issues

Miller/Benjamin/North
The Economics of Public Issues

Mills/Hamilton
Urban Economics

Mishkin
The Economics of Money, Banking, and Financial Markets*

The Economics of Money, Banking, and Financial Markets, Business School Edition*

Murray
Econometrics: A Modern Introduction

Nafziger
The Economics of Developing Countries

O'Sullivan/Sheffrin/Perez
Economics: Principles, Applications and Tools*

Parkin
Economics*

Perloff
Microeconomics*

Microeconomics: Theory and Applications with Calculus

Perman/Common/ McGilvray/Ma
Natural Resources and Environmental Economics

Phelps
Health Economics

Pindyck/Rubinfeld
Microeconomics*

Riddell/Shackelford/Stamos/ Schneider
Economics: A Tool for Critically Understanding Society

Ritter/Silber/Udell
Principles of Money, Banking & Financial Markets*

Roberts
The Choice: A Fable of Free Trade and Protection

Rohlf
Introduction to Economic Reasoning

Ruffin/Gregory
Principles of Economics

Sargent
Rational Expectations and Inflation

Sawyer/Sprinkle
International Economics

Scherer
Industry Structure, Strategy, and Public Policy

Schiller
The Economics of Poverty and Discrimination

Sherman
Market Regulation

Silberberg
Principles of Microeconomics

Stock/Watson
Introduction to Econometrics

Introduction to Econometrics, Brief Edition

Studenmund
Using Econometrics: A Practical Guide

Tietenberg/Lewis
Environmental and Natural Resource Economics

Environmental Economics and Policy

Todaro/Smith
Economic Development

Waldman
Microeconomics

Waldman/Jensen
Industrial Organization: Theory and Practice

Weil
Economic Growth

Williamson
Macroeconomics

CONTENTS

PREFACE

Econometric education is a lot like learning to fly a plane: you learn more from actually doing it than you learn from reading about it.

Using Econometrics represents an innovative approach to the understanding of elementary econometrics. It covers the topic of single-equation linear regression analysis in an easily understandable format that emphasizes real-world examples and exercises. As the subtitle *A Practical Guide* implies, the book is aimed not only at beginning econometrics students but also at regression users looking for a refresher and at experienced practitioners who want a convenient reference.

What's New in the Sixth Edition?

Using Econometrics has been praised as "one of the most important new texts of the last 30 years." We've revised the book in a way that retains the clarity and practicality of previous editions and that recognizes that Econometrics doesn't stand still.

The most exciting upgrades are:

1. **Stata:** We're delighted to offer small Stata 10 as an optional package for our readers at a discounted price when packaged with a textbook. Stata is growing rapidly in popularity among professional economists, so students will be able to learn econometrics on the same program that their professors are using for their own research. Purchasing the Stata option will allow students to use small Stata 10 for six months at a cost far below the price they'd otherwise pay.

2. **Experimental and Panel Data:** We've added a completely new chapter on experimental and panel data. The chapter covers random assignment experiments, natural experiments, difference in difference estimators, the fixed effects model, and the random effects model.

3. **PowerPoint Slides:** For the first time, we offer a complete package of downloadable PowerPoint slides for the text. These slides will make it easy for instructors to individualize their own slide packages and to mold their lecture presentations to the needs of their

students. The PowerPoint slides and online Instructor's Manual are available for download at the Instructor's Resource Center (www.pearsonhighered.com/irc) on the catalog page for *Using Econometrics.*

4. **Expanded Help for Student Projects:** We've substantially revised and upgraded Chapter 11; its title now is "Running Your Own Regression Project." The chapter covers student research projects from top to bottom, with hints on collecting data, making specification choices, and writing up a final report.

5. **Exciting New Data Sets:** We've added an average of two updated or new data sets to each chapter, with many of the data sets coming from recent articles in the economics literature. We've chosen topics that will be of real interest to students, for example, "the prices of iPods on eBay," "predicting presidential elections," "the impact of Manny Ramirez on Dodger attendance," "the impact of easy grading on RateMyProfessors.com," "attendance at Hollywood nightclubs," "how patients choose a hospital," and many more.

6. **Better Problem Sets:** At the suggestion of a number of professors, we've moved the answers to most of the text's exercises from the back of the book to the Instructor's Manual. This change frees up many excellent exercises to be used in problem sets that couldn't previously be used because the answers were in the text. Professors who want to make the answers available to their students still can do so by downloading a particular answer and circulating it to their students. The Instructor's Manual, which is available online to all adopters, also includes lecture notes, sample examinations, and an additional interactive regression learning exercise.

7. **EViews Upgrade:** EViews 4.1 has been upgraded to EViews 6.0. This means that the student version of EViews 6.0 that can be included with each copy of this text is now much more powerful. The econometric procedures have been updated and refined, and the software can handle many more variables and observations than ever before.

8. **Expanded Web Site:** The text's Web site has been modernized and made easier to use. It now includes all the text's data sets, ready for downloading, in EViews, Stata, ASCII, and Excel formats. The Web site also includes advice on using the text and two additional interactive regression learning exercises. Why not take a look? Go to www.pearsonhighered.com/studenmund.

Features

1. Our approach to the learning of econometrics is simple, intuitive, and easy to understand. We do not use matrix algebra, and we relegate proofs and calculus to the footnotes or exercises.

2. We include numerous examples and example-based exercises. We feel that the best way to get a solid grasp of applied econometrics is through an example-oriented approach.

3. Although most of this book is at a simpler level than other econometrics texts, Chapters 6 and 7 on specification choice are among the most complete in the field. We think that an understanding of specification issues is vital for regression users.

4. We use a unique kind of learning tool called an *interactive regression learning exercise* to help students simulate econometric analysis by giving them feedback on various kinds of decisions without relying on computer time or much instructor supervision.

5. We offer the student version of EViews 6.0 and small Stata 10 as options with each copy of the text at an extremely low additional cost. Although we use EViews and Stata to produce the regression results in the book, *Using Econometrics* is not tied to EViews or Stata in any way, so the text fits well with all standard regression programs.

The formal prerequisites for using this book are few. Readers are assumed to have been exposed to some microeconomic and macroeconomic theory, basic mathematical functions, and elementary statistics (even if they have forgotten most if it). Students with little statistical background are encouraged to begin their study of econometrics by reading Chapter 17, "Statistical Principles."

Because the prerequisites are few and the statistics material is self-contained, *Using Econometrics* can be used not only in undergraduate courses but also in MBA-level courses in quantitative methods. We also have been told that the book is a helpful supplement for graduate-level econometrics courses.

The EViews and Stata Options

We're delighted to be able to offer our readers the chance to purchase the student version of EViews 6.0 or small Stata 10 at discounted prices when bundled with the textbook. EViews and Stata are two of the best econometric software programs available, so it's a real advantage to be able to buy them at substantial savings.

We urge professors to make these options available to their students even if EViews or Stata aren't used in class. The advantages to students of owning their own regression software are many. They can run regressions when they're off-campus, they will add a marketable skill to their resume if they learn EViews or Stata, and they'll own a software package that will allow them to run regressions after the class is over if they choose the EViews option.

CourseSmart

For Instructors

CourseSmart goes beyond traditional expectations providing instant, online access to the textbooks and course materials you need at a lower cost to students. And, even as students save money, you can save time and hassle with a digital textbook that allows you to search the most relevant content at the very moment you need it. Whether it's evaluating textbooks or creating lecture notes to help students with difficult concepts, CourseSmart can make life a little easier. See how when you visit www.coursesmart.com/instructors.

For Students

CourseSmart goes beyond traditional expectations, providing instant, online access to the textbooks and course materials that students need at lower cost. They can also search, highlight, and take notes anywhere at any time. See all the benefits to students at www.coursesmart.com/students.

Acknowledgments

This book's spiritual parents are Henry Cassidy and Carolyn Summers. It was Henry Cassidy who saw the need for a follow-on to Rao and Miller's legendary *Applied Econometrics* and who coauthored the first edition of *Using Econometrics* as an expansion of his own work of the same name. And it was Carolyn Summers who for four straight editions was the text's superb editorial consultant, proofreader, and indexer.

Gary Smith of Pomona College once again wrote the excellent chapter on statistics. His book, *Introduction to Statistical Reasoning* (McGraw-Hill, 1998, ISBN: 0-07-059276-4) would be a perfect text for a course that acts as a prerequisite for an elementary econometrics course.

Susan Averett of Lafayette College not only was a major force behind the decision to add a chapter on experimental and panel data, but she was also kind enough to write the first draft of that chapter.

I also want to thank Nobel Prize winner Rob Engle of New York University for his help on a previous version of Chapter 12, and Peter Kennedy, the author of *A Guide to Econometrics,* for his superb advice over two editions.

In addition, this edition benefited from the evaluations of an extremely talented group of professional reviewers:

Susan Averett, Lafayette College
Niels-Hugo Blunch, Washington and Lee University
Erin Cassese, West Virginia University
W. Ken Farr, Georgia College & State University
Chulo Jung, Ohio University
Peter Kennedy, Simon Fraser University
Risa Kumazawa, Georgia Southern University
Jin Man Lee, University of Illinois
Xiaomei Li, SUNY Albany
Sita Slavov, Occidental College
Gary Smith, Pomona College
Stephen Stageberg, University of Mary Washington
Phanindra V. Wunnava, Middlebury College
Frank V. Wykoff, Pomona College

Invaluable in the editorial and production process were Adrienne D'Ambrosio, Marguerite Desornes, Kathryn Dinovo, Alison Eusden, Nancy Kotary, Holly McLean-Aldis, and Laura Murphy. Others who provided timely and useful assistance to this edition were Erdal Atukeren of the Swiss Institute for Business Cycle Research, Heather Campbell of Arizona State University, Cece Conrad of Pomona, George Jouganatos of CSU Sacramento, Manfred Keil of Claremont McKenna, Leo McGarrity of Central Arkansas, Ying Sun of Rutgers, Barbara Passerelle, Silver Oak, and my family, Jaynie, Scott, and Connell Studenmund, and Brent Morse. Finally, but perhaps most importantly, I'd like to thank my superb Occidental College colleagues and students for their feedback and encouragement. These included Lesley Chiou, John Romley, Sita Slavov, Kirsten Vandschneider, Karuna Batcha, Andrew Blythe, Ashley Flores, Richard Highsmith, Alex Lim, Gabbie McKay, Tanya Milki, Jonathan Miller, Adam O'Connor, Tyler Phillips, Thomas Pivnicny, Jake Solomon, Jacob Weiss, Robert White, Teddy Zou, and, especially, Chris Norman.

A. H. Studenmund

1 An Overview of Regression Analysis

1.1 What Is Econometrics?

"Econometrics is too mathematical; it's the reason my best friend isn't majoring in economics."

"There are two things you are better off not watching in the making: sausages and econometric estimates."[1]

"Econometrics may be defined as the quantitative analysis of actual economic phenomena."[2]

"It's my experience that 'economy-tricks' is usually nothing more than a justification of what the author believed before the research was begun."

Obviously, econometrics means different things to different people. To beginning students, it may seem as if econometrics is an overly complex obstacle to an otherwise useful education. To skeptical observers, econometric results should be trusted only when the steps that produced those

---

1. Ed Leamer, "Let's take the Con out of Econometrics," *American Economic Review*, Vol. 73, No. 1, p. 37.

2. Paul A. Samuelson, T. C. Koopmans, and J. R. Stone, "Report of the Evaluative Committee for *Econometrica*," *Econometrica*, 1954, p. 141.

results are completely known. To professionals in the field, econometrics is a fascinating set of techniques that allows the measurement and analysis of economic phenomena and the prediction of future economic trends.

You're probably thinking that such diverse points of view sound like the statements of blind people trying to describe an elephant based on what they happen to be touching, and you're partially right. Econometrics has both a formal definition and a larger context. Although you can easily memorize the formal definition, you'll get the complete picture only by understanding the many uses of and alternative approaches to econometrics.

That said, we need a formal definition. **Econometrics**—literally, "economic measurement"—is the quantitative measurement and analysis of actual economic and business phenomena. It attempts to quantify economic reality and bridge the gap between the abstract world of economic theory and the real world of human activity. To many students, these worlds may seem far apart. On the one hand, economists theorize equilibrium prices based on carefully conceived marginal costs and marginal revenues; on the other, many firms seem to operate as though they have never heard of such concepts. Econometrics allows us to examine data and to quantify the actions of firms, consumers, and governments. Such measurements have a number of different uses, and an examination of these uses is the first step to understanding econometrics.

Uses of Econometrics

Econometrics has three major uses:

1. describing economic reality
2. testing hypotheses about economic theory
3. forecasting future economic activity

The simplest use of econometrics is **description**. We can use econometrics to quantify economic activity because econometrics allows us to estimate numbers and put them in equations that previously contained only abstract symbols. For example, consumer demand for a particular commodity often can be thought of as a relationship between the quantity demanded (Q) and the commodity's price (P), the price of a substitute good (P_s), and disposable income (Yd). For most goods, the relationship between consumption and disposable income is expected to be positive, because an increase in disposable income will be associated with an increase in the consumption of the good. Econometrics actually allows us to estimate that relationship based upon past consumption, income, and prices. In other words, a general and purely theoretical functional relationship like:

$$Q = f(P, P_s, Yd) \tag{1.1}$$

can become explicit:

$$Q = 27.7 - 0.11P + 0.03P_s + 0.23Yd \tag{1.2}$$

This technique gives a much more specific and descriptive picture of the function.[3] Let's compare Equations 1.1 and 1.2. Instead of expecting consumption merely to "increase" if there is an increase in disposable income, Equation 1.2 allows us to expect an increase of a specific amount (0.23 units for each unit of increased disposable income). The number 0.23 is called an estimated regression coefficient, and it is the ability to estimate these coefficients that makes econometrics valuable.

The second and perhaps most common use of econometrics is **hypothesis testing**, the evaluation of alternative theories with quantitative evidence. Much of economics involves building theoretical models and testing them against evidence, and hypothesis testing is vital to that scientific approach. For example, you could test the hypothesis that the product in Equation 1.1 is what economists call a normal good (one for which the quantity demanded increases when disposable income increases). You could do this by applying various statistical tests to the estimated coefficient (0.23) of disposable income (Yd) in Equation 1.2. At first glance, the evidence would seem to support this hypothesis, because the coefficient's sign is positive, but the "statistical significance" of that estimate would have to be investigated before such a conclusion could be justified. Even though the estimated coefficient is positive, as expected, it may not be sufficiently different from zero to convince us that the true coefficient is indeed positive.

The third and most difficult use of econometrics is to **forecast** or predict what is likely to happen next quarter, next year, or further into the future, based on what has happened in the past. For example, economists use econometric models to make forecasts of variables like sales, profits, Gross

---

3. The results in Equation 1.2 are from a model of the demand for chicken that we will examine in more detail in Section 6.1. It's of course naïve to build a model of the demand for chicken without taking the supply of chicken into consideration. Unfortunately, it's very difficult to learn how to estimate a system of simultaneous equations until you've learned how to estimate a single equation. As a result, we will postpone our discussion of the econometrics of simultaneous equations until Chapter 14. Until then, you should be aware that we sometimes will encounter right-hand-side variables that are not truly "independent" from a theoretical point of view.

Domestic Product (GDP), and the inflation rate. The accuracy of such forecasts depends in large measure on the degree to which the past is a good guide to the future. Business leaders and politicians tend to be especially interested in this use of econometrics because they need to make decisions about the future, and the penalty for being wrong (bankruptcy for the entrepreneur and political defeat for the candidate) is high. To the extent that econometrics can shed light on the impact of their policies, business and government leaders will be better equipped to make decisions. For example, if the president of a company that sold the product modeled in Equation 1.1 wanted to decide whether to increase prices, forecasts of sales with and without the price increase could be calculated and compared to help make such a decision.

Alternative Econometric Approaches

There are many different approaches to quantitative work. For example, the fields of biology, psychology, and physics all face quantitative questions similar to those faced in economics and business. However, these fields tend to use somewhat different techniques for analysis because the problems they face aren't the same. For example, economics typically is an observational discipline rather than an experimental one. "We need a special field called econometrics, and textbooks about it, because it is generally accepted that economic data possess certain properties that are not considered in standard statistics texts or are not sufficiently emphasized there for use by economists."[4]

Different approaches also make sense within the field of economics. The kind of econometric tools used depends in part on the uses of that equation. A model built solely for descriptive purposes might be different from a forecasting model, for example.

To get a better picture of these approaches, let's look at the steps used in nonexperimental quantitative research:

1. specifying the models or relationships to be studied
2. collecting the data needed to quantify the models
3. quantifying the models with the data

The specifications used in step 1 and the techniques used in step 3 differ widely between and within disciplines. Choosing the best specification for a given model is a theory-based skill that is often referred to as the "art" of

---

4. Clive Granger, "A Review of Some Recent Textbooks of Econometrics," *Journal of Economic Literature*, Vol. 32, No. 1, p. 117.

econometrics. There are many alternative approaches to quantifying the same equation, and each approach may produce somewhat different results. The choice of approach is left to the individual econometrician (the researcher using econometrics), but each researcher should be able to justify that choice.

This book will focus primarily on one particular econometric approach: *single-equation linear regression analysis*. The majority of this book will thus concentrate on regression analysis, but it is important for every econometrician to remember that regression is only one of many approaches to econometric quantification.

The importance of critical evaluation cannot be stressed enough; a good econometrician can diagnose faults in a particular approach and figure out how to repair them. The limitations of the regression analysis approach must be fully perceived and appreciated by anyone attempting to use regression analysis or its findings. The possibility of missing or inaccurate data, incorrectly formulated relationships, poorly chosen estimating techniques, or improper statistical testing procedures implies that the results from regression analyses always should be viewed with some caution.

1.2 What Is Regression Analysis?

Econometricians use regression analysis to make quantitative estimates of economic relationships that previously have been completely theoretical in nature. After all, anybody can claim that the quantity of compact discs demanded will increase if the price of those discs decreases (holding everything else constant), but not many people can put specific numbers into an equation and estimate *by how many* compact discs the quantity demanded will increase for each dollar that price decreases. To predict the *direction* of the change, you need a knowledge of economic theory and the general characteristics of the product in question. To predict the *amount* of the change, though, you need a sample of data, and you need a way to estimate the relationship. The most frequently used method to estimate such a relationship in econometrics is regression analysis.

Dependent Variables, Independent Variables, and Causality

Regression analysis is a statistical technique that attempts to "explain" movements in one variable, the **dependent variable**, as a function of movements in a set of other variables, called the **independent** (or **explanatory**) **variables**, through the quantification of a single equation. For example, in Equation 1.1:

$$Q = f(P, P_s, Yd) \tag{1.1}$$

Q is the dependent variable and P, P_s, and Yd are the independent variables. Regression analysis is a natural tool for economists because most (though not all) economic propositions can be stated in such single-equation functional forms. For example, the quantity demanded (dependent variable) is a function of price, the prices of substitutes, and income (independent variables).

Much of economics and business is concerned with cause-and-effect propositions. If the price of a good increases by one unit, then the quantity demanded decreases on average by a certain amount, depending on the price elasticity of demand (defined as the percentage change in the quantity demanded that is caused by a one percent increase in price). Similarly, if the quantity of capital employed increases by one unit, then output increases by a certain amount, called the marginal productivity of capital. Propositions such as these pose an if-then, or causal, relationship that logically postulates that a dependent variable's movements are determined by movements in a number of specific independent variables.

> Don't be deceived by the words "dependent" and "independent," however. Although many economic relationships are causal by their very nature, a regression result, no matter how statistically significant, cannot prove causality. All regression analysis can do is test whether a significant quantitative relationship exists. Judgments as to causality must also include a healthy dose of economic theory and common sense. For example, the fact that the bell on the door of a flower shop rings just before a customer enters and purchases some flowers by no means implies that the bell causes purchases! If events A and B are related statistically, it may be that A causes B, that B causes A, that some omitted factor causes both, or that a chance correlation exists between the two.

The cause-and-effect relationship often is so subtle that it fools even the most prominent economists. For example, in the late nineteenth century, English economist Stanley Jevons hypothesized that sunspots caused an increase in economic activity. To test this theory, he collected data on national output (the dependent variable) and sunspot activity (the independent variable) and showed that a significant positive relationship existed. This result led him, and some others, to jump to the conclusion that sunspots did indeed cause output to rise. Such a conclusion was unjustified because regression analysis cannot confirm causality; it can only test the strength and direction of the quantitative relationships involved.

Single-Equation Linear Models

The simplest single-equation linear regression model is:

$$Y = \beta_0 + \beta_1 X \qquad (1.3)$$

Equation 1.3 states that Y, the dependent variable, is a single-equation linear function of X, the independent variable. The model is a single-equation model because it's the only equation specified. The model is linear because if you were to plot Equation 1.3 it would be a straight line rather than a curve.

The βs are the **coefficients** that determine the coordinates of the straight line at any point. β_0 is the **constant** or **intercept** term; it indicates the value of Y when X equals zero. β_1 is the **slope coefficient**, and it indicates the amount that Y will change when X increases by one unit. The solid line in Figure 1.1 illustrates the relationship between the coefficients and the graphical meaning of the regression equation. As can be seen from the diagram, Equation 1.3 is indeed linear.

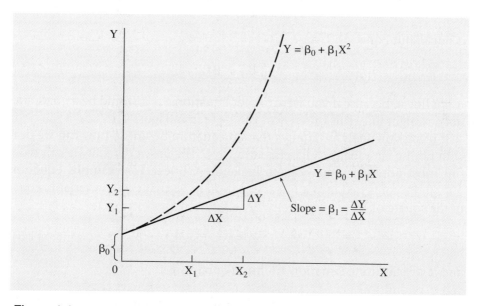

Figure 1.1 Graphical Representation of the Coefficients of the Regression Line

The graph of the equation $Y = \beta_0 + \beta_1 X$ is linear with a constant slope equal to $\beta_1 = \Delta Y / \Delta X$. The graph of the equation $Y = \beta_0 + \beta_1 X^2$, on the other hand, is nonlinear with an increasing slope (if $\beta_1 > 0$).

The slope coefficient, β_1, shows the response of Y to a one-unit increase in X. Much of the emphasis in regression analysis is on slope coefficients such as β_1. In Figure 1.1 for example, if X were to increase by one from X_1 to X_2 (ΔX), the value of Y in Equation 1.3 would increase from Y_1 to Y_2 (ΔY). For linear (i.e., straight-line) regression models, the response in the predicted value of Y due to a change in X is constant and equal to the slope coefficient β_1:

$$\frac{(Y_2 - Y_1)}{(X_2 - X_1)} = \frac{\Delta Y}{\Delta X} = \beta_1$$

where Δ is used to denote a change in the variables. Some readers may recognize this as the "rise" (ΔY) divided by the "run" (ΔX). For a linear model, the slope is constant over the entire function.

If linear regression techniques are going to be applied to an equation, that equation *must be* linear. An equation is **linear** if plotting the function in terms of X and Y generates a straight line. For example, Equation 1.3:

$$Y = \beta_0 + \beta_1 X \qquad\qquad (1.3)$$

is linear, but Equation 1.4:

$$Y = \beta_0 + \beta_1 X^2 \qquad\qquad (1.4)$$

is not linear, because if you were to plot Equation 1.4 it would be a quadratic, not a straight line. This difference[5] can be seen in Figure 1.1.

If regression analysis requires that an equation be linear, how can we deal with nonlinear equations like Equation 1.4? The answer is that we can redefine most nonlinear equations to make them linear. For example, Equation 1.4 can be converted into a linear equation if we create a new variable equal to the square of X:

$$Z = X^2 \qquad\qquad (1.5)$$

and if we substitute Equation 1.5 into Equation 1.4:

$$Y = \beta_0 + \beta_1 Z \qquad\qquad (1.6)$$

---

5. Equations 1.3 and 1.4 have the same β_0 in Figure 1.1 for comparison purposes only. If the equations were applied to the same data, the estimated β_0 values would be different. Not surprisingly, the estimated β_1 values would be different as well.

This redefined equation is now linear[6] and can be estimated by regression analysis.

The Stochastic Error Term

Besides the variation in the dependent variable (Y) that is caused by the independent variable (X), there is almost always variation that comes from other sources as well. This additional variation comes in part from omitted explanatory variables (e.g., X_2 and X_3). However, even if these extra variables are added to the equation, there still is going to be some variation in Y that simply cannot be explained by the model.[7] This variation probably comes from sources such as omitted influences, measurement error, incorrect functional form, or purely random and totally unpredictable occurrences. By *random* we mean something that has its value determined entirely by chance.

Econometricians admit the existence of such inherent unexplained variation ("error") by explicitly including a stochastic (or random) error term in their regression models. A **stochastic error term** is a term that is added to a regression equation to introduce all of the variation in Y that cannot be explained by the included Xs. It is, in effect, a symbol of the econometrician's ignorance or inability to model all the movements of the dependent variable. The error term (sometimes called a disturbance term) usually is referred to with the symbol epsilon (ϵ), although other symbols (like u or v) sometimes are used.

The addition of a stochastic error term (ϵ) to Equation 1.3 results in a typical regression equation:

$$Y = \beta_0 + \beta_1 X + \epsilon \qquad (1.7)$$

---

6. Technically, as you will learn in Chapter 7, this equation is linear in the coefficients β_0 and β_1 and linear in the variables Y and Z, but it is nonlinear in the variables Y and X. The application of regression analysis to equations that are nonlinear in the variables is covered in Chapter 7. The application of regression techniques to equations that are nonlinear in the coefficients, however, is much more difficult.

7. The exception would be the extremely rare case where the data can be explained by some sort of physical law and are measured perfectly. Here, continued variation would point to an omitted independent variable. A similar kind of problem is often encountered in astronomy, where planets can be discovered by noting that the orbits of known planets exhibit variations that can be caused only by the gravitational pull of another heavenly body. Absent these kinds of physical laws, researchers in economics and business would be foolhardy to believe that *all* variation in Y can be explained by a regression model because there are always elements of error in any attempt to measure a behavioral relationship.

Equation 1.7 can be thought of as having two components, the *deterministic* component and the *stochastic,* or random, component. The expression $\beta_0 + \beta_1 X$ is called the *deterministic* component of the regression equation because it indicates the value of Y that is determined by a given value of X, which is assumed to be nonstochastic. This deterministic component can also be thought of as the **expected value** of Y given X, the mean value of the Ys associated with a particular value of X. For example, if the average height of all 13-year-old girls is 5 feet, then 5 feet is the expected value of a girl's height given that she is 13. The deterministic part of the equation may be written:

$$E(Y|X) = \beta_0 + \beta_1 X \tag{1.8}$$

which states that the expected value of Y given X, denoted as $E(Y|X)$, is a linear function of the independent variable (or variables if there are more than one).[8]

Unfortunately, the value of Y observed in the real world is unlikely to be exactly equal to the deterministic expected value $E(Y|X)$. After all, not all 13-year-old girls are 5 feet tall. As a result, the stochastic element (ϵ) must be added to the equation:

$$Y = E(Y|X) + \epsilon = \beta_0 + \beta_1 X + \epsilon \tag{1.9}$$

The stochastic error term must be present in a regression equation because there are at least four sources of variation in Y other than the variation in the included Xs:

1. Many minor influences on Y are *omitted* from the equation (for example, because data are unavailable).

2. It is virtually impossible to avoid some sort of *measurement error* in the dependent variable.

3. The underlying theoretical equation might have a *different functional form* (or shape) than the one chosen for the regression. For example, the underlying equation might be nonlinear.

4. All attempts to generalize human behavior must contain at least some amount of unpredictable or *purely random* variation.

---

8. This property holds as long as $E(\epsilon|X) = 0$ (read as "the expected value of epsilon, given X" equals zero), which is true as long as the Classical Assumptions (to be outlined in Chapter 4) are met. It's easiest to think of $E(\epsilon)$ as the mean of ϵ, but the expected value operator E technically is a summation or integration of all the values that a function can take, weighted by the probability of each value. The expected value of a constant is that constant, and the expected value of a sum of variables equals the sum of the expected values of those variables.

To get a better feeling for these components of the stochastic error term, let's think about a consumption function (aggregate consumption as a function of aggregate disposable income). First, consumption in a particular year may have been less than it would have been because of uncertainty over the future course of the economy. Since this uncertainty is hard to measure, there might be no variable measuring consumer uncertainty in the equation. In such a case, the impact of the omitted variable (consumer uncertainty) would likely end up in the stochastic error term. Second, the observed amount of consumption may have been different from the actual level of consumption in a particular year due to an error (such as a sampling error) in the measurement of consumption in the National Income Accounts. Third, the underlying consumption function may be nonlinear, but a linear consumption function might be estimated. (To see how this incorrect functional form would cause errors, see Figure 1.2.) Fourth, the consumption function attempts to portray the behavior of people, and there is always an element of

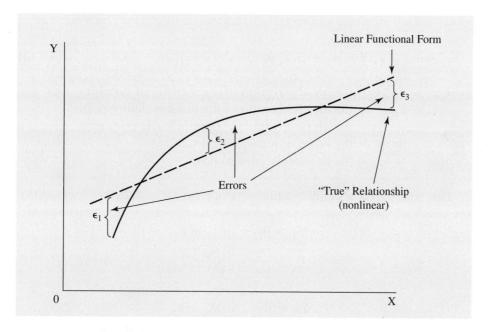

Figure 1.2 Errors Caused by Using a Linear Functional Form to Model a Nonlinear Relationship

One source of stochastic error is the use of an incorrect functional form. For example, if a linear functional form is used when the underlying relationship is nonlinear, systematic errors (the ϵs) will occur. These nonlinearities are just one component of the stochastic error term. The others are omitted variables, measurement error, and purely random variation.

unpredictability in human behavior. At any given time, some random event might increase or decrease aggregate consumption in a way that might never be repeated and couldn't be anticipated.

These possibilities explain the existence of a difference between the observed values of Y and the values expected from the deterministic component of the equation, $E(Y|X)$. These sources of error will be covered in more detail in the following chapters, but for now it is enough to recognize that in econometric research there will always be some stochastic or random element, and, for this reason, an error term must be added to all regression equations.

Extending the Notation

Our regression notation needs to be extended to allow the possibility of more than one independent variable and to include reference to the number of observations. A typical observation (or unit of analysis) is an individual person, year, or country. For example, a series of annual observations starting in 1985 would have $Y_1 = Y$ for 1985, Y_2 for 1986, etc. If we include a specific reference to the observations, the single-equation linear regression model may be written as:

$$Y_i = \beta_0 + \beta_1 X_i + \epsilon_i \qquad (i = 1, 2, \ldots, N) \qquad (1.10)$$

where:
$\begin{aligned}
Y_i &= \text{the } i\text{th observation of the dependent variable} \\
X_i &= \text{the } i\text{th observation of the independent variable} \\
\epsilon_i &= \text{the } i\text{th observation of the stochastic error term} \\
\beta_0, \beta_1 &= \text{the regression coefficients} \\
N &= \text{the number of observations}
\end{aligned}$

This equation is actually N equations, one for each of the N observations:

$$Y_1 = \beta_0 + \beta_1 X_1 + \epsilon_1$$
$$Y_2 = \beta_0 + \beta_1 X_2 + \epsilon_2$$
$$Y_3 = \beta_0 + \beta_1 X_3 + \epsilon_3$$
$$\vdots$$
$$Y_N = \beta_0 + \beta_1 X_N + \epsilon_N$$

That is, the regression model is assumed to hold for each observation. The coefficients do not change from observation to observation, but the values of Y, X, and ϵ do.

A second notational addition allows for more than one independent variable. Since more than one independent variable is likely to have an effect on the dependent variable, our notation should allow these additional explanatory Xs to be added. If we define:

X_{1i} = the ith observation of the first independent variable
X_{2i} = the ith observation of the second independent variable
X_{3i} = the ith observation of the third independent variable

then all three variables can be expressed as determinants of Y.

The resulting equation is called a **multivariate** (more than one independent variable) linear regression model:

$$Y_i = \beta_0 + \beta_1 X_{1i} + \beta_2 X_{2i} + \beta_3 X_{3i} + \epsilon_i \qquad (1.11)$$

The **meaning of the regression coefficient** β_1 in this equation is the impact of a one-unit increase in X_1 on the dependent variable Y, *holding constant* X_2 and X_3. Similarly, β_2 gives the impact of a one-unit increase in X_2 on Y, holding X_1 and X_3 constant.

These **multivariate regression coefficients** (which are parallel in nature to partial derivatives in calculus) serve to isolate the impact on Y of a change in one variable from the impact on Y of changes in the other variables. This is possible because multivariate regression takes the movements of X_2 and X_3 into account when it estimates the coefficient of X_1. The result is quite similar to what we would obtain if we were capable of conducting controlled laboratory experiments in which only one variable at a time was changed.

In the real world, though, it is very difficult to run controlled economic experiments,[9] because many economic factors change simultaneously, often in opposite directions. Thus the ability of regression analysis to measure the impact of one variable on the dependent variable, *holding constant the influence of the other variables in the equation,* is a tremendous advantage. Note that if a variable is not included in an equation, then its impact is *not* held constant in the estimation of the regression coefficients. This will be discussed further in Chapter 6.

---

9. Such experiments are difficult but not impossible. See Section 16.1.

This material is pretty abstract, so let's look at an example. Suppose we want to understand how wages are determined in a particular field, perhaps because we think that there might be discrimination in that field. The wage of a worker would be the dependent variable (WAGE), but what would be good independent variables? What variables would influence a person's wage in a given field? Well, there are literally dozens of reasonable possibilities, but three of the most common are the work experience (EXP), education (EDU), and gender (GEND) of the worker, so let's use these. To create a regression equation with these variables, we'd redefine the variables in Equation 1.11 to meet our definitions:

$$Y \ = \text{WAGE} = \text{the wage of the worker}$$
$$X_1 = \text{EXP} = \text{the years of work experience of the worker}$$
$$X_2 = \text{EDU} = \text{the years of education beyond high school of the worker}$$
$$X_3 = \text{GEND} = \text{the gender of the worker } (1 = \text{male and } 0 = \text{female})$$

The last variable, GEND, is unusual in that it can take on only two values, 0 and 1; this kind of variable is called a **dummy variable**, and it's extremely useful when we want to quantify a concept that is inherently qualitative (like gender). We'll discuss dummy variables in more depth in Sections 3.1 and 7.4.

If we substitute these definitions into Equation 1.11, we get:

$$\text{WAGE}_i = \beta_0 + \beta_1 \text{EXP}_i + \beta_2 \text{EDU}_i + \beta_3 \text{GEND}_i + \epsilon_i \qquad (1.12)$$

Equation 1.12 specifies that a worker's wage is a function of the experience, education, and gender of that worker. In such an equation, what would the meaning of β_1 be? Some readers will guess that β_1 measures the amount by which the average wage increases for an additional year of experience, but such a guess would miss the fact that there are two other independent variables in the equation that also explain wages. The correct answer is that β_1 gives us the impact on wages of a one-year increase in experience, *holding constant* education and gender. This is a significant difference, because it allows researchers to control for specific complicating factors without running controlled experiments.

Before we conclude this section, it's worth noting that the general multivariate regression model with K independent variables is written as:

$$Y_i = \beta_0 + \beta_1 X_{1i} + \beta_2 X_{2i} + \cdots + \beta_K X_{Ki} + \epsilon_i \qquad (1.13)$$

where i goes from 1 to N and indicates the observation number.

If the sample consists of a series of years or months (called a **time series**), then the subscript i is usually replaced with a t to denote time.[10]

(1.3) The Estimated Regression Equation

Once a specific equation has been decided upon, it must be quantified. This quantified version of the theoretical regression equation is called the **estimated regression equation** and is obtained from a sample of data for actual Xs and Ys. Although the theoretical equation is purely abstract in nature:

$$Y_i = \beta_0 + \beta_1 X_i + \epsilon_i \tag{1.14}$$

the estimated regression equation has actual numbers in it:

$$\hat{Y}_i = 103.40 + 6.38 X_i \tag{1.15}$$

The observed, real-world values of X and Y are used to calculate the coefficient estimates 103.40 and 6.38. These estimates are used to determine $\hat{Y}$ (read as "Y-hat"), the *estimated* or *fitted* value of Y.

Let's look at the differences between a theoretical regression equation and an estimated regression equation. First, the theoretical regression coefficients β_0 and β_1 in Equation 1.14 have been replaced with *estimates* of those coefficients like 103.40 and 6.38 in Equation 1.15. We can't actually observe the values of the true[11] regression coefficients, so instead we calculate estimates of those coefficients from the data. The **estimated regression coefficients**, more generally denoted by $\hat{\beta}_0$ and $\hat{\beta}_1$ (read as "beta-hats"), are empirical best guesses of the true regression coefficients and are obtained from data from a sample of the Ys and Xs. The expression

$$\hat{Y}_i = \hat{\beta}_0 + \hat{\beta}_1 X_i \tag{1.16}$$

---

10. The order of the subscripts doesn't matter as long as the appropriate definitions are presented. We prefer to list the variable number first (X_{1i}) because we think it's easier for a beginning econometrician to understand. However, as the reader moves on to matrix algebra and computer spreadsheets, it will become common to list the observation number first, as in X_{i1}. Often the observational subscript is deleted, and the reader is expected to understand that the equation holds for each observation in the sample.

11. Our use of the word "true" throughout the text should be taken with a grain of salt. Many philosophers argue that the concept of truth is useful only relative to the scientific research program in question. Many economists agree, pointing out that what is true for one generation may well be false for another. To us, the true coefficient is the one that you'd obtain if you could run a regression on the entire relevant population. Thus, readers who so desire can substitute the phrase "population coefficient" for "true coefficient" with no loss in meaning.

is the empirical counterpart of the theoretical regression Equation 1.14. The calculated estimates in Equation 1.15 are examples of the estimated regression coefficients $\hat{\beta}_0$ and $\hat{\beta}_1$. For each sample we calculate a different set of estimated regression coefficients.

$\hat{Y}_i$ is the *estimated value* of Y_i, and it represents the value of Y calculated from the estimated regression equation for the *i*th observation. As such, $\hat{Y}_i$ is our prediction of $E(Y_i|X_i)$ from the regression equation. The closer these $\hat{Y}$s are to the Ys in the sample, the better the fit of the equation. (The word *fit* is used here much as it would be used to describe how well clothes fit.)

The difference between the estimated value of the dependent variable $(\hat{Y}_i)$ and the actual value of the dependent variable (Y_i) is defined as the **residual (e_i)**:

$$e_i = Y_i - \hat{Y}_i \qquad (1.17)$$

Note the distinction between the residual in Equation 1.17 and the error term:

$$\epsilon_i = Y_i - E(Y_i|X_i) \qquad (1.18)$$

The *residual* is the difference between the observed Y and the estimated regression line $(\hat{Y})$, while the *error term* is the difference between the observed Y and the true regression equation (the expected value of Y). Note that the error term is a theoretical concept that can never be observed, but the residual is a real-world value that is calculated for each observation every time a regression is run. The residual can be thought of as an estimate of the error term, and e could have been denoted as $\hat{\epsilon}$. Most regression techniques not only calculate the residuals but also attempt to compute values of $\hat{\beta}_0$ and $\hat{\beta}_1$ that keep the residuals as low as possible. The smaller the residuals, the better the fit, and the closer the $\hat{Y}$s will be to the Ys.

All these concepts are shown in Figure 1.3. The (X, Y) pairs are shown as points on the diagram, and both the true regression equation (which cannot be seen in real applications) and an estimated regression equation are included. Notice that the estimated equation is close to but not equivalent to the true line. This is a typical result.

In Figure 1.3, $\hat{Y}_6$, the computed value of Y for the sixth observation, lies on the estimated (dashed) line, and it differs from Y_6, the actual observed value of Y for the sixth observation. The difference between the observed and estimated values is the residual, denoted by e_6. In addition, although we usually would not be able to see an observation of the error term, we have drawn the

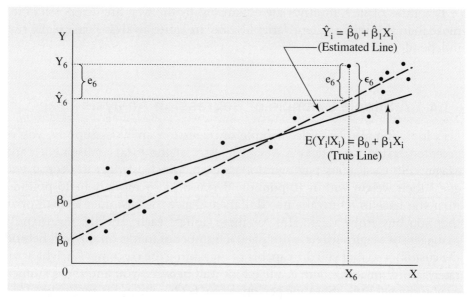

Figure 1.3 True and Estimated Regression Lines

The true relationship between X and Y (the solid line) typically cannot be observed, but the estimated regression line (the dashed line) can. The difference between an observed data point (for example, $i = 6$) and the true line is the value of the stochastic error term (ϵ_6). The difference between the observed Y_6 and the estimated value from the regression line ($\hat{Y}_6$) is the value of the residual for this observation, e_6.

assumed true regression line here (the solid line) to see the sixth observation of the error term, ϵ_6, which is the difference between the true line and the observed value of Y, Y_6.

The following table summarizes the notation used in the true and estimated regression equations:

True Regression Equation	Estimated Regression Equation
β_0	$\hat{\beta}_0$
β_1	$\hat{\beta}_1$
ϵ_i	e_i

The estimated regression model can be extended to more than one independent variable by adding the additional Xs to the right side of the equation. The multivariate estimated regression counterpart of Equation 1.13 is:

$$\hat{Y}_i = \hat{\beta}_0 + \hat{\beta}_1 X_{1i} + \hat{\beta}_2 X_{2i} + \cdots + \hat{\beta}_K X_{Ki} \qquad (1.19)$$

Diagrams of such multivariate equations, by the way, are not possible for more than two independent variables and are quite awkward for exactly two independent variables.

1.4 A Simple Example of Regression Analysis

Let's look at a fairly simple example of regression analysis. Suppose you've accepted a summer job as a weight guesser at the local amusement park, Magic Hill. Customers pay two dollars each, which you get to keep if you guess their weight within 10 pounds. If you miss by more than 10 pounds, then you have to return the two dollars and give the customer a small prize that you buy from Magic Hill for three dollars each. Luckily, the friendly managers of Magic Hill have arranged a number of marks on the wall behind the customer so that you are capable of measuring the customer's height accurately. Unfortunately, there is a five-foot wall between you and the customer, so you can tell little about the person except for height and (usually) gender.

On your first day on the job, you do so poorly that you work all day and somehow manage to lose two dollars, so on the second day you decide to collect data to run a regression to estimate the relationship between weight and height. Since most of the participants are male, you decide to limit your sample to males. You hypothesize the following theoretical relationship:

$$Y_i = f(X_i) + \epsilon_i = \beta_0 + \overset{+}{\beta_1 X_i} + \epsilon_i \qquad (1.20)$$

where: Y_i = the weight (in pounds) of the ith customer
X_i = the height (in inches above 5 feet) of the ith customer
ϵ_i = the value of the stochastic error term for the ith customer

In this case, the sign of the theoretical relationship between height and weight is believed to be positive (signified by the positive sign above X_i in the general theoretical equation), but you must quantify that relationship in order to estimate weights given heights. To do this, you need to collect a data set, and you need to apply regression analysis to the data.

The next day you collect the data summarized in Table 1.1 and run your regression on the Magic Hill computer, obtaining the following estimates:

$$\hat{\beta}_0 = 103.40 \qquad \hat{\beta}_1 = 6.38$$

This means that the equation

Estimated weight $= 103.40 + 6.38 \cdot$ Height (inches above five feet) $\qquad (1.21)$

Table 1.1   Data for and Results of the Weight-Guessing Equation

Observation i (1)	Height Above 5' X_i (2)	Weight Y_i (3)	Predicted Weight $\hat{Y}_i$ (4)	Residual e_i (5)	$ Gain or Loss (6)
1	5.0	140.0	135.3	4.7	+2.00
2	9.0	157.0	160.8	−3.8	+2.00
3	13.0	205.0	186.3	18.7	−3.00
4	12.0	198.0	179.9	18.1	−3.00
5	10.0	162.0	167.2	−5.2	+2.00
6	11.0	174.0	173.6	0.4	+2.00
7	8.0	150.0	154.4	−4.4	+2.00
8	9.0	165.0	160.8	4.2	+2.00
9	10.0	170.0	167.2	2.8	+2.00
10	12.0	180.0	179.9	0.1	+2.00
11	11.0	170.0	173.6	−3.6	+2.00
12	9.0	162.0	160.8	1.2	+2.00
13	10.0	165.0	167.2	−2.2	+2.00
14	12.0	180.0	179.9	0.1	+2.00
15	8.0	160.0	154.4	5.6	+2.00
16	9.0	155.0	160.8	−5.8	+2.00
17	10.0	165.0	167.2	−2.2	+2.00
18	15.0	190.0	199.1	−9.1	+2.00
19	13.0	185.0	186.3	−1.3	+2.00
20	11.0	155.0	173.6	−18.6	−3.00
				TOTAL	= $25.00

Note: This data set, and every other data set in the text, is available on the text's website in four formats and on the EViews CD-ROM. Datafile = HTWT1

is worth trying as an alternative to just guessing the weights of your customers. Such an equation estimates weight with a constant base of 103.40 pounds and adds 6.38 pounds for every inch of height over 5 feet. Note that the sign of $\hat{\beta}_1$ is positive, as you expected.

How well does the equation work? To answer this question, you need to calculate the residuals (Y_i minus $\hat{Y}_i$) from Equation 1.21 to see how many were greater than ten. As can be seen in the last column in Table 1.1, if you had applied the equation to these 20 people, you wouldn't exactly have gotten rich, but at least you would have earned $25.00 instead of losing $2.00. Figure 1.4 shows not only Equation 1.21 but also the weight and height data for all 20 customers used as the sample.

Equation 1.21 would probably help a beginning weight guesser, but it could be improved by adding other variables or by collecting a larger sample.

Figure 1.4 A Weight-Guessing Equation

If we plot the data from the weight-guessing example and include the estimated regression line, we can see that the estimated Ŷs come fairly close to the observed Ys for all but three observations. Find a male friend's height and weight on the graph; how well does the regression equation work?

Such an equation is realistic, though, because it's likely that every successful weight guesser uses an equation like this without consciously thinking about that concept.

Our goal with this equation was to quantify the theoretical weight/height equation, Equation 1.20, by collecting data (Table 1.1) and calculating an estimated regression, Equation 1.21. Although the true equation, like observations of the stochastic error term, can never be known, we were able to come up with an estimated equation that had the sign we expected for $\hat{\beta}_1$ and that helped us in our job. Before you decide to quit school or your job and try to make your living guessing weights at Magic Hill, there is quite a bit more to learn about regression analysis, so we'd better move on.

1.5 Using Regression to Explain Housing Prices

As much fun as guessing weights at an amusement park might be, it's hardly a typical example of the use of regression analysis. For every regression run on such an off-the-wall topic, there are literally hundreds run to *describe* the reaction of GDP to an increase in the money supply, to *test* an economic theory with new data, or to *forecast* the effect of a price change on a firm's sales.

As a more realistic example, let's look at a model of housing prices. The purchase of a house is probably the most important financial decision in an individual's life, and one of the key elements in that decision is an appraisal of the house's value. If you overvalue the house, you can lose thousands of dollars by paying too much; if you undervalue the house, someone might outbid you.

All this wouldn't be much of a problem if houses were homogeneous products, like corn or gold, that have generally known market prices with which to compare a particular asking price. Such is hardly the case in the real estate market. Consequently, an important element of every housing purchase is an appraisal of the market value of the house, and many real estate appraisers use regression analysis to help them in their work.

Suppose your family is about to buy a house in Southern California, but you're convinced that the owner is asking too much money. The owner says that the asking price of $230,000 is fair because a larger house next door sold for $230,000 about a year ago. You're not sure it's reasonable to compare the prices of different-sized houses that were purchased at different times. What can you do to help decide whether to pay the $230,000?

Since you're taking an econometrics class, you decide to collect data on all local houses that were sold within the last few weeks and to build a regression model of the sales prices of the houses as a function of their sizes.[12] Such a data set is called **cross-sectional** because all of the observations are from the same point in time and represent different individual economic entities (like countries or, in this case, houses) from that same point in time.

To measure the impact of size on price, you include the size of the house as an independent variable in a regression equation that has the price of that house as the dependent variable. You expect a positive sign for the coefficient of size, since big houses cost more to build and tend to be more desirable than small ones. Thus the theoretical model is:

$$\overset{+}{PRICE_i} = f(SIZE_i) + \epsilon_i = \beta_0 + \beta_1 SIZE_i + \epsilon_i \qquad (1.22)$$

---

12. It's unusual for an economist to build a model of price without including some measure of quantity on the right-hand side. Such models of the price of a good as a function of the attributes of that good are called *hedonic* models and will be discussed in greater depth in Section 11.8. The interested reader is encouraged to skim the first few paragraphs of that section before continuing on with this example.

where: $PRICE_i$ = the price (in thousands of \$) of the ith house
         $SIZE_i$ = the size (in square feet) of that house
         ϵ_i = the value of the stochastic error term for that house

You collect the records of all recent real estate transactions, find that 43 local houses were sold within the last 4 weeks, and estimate the following regression of those 43 observations:

$$\widehat{PRICE_i} = 40.0 + 0.138 SIZE_i \tag{1.23}$$

What do these estimated coefficients mean? The most important coefficient is $\hat{\beta}_1 = 0.138$, since the reason for the regression is to find out the impact of size on price. This coefficient means that if size increases by 1 square foot, price will increase by 0.138 thousand dollars (\$138). $\hat{\beta}_1$ thus measures the change in $PRICE_i$ associated with a one-unit increase in $SIZE_i$. It's the slope of the regression line in a graph like Figure 1.5.

What does $\hat{\beta}_0 = 40.0$ mean? $\hat{\beta}_0$ is the estimate of the constant or intercept term. In our equation, it means that price equals 40.0 when size equals zero. As can be seen in Figure 1.5, the estimated regression line intersects the price

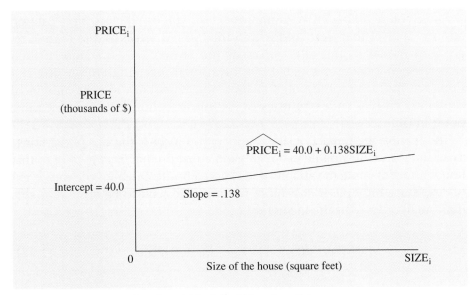

Figure 1.5 A Cross-Sectional Model of Housing Prices

A regression equation that has the price of a house in Southern California as a function of the size of that house has an intercept of 40.0 and a slope of 0.138, using Equation 1.23.

axis at 40.0. While it might be tempting to say that the average price of a vacant lot is $40,000, such a conclusion would be unjustified for a number of reasons, which will be discussed in Section 7.1. It's much safer either to interpret $\hat{\beta}_0 = 40.0$ as nothing more than the value of the estimated regression when $S_i = 0$, or to not interpret $\hat{\beta}_0$ at all.

What does $\hat{\beta}_1 = 0.138$ mean? $\hat{\beta}_1$ is the estimate of the coefficient of SIZE in Equation 1.22, and as such it's also an estimate of the slope of the line in Figure 1.5. It implies that an increase in the size of a house by one square foot will cause the estimated price of the house to go up by 0.138 thousand dollars or $138. It's a good habit to analyze estimated slope coefficients to see whether they make sense. The positive sign of $\hat{\beta}_1$ certainly is what we expected, but what about the magnitude of the coefficient? Whenever you interpret a coefficient, be sure to take the units of measurement into consideration. In this case, is $138 per square foot a plausible number? Well, it's hard to know for sure, but it certainly is a lot more reasonable than $1.38 per square foot or $13,800 per square foot!

How can you use this estimated regression to help decide whether to pay $230,000 for the house? If you calculate a $\hat{Y}$ (predicted price) for a house that is the same size (1,600 square feet) as the one you're thinking of buying, you can then compare this $\hat{Y}$ with the asking price of $230,000. To do this, substitute 1600 for $SIZE_i$ in Equation 1.23, obtaining:

$$\widehat{PRICE}_i = 40.0 + 0.138(1600) = 40.0 + 220.8 = 260.8$$

The house seems to be a good deal. The owner is asking "only" $230,000 for a house when the size implies a price of $260,800! Perhaps your original feeling that the price was too high was a reaction to the steep housing prices in Southern California in general and not a reflection of this specific price.

On the other hand, perhaps the price of a house is influenced by more than just the size of the house. (After all, what good's a house in Southern California unless it has a pool or air-conditioning?) Such multivariate models are the heart of econometrics, but we'll add more independent variables to Equation 1.23 when we return to this housing price example in Section 11.8.

1.6 Summary

1. Econometrics—literally, "economic measurement"—is a branch of economics that attempts to quantify theoretical relationships. Regression analysis is only one of the techniques used in econometrics, but it is by far the most frequently used.

2. The major uses of econometrics are description, hypothesis testing, and forecasting. The specific econometric techniques employed may vary depending on the use of the research.

3. While regression analysis specifies that a dependent variable is a function of one or more independent variables, regression analysis alone cannot prove or even imply causality.

4. A stochastic error term must be added to all regression equations to account for variations in the dependent variable that are not explained completely by the independent variables. The components of this error term include:
   a. omitted or left-out variables
   b. measurement errors in the data
   c. an underlying theoretical equation that has a different functional form (shape) than the regression equation
   d. purely random and unpredictable events

5. An estimated regression equation is an approximation of the true equation that is obtained by using data from a sample of actual Ys and Xs. Since we can never know the true equation, econometric analysis focuses on this estimated regression equation and the estimates of the regression coefficients. The difference between a particular observation of the dependent variable and the value estimated from the regression equation is called the residual.

EXERCISES

(The answer to Exercise 2 is in Appendix A.)

1. Write the meaning of each of the following terms without referring to the book (or your notes), and compare your definition with the version in the text for each:
   a. stochastic error term
   b. regression analysis
   c. linear
   d. slope coefficient
   e. multivariate regression model
   f. expected value
   g. residual
   h. time series
   i. cross-sectional data set

2. Use your own computer's regression software and the weight (Y) and height (X) data from Table 1.1 to see if you can reproduce the estimates in Equation 1.21. There are three different ways to load the data: You can type in the data yourself, you can open datafile HTWT1 on the EViews CD-ROM, or you can download datafile HTWT1 (in Excel, Stata or ASCII formats) from the text's website: www .pearsonhighered.com/studenmund. Once the datafile is loaded, run Y = f(X), and your results should match Equation 1.21. Different programs require different commands to run a regression. For help in how to do this with EViews and Stata, see the answer to this question in Appendix A.

3. Decide whether you would expect relationships between the following pairs of dependent and independent variables (respectively) to be positive, negative, or ambiguous. Explain your reasoning.
   a. Aggregate net investment in the United States in a given year and GDP in that year.
   b. The amount of hair on the head of a male professor and the age of that professor.
   c. The number of acres of wheat planted in a season and the price of wheat at the beginning of that season.
   d. Aggregate net investment and the real rate of interest in the same year and country.
   e. The growth rate of GDP in a year and the average hair length in that year.
   f. The quantity of canned tuna demanded and the price of a can of tuna.

4. Let's return to the height/weight example in Section 1.4:
   a. Go back to the data set and identify the three customers who seem to be quite a distance from the estimated regression line. Would we have a better regression equation if we dropped these customers from the sample?
   b. Measure the height of a male friend and plug it into Equation 1.21. Does the equation come within 10 pounds? If not, do you think you see why? Why does the estimated equation predict the same weight for all males of the same height when it is obvious that all males of the same height don't weigh the same?
   c. Look over the sample with the thought that it might not be randomly drawn. Does the sample look abnormal in any way? (*Hint:* Are the customers who choose to play such a game a random sample?) If the sample isn't random, would this have an effect on the regression results and the estimated weights?

d. Think of at least one other factor besides height that might be a good choice as a variable in the weight/height equation. How would you go about obtaining the data for this variable? What would the expected sign of your variable's coefficient be if the variable were added to the equation?

5. Continuing with the height/weight example, suppose you collected data on the heights and weights of 29 different male customers and estimated the following equation:

$$\hat{Y}_i = 125.1 + 4.03X_i \tag{1.24}$$

where: Y_i = the weight (in pounds) of the ith person
X_i = the height (in inches over five feet) of the ith person

a. Why aren't the coefficients in Equation 1.24 the same as those we estimated previously (Equation 1.21)?
b. Compare the estimated coefficients of Equation 1.24 with those in Equation 1.21. Which equation has the steeper estimated relationship between height and weight? Which equation has the higher intercept? At what point do the two intersect?
c. Use Equation 1.24 to "predict" the 20 original weights given the heights in Table 1.1. How many weights does Equation 1.24 miss by more than 10 pounds? Does Equation 1.24 do better or worse than Equation 1.21? Could you have predicted this result beforehand?
d. Suppose you had one last day on the weight-guessing job. What equation would you use to guess weights? (*Hint:* There is more than one possible answer.)

6. Not all regression coefficients have positive expected signs. For example, a *Sports Illustrated* article by Jaime Diaz reported on a study of golfing putts of various lengths on the Professional Golfers' Association (PGA) Tour.[13] The article included data on the percentage of putts made (P_i) as a function of the length of the putt in feet (L_i). Since the longer the putt, the less likely even a professional is to make it, we'd expect L_i to have a negative coefficient in an equation explaining P_i. Sure enough, if you estimate an equation on the data in the article, you obtain:

$$\hat{P}_i = f(\overline{L}_i) = 83.6 - 4.1L_i \tag{1.25}$$

---

13. Jaime Diaz, "Perils of Putting," *Sports Illustrated*, April 3, 1989, pp. 76–79.

a. Carefully write out the exact meaning of the coefficient of L_i.
b. Suppose someone else took the data from the article and estimated:

$$P_i = 83.6 - 4.1L_i + e_i$$

Is this the same result as that of Equation 1.25? If so, what definition do you need to use to convert this equation back to Equation 1.25?
c. Use Equation 1.25 to determine the percent of the time you'd expect a PGA golfer to make a 10-foot putt. Does this seem realistic? How about a 1-foot putt or a 25-foot putt? Do these seem as realistic?
d. Your answer to part c should suggest that there's a problem in applying a linear regression to these data. What is that problem? (*Hint:* If you're stuck, first draw the theoretical diagram you'd expect for P_i as a function of L_i, then plot Equation 1.25 onto the same diagram.)

7. Return to the housing price model of Section 1.5 and consider the following equation:

$$\widehat{SIZE}_i = -290 + 3.62\ PRICE_i \qquad (1.26)$$

where: $SIZE_i$ = the size (in square feet) of the *i*th house
$PRICE_i$ = the price (in thousands of $) of that house

a. Carefully explain the meaning of each of the estimated regression coefficients.
b. Suppose you're told that this equation explains a significant portion (more than 80 percent) of the variation in the size of a house. Have we shown that high housing prices cause houses to be large? If not, what have we shown?
c. What do you think would happen to the estimated coefficients of this equation if we had measured the price variable in dollars instead of in thousands of dollars? Be specific.

8. If an equation has more than one independent variable, we have to be careful when we interpret the regression coefficients of that equation. Think, for example, about how you might build an equation to explain the amount of money that different states spend per pupil on public education. The more income a state has, the more they probably spend on public schools, but the faster enrollment is growing, the less there would be to spend on each pupil. Thus, a reasonable equation for per pupil spending would include at least two variables: income and enrollment growth:

$$S_i = \beta_0 + \beta_1 Y_i + \beta_2 G_i + \epsilon_i \qquad (1.27)$$

where: S_i = educational dollars spent per public school student in the ith state

Y_i = per capita income in the ith state

G_i = the percent growth of public school enrollment in the ith state

a. State the economic meaning of the coefficients of Y and G. (*Hint:* Remember to hold the impact of the other variable constant.)

b. If we were to estimate Equation 1.27, what signs would you expect the coefficients of Y and G to have? Why?

c. Silva and Sonstelie estimated a cross-sectional model of per student spending by state that is very similar to Equation 1.27:[14]

$$\hat{S}_i = -183 + 0.1422Y_i - 5926G_i \qquad (1.28)$$
$$N = 49$$

Do these estimated coefficients correspond to your expectations? Explain Equation 1.28 in common sense terms.

d. The authors measured G as a decimal, so if a state had a 10 percent growth in enrollment, then G equaled .10. What would Equation 1.28 have looked like if the authors had measured G in percentage points, so that if a state had 10 percent growth, then G would have equaled 10? (*Hint:* Write out the actual numbers for the estimated coefficients.)

9. Your friend has an on-campus job making telephone calls to alumni asking for donations to your college's annual fund, and she wonders whether her calling is making any difference. In an attempt to measure the impact of student calls on fund raising, she collects data from 50 alums and estimates the following equation:

$$\widehat{GIFT}_i = 2.29 + 0.001INCOME_i + 4.62CALLS_i \qquad (1.29)$$

where: $GIFT_i$ = the 2008 annual fund donation (in dollars) from the ith alum

$INCOME_i$ = the 2008 estimated income (in dollars) of the ith alum

$CALLS_i$ = the # of calls to the ith alum asking for a donation in 2008

---

14. Fabio Silva and Jon Sonstelie, "Did Serrano Cause a Decline in School Spending?" *National Tax Review*, Vol. 48, No. 2, pp. 199–215. The authors also included the tax price for spending per pupil in the ith state as a variable.

a. Carefully explain the meaning of each estimated coefficient. Are the estimated signs what you expected?

b. Why is the left-hand variable in your friend's equation $\widehat{GIFT_i}$ and not $GIFT_i$?

c. Your friend didn't include the stochastic error term in the estimated equation. Was this a mistake? Why or why not?

d. Suppose that your friend decides to change the units of INCOME from "dollars" to "thousands of dollars." What will happen to the estimated coefficients of the equation? Be specific.

e. If you could add one more variable to this equation, what would it be? Explain.

10. Housing price models can be estimated with time-series as well as cross-sectional data. If you study aggregate time-series housing prices (see Table 1.2 for data and sources), you have:

$$
\begin{array}{c}
+ \\
\hat{P}_t = f(GDP) = 12{,}928 + 17.08Y_t \\
N = 38 \text{ (annual 1970–2007)}
\end{array}
$$

where: P_t = the nominal median price of new single-family houses in the United States in year t

Y_t = the U.S. GDP in year t (billions of current $)

a. Carefully interpret the economic meaning of the estimated coefficients.

b. What is Y_t doing on the right side of the equation? Isn't Y always supposed to be on the left side?

c. Both the price and GDP variables are measured in nominal (or current, as opposed to real, or inflation-adjusted) dollars. Thus a major portion of the excellent explanatory power of this equation (almost 99 percent of the variation in P_t can be explained by Y_t alone) comes from capturing the huge amount of inflation that took place between 1970 and 2007. What could you do to eliminate the impact of inflation in this equation?

d. GDP is included in the equation to measure more than just inflation. What factors in housing prices other than inflation does the GDP variable help capture? Can you think of a variable that might do a better job?

e. To be sure that you understand the difference between a cross-sectional data set and a time-series data set, compare the variable you thought of in part d with a variable that you could add to Equation 1.22. The dependent variable in both equations is the price of a house. Could you add the same independent variable to both equations? Explain.

Table 1.2 Data for the Time-Series Model of Housing Prices

t	Year	Price (P_t)	GDP (Y_t)
1	1970	23,400	1,038.5
2	1971	25,200	1,127.1
3	1972	27,600	1,238.3
4	1973	32,500	1,382.7
5	1974	35,900	1,500.0
6	1975	39,300	1,638.3
7	1976	44,200	1,825.3
8	1977	48,800	2,030.9
9	1978	55,700	2,294.7
10	1979	62,900	2,563.3
11	1980	64,600	2,789.5
12	1981	68,900	3,128.4
13	1982	69,300	3,255.0
14	1983	75,300	3,536.7
15	1984	79,900	3,933.2
16	1985	84,300	4,220.3
17	1986	92,000	4,462.8
18	1987	104,500	4,739.5
19	1988	112,500	5,103.8
20	1989	120,000	5,484.4
21	1990	122,900	5,803.1
22	1991	120,000	5,995.9
23	1992	121,500	6,337.7
24	1993	126,500	6,657.4
25	1994	130,000	7,072.2
26	1995	133,900	7,397.7
27	1996	140,000	7,816.9
28	1997	146,000	8,304.3
29	1998	152,500	8,747.0
30	1999	161,000	9,268.4
31	2000	169,000	9,817.0
32	2001	175,200	10,128.0
33	2002	187,600	10,469.6
34	2003	195,000	10,960.8
35	2004	221,000	11,685.9
36	2005	240,900	12,421.9
37	2006	246,500	13,178.4
38	2007	247,900	13,807.5

P_t = the nominal median price of new single-family houses in the United States in year t.
(Source: *The Statistical Abstract of the U.S.*)
Y_t = the U.S. GDP in year t (billions of current dollars). (Source: *The Economic Report of the President*)

Datafile = HOUSE1

11. The distinction between the stochastic error term and the residual is one of the most difficult concepts to master in this chapter.
    a. List at least three differences between the error term and the residual.
    b. Usually, we can never observe the error term, but we can get around this difficulty if we assume values for the true coefficients. Calculate values of the error term and residual for each of the following six observations given that the true β_0 equals 0.0, the true β_1 equals 1.5, and the estimated regression equation is $\hat{Y}_i = 0.48 + 1.32X_i$:

Y_i	2	6	3	8	5	4
X_i	1	4	2	5	3	4

    (*Hint:* To answer this question, you'll have to solve Equation 1.14 for ϵ.) Note: Datafile = EX1.

12. Let's return to the wage determination example of Section 1.2. In that example, we built a model of the wage of the *i*th worker in a particular field as a function of the work experience, education, and gender of that worker:

$$WAGE_i = \beta_0 + \beta_1 EXP_i + \beta_2 EDU_i + \beta_3 GEND_i + \epsilon_i \qquad (1.12)$$

where: Y_i = $WAGE_i$ = the wage of the *i*th worker
   X_{1i} = EXP_i = the years of work experience of the *i*th worker
   X_{2i} = EDU_i = the years of education beyond high school of the *i*th worker
   X_{3i} = $GEND_i$ = the gender of the *i*th worker (1 = male and 0 = female)

    a. What is the real-world meaning of β_2? (*Hint:* If you're unsure where to start, review Section 1.2.)
    b. What is the real-world meaning of β_3? (*Hint:* Remember that GEND is a dummy variable.)
    c. Suppose that you wanted to add a variable to this equation to measure whether there might be discrimination against people of color. How would you define such a variable? Be specific.
    d. Suppose that you had the opportunity to add another variable to the equation. Which of the following possibilities would seem best? Explain your answer.

        i. the age of the *i*th worker
        ii. the number of jobs in this field
        iii. the average wage in this field

iv. the number of "employee of the month" awards won by the ith worker

v. the number of children of the ith worker

13. Have you heard of "RateMyProfessors.com"? On this website, students evaluate a professor's overall teaching ability and a variety of other attributes. The website then summarizes these student-submitted ratings for the benefit of any student considering taking a class from the professor.

  Two of the most interesting attributes that the website tracks are how "easy" the professor is (in terms of workload and grading), and how "hot" the professor is (presumably in terms of physical attractiveness). A recently published article[15] indicates that being "hot" improves a professor's rating more than being "easy." To investigate these ideas ourselves, we created the following equation for RateMyProfessors.com:

$$RATING_i = \beta_0 + \beta_1 EASE_i + \beta_2 HOT_i + \epsilon_i \qquad (1.30)$$

where: $RATING_i$ = the overall rating (5 = best) of the ith professor
  $EASE_i$ = the easiness rating (5 = easiest) of the ith professor
  HOT_i = 1 if the ith professor is considered "hot," 0 otherwise

To estimate Equation 1.30, we need data, and Table 1.3 contains data for these variables from 25 randomly chosen professors on RateMyProfessors.com. If we estimate Equation 1.30 with the data in Table 1.3, we obtain:

$$\widehat{RATING_i} = 3.23 + 0.01 EASE_i + 0.59 HOT_i \qquad (1.31)$$

a. Take a look at Equation 1.31. Do the estimated coefficients support our expectations? Explain.

b. See if you can reproduce the results in Equation 1.31 on your own. To do this, take the data in Table 1.3 and use EViews, Stata, or your own regression program to estimate the coefficients from these data. If you do everything correctly, you should be able to verify the estimates in Equation 1.31. (If you're not sure how to get started on this question, take a look at the answer to Exercise 2 in Appendix A.)

c. This model includes two independent variables. Does it make sense to think that the teaching rating of a professor depends on

---

15. James Otto, Douglas Sanford, and Douglas Ross, "Does RateMyProfessors.com Really Rate My Professor?" *Assessment and Evaluation in Higher Education*, August 2008, pp. 355–368.

Table 1.3 RateMyProfessors.com Ratings

Observation	RATING	EASE	HOT
1	2.8	3.7	0
2	4.3	4.1	1
3	4.0	2.8	1
4	3.0	3.0	0
5	4.3	2.4	0
6	2.7	2.7	0
7	3.0	3.3	0
8	3.7	2.7	0
9	3.9	3.0	1
10	2.7	3.2	0
11	4.2	1.9	1
12	1.9	4.8	0
13	3.5	2.4	1
14	2.1	2.5	0
15	2.0	2.7	1
16	3.8	1.6	0
17	4.1	2.4	0
18	5.0	3.1	1
19	1.2	1.6	0
20	3.7	3.1	0
21	3.6	3.0	0
22	3.3	2.1	0
23	3.2	2.5	0
24	4.8	3.3	0
25	4.6	3.0	0

Datafile = RATE1

just these two variables? What other variable(s) do you think might be important?

d. Suppose that you were able to add your suggested variable(s) to Equation 1.31. What do you think would happen to the coefficients of EASE and HOT when you added the variable(s)? Would you expect them to change? Would you expect them to remain the same? Explain.

e. (optional) Go to the RateMyProfessors.com website, choose 25 observations at random, and estimate your own version of Equation 1.30. Now compare your regression results to those in Equation 1.31. Do your estimated coefficients have the same signs as those in Equation 1.31? Are your estimated coefficients exactly the same as those in Equation 1.31? Why or why not?

2 Ordinary Least Squares

The bread and butter of regression analysis is the estimation of the coefficients of econometric models with a technique called Ordinary Least Squares (OLS). The first two sections of this chapter summarize the reasoning behind and the mechanics of OLS. Regression users rely on computers to do the actual OLS calculations, so the emphasis here is on understanding what OLS attempts to do and how it goes about doing it.

How can you tell a good equation from a bad one once it has been estimated? There are a number of useful criteria, including the extent to which the estimated equation fits the actual data. A focus on fit is not without perils, however, so the chapter concludes with an example of the misuse of this criterion.

2.1 Estimating Single-Independent-Variable Models with OLS

The purpose of regression analysis is to take a purely theoretical equation like:

$$Y_i = \beta_0 + \beta_1 X_i + \epsilon_i \tag{2.1}$$

and use a set of data to create an estimated equation like:

$$\hat{Y}_i = \hat{\beta}_0 + \hat{\beta}_1 X_i \tag{2.2}$$

where each "hat" indicates a sample estimate of the true population value. (In the case of Y, the "true population value" is $E[Y|X]$.) The purpose of the estimation technique is to obtain numerical values for the coefficients of an otherwise completely theoretical regression equation.

The most widely used method of obtaining these estimates is Ordinary Least Squares (OLS), which has become so standard that its estimates are presented as a point of reference even when results from other estimation techniques are used. **Ordinary Least Squares (OLS)** is a regression estimation technique that calculates the $\hat{\beta}$s so as to minimize the sum of the squared residuals, thus:[1]

$$\text{OLS minimizes } \sum_{i=1}^{N} e_i^2 \qquad (i = 1, 2, \ldots, N) \qquad (2.3)$$

Since these residuals (e_is) are the differences between the actual Ys and the estimated Ys produced by the regression (the $\hat{Y}$s in Equation 2.2), Equation 2.3 is equivalent to saying that OLS minimizes $\sum (Y_i - \hat{Y}_i)^2$.

Why Use Ordinary Least Squares?

Although OLS is the most-used regression estimation technique, it's not the only one. Indeed, econometricians have developed what seem like zillions of different estimation techniques, a number of which we'll discuss later in this text.

There are at least three important reasons for using OLS to estimate regression models:

1. OLS is relatively easy to use.
2. The goal of minimizing $\sum e_i^2$ is quite appropriate from a theoretical point of view.
3. OLS estimates have a number of useful characteristics.

---

1. The summation symbol, $\sum$, means that all terms to its right should be added (or summed) over the range of the i values attached to the bottom and top of the symbol. In Equation 2.3, for example, this would mean adding up e_i^2 for all integer values between 1 and N:

$$\sum_{i=1}^{N} e_i^2 = e_1^2 + e_2^2 + \cdots + e_N^2$$

Often the $\sum$ notation is simply written as $\sum_i$, and it is assumed that the summation is over all observations from i = 1 to i = N. Sometimes, the i is omitted entirely and the same assumption is made implicitly. For more practice in the basics of summation algebra, see Exercise 3.

The first reason for using OLS is that it's the simplest of all econometric estimation techniques. Most other techniques involve complicated non-linear formulas or iterative procedures, many of which are extensions of OLS itself. In contrast, OLS estimates are simple enough that, if you had to, you could compute them without using a computer or a calculator (for a single-independent-variable model). Indeed, in the "dark ages" before computers and calculators, econometricians calculated OLS estimates by hand!

The second reason for using OLS is that minimizing the summed, squared residuals is a reasonable goal for an estimation technique. To see this, recall that the residual measures how close the estimated regression equation comes to the actual observed data:

$$e_i = Y_i - \hat{Y}_i \qquad (i = 1, 2, \ldots, N) \qquad (1.17)$$

Since it's reasonable to want our estimated regression equation to be as close as possible to the observed data, you might think that you'd want to minimize these residuals. The main problem with simply totaling the residuals is that e_i can be negative as well as positive. Thus, negative and positive residuals might cancel each other out, allowing a wildly inaccurate equation to have a very low $\sum e_i$. For example, if $Y = 100,000$ for two consecutive observations and if your equation predicts 1.1 million and $-900,000$, respectively, your residuals will be $+1$ million and -1 million, which add up to zero!

We could get around this problem by minimizing the sum of the absolute values of the residuals, but absolute values are difficult to work with mathematically. Luckily, minimizing the summed squared residuals does the job. Squared functions pose no unusual mathematical difficulties in terms of manipulations, and the technique avoids canceling positive and negative residuals because squared terms are always positive.

The final reason for using OLS is that its estimates have at least two useful characteristics:

1. The sum of the residuals is exactly zero.
2. OLS can be shown to be the "best" estimator possible under a set of specific assumptions. We'll define "best" in Chapter 4.

An **estimator** is a mathematical technique that is applied to a sample of data to produce real-world numerical **estimates** of the true population regression coefficients (or other parameters). Thus, OLS is an estimator, and a $\hat{\beta}$ produced by OLS is an estimate.

How Does OLS Work?

How would OLS estimate a single-independent-variable regression model like Equation 2.1?

$$Y_i = \beta_0 + \beta_1 X_i + \epsilon_i \qquad (2.1)$$

OLS selects those estimates of β_0 and β_1 that minimize the squared residuals, summed over all the sample data points.

For an equation with just one independent variable, these coefficients are:[2]

$$\hat{\beta}_1 = \frac{\sum_{i=1}^{N} [(X_i - \overline{X})(Y_i - \overline{Y})]}{\sum_{i=1}^{N} (X_i - \overline{X})^2} \qquad (2.4)$$

and, given this estimate of β_1,

$$\hat{\beta}_0 = \overline{Y} - \hat{\beta}_1 \overline{X} \qquad (2.5)$$

where $\overline{X}$ = the mean of X, or $\sum X_i / N$, and $\overline{Y}$ = the mean of Y, or $\sum Y_i / N$. Note that for each different data set, we'll get different estimates of β_1 and β_0, depending on the sample.

---

2. Since

$$\sum_{i=1}^{N} e_i^2 = \sum_{i=1}^{N} (Y_i - \hat{Y}_i)^2$$

and $\hat{Y}_i = \hat{\beta}_0 + \hat{\beta} X_{1i}$, OLS actually minimizes

$$\sum_i e_i^2 = \sum_i (Y_i - \hat{\beta}_0 - \hat{\beta}_1 X_i)^2$$

by choosing the $\hat{\beta}$s that do so. For those with a moderate grasp of calculus and algebra, the derivation of these equations is informative. See Exercise 12.

An Illustration of OLS Estimation

The equations for calculating regression coefficients might seem a little forbidding, but it's not hard to apply them yourself to data sets that have only a few observations and independent variables. Although you'll usually want to use regression software packages to do your estimation, you'll understand OLS better if you work through the following illustration.

To keep things simple, let's attempt to estimate the regression coefficients of the height and weight data given in Section 1.4. For your convenience in following this illustration, the original data are reproduced in Table 2.1. As was noted previously, the formulas for OLS estimation for a regression equation with one independent variable are Equations 2.4 and 2.5:

$$\hat{\beta}_1 = \frac{\sum\limits_{i=1}^{N} [(X_i - \bar{X})(Y_i - \bar{Y})]}{\sum\limits_{i=1}^{N} (X_i - \bar{X})^2} \tag{2.4}$$

$$\hat{\beta}_0 = \bar{Y} - \hat{\beta}_1 \bar{X} \tag{2.5}$$

If we undertake the calculations outlined in Table 2.1 and substitute them into Equations 2.4 and 2.5, we obtain these values:

$$\hat{\beta}_1 = \frac{590.20}{92.50} = 6.38$$

$$\hat{\beta}_0 = 169.4 - (6.38 \cdot 10.35) = 103.4$$

or

$$\hat{Y}_i = 103.4 + 6.38X_i \tag{2.6}$$

If you compare these estimates, you'll find that the manually calculated coefficient estimates are the same as the computer regression results summarized in Section 1.4.

As can be seen in Table 2.1, the sum of the $\hat{Y}$s (column 8) equals the sum of the Ys (column 2), so the sum of the residuals (column 9) does indeed equal zero (except for rounding errors).

Table 2.1   The Calculation of Estimated Regression Coefficients
                for the Weight/Height Example

Raw Data			Required Intermediate Calculations					
i	Y_i	X_i	$(Y_i - \bar{Y})$	$(X_i - \bar{X})$	$(X_i - \bar{X})^2$	$(X_i - \bar{X})(Y_i - \bar{Y})$	$\hat{Y}_i$	$e_i = Y_i - \hat{Y}_i$
(1)	(2)	(3)	(4)	(5)	(6)	(7)	(8)	(9)
1	140	5	−29.40	−5.35	28.62	157.29	135.3	4.7
2	157	9	−12.40	−1.35	1.82	16.74	160.8	−3.8
3	205	13	35.60	2.65	7.02	94.34	186.3	18.7
4	198	12	28.60	1.65	2.72	47.19	179.9	18.1
5	162	10	−7.40	−0.35	0.12	2.59	167.2	−5.2
6	174	11	4.60	0.65	0.42	2.99	173.6	0.4
7	150	8	−19.40	−2.35	5.52	45.59	154.4	−4.4
8	165	9	−4.40	−1.35	1.82	5.94	160.8	4.2
9	170	10	0.60	−0.35	0.12	−0.21	167.2	2.8
10	180	12	10.60	1.65	2.72	17.49	179.9	0.1
11	170	11	0.60	0.65	0.42	0.39	173.6	−3.6
12	162	9	−7.40	−1.35	1.82	9.99	160.8	1.2
13	165	10	−4.40	−0.35	0.12	1.54	167.2	2.2
14	180	12	10.60	1.65	2.72	17.49	179.9	0.1
15	160	8	−9.40	−2.35	5.52	22.09	154.4	5.6
16	155	9	−14.40	−1.35	1.82	19.44	160.8	−5.8
17	165	10	−4.40	−0.35	0.12	1.54	167.2	−2.2
18	190	15	20.60	4.65	21.62	95.79	199.1	−9.1
19	185	13	15.60	2.65	7.02	41.34	186.3	−1.3
20	155	11	−14.40	0.65	0.42	−9.36	173.6	−18.6
Sum	3388	207	0.0	0.0	92.50	590.20	3388.3	−0.3
Mean	169.4	10.35	0.0	0.0			169.4	0.0

2.2 Estimating Multivariate Regression Models with OLS

Let's face it: only a few dependent variables can be explained fully by a single independent variable. A person's weight, for example, is influenced by more than just that person's height. What about bone structure, percent body fat, exercise habits, or diet?

As important as additional explanatory variables might seem to the height/weight example, there's even more reason to include a variety of independent variables in economic and business applications. Although the quantity demanded of a product is certainly affected by price, that's not the whole story. Advertising, aggregate income, the prices of substitutes, the influence of foreign markets, the quality of customer service, possible fads, and changing tastes all are important in real-world models. As a result, it's vital to move from single-independent-variable regressions to *multivariate regression models,* or equations with more than one independent variable.

The Meaning of Multivariate Regression Coefficients

The general multivariate regression model with K independent variables can be represented by Equation 1.13:

$$Y_i = \beta_0 + \beta_1 X_{1i} + \beta_2 X_{2i} + \cdots + \beta_K X_{Ki} + \epsilon_i \qquad (1.13)$$

where i, as before, goes from 1 to N and indicates the observation number. Thus, X_{1i} indicates the *i*th observation of independent variable X_1, while X_{2i} indicates the *i*th observation of another independent variable, X_2.

The biggest difference between a single-independent-variable regression model and a multivariate regression model is in the interpretation of the latter's slope coefficients. These coefficients, often called *partial* regression coefficients,[3] are defined to allow a researcher to distinguish the impact of one variable from that of other independent variables.

> Specifically, a **multivariate regression coefficient** indicates the change in the dependent variable associated with a one-unit increase in the independent variable in question *holding constant the other independent variables in the equation.*

This last italicized phrase is a key to understanding multiple regression (as multivariate regression is often called). The coefficient β_1 measures the impact on Y of a one-unit increase in X_1, holding constant X_2, X_3, . . . and X_K but *not* holding constant any relevant variables that might have been omitted

---

3. The term "partial regression coefficient" will seem especially appropriate to those readers who have taken calculus, since multivariate regression coefficients correspond to partial derivatives. Indeed, in Equation 1.13 the partial derivative of Y_i with respect to X_{1i} is β_1, etc.

from the equation (e.g., X_{K+1}). The coefficient β_0 is the value of Y when all the Xs and the error term equal zero. As you'll learn in Section 7.1, you should always include a constant term in a regression equation, but you should not rely on estimates of β_0 for inference.

As an example, let's consider the following annual model of the per capita demand for beef in the United States:

$$\widehat{CB}_t = 37.54 - 0.88P_t + 11.9Yd_t \tag{2.7}$$

where: $\widehat{CB}_t$ = the per capita consumption of beef in year t (in pounds per person)

P_t = the price of beef in year t (in cents per pound)

Yd_t = the per capita disposable income in year t (in thousands of dollars)

The estimated coefficient of income, 11.9, tells us that beef consumption will increase by 11.9 pounds per person if per capita disposable income goes up by $1,000, holding constant the price of beef. The ability to hold price constant is crucial because we'd expect such a large increase in per capita income to stimulate demand, therefore pushing up prices and making it hard to distinguish the effect of the income increase from the effect of the price increase. The multivariate regression estimate allows us to focus on the impact of the income variable by holding the price variable constant.

Note, however, that the equation does not hold constant other possible variables (like the price of a substitute) because these variables are not included in Equation 2.7. Before you move on to the next section, take the time to think through the meaning of the estimated coefficient of P in Equation 2.7; do you agree that the sign and relative size fit with economic theory?

OLS Estimation of Multivariate Regression Models

The application of OLS to an equation with more than one independent variable is quite similar to its application to a single-independent-variable model. To see this, consider the estimation of the simplest possible multivariate model, one with just two independent variables:

$$Y_i = \beta_0 + \beta_1 X_{1i} + \beta_2 X_{2i} + \epsilon_i \tag{2.8}$$

The goal of OLS is to choose those $\hat{\beta}$s that minimize the summed square residuals. These residuals are now from a multivariate model, but they can be minimized using the same mathematical approach used in Section 2.1. Thus the

OLS estimation of multivariate models is identical in general approach to the OLS estimation of models with just one independent variable. The equations themselves are more cumbersome,[4] but the underlying principle of estimating $\hat{\beta}$s that minimize the summed squared residuals remains the same.

Luckily, user-friendly computer packages can calculate estimates with these cumbersome equations in less than a second of computer time. Indeed, only someone lost in time or stranded on a desert island would bother estimating a multivariate regression model without a computer. The rest of us will use EViews, Stata, SPSS, SAS, or any of the other commercially available regression packages.

An Example of a Multivariate Regression Model

As an example of multivariate regression, let's take a look at a model of financial aid awards at a liberal arts college. The dependent variable in such a study would be the amount, in dollars, awarded to a particular financial aid applicant:

$FINAID_i$ = the financial aid (measured in dollars of grant per year) awarded to the ith applicant

What kinds of independent variables might influence the amount of financial aid received by a given student? Well, most aid is either need-based or merit-based, so it makes sense to consider a model that includes at least these two attributes:

$$\overset{-\quad\quad\quad\quad+}{FINAID_i = f(PARENT_i, HSRANK_i)} \tag{2.9}$$

and

$$FINAID_i = \beta_0 + \beta_1 PARENT_i, + \beta_2 HSRANK_i + \epsilon_i \tag{2.10}$$

---

4. For Equation 2.8, the estimated coefficients are:

$$\hat{\beta}_1 = \frac{(\sum yx_1)(\sum x_2^2) - (\sum yx_2)(\sum x_1 x_2)}{(\sum x_1^2)(\sum x_2^2) - (\sum x_1 x_2)^2}$$

$$\hat{\beta}_2 = \frac{(\sum yx_2)(\sum x_1^2) - (\sum yx_1)(\sum x_1 x_2)}{(\sum x_1^2)(\sum x_2^2) - (\sum x_1 x_2)^2}$$

$$\hat{\beta}_0 = \bar{Y} - \hat{\beta}_1 \bar{X}_1 - \hat{\beta}_2 \bar{X}_2$$

where lowercase variables indicate deviations from the mean, as in $y = Y_i - \bar{Y}$; $x_1 = X_{1i} - \bar{X}_1$; and $x_2 = X_{2i} - \bar{X}_2$.

where: $PARENT_i$ = the amount (in dollars per year) that the parents of the ith student are judged able to contribute to college expenses

$HSRANK_i$ = the ith student's GPA rank in high school, measured as a percentage (ranging from a low of 0 to a high of 100)

Note from the signs over the independent variables in Equation 2.9 that we anticipate that the more parents can contribute to their child's education, the less the financial aid award will be. Similarly, we expect that the higher the student's rank in high school, the higher the financial aid award will be. Do you agree with these expectations?

If we estimate Equation 2.10 using OLS and the data[5] in Table 2.2, we get:

$$\widehat{FINAID_i} = 8927 - 0.36PARENT_i + 87.4HSRANK_i \qquad (2.11)$$

What do these coefficients mean? Well, the −0.36 means that the model implies that the ith student's financial aid grant will fall by $0.36 for every dollar increase in his or her parents' ability to pay, holding constant high school rank. Does the sign of the estimated coefficient meet our expectations? Yes. Does the size of the coefficient make sense? Yes.

To be sure that you understand this concept, take the time to write down the meaning of the coefficient of HSRANK in Equation 2.11. Do you agree that the model implies that the ith student's financial aid grant will increase by $87.40 for each percentage point increase in high school rank, holding constant parents' ability to pay? Does this estimated coefficient seem reasonable?

To illustrate, take a look at Figures 2.1 and 2.2. These figures contain two different views of Equation 2.11. Figure 2.1 is a diagram of the effect of PARENT on FINAID, holding HSRANK constant, and Figure 2.2 shows the effect of HSRANK on FINAID, holding PARENT constant. These two figures are graphical representations of multivariate regression coefficients, since they measure the impact on the dependent variable of a given independent variable, holding constant the other variables in the equation.

---

5. These data are from an unpublished analysis of financial aid awards at Occidental College. The fourth variable in Table 2.2 is $MALE_i$, which equals 1 if the ith student is male and 0 otherwise. This variable will be used in Exercise 11 in Chapter 6.

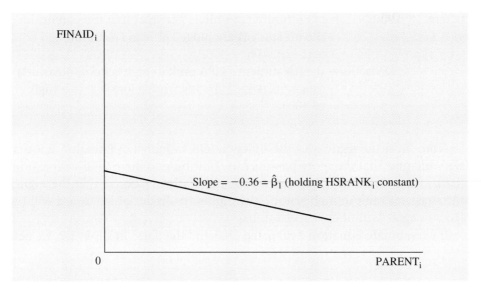

Figure 2.1 Financial Aid as a Function of Parents' Ability to Pay

In Equation 2.11, an increase of one dollar in the parents' ability to pay decreases the financial aid award by $0.36, holding constant high school rank.

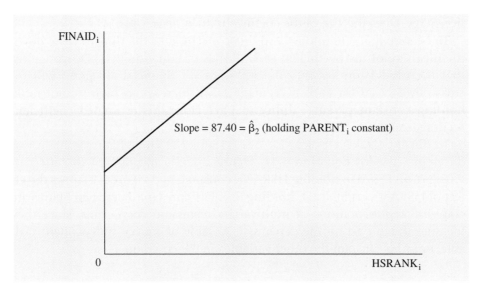

Figure 2.2 Financial Aid as a Function of High School Rank

In Equation 2.11, an increase of one percentage point in high school rank increases the financial aid award by $87.40, holding constant parents' ability to pay.

Table 2.2 Data for the Financial Aid Example

i	FINAID	PARENT	HSRANK	MALE
1	19,640	0	92	0
2	8,325	9,147	44	1
3	12,950	7,063	89	0
4	700	33,344	97	1
5	7,000	20,497	95	1
6	11,325	10,487	96	0
7	19,165	519	98	1
8	7,000	31,758	70	0
9	7,925	16,358	49	0
10	11,475	10,495	80	0
11	18,790	0	90	0
12	8,890	18,304	75	1
13	17,590	2,059	91	1
14	17,765	0	81	0
15	14,100	15,602	98	0
16	18,965	0	80	0
17	4,500	22,259	90	1
18	7,950	5,014	82	1
19	7,000	34,266	98	1
20	7,275	11,569	50	0
21	8,000	30,260	98	1
22	4,290	19,617	40	1
23	8,175	12,934	49	1
24	11,350	8,349	91	0
25	15,325	5,392	82	1
26	22,148	0	98	0
27	17,420	3,207	99	0
28	18,990	0	90	0
29	11,175	10,894	97	0
30	14,100	5,010	59	0
31	7,000	24,718	97	1
32	7,850	9,715	84	1
33	0	64,305	84	0
34	7,000	31,947	98	1
35	16,100	8,683	95	1
36	8,000	24,817	99	0
37	8,500	8,720	20	1
38	7,575	12,750	89	1
39	13,750	2,417	41	1
40	7,000	26,846	92	1
41	11,200	7,013	86	1
42	14,450	6,300	87	0

(continued)

Table 2.2 (*continued*)

i	FINAID	PARENT	HSRANK	MALE
43	15,265	3,909	84	0
44	20,470	2,027	99	1
45	9,550	12,592	89	0
46	15,970	0	57	0
47	12,190	6,249	84	0
48	11,800	6,237	81	0
49	21,640	0	99	0
50	9,200	10,535	68	0

Datafile = FINAID2

Total, Explained, and Residual Sums of Squares

Before going on, let's pause to develop some measures of how much of the variation of the dependent variable is explained by the estimated regression equation. Such comparison of the estimated values with the actual values can help a researcher judge the adequacy of an estimated regression.

Econometricians use the squared variations of Y around its mean as a measure of the amount of variation to be explained by the regression. This computed quantity is usually called the **total sum of squares,** or TSS, and is written as:

$$\text{TSS} = \sum_{i=1}^{N} (Y_i - \bar{Y})^2 \tag{2.12}$$

For Ordinary Least Squares, the total sum of squares has two components, variation that can be explained by the regression and variation that cannot:

$$\sum_i (Y_i - \bar{Y})^2 = \sum_i (\hat{Y}_i - \bar{Y})^2 + \sum_i e_i^2 \tag{2.13}$$

Total Sum	=	Explained	+	Residual
of		Sum of		Sum of
Squares		Squares		Squares
(TSS)		(ESS)		(RSS)

This is usually called the **decomposition of variance**.

Figure 2.3 illustrates the decomposition of variance for a simple regression model. The estimated values of Y_i lie on the estimated regression line

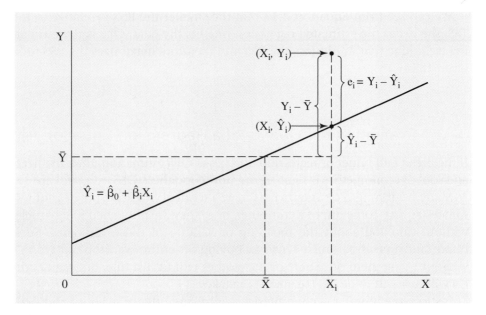

Figure 2.3 Decomposition of the Variance in Y

The variation of Y around its mean $(Y - \bar{Y})$ can be decomposed into two parts:
(1) $(\hat{Y}_i - \bar{Y})$, the difference between the estimated value of $Y(\hat{Y})$ and the mean value of
Y $(\bar{Y})$; and (2) $(Y_i - \hat{Y}_i)$, the difference between the actual value of Y and the estimated
value of Y.

$\hat{Y}_i = \hat{\beta}_0 + \hat{\beta}_1 X_i$. The variation of Y around its mean $(Y_i - \bar{Y})$ can be decomposed into two parts: (1) $(\hat{Y}_i - \bar{Y})$, the difference between the estimated
value of Y $(\hat{Y})$ and the mean value of Y $(\bar{Y})$; and (2) $(Y_i - \hat{Y}_i)$, the difference
between the actual value of Y and the estimated value of Y.

The first component of Equation 2.13 measures the amount of the
squared deviation of Y_i from its mean that is explained by the regression
line. This component of the total sum of the squared deviations, called the
explained sum of squares, or ESS, is attributable to the fitted regression
line. The unexplained portion of TSS (that is, unexplained in an empirical
sense by the estimated regression equation), is called the **residual sum of
squares,** or RSS.[6]

---

6. Note that some authors reverse the definitions of RSS and ESS (defining ESS as $\sum e_i^2$), and
other authors reverse the order of the letters, as in SSR.

We can see from Equation 2.13 that the smaller the RSS is relative to the TSS, the better the estimated regression line fits the data. OLS is the estimating technique that minimizes the RSS and therefore maximizes the ESS for a given TSS.

2.3 Evaluating the Quality of a Regression Equation

If the bread and butter of regression analysis is OLS estimation, then the heart and soul of econometrics is figuring out how good these OLS estimates are.

Many beginning econometricians have a tendency to accept regression estimates as they come out of a computer, or as they are published in an article, without thinking about the meaning or validity of those estimates. Such blind faith makes as much sense as buying an entire wardrobe of clothes without trying them on. Some of the clothes will fit just fine, but many others will turn out to be big (or small) mistakes.

Instead, the job of an econometrician is to carefully think about and evaluate every aspect of the equation, from the underlying theory to the quality of the data, before accepting a regression result as valid. In fact, most good econometricians spend quite a bit of time thinking about what to expect from an equation *before* they estimate that equation.

Once the computer estimates have been produced, however, it's time to evaluate the regression results. The list of questions that should be asked during such an evaluation is long. For example:

1. Is the equation supported by sound theory?
2. How well does the estimated regression fit the data?
3. Is the data set reasonably large and accurate?
4. Is OLS the best estimator to be used for this equation?
5. How well do the estimated coefficients correspond to the expectations developed by the researcher before the data were collected?
6. Are all the obviously important variables included in the equation?
7. Has the most theoretically logical functional form been used?
8. Does the regression appear to be free of major econometric problems?

The goal of this text is to help you develop the ability to ask and appropriately answer these kinds of questions. In fact, the number in front of each question above roughly corresponds to the chapter in which we'll address the issues raised by that question. Since this is Chapter 2, it'll come as no surprise to you to hear that the rest of the chapter will be devoted to the second of these topics—the overall fit of the estimated model.

2.4 Describing the Overall Fit of the Estimated Model

Let's face it: we expect that a good estimated regression equation will explain the variation of the dependent variable in the sample fairly accurately. If it does, we say that the estimated model fits the data well.

Looking at the overall fit of an estimated model is useful not only for evaluating the quality of the regression, but also for comparing models that have different data sets or combinations of independent variables. We can never be sure that one estimated model represents the truth any more than another, but evaluating the quality of the fit of the equation is one ingredient in a choice between different formulations of a regression model. Be careful, however! The quality of the fit is a minor ingredient in this choice, and many beginning researchers allow themselves to be overly influenced by it.

R^2

The simplest commonly used measure of fit is R^2 or the coefficient of determination. $\mathbf{R^2}$ is the ratio of the explained sum of squares to the total sum of squares:

$$R^2 = \frac{ESS}{TSS} = 1 - \frac{RSS}{TSS} = 1 - \frac{\sum e_i^2}{\sum (Y_i - \bar{Y})^2} \tag{2.14}$$

The higher R^2 is, the closer the estimated regression equation fits the sample data. Measures of this type are called "goodness of fit" measures. R^2 measures the percentage of the variation of Y around $\bar{Y}$ that is explained by the regression equation. Since OLS selects the coefficient estimates that minimize RSS, OLS provides the largest possible R^2, given a linear model. Since TSS, RSS, and ESS are all nonnegative (being squared deviations), and since ESS $\leq$ TSS, R^2 must lie in the interval $0 \leq R^2 \leq 1$, a value of R^2 close to one shows an excellent overall fit, whereas a value near zero shows a failure of the estimated regression equation to explain the values of Y_i better than could be explained by the sample mean $\bar{Y}$.

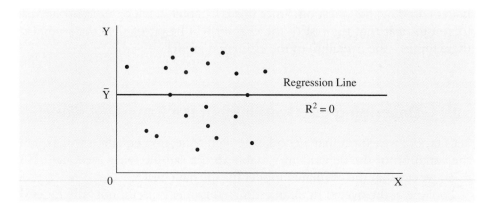

Figure 2.4
X and Y are not related; in such a case, R^2 would be 0.

Figures 2.4 through 2.6 demonstrate some extremes. Figure 2.4 shows an X and Y that are unrelated. The fitted regression line might as well be $\hat{Y} = \overline{Y}$, the same value it would have if X were omitted. As a result, the estimated linear regression is no better than the sample mean as an estimate of Y_i. The explained portion, ESS, = 0, and the unexplained portion, RSS, equals the total squared deviations TSS; thus, $R^2 = 0$.

Figure 2.5 shows a relationship between X and Y that can be "explained" quite well by a linear regression equation: the value of R^2 is .95. This kind of result is typical of a time-series regression with a good fit. Most of the variation has been explained, but there still remains a portion of the variation that is essentially random or unexplained by the model.

Goodness of fit is relative to the topic being studied. In time series data, we often get a very high R^2 because there can be significant time trends on both sides of the equation. In cross-sectional data, we often get low R^2s because the observations (say, countries) differ in ways that are not easily quantified. In such a situation, an R^2 of .50 might be considered a good fit, and researchers would tend to focus on identifying the variables that have a substantive impact on the dependent variable, not on R^2. In other words, there is no simple method of determining how high R^2 must be for the fit to be considered satisfactory. Instead, knowing when R^2 is relatively large or small is a matter of experience. It should be noted that a high R^2 does not imply that changes in X lead to changes in Y, as there may be an underlying variable whose changes lead to changes in both X and Y simultaneously.

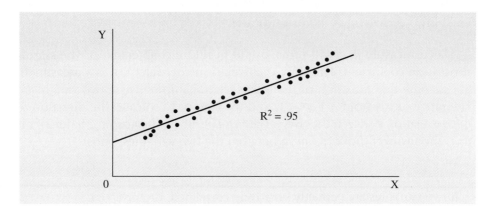

Figure 2.5
A set of data for X and Y that can be "explained" quite well with a regression line
($R^2 = .95$).

Figure 2.6 shows a perfect fit of $R^2 = 1$. Such a fit implies that no estimation is required. The relationship is completely deterministic, and the
slope and intercept can be calculated from the coordinates of any two
points. In fact, reported equations with R^2s equal to (or very near) one
should be viewed with suspicion; they very likely do not explain the movements of the dependent variable Y in terms of the causal proposition advanced, even though they explain them empirically. This caution applies to
economic applications, but not necessarily to those in fields like physics or
chemistry.

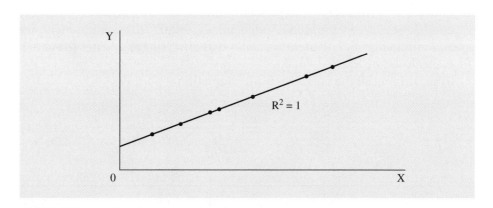

Figure 2.6
A perfect fit: all the data points are on the regression line, and the resulting R^2 is 1.

The Simple Correlation Coefficient, r

A related measure that will prove useful in future chapters is "r," the simple correlation coefficient. The **simple correlation coefficient, r**, is a measure of the strength and direction of the linear relationship between two variables.[7] The range of r is from +1 to −1, and the sign of r indicates the direction of the correlation between the two variables. The closer the absolute value of r is to 1, the stronger the correlation between the two variables. Thus:

> If two variables are perfectly positively correlated, then r = +1
>
> If two variables are perfectly negatively correlated, then r = −1
>
> If two variables are totally uncorrelated, then r = 0

We'll use the simple correlation coefficient in Chapter 6 and every chapter thereafter to describe the correlation between two variables. Interestingly, it turns out that r and R^2 are related if the estimated equation has exactly one independent variable. The square of r equals R^2 for a regression where one of the two variables is the dependent variable and the other is the only independent variable.

$\overline{R}^2$, The Adjusted R^2

A major problem with R^2 is that adding another independent variable to a particular equation can never decrease R^2. That is, if you compare two equations that are identical (same dependent variable and independent variables), except that one has an additional independent variable, the equation with the greater number of independent variables will always have a better (or equal) fit as measured by R^2.

To see this, recall the equation for R^2, Equation 2.14.

$$R^2 = \frac{ESS}{TSS} = 1 - \frac{RSS}{TSS} = 1 - \frac{\sum e_i^2}{\sum (Y_i - \overline{Y})^2} \qquad (2.14)$$

---

7. The equation for r_{12}, the simple correlation coefficient between X_1 and X_2, is:

$$r_{12} = \frac{\sum [(X_{1i} - \overline{X}_1)(X_{2i} - \overline{X}_2)]}{\sqrt{\sum (X_{1i} - \overline{X}_1)^2 \sum (X_{2i} - \overline{X}_2)^2}}$$

What will happen to R^2 if we add a variable to the equation? Adding a variable can't change TSS (can you figure out why?), but in most cases the added variable will reduce RSS, so R^2 will rise. You know that RSS will never increase because the OLS program could always set the coefficient of the added variable equal to zero, thus giving the same fit as the previous equation. The coefficient of the newly added variable being zero is the only circumstance in which R^2 will stay the same when a variable is added. Otherwise, R^2 will always increase when a variable is added to an equation.

Perhaps an example will make this clear. Let's return to our weight guessing regression, Equation 1.21:

Estimated weight $= 103.40 + 6.38 \cdot$ Height (over five feet)

The R^2 for this equation is .74. If we now add a completely nonsensical variable to the equation (say, the campus post office box number of each individual in question), then it turns out that the results become:

Estimated weight $= 102.35 + 6.36$ (Height $>$ five feet) $+ 0.02$ (Box#)

but the R^2 for this equation is .75! Thus, an individual using R^2 alone as the measure of the quality of the fit of the regression would choose the second version as better fitting.

The inclusion of the campus post office box variable not only adds a nonsensical variable to the equation, but it also requires the estimation of another coefficient. This lessens the **degrees of freedom**, or the excess of the number of observations (N) over the number of coefficients (including the intercept) estimated (K + 1). For instance, when the campus box number variable is added to the weight/height example, the number of observations stays constant at 20, but the number of estimated coefficients increases from 2 to 3, so the number of degrees of freedom falls from 18 to 17. This decrease has a cost, since the lower the degrees of freedom, the less reliable the estimates are likely to be. Thus, the increase in the quality of the fit caused by the addition of a variable needs to be compared to the decrease in the degrees of freedom before a decision can be made with respect to the statistical impact of the added variable.

To sum, R^2 is of little help if we're trying to decide whether adding a variable to an equation improves our ability to meaningfully explain the dependent variable. Because of this problem, econometricians have developed another measure of the quality of the fit of an equation. That measure is $\overline{R}^2$ (pronounced R-bar-squared), which is R^2 adjusted for degrees of freedom:

$$\overline{R}^2 = 1 - \frac{\sum e_i^2/(N - K - 1)}{\sum (Y_i - \overline{Y})^2/(N - 1)} \tag{2.15}$$

> $\overline{R}^2$ measures the percentage of the variation of Y around its mean that is explained by the regression equation, *adjusted for degrees of freedom.*

$\overline{R}^2$ will increase, decrease, or stay the same when a variable is added to an equation, depending on whether the improvement in fit caused by the addition of the new variable outweighs the loss of the degree of freedom. Indeed, the $\overline{R}^2$ for the weight-guessing equation *decreases* to .72 when the mail box variable is added. The mail box variable, since it has no theoretical relation to weight, should never have been included in the equation, and the $\overline{R}^2$ measure supports this conclusion.

The highest possible $\overline{R}^2$ is 1.00, the same as for R^2. The lowest possible $\overline{R}^2$, however, is not .00; if R^2 is extremely low, $\overline{R}^2$ can be slightly negative.

> $\overline{R}^2$ can be used to compare the fits of equations with the same dependent variable and different numbers of independent variables. Because of this property, most researchers automatically use $\overline{R}^2$ instead of R^2 when evaluating the fit of their estimated regression equations.

Finally, a warning is in order. Always remember that the quality of fit of an estimated equation is only one measure of the overall quality of that regression. As mentioned previously, the degree to which the estimated coefficients conform to economic theory and the researcher's previous expectations about those coefficients are just as important as the fit itself. For instance, an estimated equation with a good fit but with an implausible sign for an estimated coefficient might give implausible predictions and thus not be a very useful equation. Other factors, such as theoretical relevance and usefulness, also come into play. Let's look at an example of these factors.

2.5 An Example of the Misuse of $\overline{R}^2$

Section 2.4 implies that the higher the overall fit of a given equation, the better. Unfortunately, many beginning researchers assume that if a high $\overline{R}^2$ is good, then maximizing $\overline{R}^2$ is the best way to maximize the quality of an equation. Such an assumption is dangerous because a good overall fit is only one measure of the quality of an equation.

Perhaps the best way to visualize the dangers inherent in maximizing $\overline{R}^2$ without regard to the economic meaning or statistical significance of an equation is to look at an example of such misuse. This is important because it is one thing for a researcher to agree in theory that "$\overline{R}^2$ maximizing" is bad, and it is another thing entirely for that researcher to avoid subconsciously maximizing $\overline{R}^2$ on projects. It is easy to agree that the goal of regression is not to maximize $\overline{R}^2$, but many researchers find it hard to resist that temptation.

As an example, assume that you've been hired by the State of California to help the legislature evaluate a bill to provide more water to Southern California.[8] This issue is important because a decision must be made whether to ruin, through a system of dams, one of the state's best trout fishing areas. On one side of the issue are Southern Californians who claim that their desert-like environment requires more water; on the other side are nature lovers and environmentalists who want to retain the natural beauty for which California is famous. Your job is to forecast the amount of water demanded in Los Angeles County, the biggest user of water in the state.

Because the bill is about to come before the state legislature, you're forced to choose between two regressions that already have been run for you, one by the state econometrician and the other by an independent consultant. You will base your forecast on one of these two equations. The state econometrician's equation:

$$\hat{W} = 24{,}000 + 48{,}000PR + 0.40P - 370RF \qquad (2.16)$$
$$\overline{R}^2 = .859 \quad DF = 25$$

or the independent consultant's equation:

$$\hat{W} = 30{,}000 + 0.62P - 400RF \qquad (2.17)$$
$$\overline{R}^2 = .847 \quad DF = 26$$

where: W = the total amount of water consumed in Los Angeles County in a given year (measured in millions of gallons)

PR = the price of a gallon of water that year (measured in real dollars)

P = the population in Los Angeles County that year

RF = the amount of rainfall that year (measured in inches)

DF = degrees of freedom, which equal the number of observations (N = 29) minus the number of coefficients estimated

---

8. The principle involved in this section is the same one that was discussed during the actual research, but these coefficients are hypothetical because the complexities of the real equation are irrelevant to our points.

Review these two equations carefully before going on with the rest of the section. What do you think the arguments of the state econometrician were for using his equation? What case did the independent econometrician make for her work?

The question is whether the increased $\overline{R}^2$ is worth the unexpected sign in the price of water coefficient in Equation 2.16. The state econometrician argued that given the better fit of his equation, it would do a better job of forecasting water demand. The independent consultant argued that it did not make sense to expect that an increase in price in the future would, holding the other variables in the equation constant, increase the quantity of water demanded in Los Angeles. Furthermore, given the unexpected sign of the coefficient, it seemed much more likely that the demand for water was unrelated to price during the sample period or that some important variable (such as real per capita income) had been left out of both equations. Since the amount of money spent on water was fairly low compared with other expenditures during the sample years, the consultant pointed out, it was possible that the demand for water was fairly price-inelastic. The economic argument for the positive sign observed by the state econometrician is difficult to justify; it implies that as the price of water goes up, so does the quantity of water demanded.

Was this argument simply academic? The answer, unfortunately, is no. If a forecast is made with Equation 2.16, it will tend to overforecast water demand in scenarios that foresee rising prices and underforecast water demand with lower price scenarios. In essence, the equation with the better fit would do a worse job of forecasting.[9]

Thus, a researcher who uses $\overline{R}^2$ as the sole measure of the quality of an equation (at the expense of economic theory or statistical significance) increases the chances of having unrepresentative or misleading results. This practice should be avoided at all costs. No simple rule of econometric estimation is likely to work in all cases. Instead, a combination of technical competence, theoretical judgment, and common sense makes for a good econometrician.

---

9. A couple of caveats to this example are in order. First, we normally wouldn't leave price out of a demand equation, but it's appropriate to do so here because the unexpected sign for the coefficient of price would otherwise cause forecast errors. Second, average rainfall would be used in forecasts, because future rainfall would not be known. Finally, income does indeed belong in the equation, but it turns out to have a relatively small coefficient, because water expenditure is minor in relation to the overall budget.

To help avoid the natural urge to maximize $\overline{R}^2$ without regard to the rest of the equation, you might find it useful to imagine the following conversation:

You: Sometimes, it seems like the best way to choose between two models is to pick the one that gives the highest $\overline{R}^2$.

Your Conscience: But that would be wrong.

You: I know that the goal of regression analysis is to obtain the best possible estimates of the true population coefficients and not to get a high $\overline{R}^2$, but my results "look better" if my fit is good.

Your Conscience: Look better to whom? It's not at all unusual to get a high $\overline{R}^2$ but find that some of the regression coefficients have signs that are contrary to theoretical expectations.

You: Well, I guess I should be more concerned with the logical relevance of the explanatory variables than with the fit, huh?

Your Conscience: Right! If in this process we obtain a high $\overline{R}^2$, well and good, but if $\overline{R}^2$ is high, it doesn't mean that the model is good.

2.6 Summary

1. Ordinary Least Squares (OLS) is the most frequently used method of obtaining estimates of the regression coefficients from a set of data. OLS chooses those $\hat{\beta}$s that minimize the summed squared residuals $(\sum e_i^2)$ for a particular sample.

2. R-bar-squared ($\overline{R}^2$) measures the percentage of the variation of Y around its mean that has been explained by a particular regression equation, adjusted for degrees of freedom. $\overline{R}^2$ increases when a variable is added to an equation only if the improvement in fit caused by the addition of the new variable more than offsets the loss of the degree of freedom that is used up in estimating the coefficient of the new variable. As a result, most researchers will automatically use $\overline{R}^2$ when evaluating the fit of their estimated regression equations.

3. Always remember that the fit of an estimated equation is only one of the measures of the overall quality of that regression. A number of other criteria, including the degree to which the estimated coefficients conform to economic theory and expectations (developed by the researcher before the data were collected) are more important than the size of $\overline{R}^2$.

EXERCISES

(The answer to Exercise 2 is in Appendix A.)

1. Write the meaning of each of the following terms without referring to the book (or your notes), and compare your definition with the version in the text for each:
   a. Ordinary Least Squares
   b. the meaning of a multivariate regression coefficient
   c. total, explained, and residual sums of squares
   d. simple correlation coefficient
   e. degrees of freedom
   f. $\bar{R}^2$

2. Just as you are about to estimate a regression (due tomorrow), massive sunspots cause magnetic interference that ruins all electrically powered machines (e.g., computers). Instead of giving up and flunking, you decide to calculate estimates from your data (on per capita income in thousands of U.S. dollars as a function of the percent of the labor force in agriculture in 10 developed countries) using methods like those used in Section 2.1 *without* a computer. Your data are:

Country	A	B	C	D	E	F	G	H	I	J
Per Capita Income	6	8	8	7	7	12	9	8	9	10
% in Agriculture	9	10	8	7	10	4	5	5	6	7

   a. Calculate $\hat{\beta}_0$ and $\hat{\beta}_1$.
   b. Calculate R^2 and $\bar{R}^2$.
   c. If the percent of the labor force in agriculture in another developed country was 8 percent, what level of per capita income (in thousands of U.S. dollars) would you guess that country had?

3. To get more practice in the use of summation notation, use the data in Exercise 2 on per capita income (Y) and percent of the labor force in agriculture (X) to answer the following questions. (*Hint:* Before starting this exercise, reread footnote 1 in this chapter which defines $\sum X = X_1 + X_2 + \cdots + X_N$.)
   a. Calculate $\sum X$. (*Hint:* Note that N = 10.)
   b. Calculate $\sum Y$.
   c. Calculate $\sum 3X$. Does it equal $3 \sum X$?
   d. Calculate $\sum (X + Y)$. Does it equal $\sum X + \sum Y$?

4. Consider the following two least-squares estimates of the relationship between interest rates and the federal budget deficit in the United States:

$$\text{Model A: } \hat{Y}_1 = 0.103 - 0.079X_1 \qquad R^2 = .00$$

where: Y_1 = the interest rate on Aaa corporate bonds
X_1 = the federal budget deficit as a percentage of GNP (quarterly model: N = 56)

$$\text{Model T: } \hat{Y}_2 = 0.089 + 0.369X_2 + 0.887X_3 \qquad R^2 = .40$$

where: Y_2 = the interest rate on 3-month Treasury bills
X_2 = the federal budget deficit in billions of dollars
X_3 = the rate of inflation (in percent) (quarterly model: N = 38)

a. What does "least-squares estimates" mean? What is being estimated? What is being squared? In what sense are the squares "least"?
b. What does it mean to have an R^2 of .00? Is it possible for an R^2 to be negative?
c. Based on economic theory, what signs would you have expected for the estimated slope coefficients of the two models?
d. Compare the two equations. Which model has estimated signs that correspond to your prior expectations? Is Model T automatically better because it has a higher R^2? If not, which model do you prefer and why?

5. Let's return to the height-weight example on page 53 and recall what happened when we added a nonsensical variable that measured the student's campus post office box number (MAIL) to the equation. The estimated equation changed from:

$$\widehat{\text{WEIGHT}} = 103.40 + 6.38\text{HEIGHT}$$

to:

$$\widehat{\text{WEIGHT}} = 102.35 + 6.36\text{HEIGHT} + 0.02\text{MAIL}$$

a. The estimated coefficient of HEIGHT changed when we added MAIL to the equation. Does that make sense? Why?
b. In theory, someone's weight has nothing to do with their campus mail box number, yet R^2 went up from .74 to .75 when MAIL was added to the equation! How is it possible that adding a nonsensical variable to an equation can increase R^2?

    c. Adding the nonsensical variable to the equation decreased $\overline{R}^2$ from .73 to .72. Explain how it's possible that $\overline{R}^2$ can go down at the same time that R^2 goes up.

    d. If a person's campus mail box number truly is unrelated to their weight, shouldn't the estimated coefficient of that variable equal exactly 0.00? How is it possible for a nonsensical variable to get a nonzero estimated coefficient?

6. In an effort to determine whether going to class improved student academic performance, David Romer[10] developed the following equation:

$$G_i = f(ATT_i, PS_i) + \epsilon_i$$

where: G_i = the grade of the *i*th student in Romer's class (A = 4, B = 3, etc.)

         ATT_i = the percent of class lectures that the *i*th student attended

         PS_i = the percent of the problem sets that the *i*th student completed

    a. What signs do you expect for the coefficients of the independent variables in this equation? Explain your reasoning.

    b. Romer then estimated the equation:

$$\hat{G}_i = 1.07 + 1.74ATT_i + 0.60PS_i$$
$$N = 195 \quad R^2 = .33$$

    Do the estimated results agree with your expectations?

    c. It's usually easier to develop expectations about the signs of coefficients than about the *size* of those coefficients. To get an insight into the size of the coefficients, let's assume that there are 25 hours of lectures in a semester and that it takes the average student approximately 50 hours to complete all the problem sets in a semester. If a student in one of Romer's classes had only one more hour to devote to class and wanted to maximize the impact on his or her grade, should the student go to class for an extra hour or work on problem sets for an extra hour? (*Hint:* Convert the extra hour to percentage terms and then multiply those percentages by the estimated coefficients.)

    d. From the given information, it'd be easy to draw the conclusion that the bigger a variable's coefficient, the greater its impact on the

10. David Romer, "Do Students Go to Class? Should They?" *Journal of Economic Perspectives,* Vol. 7, No. 3, pp. 167–174.

dependent variable. To test this conclusion, what would your answer to part c have been if there had been 50 hours of lecture in a semester and if it had taken 10 hours for the average student to complete the problem sets? Were we right to conclude that the larger the estimated coefficient, the more important the variable?

e. What's the real-world meaning of having $R^2 = .33$? For this specific equation, does .33 seem high, low, or just about right?

f. Is it reasonable to think that only class attendance and problem-set completion affect your grade in a class? If you could add just one more variable to the equation, what would it be? Explain your reasoning. What should adding your variable to the equation do to R^2? To $\overline{R}^2$?

7. Suppose that you have been asked to estimate a regression model to explain the number of people jogging a mile or more on the school track to help decide whether to build a second track to handle all the joggers. You collect data by living in a press box for the spring semester, and you run two possible explanatory equations:

$$A: \hat{Y} = 125.0 - 15.0X_1 - 1.0X_2 + 1.5X_3 \qquad \overline{R}^2 = .75$$
$$B: \hat{Y} = 123.0 - 14.0X_1 + 5.5X_2 - 3.7X_4 \qquad \overline{R}^2 = .73$$

where: Y = the number of joggers on a given day
X_1 = inches of rain that day
X_2 = hours of sunshine that day
X_3 = the high temperature for that day (in degrees F)
X_4 = the number of classes with term papers due the next day

a. Which of the two (admittedly hypothetical) equations do you prefer? Why?

b. How is it possible to get different estimated signs for the coefficient of the same variable using the same data?

8. David Katz[11] studied faculty salaries as a function of their "productivity" and estimated a regression equation with the following coefficients:

$$\hat{S}_i = 22,310 + 460B_i + 36A_i + 204E_i + 978D_i + 378Y_i + \cdots$$

11. David A. Katz, "Faculty Salaries, Promotions, and Productivity at a Large University," *American Economic Review,* Vol. 63, No. 3, pp. 469–477. Katz's equation included other variables as well, as indicated by the "+ · · ·" at the end of the equation. Estimated coefficients have been adjusted for inflation.

where: S_i = the salary of the ith professor in dollars per year
B_i = the number of books published, lifetime
A_i = the number of articles published, lifetime
E_i = the number of "excellent" articles published, lifetime
D_i = the number of dissertations supervised
Y_i = the number of years teaching experience

a. Do the signs of the coefficients match your prior expectations?
b. Do the relative sizes of the coefficients seem reasonable? (*Hint:* Most professors think that it's much more important to write an excellent article than to supervise a dissertation.)
c. Suppose a professor had just enough time (after teaching, etc.) to write a book, write two excellent articles, or supervise three dissertations. Which would you recommend? Why?
d. Would you like to reconsider your answer to part b? Which coefficient seems out of line? What explanation can you give for that result? Is the equation in some sense invalid? Why or why not?

9. What's wrong with the following kind of thinking: "I understand that R^2 is not a perfect measure of the quality of a regression equation because it always increases when a variable is added to the equation. Once we adjust for degrees of freedom by using $\overline{R}^2$, though, it seems to me that the higher the $\overline{R}^2$, the better the equation."

10. Charles Lave[12] published a study of driver fatality rates. His overall conclusion was that the variance of driving speed (the extent to which vehicles sharing the same highway drive at dramatically different speeds) is important in determining fatality rates. As part of his analysis, he estimated an equation with cross-state data from two different years:

Year 1: $\hat{F}_i = \hat{\beta}_0 + 0.176V_i + 0.0136C_i - 7.75H_i$
$$\overline{R}^2 = .624 \qquad N = 41$$

Year 2: $\hat{F}_i = \hat{\beta}_0 + 0.190V_i + 0.0071C_i - 5.29H_i$
$$\overline{R}^2 = .532 \qquad N = 44$$

where: F_i = the fatalities on rural interstate highways (per 100 million vehicle miles traveled) in the ith state
$\hat{\beta}_0$ = an unspecified estimated intercept

---

12. Charles A. Lave, "Speeding, Coordination, and the 55 MPH Limit," *American Economic Review,* Vol. 75, No. 5, pp. 1159–1164.

V_i = the driving speed variance in the ith state
C_i = driving citations per driver in the ith state
H_i = hospitals per square mile (adjusted) in the ith state

a. Think through the theory behind each variable, and develop expected signs for each coefficient. (*Hint:* Be careful with C.) Do Lave's estimates support your expectations?

b. Should we attach much meaning to the differences between the estimated coefficients from the two years? Why or why not? Under what circumstances might you be concerned about such differences?

c. The equation for the first year has the higher $\overline{R}^2$, but which equation has the higher R^2? (*Hint:* You can calculate the R^2s with the information given, but such a calculation isn't required.)

11. In Exercise 5 in Chapter 1, we estimated a height/weight equation on a new data set of 29 male customers, Equation 1.24:

$$\hat{Y}_i = 125.1 + 4.03X_i \tag{1.24}$$

where: Y_i = the weight (in pounds) of the ith person
X_i = the height (in inches above five feet) of the ith person

Suppose that a friend now suggests adding F_i, the percent body fat of the ith person, to the equation.

a. What is the theory behind adding F_i to the equation? How does the meaning of the coefficient of X change when you add F?

b. Assume you now collect data on the percent body fat of the 29 males and estimate:

$$\hat{Y}_i = 120.8 + 4.11X_i + 0.28F_i \tag{2.18}$$

Do you prefer Equation 2.18 or Equation 1.24? Why?

c. Suppose you learn that the $\overline{R}^2$ of Equation 1.24 is .75 and the $\overline{R}^2$ of Equation 2.18 is .72. Which equation do you prefer now? Explain your answer.

d. Suppose that you learn that the mean of F for your sample is 12.0. Which equation do you prefer now? Explain your answer.

12. For students with a background in calculus, the derivation of Equations 2.4 and 2.5 is useful. Derive these two equations by carrying out the following steps. (*Hint:* Be sure to write out each step of the proof.)

a. Differentiate the second equation in footnote 2 with respect to $\hat{\beta}_0$ and then with respect to $\hat{\beta}_1$.

b. Set these two derivatives equal to zero, thus creating what are called the "normal equations."

c. Solve the normal equations for $\hat{\beta}_1$, obtaining Equation 2.4.

d. Solve the normal equations for $\hat{\beta}_0$, obtaining Equation 2.5.

13. Suppose that you work in the admissions office of a college that doesn't allow prospective students to apply by using the Common Application.[13] How might you go about estimating the number of extra applications that your college would generate if it allowed the use of the Common Application? An econometric approach to this question would be to build the best possible model of the number of college applications and then to examine the estimated coefficient of a dummy variable that equaled one if the college in question allowed the use of the "common app" (and zero otherwise).

For example, if we estimate an equation using the data in Table 2.3 for high-quality coed national liberal arts colleges, we get:

$$\widehat{APPLICATION_i} = 523.3 + 2.15SIZE_i - 32.1RANK_i \\ + 1222COMMONAPP_i \tag{2.19}$$

$$N = 49 \quad R^2 = .724 \quad \overline{R}^2 = .705$$

where: $APPLICATION_i$ = the number of applications received by the ith college in 2007

$SIZE_i$ = the total number of undergraduate students at the ith college in 2006

$RANK_i$ = the *U.S. News*[14] rank of the ith college (1 = best) in 2006

$COMMONAPP_i$ = a dummy variable equal to 1 if the ith college allowed the use of the Common Application in 2007 and 0 otherwise.

a. Take a look at the signs of each of the three estimated regression coefficients. Are they what you would have expected? Explain.

b. Carefully state the real-world meaning of the coefficients of SIZE and RANK. Does the fact that the coefficient of RANK is 15 times bigger (in absolute value) than the coefficient of SIZE mean that the ranking of a college is 15 times more important than the size

---

13. The Common Application is a computerized application form that allows high school students to apply to a number of different colleges and universities using the same basic data. For more information, go to www.commonap.org.

14. U.S. News and World Report Staff, *U.S. News Ultimate College Guide*. Naperville, Illinois: Sourcebooks, Inc., 2006–2008.

Table 2.3 Data for the College Application Example

COLLEGE	APPLICATION	COMMONAPP	RANK	SIZE
Amherst College	6680	1	2	1648
Bard College	4980	1	36	1641
Bates College	4434	1	23	1744
Bowdoin College	5961	1	7	1726
Bucknell University	8934	1	29	3529
Carleton College	4840	1	6	1966
Centre College	2159	1	44	1144
Claremont McKenna College	4140	1	12	1152
Colby College	4679	1	20	1865
Colgate University	8759	1	16	2754
College of the Holy Cross	7066	1	32	2790
Colorado College	4826	1	26	1939
Connecticut College	4742	1	39	1802
Davidson College	3992	1	10	1667
Denison University	5196	1	48	2234
DePauw University	3624	1	48	2294
Dickinson College	5844	1	41	2372
Franklin and Marshall College	5018	1	41	1984
Furman University	3879	1	41	2648
Gettysburg College	6126	1	45	2511
Grinnell College	3077	1	14	1556
Hamilton College	4962	1	17	1802
Harvey Mudd College	2493	1	14	729
Haverford College	3492	1	9	1168
Kenyon College	4626	1	32	1630
Lafayette College	6364	1	30	2322
Lawrence University	2599	1	53	1409
Macalester College	4967	1	24	1884
Middlebury College	7180	1	5	2363
Oberlin College	7014	1	22	2744
Occidental College	5275	1	36	1783
Pitzer College	3748	1	51	918
Pomona College	5907	1	7	1545
Reed College	3365	1	53	1365
Rhodes College	3709	1	45	1662
Sewanee-University of the South	2424	0	34	1498
Skidmore College	6768	1	48	2537
St. Lawrence University	4645	0	57	2148
St. Olaf College	4058	0	55	2984

(continued)

Table 2.3 (*continued*)

COLLEGE	APPLICATION	COMMONAPP	RANK	SIZE
Swarthmore College	5242	1	3	1477
Trinity College	5950	1	30	2183
Union College	4837	1	39	2178
University of Richmond	6649	1	34	2804
Vassar College	6393	1	12	2382
Washington and Lee University	3719	1	17	1749
Wesleyan University	7750	1	10	2798
Wheaton College	2160	1	55	1548
Whitman College	2892	1	36	1406
Williams College	6478	1	1	2820

Sources: U.S. News & World Report Staff, *U.S. News Ultimate College Guide*, Naperville, IL: Sourcebooks, Inc. 2006–2008.

Datafile = COLLEGE2

of that college in terms of explaining the number of applications to that college? Why or why not?

c. Now carefully state the real-world meaning of the coefficient of COMMONAPP. Does this prove that 1,222 more students would apply if your college decided to allow the Common Application? Explain. (*Hint:* There are at least two good answers to this question. Can you get them both?)

d. To get some experience with your computer's regression software, use the data in Table 2.3 to estimate Equation 2.19. Do you get the same results?

e. Now use the same data and estimate Equation 2.19 again without the COMMONAPP variable. What is the new $\overline{R}^2$? Does $\overline{R}^2$ go up or down when you drop the variable? What, if anything, does this change tell you about whether COMMONAPP belongs in the equation?

3 Learning to Use Regression Analysis

3.1 Steps in Applied Regression Analysis

3.2 Using Regression Analysis to Pick Restaurant Locations

3.3 Summary and Exercises

From a quick reading of Chapter 2, it'd be easy to conclude that regression analysis is little more than the mechanical application of a set of equations to a sample of data. Such a notion would be similar to deciding that all that matters in golf is hitting the ball well. Golfers will tell you that it does little good to hit the ball well if you have used the wrong club or have hit the ball toward a trap, tree, or pond. Similarly, experienced econometricians spend much less time thinking about the OLS estimation of an equation than they do about a number of other factors. Our goal in this chapter is to introduce some of these "real-world" concerns.

The first section, an overview of the six steps typically taken in applied regression analysis, is the most important in the chapter. We believe that the ability to learn and understand a specific topic, like OLS estimation, is enhanced if the reader has a clear vision of the role that the specific topic plays in the overall framework of regression analysis. In addition, the six steps make it hard to miss the crucial function of theory in the development of sound econometric research.

This is followed by a complete example of how to use the six steps in applied regression: a location analysis for the "Woody's" restaurant chain that is based on actual company data and to which we will return in future chapters to apply new ideas and tests.

3.1 Steps in Applied Regression Analysis

Although there are no hard and fast rules for conducting econometric research, most investigators commonly follow a standard method for applied regression analysis. The relative emphasis and effort expended on each step will vary, but normally all the steps are necessary for successful research. Note that we don't discuss the selection of the dependent variable; this choice is determined by the purpose of the research. We'll discuss choosing a dependent variable in Chapter 11. Once a dependent variable is chosen, however, it's logical to follow this sequence:

1. Review the literature and develop the theoretical model.
2. Specify the model: Select the independent variables and the functional form.
3. Hypothesize the expected signs of the coefficients.
4. Collect the data. Inspect and clean the data.
5. Estimate and evaluate the equation.
6. Document the results.

The purpose of suggesting these steps is not to discourage the use of innovative or unusual approaches but rather to develop in the reader a sense of how regression ordinarily is done by professional economists and business analysts.

Step 1: Review the Literature and Develop the Theoretical Model

The first step in any applied research is to get a good theoretical grasp of the topic to be studied. That's right: the best data analysts don't start with data, but with theory! This is because many econometric decisions, ranging from which variables to include to which functional form to employ, are determined by the underlying theoretical model. It's virtually impossible to build a good econometric model without a solid understanding of the topic you're studying.

For most topics, this means that it's smart to review the scholarly literature before doing anything else. If a professor has investigated the theory behind your topic, you want to know about it. If other researchers have estimated equations for your dependent variable, you might want to apply one of their models to your data set. On the other hand, if you disagree with the approach of previous authors, you might want to head off in a new direction. In either case, you shouldn't have to "reinvent the wheel." You should start your investigation where earlier researchers left off. Any academic paper on an empirical topic should begin with a summary of the extent and quality of previous research.

The most convenient approaches to reviewing the literature are to obtain several recent issues of the *Journal of Economic Literature* or a business-oriented publication of abstracts, or to run an Internet search or an *EconLit* search[1] on your topic. Using these resources, find and read several recent articles on your topic. Pay attention to the bibliographies of these articles. If an older article is cited by a number of current authors, or if its title hits your topic on the head, trace back through the literature and find this article as well. We'll have more advice on reviewing the literature in Chapter 11.

In some cases, a topic will be so new or so obscure that you won't be able to find any articles on it. What then? We recommend two possible strategies. First, try to transfer theory from a similar topic to yours. For example, if you're trying to build a model of the demand for a new product, read articles that analyze the demand for similar, existing products. Second, if all else fails, pick up the telephone and call someone who works in the field you're investigating. For example, if you're building a model of housing in an unfamiliar city, call a real estate agent who works there.

Step 2: Specify the Model: Select the Independent Variables and the Functional Form

The most important step in applied regression analysis is the specification of the theoretical regression model. After selecting the dependent variable, the **specification** of a model involves choosing the following components:

1. the independent variables and how they should be measured,
2. the functional (mathematical) form of the variables, and
3. the properties of the stochastic error term.

A regression equation is specified when each of these elements has been treated appropriately. We'll discuss the details of these specification decisions in Chapters 6, 7, and 4, respectively.

Each of the elements of specification is determined primarily on the basis of economic theory. A mistake in any of the three elements results in a

---

1. *EconLit* is an electronic bibliography of economics literature. *EconLit* contains abstracts, reviews, indexing, and links to full-text articles in economics journals. In addition, it abstracts books and indexes articles in books, working papers series, and dissertations. *EconLit* is available at libraries and on university websites throughout the world. For more, go to www.EconLit.org.

specification error. Of all the kinds of mistakes that can be made in applied regression analysis, specification error is usually the most disastrous to the validity of the estimated equation. Thus, the more attention paid to economic theory at the beginning of a project, the more satisfying the regression results are likely to be.

The emphasis in this text is on estimating behavioral equations, those that describe the behavior of economic entities. We focus on selecting independent variables based on the economic theory concerning that behavior. An explanatory variable is chosen because it is a theoretical determinant of the dependent variable; it is expected to explain at least part of the variation in the dependent variable. Recall that regression gives evidence but does not prove economic causality. Just as an example does not prove the rule, a regression result does not prove the theory.

There are dangers in specifying the wrong independent variables. Our goal should be to specify only relevant explanatory variables, those expected theoretically to assert a substantive influence on the dependent variable. Variables suspected of having little effect should be excluded unless their possible impact on the dependent variable is of some particular (e.g., policy) interest.

For example, an equation that explains the quantity demanded of a consumption good might use the price of the product and consumer income or wealth as likely variables. Theory also indicates that complementary and substitute goods are important. Therefore, you might decide to include the prices of complements and substitutes, but which complements and substitutes? Of course, selection of the closest complements and/or substitutes is appropriate, but how far should you go? The choice must be based on theoretical judgment, and such judgments are often quite subjective.

When researchers decide, for example, that the prices of only two other goods need to be included, they are said to impose their **priors** (i.e., previous theoretical belief) or their working hypotheses on the regression equation. Imposition of such priors is a common practice that determines the number and kind of hypotheses that the regression equation has to test. The danger is that a prior may be wrong and could diminish the usefulness of the estimated regression equation. Each of the priors therefore should be explained and justified in detail.

Some concepts (for example, gender) might seem impossible to include in an equation because they're inherently qualitative in nature and can't be quantified. Such concepts can be quantified by using dummy (or binary) variables. A **dummy variable** takes on the values of one or zero depending on whether a specified condition holds.

As an illustration of a dummy variable, suppose that Y_i represents the salary of the ith high school teacher, and that the salary level depends primarily on the experience of the teacher and the type of degree earned. All teachers have a B.A., but some also have a graduate degree, like an M.A. An equation representing the relationship between earnings and the type of degree might be:

$$Y_i = \beta_0 + \beta_1 X_{1i} + \beta_2 X_{2i} + \epsilon_i \qquad (3.1)$$

where: $X_{1i} = \begin{cases} 1 \text{ if the } i\text{th teacher has a graduate degree} \\ 0 \text{ otherwise} \end{cases}$

$X_{2i} =$ the number of years of teaching experience of the ith teacher

The variable X_1 takes on only values of zero or one, so X_1 is called a dummy variable, or just a "dummy." Needless to say, the term has generated many a pun. In this case, the dummy variable represents the condition of having a master's degree. The coefficient β_1 indicates the additional salary that can be attributed to having a graduate degree, holding teaching experience constant. We'll discuss dummy variables in detail in Chapters 7 and 13.

Step 3: Hypothesize the Expected Signs of the Coefficients

Once the variables are selected, it's important to hypothesize the expected signs of the regression coefficients. For example, in the demand equation for a final consumption good, the quantity demanded (Q_d) is expected to be inversely related to its price (P) and the price of a complementary good (P_c), and positively related to consumer income (Y) and the price of a substitute good (P_s). The first step in the written development of a regression model usually is to express the equation as a general function:

$$Q_d = f(\overset{-}{P}, \overset{+}{Y}, \overset{-}{P_c}, \overset{+}{P_s}) + \epsilon \qquad (3.2)$$

The signs above the variables indicate the hypothesized sign of the respective regression coefficient in a linear model.

In many cases, the basic theory is general knowledge, so the reasons for each sign need not be discussed. However, if any doubt surrounds the selection of an expected sign, you should document the opposing forces at work and the reasons for hypothesizing a positive or negative coefficient.

Step 4: Collect the Data. Inspect and Clean the Data

Obtaining an original data set and properly preparing it for regression is a surprisingly difficult task. This step entails more than a mechanical recording of data, because the type and size of the sample also must be chosen.

A general rule regarding sample size is "the more observations the better," as long as the observations are from the same general population. Ordinarily, researchers take all the roughly comparable observations that are readily available. In regression analysis, all the variables must have the same number of observations. They also should have the same frequency (monthly, quarterly, annual, etc.) and time period. Often, the frequency selected is determined by the availability of data.

The reason there should be as many observations as possible concerns the statistical concept of *degrees of freedom* first mentioned in Section 2.4. Consider fitting a straight line to two points on an X, Y coordinate system as in Figure 3.1. Such an exercise can be done mathematically without error. Both points lie on the line, so there is no estimation of the coefficients involved. The two points determine the two parameters, the intercept and the slope, precisely. Estimation takes place only when a straight line is fitted to three or more points that were generated by some process that is not exact. The excess of the number of observations (three) over the number of coefficients to be estimated (in this case two, the intercept and slope) is the

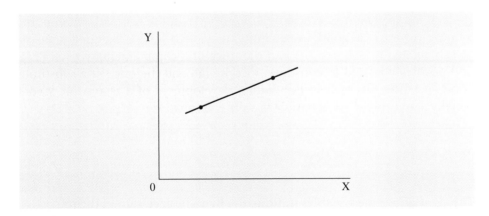

Figure 3.1 Mathematical Fit of a Line to Two Points

If there are only two points in a data set, as in Figure 3.1, a straight line can be fitted to those points mathematically without error, because two points completely determine a straight line.

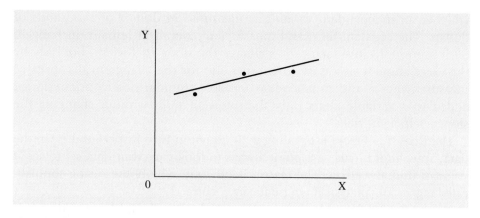

Figure 3.2 Statistical Fit of a Line to Three Points

If there are three (or more) points in a data set, as in Figure 3.2, then the line must almost always be fitted to the points statistically, using the estimation procedures of Section 2.1.

degrees of freedom.[2] All that is necessary for estimation is a single degree of freedom, as in Figure 3.2, but the more degrees of freedom there are, the better. This is because when the number of degrees of freedom is large, every positive error is likely to be balanced by a negative error. When degrees of freedom are low, the random element is likely to fail to provide such offsetting observations. For example, the more a coin is flipped, the more likely it is that the observed proportion of heads will reflect the true probability of 0.5.

Another area of concern has to do with the *units of measurement of the variables.* Does it matter if a variable is measured in dollars or thousands of dollars? Does it matter if the measured variable differs consistently from the true variable by 10 units? Interestingly, such changes don't matter in terms of regression analysis except in interpreting the scale of the coefficients. All conclusions about signs, significance, and economic theory are independent of units of measurement. For example, it makes little difference

---

2. Throughout the text, we will calculate the number of degrees of freedom (d.f.) in a regression equation as d.f. $= (N - K - 1)$, where K is the number of independent variables in the equation. Equivalently, some authors will set $K' = K + 1$ and define d.f. $= (N - K')$. Since K' equals the number of independent variables plus 1 (for the constant), it equals the number of coefficients to be estimated in the regression.

whether an independent variable is measured in dollars or thousands of dollars. The constant term and measures of overall fit remain unchanged. Such a multiplicative factor does change the slope coefficient, but only by the exact amount necessary to compensate for the change in the units of measurement of the independent variable. Similarly, a constant factor added to a variable alters only the intercept term without changing the slope coefficient itself.

The final step before estimating your equation is to inspect and clean the data. You should make it a point always to look over your data set to see if you can find any errors. The reason is obvious: why bother using sophisticated regression analysis if your data are incorrect?

To inspect the data, obtain a printout and a plot (graph) of the data and look for outliers. An **outlier** is an observation that lies outside the range of the rest of the observations, and looking for outliers is an easy way to find data entry errors. In addition, it's a good habit to look at the mean, maximum, and minimum of each variable and then think about possible inconsistencies in the data. Are any observations impossible or unrealistic? Did GDP double in one year? Does a student have a 7.0 GPA on a 4.0 scale? Is consumption negative?

Typically, the data can be cleaned of these errors by replacing an incorrect number with the correct one. In extremely rare circumstances, an observation can be dropped from the sample, but only if the correct number can't be found or if that particular observation clearly isn't from the same population as the rest of the sample. Be careful! The mere existence of an outlier is not a justification for dropping that observation from the sample. A regression needs to be able to explain all the observations in a sample, not just the well-behaved ones. For more on the details of data collection, see Sections 11.2 and 11.3. For more on generating your own data through an economic experiment, see Section 16.1.

Step 5: Estimate and Evaluate the Equation

Believe it or not, it can take months to complete steps 1–4 for a regression equation, but a computer program like EViews or Stata can estimate that equation in less than a second! Typically, estimation is done using OLS, as discussed in Section 2.1, but if another estimation technique is used, the reasons for that alternative technique should be carefully explained and evaluated.

You might think that once your equation has been estimated, your work is finished, but that's hardly the case. Instead, you need to evaluate your results in a variety of ways. How well did the equation fit the data? Were the signs and magnitudes of the estimated coefficients what you expected? Most of the rest of this book is concerned with the evaluation of estimated econometric equations, and beginning researchers should be prepared to spend a considerable amount of time doing this evaluation.

Once this evaluation is complete, don't automatically go to step 6. Regression results are rarely what one expects, and additional model development often is required. For example, an evaluation of your results might indicate that your equation is missing an important variable. In such a case, you'd go back to step 1 to review the literature and add the appropriate variable to your equation. You'd then go through each of the steps in order until you had estimated your new specification in step 5. You'd move on to step 6 only if you were satisfied with your estimated equation. Don't be too quick to make such adjustments, however, because we don't want to adjust the theory merely to fit the data. A researcher has to walk a fine line between making appropriate changes and avoiding inappropriate ones, and making these choices is one of the artistic elements of applied econometrics.

Finally, it's often worthwhile to estimate additional specifications of an equation in order to see how stable your observed results are. This approach, called *sensitivity analysis*, will be discussed in Section 6.4.

Step 6: Document the Results

A standard format usually is used to present estimated regression results:

$$\hat{Y}_i = 103.40 + 6.38X_i$$
$$(0.88)$$
$$t = 7.22$$
$$N = 20 \quad \overline{R}^2 = .73$$

(3.3)

The number in parentheses is the estimated standard error of the estimated coefficient, and the *t*-value is the one used to test the hypothesis that the true value of the coefficient is different from zero. These and other measures of the quality of the regression will be discussed in later chapters.[3] What is

---

3. The standard error of the coefficient is discussed in more detail in Section 4.2; the *t*-value is developed in Section 5.2.

important to note is that the documentation of regression results using an easily understood format is considered part of the analysis itself. For time-series data sets, the documentation also includes the frequency (e.g., quarterly or annual) and the time period of the data.

Most computer programs present statistics to eight or more digits, but it is important to recognize the difference between the number of digits computed and the number of *meaningful digits*, which may be as low as two or three.

One of the important parts of the documentation is the explanation of the model, the assumptions, and the procedures and data used. The written documentation must contain enough information so that the entire study could be replicated by others.[4] Unless the variables have been defined in a glossary or table, short definitions should be presented along with the equations. If there is a series of estimated regression equations, then tables should provide the relevant information for each equation. All data manipulations as well as data sources should be documented fully. When there is much to explain, this documentation usually is relegated to a data appendix. If the data are not available generally or are available only after computation, the data set itself might be included in this appendix.

3.2 Using Regression Analysis to Pick Restaurant Locations

To solidify your understanding of the six basic steps of applied regression analysis, let's work through a complete regression example. Suppose that you've been hired to determine the best location for the next Woody's restaurant, where Woody's is a moderately priced, 24-hour, family restaurant chain.[5] You decide to build a regression model to explain the gross sales volume at each of the restaurants in the chain as a function of various descriptors of the location of that branch. If you can come up with a sound equation to explain gross sales as a function of location, then you

---

4. For example, the *Journal of Money, Credit, and Banking* has requested authors to submit their actual data sets so that regression results can be verified. See W. G. Dewald et al., "Replication in Empirical Economics," *American Economic Review,* Vol. 76, No. 4, pp. 587–603 and Daniel S. Hamermesh, "Replication in Economics," NBER Working Paper 13026, April 2007.

5. The data in this example are real (they're from a sample of 33 Denny's restaurants in Southern California), but the number of independent variables considered is much smaller than was used in the actual research. Datafile = WOODY3

can use this equation to help Woody's decide where to build their newest eatery. Given data on land costs, building costs, and local building and restaurant municipal codes, the owners of Woody's will be able to make an informed decision.

1. *Review the literature and develop the theoretical model.* You do some reading about the restaurant industry, but your review of the literature consists mainly of talking to various experts within the firm. They give you some good ideas about the attributes of a successful Woody's location. The experts tell you that all of the chain's restaurants are identical (indeed, this is sometimes a criticism of the chain) and that all the locations are in what might be called "suburban, retail, or residential" environments (as distinguished from central cities or rural areas, for example). Because of this, you realize that many of the reasons that might help explain differences in sales volume in other chains do not apply in this case because all the Woody's locations are similar. (If you were comparing Woody's to another chain, such variables might be appropriate.)

   In addition, discussions with the people in the Woody's strategic planning department convince you that price differentials and consumption differences between locations are not as important as the number of customers a particular location attracts. This causes you concern for a while because the variable you had planned to study originally, gross sales volume, would vary as prices changed between locations. Since your company controls these prices, you feel that you would rather have an estimate of the "potential" for such sales. As a result, you decide to specify your dependent variable as the number of customers served (measured by the number of checks or bills that the waiters and waitresses handed out) in a given location in the most recent year for which complete data are available.

2. *Specify the model: Select the independent variables and the functional form.* Your discussions lead to a number of suggested variables. After a while, you realize that there are three major determinants of sales (customers) on which virtually everyone agrees. These are the number of people who live near the location, the general income level of the location, and the number of direct competitors close to the location. In addition, there are two other good suggestions for potential explanatory variables. These are the number of cars passing the location per day and the number of months that the particular restaurant has been open. After some serious consideration of your alternatives, you decide not to include the last possibilities. All the locations have been open

long enough to have achieved a stable clientele. In addition, it would be very expensive to collect data on the number of passing cars for all the locations. Should population prove to be a poor measure of the available customers in a location, you'll have to decide whether to ask your boss for the money to collect complete traffic data.

The exact definitions of the independent variables you decide to include are:

N = Competition: the number of direct market competitors within a two-mile radius of the Woody's location

P = Population: the number of people living within a three-mile radius of the Woody's location

I = Income: the average household income of the population measured in variable P

Since you have no reason to suspect anything other than a linear functional form and a typical stochastic error term, that's what you decide to use.

3. *Hypothesize the expected signs of the coefficients.* After thinking about which variables to include, you expect hypothesizing signs will be easy. For two of the variables, you're right. Everyone expects that the more competition, the fewer customers (holding constant the population and income of an area), and also that the more people who live near a particular restaurant, the more customers (holding constant the competition and income). You expect that the greater the income in a particular area, the more people will choose to eat in a family restaurant. However, people in especially high-income areas might want to eat in a restaurant that has more "atmosphere" than a family restaurant like Woody's. As a result, you worry that the income variable might be only weakly positive in its impact. To sum, you expect:

$$Y_i = f(\overset{-}{N_i}, \overset{+}{P_i}, \overset{+?}{I_i}) + \epsilon_i = \beta_0 + \beta_N N_i + \beta_P P_i + \beta_I I_i + \epsilon_i \quad (3.4)$$

where the signs above the variables indicate the expected impact of that particular independent variable on the dependent variable, holding constant the other two explanatory variables, and ϵ_i is a typical stochastic error term.

4. *Collect the data. Inspect and clean the data.* You want to include every local restaurant in the Woody's chain in your study, and, after some effort, you come up with data for your dependent variable and your independent variables for all 33 locations. You inspect the data, and you're confident that the quality of your data is excellent for three reasons: each manager measured each variable identically, you've included each restaurant in the sample, and all the information is from the same year. [The data set is included in this section, along with a sample computer output for the regression estimated by EViews (Tables 3.1 and 3.2) and Stata (Tables 3.3 and 3.4).]

5. *Estimate and evaluate the equation.* You take the data set and enter it into the computer. You then run an OLS regression on the data, but you do so only after thinking through your model once again to see if there are hints that you've made theoretical mistakes. You end up admitting that although you cannot be sure you are right, you've done the best you can, so you estimate the equation, obtaining:

$$\hat{Y}_i = 102{,}192 - 9075N_i + 0.355P_i + 1.288I_i \qquad (3.5)$$
$$(2053) \qquad (0.073) \qquad (0.543)$$
$$t = -4.42 \qquad 4.88 \qquad 2.37$$
$$N = 33 \quad \overline{R}^2 = .579$$

This equation satisfies your needs in the short run. In particular, the estimated coefficients in the equation have the signs you expected. The overall fit, although not outstanding, seems reasonable for such a diverse group of locations. To predict Y, you obtain the values of N, P, and I for each potential new location and then plug them into Equation 3.5. Other things being equal, the higher the predicted Y, the better the location from Woody's point of view.

6. *Document the results.* The results summarized in Equation 3.5 meet our documentation requirements. (Note that we include the standard errors of the estimated coefficients and *t*-values[6] for completeness,

---

6. Throughout the text, the number in parentheses below a coefficient estimate will be the standard error of that estimated coefficient. Some authors put the *t*-value in parentheses, though, so be alert when reading journal articles or other books.

Table 3.1 Data for the Woody's Restaurants Example (Using the EViews Program)

obs	Y	N	P	I
1	107919.0	3.000000	65044.00	13240.00
2	118866.0	5.000000	101376.0	22554.00
3	98579.00	7.000000	124989.0	16916.00
4	122015.0	2.000000	55249.00	20967.00
5	152827.0	3.000000	73775.00	19576.00
6	91259.00	5.000000	48484.00	15039.00
7	123550.0	8.000000	138809.0	21857.00
8	160931.0	2.000000	50244.00	26435.00
9	98496.00	6.000000	104300.0	24024.00
10	108052.0	2.000000	37852.00	14987.00
11	144788.0	3.000000	66921.00	30902.00
12	164571.0	4.000000	166332.0	31573.00
13	105564.0	3.000000	61951.00	19001.00
14	102568.0	5.000000	100441.0	20058.00
15	103342.0	2.000000	39462.00	16194.00
16	127030.0	5.000000	139900.0	21384.00
17	166755.0	6.000000	171740.0	18800.00
18	125343.0	6.000000	149894.0	15289.00
19	121886.0	3.000000	57386.00	16702.00
20	134594.0	6.000000	185105.0	19093.00
21	152937.0	3.000000	114520.0	26502.00
22	109622.0	3.000000	52933.00	18760.00
23	149884.0	5.000000	203500.0	33242.00
24	98388.00	4.000000	39334.00	14988.00
25	140791.0	3.000000	95120.00	18505.00
26	101260.0	3.000000	49200.00	16839.00
27	139517.0	4.000000	113566.0	28915.00
28	115236.0	9.000000	194125.0	19033.00
29	136749.0	7.000000	233844.0	19200.00
30	105067.0	7.000000	83416.00	22833.00
31	136872.0	6.000000	183953.0	14409.00
32	117146.0	3.000000	60457.00	20307.00
33	163538.0	2.000000	65065.00	20111.00

Correlation Matrix

	Y	N	P	I
Y	1.000000	-0.144225	0.392568	0.537022
N	-0.144225	1.000000	0.726251	-0.031534
P	0.392568	0.726251	1.000000	0.245198
I	0.537022	-0.031534	0.245198	1.000000

Table 3.2 Actual Computer Output (Using the EViews Program)

Dependent Variable: Y
Method: Least Squares
Date: 02/29/09   Time: 14:55
Sample: 1 33
Included observations: 33

Variable	Coefficient	Std. Error	t-Statistic	Prob.
C	102192.4	12799.83	7.983891	0.0000
N	-9074.674	2052.674	-4.420904	0.0001
P	0.354668	0.072681	4.879810	0.0000
I	1.287923	0.543294	2.370584	0.0246

R-squared	0.618154	Mean dependent var	125634.6
Adjusted R-squared	0.578653	S.D. dependent var	22404.09
S.E. of regression	14542.78	Akaike info criterion	22.12079
Sum squared resid	6.13E+09	Schwarz criterion	22.30218
Log likelihood	-360.9930	F-statistic	15.64894
Durbin-Watson stat	1.758193	Prob(F-statistic)	0.000003

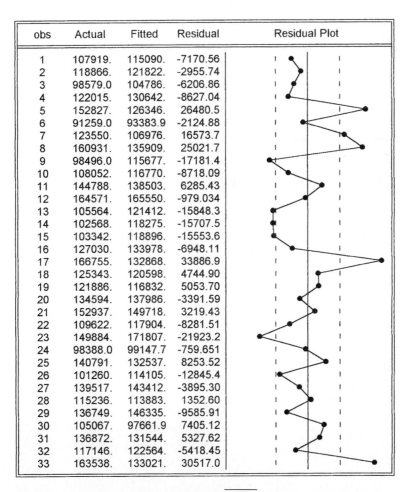

obs	Actual	Fitted	Residual	Residual Plot
1	107919.	115090.	-7170.56	
2	118866.	121822.	-2955.74	
3	98579.0	104786.	-6206.86	
4	122015.	130642.	-8627.04	
5	152827.	126346.	26480.5	
6	91259.0	93383.9	-2124.88	
7	123550.	106976.	16573.7	
8	160931.	135909.	25021.7	
9	98496.0	115677.	-17181.4	
10	108052.	116770.	-8718.09	
11	144788.	138503.	6285.43	
12	164571.	165550.	-979.034	
13	105564.	121412.	-15848.3	
14	102568.	118275.	-15707.5	
15	103342.	118896.	-15553.6	
16	127030.	133978.	-6948.11	
17	166755.	132868.	33886.9	
18	125343.	120598.	4744.90	
19	121886.	116832.	5053.70	
20	134594.	137986.	-3391.59	
21	152937.	149718.	3219.43	
22	109622.	117904.	-8281.51	
23	149884.	171807.	-21923.2	
24	98388.0	99147.7	-759.651	
25	140791.	132537.	8253.52	
26	101260.	114105.	-12845.4	
27	139517.	143412.	-3895.30	
28	115236.	113883.	1352.60	
29	136749.	146335.	-9585.91	
30	105067.	97661.9	7405.12	
31	136872.	131544.	5327.62	
32	117146.	122564.	-5418.45	
33	163538.	133021.	30517.0	

Table 3.3 Data for the Woody's Restaurant Example (Using the Stata Program)

	Y	N	P	I
1.	107919	3	65044	13240
2.	118866	5	101376	22554
3.	98579	7	124989	16916
4.	122015	2	55249	20967
5.	152827	3	73775	19576
6.	91259	5	48484	15039
7.	123550	8	138809	21857
8.	160931	2	50244	26435
9.	98496	6	104300	24024
10.	108052	2	37852	14987
11.	144788	3	66921	30902
12.	164571	4	166332	31573
13.	105564	3	61951	19001
14.	102568	5	100441	20058
15.	103342	2	39462	16194
16.	127030	5	139900	21384
17.	166755	6	171740	18800
18.	125343	6	149894	15289
19.	121886	3	57386	16702
20.	134594	6	185105	19093
21.	152937	3	114520	26502
22.	109622	3	52933	18760
23.	149884	5	203500	33242
24.	98388	4	39334	14988
25.	140791	3	95120	18505
26.	101260	3	49200	16839
27.	139517	4	113566	28915
28.	115236	9	194125	19033
29.	136749	7	233844	19200
30.	105067	7	83416	22833
31.	136872	6	183953	14409
32.	117146	3	60457	20307
33.	163538	2	65065	20111

(obs=33)

	Y	N	P	I
Y	1.0000			
N	−0.1442	1.0000		
P	0.3926	0.7263	1.0000	
I	0.5370	−0.0315	0.2452	1.0000

Table 3.4 Actual Computer Output (Using the Stata Program)

Source	SS	df	MS			
Model	9.9289e+09	3	3.3096e+09			
Residual	6.1333e+09	29	211492485			
Total	1.6062e+10	32	501943246			

Number of obs = 33
F(3, 29) = 15.65
Prob > F = 0.0000
R−squared = 0.6182
Adj R−squared = 0.5787
Root MSE = 14543

Y	Coef.	Std. Err.	t	P>|t|	[95% Conf.	Interval]
N	−9074.674	2052.674	−4.42	0.000	−13272.86	−4876.485
P	.3546684	.0726808	4.88	0.000	.2060195	.5033172
I	1.287923	.5432938	2.37	0.025	.1767628	2.399084
_cons	102192.4	12799.83	7.98	0.000	76013.84	128371

	Y	Yhat	residu~s
1.	107919	115089.6	115089.6
2.	118866	121821.7	121821.7
3.	98579	104785.9	104785.9
4.	122015	130642	130642
5.	152827	126346.5	126346.5
6.	91259	93383.88	93383.88
7.	123550	106976.3	106976.3
8.	160931	135909.3	135909.3
9.	98496	115677.4	115677.4
10.	108052	116770.1	116770.1
11.	144788	138502.6	138502.6
12.	164571	165550	165550
13.	105564	121412.3	121412.3
14.	102568	118275.5	118275.5
15.	103342	118895.6	118895.6
16.	127030	133978.1	133978.1
17.	166755	132868.1	132868.1
18.	125343	120598.1	120598.1
19.	121886	116832.3	116832.3
20.	134594	137985.6	137985.6
21.	152937	149717.6	149717.6
22.	109622	117903.5	117903.5
23.	149884	171807.2	171807.2
24.	98388	99147.65	99147.65
25.	140791	132537.5	132537.5
26.	101260	114105.4	114105.4
27.	139517	143412.3	143412.3
28.	115236	113883.4	113883.4
29.	136749	146334.9	146334.9
30.	105067	97661.88	97661.88
31.	136872	131544.4	131544.4
32.	117146	122564.5	122564.5
33.	163538	133021	133021

even though we won't make use of them until Chapter 5.) However, it's not easy for a beginning researcher to wade through a computer's regression output to find all the numbers required for documentation. You'll probably have an easier time reading your own computer system's printout if you take the time to "walk through" the sample computer output for the Woody's model in Tables 3.1–3.4. This sample output was produced by the EViews and Stata computer programs, but it's similar to those produced by SAS, SHAZAM, TSP, and others.

The first items listed are the actual data. These are followed by the simple correlation coefficients between all pairs of variables in the data set. Next comes a listing of the estimated coefficients, their estimated standard errors, and the associated t-values, and follows with R^2, $\overline{R}^2$, the standard error of the regression, RSS, the F-ratio, and other items that we will explain in later chapters. Finally, we have a listing of the observed Ys, the predicted Ys, the residuals for each observation and a graph of these residuals. Numbers followed by "E+06" or "E−01" are expressed in a scientific notation indicating that the printed decimal point should be moved six places to the right or one place to the left, respectively.

In future chapters, we'll return to this example in order to apply various tests and ideas as we learn them.

(3.3) Summary

1. Six steps typically taken in applied regression analysis for a given dependent variable are:
   a. Review the literature and develop the theoretical model.
   b. Specify the model: Select the independent variables and the functional form.
   c. Hypothesize the expected signs of the coefficients.
   d. Collect the data. Inspect and clean the data.
   e. Estimate and evaluate the equation.
   f. Document the results.

2. A dummy variable takes on only the values of 1 or 0, depending on whether some condition is met. An example of a dummy variable would be X equals 1 if a particular individual is female and 0 if the person is male.

EXERCISES

(The answer to Exercise 2 is in Appendix A.)

1. Write the meaning of each of the following terms without referring to the book (or your notes), and compare your definition with the version in the text for each:
    a. the six steps in applied regression analysis
    b. dummy variable
    c. cross-sectional data set
    d. specification error
    e. degrees of freedom

2. Contrary to their name, dummy variables are not easy to understand without a little bit of practice:
    a. Specify a dummy variable that would allow you to distinguish between undergraduate students and graduate students in your econometrics class.
    b. Specify a regression equation to explain the grade (measured on a scale of 4.0) each student in your class received on his or her first econometrics test (Y) as a function of the student's grade in a previous course in statistics (G), the number of hours the student studied for the test (H), and the dummy variable you created above (D). Are there other variables you would want to add? Explain.
    c. What is the hypothesized sign of the coefficient of D? Does the sign depend on the exact way in which you defined D? (*Hint:* In particular, suppose that you had reversed the definitions of 1 and 0 in your answer to part a.) How?
    d. Suppose that you collected the data and ran the regression and found an estimated coefficient for D that had the expected sign and an absolute value of 0.5. What would this mean in real-world terms? By the way, what would have happened if you had only undergraduates or only graduate students in your class?

3. Do liberal arts colleges pay economists more than they pay other professors? To find out, we looked at a sample of 2,929 small-college

faculty members and built a model of their salaries that included a number of variables, four of which were:

$$\hat{S}_i = 36{,}721 + 817M_i + 426A_i + 406R_i + 3539T_i + \cdots \quad (3.6)$$
$$\qquad\quad (259) \quad (456) \quad (24) \quad (458)$$
$$\overline{R}^2 = .77 \qquad N = 2929$$

where: S_i = the salary of the *i*th college professor

M_i = a dummy variable equal to 1 if the *i*th professor is a male and 0 otherwise

A_i = a dummy variable equal to 1 if the *i*th professor is African American and 0 otherwise

R_i = the years in rank of the *i*th professor

T_i = a dummy variable equal to 1 if the *i*th professor teaches economics and 0 otherwise

a. Carefully explain the meaning of the estimated coefficient of M.
b. The equation indicates that African Americans earn $426 more than members of other ethnic groups, holding constant the other variables in the equation. Does this coefficient have the sign you expected? Why or why not?
c. Is R a dummy variable? If not, what is it? Carefully explain the meaning of the coefficient of R. (*Hint:* A professor's salary typically increases each year based on rank.)
d. What's your conclusion? Do economists earn more than other professors at liberal arts colleges? Explain.
e. The fact that the equation ends with the notation "+ . . ." indicates that there were more than four independent variables in the equation. If you could add a variable to the equation, what would it be? Explain.

4. Return to the Woody's regression example of Section 3.2.
   a. In any applied regression project, there is the distinct possibility that an important explanatory variable has been omitted. Reread the discussion of the selection of independent variables and come up with a suggestion for an independent variable that has not been included in the model (other than the variables already mentioned). Why do you think this variable was not included?
   b. What other kinds of criticisms would you have of the sample or independent variables chosen in this model?

5. Suppose you were told that although data on traffic for Equation 3.5 are still too expensive to obtain, a variable on traffic, called T_i, is available that is defined as 1 if traffic is "heavy" in front of the restaurant and 0 otherwise. Further suppose that when the new variable (T_i) is added to the equation, the results are:

$$\hat{Y}_i = 95{,}236 - 7307N_i + 0.320P_i + 1.28I_i + 10{,}994T_i \qquad (3.7)$$
$$\phantom{\hat{Y}_i = 95{,}236 - } (2153) \quad (0.073) \quad (0.51) \quad (5577)$$
$$t = -3.39 \qquad 4.24 \qquad 2.47 \qquad 1.97$$
$$N = 33 \qquad \overline{R}^2 = .617$$

a. What is the expected sign of the coefficient of the new variable?
b. Would you prefer this equation to the original one? Why?
c. Does the fact that $\overline{R}^2$ is higher in Equation 3.7 mean that it is *necessarily* better than Equation 3.5?

6. Suppose that the population variable in Section 3.2 had been defined in different units, as in:

P = Population: thousands of people living within a three-mile radius of the Woody's location

a. Given this definition of P, what would the estimated slope coefficients in Equation 3.5 have been?
b. Given this definition of P, what would the estimated slope coefficients in Equation 3.7 above have been?
c. Is the estimated constant affected by this change?

7. Use EViews, Stata, or your own computer regression software to estimate Equation 3.5 using the data in Table 3.1. Can you get the same results?

8. The Graduate Record Examination (GRE) subject test in economics was a multiple-choice measure of knowledge and analytical ability in economics that was used mainly as an entrance criterion for students applying to Ph.D. programs in the "dismal science." For years, critics claimed that the GRE, like the Scholastic Aptitude Test (SAT), was biased against women and some ethnic groups. To test the possibility that the GRE subject test in economics was biased against women, Mary Hirschfeld, Robert Moore, and

Eleanor Brown estimated the following equation (standard errors in parentheses):[7]

$$\widehat{GRE}_i = 172.4 + 39.7G_i + 78.9GPA_i + 0.203SATM_i + 0.110SATV_i$$
$$(10.9) \quad (10.4) \quad\quad (0.071) \quad\quad\quad (0.058)$$
$$N = 149 \quad \overline{R}^2 = .46 \quad\quad\quad\quad\quad\quad (3.8)$$

where: GRE_i = the score of the *i*th student in the Graduate Record Examination subject test in economics

G_i = a dummy variable equal to 1 if the *i*th student was a male, 0 otherwise

GPA_i = the GPA in economics classes of the *i*th student (4 = A, 3 = B, etc.)

$SATM_i$ = the score of the *i*th student on the mathematics portion of the Scholastic Aptitude Test

$SATV_i$ = the score of the *i*th student on the verbal portion of the Scholastic Aptitude Test

a. Carefully explain the meaning of the coefficient of G in this equation. (*Hint:* Be sure to specify what 39.7 stands for.)
b. Does this result prove that the GRE is biased against women? Why or why not?
c. If you were going to add one variable to Equation 3.8, what would it be? Explain your reasoning.
d. Suppose that the authors had defined their gender variables as G_i = a dummy variable equal to 1 if the *i*th student was a female, 0 otherwise. What would the estimated Equation 3.8 have been in that case? (*Hint:* Only the intercept and the coefficient of the dummy variable change.)

9. Michael Lovell estimated the following model of the gasoline mileage of various models of cars (standard errors in parentheses):[8]

$$\hat{G}_i = 22.008 - 0.002W_i - 2.76A_i + 3.28D_i + 0.415E_i$$
$$(0.001) \quad (0.71) \quad (1.41) \quad (0.097)$$
$$\overline{R}^2 = .82$$

7. Mary Hirschfeld, Robert L. Moore, and Eleanor Brown, "Exploring the Gender Gap on the GRE Subject Test in Economics," *Journal of Economic Education*, Vol. 26, No. 1, pp. 3–15.

8. Michael C. Lovell, "Tests of the Rational Expectations Hypothesis," *American Economic Review*, Vol. 76, No. 1, pp. 110–124.

where: G_i = miles per gallon of the ith model as reported by Consumers' Union based on actual road tests
W_i = the gross weight (in pounds) of the ith model
A_i = a dummy variable equal to 1 if the ith model has an automatic transmission and 0 otherwise
D_i = a dummy variable equal to 1 if the ith model has a diesel engine and 0 otherwise
E_i = the U.S. Environmental Protection Agency's estimate of the miles per gallon of the ith model

a. Hypothesize signs for the slope coefficients of W and E. Which, if any, of the signs of the estimated coefficients are different from your expectations?
b. Carefully interpret the meanings of the estimated coefficients of A_i and D_i. (*Hint:* Remember that E is in the equation.)
c. Lovell included one of the variables in the model to test a specific hypothesis, but that variable wouldn't necessarily be in another researcher's gas mileage model. What variable do you think Lovell added? What hypothesis do you think Lovell wanted to test?

10. Your boss is about to start production of her newest box-office smash-to-be, *Invasion of the Economists, Part II*, when she calls you in and asks you to build a model of the gross receipts of all the movies produced in the last five years. Your regression is (standard errors in parentheses):[9]

$$\hat{G}_i = 781 + 15.4T_i - 992F_i + 1770J_i + 3027S_i - 3160B_i + \cdots$$
$$(5.9) \quad (674) \quad (800) \quad (1006) \quad (2381)$$
$$\overline{R}^2 = .485 \quad N = 254$$

where: G_i = the final gross receipts of the ith motion picture (in thousands of dollars)
T_i = the number of screens (theaters) on which the ith film was shown in its first week
F_i = a dummy variable equal to 1 if the star of the ith film is a female and 0 otherwise

---

9. This estimated equation (but not the question) comes from a final exam in managerial economics given at the Harvard Business School.

J_i = a dummy variable equal to 1 if the ith movie was released in June or July and 0 otherwise

S_i = a dummy variable equal to 1 if the star of the ith film is a superstar (like Tom Cruise or Milton) and 0 otherwise

B_i = a dummy variable equal to 1 if at least one member of the supporting cast of the ith film is a superstar and 0 otherwise

a. Hypothesize signs for each of the slope coefficients in the equation. Which, if any, of the signs of the estimated coefficients are different from your expectations?

b. Milton, the star of the original *Invasion of the Economists,* is demanding $4 million from your boss to appear in the sequel. If your estimates are trustworthy, should she say "yes" or hire Fred (a nobody) for $500,000?

c. Your boss wants to keep costs low, and it would cost $1.2 million to release the movie on an additional 200 screens. Assuming your estimates are trustworthy, should she spring for the extra screens?

d. The movie is scheduled for release in September, and it would cost $1 million to speed up production enough to allow a July release without hurting quality. Assuming your estimates are trustworthy, is it worth the rush?

e. You've been assuming that your estimates are trustworthy. Do you have any evidence that this is not the case? Explain your answer. (*Hint:* Assume that the equation contains no specification errors.)

11. Let's get some more experience with the six steps in applied regression. Suppose that you're interested in buying an Apple iPod (either new or used) on eBay (the auction website) but you want to avoid overbidding. One way to get an insight into how much to bid would be to run a regression on the prices[10] for which iPods have sold in previous auctions.

---

10. This is another example of a hedonic model, in which the price of an item is the dependent variable and the independent variables are the attributes of that item rather than the quantity demanded/supplied of that item. For more on hedonic models, see Section 11.8.

The first step would be to review the literature, and luckily you find some good material—particularly a 2008 article by Leonardo Rezende[11] that analyzes eBay Internet auctions and even estimates a model of the price of iPods.

The second step would be to specify the independent variables and functional form for your equation, but you run into a problem. The problem is that you want to include a variable that measures the condition of the iPod in your equation, but some iPods are new, some are used and unblemished, and some are used and have a scratch or other defect.

a. Carefully specify a variable (or variables) that will allow you to quantify the three different conditions of the iPods. Please answer this question before moving on.

b. The third step is to hypothesize the signs of the coefficients of your equation. Assume that you choose the following specification. What signs do you expect for the coefficients of NEW, SCRATCH, and BIDRS? Explain.

$$PRICE_i = \beta_0 + \beta_1 NEW_i + \beta_2 SCRATCH_i + \beta_3 BIDRS_i + \epsilon_i$$

where: $PRICE_i$ = the price at which the ith iPod sold on eBay
NEW_i = a dummy variable equal to 1 if the ith iPod was new, 0 otherwise
$SCRATCH_i$ = a dummy variable equal to 1 if the ith iPod had a minor cosmetic defect, 0 otherwise
$BIDRS_i$ = the number of bidders on the ith iPod

c. The fourth step is to collect your data. Luckily, Rezende has data for 215 silver-colored, 4 GB Apple iPod minis available on a website, so you download the data and are eager to run your first regression. Before you do, however, one of your friends points out that the iPod auctions were spread over a three-week period and worries that there's a chance that the observations are not comparable because they come from different time periods. Is this a valid concern? Why or why not?

---

11. Leonardo Rezende, "Econometrics of Auctions by Least Squares," *Journal of Applied Econometrics*, November/December 2008, pp. 925–948.

d. The fifth step is to estimate your specification using Rezende's data, producing:

$$\widehat{PRICE_i} = 109.24 + 54.99NEW_i - 20.44SCRATCH_i + 0.73BIDRS_i$$

	(5.34)	(5.11)	(0.59)
t =	10.28	−4.00	1.23

N = 215

Do the estimated coefficients correspond to your expectations? Explain.

e. The sixth step is to document your results. Look over the regression results in part d. What, if anything, is missing that should be included in our normal documentation format?

f. (optional) Estimate the equation yourself (Datafile = IPOD3), and determine the value of the item that you reported missing in your answer to part e.

4 The Classical Model

The classical model of econometrics has nothing to do with ancient Greece or even the classical economic thinking of Adam Smith. Instead, the term *classical* refers to a set of fairly basic assumptions required to hold in order for OLS to be considered the "best" estimator available for regression models. When one or more of these assumptions do not hold, other estimation techniques (such as Generalized Least Squares, to be explained in Chapter 9) sometimes may be better than OLS.

As a result, one of the most important jobs in regression analysis is to decide whether the classical assumptions hold for a particular equation. If so, the OLS estimation technique is the best available. Otherwise, the pros and cons of alternative estimation techniques must be weighed. These alternatives usually are adjustments to OLS that take account of the particular assumption that has been violated. In a sense, most of the rest of this book deals in one way or another with the question of what to do when one of the classical assumptions is not met. Since econometricians spend so much time analyzing violations of them, it is crucial that they know and understand these assumptions.

4.1 The Classical Assumptions

The **Classical Assumptions** must be met in order for OLS estimators to be the best available. Because of their importance in regression analysis, the assumptions are presented here in tabular form as well as in words. Subsequent

The Classical Assumptions

  I. The regression model is linear, is correctly specified, and has an additive error term.

  II. The error term has a zero population mean.

  III. All explanatory variables are uncorrelated with the error term.

  IV. Observations of the error term are uncorrelated with each other (no serial correlation).

  V. The error term has a constant variance (no heteroskedasticity).

  VI. No explanatory variable is a perfect linear function of any other explanatory variable(s) (no perfect multicollinearity).

  VII. The error term is normally distributed (this assumption is optional but usually is invoked).

chapters will investigate major violations of the assumptions and introduce estimation techniques that may provide better estimates in such cases.

An error term satisfying Assumptions I through V is called a **classical error term**, and if Assumption VII is added, the error term is called a **classical normal error term**.

I. *The regression model is linear, is correctly specified, and has an additive error term.* The regression model is assumed to be linear:

$$Y_i = \beta_0 + \beta_1 X_{1i} + \beta_2 X_{2i} + \cdots + \beta_K X_{Ki} + \epsilon_i \tag{4.1}$$

The assumption that the regression model is linear[1] does not require the underlying theory to be linear. For example, an exponential function:

$$Y_i = e^{\beta_0} X_i^{\beta_1} e^{\epsilon_i} \tag{4.2}$$

where e is the base of the natural log, can be transformed by taking the natural log of both sides of the equation:

$$\ln(Y_i) = \beta_0 + \beta_1 \ln(X_i) + \epsilon_i \tag{4.3}$$

---

1. The Classical Assumption that the regression model be "linear" technically requires the model to be "linear in the coefficients." You'll learn what it means for a model to be linear in the coefficients, particularly in contrast to being linear in the variables, in Section 7.2. We'll cover the application of regression analysis to equations that are nonlinear in the variables in that same section, but the application of regression analysis to equations that are nonlinear in the coefficients is beyond the scope of this textbook.

If the variables are relabeled as $Y_i^* = \ln(Y_i)$ and $X_i^* = \ln(X_i)$, then the form of the equation becomes linear:

$$Y_i^* = \beta_0 + \beta_1 X_i^* + \epsilon_i \qquad (4.4)$$

In Equation 4.4, the properties of the OLS estimator of the βs still hold because the equation is linear.

Two additional properties also must hold. First, we assume that the equation is correctly specified. If an equation has an omitted variable or an incorrect functional form, the odds are against that equation working well. Second, we assume that a stochastic error term has been added to the equation. This error term must be an additive one and cannot be multiplied by or divided into any of the variables in the equation.

II. *The error term has a zero population mean.* As was pointed out in Section 1.2, econometricians add a stochastic (random) error term to regression equations to account for variation in the dependent variable that is not explained by the model. The specific value of the error term for each observation is determined purely by chance. Probably the best way to picture this concept is to think of each observation of the error term as being drawn from a random variable distribution such as the one illustrated in Figure 4.1.

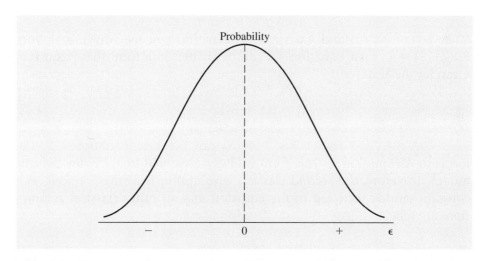

Figure 4.1 An Error Term Distribution with a Mean of Zero

Observations of stochastic error terms are assumed to be drawn from a random variable distribution with a mean of zero. If Classical Assumption II is met, the expected value (the mean) of the error term is zero.

Classical Assumption II says that the mean of this distribution is zero. That is, when the entire population of possible values for the stochastic error term is considered, the average value of that population is zero. For a small sample, it is not likely that the mean is exactly zero, but as the size of the sample approaches infinity, the mean of the sample approaches zero.

To compensate for the chance that the mean of ϵ might not equal zero, the mean of ϵ_i for any regression is forced to be zero by the existence of the constant term in the equation. In essence, the constant term equals the fixed portion of Y that cannot be explained by the independent variables, whereas the error term equals the stochastic portion of the unexplained value of Y.

Although it's true that the error term can never be observed, it's instructive to pretend that we can do so to see how the existence of a constant term forces the mean of the error term to be zero in a sample. Consider a typical regression equation:

$$Y_i = \beta_0 + \beta_1 X_i + \epsilon_i \tag{4.5}$$

Suppose that the mean of ϵ_i is 3 instead of 0, then[2] $E(\epsilon_i - 3) = 0$. If we add 3 to the constant term and subtract it from the error term, we obtain:

$$Y_i = (\beta_0 + 3) + \beta_1 X_i + (\epsilon_i - 3) \tag{4.6}$$

Since Equations 4.5 and 4.6 are equivalent (do you see why?), and since $E(\epsilon_i - 3) = 0$, then Equation 4.6 can be written in a form that has a zero mean for the error term:

$$Y_i = \beta_0^* + \beta_1 X_i + \epsilon_i^* \tag{4.7}$$

where $\beta_0^* = \beta_0 + 3$ and $\epsilon_i^* = \epsilon_i - 3$. As can be seen, Equation 4.7 conforms to Assumption II. This form is always assumed to apply for the true model. Therefore, the second classical assumption is assured as long as a constant term is included in the equation and all other classical assumptions are met.

---

2. Here, as in Chapter 1, the "E" refers to the expected value (mean) of the item in parentheses after it. Thus $E(\epsilon_i - 3)$ equals the expected value of the stochastic error term epsilon minus 3. In this specific example, since we've defined $E(\epsilon_i) = 3$, we know that $E(\epsilon_i - 3) = 0$. One way to think about expected value is as our best guess of the long-run average value a specific random variable will have.

III. *All explanatory variables are uncorrelated with the error term.* It is assumed that the observed values of the explanatory variables are independent of the values of the error term.

If an explanatory variable and the error term were instead correlated with each other, the OLS estimates would be likely to attribute to the X some of the variation in Y that actually came from the error term. If the error term and X were positively correlated, for example, then the estimated coefficient would probably be higher than it would otherwise have been (biased upward), because the OLS program would mistakenly attribute the variation in Y caused by ϵ to X instead. As a result, it's important to ensure that the explanatory variables are uncorrelated with the error term.

Classical Assumption III is violated most frequently when a researcher omits an important independent variable from an equation. As you learned in Chapter 1, one of the major components of the stochastic error term is omitted variables, so if a variable has been omitted, then the error term will change when the omitted variable changes. If this omitted variable is correlated with an included independent variable (as often happens in economics), then the error term is correlated with that independent variable as well. We have violated Assumption III! Because of this violation, OLS will attribute the impact of the omitted variable to the included variable, to the extent that the two variables are correlated.

An important economic application that violates this assumption is any model that is simultaneous in nature. In most economic applications, there are several related propositions that, when taken as a group, suggest a *system* of regression equations. In most situations, interrelated equations should be considered simultaneously instead of separately. Unfortunately, such simultaneous systems violate Classical Assumption III. This will be considered in more detail in Chapter 14.

IV. *Observations of the error term are uncorrelated with each other.* The observations of the error term are drawn independently from each other. If a systematic correlation exists between one observation of the error term and another, then it will be more difficult for OLS to get accurate estimates of the standard errors of the coefficients. For example, if the fact that the ϵ from one observation is positive increases the probability that the ϵ from another observation also is positive, then the two observations of the error term are positively correlated. Such a correlation would violate Classical Assumption IV.

In economic applications, this assumption is most important in time-series models. In such a context, Assumption IV says that an increase in the error term in one time period (a random shock, for example) does not show up in or affect in any way the error term in another time period.

In some cases, though, this assumption is unrealistic, since the effects of a random shock sometimes last for a number of time periods. For example, a natural disaster like Hurricane Katrina will have a negative impact on a region far after the time period in which it was truly a random event. If, over all the observations of the sample, ϵ_{t+1} is correlated with ϵ_t, then the error term is said to be **serially correlated** (or *autocorrelated*), and Assumption IV is violated. Violations of this assumption are considered in more detail in Chapter 9.

   V. *The error term has a constant variance.* The variance (or dispersion) of the distribution from which the observations of the error term are drawn is constant. That is, the observations of the error term are assumed to be drawn continually from identical distributions (for example, the one pictured in Figure 4.1). The alternative would be for the variance of the distribution of the error term to change for each observation or range of observations. In Figure 4.2, for example, the variance of the error term is shown to increase as

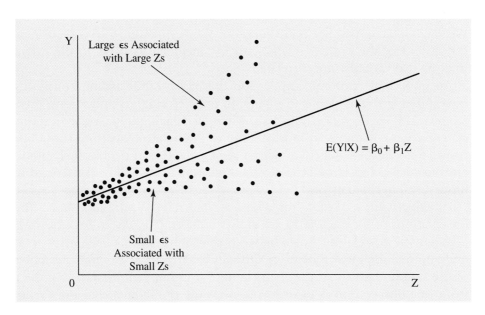

Figure 4.2 An Error Term Whose Variance Increases as Z Increases (Heteroskedasticity)

One example of Classical Assumption V not being met is when the variance of the error term increases as Z increases. In such a situation (called heteroskedasticity), the observations are on average farther from the true regression line for large values of Z than they are for small values of Z.

the variable Z increases; such a pattern violates Classical Assumption V. The actual values of the error term are not directly observable, but the lack of a constant variance for the distribution of the error term causes OLS to generate inaccurate estimates of the standard error of the coefficients.

In economic applications, Assumption V is likely to be violated in cross-sectional data sets. For example, suppose that you're studying the amount of money that the 50 states spend on education. Since New York and California are much bigger than New Hampshire and Nevada, it's probable that the variance of the stochastic error term for big states is larger than it is for small states. The amount of unexplained variation in educational expenditures seems likely to be larger in big states like New York than in small states like New Hampshire. The violation of Assumption V is referred to as **heteroskedasticity** and will be discussed in more detail in Chapter 10.

VI. *No explanatory variable is a perfect linear function of any other explanatory variable(s).* Perfect **collinearity** between two independent variables implies that they are really the same variable, or that one is a multiple of the other, and/or that a constant has been added to one of the variables. That is, the relative movements of one explanatory variable will be matched exactly by the relative movements of the other even though the absolute size of the movements might differ. Because every movement of one of the variables is matched exactly by a relative movement in the other, the OLS estimation procedure will be incapable of distinguishing one variable from the other.

Many instances of perfect collinearity (or **multicollinearity** if more than two independent variables are involved) are the result of the researcher not accounting for identities (definitional equivalences) among the independent variables. This problem can be corrected easily by dropping one of the perfectly collinear variables from the equation.

What's an example of perfect multicollinearity? Suppose that you decide to build a model of the profits of tire stores in your city and you include annual sales of tires (in dollars) at each store and the annual sales tax paid by each store as independent variables. Since the tire stores are all in the same city, they all pay the same percentage sales tax, so the sales tax paid will be a constant percentage of their total sales (in dollars). If the sales tax rate is 7%, then the total taxes paid will be exactly 7% of sales for each and every tire store. Thus sales tax will be a perfect linear function of sales, and you'll have perfect multicollinearity!

Perfect multicollinearity also can occur when two independent variables always sum to a third or when one of the explanatory variables doesn't change within the sample. With perfect multicollinearity, the OLS computer program (or any other estimation technique) will be unable to estimate the

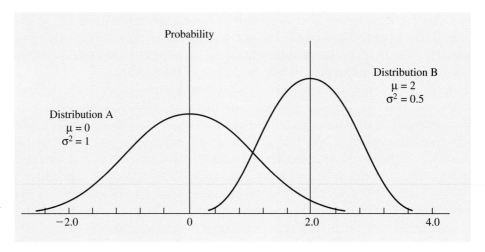

Figure 4.3 Normal Distributions

Although all normal distributions are symmetrical and bell-shaped, they do not necessarily have the same mean and variance. Distribution A has a mean of 0 and a variance of 1, whereas distribution B has a mean of 2 and a variance of 0.5. As can be seen, the whole distribution shifts when the mean changes, and the distribution gets fatter as the variance increases.

coefficients of the collinear variables (unless there is a rounding error). While it's quite unusual to encounter perfect multicollinearity in practice, even imperfect multicollinearity can cause problems for estimation, as you will see in Chapter 8.

VII. *The error term is normally distributed.* Although we have already assumed that observations of the error term are drawn independently (Assumption IV) from a distribution that has a zero mean (Assumption II) and that has a constant variance (Assumption V), we have said little about the shape of that distribution. Assumption VII states that the observations of the error term are drawn from a distribution that is normal (that is, bell-shaped, and generally following the symmetrical pattern portrayed in Figure 4.3).

This assumption of normality is not required for OLS estimation. Its major application is in **hypothesis testing**, which uses the estimated regression coefficient to investigate hypotheses about economic behavior. One example of such a test is deciding whether a particular demand curve is elastic or inelastic in a particular range. Hypothesis testing is the subject of Chapter 5, and without the normality assumption, most of the small sample tests of that chapter would be invalid.

Even though Assumption VII is optional, it's usually advisable to add the assumption of normality to the other six assumptions for two reasons:

1. The error term ϵ_i can be thought of as the sum of a number of minor influences or errors. As the number of these minor influences gets larger, the distribution of the error term tends to approach the normal distribution.[3]

2. The *t*-statistic and the *F*-statistic, which will be developed in Chapter 5, are not truly applicable unless the error term is normally distributed (or the sample is quite large).

A quick look at Figure 4.3 shows how normal distributions differ when the means and variances are different. In normal distribution A (a **Standard Normal Distribution**), the mean is 0 and the variance is 1; in normal distribution B, the mean is 2, and the variance is 0.5. When the mean is different, the entire distribution shifts. When the variance is different, the distribution becomes fatter or skinnier.

(4.2) The Sampling Distribution of $\hat{\beta}$

"It cannot be stressed too strongly how important it is for students to understand the concept of a sampling distribution."[4]

Just as the error term follows a probability distribution, so too do the estimates of β. In fact, each different sample of data typically produces a different estimate of β. The probability distribution of these $\hat{\beta}$ values across different samples is called the **sampling distribution of $\hat{\beta}$**.

Recall that an *estimator* is a formula, such as the OLS formula in Equation 2.4 that tells you how to compute $\hat{\beta}$, while an *estimate* is the value of $\hat{\beta}$ computed by the formula for a given sample. Since researchers usually have only one sample, beginning econometricians often assume that regression analysis can produce only one estimate of β for a given population. In reality, however, each different sample from the same population will produce a different estimate of β. The collection of all the possible samples has a distribution, with a

---

3. This is because of the Central Limit Theorem, which states that:

    The mean (or sum) of a number of independent, identically distributed random variables will tend to be normally distributed, regardless of their distribution, if the number of different random variables is large enough.

4. Peter Kennedy, *A Guide to Econometrics* (Malden, MA: Blackwell, 2008), p. 403.

mean and a variance, and we need to discuss the properties of this sampling distribution of $\hat{\beta}$, even though in most real applications we will encounter only a single draw from it. Be sure to remember that a sampling distribution refers to the distribution of different values of $\hat{\beta}$ across different samples, not within one. These $\hat{\beta}$s usually are assumed to be normally distributed because the normality of the error term implies that the OLS estimates of β are normally distributed as well.

Let's look at an example of a sampling distribution of $\hat{\beta}$. Suppose you decide to build a regression model to explain the starting salaries of last year's graduates of your school as a function of their GPAs at your school:

$$SALARY_i = f(\overset{+}{GPA_i}) = \beta_0 + \beta_1 GPA_i + \epsilon_i \qquad (4.8)$$

For the time being, let's focus on the sampling distribution of $\hat{\beta}_1$. If you select a sample of 25 students and get data for their salaries and grades, you can estimate Equation 4.8 with OLS and get an estimate of β_1. So far, so good.

But what will happen if you select a second sample of students and do the same thing? Will you get the same exact $\hat{\beta}_1$ that you got from the first sample? Nope! Your estimate obviously depends on the sample you pick. If your random sample includes by accident quite a few of the highest-paid graduates, the estimate will be fairly high. If another sample by chance includes an underemployed student, then the estimate will be low. As a result, you're almost certain to get a different $\hat{\beta}_1$ for every different sample you draw, because different samples are likely to have different students with different characteristics. In essence, there is a distribution of all the possible estimates that will have a mean and a variance, just as the distribution of observations of the error term does.

So, if you collect five different samples, you're extremely likely to get five different $\hat{\beta}_1$s. For instance, you might get:

First sample:	$\hat{\beta}_1 = 8,612$
Second sample:	$\hat{\beta}_1 = 8,101$
Third sample:	$\hat{\beta}_1 = 11,355$
Fourth sample:	$\hat{\beta}_1 = 6,934$
Fifth sample:	$\hat{\beta}_1 = 7,994$
Average	$\hat{\beta} = 8,599$

Each sample yields an estimate of the true population β (which is, let's say, 8,400), and the distribution of the $\hat{\beta}$s of all the possible samples has its own mean and variance. For a "good" estimation technique, we'd want the mean of the sampling distribution of the $\hat{\beta}$s to be equal to our true population β of 8,400. This is called *unbiasedness*. Although the mean $\hat{\beta}$ for our five samples is 8,599, it's likely that if we took enough samples and calculated enough $\hat{\beta}$s, the average $\hat{\beta}$ would eventually approach 8,400.

Therefore the $\hat{\beta}$s estimated by OLS for Equation 4.8 form a distribution of their own. Each sample of observations will produce a different $\hat{\beta}$, and the distribution of these estimates for all possible samples has a mean and a variance like any distribution. When we discuss the properties of estimators in the next section, it will be important to remember that we are discussing the properties of the distribution of estimates generated from a number of samples (a sampling distribution).

Properties of the Mean

A desirable property of a distribution of estimates is that its mean equals the true mean of the variable being estimated. An estimator that yields such estimates is called an unbiased estimator.

An estimator $\hat{\beta}$ is an **unbiased estimator** if its sampling distribution has as its expected value the true value of β.

$$E(\hat{\beta}) = \beta \qquad (4.9)$$

Only one value of $\hat{\beta}$ is obtained in practice, but the property of unbiasedness is useful because a single estimate drawn from an unbiased distribution is more likely to be near the true value (assuming identical variances) than one taken from a distribution not centered around the true value. If an estimator produces $\hat{\beta}$s that are not centered around the true β, the estimator is referred to as a **biased estimator**.

We cannot ensure that every estimate from an unbiased estimator is better than every estimate from a biased one, because a particular unbiased estimate[5] could, by chance, be farther from the true value than a biased estimate might be.

---

5. Technically, since an estimate has just one value, an estimate cannot be unbiased (or biased). On the other hand, the phrase "estimate produced by an unbiased estimator" is cumbersome, especially if repeated 10 times on a page. As a result, many econometricians use "unbiased estimate" as shorthand for "a single estimate produced by an unbiased estimator."

This could happen by chance or because the biased estimator had a smaller variance. Without any other information about the distribution of the estimates, however, we would always rather have an unbiased estimate than a biased one.

Properties of the Variance

Just as we would like the distribution of the $\hat{\beta}$s to be centered around the true population β, so too would we like that distribution to be as narrow (or precise) as possible. A distribution centered around the truth but with an extremely large variance might be of very little use because any given estimate would quite likely be far from the true β value. For a $\hat{\beta}$ distribution with a small variance, the estimates are likely to be close to the mean of the sampling distribution. To see this more clearly, compare distributions A and B (both of which are unbiased) in Figure 4.4. Distribution A, which has a larger variance than distribution B, is less precise than distribution B. For comparison purposes, a biased distribution (distribution C) is also pictured; note that bias implies that the expected value of the distribution is to the right or left of the true β.

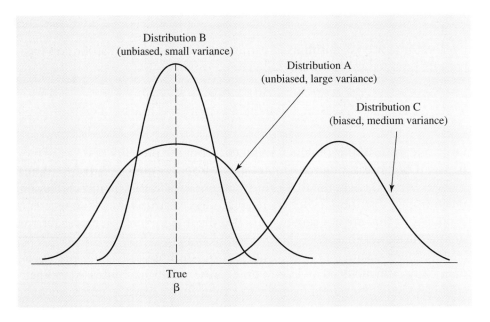

Figure 4.4 Distributions of $\hat{\beta}$

Different distributions of $\hat{\beta}$ can have different means and variances. Distributions A and B, for example, are both unbiased, but distribution A has a larger variance than does distribution B. Distribution C has a smaller variance than distribution A, but it is biased.

The variance of the distribution of the $\hat{\beta}$s can be decreased by increasing the size of the sample. This also increases the degrees of freedom, since the number of degrees of freedom equals the sample size minus the number of coefficients or parameters estimated. As the number of observations increases, other things held constant, the variance of the sampling distribution tends to decrease. Although it is not true that a sample of 15 will always produce estimates closer to the true β than a sample of 5, it is quite likely to do so; such larger samples should be sought. Figure 4.5 presents illustrative sampling distributions of $\hat{\beta}$s for 15 and 5 observations for OLS estimators of β when the true β equals 1. The larger sample does indeed produce a sampling distribution that is more closely centered around β.

In econometrics, general tendencies must be relied on. The element of chance, a random occurrence, is always present in estimating regression coefficients, and some estimates may be far from the true value no matter how good the estimating technique. However, if the distribution is centered around the

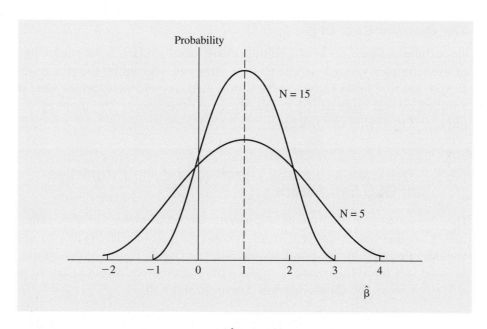

Figure 4.5 Sampling Distribution of $\hat{\beta}$ for Various Observations (N)

As the size of the sample increases, the variance of the distribution of $\hat{\beta}$s calculated from that sample tends to decrease. In the extreme case (not shown), a sample equal to the population would yield only an estimate equal to the mean of that distribution, which (for unbiased estimators) would equal the true β, and the variance of the estimates would be zero.

true value and has as small a variance as possible, the element of chance is less likely to induce a poor estimate. If the sampling distribution is centered around a value other than the true β (that is, if $\hat{\beta}$ is *biased*) then a lower variance implies that most of the sampling distribution of $\hat{\beta}$ is concentrated on the wrong value. However, if this value is not very different from the true value, which is usually not known in practice, then the greater precision will still be valuable.

One method of deciding whether this decreased variance in the distribution of the $\hat{\beta}$s is valuable enough to offset the bias is to compare different estimation techniques by using a measure called the Mean Square Error (MSE). The **Mean Square Error** is equal to the variance plus the square of the bias. The lower the MSE, the better.

A final item of importance is that as the variance of the error term increases, so too does the variance of the distribution of $\hat{\beta}$. The reason for the increased variance of $\hat{\beta}$ is that with the larger variance of ϵ_i, the more extreme values of ϵ_i are observed with more frequency, and the error term becomes more important in determining the values of Y_i.

The Standard Error of $\hat{\beta}$

Since the standard error of the estimated coefficient, $SE(\hat{\beta})$, is the square root of the estimated variance of the $\hat{\beta}$s, it is similarly affected by the size of the sample and the other factors we've mentioned. For example, an increase in sample size will cause $SE(\hat{\beta})$ to fall; the larger the sample, the more precise our coefficient estimates will be.

4.3 The Gauss–Markov Theorem and the Properties of OLS Estimators

The Gauss–Markov Theorem proves two important properties of OLS estimators. This theorem is proven in all advanced econometrics textbooks and readers interested in the proof should see Exercise 8. For a regression user, however, it's more important to know what the theorem implies than to be able to prove it. The **Gauss–Markov Theorem** states that:

> Given Classical Assumptions I through VI (Assumption VII, normality, is not needed for this theorem), the Ordinary Least Squares estimator of β_k is the minimum variance estimator from among the set of all linear unbiased estimators of β_k, for k = 0, 1, 2, . . . , K.

The Gauss–Markov Theorem is perhaps most easily remembered by stating that "OLS is BLUE" where **BLUE** stands for "*Best* (meaning minimum variance) *Linear Unbiased Estimator*." Students who might forget that "best" stands for minimum variance might be better served by remembering "OLS is MvLUE," but such a phrase is hardly catchy or easy to remember.

If an equation's coefficient estimation is unbiased (that is, if each of the estimated coefficients is produced by an unbiased estimator of the true population coefficient), then:

$$E(\hat{\beta}_k) = \beta_k \qquad (k = 0, 1, 2, \ldots, K)$$

Best means that each $\hat{\beta}_k$ has the smallest variance possible (in this case, out of all the linear unbiased estimators of β_k). An unbiased estimator with the smallest variance is called **efficient**, and that estimator is said to have the property of efficiency.

The Gauss–Markov Theorem requires that just the first six of the seven classical assumptions be met. What happens if we add in the seventh assumption, the assumption that the error term is normally distributed? In this case, the result of the Gauss–Markov Theorem is strengthened because the OLS estimator can be shown to be the best (minimum variance) unbiased estimator out of *all* the possible estimators, not just out of the linear estimators. In other words, if all seven assumptions are met, OLS is "BUE."

Given all seven classical assumptions, the OLS coefficient estimators can be shown to have the following properties:

1. *They are unbiased.* That is, $E(\hat{\beta})$ is β. This means that the OLS estimates of the coefficients are centered around the true population values of the parameters being estimated.

2. *They are minimum variance.* The distribution of the coefficient estimates around the true parameter values is as tightly or narrowly distributed as is possible for an unbiased distribution. No other unbiased estimator has a lower variance for each estimated coefficient than OLS.

3. *They are consistent.* As the sample size approaches infinity, the estimates converge to the true population parameters. Put differently, as the sample size gets larger, the variance gets smaller, and each estimate approaches the true value of the coefficient being estimated.

4. *They are normally distributed.* The $\hat{\beta}$s are $N(\beta, VAR[\hat{\beta}])$. Thus various statistical tests based on the normal distribution may indeed be applied to these estimates, as will be done in Chapter 5.

4.4 Standard Econometric Notation

This section presents the standard notation used throughout the econometrics literature. Table 4.1 presents various alternative notational devices used to represent the different population (true) parameters and their corresponding estimates (based on samples).

The measure of the central tendency of the sampling distribution of $\hat{\beta}$, which can be thought of as the mean of the $\hat{\beta}$s, is denoted as $E(\hat{\beta})$, read as "the expected value of beta-hat." The variance of $\hat{\beta}$ is the typical measure of dispersion of the sampling distribution of $\hat{\beta}$. The variance (or, alternatively, the square root of the variance, called the **standard deviation**) has several alternative notational representations, including $VAR(\hat{\beta})$ and $\sigma^2(\hat{\beta})$, read as the "variance of beta-hat."

Table 4.1 Notation Conventions

Population Parameter (True Values, but Unobserved)		Estimate (Observed from Sample)	
Name	**Symbol(s)**	**Name**	**Symbol(s)**
Regression coefficient	β_k	Estimated regression coefficient	$\hat{\beta}_k$
Expected value of the estimated coefficient	$E(\hat{\beta}_k)$		
Variance of the error term	σ^2 or $VAR(\epsilon_i)$	Estimated variance of the error term	s^2 or $\hat{\sigma}^2$
Standard deviation of the error term	σ	Standard error of the equation (estimate)	s or SE
Variance of the estimated coefficient	$\sigma^2(\hat{\beta}_k)$ or $VAR(\hat{\beta}_k)$	Estimated variance of the estimated coefficient	$s^2(\hat{\beta}_k)$ or $\widehat{VAR}(\hat{\beta}_k)$
Standard deviation of the estimated coefficient	$\sigma_{\hat{\beta}k}$ or $\sigma(\hat{\beta}_k)$	Standard error of the estimated coefficient	$\hat{\sigma}(\hat{\beta}_k)$ or $SE(\hat{\beta}_k)$
Error or disturbance term	ϵ_i	Residual (estimate of error in a loose sense)	e_i

The variance of the estimates is a population parameter that is never actually observed in practice; instead, it is estimated with $\hat{\sigma}^2(\hat{\beta}_k)$, also written as $s^2(\hat{\beta}_k)$. Note, by the way, that the variance of the true β, $\sigma^2(\beta)$, is zero, since there is only one true β_k with no distribution around it. Thus, the estimated variance of the estimated coefficient is defined and observed, the true variance of the estimated coefficient is unobservable, and the true variance of the true coefficient is zero. The square root of the estimated variance of the coefficient estimate, is the standard error of $\hat{\beta}$, $SE(\hat{\beta}_k)$, which we will use extensively in hypothesis testing.

4.5 Summary

1. The seven Classical Assumptions state that the regression model is linear with an additive error term that has a mean of zero, is uncorrelated with the explanatory variables and other observations of the error term, has a constant variance, and is normally distributed (optional). In addition, explanatory variables must not be perfect linear functions of each other.

2. The two most important properties of an estimator are unbiasedness and minimum variance. An estimator is unbiased when the expected value of the estimated coefficient is equal to the true value. Minimum variance holds when the estimating distribution has the smallest variance of all the estimators in a given class of estimators (for example, unbiased estimators).

3. Given the Classical Assumptions, OLS can be shown to be the minimum variance, linear, unbiased estimator (or BLUE, for best linear unbiased estimator) of the regression coefficients. This is the Gauss–Markov Theorem. When one or more of the classical properties do not hold (excluding normality), OLS is no longer BLUE, although it still may provide better estimates in some cases than the alternative estimation techniques discussed in subsequent chapters.

4. Because the sampling distribution of the OLS estimator of $\hat{\beta}_k$ is BLUE, it has desirable properties. Moreover, the variance, or the measure of dispersion of the sampling distribution of $\hat{\beta}_k$, decreases as the number of observations increases.

5. There is a standard notation used in the econometric literature. Table 4.1 presents this fairly complex set of notational conventions for use in regression analysis. This table should be reviewed periodically as a refresher.

EXERCISES

(The answer to Exercise 2 is in Appendix A.)

1. Write the meaning of each of the following terms without referring to the book (or to your notes), and compare your definition with the version in the text for each:
   a. the Classical Assumptions
   b. classical error term
   c. standard normal distribution
   d. $SE(\hat{\beta})$
   e. unbiased estimator
   f. BLUE
   g. sampling distribution

2. Consider the following estimated regression equation (standard errors in parentheses):

$$\hat{Y}_t = -120 + 0.10F_t + 5.33R_t \qquad \overline{R}^2 = .50$$
$$\qquad\qquad (0.05) \quad (1.00)$$

   where: Y_t = the corn yield (bushels/acre) in year t
   F_t = fertilizer intensity (pounds/acre) in year t
   R_t = rainfall (inches) in year t

   a. Carefully state the meaning of the coefficients 0.10 and 5.33 in this equation in terms of the impact of F and R on Y.
   b. Does the constant term of −120 really mean that *negative* amounts of corn are possible? If not, what is the meaning of that estimate?
   c. Suppose you were told that the true value of β_F is *known* to be 0.20. Does this show that the estimate is biased? Why or why not?
   d. Suppose you were told that the equation does not meet all the classical assumptions and, therefore, is not BLUE. Does this mean that the true β_R is definitely *not* equal to 5.33? Why or why not?

3. Which of the following pairs of independent variables would violate Assumption VI? (That is, which pairs of variables are perfect linear functions of each other?)
   a. right shoe size and left shoe size (of students in your class)
   b. consumption and disposable income (in the United States over the last 30 years)
   c. X_i and $2X_i$
   d. X_i and $(X_i)^2$

4. The Gauss–Markov Theorem shows that OLS is BLUE, so we, of course, hope and expect that our coefficient estimates will be unbiased *and* minimum variance. Suppose, however, that you had to choose one or the other.
   a. If you had to pick one, would you rather have an unbiased non-minimum variance estimate or a biased minimum variance one? Explain your reasoning.
   b. Are there circumstances in which you might change your answer to part a? (*Hint:* Does it matter *how* biased or less-than-minimum variance the estimates are?)
   c. Can you think of a way to systematically choose between estimates that have varying amounts of bias and less-than-minimum variance?

5. Edward Saunders published an article that tested the possibility that the stock market is affected by the weather on Wall Street. Using daily data from 28 years, he estimated an equation with the following significant variables (standard errors in parentheses):[6]

$$\widehat{DJ}_t = \hat{\beta}_0 + 0.10R_{t-1} + 0.0010J_t - 0.017M_t + 0.0005C_t$$
$$\qquad\quad (0.01) \qquad (0.0006) \quad (0.004) \qquad (0.0002)$$
$$N = 6{,}911 \text{ (daily)} \quad \overline{R}^2 = .02$$

where: DJ_t = the percentage change in the Dow Jones industrial average on day t
   R_t = the daily index capital gain or loss for day t
   J_t = a dummy variable equal to 1 if the *i*th day was in January, 0 otherwise

---

6. Edward M. Saunders, Jr., "Stock Prices and Wall Street Weather," *American Economic Review*, Vol. 76, No. 1, pp. 1337–1346. Saunders also estimated equations for the New York and American Stock Exchange indices, both of which had much higher R^2s than did this equation. R_{t-1} was included in the equation "to account for nonsynchronous trading effects" (p. 1341).

$$M_t = \text{a dummy variable equal to 1 if the } i\text{th day was a}$$
Monday, 0 otherwise

$$C_t = \text{a variable equal to 1 if the cloud cover was 20 per-}$$
cent or less, equal to -1 if the cloud cover was 100
percent, 0 otherwise

a. Saunders did not include an estimate of the constant term in his published regression results. Which of the Classical Assumptions supports the conclusion that you shouldn't spend much time analyzing estimates of the constant term? Explain.

b. Which of the Classical Assumptions would be violated if you decided to add a dummy variable to the equation that was equal to 1 if the ith day was a Tuesday, Wednesday, Thursday, or Friday, and equal to 0 otherwise? (*Hint:* The stock market is not open on weekends.)

c. Carefully state the meaning of the coefficients of R and M, being sure to take into account the fact that R is lagged (one time period behind) in this equation for valid theoretical reasons.

d. The variable C is a measure of the percentage of cloud cover from sunrise to sunset on the ith day and reflects the fact that approximately 85 percent of all New York's rain falls on days with 100 percent cloud cover. Is C a dummy variable? What assumptions (or conclusions) did the author have to make to use this variable? What constraints does it place on the equation?

e. Saunders concludes that these findings cast doubt on the hypothesis that security markets are entirely rational. Based just on the small portion of the author's work that we include in this question, would you agree or disagree? Why?

6. The middle third of this text (Chapters 6 through 11) concentrates on analyzing violations of the six Classical Assumptions required to prove the Gauss–Markov Theorem. If you're going to understand these chapters, it's good advice to know the Classical Assumptions *cold* before you start them. (It turns out to be fairly difficult to make sense of a whole chapter about the violation of a particular assumption if you're not really sure what that assumption is all about!) To help accomplish this task, complete the following exercises:

a. Write out the Classical Assumptions without looking at your book or notes. (*Hint:* Don't just say them to yourself in your head—put pen or pencil to paper!)

b. After you've completed writing out all six assumptions, compare your version with the text's. What differences are there? Are they important?

c. (Optional) Get together with a classmate and take turns explaining the assumptions to each other. In this exercise, try to go beyond the definition of the assumption to give your classmate a feeling for the real-world meaning of each assumption.

7. W. Bowen and T. Finegan[7] estimated the following regression equation for 78 cities (standard errors in parentheses):

$$\hat{L}_i = 94.2 - 0.24U_i + 0.20E_i - 0.69I_i - 0.06S_i + 0.002C_i - 0.80D_i$$
$$\quad\quad (0.08) \quad (0.06) \quad (0.16) \quad (0.18) \quad (0.03) \quad (0.53)$$
$$N = 78 \quad R^2 = .51$$

where: L_i = percent labor force participation (males ages 25 to 54) in the *i*th city

U_i = percent unemployment rate in the *i*th city

E_i = average earnings (hundreds of dollars/year) in the *i*th city

I_i = average other income (hundreds of dollars/year) in the *i*th city

S_i = average schooling completed (years) in the *i*th city

C_i = percent of the labor force that is nonwhite in the *i*th city

D_i = a dummy equal to 1 if the city is in the South, 0 otherwise

a. Interpret the estimated coefficients of C and D. What do they mean?

b. How likely is perfect collinearity in this equation? Explain your answer.

c. Suppose that you were told that the data for this regression were old and that estimates on new data yielded a much different coefficient of the dummy variable. Would this imply that one of the estimates was biased? If not, why not? If so, how would you determine which year's estimate was biased?

d. Comment on the following statement. "I know that these results are not BLUE because the estimated coefficient of S is wrong. It's negative when it should be positive!" Do you agree or disagree? Why?

---

7. W. G. Bowen and T. A. Finegan, "Labor Force Participation and Unemployment," in Arthur M. Ross (ed.), *Employment Policy and Labor Markets* (Berkeley: University of California Press, 1965), Table 4-2.

8. A typical exam question in a more advanced econometrics class is to prove the Gauss–Markov Theorem. How might you go about starting such a proof? What is the importance of such a proof?

9. For your first econometrics project you decide to model sales at the frozen yogurt store nearest your school. The owner of the store is glad to help you with data collection because she believes that students from your school make up the bulk of her business. After countless hours of data collection and an endless supply of frozen yogurt, you estimate the following regression equation (standard errors in parentheses):

$$\hat{Y}_t = 262.5 + 3.9T_t - 46.94P_t + 134.3A_t - 152.1C_t$$
$$(0.7) \quad (20.0) \quad (108.0) \quad (138.3)$$
$$N = 29 \quad \overline{R}^2 = .78$$

where: Y_t = the total number of frozen yogurts sold during the tth two-week time period

T_t = average high temperature (in degrees F) during period t

P_t = the price of frozen yogurt (in dollars) at the store in period t

A_t = a dummy variable equal to 1 if the owner places an ad in the school newspaper during period t, 0 otherwise

C_t = a dummy variable equal to 1 if your school is in regular session in period t (early September through early December and early January through late May), 0 otherwise

a. Does this equation appear to violate any of the Classical Assumptions? That is, do you see any evidence that a Classical Assumption is or is not met in this equation?

b. What is the real-world economic meaning of the fact that the estimated coefficient of A_t is 134.3? Be specific.

c. You and the owner are surprised at the sign of the coefficient of C_t. Can you think of any reason for this sign? (*Hint:* Assume that your school has no summer session.)

d. If you could add one variable to this equation, what would it be? Be specific.

10. In Hollywood, most nightclubs hire "promoters," or people who walk around near the nightclub and try to convince passersby to enter

the club. Recently, one of the nightclubs asked a marketing consultant to estimate the effectiveness of such promoters in terms of their ability to attract patrons to the club. The consultant did some research and found that the main entertainment at the nightclubs were attractive dancers and that the most popular nightclubs were on Hollywood Boulevard or attached to hotels, so he hypothesized the following model of nightclub attendance:

$$PEOPLE_i = \beta_0 + \beta_1 HOLLY_i + \beta_2 PROMO_i + \beta_3 HOTEL_i + \beta_4 GOGO_i + \epsilon_i$$

where: $PEOPLE_i$ = attendance at the ith nightclub at midnight on Saturday 11/24/07

$HOLLY_i$ = equal to 1 if the ith nightclub is on Hollywood Boulevard, 0 otherwise

$PROMO_i$ = number of promoters working at the ith nightclub that night

$HOTEL_i$ = equal to 1 if the ith nightclub is part of a hotel, 0 otherwise

$GOGO_i$ = number of dancers working at the ith nightclub that night

He then collected data from 25 similarly sized nightclubs on or near Hollywood Boulevard and came up with the following estimates (standard errors in parentheses):

$$\widehat{PEOPLE_i} = 162.8 + 47.4 HOLLY_i + 22.3 PROMO_i + 214.5 HOTEL_i + 26.9 GOGO_i$$
$$(21.7) \quad\quad (11.8) \quad\quad\quad (46.0) \quad\quad\quad (7.2)$$
$$N = 25 \quad \overline{R}^2 = .57$$

Let's work through the classical assumptions to see which assumptions might or might not be met by this model. As we analyze each assumption, make sure that you can state the assumption from memory and that you understand how the following questions help us understand whether the assumption has been met.

a. Assumption I: Is the equation linear with an additive error term? Is there a chance that there's an omitted variable or an incorrect functional form?

b. Assumption II: Is there a constant term in the equation to guarantee that the expected value of the error term is zero?

   c. Assumption III: Is there a chance that there's an omitted variable or that this equation is part of a simultaneous system?

   d. Assumption IV: Is the model estimated with time-series data with the chance that a random event in one time period could affect the regression in subsequent time periods?

   e. Assumption V: Is the model estimated with cross-sectional data with dramatic variations in the size of the dependent variable?

   f. Assumption VI: Is any independent variable a perfect linear function of any other independent variable?

   g. Assume that dancers earn about as much per hour as promoters. If the equation is accurate, should the nightclub hire one more promoter or one more dancer if they want to increase attendance? Explain your answer.

11. In 2001, Donald Kenkel and Joseph Terza published an article in which they investigated the impact on an individual's alcohol consumption of a physician's advice to reduce drinking.[8] In that article, Kenkel and Terza used econometric techniques well beyond the scope of this text to conclude that such physician advice can play a significant role in reducing alcohol consumption.

   We took a fifth (no pun intended) of the authors' dataset[9] and estimated the following equation (standard errors in parentheses):

$$\widehat{DRINKS_i} = 13.00 + 11.36ADVICE_i - 0.20EDUC_i + 2.85DIVSEP_i + 14.20UNEMP_i$$
$$(2.12) \qquad (0.31) \qquad (2.55) \qquad (5.16)$$
$$t = \ 5.37 \qquad\qquad -0.65 \qquad\ 1.11 \qquad\quad 2.75$$
$$N = 500 \quad \overline{R}^2 = .07$$

where: $DRINKS_i$ = drinks consumed by the ith individual in the last two weeks

             $ADVICE_i$ = 1 if a physician had advised the ith individual to cut back on drinking alcohol, 0 otherwise

             $EDUC_i$ = years of schooling of the ith individual

---

8. Donald S. Kenkel and Joseph V. Terza, "The Effect of Physician Advice on Alcohol Consumption: Count Regression with an Endogenous Treatment Effect," *Journal of Applied Econometrics*, 2001, pp. 165–184.

9. The dataset, which is available on the *JAE* website, consists of more than 20 variables for 2467 males who participated in the 1990 National Health Interview Survey and who were current drinkers with high blood pressure.

DIVSEP_i = 1 if the ith individual was divorced or separated, 0 otherwise

UNEMP_i = 1 if the ith individual was unemployed, 0 otherwise

a. Carefully state the meaning of the estimated coefficients of DIVSEP and UNEMP. Do the signs of the coefficients make sense to you? Do the relative sizes of the coefficients make sense to you? Explain.

b. Carefully state the meaning of the estimated coefficient of ADVICE. Does the sign of the coefficient make sense to you? If so, explain. If not, this unexpected sign might be related to a violation of one of the Classical Assumptions. What Classical Assumption (other than Assumption I) is this equation almost surely violating? (*Hint:* Think about what might cause a physician to advise a patient to cut back on alcohol drinking and then review the Classical Assumptions one more time.)

c. We broke up our sample of 500 observations into five different samples of 100 observations each and calculated $\hat{\beta}$s for four of the five samples. The results (for $\hat{\beta}_{\text{ADVICE}}$) were:

1st sample: $\hat{\beta}_{\text{ADVICE}} = 10.43$

2nd sample: $\hat{\beta}_{\text{ADVICE}} = 13.52$

3rd sample: $\hat{\beta}_{\text{ADVICE}} = 14.39$

4th sample: $\hat{\beta}_{\text{ADVICE}} = 8.01$

The $\hat{\beta}$s are different! Explain in your own words how it's possible to get different $\hat{\beta}$s when you're estimating identical specifications on data that are drawn from the same source. What term would you use to describe this group of $\hat{\beta}$s?

d. The data for the fifth sample of 100 observations are in Table 4.2. Use these data to estimate DRINKS = f(ADVICE, EDUC, DIVSEP, and UNEMP) with EViews, Stata, or another regression program. What value do you get for $\hat{\beta}_{\text{ADVICE}}$? How do your estimated coefficients compare to those of the entire sample of 500?

Table 4.2 Data for the Physician Advice Equation

obs	DRINKS	ADVICE	EDUC	DIVSEP	UNEMP
1	24.0	0	13	0	1
2	10.0	0	14	0	0
3	0.0	0	14	0	0
4	24.0	1	7	0	0
5	0.0	0	12	0	0
6	1.5	1	13	0	0
7	45.0	1	15	0	0
8	0.0	0	12	0	0
9	0.0	0	16	0	0
10	0.0	0	10	0	0
11	2.0	0	16	0	0
12	13.5	0	9	0	0
13	8.0	1	12	0	0
14	0.0	0	14	1	0
15	25.0	0	13	0	0
16	11.3	0	12	1	0
17	0.0	0	17	0	0
18	0.0	0	16	0	0
19	7.0	0	14	0	0
20	40.0	1	16	0	0
21	28.0	0	14	0	0
22	1.0	1	15	0	0
23	0.0	0	10	0	0
24	0.0	0	10	0	0
25	56.0	1	16	0	0
26	0.0	0	16	1	0
27	24.0	1	12	1	0
28	5.0	0	13	0	0
29	28.0	0	7	0	0
30	14.0	0	12	0	0
31	3.0	0	18	0	0
32	0.0	0	7	0	0
33	0.0	0	18	0	0
34	0.0	0	11	0	0
35	3.0	0	12	0	0
36	10.0	0	16	0	0
37	42.0	1	17	0	0
38	1.0	0	12	0	0
39	14.0	0	15	1	0
40	9.0	0	18	0	0
41	0.0	0	18	0	0
42	15.0	0	14	0	0

(continued)

Table 4.2 (*continued*)

obs	DRINKS	ADVICE	EDUC	DIVSEP	UNEMP
43	12.0	1	18	0	0
44	6.0	0	14	1	0
45	6.0	1	17	0	0
46	0.0	1	12	0	0
47	0.0	0	12	0	0
48	0.0	0	8	0	0
49	2.0	0	9	1	0
50	0.0	1	12	0	0
51	10.0	1	12	0	0
52	58.5	1	6	0	0
53	14.0	1	14	0	0
54	0.0	0	18	0	0
55	0.0	1	12	0	0
56	5.0	0	13	0	0
57	0.0	0	7	0	0
58	14.0	0	12	0	0
59	36.0	0	13	0	0
60	0.0	0	8	0	0
61	2.0	1	8	1	0
62	70.0	1	16	0	1
63	12.0	1	12	0	0
64	3.0	1	12	0	0
65	30.0	1	9	1	0
66	10.0	0	15	0	0
67	12.0	0	16	0	0
68	84.0	0	12	0	0
69	71.5	1	12	0	0
70	49.0	0	18	0	0
71	4.0	1	13	0	0
72	3.0	1	8	0	0
73	1.0	0	12	0	0
74	33.8	0	13	0	0
75	21.0	0	14	0	0
76	12.0	0	12	0	0
77	14.0	0	18	1	0
78	0.0	0	17	0	0
79	0.0	1	7	0	0
80	1.0	0	12	0	0
81	0.0	1	12	0	0
82	70.0	0	15	1	0
83	4.0	1	16	1	0
84	4.0	0	14	0	0

(*continued*)

Table 4.2 (*continued*)

obs	DRINKS	ADVICE	EDUC	DIVSEP	UNEMP
85	21.0	1	14	1	0
86	2.0	0	16	0	0
87	30.0	1	10	0	0
88	10.0	1	13	0	0
89	16.0	1	9	1	0
90	36.0	0	13	0	0
91	0.0	1	11	0	0
92	0.0	0	12	0	0
93	108.0	1	12	1	0
94	0.0	0	12	0	0
95	0.0	1	12	0	0
96	11.0	0	13	1	0
97	28.5	0	0	0	0
98	56.0	0	13	0	0
99	3.0	0	12	0	0
100	2.0	0	12	0	0

Datafile = DRINKS4

Source: Donald S. Kenkel and Joseph V. Terza, "The Effect of Physician Advice on Alcohol Consumption: Count Regression with an Endogenous Treatment Effect," *Journal of Applied Econometrics,* 2001, pp. 165–184.

5 Hypothesis Testing

In this chapter, we return to the essence of econometrics—an effort to quantify economic relationships by analyzing sample data—and ask what conclusions we can draw from this quantification. Hypothesis testing goes beyond calculating estimates of the true population parameters to a much more complex set of questions. Hypothesis testing determines what we can learn about the real world from a sample. Is it likely that our result could have been obtained by chance? Can our theories be rejected using the results generated by our sample? If our theory is correct, what is the probability that this particular sample would have been observed? This chapter starts with a brief introduction to the topic of hypothesis testing. We then examine the *t*-test, the statistical tool typically used for hypothesis tests of individual regression coefficients.

Hypothesis testing and the *t*-test should be familiar topics to readers with strong backgrounds in statistics, who are encouraged to skim this chapter and focus on only those applications that seem somewhat new. The development of hypothesis testing procedures is explained here in terms of the regression model, however, so parts of the chapter may be instructive even to those already skilled in statistics. Students with a weak background in statistics are encouraged to read Chapter 17 before beginning this chapter.

Our approach will be classical in nature, since we assume that the sample data are our best and only information about the population. An alternative,

Bayesian statistics, uses a completely different definition of probability and does not use the sampling distribution concept.[1]

5.1 What Is Hypothesis Testing?

Hypothesis testing is used in a variety of settings. The Food and Drug Administration (FDA), for example, tests new products before allowing their sale. If the sample of people exposed to the new product shows some side effect significantly more frequently than would be expected to occur by chance, the FDA is likely to withhold approval of marketing that product. Similarly, economists have been statistically testing various relationships between consumption and income for almost a century; theories developed by John Maynard Keynes and Milton Friedman, among others, have been tested on macroeconomic and microeconomic data sets.

Although researchers are always interested in learning whether the theory in question is supported by estimates generated from a sample of real-world observations, it's almost impossible to *prove* that a given hypothesis is correct. All that can be done is to state that a particular sample conforms to a particular hypothesis. Even though we cannot prove that a given theory is "correct" using hypothesis testing, we often can *reject* a given hypothesis with a certain level of significance. In such a case, the researcher concludes that it is very unlikely that the sample result would have been observed if the hypothesized theory were correct.

Classical Null and Alternative Hypotheses

The first step in hypothesis testing is to state the hypotheses to be tested. This should be done *before* the equation is estimated because hypotheses developed after estimation run the risk of being justifications of particular results rather than tests of the validity of those results.

The **null hypothesis** typically is a statement of the values that the researcher does not expect. The notation used to specify the null hypothesis is "H_0:" followed by a statement of the range of values you do not expect.

---

1. Bayesians, by being forced to state explicitly their prior expectations, tend to do most of their thinking before estimation, which is a good habit for a number of important reasons. For more on this approach, see Peter Kennedy, *A Guide to Econometrics* (Malden, MA: Blackwell, 2008), pp. 213–231. For more advanced coverage, see Tony Lancaster, *An Introduction to Bayesian Econometrics* (Oxford: Blackwell Publishing, 2004).

For example, if you expect a positive coefficient, then you don't expect a zero or negative coefficient, and the null hypothesis is:

Null hypothesis H_0: $\beta \leq 0$ (the values you do not expect)

The **alternative hypothesis** typically is a statement of the values that the researcher expects. The notation used to specify the alternative hypothesis is "H_A:" followed by a statement of the range of values you expect. To continue our previous example, if you expect a positive coefficient, then the alternative hypothesis is:

Alternative hypothesis H_A: $\beta > 0$ (the values you expect)

To test yourself, take a moment and think about what the null and alternative hypotheses will be if you expect a negative coefficient. That's right, they're:

$$H_0: \beta \geq 0$$
$$H_A: \beta < 0$$

The above hypotheses are for a **one-sided test** because the alternative hypotheses have values on only one side of the null hypothesis. Another approach is to use a **two-sided test** (or a **two-tailed test**) in which the alternative hypothesis has values on both sides of the null hypothesis. For a two-sided test around zero, the null and alternative hypotheses are:

$$H_0: \beta = 0$$
$$H_A: \beta \neq 0$$

We should note that there are a few rare cases in which we must violate our rule that the value you expect goes in the alternative hypothesis. Classical hypothesis testing requires that the null hypothesis contain the equal sign in some form (whether it be $=$, $\leq$, or $\geq$). This requirement means that researchers are forced to put the value they expect in the null hypothesis if their expectation includes an equal sign. This typically happens when the researcher specifies a specific value rather than a range. Luckily, such exceptions are unusual in elementary applications.

With the exception of the unusual cases previously mentioned, economists always put what they expect in the alternative hypothesis. This allows us to make rather strong statements when we reject a null hypothesis. However, we can never say that we *accept* the null hypothesis; we must always say that we *cannot reject* the null hypothesis. As put by Jan Kmenta:

> Just as a court pronounces a verdict as *not guilty* rather than *innocent,* so the conclusion of a statistical test is *do not reject* rather than *accept.*[2]

Type I and Type II Errors

The typical testing technique in econometrics is to hypothesize an expected sign (or value) for each regression coefficient (except the constant term) and then to determine whether to reject the null hypothesis. Since the regression coefficients are only estimates of the true population parameters, it would be unrealistic to think that conclusions drawn from regression analysis will always be right.

There are two kinds of errors we can make in such hypothesis testing:

Type I: We reject a true null hypothesis.
Type II: We do not reject a false null hypothesis.

We will refer to these errors as **Type I** and **Type II Errors**, respectively.

Suppose we have the following null and alternative hypotheses:

$$H_0: \beta \leq 0$$
$$H_A: \beta > 0$$

Even if the true parameter β is not positive, the particular estimate obtained by a researcher may be sufficiently positive to lead to the rejection of the null hypothesis that $\beta \leq 0$. This is a Type I Error; we have rejected the truth! A Type I Error is graphed in Figure 5.1.

Alternatively, it's possible to obtain an estimate of β that is close enough to zero (or negative) to be considered "not significantly positive." Such a result may lead the researcher to "accept"[3] the hypothesis that $\beta \leq 0$ when in truth $\beta > 0$. This is a Type II Error; we have failed to reject a false null hypothesis! A Type II Error is graphed in Figure 5.2. (The specific value of $\beta = 1$ was selected as the true value in that figure purely for illustrative purposes.)

---

2. Jan Kmenta, *Elements of Econometrics* (Ann Arbor: University of Michigan Press, 1986), p. 112. (Emphasis added.)

3. We will consistently put the word accept in quotes whenever we use it. In essence, "accept" means *do not reject.*

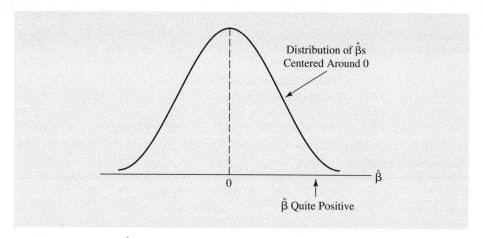

Figure 5.1 Rejecting a True Null Hypothesis Is a Type I Error

If $\beta = 0$, but you observe a $\hat{\beta}$ that is very positive, you might reject a true null hypothesis, H_0: $\beta \leq 0$, and conclude incorrectly that the alternative hypothesis H_A: $\beta > 0$ is true.

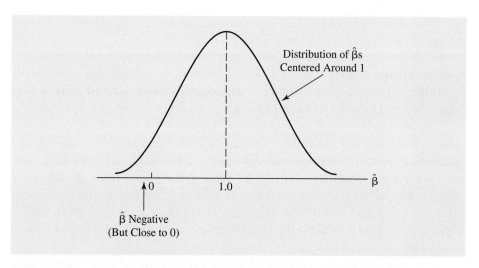

Figure 5.2 Failure to Reject a False Null Hypothesis Is a Type II Error

If $\beta = 1$, but you observe a $\hat{\beta}$ that is negative but close to zero, you might fail to reject a false null hypothesis, H_0: $\beta \leq 0$, and incorrectly ignore the fact that the alternative hypothesis, H_A: $\beta > 0$, is true.

As an example of Type I and Type II Errors, let's suppose that you're on a jury in a murder case.[4] In such a situation, the presumption of "innocent until proven guilty" implies that:

H_0: *The defendant is innocent.*
H_A: *The defendant is guilty.*

What would a Type I Error be? Rejecting the null hypothesis would mean sending the defendant to jail, so a Type I Error, rejecting a true null hypothesis, would mean:

Type I Error = Sending an innocent defendant to jail.

Similarly,

Type II Error = Freeing a guilty defendant.

Most reasonable jury members would want both levels of error to be quite small, but such certainty is almost impossible. After all, couldn't there be a mistaken identification or a lying witness? In the real world, decreasing the probability of a Type I Error (sending an innocent defendant to jail) means increasing the probability of a Type II Error (freeing a guilty defendant). If we never sent an innocent defendant to jail, we'd be freeing quite a few murderers!

Decision Rules of Hypothesis Testing

A **decision rule** is a method of deciding whether to reject a null hypothesis. Typically, a decision rule involves comparing a sample statistic with a pre-selected *critical value* found in tables such as those in the end of this text.

A decision rule should be formulated before regression estimates are obtained. The range of possible values of $\hat{\beta}$ is divided into two regions, an "*acceptance*" region and a *rejection region*, where the terms are expressed relative to the null hypothesis. To define these regions, we must determine a *critical value* (or, for a two-tailed test, two critical values) of $\hat{\beta}$. Thus, a **critical value** is a value that divides the "acceptance" region from the rejection region when testing a null hypothesis. Graphs of these "acceptance" and rejection regions are presented in Figures 5.3 and 5.4.

To use a decision rule, we need to select a critical value. Let's suppose that the critical value is 1.8. If the observed $\hat{\beta}$ is greater than 1.8, we can reject the

---

4. This example comes from and is discussed in much more detail in Ed Leamer, *Specification Searches* (New York: John Wiley and Sons, 1978), pp. 93–98.

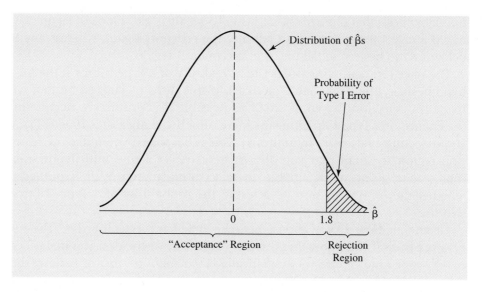

Figure 5.3 "Acceptance" and Rejection Regions for a One-Sided Test of β

For a one-sided test of H_0: $\beta \leq 0$ vs. H_A: $\beta > 0$, the critical value divides the distribution of $\hat{\beta}$ (centered around zero on the assumption that H_0 is true) into "acceptance" and rejection regions.

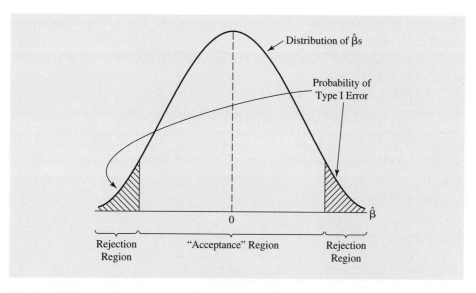

Figure 5.4 "Acceptance" and Rejection Regions for a Two-Sided Test of β

For a two-sided test of H_0: $\beta = 0$ vs. H_A: $\beta \neq 0$, we divided the distribution of $\hat{\beta}$ into an "acceptance" region and *two* rejection regions.

null hypothesis that β is zero or negative. To see this, take a look at Figure 5.3. Any $\hat{\beta}$ above 1.8 can be seen to fall into the rejection region, whereas any $\hat{\beta}$ below 1.8 can be seen to fall into the "acceptance" region.

The rejection region measures the probability of a Type I Error if the null hypothesis is true. Some students react to this news by suggesting that we make the rejection region as small as possible. Unfortunately, decreasing the chance of a Type I Error means increasing the chance of a Type II Error (not rejecting a false null hypothesis). This is because if you make the rejection region so small that you almost never reject a true null hypothesis, then you're going to be unable to reject almost every null hypothesis, whether they're true or not! As a result, the probability of a Type II Error will rise.

Given that, how do you choose between Type I and Type II Errors? The answer is easiest if you know that the cost (to society or the decision maker) of making one kind of error is dramatically larger than the cost of making the other. If you worked for the FDA, for example, you'd want to be very sure that you hadn't released a product that had horrible side effects. We'll discuss this dilemma for the t-test on page 132.

5.2   The t-Test

The t-test is the test that econometricians usually use to test hypotheses about individual regression slope coefficients. Tests of more than one coefficient at a time (joint hypotheses) are typically done with the F-test, presented in Section 5.6.

The t-test is easy to use because it accounts for differences in the units of measurement of the variables and in the standard deviations of the estimated coefficients. More important, the t-statistic is the appropriate test to use when the stochastic error term is normally distributed and when the variance of that distribution must be estimated. Since these usually are the case, the use of the t-test for hypothesis testing has become standard practice in econometrics.

The t-Statistic

For a typical multiple regression equation:

$$Y_i = \beta_0 + \beta_1 X_{1i} + \beta_2 X_{2i} + \epsilon_i \tag{5.1}$$

we can calculate t-values for each of the estimated coefficients in the equation. For reasons that will be explained in Section 7.1, t-tests are usually done only on the slope coefficients; for these, the relevant form of the *t*-statistic for the *k*th coefficient is

$$t_k = \frac{(\hat{\beta}_k - \beta_{H_0})}{SE(\hat{\beta}_k)} \qquad (k = 1, 2, \ldots, K) \qquad (5.2)$$

where: $\hat{\beta}_k$ = the estimated regression coefficient of the *k*th variable

         β_{H_0} = the border value (usually zero) implied by the null hypothesis for β_k

         $SE(\hat{\beta}_k)$ = the estimated standard error of $\hat{\beta}_k$ (that is, the square root of the estimated variance of the distribution of the $\hat{\beta}_k$; note that there is no "hat" attached to SE because SE is already defined as an estimate)

How do you decide what *border* is implied by the null hypothesis? Some null hypotheses specify a particular value. For these, β_{H_0} is simply that value; if $H_0: \beta = S$, then $\beta_{H_0} = S$. Other null hypotheses involve ranges, but we are concerned only with the value in the null hypothesis that is closest to the border between the "acceptance" region and the rejection region. This border value then becomes the β_{H_0}. For example, if $H_0: \beta \geq 0$ and $H_A: \beta < 0$, then the value in the null hypothesis closest to the border is zero, and $\beta_{H_0} = 0$.

Since most regression hypotheses test whether a particular regression coefficient is significantly different from zero, β_{H_0} is typically zero, and the most-used form of the *t*-statistic becomes

$$t_k = \frac{(\hat{\beta}_k - 0)}{SE(\hat{\beta}_k)} \qquad (k = 1, 2, \ldots, K)$$

which simplifies to

$$t_k = \frac{\hat{\beta}_k}{SE(\hat{\beta}_k)} \qquad (k = 1, 2, \ldots, K) \qquad (5.3)$$

or the estimated coefficient divided by the estimate of its standard error. This is the *t*-statistic formula used by most computer programs.

For an example of this calculation, let's consider the equation for the check volume at Woody's restaurants from Section 3.2:

$$\hat{Y}_i = 102{,}192 - 9075N_i + 0.3547P_i + 1.288I_i \qquad (5.4)$$
$$(2053) \qquad (0.0727) \quad (0.543)$$
$$t = -4.42 \qquad 4.88 \qquad 2.37$$
$$N = 33 \qquad \overline{R}^2 = .579$$

In Equation 5.4, the numbers in parentheses underneath the estimated regression coefficients are the estimated standard errors of the estimated $\hat{\beta}$s, and the numbers below them are t-values calculated according to Equation 5.3. The format used to document Equation 5.4 is the one we'll use whenever possible throughout this text. Note that the sign of the t-value is always the same as that of the estimated regression coefficient, and the standard error is always positive.

Using the regression results in Equation 5.4, let's calculate the t-value for the estimated coefficient of P, the population variable. Given the values in Equation 5.4 of 0.3547 for $\hat{\beta}_P$ and 0.0727 for $SE(\hat{\beta}_P)$, and given H_0: $\beta_P \leq 0$, the relevant t-value is indeed 4.88, as specified in Equation 5.4:

$$t_P = \frac{\hat{\beta}_P}{SE(\hat{\beta}_P)} = \frac{0.3547}{0.0727} = 4.88$$

The larger in absolute value this t-value is, the greater the likelihood that the estimated regression coefficient is significantly different from zero.

The Critical t-Value and the t-Test Decision Rule

To decide whether to reject or not to reject a null hypothesis based on a calculated t-value, we use a critical t-value. A **critical t-value** is the value that distinguishes the "acceptance" region from the rejection region. The critical t-value, t_c, is selected from a t-table (see Statistical Table B-1 in the back of the book) depending on whether the test is one-sided or two-sided, on the level of Type I Error you specify and on the degrees of freedom, which we have defined as the number of observations minus the number of coefficients estimated (including the constant) or $N - K - 1$. The level of Type I Error in a hypothesis test is also called the *level of significance* of that test and will be discussed in more detail later in this section. The t-table was created to save time during research; it consists of critical t-values given specific areas underneath curves such as those in Figure 5.3 for Type I Errors. A critical t-value is thus a function of the probability of Type I Error that the researcher wants to specify.

Once you have obtained a calculated t-value t_k and a critical t-value t_c, you reject the null hypothesis if the calculated t-value is greater in absolute value than the critical t-value and if the calculated t-value has the sign implied by H_A.

Thus, the rule to apply when testing a single regression coefficient is that you should:

Reject H_0 if $|t_k| > t_c$ and if t_k also has the sign implied by H_A. Do not reject H_0 otherwise.

This decision rule works for calculated *t*-values and critical *t*-values for one-sided hypotheses around zero:

$$H_0: \beta_k \leq 0$$
$$H_A: \beta_k > 0$$

$$H_0: \beta_k \geq 0$$
$$H_A: \beta_k < 0$$

for two-sided hypotheses around zero:

$$H_0: \beta_k = 0$$
$$H_A: \beta_k \neq 0$$

for one-sided hypotheses based on hypothesized values other than zero:

$$H_0: \beta_k \leq S$$
$$H_A: \beta_k > S$$

$$H_0: \beta_k \geq S$$
$$H_A: \beta_k < S$$

and for two-sided hypotheses based on hypothesized values other than zero:

$$H_0: \beta_k = S$$
$$H_A: \beta_k \neq S$$

The decision rule is the same: Reject the null hypothesis if the appropriately calculated *t*-value, t_k, is greater in absolute value than the critical *t*-value, t_c, as long as the sign of t_k is the same as the sign of the coefficient implied in H_A. Otherwise, do not reject H_0. Always use Equation 5.2 whenever the hypothesized value is not zero.

Statistical Table B-1 contains the critical values t_c for varying degrees of freedom and levels of significance. The columns indicate the levels of significance according to whether the test is one-sided or two-sided, and the rows indicate the degrees of freedom. For an example of the use of this table and the decision rule, let's return to the Woody's restaurant example and, in particular, to the *t*-value for $\hat{\beta}_P$ calculated in the previous section. Recall that we hypothesized that population's coefficient would be positive, so this is a one-sided test:

$$H_0: \beta_p \leq 0$$
$$H_A: \beta_p > 0$$

There are 29 degrees of freedom (equal to $N - K - 1$, or $33 - 3 - 1$) in this regression, so the appropriate t-value with which to test the calculated t-value is a one-tailed critical t-value with 29 degrees of freedom. To find this value, pick a level of significance, say 5 percent, and turn to Statistical Table B-1. Take a look for yourself. Do you agree that the number there is 1.699?

Given that, should you reject the null hypothesis? The decision rule is to reject H_0 if $|t_k| > t_c$ and if t_k has the sign implied by H_A. Since the 5-percent, one-sided, 29 degrees of freedom critical t-value is 1.699, and since the sign implied by H_A is positive, the decision rule (for this specific case) becomes:

$$\text{Reject } H_0 \text{ if } |t_P| > 1.699 \text{ and if } t_P \text{ is positive}$$

or, combining the two conditions:

$$\text{Reject } H_0 \text{ if } t_P > 1.699$$

What is t_P? In the previous section, we found that t_P was $+4.88$, so we would reject the null hypothesis and conclude that population does indeed tend to have a positive relationship with Woody's check volume (holding the other variables in the equation constant).

Note from Statistical Table B-1 that the critical t-value for a one-tailed test at a given level of significance is exactly equal to the critical t-value for a two-tailed test at twice the level of significance as the one-tailed test. This relationship between one-sided and two-sided tests is illustrated in Figure 5.5. The critical value $t_c = 1.699$ is for a one-sided, 5-percent level of significance, but it also represents a two-sided, 10-percent level of significance because if one tail represents 5 percent, then both tails added together represent 10 percent.

Choosing a Level of Significance

To complete the previous example, it was necessary to pick a level of significance before a critical t-value could be found in Statistical Table B-1. The words "significantly positive" usually carry the statistical interpretation that H_0 ($\beta \leq 0$) was rejected in favor of H_A ($\beta > 0$) according to the pre-established decision rule, which was set up with a given level of significance. The **level of significance** indicates the probability of observing an estimated t-value greater than the critical t-value if the null hypothesis were correct. It measures the amount of Type I Error implied by a particular critical t-value. If the level of significance is 10 percent and we reject the null hypothesis at that level, then this result would have occurred only 10 percent of the time that the null hypothesis was indeed correct.

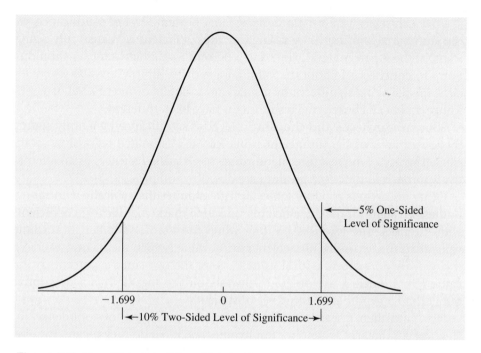

Figure 5.5 One-Sided and Two-Sided *t*-Tests

The t_c for a one-sided test at a given level of significance is equal exactly to the t_c for a two-sided test with twice the level of significance of the one-sided test. For example, $t_c = 1.699$ for a 10-percent two-sided *and* for a 5-percent one-sided test (for 29 degrees of freedom).

How should you choose a level of significance? Most beginning econometricians (and many published ones, too) assume that the lower the level of significance, the better. After all, they say, doesn't a low level of significance guarantee a low probability of making a Type I Error? Unfortunately, an extremely low level of significance also dramatically increases the probability of making a Type II Error. Therefore, unless you're in the unusual situation of not caring about mistakenly "accepting" a false null hypothesis, minimizing the level of significance is *not* good standard practice.

Instead, we recommend using a 5-percent level of significance except in those circumstances when you know something unusual about the relative costs of making Type I and Type II Errors. If you know that a Type II Error will be extremely costly, for example, then it makes sense to consider using a 10-percent level of significance when you determine your critical value. Such judgments are difficult, however, so we encourage beginning researchers to adopt a 5-percent level of significance as standard.

If we can reject a null hypothesis at the 5-percent level of significance, we can summarize our results by saying that the coefficient is "statistically significant" at the 5-percent level. Since the 5-percent level is arbitrary, we shouldn't jump to conclusions about the value of a variable simply because its coefficient misses being significant by a small amount; if a different level of significance had been chosen, the result might have been different.

Some researchers avoid choosing a level of significance by simply stating the lowest level of significance possible for each estimated regression coefficient. The use of the resulting significance levels, called *p-values*, is an alternative approach to the *t*-test. *p*-values are described on pages 135–137.

Other researchers produce tables of regression results, typically without hypothesized signs for their coefficients, and then mark "significant" coefficients with asterisks. The asterisks indicate when the *t*-score is larger in absolute value than the two-sided 10-percent critical value (which merits one asterisk), the two-sided 5-percent critical value (**), or the two-sided 1-percent critical value (***). Such a use of the *t*-value should be regarded as a descriptive rather than a hypothesis-testing use of statistics.

Now and then researchers will use the phrase "degree of confidence" or "level of confidence" when they test hypotheses. What do they mean? The *level of confidence* is nothing more than 100 percent minus the level of significance. Thus a *t*-test for which we use a 5-percent level of significance can also be said to have a 95-percent level of confidence. Since the two terms have identical meanings, we will use level of significance throughout this text. Another reason we prefer the term level of significance to level of confidence is to avoid any possible confusion with the related concept of confidence intervals.

Confidence Intervals

A **confidence interval** is a range that contains the true value of an item a specified percentage of the time.[5] This percentage is the level of confidence associated with the level of significance used to choose the critical *t*-value in the interval. For an estimated regression coefficient, the confidence interval can be calculated using the two-sided critical *t*-value and the standard error of the estimated coefficient:

$$\text{Confidence interval} = \hat{\beta} \pm t_c \cdot SE(\hat{\beta}) \tag{5.5}$$

---

5. Technically, if we could take repeated samples, a 90-percent confidence interval would contain the true value in 90 out of 100 of these repeated samples.

As an example, let's return to Equation 5.4 and our *t*-test of the significance of the estimate of the coefficient of population in that equation:

$$\hat{Y}_i = 102{,}192 - 9075N_i + 0.3547P_i + 1.288I_i \qquad (5.4)$$
$$\phantom{\hat{Y}_i = 102{,}192} (2053) \quad (0.0727) \quad (0.543)$$
$$t = -4.42 \qquad 4.88 \qquad 2.37$$
$$N = 33 \qquad \overline{R}^2 = .579$$

What would a 90 percent confidence interval for $\hat{\beta}_p$ look like? Well, $\hat{\beta}_p = 0.3547$ and $SE(\hat{\beta}_p) = 0.0727$, so all we need is a 90-percent two-sided critical *t*-value for 29 degrees of freedom. As can be seen in Statistical Table B-1, this $t_c = 1.699$. Substituting these values into Equation 5.5, we get:

$$\text{90-percent confidence interval around } \hat{\beta}_p = 0.3547 \pm 1.699 \cdot 0.0727$$
$$= 0.3547 \pm 0.1235$$

In other words, we are confident that the true coefficient will fall between 0.2312 and 0.4782 90 percent of the time.

What's the relationship between confidence intervals and two-sided hypothesis testing? It turns out that if a hypothesized border value, β_{H_0}, falls within the 90-percent confidence interval for an estimated coefficient, then we will not be able to reject the null hypothesis at the 10-percent level of significance in a two-sided test. If, on the other hand, β_{H_0} falls outside the 90-percent confidence interval, then we can reject the null hypothesis.

Perhaps the most important econometric use of confidence intervals is in forecasting. Many decision makers find it practical to be given a forecast of a range of values because they find that a specific point forecast provides them with little information about the reliability or variability of the forecast. For more on this application of confidence intervals, see Section 15.2.

p-Values

There's an alternative approach to the *t*-test. This alternative, based on a measure called the *p*-value, or *marginal significance level*, is growing in popularity. A **p-value** for a *t*-score is the probability of observing a *t*-score that size or larger (in absolute value) if the null hypothesis were true. Graphically, it's the area under the curve of the *t*-distribution between the actual *t*-score and infinity (assuming that the sign of $\hat{\beta}$ is as expected).

A *p*-value is a probability, so it runs from 0 to 1. It tells us the lowest level of significance at which we could reject the null hypothesis (assuming that the estimate is in the expected direction). A small p-value casts doubt on the null hypothesis, so to reject a null hypothesis, we need a low p-value.

How do we calculate a p-value? One option would be to comb through pages and pages of statistical tables, looking for the level of significance that exactly matches the regression result. That could take days! Luckily, standard regression software packages calculate p-values automatically and print them out for every estimated coefficient.[6] You're thus able to read p-values off your regression output just as you would your $\hat{\beta}$s. Be careful, however, because virtually every regression package prints out p-values for two-sided alternative hypotheses. Such two-sided p-values include the area in both "tails," so two-sided p-values are twice the size of one-sided ones. If your test is one-sided, you need to divide the p-value in your regression output by 2 before doing any tests.

How would you use a p-value to run a t-test? If your chosen level of significance is 5 percent and the p-value is less than .05, then you can reject your null hypothesis as long as the sign is in the expected direction. Thus the p-value decision rule is:

> Reject H_0 if p-value$_K$ < the level of significance and if $\hat{\beta}_K$ has the sign implied by H_A.

Let's look at an example of the use of a p-value to run a t-test. If we return to the Woody's example of Equation 5.4 and run a one-sided test on the coefficient of I, the income variable, we have the following null and alternative hypotheses:

$$H_0: \beta_I \leq 0$$
$$H_A: \beta_I > 0$$

As you can see from the regression output for the Woody's equation on page 81 or 83 the p-value for $\hat{\beta}_I$ is .0246. This is a two-sided p-value and we're running a one-sided test, so we need to divide .0246 by 2, getting .0123. Since .0123 is lower than our chosen level of significance of .05, and since the sign of $\hat{\beta}_I$ agrees with that in H_A, we can reject H_0. Not surprisingly, this is the same result we'd get if we ran a conventional t-test.

---

6. Different software packages use different names for p-values. EViews, for example, uses the term "Prob." To see this, turn to page 81 and look in the upper-right-hand corner of the regression output. Stata, on the other hand, uses P > |t|. To see this, turn to page 83 and look in the center of the top of the page. Note that such p-values are for $H_0: \beta = 0$.

p-values have a number of advantages. They're easy to use, and they allow readers of research to choose their own levels of significance instead of being forced to use the level chosen by the original researcher. In addition, *p*-values convey information to the reader about the relative strength with which we can reject a null hypothesis. Because of these benefits, many researchers use *p*-values on a consistent basis.

Despite these advantages, we will not use *p*-values in this text. We think that beginning researchers benefit from learning the standard *t*-test procedure, particularly since it's more likely to force them to remember to hypothesize the sign of the coefficient and to use a one-sided test when a particular sign can be hypothesized. In addition, if you know how to use the standard *t*-test approach, it's easy to switch to the *p*-value approach, but the reverse isn't necessarily true.

However, we acknowledge that practicing econometricians today spend far more energy estimating models and coefficients than they spend testing hypotheses. This is because most researchers are more confident in their theories (say, that demand curves slope downward) than they are in the quality of their data or their regression methods.[7] In such situations, where the statistical tools are being used more for descriptive purposes than for hypothesis testing purposes, it's clear that the use of *p*-values saves time and conveys more information than does the standard *t*-test procedure.

5.3   Examples of *t*-Tests

Examples of One-Sided *t*-Tests

The most common use of the one-sided *t*-test is to determine whether a regression coefficient is significantly different from zero in the direction predicted by theory. Let's face it: if you expect a positive sign for a coefficient and you get a negative $\hat{\beta}$, it's hard to reject the possibility that the true β might be negative (or zero). On the other hand, if you expect a positive sign and get a positive $\hat{\beta}$, things get a bit tricky. If $\hat{\beta}$ is positive but fairly close to zero, then a one-sided *t*-test should be used to determine whether the $\hat{\beta}$ is different enough from zero to allow the rejection of the null hypothesis. Recall that in order to be able to control the amount of Type I Error we make, such a theory implies an alternative hypothesis of H_A: $\beta > 0$ (the expected sign) and a null hypothesis of H_0: $\beta \leq 0$. Let's look at some complete examples of these kinds of one-sided *t*-tests.

---

7. With thanks to Frank Wykoff.

Consider a simple model of the aggregate retail sales of new cars that hypothesizes that sales of new cars (Y) are a function of real disposable income (X_1) and the average retail price of a new car adjusted by the consumer price index (X_2). Suppose you spend some time reviewing the literature on the automobile industry and are inspired to test a new theory. You decide to add a third independent variable, the number of sports utility vehicles sold (X_3), to take account of the fact that some potential new car buyers now buy car-like trucks instead. You therefore hypothesize the following model:

$$Y = f(\overset{+}{X}_1, \overset{-}{X}_2, \overset{-}{X}_3) + \epsilon \qquad (5.6)$$

β_1 is expected to be positive and β_2 and β_3 negative. This makes sense, since you'd expect higher incomes, lower prices, or lower numbers of sports utility vehicles sold to increase new car sales, holding the other variables in the equation constant. The four steps to use when working with the t-test are:

1. Set up the null and alternative hypotheses.

2. Choose a level of significance and therefore a critical t-value.

3. Run the regression and obtain an estimated t-value (or t-score).

4. Apply the decision rule by comparing the calculated t-value with the critical t-value in order to reject or not reject the null hypothesis.

Let's look at each step in more detail.

1. *Set up the null and alternative hypotheses.*[8] From Equation 5.6, the one-sided hypotheses are set up as:

1. $H_0: \beta_1 \leq 0$
   $H_A: \beta_1 > 0$

2. $H_0: \beta_2 \geq 0$
   $H_A: \beta_2 < 0$

3. $H_0: \beta_3 \geq 0$
   $H_A: \beta_3 < 0$

---

8. The null hypothesis can be stated either as $H_0: \beta \leq 0$ or $H_0: \beta = 0$ because the value used to test $H_0: \beta \leq 0$ is the value in the null hypothesis closest to the border between the acceptance and the rejection regions. When the amount of Type I Error is calculated, this border value of β is the one that is used, because over the whole range of $\beta \leq 0$, the value $\beta = 0$ gives the maximum amount of Type I Error. The classical approach limits this maximum amount to a preassigned level—the chosen level of significance.

Remember that a *t*-test typically is not run on the estimate of the constant term β_0.

2. *Choose a level of significance and therefore a critical t-value.* Assume that you have considered the various costs involved in making Type I and Type II Errors and have chosen 5 percent as the level of significance with which you want to test. There are 10 observations in the data set that is going to be used to test these hypotheses, and so there are $10 - 3 - 1 = 6$ degrees of freedom. At a 5-percent level of significance, the critical *t*-value, t_c, can be found in Statistical Table B-1 to be 1.943. Note that the level of significance does not have to be the same for all the coefficients in the same regression equation. It could well be that the costs involved in an incorrectly rejected null hypothesis for one coefficient are much higher than for another, so lower levels of significance would be used. In this equation, though, for all three variables:

$$t_c = 1.943$$

3. *Run the regression and obtain an estimated t-value.* You now use the data (annual from 2000 to 2009) to run the regression on your OLS computer package, getting:

$$\hat{Y}_t = 1.30 + 4.91X_{1t} + 0.00123X_{2t} - 7.14X_{3t} \tag{5.7}$$
$$(2.38) \quad (0.00022) \quad (71.38)$$
$$t = 2.1 \qquad 5.6 \qquad\quad -0.1$$

where: Y = new car sales (in hundreds of thousands of units) in year t

X_1 = real U.S. disposable income (in hundreds of billions of dollars)

X_2 = the average retail price of a new car in year t (in dollars)

X_3 = the number of sports utility vehicles sold in year t (in millions)

Once again, we use our standard documentation notation, so the figures in parentheses are the estimated standard errors of the $\hat{\beta}$s. The *t*-values to be used in these hypothesis tests are printed out by standard OLS programs:

$$t_k = \frac{\hat{\beta}_k}{SE(\hat{\beta}_k)} \qquad (k = 1, 2, \ldots, K) \tag{5.3}$$

For example, the estimated coefficient of X_3 divided by its estimated standard error is $-7.14/71.38 = -0.1$. Note that since standard errors are always positive, a negative estimated coefficient implies a negative t-value.

4. *Apply the decision rule by comparing the calculated t-value with the critical t-value in order to reject or not reject the null hypothesis.* As stated in Section 5.2, the decision rule for the t-test is to

> Reject H_0 if $|t_k| > t_c$ and if t_k also has the sign implied by H_A.
> Do not reject H_0 otherwise.

What would these decision rules be for the three hypotheses, given the relevant critical t-value (1.943) and the calculated t-values?

> For β_1: Reject H_0 if $|2.1| > 1.943$ and if 2.1 is positive.

In the case of disposable income, you reject the null hypothesis that $\beta_1 \leq 0$ since 2.1 is indeed greater than 1.943. The result (that is, $H_A: \beta_1 > 0$) is as you expected on the basis of theory, since the more income in the country, the more new car sales you'd expect.

> For β_2: Reject H_0: if $|5.6| > 1.943$ and if 5.6 is negative.

For prices, the t-statistic is large in absolute value (being greater than 1.943) but has a sign that is contrary to our expectations, since the alternative hypothesis implies a negative sign. Since both conditions in the decision rule must be met before we can reject H_0, you cannot reject the null hypothesis that $\beta_2 \geq 0$. That is, you cannot reject the hypothesis that prices have a zero or positive effect on new car sales! This is an extremely small data set that covers a time period of dramatic economic swings, but even so, you're surprised by this result. Despite your surprise, you stick with your contention that prices belong in the equation and that their expected impact should be negative.

Notice that the coefficient of X_2 is quite small, 0.00123, but that this size has no effect on the t-calculation other than its relationship to the standard error of the estimated coefficient. In other words, the absolute magnitude of any $\hat{\beta}$ is of no particular importance in determining statistical significance because a change in the units of measurement of X_2 will change both $\hat{\beta}_2$ and $SE(\hat{\beta}_2)$ in exactly the same way, so the calculated t-value (the ratio of the two) is unchanged.

> For β_3: Reject H_0 if $|-0.1| > 1.943$ and if -0.1 is negative.

For sales of sports utility vehicles, the coefficient $\hat{\beta}_3$ is not statistically different from zero, since $|-0.1| < 1.943$, and you cannot reject the null hypothesis

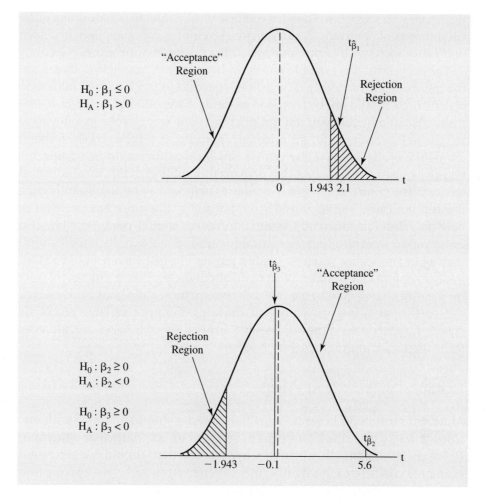

Figure 5.6 One-Sided *t*-Tests of the Coefficients of the New
Car Sales Model

Given the estimates in Equation 5.7 and the critical *t*-value of 1.943 for a 5-percent
level of significance, one-sided, 6 degrees of freedom *t*-test, we can reject the null hypothesis for $\hat{\beta}_1$, but not for $\hat{\beta}_2$ or $\hat{\beta}_3$.

that $\beta \geq 0$ even though the estimated coefficient has the sign implied by the alternative hypothesis. After thinking this model over again, you come to the conclusion that you were hasty in adding the variable to the equation.

Figure 5.6 illustrates all three of these outcomes by plotting the critical *t*-value and the calculated *t*-values for all three null hypotheses on a *t*-distribution that is centered around zero (the value in the null hypothesis closest to the border between the acceptance and rejection regions). Students are urged to analyze the results of tests on the estimated coefficients of Equation 5.7 assuming different numbers of observations and different levels of significance. Exercise 2 has a number of such specific combinations, with answers in Appendix A.

The purpose of this example is to provide practice in testing hypotheses, and the results of such a poorly thought-out equation for such a small number of observations should not be taken too seriously. Given all that, however, it's still instructive to note that you did not react the same way to your inability to reject the null hypotheses for the price and sports utility vehicle variables. That is, the failure of the sports utility vehicle variable's coefficient to be significantly negative caused you to realize that perhaps the addition of this variable was ill-advised. The failure of the price variable's coefficient to be significantly negative did not cause you to consider the possibility that price has no effect on new car sales. Put differently, estimation results should never be allowed to cause you to want to adjust theoretically sound variables or hypotheses, but if they make you realize you have made a serious mistake, then it would be foolhardy to ignore that mistake. What to do about the positive coefficient of price, on the other hand, is what the "art" of econometrics is all about. Surely a positive coefficient is unsatisfactory, but throwing the price variable out of the equation seems even more so. Possible answers to such issues are addressed more than once in the chapters that follow.

Examples of Two-Sided *t*-Tests

Although most hypotheses in regression analysis should be tested with one-sided *t*-tests, two-sided *t*-tests are appropriate in particular situations. Researchers sometimes encounter hypotheses that should be rejected if estimated coefficients are significantly different from zero, or a specific nonzero value, in either direction. This situation requires a two-sided *t*-test. The kinds of circumstances that call for a two-sided test fall into two categories:

1. Two-sided tests of whether an estimated coefficient is significantly different from zero, and

2. Two-sided tests of whether an estimated coefficient is significantly different from a specific nonzero value.

Let's take a closer look at these categories:

1. **Testing whether a $\hat{\beta}$ is statistically different from zero.** The first case for a two-sided test of $\hat{\beta}$ arises when there are two or more conflicting hypotheses about the expected sign of a coefficient. For example, in the Woody's restaurant equation of Section 3.2, the impact of the average income of an area on the expected number of Woody's customers in

that area is ambiguous. A high-income neighborhood might have more total customers going out to dinner, but those customers might decide to eat at a more formal restaurant than Woody's. As a result, you might run a two-sided *t*-test around zero to determine whether the estimated coefficient of income is significantly different from zero in *either* direction. In other words, since there are reasonable cases to be made for either a positive or a negative coefficient, it is appropriate to test the $\hat{\beta}$ for income with a two-sided *t*-test:

$$H_0: \beta_I = 0$$
$$H_A: \beta_I \neq 0$$

As Figure 5.7 illustrates, a two-sided test implies two different rejection regions (one positive and one negative) surrounding the acceptance region. A critical *t*-value, t_c, must be increased in order to achieve the

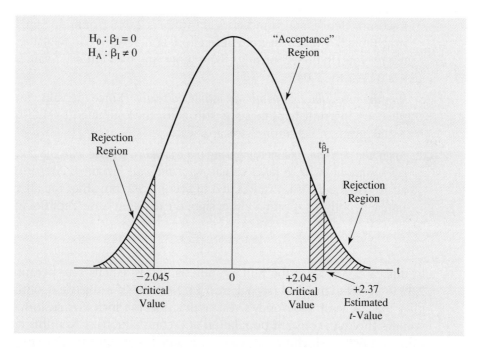

Figure 5.7 Two-Sided *t*-Test of the Coefficient of Income in the Woody's Model

Given the estimates of Equation 5.4 and the critical *t*-values of ± 2.045 for a 5-percent level of significance, two-sided, 29 degrees of freedom *t*-test, we can reject the null hypothesis that $\beta_I = 0$.

same level of significance with a two-sided test as can be achieved with a one-sided test.[9] As a result, there is an advantage to testing hypotheses with a one-sided test if the underlying theory allows because, for the same t-values, the possibility of Type I Error is half as much for a one-sided test as for a two-sided test. In cases where there are powerful theoretical arguments on both sides, however, the researcher has no alternative to using a two-sided t-test around zero. To see how this works, let's follow through the Woody's income variable example in more detail.

a. *Set up the null and alternative hypotheses.*

$$H_0: \beta_I = 0$$
$$H_A: \beta_I \neq 0$$

b. *Choose a level of significance and therefore a critical t-value.* You decide to keep the level of significance at 5 percent, but now this amount must be distributed between two rejection regions for 29 degrees of freedom. Hence, the correct critical t-value is 2.045 (found in Statistical Table B-1 for 29 degrees of freedom and a 5-percent, two-sided test). Note that, technically, there now are two critical t-values, $+2.045$ and -2.045.

c. *Run the regression and obtain an estimated t-value.* Since the value implied by the null hypothesis is still zero, the estimated t-value of $+2.37$ given in Equation 5.4 is applicable.

d. *Apply the decision rule by comparing the calculated t-value with the critical t-value in order to reject or not reject the null hypothesis.* We once again use the decision rule stated in Section 5.2, but since the alternative hypothesis specifies either sign, the decision rule simplifies to:

$$\text{For } \beta_I \quad \text{Reject } H_0 \text{ if } |2.37| > 2.045$$

In this case, you reject the null hypothesis that β_I equals zero because 2.37 is greater than 2.045 (see Figure 5.7). Note that the positive sign implies that, at least for Woody's restaurants, income increases customer volume (holding constant population and competition). Given this result, we might well choose to run a one-sided t-test on the next year's Woody's data set. For more practice with two-sided t-tests, see Exercise 6.

---

9. See Figure 5.5. In that figure, the same critical t-value has double the level of significance for a two-sided test as for a one-sided test.

2. **Two-sided *t*-tests of a specific nonzero coefficient value.** The second case for a two-sided *t*-test arises when there is reason to expect a specific nonzero value for an estimated coefficient. For example, if a previous researcher has stated that the true value of some coefficient almost surely equals a particular number, β_{H_0}, then that number would be the one to test by creating a two-sided *t*-test around the hypothesized value, β_{H_0}. To the extent that you feel that the hypothesized value is theoretically correct, you also violate the normal practice of using the null hypothesis to state the hypothesis you expect to reject.[10]

In such a case, the null and alternative hypotheses become:

$$H_0: \beta_k = \beta_{H_0}$$
$$H_A: \beta_k \neq \beta_{H_0}$$

where β_{H_0} is the specific nonzero value hypothesized.

Since the hypothesized β value is no longer zero, the formula with which to calculate the estimated *t*-value is Equation 5.2, repeated here:

$$t_k = \frac{(\hat{\beta}_k - \beta_{H_0})}{SE(\hat{\beta}_k)} \qquad (k = 1, 2, \ldots, K) \qquad (5.2)$$

This *t*-statistic is still distributed around zero if the null hypothesis is correct, because we have subtracted β_{H_0} from the estimated regression coefficient whose expected value is supposed to be β_{H_0} when H_0 is true. Since the *t*-statistic is still centered around zero, the decision rule developed earlier still is applicable. For practice with this kind of *t*-test, see Exercise 6.

5.4 Limitations of the *t*-Test

A problem with the *t*-test is that it is easy to misuse; *t*-scores are printed out by computer regression packages and the *t*-test seems easy to work with, so beginning researchers sometimes attempt to use the *t*-test to "prove" things

---

10. Instead of being able to reject an incorrect theory based on the evidence, the researcher who violates the normal practice is reduced to "not rejecting" the β value expected to be true. However, there are many theories that are not rejected by the data, and the researcher is left with a regrettably weak conclusion. One way to accommodate such violations is to increase the level of significance, thereby increasing the likelihood of a Type I Error.

that it was never intended to even test. For that reason, it's probably just as important to know the limitations of the t-test[11] as it is to know the applications of that test. Perhaps the most important of these limitations, that the usefulness of the t-test diminishes rapidly as more and more specifications are estimated and tested, is the subject of Section 6.4. The purpose of the present section is to give additional examples of how the t-test should *not* be used.

The t-Test Does Not Test Theoretical Validity

Recall that the purpose of the t-test is to help the researcher make inferences about a particular population coefficient based on an estimate obtained from a sample of that population. Some beginning researchers conclude that any *statistically* significant result is also a *theoretically* correct one. This is dangerous because such a conclusion confuses statistical significance with theoretical validity.

Consider for instance, the following estimated regression that explains the consumer price index in the United Kingdom:[12]

$$\hat{P} = 10.9 - 3.2C + 0.39C^2 \qquad (5.8)$$
$$(0.23) \quad (0.02)$$
$$t = -13.9 \quad 19.5$$
$$\overline{R}^2 = .982 \quad N = 21$$

Apply the t-test to these estimates. Do you agree that the two slope coefficients are statistically significant? As a quick check of Statistical Table B-1 shows, the critical t-value for 18 degrees of freedom and a 5-percent two-tailed level of significance is 2.101, so we can reject the null hypothesis of no effect in these cases and conclude that C and C^2 are indeed statistically significant variables in explaining P.

The catch is that P is the consumer price index and C is the cumulative amount of rainfall in the United Kingdom! We have just shown that rain is statistically significant in explaining consumer prices; does that also show that the underlying theory is valid? Of course not. Why is the statistical result so significant? The answer is that by chance there is a common trend on both

---

11. These limitations also apply to the use of p-values. For example, many beginning students conclude that the variable with the lowest p-value is the most important variable in an equation, but this is just as false for p-values as it is for the t-test.

12. These results, and others similar to them, can be found in David F. Hendry, "Econometrics—Alchemy or Science?" *Economica*, Vol. 47, pp. 383–406.

sides of the equation. This common trend does *not* have any meaning. The moral should be clear: Never conclude that statistical significance, as shown by the *t*-test, is the same as theoretical validity.

Occasionally, estimated coefficients will be significant in the direction opposite from that hypothesized, and some beginning researchers may be tempted to change their hypotheses. For example, a student might run a regression in which the hypothesized sign is positive, get a "statistically significant" negative sign, and be tempted to change the theoretical expectations to "expect" a negative sign after "rethinking" the issue. Although it is admirable to be willing to reexamine incorrect theories on the basis of new evidence, that evidence should be, for the most part, theoretical in nature. If the evidence causes a researcher to go back to the theoretical underpinnings of a model and find a mistake, then the null hypothesis should be changed, but then this new hypothesis should be tested using a completely different data set. After all, we already know what the result will be if the hypothesis is tested on the old one.

The *t*-Test Does Not Test "Importance"

One possible use of a regression equation is to help determine which independent variable has the largest relative effect (importance) on the dependent variable. Some beginning researchers draw the unwarranted conclusion that the most statistically significant variable in their estimated regression is also the most important in terms of explaining the largest portion of the movement of the dependent variable. Statistical significance indicates the likelihood that a particular sample result could have been obtained by chance, but it says little—if anything—about which variables determine the major portion of the variation in the dependent variable. To determine importance, a measure such as the size of the coefficient multiplied by the average size of the independent variable or the standard error of the independent variable would make much more sense. Consider the following hypothetical equation:

$$\hat{Y} = 300.0 + 10.0X_1 + 200.0X_2 \qquad (5.9)$$
$$(1.0) \qquad (25.0)$$
$$t = 10.0 \qquad 8.0$$
$$\overline{R}^2 = .90 \qquad N = 30$$

where: Y = mail-order sales of *O'Henry's Oyster Recipes*
   X_1 = hundreds of dollars of advertising expenditures in *Gourmets' Magazine*
   X_2 = hundreds of dollars of advertising expenditures on the *Julia Adult TV Cooking Show*

(Assume that all other factors, including prices, quality, and competition, remain constant during the estimation period.)

Where should O'Henry be spending his advertising money? That is, which independent variable has the biggest impact per dollar on Y? Given that X_2's coefficient is 20 times X_1's coefficient, you'd have to agree that X_2 is more important as defined, and yet which coefficient is more statistically significantly different from zero? With a t-score of 10.0, X_1 is more statistically significant than X_2 and its 8.0, but all that means is that we have more evidence that the coefficient is positive, not that the variable itself is necessarily more important in determining Y.

The t-Test Is Not Intended for Tests of the Entire Population

The t-test helps make inferences about the true value of a parameter from an estimate calculated from a sample of the *population* (the group from which the sample is being drawn). As the size of the sample approaches the size of the population, an unbiased estimated coefficient approaches the true population value. If a coefficient is calculated from the entire population, then an unbiased estimate already measures the population value and a significant t-test adds nothing to this knowledge. One might forget this property and attach too much importance to t-scores that have been obtained from samples that approximate the population in size. All the t-test does is help decide how likely it is that a particular small sample will cause a researcher to make a mistake in rejecting hypotheses about the true population parameters.

This point can perhaps best be seen by remembering that the t-score is the estimated regression coefficient divided by the standard error of the estimated regression coefficient. If the sample size is large enough to approach the population, then the standard error will fall close to zero because the distribution of estimates becomes more and more narrowly distributed around the true parameter (if this is an unbiased estimate). The standard error will approach zero as the sample size approaches infinity. Thus, the t-score will eventually become:

$$t = \frac{\hat{\beta}}{0} = \infty$$

The mere existence of a large t-score for a huge sample has no real substantive significance, because if the sample size is large enough, you can reject almost any null hypothesis! It is true that sample sizes in econometrics can never approach infinity, but many are quite large; and others contain the entire population in one data set.[13]

5.5 Summary

1. Hypothesis testing makes inferences about the validity of specific economic (or other) theories from a sample of the population for which the theories are supposed to be true. The four basic steps of hypothesis testing (using a *t*-test as an example) are:
   a. Set up the null and alternative hypotheses.
   b. Choose a level of significance and, therefore, a critical *t*-value.
   c. Run the regression and obtain an estimated *t*-value.
   d. Apply the decision rule by comparing the calculated *t*-value with the critical *t*-value in order to reject or not reject the null hypothesis.

2. The null hypothesis states the range of values that the regression coefficient is expected to take on if the researcher's theory is not correct. The alternative hypothesis is a statement of the range of values that the regression coefficient is expected to take if the researcher's theory is correct.

3. The two kinds of errors we can make in such hypothesis testing are:

   Type I: We reject a null hypothesis that is true.
   Type II: We do not reject a null hypothesis that is false.

4. The *t*-test tests hypotheses about individual coefficients from regression equations. The form for the *t*-statistic is

$$t_k = \frac{(\hat{\beta}_k - \beta_{H_0})}{SE(\hat{\beta}_k)} \qquad (k = 1, 2, \ldots, K)$$

   In many regression applications, β_{H_0} is zero. Once you have calculated a *t*-value and chosen a critical *t*-value, you reject the null hypothesis if the *t*-value is greater in absolute value than the critical *t*-value and if the *t*-value has the sign implied by the alternative hypothesis.

---

13. D. N. McCloskey, "The Loss Function Has Been Mislaid: The Rhetoric of Significance Tests," *American Economic Review*, Vol. 75, No. 2, p. 204.

5. The *t*-test is easy to use for a number of reasons, but care should be taken when using the *t*-test to avoid confusing statistical significance with theoretical validity or empirical importance.

EXERCISES

(The answer to Exercise 2 is in Appendix A.)

1. Write the meaning of each of the following terms without referring to the book (or your notes), and compare your definition with the version in the text for each.
   a. null hypothesis
   b. alternative hypothesis
   c. Type I Error
   d. level of significance
   e. two-sided test
   f. decision rule
   g. critical value
   h. *t*-statistic
   i. confidence interval
   j. *p*-value

2. Return to Section 5.3 and test the hypotheses implied by Equation 5.6 with the results in Equation 5.7 for all three coefficients under the following circumstances:
   a. 10 percent significance and 15 observations
   b. 10 percent significance and 28 observations
   c. 1 percent significance and 10 observations

3. Create null and alternative hypotheses for the following coefficients:
   a. the impact of height on weight (Section 1.4)
   b. all the coefficients in Equation A in Exercise 7, Chapter 2
   c. all the coefficients in $Y = f(X_1, X_2, \text{ and } X_3)$ where Y is total gasoline used on a particular trip, X_1 is miles traveled, X_2 is the weight of the car, and X_3 is the average speed traveled
   d. the impact of the decibel level of the grunt of a shot-putter on the length of the throw involved (shot-putters are known to make loud noises when they throw, but there is little theory about the impact of this yelling on the length of the put). Assume all relevant "non-grunt" variables are included in the equation.

4. Think of examples other than the ones in this chapter in which:
   a. It would be more important to keep the likelihood of a Type I Error low than to keep the likelihood of a Type II Error low.
   b. It would be more important to keep the likelihood of a Type II Error low than to keep the likelihood of a Type I Error low.

5. Return to Section 5.2 and test the appropriate hypotheses with the results in Equation 5.4 for all three coefficients under the following circumstances:
   a. 5 percent significance and 6 degrees of freedom
   b. 10 percent significance and 29 degrees of freedom
   c. 1 percent significance and 2 degrees of freedom

6. Using the techniques of Section 5.3, test the following two-sided hypotheses:
   a. For Equation 5.9, test the hypothesis that:

$$H_0: \beta_2 = 160.0$$
$$H_A: \beta_2 \neq 160.0$$

   at the 5-percent level of significance.
   b. For Equation 5.4, test the hypothesis that:

$$H_0: \beta_3 = 0$$
$$H_A: \beta_3 \neq 0$$

   at the 1-percent level of significance.
   c. For Equation 5.7, test the hypothesis that:

$$H_0: \beta_2 = 0$$
$$H_A: \beta_2 \neq 0$$

   at the 5-percent level of significance.

7. For all three tests in Exercise 6, under what circumstances would you worry about possible violations of the principle that the null hypothesis contains that which you do not expect to be true? In particular, what would your theoretical expectations have to be in order to avoid violating this principle in Exercise 6a?

8. Consider the following hypothetical equation for a sample of divorced men who failed to make at least one child support payment in the last four years (standard errors in parentheses):

$$\hat{P}_i = 2.0 + 0.50M_i + 25.0Y_i + 0.80A_i + 3.0B_i - 0.15C_i$$
$$\quad\quad\quad (0.10) \quad\quad (20.0) \quad (1.00) \quad (3.0) \quad\quad (0.05)$$

where: P_i = the number of monthly child support payments that the ith man missed in the last four years

M_i = the number of months the ith man was unemployed in the last four years

Y_i = the percentage of disposable income that goes to child support payments for the ith man

A_i = the age in years of the ith man

B_i = the religious beliefs of the ith man (a scale of 1 to 4, with 4 being the most religious)

C_i = the number of children the ith man has fathered

a. Your friend expects the coefficients of M and Y to be positive. Test these hypotheses. (Use the 5-percent level and N = 20.)

b. Test the hypothesis that the coefficient of A is different from zero. (Use the 1-percent level and N = 25.)

c. Develop and test hypotheses for the coefficients of B and C. (Use the 10-percent level and N = 17.)

9. Suppose that you estimate a model of house prices to determine the impact of having beach frontage on the value of a house.[14] You do some research, and you decide to use the size of the lot instead of the size of the house for a number of theoretical and data availability reasons. Your results (standard errors in parentheses) are:

$$\widehat{PRICE}_i = 40 + 35.0\,LOT_i - 2.0\,AGE_i + 10.0\,BED_i - 4.0\,FIRE_i + 100\,BEACH_i$$
$$\qquad\qquad (5.0) \qquad (1.0) \qquad (10.0) \qquad (4.0) \qquad (10)$$
$$\qquad N = 30 \qquad\qquad\qquad \overline{R}^2 = .63$$

where: $PRICE_i$ = the price of the ith house (in thousands of dollars)

LOT_i = the size of the lot of the ith house (in thousands of square feet)

AGE_i = the age of the ith house in years

BED_i = the number of bedrooms in the ith house

$FIRE_i$ = a dummy variable for a fireplace (1 = yes for the ith house)

$BEACH_i$ = a dummy for having beach frontage (1 = yes for the ith house)

---

14. This hypothetical result draws on Rachelle Rush and Thomas H. Bruggink, "The Value of Ocean Proximity on Barrier Island Houses," *The Appraisal Journal*, April 2000, pp. 142–150.

a. You expect the variables LOT, BED, and BEACH to have positive co-efficients. Create and test the appropriate hypotheses to evaluate these expectations at the 5-percent level.

b. You expect AGE to have a negative coefficient. Create and test the appropriate hypotheses to evaluate these expectations at the 10-percent level.

c. At first you expect FIRE to have a positive coefficient, but one of your friends says that fireplaces are messy and are a pain to keep clean, so you're not sure. Run a two-sided t-test around zero to test these expectations at the 5-percent level.

d. What problems appear to exist in your equation? (*Hint:* Do you have any unexpected signs? Do you have any coefficients that are not significantly different from zero?)

e. Which of the problems that you outline in part d is the most worri-some? Explain your answer.

f. What explanation or solution can you think of for this problem?

10. Suppose that you've been asked by the San Diego Padres baseball team to evaluate the economic impact of their new stadium by ana-lyzing the team's attendance per game in the last year at their old sta-dium. After some research on the topic, you build the following model (standard errors in parentheses):

$$\widehat{ATT_i} = 25000 + 15000\,WIN_i + 4000\,FREE_i - 3000\,DAY_i - 12000\,WEEK_i$$
$$(15000) \qquad (2000) \qquad (3000) \qquad (3000)$$
$$N = 35 \qquad \overline{R}^2 = .41$$

where: ATT_i = the attendance at the ith game

WIN_i = the winning percentage of the opponent in the ith game

$FREE_i$ = a dummy variable equal to 1 if the ith game was a "promotion" game at which something was given free to each fan, 0 otherwise

DAY_i = a dummy variable equal to 1 if the ith game was a day game and equal to 0 if the game was a night or twilight game

$WEEK_i$ = a dummy variable equal to 1 if the ith game was during the week and equal to 0 if it was on the weekend

a. You expect the variables WIN and FREE to have positive coeffi-cients. Create and test the appropriate hypotheses to evaluate these expectations at the 5-percent level.

b. You expect WEEK to have a negative coefficient. Create and test the appropriate hypotheses to evaluate these expectations at the 1-percent level.

c. You've included the day game variable because your boss thinks it's important, but you're not sure about the impact of day games on attendance. Run a two-sided t-test around zero to test these expectations at the 5-percent level.

d. What problems appear to exist in your equation? (*Hint:* Do you have any unexpected signs? Do you have any coefficients that are not significantly different from zero?)

e. Which of the problems that you outlined in part d is the most worrisome? Explain your answer.

f. What explanation or solution can you think of for this problem? (*Hint:* You don't need to be a sports fan to answer this question. If you like music, think about attendance at outdoor concerts.)

11. Thomas Bruggink and David Rose[15] estimated a regression for the annual team revenue for Major League Baseball franchises:

$$\hat{R}_i = -1522.5 + 53.1P_i + 1469.4M_i + 1322.7S_i - 7376.3T_i$$
$$\phantom{\hat{R}_i = -1522.5 +} (9.1) \quad\;\; (233.6) \quad\;\; (1363.6) \quad\;\; (2255.7)$$
$$\phantom{\hat{R}_i = -152} t = 5.8 \qquad\quad 6.3 \qquad\quad\;\; 1.0 \qquad\quad -3.3$$
$$\overline{R}^2 = .682 \quad N = 78\,(1984-1986)$$

where: R_i = team revenue from attendance, broadcasting, and concessions (in thousands of dollars)

P_i = the ith team's winning rate (their winning percentage multiplied by a thousand, $1{,}000$ = high)

M_i = the population of the ith team's metropolitan area (in millions)

S_i = a dummy equal to 1 if the ith team's stadium was built before 1940, 0 otherwise

T_i = a dummy equal to 1 if the ith team's city has two Major League Baseball teams, 0 otherwise

a. Develop and test appropriate hypotheses about the individual coefficients at the 5 percent level. (*Hint:* You do not have to be a sports fan to do this question correctly.)

b. The authors originally expected a negative coefficient for S. Their explanation for the unexpected positive sign was that teams in older stadiums have greater revenue because they're better known and have more faithful fans. Since this $\hat{\beta}$ is just one observation from the sampling distribution of $\hat{\beta}$s, do you think they should have changed their expected sign?

c. On the other hand, Keynes reportedly said, "When I'm wrong, I change my mind; what do you do?" If one $\hat{\beta}$ lets you realize an error, shouldn't you be allowed to change your expectation? How would you go about resolving this difficulty?

d. Assume that your team is in last place with P = 350. According to this regression equation, would it be profitable to pay $7 million a year to a free agent who would raise the team's winning rate (P) to 500? Be specific.

12. To get some practice with the *t*-test, let's return to the model of iPod prices on eBay that was developed in Exercise 11 in Chapter 3. That equation was:

$$\widehat{PRICE}_i = 109.24 + 54.99NEW_i - 20.44SCRATCH_i + 0.73BIDRS_i$$
$$(5.34) \qquad\quad (5.11) \qquad\qquad (0.59)$$
$$t = 10.28 \qquad\quad -4.00 \qquad\qquad 1.23$$
$$N = 215$$

where: PRICE$_i$ = the price at which the *i*th iPod sold on eBay

NEW$_i$ = a dummy variable equal to 1 if the *i*th iPod was new, 0 otherwise

SCRATCH$_i$ = a dummy variable equal to 1 if the *i*th iPod had a minor cosmetic defect, 0 otherwise

BIDRS$_i$ = the number of bidders on the *i*th iPod

a. Create and test hypothesis for the coefficients of NEW and SCRATCH at the 5-percent level. (*Hint:* Use the critical value for 120 degrees of freedom.)

b. In theory, the more bidders there are on a given iPod, the higher the price should be. Create and test hypotheses at the 1-percent level to see if this theory can be supported by the results.

c. Based on the hypothesis tests you conducted in parts a and b, are there any variables that you think should be dropped from the equation? Explain.

d. If you could add one variable to this equation, what would it be? Explain. (*Hint:* All the iPods in the sample are silver-colored, 4 GB Apple iPod minis.)

13. To get more experience with the *t*-test, let's return to the model of alcohol consumption that we developed in Exercise 11 of Chapter 4. That equation was:

$$\widehat{DRINKS_i} = 13.00 + 11.36ADVICE_i - 0.20EDUC_i + 2.85DIVSEP_i + 14.20UNEMP_i$$
$$\qquad\qquad (2.12)\qquad\quad (0.31)\qquad\quad (2.55)\qquad\quad (5.16)$$
$$\qquad\quad t = 5.37\qquad\quad -0.65\qquad\quad 1.11\qquad\quad 2.75$$
$$\qquad\qquad N = 500\qquad \overline{R}^2 = .07$$

where: $DRINKS_i$ = drinks consumed by the *i*th individual in the last two weeks
   $ADVICE_i$ = 1 if a physician had advised the *i*th individual to cut back on drinking alcohol, 0 otherwise
   $EDUC_i$ = years of schooling of the *i*th individual
   $DIVSEP_i$ = 1 if the *i*th individual was divorced or separated, 0 otherwise
   $UNEMP_i$ = 1 if the *i*th individual was unemployed, 0 otherwise

a. It seems reasonable to expect positive coefficients for DIVSEP and UNEMP. Create and test appropriate hypotheses for the coefficients of DIVSEP and UNEMP at the 5-percent level. (*Hint:* Use the critical value for 120 degrees of freedom.)
b. Create and run a two-sided hypothesis test around zero of the coefficient of EDUC at the 1-percent level. Why might a two-sided test be appropriate for this coefficient?
c. Most physicians would expect that if they urged patients to drink less alcohol, that's what the patients actually would do (holding constant the other variables in the equation). Create and test appropriate hypotheses for the coefficient of ADVICE at the 10-percent level.
d. Does your answer to part c cause you to wonder if perhaps you should change your hypotheses in part c? Explain.

14. Frederick Schut and Peter VanBergeijk[16] published an article in which they attempted to see if the pharmaceutical industry practiced international price discrimination by estimating a model of the prices of pharmaceuticals in a cross section of 32 countries. The authors felt

---

16. Frederick T. Schut and Peter A. G. VanBergeijk, "International Price Discrimination: The Pharmaceutical Industry," *World Development*, Vol. 14, No. 9, pp. 1141–1150. The estimated coefficients we list are those produced by EViews using the original data and differ slightly from those in the original article.

that if price discrimination existed, then the coefficient of per capita income in a properly specified price equation would be strongly positive. The reason they felt that the coefficient of per capita income would measure price discrimination went as follows: the higher the ability to pay, the lower (in absolute value) the price elasticity of demand for pharmaceuticals and the higher the price a price discriminator could charge. In addition, the authors expected that prices would be higher if pharmaceutical patents were allowed and that prices would be lower if price controls existed, if competition was encouraged, or if the pharmaceutical market in a country was relatively large. Their estimates were (standard errors in parentheses):

$$\hat{P}_i = 38.22 + 1.43GDPN_i - 0.6CVN_i + 7.31PP_i \qquad (5.10)$$
$$\phantom{\hat{P}_i = 38.22 + } (0.21) \qquad\quad (0.22) \qquad (6.12)$$
$$t = \qquad\quad 6.69 \qquad\qquad -2.66 \qquad 1.19$$

$$ - 15.63DPC_i - 11.38IPC_i$$
$$ (6.93) \qquad\qquad (7.16)$$
$$t = -2.25 \qquad\quad -1.59$$
$$N = 32 \qquad \overline{R}^2 = .775$$

where: P_i = the pharmaceutical price level in the ith country divided by that of the United States

$GDPN_i$ = per capita domestic product in the ith country divided by that of the United States

CVN_i = per capita volume of consumption of pharmaceuticals in the ith country divided by that of the United States

PP_i = a dummy variable equal to 1 if patents for pharmaceutical products are recognized in the ith country, 0 otherwise

DPC_i = a dummy variable equal to 1 if the ith country applied strict price controls, 0 otherwise

IPC_i = a dummy variable equal to 1 if the ith country encouraged price competition, 0 otherwise

a. Develop and test appropriate hypotheses concerning the regression coefficients using the t-test at the 5-percent level.
b. Set up 90-percent confidence intervals for each of the estimated slope coefficients.
c. Do you think Schut and VanBergeijk concluded that international price discrimination exists? Why or why not?
d. How would the estimated results have differed if the authors had not divided each country's prices, per capita income, and per capita

pharmaceutical consumption by that of the United States? Explain your answer.

e. Reproduce their regression results by using the EViews computer program (datafile DRUGS5) or your own computer program and the data from Table 5.1.

Table 5.1 Data for the Pharmaceutical Price Discrimination Exercise

Country	P	GDPN	CV	N	CVN	PP	IPC	DPC
Malawi	60.83	4.9	0.014	2.36	0.6	1	0	0
Kenya	50.63	6.56	0.07	6.27	1.1	1	0	0
India	31.71	6.56	18.66	282.76	6.6	0	0	1
Pakistan	38.76	8.23	3.42	32.9	10.4	0	1	1
Sri Lanka	15.22	9.3	0.42	6.32	6.7	1	1	1
Zambia	96.58	10.3	0.05	2.33	2.2	1	0	0
Thailand	48.01	13.0	2.21	19.60	11.3	0	0	0
Philippines	51.14	13.2	0.77	19.70	3.9	1	0	0
South Korea	35.10	20.7	2.20	16.52	13.3	0	0	0
Malaysia	70.74	21.5	0.50	5.58	8.9	1	0	0
Colombia	48.07	22.4	1.56	11.09	14.1	0	1	0
Jamaica	46.13	24.0	0.21	0.96	22.0	1	0	0
Brazil	63.83	25.2	10.48	50.17	21.6	0	1	0
Mexico	69.68	34.7	7.77	28.16	27.6	0	0	0
Yugoslavia	48.24	36.1	3.83	9.42	40.6	0	1	1
Iran	70.42	37.7	3.27	15.33	21.3	0	0	0
Uruguay	65.95	39.6	0.44	1.30	33.8	0	0	0
Ireland	73.58	42.5	0.57	1.49	38.0	1	0	0
Hungary	57.25	49.6	2.36	4.94	47.8	0	1	1
Poland	53.98	50.1	8.08	15.93	50.7	0	1	1
Italy	69.01	53.8	12.02	26.14	45.9	0	0	1
Spain	69.68	55.9	9.01	16.63	54.2	0	0	0
United Kingdom	71.19	63.9	9.96	26.21	38.0	1	1	1
Japan	81.88	68.4	28.58	52.24	54.7	0	0	1
Austria	139.53	69.6	1.24	3.52	35.2	0	0	0
Netherlands	137.29	75.2	1.54	6.40	24.1	1	0	0
Belgium	101.73	77.7	3.49	4.59	76.0	1	0	1
France	91.56	81.9	25.14	24.70	101.8	1	0	1
Luxembourg	100.27	82.0	0.10	0.17	60.5	1	0	1
Denmark	157.56	82.4	0.70	2.35	29.5	1	0	0
Germany, West	152.52	83.0	24.29	28.95	83.9	1	0	0
United States	100.00	100.0	100.00	100.00	100.0	1	1	0

Source: Frederick T. Schut and Peter A. G. VanBergeijk, "International Price Discrimination: The Pharmaceutical Industry," *World Development,* Vol. 14, No. 9, p. 1144.

Datafile = DRUGS5

$\boxed{5.6}$ **Appendix: The *F*-Test**

Although the *t*-test is invaluable for hypotheses about individual regression coefficients, it can't be used to test multiple hypotheses simultaneously. Such a limitation is unfortunate because many interesting ideas involve a number of hypotheses or involve one hypothesis about multiple coefficients. For example, suppose that you want to test the null hypothesis that there is no seasonal variation in a quarterly regression equation that has dummy variables for the seasons. To test such a hypothesis, most researchers would use the *F*-test.

What Is the *F*-Test?

The **F-test** is a formal hypothesis test that is designed to deal with a null hypothesis that contains multiple hypotheses or a single hypothesis about a group of coefficients.[17] Such "joint" or "compound" null hypotheses are appropriate whenever the underlying economic theory specifies values for multiple coefficients simultaneously.

The way in which the *F*-test works is fairly ingenious. The first step is to translate the particular null hypothesis in question into constraints that will be placed on the equation. The resulting constrained equation can be thought of as what the equation would look like if the null hypothesis were correct; you substitute the hypothesized values into the regression equation in order to see what would happen if the equation were constrained to agree with the null hypothesis. As a result, in the *F*-test the null hypothesis always leads to a constrained equation, even if this violates our standard practice that the alternative hypothesis contains what we expect is true.

The second step in an *F*-test is to estimate this constrained equation with OLS and compare the fit of this constrained equation with the fit of the unconstrained equation. If the fits of the constrained equation and the unconstrained equation are not significantly different, the null hypothesis should not be rejected. If the fit of the unconstrained equation is significantly better than that of the constrained equation, then we reject the null hypothesis. The fit of the constrained equation is never superior to the fit of the unconstrained equation, as we'll explain next.

---

17. As you will see, the *F*-test works by placing constraints or restrictions on the equation to be tested. Because of this, it's equivalent to say that the *F*-test is for tests that involve multiple linear restrictions.

The fits of the equations are compared with the general *F*-statistic:

$$F = \frac{(RSS_M - RSS)/M}{RSS/(N - K - 1)} \qquad (5.11)$$

where: RSS   = residual sum of squares from the unconstrained equation

RSS_M equation   = residual sum of squares from the constrained

M   = number of constraints placed on the equation (usually equal to the number of βs eliminated from the unconstrained equation)

(N − K − 1) = degrees of freedom in the unconstrained equation

RSS_M is always greater than or equal to RSS; imposing constraints on the coefficients instead of allowing OLS to select their values can never decrease the summed squared residuals. (Recall that OLS selects that combination of values of the coefficients that minimizes RSS.) At the extreme, if the unconstrained regression yields exactly the same estimated coefficients as does the constrained regression, then the RSS are equal, and the *F*-statistic is zero. In this case, H_0 is not rejected because the data indicate that the constraints appear to be correct. As the difference between the constrained coefficients and the unconstrained coefficients increases, the data indicate that the null hypothesis is less likely to be true. Thus, when F gets larger than the critical *F*-value, the hypothesized restrictions specified in the null hypothesis are rejected by the test.

The decision rule to use in the *F*-test is to reject the null hypothesis if the calculated *F*-value (F) from Equation 5.11 is greater than the appropriate critical *F*-value (F_c):

Reject H_0 if $F > F_c$

Do not reject H_0 if $F \le F_c$

The critical *F*-value, F_c, is determined from Statistical Table B-2 or B-3 depending on a level of significance chosen by the researcher and on the degrees of freedom. The *F*-statistic has two types of degrees of freedom: the degrees of freedom for the numerator of Equation 5.11 (M, the number of constraints implied by the null hypothesis) and the degrees of freedom for the denominator of Equation 5.11 ($N - K - 1$, the degrees of freedom in the regression equation). The underlying principle here is that if the calculated *F*-value (or *F*-ratio) is greater than the critical value, then the estimated equation's fit is significantly better than the constrained equation's fit, and we can reject the null hypothesis of no effect.

The *F*-Test of Overall Significance

Although R^2 and $\overline{R}^2$ measure the overall degree of fit of an equation, they don't provide a formal hypothesis test of that overall fit. Such a test is provided by the *F*-test. The null hypothesis in an *F*-test of overall significance is that all the slope coefficients in the equation equal zero simultaneously. For an equation with K independent variables, this means that the null and alternative hypotheses would be[18]:

$$H_0: \beta_1 = \beta_2 = \cdots = \beta_K = 0$$
$$H_A: H_0 \text{ is not true}$$

To show that the overall fit of the estimated equation is statistically significant, we must be able to reject this null hypothesis using the *F*-test.

For the *F*-test of overall significance, Equation 5.11 simplifies to:

$$F = \frac{ESS/K}{RSS/(N - K - 1)} = \frac{\sum (\hat{Y}_i - \overline{Y})^2/K}{\sum e_i^2/(N - K - 1)} \tag{5.12}$$

This is the ratio of the explained sum of squares (ESS) to the residual sum of squares (RSS), adjusted for the number of independent variables (K) and the number of observations in the sample (N). In this case, the "constrained equation" to which we're comparing the overall fit is:

$$Y_i = \beta_0 + \epsilon_i \tag{5.13}$$

which is nothing more than saying $\hat{Y}_i = \overline{Y}$. Thus the *F*-test of overall significance is really testing the null hypothesis that the fit of the equation isn't significantly better than that provided by using the mean alone.

---

18. Note that we don't hypothesize that $\beta_0 = 0$. This would imply that $E(\overline{Y}) = 0$. Note also that for the test of overall significance, M = K.

To see how this works, let's test the overall significance of the Woody's restaurant model of Equation 3.4. Since there are three independent variables, the null and alternative hypotheses are:

$$H_0: \beta_N = \beta_P = \beta_I = 0$$
$$H_A: H_0 \text{ is not true}$$

To decide whether to reject or not reject this null hypothesis, we need to calculate Equation 5.12 for the Woody's example. There are three constraints in the null hypothesis, so K = 3. If we check the EViews computer output for the Woody's equation on pages 81 and 83, we can see that N = 33 and RSS = 6,130,000,000. In addition, it can be calculated that ESS equals 9,929,450,000.[19] Thus the appropriate F-ratio is:

$$F = \frac{ESS/K}{RSS/(N - K - 1)} = \frac{9,929,450,000/3}{6,130,000,000/29} = 15.65 \qquad (5.14)$$

In practice, this calculation is never necessary, since virtually every computer regression package routinely provides the computed F-ratio for a test of overall significance as a matter of course. On the Woody's computer output, the value of the F-statistic can be found in the right-hand column.

Our decision rule tells us to reject the null hypothesis if the calculated F-value is greater than the critical F-value. To determine that critical F-value, we need to know the level of significance and the degrees of freedom. If we assume a 5-percent level of significance, the appropriate table to use is Statistical Table B-2. The numerator degrees of freedom equal 3 (K), and the denominator degrees of freedom equal 29 (N − K − 1), so we need to look in Statistical Table B-2 for the critical F-value for 3 and 29 degrees of freedom. As the reader can verify,[20] $F_c = 2.93$ is well below the calculated F-value of 15.65, so we can reject the null hypothesis and conclude that the Woody's equation does indeed have a significant overall fit.

---

19. To do this calculation, note that $R^2 = ESS/TSS$ and that $TSS = ESS + RSS$. If you substitute the second equation into the first and solve for ESS, you obtain $ESS = RSS \cdot (R^2)/(1 - R^2)$. Since both RSS and R^2 are included in the computer output on pages 81 and 83, you can then calculate ESS.

20. Note that this critical F-value must be interpolated. The critical value for 30 denominator degrees of freedom is 2.92, and the critical value for 25 denominator degrees of freedom is 2.99. Since both numbers are well below the calculated F-value of 15.65, however, the interpolation isn't necessary to reject the null hypothesis. As a result, many researchers don't bother with such interpolations unless the calculated F-value is inside the range of the interpolation.

Just as *p*-values provide an alternative approach to the *t*-test, so too can *p*-values provide an alternative approach to the *F*-test of overall significance. Most standard regression estimation programs report not only the *F*-value for the test of overall significance but also the *p*-value associated with that test. To see this for the Woody's output, look for "Prob" in the right-hand column on the top of pages 81 and 83. If the *p*-value is less than your chosen level of significance, you can reject the null hypothesis.

Other Uses of the *F*-Test

There are many other uses of the *F*-test besides the test of overall significance. For example, let's look at a Cobb–Douglas production function.

$$Q_t = \beta_0 + \beta_1 L_t + \beta_2 K_t + \epsilon_t \tag{5.15}$$

where: Q_t = the natural log of total output in the United States in year t
   L_t = the natural log of labor input in the United States in year t
   K_t = the natural log of capital input in the United States in year t
   ϵ_t = a well-behaved stochastic error term

As you'll learn in Chapter 7, this is a double-log functional form, and one of the properties of a double-log equation is that the coefficients of Equation 5.15 can be used to test for constant returns to scale. (Constant returns to scale refers to a situation in which a given percentage increase in inputs translates to exactly that percentage increase in output.) It can be shown that a Cobb–Douglas production function with constant returns to scale is one where β_1 and β_2 add up to exactly 1, so the null hypothesis to be tested is:

$$H_0: \beta_1 + \beta_2 = 1$$
$$H_A: \text{otherwise}$$

To test this null hypothesis with the *F*-test, we must run regressions on the unconstrained Equation 5.15 and an equation that is constrained to conform to the null hypothesis. To create such a constrained equation, we solve the null hypothesis for β_2 and substitute it into Equation 5.15, obtaining:

$$\begin{aligned} Q_t &= \beta_0 + \beta_1 L_t + (1 - \beta_1) K_t + \epsilon_t \\ &= \beta_0 + \beta_1 (L_t - K_t) + K_t + \epsilon_t \end{aligned} \tag{5.16}$$

If we move K_t to the left-hand side of the equation, we obtain our constrained equation:

$$(Q_t - K_t) = \beta_0 + \beta_1(L_t - K_t) + \epsilon_t \qquad (5.17)$$

Equation 5.17 is the equation that would hold if our null hypothesis were correct.

To run an F-test on our null hypothesis of constant returns to scale, we need to run regressions on the constrained Equation 5.17 and the unconstrained Equation 5.15 and compare the fits of the two equations with the F-ratio from Equation 5.14. If we use annual U.S. data, we obtain an unconstrained equation of:

$$\hat{Q}_t = -38.08 + 1.28L_t + 0.72K_t \qquad (5.18)$$
$$(0.30) \quad (0.05)$$
$$t = \quad 4.24 \quad 13.29$$
$$N = 24 \text{ (annual U.S. data)} \quad \overline{R}^2 = .997 \quad F = 4{,}118.9$$

If we run the constrained equation and substitute the appropriate RSS into Equation 5.14, with $M = 1$, we obtain $F = 16.26$. When this F is compared to a 5-percent critical F-value of only 4.32 (for 1 and 21 degrees of freedom) we must reject the null hypothesis that constant returns to scale characterize the U.S. economy. Note that $M = 1$ and the degrees of freedom in the numerator equal one because only one coefficient (β_2) has been eliminated from the equation by the constraint.

Interestingly, the estimate of $\hat{\beta}_1 + \hat{\beta}_2 = 1.28 + 0.72 = 2.00$ indicates drastically increasing returns to scale. However, since $\hat{\beta}_1 = 1.28$, and since economic theory suggests that the slope coefficient of a Cobb–Douglas production function should be between 0 and 1, we should be extremely cautious. There are problems in the equation that need to be resolved before we can feel comfortable with this conclusion.

Finally, let's take a look at the problem of testing the significance of seasonal dummies. **Seasonal dummies** are dummy variables that are used to account for seasonal variation in the data in time-series models. In a quarterly model, if:

$$X_{1t} = \begin{cases} 1 \text{ in quarter 1} \\ 0 \text{ otherwise} \end{cases}$$

$$X_{2t} = \begin{cases} 1 \text{ in quarter 2} \\ 0 \text{ otherwise} \end{cases}$$

$$X_{3t} = \begin{cases} 1 \text{ in quarter 3} \\ 0 \text{ otherwise} \end{cases}$$

then:

$$Y_t = \beta_0 + \beta_1 X_{1t} + \beta_2 X_{2t} + \beta_3 X_{3t} + \beta_4 X_{4t} + \epsilon_t \qquad (5.19)$$

where X_4 is a nondummy independent variable and t is quarterly. Notice that only three dummy variables are required to represent four seasons. In this formulation β_1 shows the extent to which the expected value of Y in the first quarter differs from its expected value in the fourth quarter, the omitted condition. β_2 and β_3 can be interpreted similarly.

Inclusion of a set of seasonal dummies "deseasonalizes" Y. This procedure may be used as long as Y and X_4 are not "seasonally adjusted" prior to estimation. Many researchers avoid the type of seasonal adjustment done prior to estimation because they think it distorts the data in unknown and arbitrary ways, but seasonal dummies have their own limitations such as remaining constant for the entire time period. As a result, there is no unambiguously best approach to deseasonalizing data.

To test the hypothesis of significant seasonality in the data, one must test the hypothesis that all the dummies equal zero simultaneously rather than test the dummies one at a time. In other words, the appropriate test of seasonality in a regression model using seasonal dummies involves the use of the *F*-test instead of the *t*-test.

In this case, the null hypothesis is that there is *no* seasonality:

$$H_0: \beta_1 = \beta_2 = \beta_3 = 0$$
$$H_A: H_0 \text{ is not true}$$

The constrained equation would then be $Y = \beta_0 + \beta_4 X_4 + \epsilon$. To determine whether the whole set of seasonal dummies should be included, the fit of the estimated constrained equation would be compared to the fit of the estimated unconstrained equation by using the *F*-test in equation 5.11. Note that this example uses the *F*-test to test null hypotheses that include only a subset of the slope coefficients. Also note that in this case M = 3, because three coefficients (β_1, β_2, and β_3) have been eliminated from the equation.

The exclusion of some seasonal dummies because their estimated coefficients have low *t*-scores is not recommended. Seasonal dummy coefficients should be tested with the *F*-test instead of with the *t*-test because seasonality is usually a single compound hypothesis rather than 3 individual hypotheses (or 11 with monthly data) having to do with each quarter (or month). To the extent that a hypothesis is a joint one, it should be tested with the *F*-test. If the hypothesis of seasonal variation can be summarized into a single dummy variable, then the use of the *t*-test will cause no problems. Often, where seasonal dummies are unambiguously called for, no hypothesis testing at all is undertaken.

6 Specification: Choosing the Independent Variables

Before any equation can be estimated, it must be completely specified. **Specifying** an econometric equation consists of three parts: choosing the correct independent variables, the correct functional form, and the correct form of the stochastic error term.

A **specification error** results when any one of these choices is made incorrectly. This chapter is concerned with only the first of these, choosing the variables; the second and third will be taken up in later chapters.

That researchers can decide which independent variables to include in regression equations is a source of both strength and weakness in econometrics. The strength is that the equations can be formulated to fit individual needs, but the weakness is that researchers can estimate many different specifications until they find the one that "proves" their point, even if many other results disprove it. A major goal of this chapter is to help you understand how to choose variables for your regressions without falling prey to the various errors that result from misusing the ability to choose.

The primary consideration in deciding whether an independent variable belongs in an equation is whether the variable is essential to the regression on the basis of theory. If the answer is an unambiguous yes, then the variable definitely should be included in the equation, even if it seems to be lacking in statistical significance. If theory is ambivalent or less emphatic, a dilemma arises. Leaving a relevant variable out of an equation is likely to bias the remaining estimates, but including an irrelevant variable leads to higher variances of the estimated coefficients. Although we'll develop statistical tools to help us deal with this decision, it's difficult in practice to be sure that a variable is relevant, and so the problem often remains unresolved.

We devote the fourth section of the chapter to specification searches and the pros and cons of various approaches to such searches. For example, poorly done specification searches often cause bias or make the usual tests of significance inapplicable. Instead, we suggest trying to minimize the number of regressions estimated and relying as much as possible on theory rather than statistical fit when choosing variables. There are no pat answers, however, and so the final decisions must be left to each individual researcher.

6.1 Omitted Variables

Suppose that you forget to include one of the relevant independent variables when you first specify an equation (after all, no one's perfect!). Or suppose that you can't get data for one of the variables that you *do* think of. The result in both these situations is an **omitted variable**, defined as an important explanatory variable that has been left out of a regression equation.

Whenever you have an omitted (or *left-out*) variable, the interpretation and use of your estimated equation become suspect. Leaving out a relevant variable, like price from a demand equation, not only prevents you from getting an estimate of the coefficient of price but also usually causes bias in the estimated coefficients of the variables that are in the equation.

The bias caused by leaving a variable out of an equation is called **omitted variable bias** (or, more generally, **specification bias**). In an equation with more than one independent variable, the coefficient β_k represents the change in the dependent variable Y caused by a one-unit increase in the independent variable X_k, holding constant the other independent variables in the equation. If a variable is omitted, then it is not included as an independent variable, and it is not held constant for the calculation and interpretation of $\hat{\beta}_k$. This omission can cause bias: It can force the expected value of the estimated coefficient away from the true value of the population coefficient.

Thus, omitting a relevant variable is usually evidence that the entire estimated equation is suspect, because of the likely bias in the coefficients of the variables that remain in the equation. Let's look at this issue in more detail.

The Consequences of an Omitted Variable

What happens if you omit an important variable from your equation (perhaps because you can't get the data for the variable or didn't even think of the variable in the first place)? The major consequence of omitting a relevant independent variable from an equation is to cause bias in the regression coefficients that remain in the equation. Suppose that the true regression model is:

$$Y_i = \beta_0 + \beta_1 X_{1i} + \beta_2 X_{2i} + \epsilon_i \qquad (6.1)$$

where ϵ_i is a classical error term. If you omit X_2 from the equation, then the equation becomes:

$$Y_i = \beta_0 + \beta_1 X_{1i} + \epsilon_i^* \qquad (6.2)$$

where ϵ_i^* equals:

$$\epsilon_i^* = \epsilon_i + \beta_2 X_{2i} \qquad (6.3)$$

because the stochastic error term includes the effects of any omitted variables, as mentioned in Section 1.2. From Equations 6.2 and 6.3, it might seem as though we could get unbiased estimates of β_0 and β_1 even if we left X_2 out of the equation. Unfortunately, this is not the case,[1] because the included coefficients almost surely pick up some of the effect of the omitted variable and therefore will change, causing bias. To see why, take another look at Equations 6.2 and 6.3. Most pairs of variables are correlated to some degree, even if that correlation is random, so X_1 and X_2 almost surely are correlated. When X_2 is omitted from the equation, the impact of X_2 goes into ϵ^*, so ϵ^* and X_2 are correlated. Thus if X_2 is omitted from the equation and X_1 and X_2 are correlated, both X_1 and ϵ^* will change when X_2 changes, and the error term will no longer be independent of the explanatory variable. That violates Classical Assumption III!

In other words, if we leave an important variable out of an equation, we violate Classical Assumption III (that the explanatory variables are independent of the error term), unless the omitted variable is uncorrelated with all the included independent variables (which is extremely unlikely). In general, when there is a violation of one of the Classical Assumptions, the Gauss–Markov Theorem does not hold, and the OLS estimates are not BLUE. Given linear estimators, this means that the estimated coefficients are

---

1. To avoid bias, X_1 and X_2 must be perfectly uncorrelated—an extremely unlikely result.

no longer unbiased or are no longer minimum variance (for all linear unbiased estimators), or both. In such a circumstance, econometricians first determine the exact property (unbiasedness or minimum variance) that no longer holds and then suggest an alternative estimation technique that might be better than OLS.

An omitted variable causes Classical Assumption III to be violated in a way that causes bias. Estimating Equation 6.2 when Equation 6.1 is the truth will cause bias. This means that:

$$E(\hat{\beta}_1) \neq \beta_1 \tag{6.4}$$

Instead of having an expected value equal to the true β_1, the estimate will compensate for the fact that X_2 is missing from the equation. If X_1 and X_2 are correlated and X_2 is omitted from the equation, then the OLS estimation procedure will attribute to X_1 variations in Y actually caused by X_2, and a biased estimate of $\hat{\beta}_1$ will result.

To see how a left-out variable can cause bias, picture a production function that states that output (Y) depends on the amount of labor (X_1) and capital (X_2) used. What would happen if data on capital were unavailable for some reason and X_2 was omitted from the equation? In this case, we would be leaving out the impact of capital on output in our model. This omission would almost surely bias the estimate of the coefficient of labor because it is likely that capital and labor are positively correlated (an increase in capital usually requires at least some labor to utilize it and vice versa). As a result, the OLS program would attribute to labor the increase in output actually caused by capital to the extent that labor and capital were correlated. Thus the bias would be a function of the impact of capital on output (β_2) and the correlation between capital and labor.

To generalize for a model with two independent variables, the expected value of the coefficient of an included variable (X_1) when a relevant variable (X_2) is omitted from the equation equals:

$$E(\beta_1) = \beta_1 + \beta_2 \cdot \alpha_1 \tag{6.5}$$

where α_1 is the slope coefficient of the secondary regression that relates X_2 to X_1:

$$X_{2i} = \alpha_0 + \alpha_1 X_{1i} + u_i \tag{6.6}$$

where u_i is a classical error term. α_1 can be expressed as a function of the correlation between X_1 and X_2, the included and excluded variables, or $f(r_{12})$.

Let's take a look at Equation 6.5. It states that the expected value of the included variable's coefficient is equal to its true value plus the omitted variable's true coefficient times a function of the correlation between the included (in) and omitted (om) variables.[2] Since the expected value of an unbiased estimate equals the true value, the right-hand term in Equation 6.5 measures the omitted variable bias in the equation:

$$\text{Bias} = \beta_2\alpha_1 \quad \text{or} \quad \text{Bias} = \beta_{om}f(r_{in,om}) \tag{6.7}$$

In general terms, the bias thus equals β_{om}, the coefficient of the omitted variable, times $f(r_{in,om})$, a function of the correlation between the included and omitted variables.

This bias exists unless:

1. the true coefficient equals zero, or
2. the included and omitted variables are uncorrelated.

The term $\beta_{om}f(r_{in,om})$ is the amount of specification bias introduced into the estimate of the coefficient of the included variable by leaving out the omitted variable. Although it's true that there is no bias if the included and excluded variables are uncorrelated, there almost always is some correlation between any two variables in the real world (even if it's just random), and so bias is almost always caused by the omission of a relevant variable. Although the omission of a relevant variable almost always produces bias in the estimators of the coefficients of the included variables, the variances of these estimators are generally lower than they otherwise would be.

An Example of Specification Bias

As an example of specification bias, let's take a look at a simple model of the annual consumption of chicken in the United States. There are a variety of variables that might make sense in such an equation, and at least three variables seem obvious. We'd expect the demand for chicken to be a negative

---

2. Equations 6.5 and 6.7 hold when there are exactly two independent variables, but the more general equations are quite similar.

function of the price of chicken and a positive function of the price of beef (its main substitute) and income:

$$Y_t = f(\overset{-}{PC_t}, \overset{+}{PB_t}, \overset{+}{YD_t}) + \epsilon_t$$

where: Y_t = per capita chicken consumption (in pounds) in year t
PC_t = the price of chicken (in cents per pound) in year t
PB_t = the price of beef (in cents per pound) in year t
YD_t = U.S. per capita disposable income (in hundreds of dollars) in year t

If we collect data for these variables for the years 1974 through 2002, we can estimate the following equation. (The data for this example are included in Exercise 5; t-scores differ because of rounding.)

$$\hat{Y}_t = 27.7 - 0.11PC_t + 0.03PB_t + 0.23YD_t \qquad (6.8)$$
$$(0.03) \qquad (0.02) \qquad (0.01)$$
$$t = \quad -3.38 \qquad +1.86 \qquad +15.7$$
$$\overline{R}^2 = .9904 \quad N = 29 \text{ (annual 1974–2002)}$$

How does our estimated equation look? The overall fit of Equation 6.8 is excellent, and each of the individual regression coefficients is significantly different from zero in the expected direction. The price of chicken does indeed have a significant negative effect (holding the price of beef and disposable income constant), and the price of beef and disposable income do indeed have positive effects (holding the other independent variables constant). If we estimate this equation without the price of the substitute, we obtain:

$$\hat{Y}_t = 30.7 - 0.09PC_t + 0.25YD_t \qquad (6.9)$$
$$(0.03) \qquad (0.005)$$
$$t = \quad -2.76 \qquad +46.1$$
$$\overline{R}^2 = .9895 \quad N = 29 \text{ (annual 1974–2002)}$$

Let's compare Equations 6.8 and 6.9 to see if dropping the beef price variable had an impact on the estimated equations. If you compare the overall fit, for example, you can see that $\overline{R}^2$ fell from .9904 to .9895 when PB was dropped, exactly what we'd expect to occur when a relevant variable is omitted.

More important, from the point of view of showing that an omitted variable causes bias, let's see if the coefficient estimates of the remaining variables changed. Sure enough, dropping PB caused $\hat{\beta}_{PC}$ to go from −0.11 to −0.09 and caused $\hat{\beta}_{YD}$ to go from 0.23 to 0.25. The direction of this bias, by the way, is considered positive because the biased coefficient of PC (−0.11) is more positive (less negative) than the suspected unbiased one (−0.09) and the biased coefficient of YD (0.25) is more positive than the suspected unbiased one of (0.23).

The fact that the bias is positive could have been guessed before any regressions were run if Equation 6.7 had been used. The specification bias caused by omitting the price of beef is expected[3] to be positive because the expected sign of the coefficient of PB is positive and because the expected correlation between the price of beef and the price of chicken itself is positive:

$$\text{Expected bias in } \hat{\beta}_{PC} = \beta_{PB} \cdot f(r_{PC,PB}) = (+) \cdot (+) = (+)$$

Similarly for YD:

$$\text{Expected bias in } \hat{\beta}_{YD} = \beta_{PB} \cdot f(r_{YD,PB}) = (+) \cdot (+) = (+)$$

Note that both correlation coefficients are anticipated to be (and actually are) positive. To see this, think of the impact of an increase in the price of chicken on the price of beef and then follow through the impact of any increase in income on the price of beef.

To sum, if a relevant variable is left out of a regression equation,

1. there is no longer an estimate of the coefficient of that variable in the equation, and

2. the coefficients of the remaining variables are likely to be biased.

Although the amount of the bias might not be very large in some cases (when, for instance, there is little correlation between the included and excluded variables), it is extremely likely that at least a small amount of specification bias will be present in all such situations.

Correcting for an Omitted Variable

In theory, the solution to a problem of specification bias seems easy: add the omitted variable to the equation! Unfortunately, that's easier said than done, for a couple of reasons.

First, omitted variable bias is hard to detect. As mentioned earlier, the amount of bias introduced can be small and not immediately detectable.

---

3. It is important to note the distinction between expected bias and any actual observed differences between coefficient estimates. Because of the random nature of the error term (and hence the $\hat{\beta}$s), the change in an estimated coefficient brought about by dropping a relevant variable from the equation will not necessarily be in the expected direction. Biasedness refers to the central tendency of the sampling distribution of the $\hat{\beta}$s, not to every single drawing from that distribution. However, we usually (and justifiably) rely on these general tendencies. Note also that Equation 6.8 has three independent variables, whereas Equation 6.7 was derived for use with equations with exactly two. However, Equation 6.7 represents a general tendency that is still applicable.

This is especially true when there is no reason to believe that you have mis-specified the model. Some indications of specification bias are obvious (such as an estimated coefficient that is significant in the direction opposite from that expected), but others are not so clear. Could you tell from Equation 6.9 alone that a variable was missing? The best indicators of an omitted relevant variable are the theoretical underpinnings of the model itself. What variables *must* be included? What signs do you expect? Do you have any notions about the range into which the coefficient values should fall? Have you accidentally left out a variable that most researchers would agree is important? The best way to avoid omitting an important variable is to invest the time to think carefully through the equation before the data are entered into the computer.

A second source of complexity is the problem of choosing which variable to add to an equation once you decide that it is suffering from omitted variable bias. That is, a researcher faced with a clear case of specification bias (like an estimated $\hat{\beta}$ that is significantly different from zero in the unexpected direction) will often have no clue as to what variable could be causing the problem. Some beginning researchers, when faced with this dilemma, will add all the possible relevant variables to the equation at once, but this process leads to less precise estimates, as will be discussed in the next section. Other beginning researchers will test a number of different variables and keep the one in the equation that does the best statistical job of appearing to reduce the bias (by giving plausible signs and satisfactory *t*-values). This technique, adding a "left-out" variable to "fix" a strange-looking regression result, is invalid because the variable that best corrects a case of specification bias might do so only by chance rather than by being the true solution to the problem. In such an instance, the "fixed" equation may give superb statistical results for the sample at hand but then do terribly when applied to other samples because it does not describe the characteristics of the true population.

Dropping a variable will not help cure omitted variable bias. If the sign of an estimated coefficient is different from expected, it cannot be changed to the expected direction by dropping a variable that has a *t*-score lower (in absolute value) than the *t*-score of the coefficient estimate that has the unexpected sign. Furthermore, the sign in general will not likely change even if the variable to be deleted has a large *t*-score.[4]

If an unexpected result leads you to believe that you have an omitted variable, one way to decide which variable to add to the equation is to use

---

4. Ignazio Visco, "On Obtaining the Right Sign of a Coefficient Estimate by Omitting a Variable from the Regression," *Journal of Econometrics*, Vol. 7, No. 1, pp. 115–117.

expected bias analysis. **Expected bias** is the likely bias that omitting a particular variable would have caused in the estimated coefficient of one of the included variables. It can be estimated with Equation 6.7:

$$\text{Expected bias} = \beta_{om} \cdot f(r_{in,om}) \tag{6.7}$$

If the sign of the expected bias is the same as the sign of your unexpected result, then the variable might be the source of the apparent bias. If the sign of the expected bias is *not* the same as the sign of your unexpected result, however, then the variable is extremely unlikely to have caused your unexpected result. Expected bias analysis should be used only when you're choosing between theoretically sound potential variables.

As an example of expected bias analysis, let's return to Equation 6.9, the chicken demand equation without the beef price variable. Let's assume that you had expected the coefficient of β_{PC} to be in the range of -1.0 and that you were surprised by the unexpectedly positive coefficient of PC in Equation 6.9.

This unexpectedly positive result could have been caused by an omitted variable with positive expected bias. One such variable is the price of beef. The expected bias in $\hat{\beta}_{PC}$ due to leaving out PB is positive, since both the expected coefficient of PB and the expected correlation between PC and PB are positive:

$$\text{Expected bias in } \hat{\beta}_{PC} = \beta_{PB} \cdot f(r_{PC,PB}) = (+) \cdot (+) = (+)$$

Hence the price of beef is a reasonable candidate to be an omitted variable in Equation 6.9.

Although you can never actually observe bias (since you don't know the true β), the use of this technique to screen potential causes of specification bias should reduce the number of regressions run and therefore increase the statistical validity of the results.

A brief warning: It may be tempting to conduct what might be called "residual analysis" by examining a plot of the residuals in an attempt to find patterns that suggest variables that have been accidentally omitted. A major problem with this approach is that the coefficients of the estimated equation will possibly have some of the effects of the left-out variable already altering their estimated values. Thus, residuals may show a pattern that only vaguely resembles the pattern of the actual omitted variable. The chances are high that the pattern shown in the residuals may lead to the selection of an incorrect variable. In addition, care should be taken to use residual analysis only to choose between theoretically sound candidate variables rather than to generate those candidates.

6.2 Irrelevant Variables

What happens if you include a variable in an equation that doesn't belong there? This case, **irrelevant variables**, is the converse of omitted variables and can be analyzed using the model we developed in Section 6.1. The addition of a variable to an equation where it doesn't belong does not cause bias, but it does increase the variances of the estimated coefficients of the included variables.

Impact of Irrelevant Variables

If the true regression specification is:

$$Y_i = \beta_0 + \beta_1 X_{1i} + \epsilon_i \tag{6.10}$$

but the researcher for some reason includes an extra variable,

$$Y_i = \beta_0 + \beta_1 X_{1i} + \beta_2 X_{2i} + \epsilon_i^{**} \tag{6.11}$$

the misspecified equation's error term can be seen to be:

$$\epsilon_i^{**} = \epsilon_i - \beta_2 X_{2i} \tag{6.12}$$

Such a mistake will not cause bias if the true coefficient of the extra (or irrelevant) variable is zero. That is, $\hat{\beta}_1$ in Equation 6.11 is unbiased when $\beta_2 = 0$.

However, the inclusion of an irrelevant variable will increase the variance of the estimated coefficients, and this increased variance will tend to decrease the absolute magnitude of their t-scores. Also, an irrelevant variable usually will decrease the $\overline{R}^2$ (but not the R^2).

Thus, although the irrelevant variable causes no bias, it causes problems for the regression because it reduces the t-scores and $\overline{R}^2$.

Table 6.1 summarizes the consequences of the omitted variable and the included irrelevant variable cases (unless $r_{12} = 0$).

Table 6.1 Effect of Omitted Variables and Irrelevant Variables on the Coefficient Estimates

Effect on Coefficient Estimates	Omitted Variable	Irrelevant Variable
Bias	Yes	No
Variance	Decreases	Increases

An Example of an Irrelevant Variable

Let's return to the equation from Section 6.1 for the annual consumption of chicken and see what happens when we add an irrelevant variable to the equation. The original equation was:

$$\hat{Y}_t = 27.7 - 0.11PC_t + 0.03PB_t + 0.23YD_t \qquad (6.8)$$
$$(0.03) \quad (0.02) \quad (0.01)$$
$$t = \quad -3.38 \quad +1.86 \quad +15.7$$
$$\overline{R}^2 = .9904 \quad N = 29 \text{ (annual 1974–2002)}$$

Suppose you hypothesize that the demand for chicken also depends on TEMP, the average annual change in temperature in tenths of a degree (included, perhaps, on the dubious theory that demand for chicken might heat up when temperatures are rising). If you now estimate the equation with TEMP included, you obtain:

$$\hat{Y}_t = 26.9 - 0.11PC_t + 0.03PB_t + 0.23YD_t - 0.02TEMP_t \qquad (6.13)$$
$$(0.03) \quad (0.02) \quad (0.015) \quad (0.02)$$
$$t = \quad -3.38 \quad +1.99 \quad +14.99 \quad -0.93$$
$$\overline{R}^2 = .9903 \quad N = 29 \text{ (annual 1974–2002)}$$

A comparison of Equations 6.8 and 6.13 will make the theory in Section 6.2 come to life. First of all, $\overline{R}^2$ has fallen slightly, indicating the reduction in fit adjusted for degrees of freedom. Second, none of the regression coefficients from the original equation changed; compare these results with the larger differences between Equations 6.8 and 6.9. Further, the standard errors of the estimated coefficients increased or remained constant. Finally, the t-score for the potential variable (TEMP) is small, indicating that it is not significantly different from zero. Given the theoretical shakiness of the new variable, these results indicate that it is irrelevant and never should have been included in the regression.

Four Important Specification Criteria

We have now discussed at least four valid criteria to help decide whether a given variable belongs in the equation. We think these criteria are so important that we urge beginning researchers to work through them every time a variable is added or subtracted.

1. *Theory:* Is the variable's place in the equation unambiguous and theoretically sound?

2. *t-Test:* Is the variable's estimated coefficient significant in the expected direction?

3. $\overline{R}^2$: Does the overall fit of the equation (adjusted for degrees of freedom) improve when the variable is added to the equation?

4. *Bias:* Do other variables' coefficients change significantly when the variable is added to the equation?

If all these conditions hold, the variable belongs in the equation; if none of them do, the variable is irrelevant and can be safely excluded from the equation. When a typical omitted relevant variable is included in the equation, its inclusion probably will increase $\overline{R}^2$ and change at least one other coefficient. If an irrelevant variable, on the other hand, is included, it will reduce $\overline{R}^2$, have an insignificant *t*-score, and have little impact on the other variables' coefficients.

In many cases, all four criteria do not agree. It is possible for a variable to have an insignificant *t*-score that is greater than one, for example. In such a case, it can be shown that $\overline{R}^2$ will go up when the variable is added to the equation and yet the *t*-score still will be insignificant.

Whenever our four specification criteria disagree, the econometrician must use careful judgment and should not rely on a single criterion like $\overline{R}^2$ to determine the specification. Researchers should not misuse this freedom by testing various combinations of variables until they find the results that appear to statistically support the point they want to make. All such decisions are a bit easier when you realize that the single most important determinant of a variable's relevance is its theoretical justification. No amount of statistical evidence should make a theoretical necessity into an "irrelevant" variable. Once in a while, a researcher is forced to leave a theoretically important variable out of an equation for lack of data; in such cases, the usefulness of the equation is limited.

6.3 An Illustration of the Misuse of Specification Criteria

At times, the four specification criteria outlined in the previous section will lead the researcher to an incorrect conclusion if those criteria are applied to a problem without proper concern for economic principles or common sense.

In particular, a *t*-score can often be insignificant for reasons other than the presence of an irrelevant variable. Since economic theory is the most important test for including a variable, an example of why a variable should not be dropped from an equation simply because it has an insignificant *t*-score is in order.

Suppose you believe that the demand for Brazilian coffee in the United States is a negative function of the real price of Brazilian coffee (P_{bc}) and a positive function of both the real price of tea (P_t) and real disposable income in the United States (Y_d).[5] Suppose further that you obtain the data, run the implied regression, and observe the following results:

$$\widehat{\text{COFFEE}} = 9.1 + 7.8P_{bc} + 2.4P_t + 0.0035Y_d \qquad (6.14)$$
$$(15.6) \qquad (1.2) \qquad (0.0010)$$
$$t = 0.5 \qquad 2.0 \qquad 3.5$$
$$\overline{R}^2 = .60 \quad N = 25$$

The coefficients of the second and third variables, P_t and Y_d, appear to be fairly significant in the direction you hypothesized, but the first variable, P_{bc}, appears to have an insignificant coefficient with an unexpected sign. If you think there is a possibility that the demand for Brazilian coffee is perfectly price-inelastic (that is, its coefficient is zero), you might decide to run the same equation without the price variable, obtaining:

$$\widehat{\text{COFFEE}} = 9.3 + 2.6P_t + 0.0036Y_d \qquad (6.15)$$
$$(1.0) \qquad (0.0009)$$
$$t = 2.6 \qquad 4.0$$
$$\overline{R}^2 = .61 \quad N = 25$$

By comparing Equations 6.14 and 6.15, we can apply our four specification criteria for the inclusion of a variable in an equation that were outlined in the previous section:

1. *Theory:* Since the demand for coffee could possibly be perfectly price-inelastic, the theory behind dropping the variable seems plausible.

2. *t-Test:* The *t*-score of the possibly irrelevant variable is 0.5, insignificant at any level.

---

5. This example was inspired by a similar one concerning Ceylonese tea published in Potluri Rao and Roger LeRoy Miller, *Applied Econometrics* (Belmont, CA: Wadsworth, 1971), pp. 38–40. This wonderful book is now out of print.

3. $\overline{R}^2$: $\overline{R}^2$ increases when the variable is dropped, indicating that the variable is irrelevant. (Since the t-score is less than 1, this is to be expected.)

4. *Bias:* The remaining coefficients change only a small amount when P_{bc} is dropped, suggesting that there is little—if any—bias caused by excluding the variable.

Based upon this analysis, you might conclude that the demand for Brazilian coffee is indeed perfectly price-inelastic and that the variable is therefore irrelevant and should be dropped from the model. As it turns out, this conclusion would be unwarranted. Although the elasticity of demand for coffee in general might be fairly low (actually, the evidence suggests that it is inelastic only over a particular range of prices), it is hard to believe that Brazilian coffee is immune to price competition from other kinds of coffee. Indeed, one would expect quite a bit of sensitivity in the demand for Brazilian coffee with respect to the price of, for example, Colombian coffee. To test this hypothesis, the price of Colombian coffee (P_{cc}) should be added to the original Equation 6.14:

$$\widehat{\text{COFFEE}} = 10.0 + 8.0P_{cc} - 5.6P_{bc} + 2.6P_t + 0.0030Y_d \qquad (6.16)$$
$$\phantom{\widehat{\text{COFFEE}} = 10.0 + } (4.0) \quad\; (2.0) \quad\;\; (1.3) \quad\; (0.0010)$$
$$\phantom{\widehat{\text{COFFEE}} = } t = 2.0 \quad\;\; -2.8 \quad\;\; 2.0 \quad\;\; 3.0$$
$$\phantom{\widehat{\text{COFFEE}} = } \overline{R}^2 = .65 \quad N = 25$$

By comparing Equations 6.14 and 6.16, we can once again apply our four specification criteria:

1. *Theory:* Both prices should always have been included in the model; their logical justification is quite strong.

2. *t-Test:* The t-score of the new variable, the price of Colombian coffee, is 2.0, significant at most levels.

3. $\overline{R}^2$: $\overline{R}^2$ increases with the addition of the variable, indicating that the variable was an omitted variable.

4. *Bias:* Although two of the coefficients remain virtually unchanged, indicating that the correlations between these variables and the price of Colombian coffee variable are low, the coefficient for the price of Brazilian coffee does change significantly, indicating bias in the original result.

The moral to be drawn is that theoretical considerations never should be discarded, even in the face of statistical insignificance. If a variable known to be extremely important from a theoretical point of view turns out to be statistically insignificant in a particular sample, that variable should be left in the equation despite the fact that it makes the results look bad.

Don't conclude that the particular path outlined in this example is the correct way to specify an equation. Trying a long string of possible variables until you get the particular one that makes the coefficient of P_{bc} turn negative and significant is not the way to obtain a result that will stand up well to other samples or alternative hypotheses. The original equation should never have been run without the Colombian coffee price variable. Instead, the problem should have been analyzed enough so that such errors of omission were unlikely before any regressions were attempted at all. The more thinking that's done before the first regression is run, and the fewer alternative specifications that are estimated, the better the regression results are likely to be.

6.4 Specification Searches

One of the weaknesses of econometrics is that a researcher potentially can manipulate a data set to produce almost *any* result by specifying different regressions until estimates with the desired properties are obtained. Because the integrity of all empirical work is thus open to question, the subject of how to search for the best specification is quite controversial among econometricians.[6] Our goal in this section isn't to summarize or settle this controversy; instead, I hope to provide some guidance and insight for beginning researchers.

Best Practices in Specification Searches

The issue of how best to choose a specification from among alternative possibilities is a difficult one, but our experience leads us to make the following recommendations:

1. Rely on theory rather than statistical fit as much as possible when choosing variables, functional forms, and the like.
2. Minimize the number of equations estimated (except for sensitivity analysis, to be discussed later in this section).
3. Reveal, in a footnote or appendix, all alternative specifications estimated.

---

6. For an excellent summary of this controversy and the entire subject of specification, see Peter Kennedy, *A Guide to Econometrics* (Malden, MA: Blackwell), pp. 71–92.

If theory, not $\overline{R}^2$ or t-scores, is the most important criterion for the inclusion of a variable in a regression equation, then it follows that most of the work of specifying a model should be done before you attempt to estimate the equation. Since it's unreasonable to expect researchers to be perfect, there will be times when additional specifications must be estimated. However, these new estimates should be few in number and should be thoroughly grounded in theory. In addition, they should be explicitly taken into account when testing for significance and/or summarizing results. In this way, the danger of misleading the reader about the statistical properties of the final equation will be reduced.

Sequential Specification Searches

Most econometricians tend to specify equations by estimating an initial equation and then sequentially dropping or adding variables (or changing functional forms) until a plausible equation is found with "good statistics." Faced with knowing that a few variables are relevant (on the basis of theory) but not knowing whether other additional variables are relevant, inspecting $\overline{R}^2$ and t-tests for all variables for each specification appears to be the generally accepted practice. Indeed, casual reading of the previous section might make it seem as if such a sequential specification search is the best way to go about finding the "truth." Instead, as we shall see, there is a vast difference between a sequential specification search and our recommended approach.

The **sequential specification search** technique allows a researcher to estimate an undisclosed number of regressions and then present a final choice (which is based upon an unspecified set of expectations about the signs and significance of the coefficients) as if it were the only specification estimated. Such a method misstates the statistical validity of the regression results for two reasons:

1. The statistical significance of the results is overestimated because the estimations of the previous regressions are ignored.

2. The expectations used by the researcher to choose between various regression results rarely, if ever, are disclosed. Thus the reader has no way of knowing whether all the other regression results had opposite signs or insignificant coefficients for the important variables.

Unfortunately, there is no universally accepted way of conducting sequential searches, primarily because the appropriate test at one stage in the procedure depends on which tests previously were conducted, and also because the tests have been very difficult to invent.

Instead we recommend trying to keep the number of regressions estimated as low as possible; to focus on theoretical considerations when choosing variables or functional forms; and to document all the various specifications investigated. That is, we recommend combining parsimony (using theory and analysis to limit the number of specifications estimated) with disclosure (reporting all the equations estimated).

Not everyone agrees with our advice. Some researchers feel that the true model will show through if given the chance and that the best statistical results (including signs of coefficients, etc.) are most likely to have come from the true specification. In addition, reasonable people often disagree as to what the "true" model should look like. As a result, different researchers can look at the same data set and come up with very different "best" equations. Because this can happen, the distinction between good and bad econometrics is not always as clear-cut as is implied by the previous paragraphs. As long as researchers have a healthy respect for the dangers inherent in specification searches, they are very likely to proceed in a reasonable way.

Bias Caused by Relying on the *t*-Test to Choose Variables

In the previous section, we stated that sequential specification searches are likely to mislead researchers about the statistical properties of their results. In particular, the practice of dropping a potential independent variable simply because its coefficient has a low *t*-score will cause systematic bias in the estimated coefficients (and their *t*-scores) of the remaining variables.

Let's say the hypothesized model is:

$$Y_i = \beta_0 + \beta_1 X_{1i} + \beta_2 X_{2i} + \epsilon_i \qquad (6.17)$$

Assume further that, on the basis of theory, we are certain that X_1 belongs in the equation but that we are not as certain that X_2 belongs. Many inexperienced researchers use only the *t*-test on $\hat{\beta}_2$ to determine whether X_2 should be included. If this preliminary *t*-test indicates that $\hat{\beta}_2$ is significantly different from zero, then these researchers leave X_2 in the equation. If, however, the *t*-test does *not* indicate that $\hat{\beta}_2$ is significantly different from zero, then such researchers drop X_2 from the equation and consider Y to be a function of X_1.

Two kinds of mistakes can be made using such a system. First, X_2 sometimes can be left in the equation when it does not belong there, but such a mistake does not change the expected value of $\hat{\beta}_1$.

Second, X_2 sometimes can be dropped from the equation when it belongs. In this second case, the estimated coefficient of X_1 will be biased. In other words, $\hat{\beta}_1$ will be biased every time X_2 belongs in the equation and is left out, and X_2 will be left out every time that its estimated coefficient is not significantly different from zero. We will have systematic bias in our equation!

To summarize, the *t*-test is biased by sequential specification searches. Since most researchers consider a number of different variables before settling on the final model, someone who relies on the *t*-test alone is likely to encounter this problem systematically.

Sensitivity Analysis

Throughout this text, we've encouraged you to estimate as few specifications as possible and to avoid depending on fit alone to choose between those specifications. If you read the current economics literature, however, it won't take you long to find well-known researchers who have estimated five or more specifications and then have listed all their results in an academic journal article. What's going on?

In almost every case, these authors have employed a technique called sensitivity analysis.

Sensitivity analysis consists of purposely running a number of alternative specifications to determine whether particular results are *robust* (not statistical flukes). In essence, we're trying to determine how sensitive a potential "best" equation is to a change in specification because the true specification isn't known. Researchers who use sensitivity analysis run (and report on) a number of different reasonable specifications and tend to discount a result that appears significant in some specifications and insignificant in others. Indeed, the whole purpose of sensitivity analysis is to gain confidence that a particular result is significant in a variety of alternative specifications, functional forms, variable definitions, and/or subsets of the data.

Data Mining

In contrast to sensitivity analysis, which consists of estimating a variety of alternative specifications after a potential "best" equation has been identified, **data mining** involves estimating a variety of alternative specifications *before* that "best" equation has been chosen. Readers of this text will not be surprised to hear that we urge extreme caution when data mining. Improperly done data mining is worse than doing nothing at all.

Done properly, data mining involves exploring a data set not for the purpose of testing hypotheses or finding a specification, but for the purpose of uncovering empirical regularities that can inform economic theory.[7] After all, we can't expect economic theorists to think of everything!

Be careful, however! If you develop a hypothesis using data mining techniques, you must test that hypothesis on a *different* data set (or in a different context) than the one you used to develop the hypothesis. A new data set must be used because our typical statistical tests have little meaning if the new hypothesis is tested on the data set that was used to generate it. After all, the researcher already knows ahead of time what the results will be! The use of dual data sets is easiest when there is a plethora of data. This sometimes is the case in cross-sectional research projects but rarely is the case for time series research.

Data mining without using dual data sets is almost surely the worst way to choose a specification. In such a situation, a researcher could estimate virtually every possible combination of the various alternative independent variables, could choose the results that "look" the best, and then could report the "best" equation as if no data mining had been done. This improper use of data mining ignores the fact that a number of specifications have been examined before the final one is reported.

In addition, data mining will cause you to choose specifications that reflect the peculiarities of your particular data set. How does this happen? Suppose you have 100 true null hypotheses and you run 100 tests of these hypotheses. At the 5-percent level of significance, you'd expect to reject about five true null hypotheses and thus make about five Type I Errors. By looking for high *t*-values, a data mining search procedure will find these Type I Errors and incorporate them into your specification. As a result, the reported *t*-scores will overstate the statistical significance of the estimated coefficients.

In essence, improper data mining to obtain desired statistics for the final regression equation is a potentially unethical empirical research method. Whether the improper data mining is accomplished by estimating one equation at a time or by estimating batches of equations or by techniques like stepwise regression procedures,[8] the conclusion is the same. Hypotheses developed

---

7. For an excellent presentation of this approach, see Lawrence H. Summers, "The Scientific Illusion in Empirical Macroeconomics," *Scandinavian Journal of Economics*, Vol. 93, No. 2, pp. 129–148.

8. A stepwise regression involves the use of an automated computer program to choose the independent variables in an equation. The researcher specifies a "shopping list" of possible independent variables, and then the computer estimates a number of equations until it finds the one that maximizes $\overline{R}^2$. Such stepwise techniques are deficient in the face of multicollinearity (to be discussed in Chapter 8) and they run the risk that the chosen specification will have little theoretical justification and/or will have coefficients with unexpected signs. Because of these pitfalls, econometricians avoid stepwise procedures.

by data mining should always be tested on a data set different from the one that was used to develop the hypothesis. Otherwise, the researcher hasn't found any scientific evidence to support the hypothesis; rather, a specification has been chosen in a way that is essentially misleading. As put by one econometrician, "if you torture the data long enough, they will confess."[9]

6.5   An Example of Choosing Independent Variables

It's time to get some experience choosing independent variables. After all, every equation so far in the text has come with the specification already determined, but once you've finished this course you'll have to make all such specification decisions on your own. In future chapters, we'll use a technique called "interactive regression learning exercises" to allow you to make your own actual specification choices and get feedback on your choices. To start, though, let's work through a specification together.

To keep things as simple as possible, we'll begin with a topic near and dear to your heart—your GPA! Suppose a friend who attends a small liberal arts college surveys all 25 members of her econometrics class, obtains data on the variables listed here, and asks for your help in choosing a specification:

GPA_i = the cumulative college grade point average on the ith student on a four-point scale

$HGPA_i$ = the cumulative high school grade point average of the ith student on a four-point scale

$MSAT_i$ = the highest score earned by the ith student on the math section of the SAT test (800 maximum)

$VSAT_i$ = the highest score earned by the ith student on the verbal section of the SAT test (800 maximum)

SAT_i = $MSAT_i + VSAT_i$

$GREK_i$ = a dummy variable equal to 1 if the ith student is a member of a fraternity or sorority, 0 otherwise

HRS_i = the ith student's estimate of the average number of hours spent studying per course per week in college

---

9. Thomas Mayer, "Economics as a Hard Science: Realistic Goal or Wishful Thinking?" *Economic Inquiry*, Vol. 18, No. 2, p. 175. (This quote also has been attributed to Ronald Coase.)

$PRIV_i$ = a dummy variable equal to 1 if the ith student graduated from a private high school, 0 otherwise

$JOCK_i$ = a dummy variable equal to 1 if the ith student is or was a member of a varsity intercollegiate athletic team for at least one season, 0 otherwise

$lnEX_i$ = the natural log of the number of full courses that the ith student has completed in college.

Assuming that GPA_i is the dependent variable, which independent variables would you choose? Before you answer, think through the possibilities carefully. What does the literature tell us on this subject? (Is there literature?) What are the expected signs of each of the coefficients? How strong is the theory behind each variable? Which variables seem obviously important? Which variables seem potentially irrelevant or redundant? Are there any other variables that you wish your friend had collected?

To get the most out of this example, you should take the time to *write down* the exact specification that you would run:

$$GPA_i = f(?, ?, ?, ?, ?) + \epsilon$$

It's hard for most beginning econometricians to avoid the temptation of including *all* of these variables in a GPA equation and then dropping any variables that have insignificant t-scores. Even though we mentioned in the previous section that such a specification search procedure will result in biased coefficient estimates, most beginners don't trust their own judgment and tend to include too many variables. With this warning in mind, do you want to make any changes in your proposed specification?

No? OK, let's compare notes. We believe that grades are a function of a student's ability, how hard the student works, and the student's experience taking college courses. Consequently, our specification would be:

$$GPA_i = f(\overset{+}{HGPA_i}, \overset{+}{HRS_i}, \overset{+}{lnEX_i}) + \epsilon$$

We can already hear you complaining! What about SATs, you say? Everyone knows they're important. How about jocks and Greeks? Don't they have lower GPAs? Don't prep schools grade harder and prepare students better than public high schools?

Before we answer, it's important to note that we think of specification choice as choosing which variables to *include*, not which variables to *exclude*. That is, we don't assume automatically that a given variable should be included in an equation simply because we can't think of a good reason for dropping it.

Given that, however, why did we choose the variables we did? First, we think that the best predictor of a student's college GPA is his or her high school GPA. We have a hunch that once you know HGPA, SATs are redundant, at least at a liberal arts college where there are few multiple choice tests. In addition, we're concerned that possible racial and gender bias in the SAT test makes it a questionable measure of academic potential, but we recognize that we could be wrong on this issue.

As for the other variables, we're more confident. For example, we feel that once we know how many hours a week a student spends studying, we couldn't care less what that student does with the rest of his or her time, so JOCK and GREK are superfluous once HRS is included. In addition, the higher LnEX is, the better student study habits are and the more likely students are to be taking courses in their major. Finally, while we recognize that some private schools are superb and that some public schools are not, we'd guess that PRIV is irrelevant; it probably has only a minor effect.

If we estimate this specification on the 25 students, we obtain:

$$\widehat{GPA}_i = -0.26 + 0.49HGPA_i + 0.06HRS_i + 0.42lnEX_i \qquad (6.18)$$
$$\phantom{\widehat{GPA}_i = -0.26 + } (0.21) \qquad\quad (0.02) \qquad\quad (0.14)$$
$$\phantom{\widehat{GPA}_i = -0.26 + } t = 2.33 \qquad\qquad 3.00 \qquad\quad 3.00$$
$$\phantom{\widehat{GPA}_i = } N = 25 \quad \overline{R}^2 = .585$$

Since we prefer this specification on theoretical grounds, since the overall fit seems reasonable, and since each coefficient meets our expectations in terms of sign, size, and significance, we consider this an acceptable equation. The only circumstance under which we'd consider estimating a second specification would be if we had theoretical reasons to believe that we had omitted a relevant variable. The only variable that might meet this description is SAT_i (which we prefer to the individual MSAT and VSAT):

$$\widehat{GPA}_i = -0.92 + 0.47HGPA_i + 0.05HRS_i \qquad (6.19)$$
$$\phantom{\widehat{GPA}_i = -0.92 + } (0.22) \qquad\quad (0.02)$$
$$\phantom{\widehat{GPA}_i = -0.92 + } t = 2.12 \qquad\qquad 2.50$$
$$\phantom{\widehat{GPA}_i = } + 0.44lnEX_i \quad + 0.00060SAT_i$$
$$\phantom{\widehat{GPA}_i = } (0.14) \qquad\qquad (0.00064)$$
$$\phantom{\widehat{GPA}_i = } t = 3.12 \qquad\qquad 0.93$$
$$\phantom{\widehat{GPA}_i = } N = 25 \quad \overline{R}^2 = .583$$

Let's use our four specification criteria to compare Equations 6.18 and 6.19:

1. *Theory:* As discussed previously, the theoretical validity of SAT tests is a matter of some academic controversy, but they still are one of the most-cited measures of academic potential in this country.

2. *t-Test:* The coefficient of SAT is positive, as we'd expect, but it's not significantly different from zero.

3. $\overline{R}^2$: As you'd expect (since SAT's *t*-score is under 1), $\overline{R}^2$ falls slightly when SAT is added.

4. *Bias:* None of the estimated slope coefficients changes significantly when SAT is added, though some of the *t*-scores do change because of the increase in the $SE(\hat{\beta})$s caused by the addition of SAT.

Thus, the statistical criteria support our theoretical contention that SAT is irrelevant.

Finally, it's important to recognize that different researchers could come up with different final equations on this topic. A researcher whose prior expectation was that SAT unambiguously belonged in the equation would have estimated Equation 6.19 and accepted that equation without bothering to estimate Equation 6.18. Other researchers, in the spirit of sensitivity analysis, would report both equations.

6.6 Summary

1. The omission of a variable from an equation will cause bias in the estimates of the remaining coefficients to the extent that the omitted variable is correlated with included variables.

2. The bias to be expected from leaving a variable out of an equation equals the coefficient of the excluded variable times a function of the simple correlation coefficient between the excluded variable and the included variable in question.

3. Including a variable in an equation in which it is actually irrelevant does not cause bias, but it will usually increase the variances of the included variables' estimated coefficients, thus lowering their *t*-values and lowering $\overline{R}^2$.

4. Four useful criteria for the inclusion of a variable in an equation are:
    a. theory
    b. t-test
    c. $\overline{R}^2$
    d. bias

5. Theory, not statistical fit, should be the most important criterion for the inclusion of a variable in a regression equation. To do otherwise runs the risk of producing incorrect and/or disbelieved results.

EXERCISES

(The answer to Exercise 2 is in Appendix A.)

1. Write the meaning of each of the following terms without referring to the book (or your notes), and compare your definition with the version in the text for each:
    a. omitted variable
    b. irrelevant variable
    c. specification bias
    d. sequential specification search
    e. specification error
    f. the four specification criteria
    g. expected bias
    h. sensitivity analysis

. 2. You've been hired by "Indo," the new Indonesian automobile manufacturer, to build a model of U.S. car prices in order to help the company undercut U.S. prices. Allowing Friedmaniac zeal to overwhelm any patriotic urges, you build the following model of the price of 35 different American-made 2004 U.S. sedans (standard errors in parentheses):

$$\text{Model A: } \hat{P}_i = 3.0 + 0.28W_i + 1.2T_i + 5.8C_i + 0.19L_i$$
$$\qquad\qquad (0.07) \quad (0.4) \quad (2.9) \quad (0.20)$$
$$\overline{R}^2 = .92$$

where: P_i = the list price of the ith car (thousands of dollars)
    W_i = the weight of the ith car (hundreds of pounds)
    T_i = a dummy equal to 1 if the ith car has an automatic transmission, 0 otherwise

C_i = a dummy equal to 1 if the ith car has cruise control, 0 otherwise

L_i = the size of the engine of the ith car (in liters)

a. Your firm's pricing expert hypothesizes positive signs for all the slope coefficients in Model A. Test her expectations at the 5-percent level.

b. What econometric problems appear to exist in Model A? In particular, does the size of the coefficient of C cause any concern? Why? What could be the problem?

c. You decide to test the possibility that L is an irrelevant variable by dropping it and rerunning the equation, obtaining the following Model T equation. Which model do you prefer? Why? (*Hint:* Be sure to use our four specification criteria.)

$$\text{Model T: } \hat{P} = 18 + 0.29W_i + 1.2T_i + 5.9C_i$$
$$(0.07) \quad (0.30) \quad (2.9)$$
$$\overline{R}^2 = .93$$

·3. Consider the following annual model of the death rate (per million population) due to coronary heart disease in the United States (Y_t):

$$\hat{Y}_t = 140 + 10.0C_t + 4.0E_t - 1.0M_t$$
$$(2.5) \quad (1.0) \quad (0.5)$$
$$t = 4.0 \quad 4.0 \quad -2.0$$
$$N = 31 \ (1975-2005) \quad \overline{R}^2 = .678$$

where: C_t = per capita cigarette consumption (pounds of tobacco) in year t

E_t = per capita consumption of edible saturated fats (pounds of butter, margarine, and lard) in year t

M_t = per capita consumption of meat (pounds) in year t

a. Create and test appropriate hypotheses at the 10-percent level. What, if anything, seems to be wrong with the estimated coefficient of M?

b. The most likely cause of a coefficient that is significant in the unexpected direction is omitted variable bias. Which of the following variables could possibly be an omitted variable that is causing $\hat{\beta}_M$'s unexpected sign? Explain. (*Hint:* Be sure to analyze expected bias in your explanation.)

B_t = per capita consumption of hard liquor (gallons) in year t

F_t = the average fat content (percentage) of the meat that was consumed in year t

W_t = per capita consumption of wine and beer (gallons) in year t
R_t = per capita number of miles run in year t
H_t = per capita open-heart surgeries in year t
O_t = per capita amount of oat bran eaten in year t

c. If you had to choose a variable not listed in part b to add to the equation, what would it be? Explain your answer.

4. Assume that you've been hired by the surgeon general of the United States to study the determinants of smoking behavior and that you estimate the following cross-sectional model based on data for all 50 states (standard errors in parentheses):[10]

$$\hat{C}_i = 100 - 9.0E_i + 1.0I_i - 0.04T_i - 3.0V_i + 1.5R_i \qquad (6.20)$$
$$\phantom{\hat{C}_i = 100} (3.0) \quad (1.0) \quad (0.04) \quad (1.0) \quad (0.5)$$
$$t = -3.0 \quad\ 1.0 \quad -1.0 \quad -3.0 \quad\ 3.0$$
$$\bar{R}^2 = .40 \quad N = 50 \text{ (states)}$$

where: C_i = the number of cigarettes consumed per day per person in the *i*th state
E_i = the average years of education for persons over 21 in the *i*th state
I_i = the average income in the *i*th state (thousands of dollars)
T_i = the tax per package of cigarettes in the *i*th state (cents)
V_i = the number of video ads against smoking aired on the three major networks in the *i*th state.
R_i = the number of radio ads against smoking aired on the five largest radio networks in the *i*th state

a. Develop and test (at the 5-percent level) appropriate hypotheses for the coefficients of the variables in this equation.
b. Do you appear to have any irrelevant variables? Do you appear to have any omitted variables? Explain your answer.
c. Let's assume that your answer to part b was yes to both. Which problem is more important to solve first—irrelevant variables or omitted variables? Why?
d. One of the purposes of running the equation was to determine the effectiveness of antismoking advertising on television and radio. What is your conclusion?

---

10. This question is generalized from a number of similar studies, including John A. Bishop and Jang H. Yoo, "Health Scare, Excise Taxes, and Advertising Ban in the Cigarette Demand and Supply," *Southern Economic Journal*, Vol. 52, No. 1, pp. 402–411.

e. The surgeon general decides that tax rates are irrelevant to cigarette smoking and orders you to drop the variable from your equation. Given the following results, use our four specification criteria to decide whether you agree with her conclusion. Carefully explain your reasoning (standard errors in parentheses).

$$\hat{C}_i = 101 - 9.1E_i + 1.0I_i - 3.5V_i + 1.6R_i \qquad (6.21)$$
$$(3.0) \quad (0.9) \quad (1.0) \quad (0.5)$$
$$\overline{R}^2 = .40 \quad N = 50 \text{ (states)}$$

f. In answering part e, you surely noticed that the $\overline{R}^2$ figures were identical. Did this surprise you? Why or why not?

5. The data set in Table 6.2 is the one that was used to estimate the chicken demand examples of Sections 6.1 and 6.2.
   a. Use these data to reproduce the specifications in the chapter (datafile = CHICK6).
   b. Find data in Table 6.2 for the price of pork (another substitute for chicken) and add that variable to Equation 6.8. Analyze your results. In particular, apply the four criteria for the inclusion of a variable to determine whether the price of pork is irrelevant or previously was an omitted variable.

· 6. You have been retained by the "Expressive Expresso" company to help them decide where to build their next "Expressive Expresso" store. You decide to run a regression on the sales of the 30 existing "Expressive Expresso" stores as a function of the characteristics of the locations they are in and then use the equation to predict the sales at the various locations you are considering for the newest store. You end up estimating (standard errors in parentheses):

$$\hat{Y}_i = 30 + 0.1X_{1i} + 0.01X_{2i} + 10.0X_{3i} + 3.0X_{4i}$$
$$(0.02) \quad (0.01) \quad (1.0) \quad (1.0)$$

where: Y_i = average daily sales (in hundreds of dollars) of the ith store
   X_{1i} = the number of cars that pass the ith location per hour
   X_{2i} = average income in the area of the ith store
   X_{3i} = the number of tables in the ith store
   X_{4i} = the number of competing shops in the area of the ith store

Table 6.2 Data for the Chicken Demand Equation

Year	Y	PC	PB	YD	TEMP	PRP
1974	39.70	42.30	143.80	50.10	−16	107.80
1975	38.69	49.40	152.20	54.98	−4	134.60
1976	42.02	45.50	145.70	59.72	−24	134.00
1977	42.71	45.30	145.90	65.17	16	125.40
1978	44.75	49.30	178.80	72.24	5	143.60
1979	48.35	50.00	222.40	79.67	13	152.50
1980	48.47	53.50	233.60	88.22	21	147.50
1981	50.37	53.80	234.70	97.65	49	161.20
1982	51.52	51.50	238.40	104.26	4	185.60
1983	52.55	56.00	234.10	111.31	35	179.70
1984	54.61	61.50	235.50	123.19	11	171.40
1985	56.42	56.20	228.60	130.37	4	170.80
1986	57.70	63.10	226.80	136.49	18	188.80
1987	61.94	53.10	238.40	142.41	35	199.40
1988	63.80	62.10	250.30	152.97	46	194.00
1989	66.88	64.20	265.70	162.57	32	193.50
1990	70.34	60.50	281.00	171.31	64	224.90
1991	73.26	57.70	288.30	176.09	52	224.20
1992	76.39	59.00	284.60	184.94	18	209.50
1993	78.27	27.10	293.40	188.72	27	209.10
1994	79.65	26.20	282.90	195.55	48	209.50
1995	79.27	26.90	284.30	202.87	71	206.10
1996	80.61	28.00	280.20	210.91	36	233.70
1997	83.10	33.20	279.50	219.40	60	245.00
1998	83.76	33.40	277.10	231.61	89	242.70
1999	88.98	39.50	287.80	239.68	60	241.40
2000	90.08	43.00	306.40	254.69	62	258.20
2001	89.71	43.40	337.70	262.24	74	269.40
2002	94.37	43.90	331.50	271.45	85	265.80

Sources: U.S. Department of Agriculture. *Agricultural Statistics*; U.S. Bureau of the Census. *Historical Statistics of the United States*, U.S. Bureau of the Census. *Statistical Abstract of the United States*. (Datafile = CHICK6)

a. Hypothesize expected signs, calculate the correct *t*-scores, and test the significance at the 1-percent level for each of the coefficients.
b. What problems appear to exist in the equation? What evidence of these problems do you have?
c. What suggestions would you make for a possible second run of this admittedly hypothetical equation? (*Hint*: Before recommending the inclusion of a potentially omitted variable, consider whether the exclusion of the variable could possibly have caused any observed bias.)

7. Discuss the topic of specification searches with various members of your econometrics class. What is so wrong with not mentioning previous (probably incorrect) estimates? Why should readers be suspicious when researchers attempt to find results that support their hypotheses? Who would try to do the opposite? Do these concerns have any meaning in the world of business? In particular, if you're not trying to publish a paper, couldn't you use any specification search techniques you want to find the best equation?

8. For each of the following situations, determine the *sign* (and, if possible, comment on the likely size) of the expected bias introduced by omitting a variable:
   a. In an equation for the demand for peanut butter, the impact on the coefficient of disposable income of omitting the price of peanut butter variable. (*Hint:* Start by hypothesizing signs.)
   b. In an earnings equation for workers, the impact on the coefficient of experience of omitting the variable for age.
   c. In a production function for airplanes, the impact on the coefficient of labor of omitting the capital variable.
   d. In an equation for daily attendance at outdoor concerts, the impact on the coefficient of the weekend dummy variable (1 = weekend) of omitting a variable that measures the probability of precipitation at concert time.

9. Most of the examples in the text so far have been demand-side equations or production functions, but economists often also have to quantify supply-side equations that are not true production functions. These equations attempt to explain the production of a product (for example, Brazilian coffee) as a function of the price of the product and various other attributes of the market that might have an impact on the total output of growers.
   a. What sign would you expect the coefficient of price to have in a supply-side equation? Why?
   b. What other variables can you think of that might be important in a supply-side equation?
   c. Many agricultural decisions are made months (if not a full year or more) before the results of those decisions appear in the market. How would you adjust your hypothesized equation to take account of these lags?
   d. Using the information given so far, carefully specify the exact equation you would use to attempt to explain Brazilian coffee production. Be sure to hypothesize the expected signs, be specific with respect to lags, and try to make sure that you have not omitted an important independent variable.

10. If you think about the previous question, you'll realize that the *same* dependent variable (quantity of Brazilian coffee) can have different expected signs for the coefficient of the *same* independent variable (the price of Brazilian coffee), depending on what other variables are in the regression.

    a. How is this possible? That is, how is it possible to expect different signs in demand-side equations from what you would expect in supply-side ones?

    b. Given that we will not discuss how to estimate simultaneous equations until Chapter 14, what can be done to avoid getting the price coefficient from the demand equation in the supply equation and vice versa?

    c. What can you do to systematically ensure that you do not have supply-side variables in your demand equation or demand-side variables in your supply equation?

11. Let's return to the model of financial aid awards at a liberal arts college that was first introduced in Section 2.2. In that section, we estimated the following equation (standard errors in parentheses):

$$\widehat{FINAID_i} = 8927 - 0.36 \ PARENT_i + 87.4 \ HSRANK_i \qquad (6.22)$$
$$\phantom{\widehat{FINAID_i} = 8927 -} (0.03) (20.7)$$
$$t = -11.26 4.22$$
$$\overline{R}^2 = 0.73 \qquad N = 50$$

where: $FINAID_i$ = the financial aid (measured in dollars of grant) awarded to the *i*th applicant

   $PARENT_i$ = the amount (in dollars) that the parents of the *i*th student are judged able to contribute to college expenses

   $HSRANK_i$ = the *i*th student's GPA rank in high school, measured as a percentage (ranging from a low of 0 to a high of 100)

    a. Create and test hypotheses for the coefficients of the independent variables.

    b. What econometric problems do you see in the equation? Are there any signs of an omitted variable? Of an irrelevant variable? Explain your answer.

    c. Suppose that you now hear a charge that financial aid awards at the school are unfairly tilted toward males, so you decide to attempt to test this charge by adding a dummy variable for gender ($MALE_i = 1$

if the ith student is a male, 0 if female) to your equation, getting the following results:

$$\widehat{FINAID_i} = 9813 - 0.34 \, PARENT_i + 83.3 \, HSRANK_i - 1570 \, MALE_i \quad (6.23)$$

$$\begin{array}{cccc} & (0.03) & (20.1) & (784) \\ t = & -10.88 & 4.13 & -2.00 \\ & \overline{R}^2 = 0.75 & N = 50 & \end{array}$$

d. Carefully explain the real-world meaning of the estimated coefficient of MALE.

e. Which equation is better, Equation 6.22 or Equation 6.23? Carefully use our four specification criteria to make your decision, being sure to state which criteria support which equation and why.

12. Determine the sign (and, if possible, comment on the likely size) of the bias introduced by leaving a variable out of an equation in each of the following cases:

a. In an annual equation for corn yields per acre (in year t), the impact on the coefficient of rainfall in year t of omitting average temperature that year. (*Hint:* Drought and cold weather both hurt corn yields.)

b. In an equation for daily attendance at Los Angeles Lakers' home basketball games, the impact on the coefficient of the winning percentage of the opponent (as of the game in question) of omitting a dummy variable that equals 1 if the opponent's team includes a superstar.

c. In an equation for annual consumption of apples in the United States, the impact on the coefficient of the price of bananas of omitting the price of oranges.

d. In an equation for student grades on the first midterm in this class, the impact on the coefficient of total hours studied (for the test) of omitting hours slept the night before the test.

13. Suppose that you run a regression to determine whether gender or race has any significant impact on scores on a test of the economic understanding of children.[11] You model the score of the ith student on the test of elementary economics (S_i) as a function of the composite score on the Iowa Tests of Basic Skills of the ith student, a dummy variable equal to 1 if the ith student is female (0 otherwise), the average number of years of education of the parents of the ith student, and a

---

11. These results have been jiggled to meet the needs of this question, but this research actually was done. See Stephen Buckles and Vera Freeman, "Male-Female Differences in the Stock and Flow of Economic Knowledge," *Review of Economics and Statistics*, Vol. 65, No. 2, pp. 355–357.

dummy variable equal to 1 if the ith student is nonwhite (0 otherwise). Unfortunately, a rainstorm floods the computer center and makes it impossible to read the part of the computer output that identifies which variable is which. All you know is that the regression results are (standard errors in parentheses):

$$\hat{S}_i = 5.7 - 0.63X_{1i} - 0.22X_{2i} + 0.16X_{3i} + 1.20X_{4i}$$
$$(0.63) \quad (0.88) \quad (0.08) \quad (0.10)$$
$$N = 24 \quad \overline{R}^2 = .54$$

a. Attempt to identify which result corresponds to which variable. Be specific.
b. Explain the reasoning behind your answer to part a.
c. Assuming that your answer is correct, create and test appropriate hypotheses (at the 5-percent level) and come to conclusions about the effects of gender and race on the test scores of this particular sample.
d. Did you use a one-tailed or two-tailed test in part c? Why?

· 14. Let's return to the model of Exercises 3-11 and 5-12 of the auction price of iPods on eBay. In that model, we used datafile IPOD3 to estimate the following equation:

$$\widehat{PRICE}_i = 109.24 + 54.99NEW_i - 20.44SCRATCH_i + 0.73BIDRS_i \quad (6.24)$$
$$(5.34) \qquad\quad (5.11) \qquad\qquad (0.59)$$
$$t = \qquad\qquad 10.28 \qquad\quad -4.00 \qquad\qquad 1.23$$
$$N = 215$$

where: $PRICE_i$ = the price at which the ith iPod sold on eBay
NEW_i = a dummy variable equal to 1 if the ith iPod was new, 0 otherwise
$SCRATCH_i$ = a dummy variable equal to 1 if the ith iPod had a minor cosmetic defect, 0 otherwise
$BIDRS_i$ = the number of bidders on the ith iPod

The dataset also includes a variable ($PERCENT_i$) that measures the percentage of customers of the seller of the ith iPod who gave that seller a positive rating for quality and reliability in previous transactions.[12] In theory, the higher the rating of a seller, the more a potential bidder

---

12. For more on this dataset and this variable, see Leonardo Rezende, "Econometrics of Auctions by Least Squares," *Journal of Applied Econometrics*, November/December 2008, pp. 925–948.

would trust that seller, and the more that potential bidder would be willing to bid. If you add PERCENT to the equation, you obtain

$$\widehat{PRICE}_i = 82.67 + 55.42NEW_i - 20.95SCRATCH_i + 0.63BIDRS_i + 0.28PERCENT_i$$
$$\qquad\qquad\quad (5.34)\qquad\quad (5.12)\qquad\qquad (0.59)\qquad\quad (0.20)$$
$$t = \qquad\quad 10.38\qquad\quad -4.10\qquad\qquad\quad 1.07\qquad\qquad 1.40\quad (6.25)$$
$$N = 215$$

a. Use our four specification criteria to decide whether you think PERCENT belongs in the equation. Be specific. (*Hint:* $\overline{R}^2$ isn't given, but you're capable of determining which equation had the higher $\overline{R}^2$.)

b. Do you think that PERCENT is an accurate measure of the quality and reliability of the seller? Why or why not? (*Hint:* Among other things, consider the case of a seller with very few previous transactions.)

c. (optional) With datafile IPOD3, use EViews, Stata, or your own regression program to estimate the equation with and without PERCENT. What are the $\overline{R}^2$ figures for the two specifications? Were you correct in your determination (in part a) as to which equation had the higher $\overline{R}^2$?

15. Look back at Exercise 14 in Chapter 5, the equation on international price discrimination in pharmaceuticals. In that cross-sectional study, Schut and VanBergeijk estimated two equations in addition to the one cited in the exercise.[13] These two equations tested the possibility that CV_i, total volume of consumption of pharmaceuticals in the ith country, and N_i, the population of the ith country, belonged in the original equation, Equation 5.10, repeated here:

$$\hat{P}_i = 38.22 + 1.43GDPN_i - 0.6CVN_i + 7.31PP_i \qquad (5.10)$$
$$\qquad\qquad\quad (0.21)\qquad\quad (0.22)\qquad (6.12)$$
$$t = \qquad\qquad 6.69\qquad\quad -2.66\qquad 1.19$$

$$\qquad\qquad\quad -15.63DPC_i - 11.38IPC_i$$
$$\qquad\qquad\qquad (6.93)\qquad\quad (7.16)$$
$$t = \qquad\qquad -2.25\qquad\quad -1.59$$
$$N = 32 \quad \overline{R}^2 = .775$$

13. Frederick T. Schut and Peter A. G. VanBergeijk, "International Price Discrimination: The Pharmaceutical Industry," *World Development*, Vol. 14, No. 9, pp. 1141–1150.

where: P_i = the pharmaceutical price level in the ith country divided by that of the United States

$GDPN_i$ = per capita domestic product in the ith country divided by that of the United States

CVN_i = per capita volume of consumption of pharmaceuticals in the ith country divided by that of the United States

PP_i = a dummy variable equal to 1 if patents for pharmaceutical products are recognized in the ith country, 0 otherwise

DPC_i = a dummy variable equal to 1 if the ith country applied strict price controls, 0 otherwise

IPC_i = a dummy variable equal to 1 if the ith country encouraged price competition, 0 otherwise

a. Using EViews, Stata (or your own computer program), and datafile DRUG5 (or Table 5.1), estimate:
   i. Equation 5.10 with CV_i added, and
   ii. Equation 5.10 with N_i added
b. Use our four specification criteria to determine whether CV and N are irrelevant or omitted variables. (*Hint:* The authors expected that prices would be lower if market size were larger because of possible economies of scale and/or enhanced competition.)
c. Why didn't the authors run Equation 5.10 with *both* CV and N included? (*Hint:* While you can estimate this equation yourself, you don't have to do so to answer the question.)
d. Why do you think that the authors reported all three estimated specifications in their results when they thought that Equation 5.10 was the best?

· 16. You've just been promoted to be the product manager for "Amish Oats Instant Oatmeal," and your first assignment is to decide whether to raise prices for next year. (Instant oatmeal is a product that can be mixed with hot water to create a hot breakfast cereal in much less time than it takes to make the same cereal using regular oatmeal.) In keeping with your reputation as the econometric expert at Amish Oats, you decide to build a model of the impact of price on sales, and you estimate the following hypothetical equation (standard errors in parentheses):

$$\widehat{OAT}_t = 30 + 20PR_t + 18PRCOMP_t + 30ADS_t + 0.0015YD_t$$
$$\phantom{\widehat{OAT}_t = 30 +} (20) \qquad (6) \qquad\qquad (10) \qquad\quad (0.0005)$$
$$\phantom{\widehat{OAT}_t = 30 +} t = 1.00 \quad\ 3.00 \qquad\qquad 3.00 \qquad\quad 3.00$$
$$\phantom{\widehat{OAT}_t =} \overline{R}^2 = .78 \quad\ N = 29 \text{ (annual model)}$$

where: OAT_t = U.S. sales of Amish Oats instant oatmeal in year t

PR_t = the U.S. price of Amish Oats instant oatmeal in year t

$PRCOMP_t$ = the U.S. price of the competing instant oatmeal in year t

ADS_t = U.S. advertising for Amish Oats instant oatmeal in year t

YD_t = U.S. disposable income in year t

a. Create and test appropriate hypotheses about the slope coefficients of this equation at the 5-percent level.
b. What econometric problems, if any, appear to be in this equation? Do you see any indications that there is an omitted variable? Do you see any indications that there is an irrelevant variable? Explain.
c. If you could add one variable to this equation, what would it be? Explain your answer.
d. Suddenly it hits you! You've made a horrible mistake! What is it? (*Hint:* Think about substitutes for OAT.)

6.7 Appendix: Additional Specification Criteria

So far in this chapter, we've suggested four criteria for choosing the independent variables (economic theory, $\overline{R}^2$, the t-test, and possible bias in the coefficients). Sometimes, however, these criteria don't provide enough information for a researcher to feel confident that a given specification is best. For instance, there can be two different specifications that both have excellent theoretical underpinnings. In such a situation, many econometricians use additional, often more formal, specification criteria to provide comparisons of the properties of the alternative estimated equations.

The use of formal specification criteria is not without problems, however. First, no test, no matter how sophisticated, can "prove" that a particular specification is the true one. The use of specification criteria, therefore, must be tempered with a healthy dose of economic theory and common sense. A second problem is that more than 20 such criteria have been proposed; how do we decide which one(s) to use? Because many of these criteria overlap with one another or have varying levels of complexity, a choice between the alternatives is a matter of personal preference.

In this section, we'll describe the use of three of the most popular specification criteria, J. B. Ramsey's RESET test, Akaike's Information Criterion, and the Schwarz Criterion. Our inclusion of just these techniques does not imply that other tests and criteria are not appropriate or useful. Indeed, the reader will find that most other formal specification criteria have quite a bit in common with at least one of the techniques that we include. We think that you'll be better able to use and understand other formal specification criteria[14] once you've mastered these three.

Ramsey's Regression Specification Error Test (RESET)

One of the most-used formal specification criteria other than $\bar{R}^2$ is the Ramsey Regression Specification Error Test (RESET).[15] The **Ramsey RESET test** is a general test that determines the likelihood of an omitted variable or some other specification error by measuring whether the fit of a given equation can be significantly improved by the addition of $\hat{Y}^2$, $\hat{Y}^3$, and $\hat{Y}^4$ terms.

What's the intuition behind RESET? The additional terms act as proxies for any possible (unknown) omitted variables or incorrect functional forms. If the proxies can be shown by the *F*-test to have improved the overall fit of the original equation, then we have evidence that there is some sort of specification error in our equation. As you'll learn in Chapter 7, the $\hat{Y}^2$, $\hat{Y}^3$, and $\hat{Y}^4$ terms form a *polynomial* functional form. Such a polynomial is a powerful curve-fitting device that has a good chance of acting as a proxy for a specification error if one exists. If there is no specification error, then we'd expect the coefficients of the added terms to be insignificantly different from zero because there is nothing for them to act as a proxy for.

The Ramsey RESET test involves three steps:

1. Estimate the equation to be tested using OLS:

$$\hat{Y}_i = \hat{\beta}_0 + \hat{\beta}_1 X_{1i} + \hat{\beta}_2 X_{2i} \tag{6.26}$$

2. Take the $\hat{Y}_i$ values from Equation 6.26 and create $\hat{Y}_i^2$, $\hat{Y}_i^3$, and $\hat{Y}_i^4$ terms. Then add these terms to Equation 6.26 as additional explanatory variables and estimate the new equation with OLS:

$$Y_i = \beta_0 + \beta_1 X_{1i} + \beta_2 X_{2i} + \beta_3 \hat{Y}_i^2 + \beta_4 \hat{Y}_i^3 + \beta_5 \hat{Y}_i^4 + \epsilon_i \tag{6.27}$$

---

14. In particular, the likelihood ratio test, versions of which will be covered in Section 12.2, can be used as a specification test. For an introductory level summary of six other specification criteria, see Ramu Ramanathan, *Introductory Econometrics* (Fort Worth: Harcourt Brace Jovanovich, 1998, pp. 164–166).

15. J. B. Ramsey, "Tests for Specification Errors in Classical Linear Squares Regression Analysis," *Journal of the Royal Statistical Society,* Vol. 31, No. 2, pp. 350–371.

3. Compare the fits of Equations 6.26 and 6.27 using the *F*-test. If the two equations are significantly different in overall fit, we can conclude that it's likely that Equation 6.26 is misspecified.

While the Ramsey RESET test is fairly easy to use, it does little more than signal *when* a major specification error might exist. If you encounter a significant Ramsey RESET test, then you face the daunting task of figuring out exactly *what* the error is! Thus, the test often ends up being more useful in "supporting" (technically, not refuting) a researcher's contention that a given specification has no major specification errors than it is in helping find an otherwise undiscovered flaw.[16]

As an example of the Ramsey RESET test, let's return to the chicken demand model of this chapter to see if RESET can detect the known specification error (omitting the price of beef) in Equation 6.9. Step one involves running the original equation without PB.

$$\hat{Y}_t = 30.7 - 0.09PC_t + 0.25YD_t \tag{6.9}$$
$$\phantom{\hat{Y}_t = 30.7 -}(0.03)(0.005)$$
$$t = -2.76+46.1$$
$$\overline{R}^2 = .9895 \quad N = 29 \text{ (annual 1974–2002)} \quad RSS = 83.22$$

For step two, we take $\hat{Y}_t$ from Equation 6.9, calculate $\hat{Y}_t^2$, $\hat{Y}_t^3$, and $\hat{Y}_t^4$, and then reestimate Equation 6.9 with the three new terms added in:

$$Y_t = -41.4 + 0.40PC_t - 1.09YD_t + 0.11\hat{Y}_t^2 \tag{6.28}$$
$$(0.59)(1.77)(0.17)$$
$$-0.001\hat{Y}_t^3 + 0.000002\hat{Y}_t^4 + e_t$$
$$(0.002)(0.000006)$$
$$\overline{R}^2 = .991 \quad N = 29 \text{ (annual 1974–2002)} \quad RSS = 57.43$$

In step three, we compare the fits of the two equations by using the *F*-test. Specifically, we test the hypothesis that the coefficients of all three of the added terms are equal to zero:

$$H_0: \beta_3 = \beta_4 = \beta_5 = 0$$
$$H_A: \text{otherwise}$$

---

16. The particular version of the Ramsey RESET test we describe in this section is only one of a number of possible formulations of the test. For example, some researchers delete the $\hat{Y}^4$ term from Equation 6.27. In addition, versions of the Ramsey RESET test are useful in testing for functional form errors (to be described in Chapter 7) and serial correlation (to be described in Chapter 9).

The appropriate F-statistic to use is one that is presented in Section 5.6.

$$F = \frac{(RSS_M - RSS)/M}{RSS/(N - K - 1)} \tag{6.29}$$

where RSS_M is the residual sum of squares from the restricted equation (Equation 6.9), RSS is the residual sum of squares from the unrestricted equation[17] (Equation 6.28), M is the number of restrictions (3), and $(N - K - 1)$ is the number of degrees of freedom in the unrestricted equation (34):

$$F = \frac{(83.22 - 57.43)/3}{57.43/23} = 3.44$$

The critical F-value to use, 3.03, is found in Statistical Table B-2 at the 5-percent level of significance with 3 numerator and 23 denominator degrees of freedom. Since 3.44 is greater than 3.03, we can reject the null hypothesis that the coefficients of the added variables are jointly zero, allowing us to conclude that there is indeed a specification error in Equation 6.9. Such a conclusion is no surprise, since we know that the price of beef was left out of the equation. Note, however, that the Ramsey RESET test tells us only that a specification error is likely to exist in Equation 6.9; it does not specify the details of that error.

Akaike's Information Criterion and the Schwarz Criterion

A second category of formal specification criteria involves adjusting the summed squared residuals (RSS) by one factor or another to create an index of the fit of an equation. The most popular criterion of this type is $\overline{R}^2$, but a number of interesting alternatives have been proposed.

Akaike's Information Criterion (AIC) and the **Schwarz Criterion (SC)** are methods of comparing alternative specifications by adjusting RSS for the sample size (N) and the number of independent variables (K).[18] These criteria can be used to augment our four basic specification criteria when we try

---

17. Because of the obvious correlation between the three $\hat{Y}$ values, Equation 6.28 (with most RESET equations) suffers from extreme multicollinearity. Since the purpose of the RESET equation is to see whether the overall fit can be improved by adding in proxies for an omitted variable (or other specification error), this extreme multicollinearity is not a concern.

18. Hirotogu Akaike, "Likelihood of a Model and Information Criteria," *Journal of Econometrics,* Vol. 16, No. 1, pp. 3–14 and G. Schwarz, "Estimating the Dimension of a Model," *The Annals of Statistics,* Vol. 6, pp. 461–464. The definitions of AIC and SC we use in Equations 6.30 and 6.31 produce slightly different numbers than the versions used by EViews, but the versions map on a one-to-one basis and therefore produce identical conclusions.

to decide if the improved fit caused by an additional variable is worth the decreased degrees of freedom and increased complexity caused by the addition. Their equations are:

$$AIC = Log(RSS/N) + 2(K + 1)/N \qquad (6.30)$$

$$SC = Log(RSS/N) + Log(N)(K + 1)/N \qquad (6.31)$$

To use AIC and SC, estimate two alternative specifications and calculate AIC and SC for each equation. The lower AIC or SC are, the better the specification. Note that even though the two criteria were developed independently to maximize different object functions, their equations are quite similar. Both criteria tend to penalize the addition of another explanatory variable more than $\overline{R}^2$ does. As a result, AIC and SC will quite often[19] be minimized by an equation with fewer independent variables than the ones that maximize $\overline{R}^2$.

Let's apply Akaike's Information Criterion and the Schwarz Criterion to the same chicken demand example we used for Ramsey's RESET. To see whether AIC and/or SC can detect the specification error we already know exists in Equation 6.9 (the omission of the price of beef), we need to calculate AIC and SC for equations with and without the price of beef. The equation with the lower AIC and SC values will, other things being equal, be our preferred specification.

The original chicken demand model, Equation 6.8, was:

$$\hat{Y}_t = 27.7 - 0.11PC_t + 0.03PB_t + 0.23YD_t \qquad (6.8)$$
$$(0.03) \qquad (0.02) \qquad (0.01)$$
$$t = \quad -3.38 \qquad +1.86 \qquad +15.7$$
$$\overline{R}^2 = .9904 \quad N = 29 \text{ (annual 1974–2002)} \quad RSS = 73.11$$

Plugging the numbers from Equation 6.8 into Equations 6.30 and 6.31, AIC and SC can be seen to be:

$$AIC = Log(73.11/29) + 2(4)/29 = 1.20$$
$$SC = Log(73.11/29) + Log(29)*4/29 = 1.39$$

---

19. Using a Monte Carlo study, Judge et al. showed that (given specific simplifying assumptions) a specification chosen by maximizing $\overline{R}^2$ is more than 50 percent more likely to include an irrelevant variable than is one chosen by minimizing AIC or SC. See George C. Judge, R. Carter Hill, W. E. Griffiths, Helmut Lutkepohl, and Tsoung-Chao Lee, *Introduction to the Theory and Practice of Econometrics* (New York: Wiley, 1988), pp. 849–850. At the same time, minimizing AIC or SC will omit a relevant variable more frequently than will maximizing $\overline{R}^2$.

Equation 6.9 (see page 203) which omits the price of beef, has an RSS of 83.22 and two independent variables, so:

$$AIC = Log(83.22/29) + 2(3)/29 = 1.26$$
$$SC = Log(83.22/29) + Log(29)*3/29 = 1.40$$

For AIC, $1.20 < 1.26$, and for SC, $1.39 < 1.40$, so both Akaike's Information Criterion and the Schwarz Criterion provide evidence that Equation 6.8 is preferable to Equation 6.9. That is, the price of beef appears to belong in the equation. In practice, these calculations may not be necessary because AIC and SC are automatically calculated by some regression software packages, including EViews.

As it turns out, then, all three new specification criteria indicate the presence of a specification error when we leave the price of beef out of the equation. This result is not surprising, since we purposely omitted a theoretically justified variable, but it provides an example of how useful these specification criteria could be when we're less than sure about the underlying theory.

Note that AIC and SC require the researcher to come up with a particular alternative specification, whereas Ramsey's RESET does not. Such a distinction makes RESET easier to use, but it makes AIC and SC more informative if a specification error is found. Thus our additional specification criteria serve different purposes. RESET is useful as a general test of the existence of a specification error, whereas AIC and SC are useful as means of comparing two or more alternative specifications.

7 Specification: Choosing a Functional Form

Even after you've chosen your independent variables, the job of specifying the equation is not over. The next step is to choose the functional form of the relationship between each independent variable and the dependent variable. Should the equation go through the origin? Do you expect a curve instead of a straight line? Does the effect of a variable peak at some point and then start to decline? An affirmative answer to any of these questions suggests that an equation other than the standard linear model of the previous chapters might be appropriate. Such alternative specifications are important for two reasons: a correct explanatory variable may well appear to be insignificant or to have an unexpected sign if an inappropriate functional form is used, and the consequences of an incorrect functional form for interpretation and forecasting can be severe.

Theoretical considerations usually dictate the form of a regression model. The basic technique involved in deciding on a functional form is to choose the shape that best exemplifies the expected underlying economic or business principles and then to use the mathematical form that produces that shape. To help with that choice, this chapter contains plots of the most commonly used functional forms along with the mathematical equations that correspond to each.

The chapter begins with a brief discussion of the constant term. In particular, we suggest that the constant term should be retained in equations even if theory suggests otherwise and that estimates of the constant term should not be relied on for inference or analysis. The chapter concludes with a discussion of dummy variables.

7.1 The Use and Interpretation of the Constant Term

In the linear regression model, β_0 is the intercept or constant term. It is the expected value of Y when all the explanatory variables (and the error term) equal zero. An estimate of β_0 has at least three components:

1. the true β_0,

2. the constant impact of any specification errors (an omitted variable, for example), and

3. the mean of ϵ for the correctly specified equation (if not equal to zero).

Unfortunately, these components can't be distinguished from one another because we can observe only β_0, the sum of the three components. The result is that we have to analyze β_0 differently from the way we analyze the other coefficients in the equation.[1]

At times, β_0 is of theoretical importance. Consider, for example, the following cost equation:

$$C_i = \beta_0 + \beta_1 Q_i + \epsilon_i$$

where C_i is the total cost of producing output Q_i. The term $\beta_1 Q_i$ represents the total variable cost associated with output level Q_i, and β_0 represents the total fixed cost, defined as the cost when output $Q_i = 0$. Thus, a regression equation might seem useful to a researcher who wanted to determine the relative magnitudes of fixed and variable costs. This would be an example of relying on the constant term for inference.

---

1. If the second and third components of β_0 are small compared to the first component, then this difference diminishes. See R. C. Allen and J. H. Stone, "Textbook Neglect of the Constant Coefficient," *The Journal of Economic Education*, Fall 2005, pp. 379–384.

On the other hand, the product involved might be one for which it is known that there are few—if any—fixed costs. In such a case, a researcher might want to eliminate the constant term; to do so would conform to the notion of zero fixed costs and would conserve a degree of freedom (which would presumably make the estimate of β_1 more precise). This would be an example of suppressing the constant term.

Neither suppressing the constant term nor relying on it for inference is advisable, however, and reasons for these conclusions are explained in the following sections.

Do Not Suppress the Constant Term

Suppressing the constant term leads to a violation of the Classical Assumptions. This is because Classical Assumption II (that the error term has an expected value of zero) can be met only if the constant term absorbs any nonzero mean that the observations of the error might have in a given sample.[2]

If you omit the constant term, then the impact of the constant is forced into the estimates of the other coefficients, causing potential bias. This is demonstrated in Figure 7.1. Given the pattern of the X and Y observations, estimating a regression equation with a constant term would likely produce an estimated regression line very similar to the true regression line, which has a constant term (β_0) quite different from zero. The slope of this estimated line is very low, and the t-score of the estimated slope coefficient may be very close to zero.

However, if the researcher were to suppress the constant term, which implies that the estimated regression line must pass through the origin, then the estimated regression line shown in Figure 7.1 would result. The slope coefficient is biased upward compared with the true slope coefficient. The t-score is biased upward as well, and it may very well be large enough to indicate that the estimated slope coefficient is statistically significantly positive. Such a conclusion would be incorrect.

Thus, even though some regression packages allow the constant term to be suppressed (set to zero), the general rule is: *Don't*, even if theory specifically calls for it.

---

2. The only time that Classical Assumption II isn't violated by omitting the constant term is when the mean of the unobserved error term equals zero (exactly) over all the observations. This result is extremely unlikely.

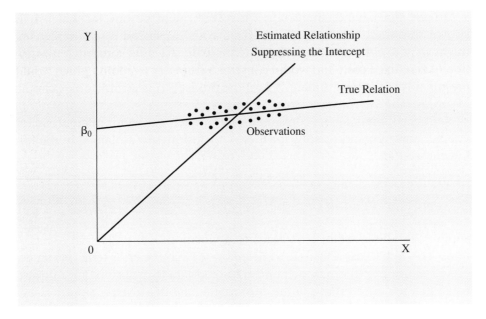

Figure 7.1 The Harmful Effect of Suppressing the Constant Term

If the constant (or intercept) term is suppressed, the estimated regression will go through the origin. Such an effect potentially biases the $\hat{\beta}$s and inflates their t-scores. In this particular example, the true slope is close to zero in the range of the sample, but forcing the regression through the origin makes the slope appear to be significantly positive.

Do Not Rely on Estimates of the Constant Term

It would seem logical that if it's a bad idea to suppress the constant term, then the constant term must be an important analytical tool to use in evaluating the results of the regression. Unfortunately, there are at least two reasons that suggest that the intercept should *not* be relied on for purposes of analysis or inference.

First, the error term is generated, in part, by the omission of a number of marginal independent variables, the mean effect of which is placed in the constant term. The constant term acts as a garbage collector, with an unknown amount of this mean effect being dumped into it. The constant term's estimated coefficient may be different from what it would have been without performing this task, which is done for the sake of the equation as a whole. As a result, it's meaningless to run a t-test on $\hat{\beta}_0$.

Second, the constant term is the value of the dependent variable when all the independent variables and the error term are zero, but the variables used for economic analysis are usually positive. Thus, the origin often lies *outside* the range of sample observations (as can be seen in Figure 7.1). Since the constant term is an estimate of Y when the Xs are outside the range of the sample observations, estimates of it are tenuous.

7.2 Alternative Functional Forms

The choice of a functional form for an equation is a vital part of the specification of that equation. Before we can talk about those functional forms, however, we need to make a distinction between an equation that is linear in the coefficients and one that is linear in the variables.

An equation is **linear in the variables** if plotting the function in terms of X and Y generates a straight line. For example, Equation 7.1:

$$Y = \beta_0 + \beta_1 X + \epsilon \tag{7.1}$$

is linear in the variables, but Equation 7.2:

$$Y = \beta_0 + \beta_1 X^2 + \epsilon \tag{7.2}$$

is not linear in the variables, because if you were to plot Equation 7.2 it would be a quadratic, not a straight line.

An equation is **linear in the coefficients** only if the coefficients (the βs) appear in their simplest form—they are not raised to any powers (other than one), are not multiplied or divided by other coefficients, and do not themselves include some sort of function (like logs or exponents). For example, Equation 7.1 is linear in the coefficients, but Equation 7.3:

$$Y = \beta_0 + X^{\beta_1} \tag{7.3}$$

is not linear in the coefficients β_0 and β_1. Equation 7.3 is not linear because there is no rearrangement of the equation that will make it linear in the βs of original interest, β_0 and β_1. In fact, of all possible equations for a single explanatory variable, *only* functions of the general form:

$$f(Y) = \beta_0 + \beta_1 f(X) \tag{7.4}$$

are linear in the coefficients β_0 and β_1. Linear regression analysis can be applied to an equation that is nonlinear in the variables as long as the equation is linear in the coefficients. Indeed, when econometricians use the phrase "linear regression"(for example, in the Classical Assumptions) they usually mean "regression that is linear in the coefficients."

The use of OLS requires that the equation be linear in the coefficients, but there is a wide variety of functional forms that are linear in the coefficients while being nonlinear in the variables. Indeed, in previous chapters we've already used several equations that are linear in the coefficients and nonlinear in the variables, but we've said little about when to use such nonlinear equations. The purpose of the current section is to present the details of the most frequently used functional forms to help the reader develop the ability to choose the correct one when specifying an equation.

The choice of a functional form almost always should be based on the underlying theory and only rarely on which form provides the best fit. The logical form of the relationship between the dependent variable and the independent variable in question should be compared with the properties of various functional forms, and the one that comes closest to that underlying theory should be chosen. To allow such a comparison, the paragraphs that follow characterize the most frequently used forms in terms of graphs, equations, and examples. In some cases, more than one functional form will be applicable, but usually a choice between alternative functional forms can be made on the basis of the information we'll present.

Linear Form

The linear regression model, used almost exclusively in this text thus far, is based on the assumption that the slope of the relationship between the independent variable and the dependent variable is constant:[3]

$$\frac{\Delta Y}{\Delta X_k} = \beta_k \qquad k = 1, 2, \ldots, K$$

---

3. Throughout this section, the "delta" notation (Δ) will be used instead of the calculus notation to make for easier reading. The specific definition of Δ is "change," and it implies a small change in the variable it is attached to. For example, the term ΔX should be read as "change in X." Since a regression coefficient represents the change in the expected value of Y brought about by a one-unit increase in X_k (holding constant all other variables in the equation), then $\beta_k = \Delta Y/\Delta X_k$. Those comfortable with calculus should substitute partial derivative signs for Δs.

If the hypothesized relationship between Y and X is such that the slope of the relationship can be expected to be constant, then the linear functional form should be used.

Since the slope is constant, the **elasticity** of Y with respect to X (the percentage change in the dependent variable caused by a 1-percent increase in the independent variable, holding the other variables in the equation constant) can be calculated fairly easily:

$$\text{Elasticity}_{Y,X_k} = \frac{\Delta Y/Y}{\Delta X_k/X_k} = \frac{\Delta Y}{\Delta X_k} \cdot \frac{X_k}{Y} = \beta_k \frac{X_k}{Y}$$

Unless theory, common sense, or experience justifies using some other functional form, you should use the linear model. Because, in effect, it's being used by default, the linear model is sometimes referred to as the *default* functional form.

Double-Log Form

The double-log form is the most common functional form that is nonlinear in the variables while still being linear in the coefficients. Indeed, the double-log form is so popular that some researchers use it as their default functional form instead of the linear form. In a **double-log functional form**, the natural log of Y is the dependent variable and the natural log of X is the independent variable:

$$\ln Y = \beta_0 + \beta_1 \ln X_1 + \beta_2 \ln X_2 + \epsilon \tag{7.5}$$

where lnY refers to the natural log of Y, and so on. For a brief review of the meaning of a log, see the boxed feature on the following pages.

The double-log form, sometimes called the log-log form, often is used because a researcher has specified that the elasticities of the model are constant and the slopes are not. This is in contrast to the linear model, in which the slopes are constant but the elasticities are not.

In a double-log equation, an individual regression coefficient can be interpreted as an elasticity because:

$$\beta_k = \frac{\Delta(\ln Y)}{\Delta(\ln X_k)} = \frac{\Delta Y/Y}{\Delta X_k/X_k} = \text{Elasticity}_{Y,X_k} \tag{7.6}$$

Since regression coefficients are constant, the condition that the model have a constant elasticity is met by the double-log equation.

The way to interpret β_k in a double-log equation is that if X_k increases by 1 percent while the other Xs are held constant, then Y will change by β_k percent. Since elasticities are constant, the slopes are now no longer constant.

Figure 7.2 is a graph of the double-log function (ignoring the error term). The panel on the left shows the economic concept of an isoquant or an indifference curve. Isoquants from production functions show the different combinations of factors X_1 and X_2, probably capital and labor, that can be used to produce a given level of output Y. The panel on the right of Figure 7.2 shows the relationship between Y and X_1 that would exist if X_2 were held constant or were not included in the model. Note that the shape of the curve depends on the sign and magnitude of coefficient β_1. If β_1 is negative, a double-log functional form can be used to model a typical demand curve.

Double-log models should be run only when the logged variables take on positive values. Dummy variables, which can take on the value of zero, should not be logged but still can be used in a double-log

---

What Is a Log?

What the heck is a log? If e (a constant equal to 2.71828) to the "*b*th power" produces x, then b is the log of x:

$$b \text{ is the log of x to the base e if:} \quad e^b = x$$

Thus, a **log** (or logarithm) is the exponent to which a given base must be taken in order to produce a specific number. While logs come in more than one variety, we'll use only *natural* logs (logs to the base e) in this text. The symbol for a natural log is "ln," so $\ln(x) = b$ means that $(2.71828)^b = x$ or, more simply,

$$\ln(x) = b \quad \text{means that} \quad e^b = x$$

For example, since $e^2 = (2.71828)^2 = 7.389$, we can state that:

$$\ln(7.389) = 2$$

Thus, the natural log of 7.389 is 2! Two is the power of e that produces 7.389. Let's look at some other natural log calculations:

$$\ln(100) = 4.605$$
$$\ln(1000) = 6.908$$

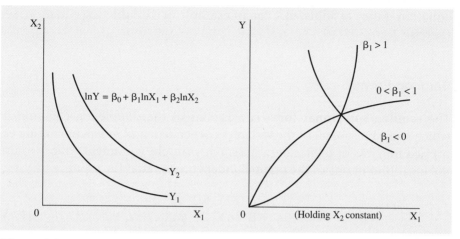

Figure 7.2 Double-Log Functions

Depending on the values of the regression coefficients, the double-log functional form can take on a number of shapes. The left panel shows the use of a double-log function to depict a shape useful in describing the economic concept of an isoquant or an indifference curve. The right panel shows various shapes that can be achieved with a double-log function if X_2 is held constant or is not included in the equation.

$$\ln(10000) = 9.210$$
$$\ln(100000) = 11.513$$
$$\ln(1000000) = 13.816$$

Note that as a number goes from 100 to 1,000,000, its natural log goes from 4.605 to only 13.816! Since logs are exponents, even a small change in a log can mean a big change in impact. As a result, logs can be used in econometrics if a researcher wants to reduce the absolute size of the numbers associated with the same actual meaning.

One useful property of natural logs in econometrics is that they make it easier to figure out impacts in percentage terms. If you run a double-log regression, the meaning of a slope coefficient is the percentage change in the dependent variable caused by a one percentage point increase in the independent variable, holding the other independent variables in the equation constant.[4] It's because of this percentage change property that the slope coefficients in a double-log equation are elasticities.

---

4. This is because the derivative of a natural log of X equals dX/X (or $\Delta X/X$), which is the same as percentage change.

equation if they're adjusted.[5] For an example of a double-log equation, see Exercise 7.

Semilog Form

The **semilog functional form** is a variant of the double-log equation in which some but not all of the variables (dependent and independent) are expressed in terms of their natural logs. For example, you might choose to use the logarithm of one of the original independent variables, as in:

$$Y_i = \beta_0 + \beta_1 \ln X_{1i} + \beta_2 X_{2i} + \epsilon_i \tag{7.7}$$

In this case, the economic meanings of the two slope coefficients are different, since X_2 is linearly related to Y while X_1 is nonlinearly related to Y.

The right-hand side of Figure 7.3 shows the relationship between Y and X_1 in this kind of semilog equation when X_2 is held constant. Note that if β_1 is greater than zero, the impact of changes in X_1 on Y decreases as X_1 gets bigger. Thus, the semilog functional form should be used when the relationship between X_1 and Y is hypothesized to have this "increasing at a decreasing rate" form.

Applications of the semilog form are quite frequent. For example, most consumption functions tend to increase at a decreasing rate past some level of income. These *Engel curves* tend to flatten out because as incomes get higher, a smaller percentage of income goes to consumption and a greater percentage goes to saving. Consumption thus increases at a decreasing rate. If Y is the consumption of an item and X_1 is disposable income (with X_2 standing for all the other independent variables), then the use of the semilog functional form is justified whenever the item's consumption can be expected to increase at a decreasing rate as income increases.

---

5. If it is necessary to take the log of a dummy variable, that variable needs to be transformed to avoid the possibility of taking the log of zero. The best way is to redefine the entire dummy variable so that instead of taking on the values of 0 and 1, it takes on the values of 1 and e (the base of the natural logarithm). The log of this newly defined dummy then takes on the values of 0 and 1, and the interpretation of β remains the same as in a linear equation. Such a transformation changes the coefficient value but not the usefulness or theoretical validity of the dummy variable.

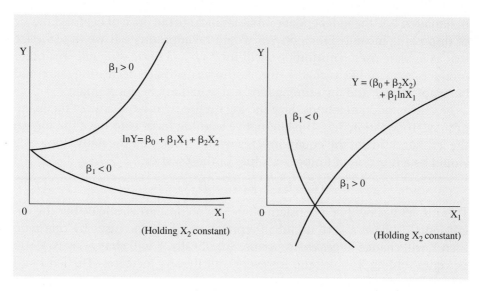

Figure 7.3 Semilog Functions

The semilog functional form on the right ($\ln X$) can be used to depict a situation in which the impact of X_1 on Y is expected to increase at a decreasing rate as X_1 gets bigger as long as β_1 is greater than zero (holding X_2 constant). The semilog functional form on the left ($\ln Y$) can be used to depict a situation in which an increase in X_1 causes Y to increase at an increasing rate.

For example, recall the beef demand equation, Equation 2.7, from Chapter 2:

$$\widehat{CB}_t = 37.54 - 0.88P_t + 11.9Yd_t \qquad (2.7)$$
$$(0.16) \qquad (1.76)$$
$$t = \qquad -5.36 \qquad 6.75$$
$$\overline{R}^2 = 0.631 \quad N = 28 \text{ (annual)}$$

where: CB = per capita consumption of beef
P = the price of beef in cents per pound
Yd = U.S. disposable income in thousands of dollars

If we substitute the log of disposable income ($\ln Yd_t$) for disposable income in Equation 2.7, we get:

$$\widehat{BC}_t = -71.75 - 0.87P_t + 98.87\ln Yd_t \qquad (7.8)$$
$$(0.13) \quad (11.11)$$
$$t = \qquad -6.93 \qquad 8.90$$
$$\overline{R}^2 = .750 \quad N = 28 \text{ (annual)}$$

In Equation 7.8, the independent variables include the price of beef and the *log* of disposable income. Equation 7.8 would be appropriate if we hypothesize that as income rises, consumption will increase at a decreasing rate. For other products, perhaps like yachts or summer homes, no such decreasing rate could be hypothesized, and the semilog function would not be appropriate.

Not all semilog functions have the log on the right-hand side of the equation, as in Equation 7.7. The alternative semilog form is to have the log on the left-hand side of the equation. This would mean that the natural log of Y would be a function of unlogged values of the Xs, as in:

$$\ln Y = \beta_0 + \beta_1 X_1 + \beta_2 X_2 + \epsilon \tag{7.9}$$

This model has neither a constant slope nor a constant elasticity, but the co-efficients do have a very useful interpretation. If X_1 increases by one *unit*, then Y will change in *percentage* terms. Specifically, Y will change by $\beta_1 \cdot 100$ percent, holding X_2 constant, for every unit that X_1 increases. The left-hand side of Figure 7.3 shows such a semilog function.

This fact means that the lnY semilog function of Equation 7.9 is perfect for any model in which the dependent variable adjusts in percentage terms to a unit change in an independent variable. The most common economic and business application of Equation 7.9 is in a model of the earnings of individuals, where firms often give annual raises in percentage terms. In such a model Y would be the salary or wage of the *i*th employee, and X_1 would be the experience of the *i*th worker. Each year X_1 would increase by one, and β_1 would measure the percentage raises given by the firm. For more on this example of a left-side semilog functional form, see Exercise 4 at the end of the chapter.

Note that we now have two different kinds of semilog functional forms, creating possible confusion. As a result, many econometricians use phrases like "right-side semilog" or "lin-log functional form" to refer to Equation 7.7 while using "left-side semilog" or "log-lin functional form" to refer to Equation 7.9.

Polynomial Form

In most cost functions, the slope of the cost curve changes sign as output changes. If the slopes of a relationship are expected to depend on the level of the variable itself, then a polynomial model should be considered. **Polynomial functional forms** express Y as a function of independent variables, some of which are raised to powers other than 1. For example, in a second-degree poly-nomial (also called a quadratic) equation, at least one independent variable is squared:

$$Y_i = \beta_0 + \beta_1 X_{1i} + \beta_2 (X_{1i})^2 + \beta_3 X_{2i} + \epsilon_i \tag{7.10}$$

Such a model can indeed produce slopes that change sign as the independent variables change. The slope of Y with respect to X_1 in Equation 7.10 is:

$$\frac{\Delta Y}{\Delta X_1} = \beta_1 + 2\beta_2 X_1 \qquad (7.11)$$

Note that the slope depends on the level of X_1. For small values of X_1, β_1 might dominate, but for large values of X_1, β_2 will always dominate. If this were a cost function, with Y being the average cost of production and X_1 being the level of output of the firm, then we would expect β_1 to be negative and β_2 to be positive if the firm has the typical U-shaped cost curve depicted in the left half of Figure 7.4.

For another example, consider a model of annual employee earnings as a function of the age of each employee and a number of other measures of productivity such as education. What is the expected impact of age on earnings? As a young worker gets older, his or her earnings will typically increase. Beyond some point, however, an increase in age will not increase earnings by very much at all, and around retirement we expect earnings to start to fall

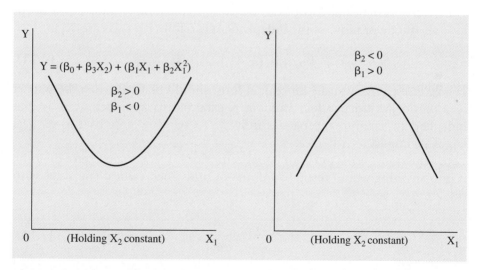

Figure 7.4 Polynomial Functions

Quadratic functional forms (polynomials with squared terms) take on U or inverted U shapes, depending on the values of the coefficients (holding X_2 constant). The left panel shows the shape of a quadratic function that could be used to show a typical cost curve; the right panel allows the description of an impact that rises and then falls (like the impact of age on earnings).

abruptly with age. As a result, a logical relationship between earnings and age might look something like the right half of Figure 7.4; earnings would rise, level off, and then fall as age increased. Such a theoretical relationship could be modeled with a quadratic equation:

$$\text{Earnings}_i = \beta_0 + \beta_1 \text{Age}_i + \beta_2 \text{Age}_i^2 + \cdots + \epsilon_i \qquad (7.12)$$

What would the expected signs of $\hat{\beta}_1$ and $\hat{\beta}_2$ be? Since you expect the impact of age to rise and fall, you'd thus expect $\hat{\beta}_1$ to be positive and $\hat{\beta}_2$ to be negative (all else being equal). In fact, this is exactly what many researchers in labor economics have observed.

With polynomial regressions, the interpretation of the individual regression coefficients becomes difficult, and the equation may produce unwanted results for particular ranges of X. Great care must be taken when using a polynomial regression equation to ensure that the functional form will achieve what is intended by the researcher and no more.

Inverse Form

The **inverse functional form** expresses Y as a function of the reciprocal (or inverse) of one or more of the independent variables (in this case, X_1):

$$Y_i = \beta_0 + \beta_1(1/X_{1i}) + \beta_2 X_{2i} + \epsilon_i \qquad (7.13)$$

The inverse (or reciprocal) functional form should be used when the impact of a particular independent variable is expected to approach zero as that independent variable approaches infinity. To see this, note that as X_1 gets larger, its impact on Y decreases.

In Equation 7.13, X_1 cannot equal zero, since if X_1 equaled zero, dividing it into anything would result in infinite or undefined values. The slope with respect to X_1 is:

$$\frac{\Delta Y}{\Delta X_1} = \frac{-\beta_1}{X_1^2} \qquad (7.14)$$

The slopes for X_1 fall into two categories, both of which are depicted in Figure 7.5:

1. When β_1 is positive, the slope with respect to X_1 is negative and decreases in absolute value as X_1 increases. As a result, the relationship between Y and X_1 holding X_2 constant approaches $\beta_0 + \beta_2 X_2$ as X_1 increases (ignoring the error term).

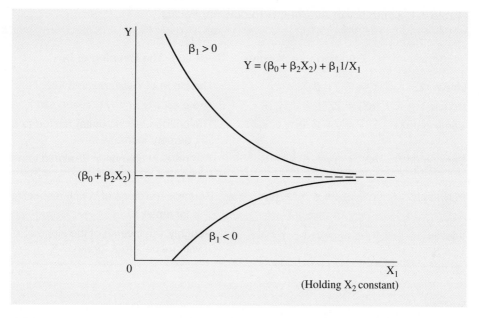

Figure 7.5 Inverse Functions

Inverse (or reciprocal) functional forms allow the impact of an X_1 on Y to approach zero as X_1 increases in size. The inverse function approaches the same value (the asymptote) from the top or bottom depending on the sign of β_1.

2. When β_1 is negative, the relationship intersects the X_1 axis at $-\beta_1/(\beta_0 + \beta_2 X_2)$ and slopes upward toward the same horizontal line (called an asymptote) that it approaches when β_1 is positive.

Applications of reciprocals or inverses exist in a number of areas in economic theory and the real world. For example, the once-popular Phillips curve originally was estimated with an inverse function.

Choosing a Functional Form

The best way to choose a functional form for a regression model is to choose a specification that matches the underlying theory of the equation. In a majority of cases, the linear form will be adequate, and for most of the rest, common sense will point out a fairly easy choice from among the alternatives outlined above. Table 7.1 contains a summary of the properties of the various alternative functional forms.

Table 7.1 Summary of Alternative Functional Forms

Functional Form	Equation (one X only)	The Meaning of β_1
Linear	$Y_i = \beta_0 + \beta_1 X_i + \epsilon_i$	The slope of Y with respect to X
Double-log	$\ln Y_i = \beta_0 + \beta_1 \ln X_i + \epsilon_i$	The elasticity of Y with respect to X
Semilog (lnX)	$Y_i = \beta_0 + \beta_1 \ln X_i + \epsilon_i$	The change in Y (in units) related to a 1 percent increase in X
Semilog (lnY)	$\ln Y_i = \beta_0 + \beta_1 X_i + \epsilon_i$	The percent change in Y related to a one-unit increase in X
Polynomial	$Y_i = \beta_0 + \beta_1 X_i + \beta_2 X_i^2 + \epsilon_i$	Roughly, the slope of Y with respect to X for small X
Inverse	$Y_i = \beta_0 + \beta_1\left(\dfrac{1}{X_i}\right) + \epsilon_i$	Roughly, the inverse of the slope of Y with respect to X for small X

7.3 Lagged Independent Variables

Virtually all the regressions we've studied so far have been "instantaneous" in nature. In other words, they have included independent and dependent variables from the same time period, as in:

$$Y_t = \beta_0 + \beta_1 X_{1t} + \beta_2 X_{2t} + \epsilon_t \qquad (7.15)$$

where the subscript t is used to refer to a particular point in time. If all variables have the same subscript, then the equation is instantaneous.

However, not all economic or business situations imply such instantaneous relationships between the dependent and independent variables. In many cases time elapses between a change in the independent variable and the resulting change in the dependent variable. The length of this time between cause and effect is called a **lag**. Many econometric equations include one or more *lagged independent variables* like X_{1t-1}, where the subscript $t - 1$ indicates that the observation of X_1 is from the time period previous to time period t, as in the following equation:

$$Y_t = \beta_0 + \beta_1 X_{1t-1} + \beta_2 X_{2t} + \epsilon_t \qquad (7.16)$$

In this equation, X_1 has been lagged by one time period, but the relationship between Y and X_2 is still instantaneous.

For example, think about the process by which the supply of an agricultural product is determined. Since agricultural goods take time to grow, decisions on how many acres to plant or how many eggs to let hatch into egg-producing hens (instead of selling them immediately) must be made months, if not years, before the product is actually supplied to the consumer. Any change in an agricultural market, such as an increase in the price that the farmer can earn for providing cotton, has a lagged effect on the supply of that product:

$$C_t = f(\overset{+}{P}C_{t-1}, \overset{-}{P}F_t) + \epsilon_t = \beta_0 + \beta_1 PC_{t-1} + \beta_2 PF_t + \epsilon_t \qquad (7.17)$$

where: C_t = the quantity of cotton supplied in year t
PC_{t-1} = the price of cotton in year t − 1
PF_t = the price of farm labor in year t

Note that this equation hypothesizes a lag between the price of cotton and the production of cotton, but not between the price of farm labor and the production of cotton. It's reasonable to think that if cotton prices change, farmers won't be able to react immediately because it takes a while for cotton to be planted and to grow.

The meaning of the regression coefficient of a lagged variable is not the same as the meaning of the coefficient of an unlagged variable. The estimated coefficient of a lagged X measures the change in *this year's* Y attributed to a one-unit increase in *last year's* X (holding constant the other Xs in the equation). Thus β_1 in Equation 7.17 measures the extra number of units of cotton that would be produced this year as a result of a one-unit increase in last year's price of cotton, holding this year's price of farm labor constant.

If the lag structure is hypothesized to take place over more than one time period, or if a lagged dependent variable is included on the right-hand side of an equation, the question becomes significantly more complex. Such cases, called *distributed lags,* will be dealt with in Chapter 12.

(7.4) Using Dummy Variables

In Section 3.1 we introduced the concept of a dummy variable, which we defined as one that takes on the values of 0 or 1, depending on a qualitative attribute such as gender. In that section our sole focus was on the use of a dummy variable as an **intercept dummy**, a dummy variable that changes the constant or intercept term, depending on whether the qualitative condition is met. These take the general form:

$$Y_i = \beta_0 + \beta_1 X_i + \beta_2 D_i + \epsilon_i \qquad (7.18)$$

where $D_i = \begin{cases} 1 \text{ if the } ith \text{ observation meets a particular condition} \\ 0 \text{ otherwise} \end{cases}$

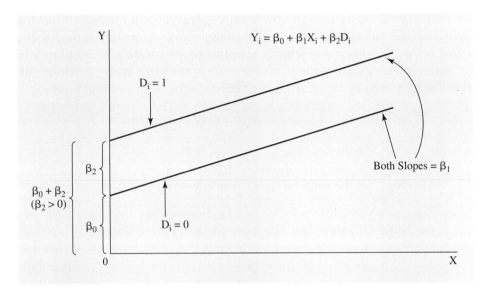

Figure 7.6 An Intercept Dummy

If an intercept dummy ($\beta_2 D_i$) is added to an equation, a graph of the equation will have different intercepts for the two qualitative conditions specified by the dummy variable. The difference between the two intercepts is β_2. The slopes are constant with respect to the qualitative condition.

As can be seen in Figure 7.6, the intercept dummy does indeed change the intercept depending on the value of D, but the slopes remain constant no matter what value D takes. This is true even if we define the dummy variable "backwards" and have $D = 0$ if the particular condition is met and $D = 1$ otherwise. The slopes still remain constant.

Note that in this example only one dummy variable is used even though there were two conditions. This is because one fewer dummy variable is constructed than conditions. The event not explicitly represented by a dummy variable, the **omitted condition**, forms the basis against which the included conditions are compared. Thus, for dual situations only one dummy variable is entered as an independent variable; the coefficient is interpreted as the effect of the included condition relative to the omitted condition.

What happens if you use two dummy variables to describe the two conditions? For example, suppose you decide to include gender in an equation by specifying that $X_1 = 1$ if a person is male and $X_2 = 1$ if a person is female. In such a situation, X_1 plus X_2 would always add up to 1—do you see why?

Thus X_1 would be perfectly, linearly correlated with X_2, and the equation would violate Classical Assumption VI! If you were to make this mistake, sometimes called a *dummy variable trap*, you'd have perfect multicollinearity (to be described in Section 8.1), and OLS almost surely would fail to estimate the equation.

For an example of the meaning of the coefficient of a dummy variable, let's look at a study of the relationship between fraternity/sorority membership and grade point average (GPA). Most noneconometricians would approach this research problem by calculating the mean grades of fraternity/sorority (so-called Greek) members and comparing them to the mean grades of nonmembers. However, such a technique ignores the relationship that grades have to characteristics other than Greek membership.

Instead, we'd want to build a regression model that explains college GPA. Independent variables would include not only Greek membership but also other predictors of academic performance such as SAT scores and high school grades. Being a member of a social organization is a qualitative variable, however, so we'd have to create a dummy variable to represent fraternity or sorority membership quantitatively in a regression equation:

$$G_i = \begin{cases} 1 & \text{if the } i\text{th student is an active member of} \\ & \quad \text{a fraternity or sorority} \\ 0 & \text{otherwise} \end{cases}$$

If we collect data from all the students in our class and estimate the equation implied in this example, we obtain:

$$\widehat{CG_i} = 0.37 + 0.81HG_i + 0.00001S_i - 0.38G_i \qquad (7.19)$$
$$\overline{R}^2 = .45 \quad N = 25$$

where: CG_i = the cumulative college GPA (4-point scale) of the ith student
    HG_i = the cumulative high school GPA (4-point scale) of the ith student
    S_i = the sum of the highest verbal and mathematics SAT scores earned by the ith student

The meaning of the estimated coefficient of G_i in Equation 7.19 is very specific. Stop for a second and figure it out for yourself. What is it? The estimate that $\hat{\beta}_G = -0.38$ means that, for this sample, the GPA of fraternity/sorority members is 0.38 lower than for nonmembers, holding SATs and high school GPA constant. Thus, Greek members are doing about a third of a grade worse than otherwise might be expected. To understand this example better, try using Equation 7.19 to predict your own GPA; how close does it come?

Before you rush out and quit whatever social organization you're in, however, note that this sample is quite small and that we've surely omitted some important determinants of academic success from the equation. As a result, we shouldn't be too quick to conclude that Greeks are dummies.

To this point, we've used dummy variables to represent just those qualitative variables that have exactly two possibilities (such as gender). What about situations where a qualitative variable has three or more alternatives? For example, what if you're trying to measure the impact of education on salaries in business and you want to distinguish high school graduates from holders of B.A.s *and* M.B.A.s? The answer certainly isn't to have MBA = 2, BA = 1, and 0 otherwise, because we have no reason to think that the impact of having an M.B.A. is exactly twice that of having a B.A. If not that, then what?

The answer is to create one less dummy variable than there are alternatives and to use each dummy to represent just one of the possible conditions. In the salary case, for example, you'd create two variables, the first equal to 1 if the employee had an M.B.A. (0 otherwise) and the second equal to 1 if the employee's highest degree was a B.A. (and 0 otherwise). As before, the omitted condition is represented by having both dummies equal to 0. This way you can measure the impact of each degree independently without having to link the impacts of having an M.B.A. and a B.A.

A dummy variable that has only a single observation with a value of 1 while the rest of the observations are 0 (or vice versa) is to be avoided unless the variable is required by theory. Such a "one-time dummy" acts merely to eliminate that observation from the data set, improving the fit artificially by setting the dummy's coefficient equal to the residual for that observation. One would obtain exactly the same estimates of the other coefficients if that observation were deleted, but the deletion of an observation is rarely, if ever, appropriate. Finally, dummy variables can be used as *dependent* variables; this possibility is covered in an entire chapter, Chapter 13.

7.5 Slope Dummy Variables

Until now, every independent variable in this text has been multiplied by exactly one other item: the slope coefficient. To see this, take another look at Equation 7.18:

$$Y_i = \beta_0 + \beta_1 X_i + \beta_2 D_i + \epsilon_i \qquad (7.18)$$

In this equation X is multiplied only by β_1, and D is multiplied only by β_2, and there are no other factors involved.

This restriction does not apply to a new kind of variable called an interaction term. An **interaction term** is an independent variable in a regression equation that is the *multiple* of two or more other independent variables. Each interaction term has its own regression coefficient, so the end result is that the interaction term has three or more components, as in $\beta_3 X_i D_i$. Such interaction terms are used when the change in Y with respect to one independent variable (in this case X) depends on the level of another independent variable (in this case D). For an example of the use of interaction terms, see Exercise 14.

Interaction terms can involve two quantitative variables ($B_3 X_1 X_2$) or two dummy variables ($B_3 D_1 D_2$), but the most frequent application of interaction terms involves one quantitative variable and one dummy variable ($B_3 X_1 D_1$), a combination that is typically called a *slope dummy*. **Slope dummy variables** allow the slope of the relationship between the dependent variable and an independent variable to be different depending on whether the condition specified by a dummy variable is met. This is in contrast to an intercept dummy variable, which changes the intercept, but does not change the slope, when a particular condition is met.

In general, a slope dummy is introduced by adding to the equation a variable that is the multiple of the independent variable that has a slope you want to change and the dummy variable that you want to cause the changed slope. The general form of a slope dummy equation is:

$$Y_i = \beta_0 + \beta_1 X_i + \beta_2 D_i + \beta_3 X_i D_i + \epsilon_i \qquad (7.20)$$

Note the difference between Equations 7.18 and 7.20. Equation 7.20 is the same as Equation 7.18, except that we have added an interaction term in which the dummy variable is multiplied by an independent variable ($\beta_3 X_i D_i$). Let's check to make sure that the slope of Y with respect to X does indeed change if D changes:

$$\text{When } D = 0, \quad \Delta Y / \Delta X = \beta_1$$
$$\text{When } D = 1, \quad \Delta Y / \Delta X = (\beta_1 + \beta_3)$$

In essence, the coefficient of X *changes* when the condition specified by D is met. To see this, substitute $D = 0$ and $D = 1$, respectively, into Equation 7.20 and factor out X.

Note that Equation 7.20 includes both a slope dummy and an intercept dummy. It turns out that whenever a slope dummy is used, it's vital to also have $\beta_1 X_i$ and $\beta_2 D$ in the equation to avoid bias in the estimate of the coefficient of the slope dummy term. If there are other Xs in an equation, they should not be multiplied by D unless you hypothesize that their slopes change with respect to D as well.

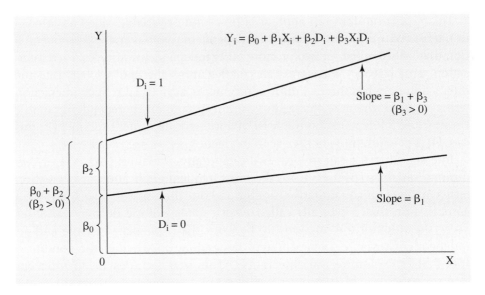

Figure 7.7 Slope and Intercept Dummies

If slope dummy ($\beta_3 X_i D_i$) and intercept dummy ($\beta_2 D_i$) terms are added to an equation, a graph of the equation will have different intercepts *and* different slopes depending on the value of the qualitative condition specified by the dummy variable. The difference between the two intercepts is β_2, whereas the difference between the two slopes is β_3.

Take a look at Figure 7.7, which has both a slope dummy and an intercept dummy. In Figure 7.7 the intercept will be β_0 when $D = 0$ and $\beta_0 + \beta_2$ when $D = 1$. In addition, the slope of Y with respect to X will be β_1 when $D = 0$ and $\beta_1 + \beta_3$ when $D = 1$. As a result, there really are two equations:

$$Y_i = \beta_0 \qquad\qquad + \beta_1 X_i + \epsilon_i \qquad [\text{when } D = 0]$$
$$Y_i = (\beta_0 + \beta_2) + (\beta_1 + \beta_3) X_i + \epsilon_i \qquad [\text{when } D = 1]$$

In practice, slope dummies have many realistic uses. For example, consider the question of earnings differentials between men and women. Although there is little argument that these differentials exist, there is quite a bit of controversy over the extent to which these differentials are caused by sexual discrimination (as opposed to other factors). Suppose you decide to build a model of earnings to get a better view of this controversy. If you hypothesized that men earn more than women on average, then you would want to use an intercept dummy variable for gender in an earnings equation that included measures of experience, special skills, education, and so on, as independent variables:

$$\ln(\text{Earnings}_i) = \beta_0 + \beta_1 D_i + \beta_2 \text{EXP}_i + \cdots + \epsilon_i \qquad (7.21)$$

where: D_i = 1 if the ith worker is male and 0 otherwise
$\quad\quad\quad$ EXP_i = the years experience of the ith worker
$\quad\quad\quad$ ϵ_i = a classical error term

In Equation 7.21, $\hat{\beta}_1$ would be an estimate of the average difference between males and females, holding constant their experience and the other factors in the equation. Equation 7.21 also forces the impact of increases in experience (and the other factors in the equation) to have the same effect for females as for males because the slopes are the same for both genders.

If you hypothesized that men also increase their earnings more per year of experience than women, then you would include a slope dummy as well as an intercept dummy in such a model:

$$\ln(\text{Earnings}_i) = \beta_0 + \beta_1 D_i + \beta_2 EXP_i + \beta_3 D_i EXP_i + \cdots + \epsilon_i \quad (7.22)$$

In Equation 7.22, $\hat{\beta}_3$ would be an estimate of the differential impact of an extra year of experience on earnings between men and women. We could test the possibility of a positive true β_3 by running a one-tailed t-test on $\hat{\beta}_3$. If $\hat{\beta}_3$ were significantly different from zero in a positive direction, then we could reject the null hypothesis of no difference due to gender in the impact of experience on earnings, holding constant the other variables in the equation.

7.6 Problems with Incorrect Functional Forms

Once in a while a circumstance will arise in which the model is logically nonlinear in the variables, but the exact form of this nonlinearity is hard to specify. In such a case, the linear form is not correct, and yet a choice between the various nonlinear forms cannot be made on the basis of economic theory. Even in these cases, however, it still pays (in terms of understanding the true relationships) to avoid choosing a functional form on the basis of fit alone.

If functional forms are similar, and if theory does not specify exactly which form to use, why should we try to avoid using goodness of fit over the sample to determine which equation to use? This section will highlight two answers to this question:

1. $\overline{R}^2$s are difficult to compare if the dependent variable is transformed.
2. An incorrect functional form may provide a reasonable fit within the sample but have the potential to make large forecast errors when used outside the range of the sample.

$\overline{R}^2$s Are Difficult to Compare When Y Is Transformed

When the dependent variable is transformed from its linear version, the overall measure of fit, the $\overline{R}^2$, cannot be used for comparing the fit of the nonlinear equation with the original linear one. This problem is not especially important in most cases because the emphasis in applied regression analysis is usually on the coefficient estimates. However, if $\overline{R}^2$s are ever used to compare the fit of two different functional forms, then it becomes crucial that this lack of comparability be remembered. For example, suppose you were trying to compare a linear equation:

$$Y = \beta_0 + \beta_1 X_1 + \beta_2 X_2 + \epsilon \qquad (7.23)$$

with a semilog version of the same equation (using the version of a semilog function that takes the log of the dependent variable):

$$\ln Y = \beta_0 + \beta_1 X_1 + \beta_2 X_2 + \epsilon \qquad (7.24)$$

Notice that the only difference between Equations 7.23 and 7.24 is the functional form of the dependent variable. The reason that the $\overline{R}^2$s of the respective equations cannot be used to compare overall fits of the two equations is that the total sum of squares (TSS) of the dependent variable around its mean is different in the two formulations. That is, the $\overline{R}^2$s are not comparable because the dependent variables are different. There is no reason to expect that different dependent variables will have the identical (or easily comparable) degrees of dispersion around their means.

Incorrect Functional Forms Outside the Range of the Sample

If an incorrect functional form is used, then the probability of mistaken inferences about the true population parameters will increase. Using an incorrect functional form is a kind of specification error that is similar to the omitted variable bias discussed in Section 6.1. Even if an incorrect functional form provides good statistics within a sample, large residuals almost surely will arise when the misspecified equation is used on data that were not part of the sample used to estimate the coefficients.

In general, the extrapolation of a regression equation to data that are outside the range over which the equation was estimated runs increased risks of large forecasting errors and incorrect conclusions about population values. This risk is heightened if the regression uses a functional form that is inappropriate for the particular variables being studied.

Two functional forms that behave similarly over the range of the sample may behave quite differently outside that range. If the functional form is chosen on the basis of theory, then the researcher can take into account how the equation would act over any range of values, even if some of those values are

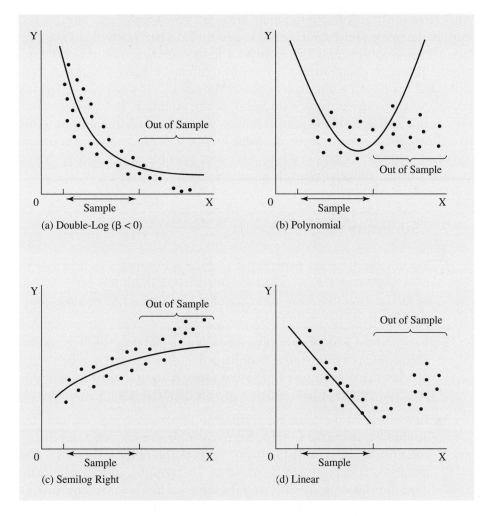

Figure 7.8 Incorrect Functional Forms Outside the Sample Range

If an incorrect form is applied to data outside the range of the sample on which it was estimated, the probability of large mistakes increases. In particular, note how the polynomial functional form can change slope rapidly outside the sample range (panel b) and that even a linear form can cause mistakes if the true functional form is nonlinear (panel d).

outside the range of the sample. If functional forms are chosen on the basis of fit, then extrapolating outside the sample becomes tenuous.

Figure 7.8 contains a number of hypothetical examples. As can be seen, some functional forms have the potential to fit quite poorly outside the sample range. Such graphs are meant as examples of what could happen, not as statements of what necessarily will happen, when incorrect functional forms are pushed outside the range of the sample over which they were estimated. Do not conclude from these diagrams that nonlinear functions should be avoided completely. If the true relationship is nonlinear, then the *linear* functional form will make large forecasting errors outside the sample. Instead, the researcher must take the time to think through how the equation will act for values both inside and outside the sample before choosing a functional form to use to estimate the equation. If the theoretically appropriate nonlinear equation appears to work well over the relevant range of possible values, then it should be used without concern over this issue.

7.7 Summary

1. Do not suppress the constant term even if it appears to be theoretically likely to equal zero. On the other hand, don't rely on estimates of the constant term for inference even if it appears to be statistically significant.

2. The choice of a functional form should be based on the underlying economic theory to the extent that theory suggests a shape similar to that provided by a particular functional form. A form that is linear in the variables should be used unless a specific hypothesis suggests otherwise.

3. Functional forms that are nonlinear in the variables include the double-log form, the semilog form, the polynomial form, and the inverse form. The double-log form is especially useful if the elasticities involved are expected to be constant. The semilog and inverse forms have the advantage of allowing the effect of an independent variable to tail off as that variable increases. The polynomial form is useful if the slopes are expected to change sign, depending on the level of an independent variable.

4. A slope dummy is a dummy variable that is multiplied by an independent variable to allow the slope of the relationship between the dependent variable and the particular independent variable to change, depending on whether a particular condition is met.

5. The use of nonlinear functional forms has a number of potential problems. In particular, the $\overline{R}^2$s are difficult to compare if Y has been transformed, and the residuals are potentially large if an incorrect functional form is used for forecasting outside the range of the sample.

EXERCISES

(The answer to Exercise 2 is in Appendix A.)

1. Write out the meaning of each of the following terms without referring to the book (or your notes), and compare your definition with
   the version in the text for each:
   a. elasticity
   b. double-log functional form
   c. semilog functional form
   d. polynomial functional form
   e. inverse functional form
   f. slope dummy
   g. natural log
   h. omitted condition
   i. interaction term
   j. linear in the variables
   k. linear in the coefficients

2. For each of the following pairs of dependent (Y) and independent (X)
   variables, pick the functional form that you think is likely to be
   appropriate, and then explain your reasoning (assume that all other
   relevant independent variables are included in the equation):
   a. Y = sales of shoes
      X = disposable income
   b. Y = the attendance at the Hollywood Bowl outdoor symphony
         concerts on a given night
      X = whether the orchestra's most famous conductor was scheduled
         to conduct that night
   c. Y = aggregate consumption of goods and services in the United States
      X = aggregate disposable income in the United States
   d. Y = the money supply in the United States
      X = the interest rate on Treasury Bills (in a demand function)
   e. Y = the average production cost of a box of pasta
      X = the number of boxes of pasta produced

3. Look over the following equations and decide whether they are linear
   in the variables, linear in the coefficients, both, or neither:
   a. $Y_i = \beta_0 + \beta_1 X_i^3 + \epsilon_i$
   b. $Y_i = \beta_0 + \beta_1 \ln X_i + \epsilon_i$

   c. $\ln Y_i = \beta_0 + \beta_1 \ln X_i + \epsilon_i$

   d. $Y_i = \beta_0 + \beta_1 X_i^{\beta_2} + \epsilon_i$

   e. $Y_i^{\beta_0} = \beta_1 + \beta_2 X_i^2 + \epsilon_i$

4. Consider the following estimated semilog equation (standard errors in parentheses):

$$\widehat{\ln SAL_i} = -8.10 + 0.100 ED_i + 0.110 EXP_i$$
$$(0.025) \qquad (0.050)$$
$$\overline{R}^2 = .48 \qquad N = 28$$

where: $\ln SAL_i$ = the log of the salary of the ith worker
          ED_i = the years of education of the ith worker
         EXP_i = the years of experience of the ith worker

   a. Make appropriate hypotheses for signs, calculate t-scores, and test your hypotheses.

   b. What is the economic meaning of the constant in this equation?

   c. Why do you think a left-side semilog functional form is used in this model? (*Hint:* What are the slopes of salary with respect to education and experience?)

   d. Suppose you ran the linear version of this equation and obtained an $\overline{R}^2$ of .46. What can you conclude from this result?

5. In 2003, Ray Fair[6] analyzed the relationship between stock prices and risk aversion by looking at the 1996–2000 performance of the 65 companies that had been a part of Standard and Poor's famous index (the S&P 500) since its inception in 1957. Fair focused on the P/E ratio (the ratio of a company's stock price to its earnings per share) and its relationship to the β coefficient (a measure of a company's riskiness—a high β implies high risk). Hypothesizing that the stock price would be a positive function of earnings growth and dividend growth, he estimated the following equation:

$$\widehat{LNPE_i} = 2.74 - 0.22 BETA_i + 0.83 EARN_i + 2.81 DIV_i$$
$$(0.11) \qquad (0.57) \qquad (0.84)$$
$$t = \qquad -1.99 \qquad 1.45 \qquad 3.33$$
$$N = 65 \quad R^2 = .232 \quad \overline{R}^2 = .194$$

6. Ray C. Fair, "Risk Aversion and Stock Prices," Cowles Foundation Discussion Papers 1382, Cowles Foundation: Yale University, revised February 2003. Most of the article is well beyond the scope of this text, but Fair generously included the data (including proprietary data that he generated) necessary to replicate his regression results.

where: $LNPE_i$ = the log of the median P/E ratio of the ith company from 1996 to 2000

$BETA_i$ = the mean β of the ith company from 1958 to 1994

$EARN_i$ = the median percentage earnings growth rate for the ith company from 1996 to 2000

DIV_i = the median percentage dividend growth rate for the ith company from 1996 to 2000

a. Create and test appropriate hypotheses about the slope coefficients of this equation at the 5-percent level.

b. One of these variables is lagged and yet this is a cross-sectional equation. Explain which variable is lagged and why you think Fair lagged it.

c. Is one of Fair's variables potentially irrelevant? Which one? Use EViews, Stata, or your own regression program on the data in Table 7.2 to estimate Fair's equation without your potentially irrelevant variable and then use our four specification criteria to determine whether the variable is indeed irrelevant.

d. What functional form does Fair use? Does this form seem appropriate on the basis of theory? (*Hint:* A review of the literature would certainly help you answer this question, but before you start that review, think through the meaning of slope coefficients in this functional form.)

e. (optional) Suppose that your review of the literature makes you concerned that Fair should have used a double-log functional form for his equation. Use the data in Table 7.2 to estimate that functional form on Fair's data. What is your estimated result? Does it support your concern? Explain.

6. In an effort to explain regional wage differentials, you collect wage data from 7,338 unskilled workers, divide the country into four regions (Northeast, South, Midwest, and West), and estimate the following equation (standard errors in parentheses):

$$\hat{Y}_i = 4.78 - 0.038E_i - 0.041S_i - 0.048W_i$$
$$\phantom{\hat{Y}_i = 4.78} (0.019) \quad (0.010) \quad (0.012)$$
$$\overline{R}^2 = .49 \qquad N = 7{,}338$$

where: Y_i = the hourly wage (in dollars) of the ith unskilled worker

E_i = a dummy variable equal to 1 if the ith worker lives in the Northeast, 0 otherwise

S_i = a dummy variable equal to 1 if the ith worker lives in the South, 0 otherwise

W_i = a dummy variable equal to 1 if the ith worker lives in the West, 0 otherwise

Table 7.2 Data for the Stock Price Example

	COMPANY	PE	BETA	EARN	DIV
1	Alcan	12.64	0.466	0.169	−0.013
2	TXU Corp.	10.80	0.545	0.016	0.014
3	Procter & Gamble	19.90	0.597	0.066	0.050
4	PG&E	11.30	0.651	0.021	0.014
5	Phillips Petroleum	13.27	0.678	0.071	0.006
6	AT&T	13.71	0.697	−0.004	−0.008
7	Minnesota Mining & Mfg.	17.61	0.781	0.054	0.051
8	Alcoa	15.97	0.795	0.120	−0.015
9	American Electric Power	10.68	0.836	−0.001	−0.021
10	Public Service Entrp	9.63	0.845	−0.018	−0.011
11	Hercules	16.07	0.851	0.077	−0.008
12	Air Products & Chemicals	16.20	0.865	0.051	0.074
13	Bristol Myers Squibb	17.01	0.866	0.068	0.110
14	Kimberly-Clark	13.42	0.869	0.063	0.018
15	Aetna	8.98	0.894	−0.137	0.007
16	Wrigley	14.49	0.898	0.062	0.044
17	Halliburton	17.84	0.906	0.120	−0.011
18	Deere & Co.	12.15	0.916	−0.010	0.004
19	Kroger	11.82	0.931	0.010	0.000
20	Intl Business Machines	16.08	0.944	0.081	0.045
21	Caterpillar	16.95	0.952	−0.043	−0.005
22	Goodrich	12.06	0.958	0.028	−0.015
23	General Mills	17.16	0.965	0.060	0.048
24	Winn-Dixie Stores	16.10	0.973	0.045	0.047
25	Heinz (H J)	13.49	0.979	0.079	0.079
26	Eastman Kodak	28.28	0.983	0.023	0.009
27	Campbell Soup	16.33	0.986	0.028	0.025
28	Philip Morris	12.25	0.993	0.129	0.130
29	Southern Co.	11.26	0.995	0.034	0.000
30	Du Pont	14.16	0.996	0.099	0.001
31	Phelps Dodge	11.47	1.008	0.186	−0.011
32	Pfizer Inc.	17.63	1.019	0.052	0.062
33	Hershey Foods	14.66	1.022	0.025	0.058
34	Ingersoll-Rand	14.24	1.024	0.045	−0.018
35	FPL Group	11.86	1.048	0.038	0.019
36	Pitney Bowes	16.11	1.064	0.049	0.086
37	Archer-Daniels-Midland	14.43	1.073	0.073	−0.011

(*continued*)

Table 7.2 (*continued*)

	COMPANY	PE	BETA	EARN	DIV
38	Rockwell	9.42	1.075	0.062	0.020
39	Dow Chemical	15.25	1.081	0.042	0.026
40	General Electric	15.16	1.091	0.051	0.015
41	Abbott Laboratories	17.58	1.097	0.114	0.098
42	Merck & Co.	23.29	1.122	0.066	0.072
43	J C Penney	13.14	1.133	0.094	−0.003
44	Union Pacific Corp.	12.99	1.136	0.010	0.021
45	Schering-Plough	18.18	1.137	0.112	0.060
46	Pepsico	18.94	1.147	0.082	0.046
47	McGraw-Hill	16.93	1.150	0.051	0.052
48	Household International	8.36	1.184	0.019	0.008
49	Emerson Electric	17.52	1.196	0.047	0.044
50	General Motors	11.21	1.206	0.052	−0.023
51	Colgate-Palmolive	16.60	1.213	0.067	0.025
52	Eaton Corp.	10.64	1.216	0.137	0.001
53	Dana Corp.	10.26	1.222	0.069	−0.011
54	Sears Roebuck	12.41	1.256	0.030	−0.014
55	Corning Inc.	19.33	1.258	0.052	−0.013
56	General Dynamics	9.06	1.285	0.056	−0.023
57	Coca-Cola	21.68	1.290	0.085	0.055
58	Boeing	11.93	1.306	0.169	0.017
59	Ford	8.62	1.308	0.016	0.026
60	Peoples Energy	9.58	1.454	0.000	0.005
61	Goodyear	12.02	1.464	0.022	0.012
62	May Co.	11.32	1.525	0.050	0.006
63	ITT Industries	9.92	1.630	0.038	0.018
64	Raytheon	11.75	1.821	0.112	0.050
65	Cooper Industries	12.41	1.857	0.108	0.037

Source: Ray C. Fair, "Risk Aversion and Stock Prices," Cowles Foundation Discussion Papers 1382, Cowles Foundation: Yale University, revised February 2003.

Datafile = STOCK7

a. What is the omitted condition in this equation?
b. If you add a dummy variable for the omitted condition to the equation without dropping E_i, S_i, or W_i, what will happen?
c. If you add a dummy variable for the omitted condition to the equation and drop E_i, what will the sign of the new variable's estimated coefficient be?

d. Which of the following three statements is most correct? Least correct? Explain your answer.
   i. The equation explains 49 percent of the variation of Y around its mean with regional variables alone, so there must be quite a bit of wage variation by region.
   ii. The coefficients of the regional variables are virtually identical, so there must not be much wage variation by region.
   iii. The coefficients of the regional variables are quite small compared with the average wage, so there must not be much wage variation by region.
e. If you were going to add one variable to this model, what would it be? Justify your choice.

7. V. N. Murti and V. K. Sastri[7] investigated the production characteristics of various Indian industries, including cotton and sugar. They specified Cobb–Douglas production functions for output (Q) as a double-log function of labor (L) and capital (K):

$$\ln Q_i = \beta_0 + \beta_1 \ln L_i + \beta_2 \ln K_i + \epsilon_i$$

and obtained the following estimates (standard errors in parentheses):

Industry	$\hat{\beta}_0$	$\hat{\beta}_1$	$\hat{\beta}_2$	R^2
Cotton	0.97	0.92 (0.03)	0.12 (0.04)	.98
Sugar	2.70	0.59 (0.14)	0.33 (0.17)	.80

a. What are the elasticities of output with respect to labor and capital for each industry?
b. What economic significance does the sum $(\hat{\beta}_1 + \hat{\beta}_2)$ have?
c. Murti and Sastri expected positive slope coefficients. Test their hypotheses at the 5-percent level of significance. (*Hint:* This is much harder than it looks!)

8. Suppose you are studying the rate of growth of income in a country as a function of the rate of growth of capital in that country and of the per capita income of that country. You're using a cross-sectional data set that includes both developed and developing countries. Suppose further that the underlying theory suggests that income growth rates

7. V. N. Murti and V. K. Sastri, "Production Functions for Indian Industry," *Econometrica*, Vol. 25, No. 2, pp. 205–221.

will increase as per capita income increases and then start decreasing past a particular point. Describe how you would model this relationship with each of the following functional forms:

a. a quadratic function

b. a semilog function

c. a slope dummy equation

9. A study of hotel investments in Waikiki estimated this revenue production function:

$$\ln R = \beta_0 + \beta_1 \ln L + \beta_2 \ln K + \epsilon$$

where: R = the annual net revenue of the hotel (in thousands of dollars)

L = land input (site area in square feet)

K = capital input (construction cost in thousands of dollars)

a. Create specific null and alternative hypotheses for this equation.

b. Calculate the appropriate t-values and run t-tests given the following regression result (standard errors in parentheses):

$$\widehat{\ln R} = -0.91750 + 0.273 \ln L + 0.733 \ln K$$
$$(0.135) \qquad (0.125)$$
$$N = 25$$

c. If you were going to build a Waikiki hotel, what input would you most want to use? Is there an additional piece of information you would need to know before you could answer?

10. William Comanor and Thomas Wilson[8] specified the following regression in their study of advertising's effect on the profit rates of 41 consumer goods firms:

$$PR_i = \beta_0 + \beta_1 ADV_i/SALES_i + \beta_2 \ln CAP_i + \beta_3 \ln ES_i + \beta_4 \ln DG_i + \epsilon_i$$

where: PR_i = the profit rate of the ith firm

ADV_i = the advertising expenditures in the ith firm (in dollars)

$SALES_i$ = the total gross sales of the ith firm (in dollars)

CAP_i = the capital needed to enter the ith firm's market at an efficient size

8. William S. Comanor and Thomas A. Wilson, "Advertising, Market Structure and Performance," *Review of Economics and Statistics,* Vol. 49, p. 432.

ES_i = the degree to which economies of scale exist in the ith firm's industry

DG_i = percent growth in sales (demand) of the ith firm over the last 10 years

ln = natural logarithm

ϵ_i = a classical error term

a. Hypothesize expected signs for each of the slope coefficients.

b. Note that there are two different kinds of nonlinear (in the variables) relationships in this equation. For each independent variable, determine the shape that the chosen functional form implies, and state whether you agree or disagree with this shape. Explain your reasoning in each case.

c. Comanor and Wilson state that the simple correlation coefficient between $ADV_i/SALES_i$ and each of the other independent variables is positive. If one of these other variables were omitted, in which direction would $\hat{\beta}_1$ likely be biased?

11. Suggest the appropriate functional forms for the relationships between the following variables. Be sure to explain your reasoning:

a. The age of the ith house in a cross-sectional equation for the sales price of houses in Cooperstown, New York. (*Hint:* Cooperstown is known as a lovely town with a number of elegant historic homes.)

b. The price of natural gas in year t in a demand-side time-series equation for the consumption of natural gas in the United States.

c. The income of the ith individual in a cross-sectional equation for the number of suits owned by individuals.

d. A dummy variable for being a student (1 = yes) in the equation specified in part c.

e. The number of long-distance telephone calls handled per year in a cross-sectional equation for the marginal cost of a telephone call faced by various competing long-distance telephone carriers.

12. Suppose you've been hired by a union that wants to convince workers in local dry cleaning establishments that joining the union will improve their well-being. As your first assignment, your boss asks you to build a model of wages for dry cleaning workers that measures the impact of union membership on those wages. Your first equation (standard errors in parentheses) is:

$$\hat{W}_i = -11.40 + 0.30A_i - 0.003A_i^2 + 1.00S_i + 1.20U_i$$
$$(0.10) \quad (0.002) \quad (0.20) \quad (1.00)$$
$$N = 34 \qquad \overline{R}^2 = .14$$

where: W_i = the hourly wage (in dollars) of the *i*th worker
A_i = the age of the *i*th worker
S_i = the number of years of education of the *i*th worker
U_i = a dummy variable = 1 if the *i*th worker is a union member, 0 otherwise

a. Evaluate the equation. How do $\overline{R}^2$ and the signs and significance of the coefficients compare with your expectations?
b. What is the meaning of the A^2 term? What relationship between A and W does it imply? Why doesn't the inclusion of A and A^2 violate Classical Assumption VI of no perfect collinearity between two independent variables?
c. Do you think you should have used the log of W as your dependent variable? Why or why not? (*Hint:* Compare this equation to the one in Exercise 4.)
d. Even though we've been told not to analyze the value of the intercept, isn't −$11.40 too low to ignore? What should be done to correct this problem?
e. On the basis of your regression, should the workers be convinced that joining the union will improve their well-being? Why or why not?

13. Your boss manages to use the regression results in Exercise 12 to convince the dry cleaning workers to join your union. About a year later, they go on strike, a strike that turns violent. Now your union is being sued by all the local dry cleaning establishments for some of the revenues lost during the strike. Their claim is that the violence has intimidated replacement workers, thus decreasing production. Your boss doesn't believe that the violence has had a significant impact on production efficiency and asks you to test his hypothesis with a regression. Your results (standard errors in parentheses) are:

$$\widehat{LE}_t = 3.08 + 0.16LQ_t - 0.020A_t - 0.0001V_t$$
$$(0.04) \qquad (0.010) \qquad (0.0008)$$
$$N = 24 \qquad \overline{R}^2 = .855$$

where: LE_t = the natural log of the efficiency rate (defined as the ratio of actual total output to the goal output in week t)
LQ_t = the natural log of actual total output in week t
A_t = the absentee rate (%) during week t
V_t = the number of incidents of violence during week t

a. Hypothesize signs and develop and test the appropriate hypotheses for the individual estimated coefficients (5-percent level).
b. If the functional form is correct, what does its use suggest about the theoretical elasticity of E with respect to Q compared with the elasticities of E with respect to A and V?
c. On the basis of this result, do you think the court will conclude that the violence had a significant impact on the efficiency rate? Why or why not?
d. What problems appear to exist in this equation? (*Hint:* The problems may be theoretical as well as econometric.) If you could make one change in the specification of this equation, what would it be?

14. Richard Fowles and Peter Loeb studied the interactive effect of drinking and altitude on traffic deaths.[9] The authors hypothesized that drunk driving fatalities are more likely at high altitude than at low altitude because higher elevations diminish the oxygen intake of the brain, increasing the impact of a given amount of alcohol. To test this hypothesis, they used an interaction variable between altitude and beer consumption. They estimated the following cross-sectional model (by state for the continental United States) of the motor vehicle fatality rate (*t*-scores in parentheses):

$$\hat{F}_i = -3.36 - 0.002B_i + 0.17S_i - 0.31D_i + 0.011B_iA_i \quad (7.25)$$
$$\quad\quad (-0.08) \quad (1.85) \;\; (-1.29) \quad\;\; (4.05)$$
$$N = 48 \quad\quad \overline{R}^2 = .499$$

where: F_i = traffic fatalities per motor vehicle mile driven in the *i*th state
B_t = per capita consumption of beer (malt beverages) in state *i*
S_i = average highway driving speed in state *i*
D_i = a dummy variable equal to 1 if the *i*th state had a vehicle safety inspection program, 0 otherwise
A_i = the average altitude of metropolitan areas in state *i* (in thousands)

---

9. Richard Fowles and Peter D. Loeb, "The Interactive Effect of Alcohol and Altitude on Traffic Fatalities," *Southern Economic Journal*, Vol. 59, pp. 108–111. To focus the analysis, we have omitted the coefficients of three other variables (the minimum legal drinking age, the percent of the population between 18 and 24, and the variability of highway driving speeds) that were insignificant in Equations 7.25 and 7.26.

a. Carefully state and test appropriate hypotheses about the coefficients of B, S, and D at the 5-percent level. Do these results give any indication of econometric problems in the equation? Explain.

b. Think through the interaction variable. What is it measuring? Carefully state the meaning of the coefficient of B*A.

c. Create and test appropriate hypotheses about the coefficient of the interaction variable at the 5-percent level.

d. Note that A_i is included in the equation in the interaction variable but not as an independent variable on its own. If an equation includes an interaction variable, should both components of the interaction be independent variables in the equation as a matter of course? Why or why not? (*Hint:* Recall that with slope dummies, we emphasized that both the intercept dummy term and the slope dummy variable term should be in the equation.)

e. When the authors included A_i in their model, the results were as in Equation 7.26. Which equation do you prefer? Explain.

$$\hat{F}_i = -2.33 - 0.024B_i + 0.14S_i - 0.24D_i - 0.35A_i + 0.023B_i A_i \quad (7.26)$$
$$(-0.80) \quad (1.53)(-0.96) \quad (-1.07) \quad (1.97)$$
$$N = 48 \quad \overline{R}^2 = .501$$

15. Walter Primeaux used slope dummies to help test his hypothesis that monopolies tend to advertise less intensively than do duopolies in the electric utility industry.[10] His estimated equation (which also included a number of geographic dummies and a time variable) was (*t*-scores in parentheses):

$$\hat{Y}_i = 0.15 + 5.0S_i + 0.015G_i + 0.35D_i$$
$$(4.5) \quad (0.4) \quad (2.9)$$
$$- 20.0S_i \cdot D_i + 0.49G_i \cdot D_i$$
$$(-5.0) \quad (2.3)$$
$$\overline{R}^2 = .456 \quad N = 350$$

where: Y_i = advertising and promotional expense (in dollars) per 1,000 residential kilowatt hours (KWH) of the *i*th electric utility

---

10. Walter J. Primeaux, Jr., "An Assessment of the Effects of Competition on Advertising Intensity," *Economic Inquiry,* Vol. 19, No. 4, pp. 613–625.

S_i = number of residential customers of the ith utility (hundreds of thousands)

G_i = annual percentage growth in residential KWH of the ith utility

D_i = a dummy variable equal to 1 if the ith utility is a duopoly, 0 if a monopoly

a. Carefully explain the economic meaning of each of the five slope coefficients. Note that *both* independent variables have slope dummies.

b. Hypothesize and test the relevant null hypotheses with the *t*-test at the 5-percent level of significance. (*Hint:* Primeaux expected positive coefficients for all five.)

c. Assuming that Primeaux's equation is correct, graph the relationship between advertising (Y_i) and size (S_i) for monopolies and for duopolies.

d. Assuming that Primeaux's equation is correct, graph the relationship between advertising and growth (G_i) for monopolies and for duopolies.

16. What attributes make a car accelerate well? If you're like most people, you'd answer that the fastest accelerators are high-powered, light cars with aerodynamic shapes. To test this, we used the data in Table 7.3 for 2009 model vehicles to estimate the following equation (standard errors in parentheses):

$$\widehat{TIME}_i = 7.43 - 1.90 TOP_i + 0.0007 WEIGHT_i - 0.005 HP_i \qquad (7.27)$$
$$\quad\quad\quad (0.29) \qquad\quad (0.0003) \qquad\quad\quad (0.00060)$$
$$t = \quad -6.49 \qquad\quad 2.23 \qquad\quad\quad\quad -7.74$$
$$N = 30 \quad \overline{R}^2 = .877$$

where: $TIME_i$ = the time (in seconds) it takes the ith car to accelerate from 0 to 60 miles per hour

TOP_i = a dummy equal to 1 if the ith car has a hard top, 0 if it has a soft top (convertible)

$WEIGHT_i$ = the curb weight (in pounds) of the ith car

HP_i = the base horsepower of the ith car

a. Create and test appropriate hypotheses about the slope coefficients of the equation at the 1-percent level.

b. What possible econometric problems, out of omitted variables, irrelevant variables, or incorrect functional form, does Equation 7.27 appear to have? Explain.

Table 7.3 Acceleration Times for 2009 Model Vehicles

	MAKE	MODEL	TIME	SPEED	TOP	WEIGHT	HP
1	Audi	TT Roadster	8.9	133	0	1335	150
2	Mini	Cooper S	7.4	134	0	1240	168
3	Volvo	C70 T5 Sport	7.4	150	0	1711	220
4	Saab	Nine-Three	7.9	149	0	1680	247
5	Mercedes-Benz	SL350	6.6	155	0	1825	268
6	Jaguar	XK8	6.7	154	0	1703	290
7	Bugatti	Veyron 16.4	2.4	253	1	1950	1000
8	Lotus	Exige	4.9	147	1	875	189
9	BMW	M3 (E30)	6.7	144	1	1257	220
10	BMW	330i Sport	5.9	155	1	1510	231
11	Porsche	Cayman S	5.3	171	1	1350	291
12	Nissan	Skyline GT-R (R34)	4.7	165	1	1560	276
13	Porsche	911 RS	4.7	172	1	1270	300
14	Ford	Shelby GT	5	150	1	1584	319
15	Mitsubishi	Evo VII RS Sprint	4.4	150	1	1260	320
16	Aston Martin	V8 Vantage	5.2	175	1	1630	380
17	Mercedes-Benz	SLK55 AMG	4.8	155	1	1540	355
18	Maserati	Quattroporte Sport GT	5.1	171	1	1930	394
19	Spyker	C8	4.5	187	1	1275	400
20	Ferrari	288GTO	4.9	189	1	1161	400
21	Mosler	MT900	3.9	190	1	1130	435
22	Lamborghini	Countach QV	4.9	180	1	1447	455
23	Chrysler	Viper GTS-R	4	190	1	1290	460
24	Bentley	Arnage T	5.2	179	1	2585	500
25	Ferrari	430 Scuderia	3.5	198	1	1350	503
26	Saleen	S7	3.3	240	1	1247	550
27	Lamborghini	Murcielago	4	205	1	1650	570
28	Pagani	Zonda F	3.6	214	1	1230	602
29	McLaren	F1	3.2	240	1	1140	627
30	Koenigsegg	CCR	3.2	242	1	1180	806

Source: StrikeEngine. "Performance Car Specs: 0–60, 0–100, Power to Weight Ratio, Top Speed." StrikeEngine.com. 2009.

c. Suppose that your next-door neighbor is a physics major who tells you that horsepower can be expressed in terms of the following equation: HP = MDA/TIME where M = mass, D = distance, A = acceleration, and TIME and HP are as defined previously. Does this change your answer to part b? How? Why?

d. On the basis of your answer to part c, you decide to change the functional form of the relationship between TIME and HP to an inverse because that's the appropriate theoretical relationship between the two variables. What would the expected sign of the coefficient of 1/HP be? Explain.

e. Equation 7.28 shows what happens if you switch your horsepower functional form to an inverse. Which equation do you prefer? Why? If Equation 7.28 had a higher $\overline{R}^2$ and higher t-scores, would that change your answer? Why or why not?

$$\widehat{TIME}_i = 2.26 - 1.26TOP_i + 0.001WEIGHT_i + 765.44(1/HP_i) \quad (7.28)$$
$$(0.33) \qquad (0.0003) \qquad (99.61)$$
$$t = \quad -3.74 \qquad 3.06 \qquad 7.68$$
$$N = 30 \quad \overline{R}^2 = .875$$

f. Since the two equations have different functional forms, can $\overline{R}^2$ be used to compare the overall fit of the equations? Why or why not?

g. (optional) Note that Table 7.3 also includes data on $SPEED_i$, defined as the top speed of the ith vehicle. Use EViews, Stata, or your computer's regression program to estimate Equations 7.27 and 7.28 with SPEED as the dependent variable instead of TIME, and then answer parts a–f of this exercise for the new dependent variable.

8 Multicollinearity

The next three chapters deal with violations of the Classical Assumptions and remedies for those violations. This chapter addresses multicollinearity; the next two chapters are on serial correlation and heteroskedasticity. For each of these three problems, we will attempt to answer the following questions:

1. What is the nature of the problem?
2. What are the consequences of the problem?
3. How is the problem diagnosed?
4. What remedies for the problem are available?

Strictly speaking, **perfect multicollinearity** is the violation of Classical Assumption VI—that no independent variable is a perfect linear function of one or more other independent variables. Perfect multicollinearity is rare, but severe imperfect multicollinearity, although not violating Classical Assumption VI, still causes substantial problems.

Recall that the coefficient β_k can be thought of as the impact on the dependent variable of a one-unit increase in the independent variable X_k, holding constant the other independent variables in the equation. But if two explanatory variables are significantly related, then the OLS computer program will find it difficult to distinguish the effects of one variable from the effects of the other.

In essence, the more highly correlated two (or more) independent variables are, the more difficult it becomes to accurately estimate the coefficients of the true model. If two variables move identically, then there is no hope of distinguishing between the impacts of the two; but if the variables are only roughly correlated, then we still might be able to estimate the two effects accurately enough for most purposes.

8.1 Perfect versus Imperfect Multicollinearity

Perfect Multicollinearity

Perfect multicollinearity[1] violates Classical Assumption VI, which specifies that no explanatory variable is a perfect linear function of any other explanatory variables. The word *perfect* in this context implies that the variation in one explanatory variable can be *completely* explained by movements in another explanatory variable. Such a perfect linear function between two independent variables would be:

$$X_{1i} = \alpha_0 + \alpha_1 X_{2i} \tag{8.1}$$

where the αs are constants and the Xs are independent variables in:

$$Y_i = \beta_0 + \beta_1 X_{1i} + \beta_2 X_{2i} + \epsilon_i \tag{8.2}$$

Notice that there is no error term in Equation 8.1. This implies that X_1 can be exactly calculated given X_2 and the equation. Examples of such perfect linear relationships would be:

$$X_{1i} = 3X_{2i} \tag{8.3}$$

$$X_{1i} = 2 + 4X_{2i} \tag{8.4}$$

Figure 8.1 shows a graph of explanatory variables that are perfectly correlated. As can be seen in Figure 8.1, a perfect linear function has all data points on the same straight line. There is none of the variation that accompanies the data from a typical regression.

---

1. The word *collinearity* describes a linear correlation between two independent variables, and *multicollinearity* indicates that more than two independent variables are involved. In common usage, multicollinearity is used to apply to both cases, and so we'll typically use that term in this text even though many of the examples and techniques discussed relate, strictly speaking, to collinearity.

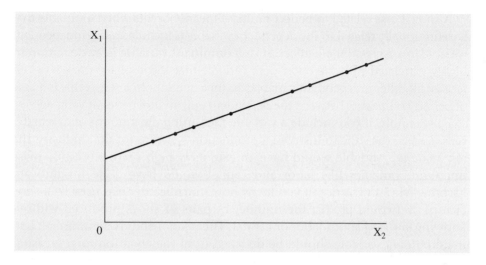

Figure 8.1 Perfect Multicollinearity

With perfect multicollinearity, an independent variable can be completely explained by the movements of one or more other independent variables. Perfect multicollinearity can usually be avoided by careful screening of the independent variables before a regression is run.

What happens to the estimation of an econometric equation where there is perfect multicollinearity? OLS is incapable of generating estimates of the regression coefficients, and most OLS computer programs will print out an error message in such a situation. Using Equation 8.2 as an example, we theoretically would obtain the following estimated coefficients and standard errors:

$$\hat{\beta}_1 = \text{indeterminate} \qquad \text{SE}(\hat{\beta}_1) = \infty \qquad (8.5)$$

$$\hat{\beta}_2 = \text{indeterminate} \qquad \text{SE}(\hat{\beta}_2) = \infty \qquad (8.6)$$

Perfect multicollinearity ruins our ability to estimate the coefficients because the two variables cannot be distinguished. You cannot "hold all the other independent variables in the equation constant" if every time one variable changes, another changes in an identical manner.

Fortunately, instances in which one explanatory variable is a perfect linear function of another are rare. More important, perfect multicollinearity should be fairly easy to discover before a regression is run. You can detect perfect multicollinearity by asking whether one variable equals a multiple of another or if one variable can be derived by adding a constant to another or if a variable equals the sum of two other variables. If so, then one of the variables should be dropped because there is no essential difference between the two.

A special case related to perfect multicollinearity occurs when a variable that is definitionally related to the dependent variable is included as an independent variable in a regression equation. Such a **dominant variable** is by definition so highly correlated with the dependent variable that it completely masks the effects of all other independent variables in the equation. In a sense, this is a case of perfect collinearity between the dependent and an independent variable.

For example, if you include a variable measuring the amount of raw materials used by the shoe industry in a production function for that industry, the raw materials variable would have an extremely high *t*-score, but otherwise important variables like labor and capital would have quite insignificant *t*-scores. Why? In essence, if you knew how much leather was used by a shoe factory, you could predict the number of pairs of shoes produced without knowing *anything* about labor or capital. The relationship is definitional, and the dominant variable should be dropped from the equation to get reasonable estimates of the coefficients of the other variables.

Be careful, though! Dominant variables shouldn't be confused with highly significant or important explanatory variables. Instead, they should be recognized as being virtually identical to the dependent variable. While the fit between the two is superb, knowledge of that fit could have been obtained from the definitions of the variables without any econometric estimation.

Imperfect Multicollinearity

Since perfect multicollinearity is fairly easy to avoid, econometricians almost never talk about it. Instead, when we use the word multicollinearity, we really are talking about severe imperfect multicollinearity. **Imperfect multicollinearity** can be defined as a linear functional relationship between two or more independent variables that is so strong that it can significantly affect the estimation of the coefficients of the variables.

In other words, imperfect multicollinearity occurs when two (or more) explanatory variables are imperfectly linearly related, as in:

$$X_{1i} = \alpha_0 + \alpha_1 X_{2i} + u_i \qquad (8.7)$$

Compare Equation 8.7 to Equation 8.1; notice that Equation 8.7 includes u_i, a stochastic error term. This implies that although the relationship between X_1 and X_2 might be fairly strong, it is not strong enough to allow X_1 to be completely explained by X_2; some unexplained variation still remains. Figure 8.2 shows the graph of two explanatory variables that might be considered imperfectly multicollinear. Notice that although all the observations in the sample are fairly close to the straight line, there is still some variation in X_1 that cannot be explained by X_2.

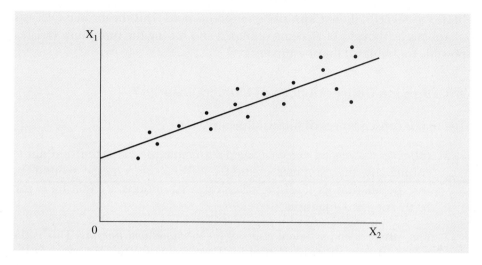

Figure 8.2 Imperfect Multicollinearity

With imperfect multicollinearity, an independent variable is a strong but not perfect linear function of one or more other independent variables. Imperfect multicollinearity varies in degree from sample to sample.

Imperfect multicollinearity is a strong linear relationship between the explanatory variables. The stronger the relationship between the two (or more) explanatory variables, the more likely it is that they'll be considered significantly multicollinear. Two variables that might be only slightly related in one sample might be so strongly related in another that they could be considered to be imperfectly multicollinear. In this sense, it is fair to say that multicollinearity is a sample phenomenon as well as a theoretical one. This contrasts with perfect multicollinearity because two variables that are perfectly related probably can be detected on a logical basis. The detection of multicollinearity will be discussed in more detail in Section 8.3.

(8.2) The Consequences of Multicollinearity

If the multicollinearity in a particular sample is severe, what will happen to estimates calculated from that sample? The purpose of this section is to explain the consequences of multicollinearity and then to explore some examples of such consequences.

Recall the properties of OLS estimators that might be affected by this or some other econometric problem. In Chapter 4, we stated that the OLS estimators are

BLUE (or MvLUE) if the Classical Assumptions hold. This means that OLS estimates can be thought of as being unbiased and having the minimum variance possible for unbiased linear estimators.

What Are the Consequences of Multicollinearity?

The major consequences of multicollinearity are:

1. *Estimates will remain unbiased.* Even if an equation has significant multicollinearity, the estimates of the βs still will be centered around the true population βs if all the Classical Assumptions are met for a correctly specified equation.

2. *The variances and standard errors of the estimates will increase.* This is the principal consequence of multicollinearity. Since two or more of the explanatory variables are significantly related, it becomes difficult to precisely identify the separate effects of the multicollinear variables. When it becomes hard to distinguish the effect of one variable from the effect of another, then we're much more likely to make large errors in estimating the βs than we were before we encountered multicollinearity. As a result, the estimated coefficients, although still unbiased, now come from distributions with much larger variances and, therefore, larger standard errors.[2]

   Figure 8.3 compares a distribution of β̂s from a sample with severe multicollinearity to one with virtually no correlation between any of the independent variables. Notice that the two distributions have the same mean, indicating that multicollinearity does not cause bias. Also note how much wider the distribution of β̂ becomes when multicollinearity is severe; this is the result of the increase in the standard error of β̂ that is caused by multicollinearity.

   Because of this larger variance, multicollinearity increases the likelihood of obtaining an unexpected sign[3] for a coefficient even though, as mentioned earlier, multicollinearity causes no bias.

---

2. Even though the variances and standard errors are larger with multicollinearity than they are without it, OLS is still BLUE when multicollinearity exists. That is, no other linear unbiased estimation technique can get lower variances than OLS even in the presence of multicollinearity. Thus, although the effect of multicollinearity is to increase the variance of the estimated coefficients, OLS still has the property of minimum variance. These "minimum variances" are just fairly large.

3. These unexpected signs generally occur because the distribution of the β̂s with multicollinearity is wider than without it, increasing the chance that a particular observed β̂ will be on the other side of zero from the true β (have an unexpected sign).

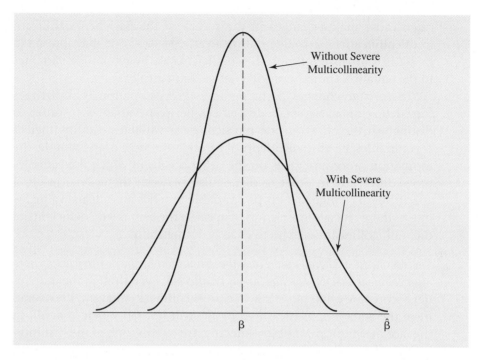

Figure 8.3 Severe Multicollinearity Increases the Variances of the $\hat{\beta}$s

Severe multicollinearity produces a distribution of the $\hat{\beta}$s that is centered around the true β but that has a much wider variance. Thus, the distribution of $\hat{\beta}$s with multicollinearity is much wider than otherwise.

3. *The computed t-scores will fall.* Multicollinearity tends to decrease the *t*-scores of the estimated coefficients mainly because of the formula for the *t*-statistic:

$$t_k = \frac{(\hat{\beta}_k - \hat{\beta}_{H_0})}{SE(\hat{\beta}_k)} \qquad (8.8)$$

Notice that this equation is divided by the standard error of the estimated coefficient. Multicollinearity increases the standard error of the estimated coefficient, and if the standard error increases, then the *t*-score must fall, as can be seen from Equation 8.8. Not surprisingly, it's quite common to observe low *t*-scores in equations with severe multicollinearity.

4. *Estimates will become very sensitive to changes in specification.* The addition or deletion of an explanatory variable or of a few observations will

often cause major changes in the values of the $\hat{\beta}$s when significant multicollinearity exists. If you drop a variable, even one that appears to be statistically insignificant, the coefficients of the remaining variables in the equation sometimes will change dramatically.

These large changes occur because OLS estimation is sometimes forced to emphasize small differences between variables in order to distinguish the effect of one multicollinear variable from another. If two variables are virtually identical throughout most of the sample, the estimation procedure relies on the observations in which the variables move differently in order to distinguish between them. As a result, a specification change that drops a variable that has an unusual value for one of these crucial observations can cause the estimated coefficients of the multicollinear variables to change dramatically.

5. *The overall fit of the equation and the estimation of the coefficients of non-multicollinear variables will be largely unaffected.* Even though the individual t-scores are often quite low in a multicollinear equation, the overall fit of the equation, as measured by $\overline{R}^2$, will not fall much, if at all, in the face of significant multicollinearity. Given this, one of the first indications of severe multicollinearity is the combination of a high $\overline{R}^2$ with no statistically significant individual regression coefficients. Similarly, if an explanatory variable in an equation is not multicollinear with the other variables, then the estimation of its coefficient and standard error usually will not be affected.

Because multicollinearity has little effect on the overall fit of the equation, it will also have little effect on the use of that equation for prediction or forecasting, as long as the independent variables maintain the same pattern of multicollinearity in the forecast period that they demonstrated in the sample.

Two Examples of the Consequences of Multicollinearity

To see what severe multicollinearity does to an estimated equation, let's look at a hypothetical example. Suppose you decide to estimate a "student consumption function." After the appropriate preliminary work, you come up with the following hypothesized equation:

$$CO_i = f(\overset{+}{Yd_i}, \overset{+}{LA_i}) + \epsilon_i = \beta_0 + \beta_1 Yd_i + \beta_2 LA_i + \epsilon_i \qquad (8.9)$$

where: CO_i = the annual consumption expenditures of the ith student on items other than tuition and room and board

Yd_i = the annual disposable income (including gifts) of that student

LA_i = the liquid assets (savings, etc.) of the ith student

ϵ_i = a stochastic error term

You then collect a small amount of data from people who are sitting near you in class:

Student	CO_i	Yd_i	LA_i
Mary	$2000	$2500	$25000
Robby	2300	3000	31000
Jim	2800	3500	33000
Lesley	3800	4000	39000
Sita	3500	4500	48000
Jerry	5000	5000	54000
Harwood	4500	5500	55000

Datafile = CONS8

If you run an OLS regression on your data set for Equation 8.9, you obtain:

$$\widehat{CO}_i = -367.83 + 0.5113Yd_i + 0.0427LA_i \qquad (8.10)$$
$$(1.0307) \qquad (0.0942)$$
$$t = 0.496 \qquad 0.453$$
$$\overline{R}^2 = .835$$

On the other hand, if you had consumption as a function of disposable income alone, then you would have obtained:

$$\widehat{CO}_i = -471.43 + 0.9714Yd_i \qquad (8.11)$$
$$(0.157)$$
$$t = 6.187$$
$$\overline{R}^2 = .861$$

Notice from Equations 8.10 and 8.11 that the t-score for disposable income increases more than tenfold when the liquid assets variable is dropped from the equation. Why does this happen? First of all, the simple correlation coefficient between Yd and LA is quite high: $r_{Yd,LA} = .986$. This high degree of correlation causes the standard errors of the estimated coefficients to be very high when both variables are included. In the case of $\hat{\beta}_{Yd}$, the standard error goes from 0.157 to 1.03 with the inclusion of LA!

In addition, the coefficient estimate itself changes somewhat. Further, note that the $\overline{R}^2$s of the two equations are quite similar despite the large differences in the significance of the explanatory variables in the two equations. It's quite common for $\overline{R}^2$ to stay virtually unchanged when multicollinear variables are dropped. All of these results are typical of equations with multicollinearity.

Which equation is better? If the liquid assets variable theoretically belongs in the equation, then to drop it will run the risk of omitted variable bias, but to include the variable will mean certain multicollinearity. There is no automatic answer when dealing with multicollinearity. We'll discuss this issue in more detail in Sections 8.4 and 8.5.

A second example of the consequences of multicollinearity is based on actual rather than hypothetical data. Suppose you've decided to build a cross-sectional model of the demand for gasoline by state:

$$PCON_i = f(\overset{+}{UHM_i}, \overset{-}{TAX_i}, \overset{+}{REG_i}) + \epsilon_i \qquad (8.12)$$

where: $PCON_i$ = petroleum consumption in the ith state (trillions of BTUs)
UHM_i = urban highway miles within the ith state
TAX_i = the gasoline tax rate in the ith state (cents per gallon)
REG_i = motor vehicle registrations in the ith state (thousands)

Given the definitions, let's move on to the estimation of Equation 8.12 using a linear functional form (assuming a classical error term):

$$\widehat{PCON_i} = 389.6 + 60.8UHM_i - 36.5TAX_i - 0.061REG_i \qquad (8.13)$$
$$\phantom{\widehat{PCON_i} = 389.6 + } (10.3) \qquad (13.2) \qquad (0.043)$$
$$\phantom{\widehat{PCON_i} = 389.6 + } t = 5.92 \qquad -2.77 \qquad -1.43$$
$$\phantom{\widehat{PCON_i} = 389.6 + } N = 50 \qquad \overline{R}^2 = .919$$

What's wrong with this equation? The motor vehicle registrations variable has an insignificant coefficient with an unexpected sign, but it's hard to believe that the variable is irrelevant. Is an omitted variable causing bias? It's possible, but adding a variable is unlikely to fix things. Does it help to know that the simple correlation coefficient between REG and UHM is 0.98? Given that, it seems fair to say that one of the two variables is redundant; both variables are really measuring the *size* of the state, so we have multicollinearity.

Notice the impact of the multicollinearity on the equation. The coefficient of a variable such as motor vehicle registrations, which has a very strong theoretical relationship to petroleum consumption, is insignificant and has a sign contrary to our expectations. This is mainly because the multicollinearity has increased the variance of the distribution of the estimated $\hat{\beta}$s.

What would happen if we were to drop one of the multicollinear variables?

$$\widehat{PCON}_i = 551.7 - 53.6TAX_i + 0.186REG_i \qquad (8.14)$$
$$(16.9) \qquad (0.012)$$
$$t = -3.18 \qquad 15.88$$
$$N = 50 \qquad \overline{R}^2 = .861$$

Dropping UHM has made REG extremely significant. Why did this occur? The answer is that the standard error of the coefficient of REG has fallen substantially (from 0.043 to 0.012) now that the multicollinearity has been removed from the equation. Also note that the sign of the estimated coefficient has now become positive as hypothesized. The reason is that REG and UHM are virtually indistinguishable from an empirical point of view, and so the OLS program latched onto minor differences between the variables to explain the movements of PCON. Once the multicollinearity was removed, the direct positive relationship between REG and PCON was obvious.

Either UHM or REG could have been dropped with similar results because the two variables are, in a quantitative sense, virtually identical. In this case, REG was judged to be theoretically superior to UHM. Even though $\overline{R}^2$ fell when UHM was dropped, Equation 8.14 should be considered superior to Equation 8.13. This is an example of the point, first made in Chapter 3, that the fit of the equation is not the most important criterion to be used in determining its overall quality.

8.3 The Detection of Multicollinearity

How do we decide whether an equation has a severe multicollinearity problem? A first step is to recognize that some multicollinearity exists in every equation. It's virtually impossible in a real-world example to find a set of explanatory variables that are totally uncorrelated with each other (except for designed experiments). Our main purpose in this section will be to learn to determine *how much* multicollinearity exists in an equation, not *whether* any multicollinearity exists.

A second key point is that the severity of multicollinearity in a given equation can change from sample to sample depending on the characteristics of the sample. As a result, the theoretical underpinnings of the equation are not quite as important in the detection of multicollinearity as they are in the detection of an omitted variable or an incorrect functional form. Instead, we tend to rely more on data-oriented techniques to determine the severity of the multicollinearity in a given sample. Of course, we can never ignore the theory behind an equation. The trick is to find variables that are theoretically relevant (for meaningful interpretation) and that are also statistically nonmulticollinear (for meaningful inference).

Because multicollinearity is a sample phenomenon, and the level of damage of its impact is a matter of degree, many of the methods used to detect it are informal tests without critical values or levels of significance. Indeed, there are no generally accepted, true statistical tests for multicollinearity. Most researchers develop a general feeling for the severity of multicollinearity in an estimated equation by looking at a number of the characteristics of that equation. Let's examine two of the most-used of those characteristics.

High Simple Correlation Coefficients

One way to detect severe multicollinearity is to examine the simple correlation coefficients between the explanatory variables. If an r is high in absolute value, then we know that these two particular Xs are quite correlated and that multicollinearity is a potential problem. For example, in Equation 8.10, the simple correlation coefficient between disposable income and liquid assets is 0.986. A simple correlation coefficient this high, especially in an equation with only two independent variables, is a certain indication of severe multicollinearity.

How high is high? Some researchers pick an arbitrary number, such as 0.80, and become concerned about multicollinearity any time the absolute value of a simple correlation coefficient exceeds 0.80. A better answer might be that r is high if it causes unacceptably large variances in the coefficient estimates in which we're interested.

Be careful; the use of simple correlation coefficients as an indication of the extent of multicollinearity involves a major limitation if there are more than two explanatory variables. It is quite possible for groups of independent variables, acting together, to cause multicollinearity without any single simple correlation coefficient being high enough to indicate that multicollinearity is in fact severe. As a result, simple correlation coefficients must be considered to be sufficient but not necessary tests for multicollinearity. Although a high r does indeed indicate the probability of severe multicollinearity, a low r by no means proves otherwise.[4]

High Variance Inflation Factors (VIFs)

The use of tests to give an indication of the severity of multicollinearity in a particular sample is controversial. Some econometricians reject even the simple indicator described previously, mainly because of the limitations cited. Others tend to use a variety of more formal tests.[5]

One measure of the severity of multicollinearity that is easy to use and that is gaining in popularity is the variance inflation factor. The **variance inflation factor (VIF)** is a method of detecting the severity of multicollinearity by looking at the extent to which a given explanatory variable can be explained by all the other explanatory variables in the equation. There is a VIF for each explanatory variable in an equation. The VIF is an index of how much multicollinearity has increased the variance of an estimated coefficient. A high VIF indicates that multicollinearity has increased the estimated variance of the estimated coefficient by quite a bit, yielding a decreased t-score.

Suppose you want to use the VIF to attempt to detect multicollinearity in an original equation with K independent variables:

$$Y = \beta_0 + \beta_1 X_1 + \beta_2 X_2 + \cdots + \beta_K X_K + \epsilon$$

Doing so requires calculating K different VIFs, one for each X_i. Calculating the VIF for a given X_i involves two steps:

1. *Run an OLS regression that has X_i as a function of all the other explanatory variables in the equation.* For i = 1, this equation would be:

$$X_1 = \alpha_1 + \alpha_2 X_2 + \alpha_3 X_3 + \cdots + \alpha_K X_K + v \qquad (8.15)$$

where v is a classical stochastic error term. Note that X_1 is not included on the right-hand side of Equation 8.15, which is referred to as an

---

4. Most authors criticize the use of simple correlation coefficients to detect multicollinearity in equations with large numbers of explanatory variables, but many researchers continue to do so because a scan of the simple correlation coefficients is a "quick and dirty" way to get a feel for the degree of multicollinearity in an equation.

5. Perhaps the best of these is the Condition number. For more on the Condition number, which is a single index of the degree of multicollinearity in the overall equation, see D. A. Belsley, *Conditioning Diagnostics* (New York: Wiley, 1991).

auxiliary or secondary regression. Thus there are K auxiliary regressions, one for each independent variable in the original equation.

2. *Calculate the variance inflation factor for $\hat{\beta}_i$:*

$$VIF(\hat{\beta}_i) = \frac{1}{(1 - R_i^2)} \tag{8.16}$$

where R_i^2 is the coefficient of determination (the unadjusted R^2) of the auxiliary regression in step one. Since there is a separate auxiliary regression for each independent variable in the original equation, there also is an R_i^2 and a $VIF(\hat{\beta}_i)$ for each X_i. The higher the VIF, the more severe the effects of multicollinearity.

How high is high? An R_i^2 of 1, indicating perfect multicollinearity, produces a VIF of infinity, whereas an R_i^2 of 0, indicating no multicollinearity at all, produces a VIF of 1. While there is no table of formal critical VIF values, a common rule of thumb is that if $VIF(\hat{\beta}_i) > 5$, the multicollinearity is severe. As the number of independent variables increases, it makes sense to increase this number slightly.

For example, let's return to Equation 8.10 and calculate the VIFs for both independent variables. Both VIFs equal 36, confirming the quite severe multicollinearity we already know exists. It's no coincidence that the VIFs for the two variables are equal. In an equation with exactly two independent variables, the two auxiliary equations will have identical R_i^2s, leading to equal VIFs.[6]

Some authors and statistical software programs replace the VIF with its reciprocal, $(1 - R_i^2)$, called *tolerance*, or TOL. Whether we calculate VIF or TOL is a matter of personal preference, but either way, the general approach is the most comprehensive multicollinearity detection technique we've discussed in this text.

Unfortunately, there are a couple of problems with using VIFs. First, as mentioned, there is no hard-and-fast VIF decision rule. Second, it's possible to have multicollinear effects in an equation that has no large VIFs. For instance, if the simple correlation coefficient between X_1 and X_2 is 0.88, multicollinear effects are quite likely, and yet the VIF for the equation (assuming no other Xs) is only 4.4.

---

6. Another use for the R^2s of these auxiliary equations is to compare them with the overall equation's R^2. If an auxiliary equation's R^2 is higher, it's yet another sign of multicollinearity.

In essence, then, the VIF is a sufficient but not necessary test for multicollinearity, just like the other test described in this section. Indeed, as is probably obvious to the reader by now, there is no test that allows a researcher to reject the possibility of multicollinearity with any real certainty.

8.4 Remedies for Multicollinearity

What can be done to minimize the consequences of severe multicollinearity? There is no automatic answer to this question because multicollinearity is a phenomenon that could change from sample to sample even for the same specification of a regression equation. The purpose of this section is to outline a number of alternative remedies for multicollinearity that might be appropriate under certain circumstances.

Do Nothing

The first step to take once severe multicollinearity has been diagnosed is to decide whether anything should be done at all. As we'll see, it turns out that every remedy for multicollinearity has a drawback of some sort, and so it often happens that doing nothing is the correct course of action.

One reason for doing nothing is that multicollinearity in an equation will not always reduce the t-scores enough to make them insignificant or change the $\hat{\beta}$s enough to make them differ from expectations. In other words, the mere existence of multicollinearity does not necessarily mean anything. A remedy for multicollinearity should be considered only if the consequences cause insignificant t-scores or unreliable estimated coefficients. For example, it's possible to observe a simple correlation coefficient of .97 between two explanatory variables and yet have each individual t-score be significant. It makes no sense to consider remedial action in such a case, because any remedy for multicollinearity would probably cause other problems for the equation. In a sense, multicollinearity is similar to a non-life-threatening human disease that requires general anesthesia to operate on the patient: The risk of the operation should be undertaken only if the disease is causing a significant problem.

A second reason for doing nothing is that the deletion of a multicollinear variable that belongs in an equation will cause specification bias. If we drop such a variable, then we are *purposely* creating bias. Given all the effort typically spent avoiding omitted variables, it seems foolhardy to consider running that risk on purpose. As a result, experienced econometricians often will leave multicollinear variables in equations despite low t-scores.

The final reason for considering doing nothing to offset multicollinearity is that every time a regression is rerun, we risk encountering a specification that fits because it accidentally works for the particular data set involved, not because it is the truth. The larger the number of experiments, the greater the chances of finding the accidental result. To make things worse, when there is significant multicollinearity in the sample, the odds of strange results increase rapidly because of the sensitivity of the coefficient estimates to slight specification changes.

To sum, it is often best to leave an equation unadjusted in the face of all but extreme multicollinearity. Such advice might be difficult for beginning researchers to take, however, if they think that it's embarrassing to report that their final regression is one with insignificant t-scores. Compared to the alternatives of possible omitted variable bias or accidentally significant regression results, the low t-scores seem like a minor problem. For an example of "doing nothing" in the face of severe multicollinearity, see Section 8.5.

Drop a Redundant Variable

On occasion, the simple solution of dropping one of the multicollinear variables is a good one. For example, some inexperienced researchers include too many variables in their regressions, not wanting to face omitted variable bias. As a result, they often have two or more variables in their equations that are measuring essentially the same thing. In such a case the multicollinear variables are not irrelevant, since any one of them is quite probably theoretically and statistically sound. Instead, the variables might be called **redundant**; only one of them is needed to represent the effect on the dependent variable that all of them currently represent. For example, in an aggregate demand function, it would not make sense to include disposable income and GDP because both are measuring the same thing: income. A bit more subtle is the inference that population and disposable income should not both be included in the same aggregate demand function because, once again, they really are measuring the same thing: the size of the aggregate market. As population rises, so too will income. Dropping these kinds of redundant multicollinear variables is doing nothing more than making up for a specification error; the variables should never have been included in the first place.

To see how this solution would work, let's return to the student consumption function example of Equation 8.10:

$$\widehat{CO}_i = -367.83 + 0.5113Yd_i + 0.0427LA_i \qquad (8.10)$$
$$(1.0307) \qquad (0.0942)$$
$$t = 0.496 \qquad 0.453 \qquad \overline{R}^2 = .835$$

where CO = consumption, Yd = disposable income, and LA = liquid assets. When we first discussed this example, we compared this result to the same equation without the liquid assets variable:

$$\widehat{CO}_i = -471.43 + 0.9714Yd_i \qquad\qquad (8.11)$$
$$(0.157)$$
$$t = 6.187 \qquad \overline{R}^2 = .861$$

If we had instead dropped the disposable income variable, we would have obtained:

$$\widehat{CO}_i = -199.44 + 0.08876LA_i \qquad\qquad (8.17)$$
$$(0.01443)$$
$$t = 6.153 \qquad \overline{R}^2 = .860$$

Note that dropping one of the multicollinear variables has eliminated both the multicollinearity between the two explanatory variables and also the low t-score of the coefficient of the remaining variable. By dropping Yd, we were able to increase t_{LA} from 0.453 to 6.153. Since dropping a variable changes the meaning of the remaining coefficient (because the dropped variable is no longer being held constant), such dramatic changes are not unusual. The coefficient of the remaining included variable also now measures almost all of the joint impact on the dependent variable of the multicollinear explanatory variables.

Assuming you want to drop a variable, how do you decide which variable to drop? In cases of severe multicollinearity, it makes no statistical difference which variable is dropped. As a result, it doesn't make sense to pick the variable to be dropped on the basis of which one gives superior fit or which one is more significant (or has the expected sign) in the original equation. Instead, the theoretical underpinnings of the model should be the basis for such a decision. In the example of the student consumption function, there is more theoretical support for the hypothesis that disposable income determines consumption than there is for the liquid assets hypothesis. Therefore, Equation 8.11 should be preferred to Equation 8.17.

Increase the Size of the Sample

Another way to deal with multicollinearity is to attempt to increase the size of the sample to reduce the degree of multicollinearity. Although such an increase may be impossible, it's a useful alternative to be considered when feasible.

The idea behind increasing the size of the sample is that a larger data set (often requiring new data collection) will allow more accurate estimates than a small one, since the larger sample normally will reduce the variance of the estimated coefficients, diminishing the impact of the multicollinearity.

For most time series data sets, however, this solution isn't feasible. After all, samples typically are drawn by getting all the available data that seem similar. As a result, new data are generally impossible or quite expensive to find. Going out and generating new data is much easier with a cross-sectional or experimental data set than it is when the observations must be generated by the passage of time.

8.5 An Example of Why Multicollinearity Often Is Best Left Unadjusted

Let's look at an example of the idea that multicollinearity often should be left unadjusted. Suppose you work in the marketing department of a hypothetical soft drink company and you build a model of the impact on sales of your firm's advertising:

$$\hat{S}_t = 3080 - 75{,}000P_t + 4.23A_t - 1.04B_t \qquad (8.18)$$
$$(25{,}000) \quad (1.06) \quad (0.51)$$
$$t = -3.00 \quad 3.99 \quad -2.04$$
$$\overline{R}^2 = .825 \quad N = 28$$

where: S_t = sales of the soft drink in year t
P_t = average relative price of the drink in year t
A_t = advertising expenditures for the company in year t
B_t = advertising expenditures for the company's main competitor in year t

Assume that there are no omitted variables. All variables are measured in real dollars; that is, the nominal values are divided, or deflated, by a price index.

On the face of it, this is a reasonable-looking result. Estimated coefficients are significant in the directions implied by the underlying theory, and both the overall fit and the size of the coefficients seem acceptable. Suppose you now were told that advertising in the soft drink industry is cut-throat in nature and that firms tend to match their main competitor's advertising expenditures. This would lead you to suspect that significant multicollinearity was possible. Further suppose that the simple correlation coefficient between the two advertising variables is .974 and that their respective VIFs are well over 5.

Such a correlation coefficient is evidence that there is severe multicollinearity in the equation, but there is no reason even to consider doing anything about it, because the coefficients are so powerful that their *t*-scores remain significant, even in the face of severe multicollinearity. Unless multi-collinearity causes problems in the equation, it should be left unadjusted. To change the specification might give us better-looking results, but the adjust-ment would decrease our chances of obtaining the best possible estimates of the true coefficients. Although it's certainly lucky that there were no major problems due to multicollinearity in this example, that luck is no reason to try to fix something that isn't broken.

When a variable is dropped from an equation, its effect will be absorbed by the other explanatory variables to the extent that they are correlated with the newly omitted variable. It's likely that the remaining multicollinear vari-able(s) will absorb virtually all the bias, since the variables are highly corre-lated. This bias may destroy whatever usefulness the estimates had before the variable was dropped.

For example, if a variable, say B, is dropped from the equation to fix the multicollinearity, then the following might occur:

$$\hat{S}_t = 2586 - 78{,}000P_t + 0.52A_t \qquad (8.19)$$
$$(24{,}000) \quad (4.32)$$
$$t = -3.25 \quad 0.12$$
$$\overline{R}^2 = .531 \qquad N = 28$$

What's going on here? The company's advertising coefficient becomes less in-stead of more significant when one of the multicollinear variables is dropped. To see why, first note that the expected bias on $\hat{\beta}_A$ is negative be-cause the product of the expected sign of the coefficient of B and of the corre-lation between A and B is negative:

$$\text{Bias} = \beta_B \cdot f(r_{A,B}) = (-) \cdot (+) = - \qquad (8.20)$$

Second, this negative bias is strong enough to decrease the estimated coeffi-cient of A until it is insignificant. Although this problem could have been avoided by using a relative advertising variable (A divided by B, for instance), that formulation would have forced identical absolute coefficients on A and 1/B. Such identical coefficients will sometimes be theoretically expected or empirically reasonable but, in most cases, these kinds of constraints will force bias onto an equation that previously had none.

This example is simplistic, but its results are typical in cases in which equations are adjusted for multicollinearity by dropping a variable with-out regard to the effect that the deletion is going to have. The point here is that it's quite often theoretically or operationally unwise to drop a variable from an equation and that multicollinearity in such cases is best left unadjusted.

8.6 Summary

1. Perfect multicollinearity is the violation of the assumption that no explanatory variable is a perfect linear function of other explanatory variable(s). Perfect multicollinearity results in indeterminate estimates of the regression coefficients and infinite standard errors of those estimates.

2. Imperfect multicollinearity, which is what is typically meant when the word "multicollinearity" is used, is a linear relationship between two or more independent variables that is strong enough to significantly affect the estimation of that equation. Multicollinearity is a sample phenomenon as well as a theoretical one. Different samples can exhibit different degrees of multicollinearity.

3. The major consequence of severe multicollinearity is to increase the variances of the estimated regression coefficients and therefore decrease the calculated t-scores of those coefficients. Multicollinearity causes no bias in the estimated coefficients, and it has little effect on the overall significance of the regression or on the estimates of the coefficients of any nonmulticollinear explanatory variables.

4. Since multicollinearity exists, to one degree or another, in virtually every data set, the question to be asked in detection is how severe the multicollinearity in a particular sample is.

5. Two useful methods for the detection of severe multicollinearity are:
   a. Are the simple correlation coefficients between the explanatory variables high?
   b. Are the variance inflation factors high?

   If either of these answers is yes, then multicollinearity certainly exists, but multicollinearity can also exist even if the answers are no.

6. The three most common remedies for multicollinearity are:
   a. Do nothing (and thus avoid specification bias).
   b. Drop a redundant variable.
   c. Increase the size of the sample.

7. Quite often, doing nothing is the best remedy for multicollinearity. If the multicollinearity has not decreased t-scores to the point of insignificance, then no remedy should even be considered. Even if the t-scores are insignificant, remedies should be undertaken cautiously, because all impose costs on the estimation that may be greater than the potential benefit of ridding the equation of multicollinearity.

EXERCISES

(The answer to Exercise 2 is in Appendix A.)

1. Write the meaning of each of the following terms without referring to the book (or your notes), and then compare your definition with the version in the text for each:
   a. perfect multicollinearity
   b. severe imperfect multicollinearity
   c. dominant variable
   d. auxiliary (or secondary) equation
   e. variance inflation factor
   f. redundant variable

2. A recent study of the salaries of elementary school teachers in a small school district in Northern California came up with the following estimated equation (note: t-scores in parentheses!):

$$\widehat{\ln SAL_i} = 10.5 - 0.006 EMP_i + 0.002 UNITS_i + 0.079 LANG_i + 0.020 EXP_i$$
$$ (-0.98) \qquad (2.39) \qquad (2.08) \qquad (4.97)$$
$$\overline{R}^2 = .866 \quad N = 25 \tag{8.21}$$

where: SAL_i = the salary of the ith teacher (in dollars)
EMP_i = the years that the ith teacher has worked in this school district
$UNITS_i$ = the units of graduate work completed by the ith teacher
$LANG_i$ = a dummy variable equal to 1 if the ith teacher speaks two languages
EXP_i = the total years of teaching experience of the ith teacher

    a. Make up and test appropriate hypotheses for the coefficients of this equation at the 5-percent level.

    b. What is the functional form of this equation? Does it seem appropriate? Explain.

    c. What econometric problems (out of irrelevant variables, omitted variables, and multicollinearity) does this equation appear to have? Explain.

    d. Suppose that you now are told that the simple correlation coefficient between EMP and EXP is .89 and that the VIFs for EMP and EXP are both just barely over 5. Does this change your answer to part c above? How?

    e. What remedy for the problem you identify in part d do you recommend? Explain.

    f. If you drop EMP from the equation, the estimated equation becomes Equation 8.22. Use our four specification criteria to decide whether you prefer Equation 8.21 or Equation 8.22. Which do you like better? Why?

$$\widehat{\ln SAL_i} = 10.5 + 0.002 UNITS_i + 0.081 LANG_i + 0.015 EXP_i \quad\quad (8.22)$$
$$(2.47) \quad\quad\quad (2.09) \quad\quad\quad (8.65)$$
$$\overline{R}^2 = .871 \quad\quad N = 25$$

3. A researcher once attempted to estimate an asset demand equation that included the following three explanatory variables: current wealth W_t, wealth in the previous quarter W_{t-1}, and the change in wealth $\Delta W_t = W_t - W_{t-1}$. What problem did this researcher encounter? What should have been done to solve this problem?

4. In each of the following situations, determine whether the variable involved is a dominant variable:

    a. games lost in year t in an equation for the number of games won in year t by a baseball team that plays the same number of games each year

    b. number of Woody's restaurants in a model of the total sales of the entire Woody's chain of restaurants

    c. disposable income in an equation for aggregate consumption expenditures

    d. number of tires purchased in an annual model of the number of automobiles produced by an automaker that does not make its own tires

    e. number of acres planted in an agricultural supply function

5. Beginning researchers quite often believe that they have multi-collinearity when they've accidentally included in their equation two or more explanatory variables that basically serve the same purpose or are, in essence, measuring the same thing. Which of the following pairs of variables are likely to include such a redundant variable?
   a. GDP and NDP in a macroeconomic equation of some sort
   b. the price of refrigerators and the price of washing machines in a durable goods demand function
   c. the number of acres harvested and the amount of seed used in an agricultural supply function
   d. long-term interest rates and the money supply in an investment function

6. You've been hired by the Dean of Students Office to help reduce damage done to dorms by rowdy students, and your first step is to build a cross-sectional model of last term's damage to each dorm as a function of the attributes of that dorm (standard errors in parentheses):

$$\hat{D}_i = 210 + 733F_i - 0.805S_i + 74.0A_i$$
$$\qquad\quad (253) \quad (0.752) \quad (12.4)$$
$$\qquad N = 33 \qquad \overline{R}^2 = .84$$

where: D_i = the amount of damage (in dollars) done to the ith dorm last term

   F_i = the percentage of the ith dorm residents who are frosh

   S_i = the number of students who live in the ith dorm

   A_i = the number of incidents involving alcohol that were reported to the Dean of Students Office from the ith dorm last term (incidents involving alcohol may or may not involve damage to the dorm)

   a. Hypothesize signs, calculate t-scores, and test hypotheses for this result (5-percent level).
   b. What problems (omitted variables, irrelevant variables, or multicollinearity) appear to exist in this equation? Why?
   c. Suppose you were now told that the simple correlation coefficient between S_i and A_i was .94; would that change your answer? How?
   d. Is it possible that the unexpected sign of $\hat{\beta}_S$ could have been caused by multicollinearity? Why?

7. Suppose that your friend was modeling the impact of income on consumption in a quarterly model and discovered that income's impact

on consumption lasts at least a year. As a result, your friend estimated the following model:

$$C_t = \beta_0 + \beta_1 Yd_t + \beta_2 Yd_{t-1} + \beta_3 Yd_{t-2} + \beta_4 Yd_{t-3} + \epsilon_t$$

a. Would this equation be subject to perfect multicollinearity?
b. Would this equation be subject to imperfect multicollinearity?
c. What, if anything, could be done to rid this equation of any multicollinearity it might have? (One answer to this question, the autoregressive approach to distributed lags, will be covered in Chapter 12.)

8. In 1998, Mark McGwire hit 70 homers to break Roger Maris's old record of 61, and yet McGwire wasn't voted the Most Valuable Player (MVP) in his league. To try to understand how this happened, you collect the following data on MVP votes, batting average (BA), home runs (HR), and runs batted in (RBI) from the 1998 National League:

Name	Votes (V)	BA	HR	RBI
Sosa	438	.308	66	158
McGwire	272	.299	70	147
Alou	215	.312	38	124
Vaughn	185	.272	50	119
Biggio	163	.325	20	88
Galarraga	147	.305	44	121
Bonds	66	.303	37	122
Jones	56	.313	34	107

Datafile = MVP8

Just as you are about to run the regression, your friend (trying to get back at you for your comments on Exercise 7) warns you that you probably have multicollinearity.

a. What should you do about your friend's warning before running the regression?
b. Run the regression implied in this example: $V = f(\overset{+}{BA}, \overset{+}{HR}, \overset{+}{RBI}) + \epsilon$ on the data given. What signs of multicollinearity are there?
c. What suggestions would you make for another run of this equation? In particular, what would you do about multicollinearity?

9. A full-scale regression model for the total annual gross sales in thousands of dollars of J. C. Quarter's durable goods for the last 26 years

produces the following result (all measurements are in real dollars—or billions of real dollars; standard errors in parentheses):

$$\widehat{SQ_t} = -7.2 + 200.3PC_t - 150.6PQ_t + 20.6Y_t$$
$$\phantom{\widehat{SQ_t} = -7.2 +} (250.1) \quad\;\; (125.6) \quad\;\; (40.1)$$
$$\phantom{\widehat{SQ_t} = -7.2 +} -15.8C_t + 201.1N_t$$
$$\phantom{\widehat{SQ_t} = -7.2 +} (10.6) \quad\;\; (103.8)$$

where: SQ_t = sales of durable goods at J. C. Quarter's in year t
         PC_t = average price of durables in year t at J. C. Quarter's main competition
         PQ_t = the average price of durables at J. C. Quarter's in year t
         Y_t = U.S. gross domestic product in year t
         C_t = U.S. aggregate consumption in year t
         N_t = the number of J. C. Quarter's stores open in year t

a. Hypothesize signs, calculate t-scores, and test hypotheses for this result (5-percent level).
b. What problems (out of omitted variables, irrelevant variables, and multicollinearity) appear to exist in this equation? Explain.
c. Suppose you were now told that the $\overline{R}^2$ was .821, that $r_{Y,C}$ was .993, and that $r_{PC,PQ}$ was .813. Would this change your answer to the previous question? How?
d. What recommendation would you make for a rerun of this equation with different explanatory variables? Why?

10. A cross-sectional regression was run on a sample of 44 states in an effort to understand federal defense spending by state (standard errors in parentheses):

$$\hat{S_i} = -148.0 + 0.841C_i - 0.0115P_i - 0.0078E_i$$
$$\phantom{\hat{S_i} = -148.0 +} (0.027) \quad (0.1664) \quad (0.0092)$$

where: S_i = annual spending (millions of dollars) on defense in the ith state
         C_i = contracts (millions of dollars) awarded in the ith state (contracts are often for many years of service) per year
         P_i = annual payroll (millions of dollars) for workers in defense-oriented industries in the ith state
         E_i = the number of civilians employed in defense-oriented industries in the ith state

a. Hypothesize signs, calculate t-scores, and test hypotheses for this result (5-percent level).
b. The VIFs for this equation are all above 20, and those for P and C are above 30. What conclusion does this information allow you to draw?
c. What recommendation would you make for a rerun of this equation with a different specification? Explain your answer.

11. Consider the following regression result paraphrased from a study conducted by the admissions office at the Stanford Business School (standard errors in parentheses):

$$\hat{G}_i = 1.00 + 0.005M_i + 0.20B_i - 0.10A_i + 0.25S_i$$
$$\phantom{\hat{G}_i = 1.00 +}(0.001)\quad(0.20)\quad(0.10)\quad(0.10)$$
$$\overline{R}^2 = 0.20 \qquad N = 1000$$

where: G_i = the Stanford Business School GPA of the ith student (4 = high)
M_i = the score on the graduate management admission test of the ith student (800 = high)
B_i = the number of years of business experience of the ith student
A_i = the age of the ith student
S_i = dummy equal to 1 if the ith student was an economics major, 0 otherwise

a. Theorize the expected signs of all the coefficients (try not to look at the results) and test these expectations with appropriate hypotheses (including choosing a significance level).
b. Do any problems appear to exist in this equation? Explain your answer.
c. How would you react if someone suggested a polynomial functional form for A? Why?
d. What suggestions (if any) would you have for another run of this equation?

12. Calculating VIFs typically involves running sets of auxiliary regressions, one regression for each independent variable in an equation. To get practice with this procedure, calculate the following:
a. the VIFs for N, P, and I from the Woody's data in Table 3.1
b. the VIFs for PB, PC, and YD from the chicken demand data in Table 6.2 (using Equation 6.8)

   c. the VIF for X_1 in an equation where X_1 and X_2 are the only independent variables, given that the VIF for X_2 is 3.8 and $N = 28$

   d. the VIF for X_1 in an equation where X_1 and X_2 are the only independent variables, given that the simple correlation coefficient between X_1 and X_2 is 0.80 and $N = 15$

13. Let's take a look at a classic example, a model of the demand for fish in the United States from 1946 to 1970. This time period is interesting because it includes the Pope's 1966 decision to allow Catholics to eat meat on non-Lent Fridays. Before the Pope's decision, many Catholics ate fish on Fridays (when they weren't allowed to eat meat), and the purpose of the research is to determine whether the Pope's decision decreased the demand for fish or simply changed the days of the week when fish was eaten.

   If you use the data in Table 8.1, you can estimate the following equation:

$$\hat{F}_t = 7.96 + 0.03PF_t + 0.0047PB_t + 0.36\ln Yd_t - 0.12P_t \qquad (8.23)$$
$$\phantom{\hat{F}_t = 7.96 + } (0.03) \quad (0.019) \qquad (1.15) \qquad (0.26)$$
$$t = \quad 0.98 \qquad 0.24 \qquad\quad 0.31 \qquad\quad -0.48$$
$$\overline{R}^2 = .667 \qquad N = 25$$

where:
   F_t = average pounds of fish consumed per capita in year t
   PF_t = price index for fish in year t
   PB_t = price index for beef in year t
   Yd_t = real per capita disposable income in year t (in billions of dollars)
   P_t = a dummy variable equal to 1 after the Pope's 1966 decision and 0 otherwise

   a. Create and test appropriate hypotheses about the slope coefficients of Equation 8.23 at the 5-percent level.

   b. What's going on here? How is it possible to have a reasonably high $\overline{R}^2$ and have t-scores of less than 1 for all the slope coefficients?

   c. One possibility is an omitted variable, and a friend suggests adding a variable (N) that measures the number of Catholics in the United States in year t. Do you agree with this suggestion? Explain your reasoning.

   d. A second possibility is an irrelevant variable, and another friend suggests dropping P. Do you agree with this suggestion? Explain your reasoning.

Table 8.1 Data for the Fish/Pope Example

Year	F	PF	PB	N	Yd
1946	12.8	56.0	50.1	24402	1606
1947	12.3	64.3	71.3	25268	1513
1948	13.1	74.1	81.0	26076	1567
1949	12.9	74.5	76.2	26718	1547
1950	13.8	73.1	80.3	27766	1646
1951	13.2	83.4	91.0	28635	1657
1952	13.3	81.3	90.2	29408	1678
1953	13.6	78.2	84.2	30425	1726
1954	13.5	78.7	83.7	31648	1714
1955	12.9	77.1	77.1	32576	1795
1956	12.9	77.0	74.5	33574	1839
1957	12.8	78.0	82.8	34564	1844
1958	13.3	83.4	92.2	36024	1831
1959	13.7	84.9	88.8	39505	1881
1960	13.2	85.0	87.2	40871	1883
1961	13.7	86.9	88.3	42105	1909
1962	13.6	90.5	90.1	42882	1969
1963	13.7	90.3	88.7	43847	2015
1964	13.5	88.2	87.3	44874	2126
1965	13.9	90.8	93.9	45640	2239
1966	13.9	96.7	102.6	46246	2335
1967	13.6	100.0	100.0	46864	2403
1968	14.0	101.6	102.3	47468	2486
1969	14.2	107.2	111.4	47873	2534
1970	14.8	118.0	117.6	47872	2610

Source: *Historical Statistics of the U.S., Colonial Times to 1970* (Washington, D.C.: U.S. Bureau of the Census, 1975).

Datafile = FISH8

e. A third possibility is multicollinearity, and the simple correlation coefficient of .958 between PF and PB certainly is high! Are the two price variables redundant? Should you drop one? If so, which one? Explain your reasoning.

f. (optional) Using the data in Table 8.1, calculate the VIFs for Equation 8.23. Do they support the possibility of multicollinearity? Explain.

g. You decide to replace the individual price variables with a relative price variable:

$$RP_t = PF_t/PB_t$$

Such a variable would make sense if theory calls for keeping both prices in the equation and if the two price coefficients are expected to be close in absolute value with opposite signs. (Opposite expected signs are required because an increase in PF will increase RP while an increase in PB will decrease it.) What is the expected sign of the coefficient of RP?

h. You replace PF and PB with RP and estimate:

$$\hat{F}_t = -5.17 - 1.93 RP_t + 2.71 \ln Yd_t + 0.0052 P_t \qquad (8.24)$$
$$\phantom{\hat{F}_t = -5.17} (1.43) \quad\quad (0.66) \quad\quad\quad (0.2801)$$
$$t = -1.35 \quad\quad 4.13 \quad\quad\quad\quad 0.019$$
$$\bar{R}^2 = .588 \quad\quad N = 25$$

Which equation do you prefer, Equation 8.23 or Equation 8.24? Explain your reasoning.

i. What's your conclusion? Did the Pope's decision reduce the overall demand for fish?

14. Let's assume that you were hired by the Department of Agriculture to do a cross-sectional study of weekly expenditures for food consumed at home by the ith household (F_i) and that you estimated the following equation (standard errors in parentheses):

$$\hat{F}_i = -10.50 + 2.1 Y_i - .04 Y_i^2 + 13.0 H_i - 2.0 A_i$$
$$\phantom{\hat{F}_i = -10.50} (0.7) \quad (.05) \quad\quad (2.0) \quad\quad (2.0)$$
$$\bar{R}^2 = .46 \quad\quad N = 235$$

where: Y_i = the weekly disposable income of the ith household
H_i = the number of people in the ith household
A_i = the number of children (under 19) in the ith household

a. Create and test appropriate hypotheses at the 10-percent level.
b. Isn't the estimated coefficient for Y impossible? (There's no way that people can spend twice their income on food.) Explain your answer.
c. Which econometric problems (omitted variables, irrelevant variables, or multicollinearity) appear to exist in this equation? Explain your answer.
d. Suppose that you were now told that the VIFs for A and H were both between 5 and 10. How does this change your answer to part c?
e. Would you suggest changing this specification for one final run of this equation? How? Why? What are the possible econometric costs of estimating another specification?

15. Suppose you hear that because of the asymmetry of the human heart, the heartbeat of any individual is a function of the difference between the lengths of that individual's legs rather than of the length of either leg. You decide to collect data and build a regression model to test this hypothesis, but you can't decide which of the following two models to estimate[7]:

$$\text{Model A: } H_i = \alpha_0 + \alpha_1 R_i + \alpha_2 L_i + \epsilon_i$$
$$\text{Model B: } H_i = \beta_0 + \beta_1 R_i + \beta_2(L_i - R_i) + \epsilon_i$$

where: H_i = the heartbeat of the ith cardiac patient
R_i = the length of the ith patient's right leg
L_i = the length of the ith patient's left leg

a. Model A seems more likely to encounter multicollinearity than does Model B, at least as measured by the simple correlation coefficient. Why? What remedy for this multicollinearity would you recommend?
b. Suppose you estimate a set of coefficients for Model A. Can you calculate estimates of the coefficients of Model B from this information? If so, how? If not, why?
c. What does your answer to part b tell you about which of the two models is more vulnerable to multicollinearity?
d. Suppose you had dropped L_i from Model A because of the high simple correlation coefficient between L_i and R_i. What would this deletion have done to your answers to parts b and c?

8.7 Appendix: The SAT Interactive Regression Learning Exercise

Econometrics is difficult to learn by reading examples, no matter how good they are. Most econometricians, the author included, had trouble understanding how to use econometrics, particularly in the area of specification choice, until they ran their own regression projects. This is because there's an element of econometric understanding that is better learned by *doing* than by reading about what someone else is doing.

Unfortunately, mastering the art of econometrics by running your own regression projects without any feedback is also difficult because it takes quite a

---

7. Potluri Rao and Roger Miller, *Applied Econometrics* (Belmont, CA: Wadsworth, 1971), p. 48.

while to learn to avoid some fairly simple mistakes. Probably the best way to learn is to work on your own regression project, analyzing your own problems and making your own decisions, but with a more experienced econometrician nearby to give you one-on-one feedback on exactly which of your decisions were inspired and which were flawed (and why).

This section is an attempt to give you an opportunity to make independent specification decisions and to then get feedback on the advantages or disadvantages of those decisions. Using the interactive learning exercise of this section requires neither a computer nor a tutor, although either would certainly be useful. Instead, we have designed an exercise that can be used on its own to help to bridge the gap between the typical econometrics examples (which require no decision making) and the typical econometrics projects (which give little feedback). An additional interactive learning exercise is presented in Chapter 11.

STOP!

To get the most out of the exercise, it's important to follow the instructions carefully. Reading the pages in order as with any other example will waste your time, because once you have seen even a few of the results, the benefits to you of making specification decisions will diminish. In addition, you shouldn't look at any of the regression results until you have specified your first equation.

Building a Model of Scholastic Aptitude Test Scores

The dependent variable for this interactive learning exercise is the combined "two-test" SAT score, math plus verbal, earned by students in the senior class at Arcadia High School. Arcadia is an upper-middle-class suburban community located near Los Angeles, California. Out of a graduating class of about 640, a total of 65 students who had taken the SATs were randomly selected for inclusion in the data set. In cases in which a student had taken the test more than once, the highest score was recorded.

A review of the literature on the SAT shows many more psychological studies and popular press articles than econometric regressions. Many articles have been authored by critics of the SAT, who maintain (among other things) that it is biased against women and minorities. In support of this argument, these critics have pointed to national average scores for women and some minorities, which in recent years have been significantly lower than the national averages for white males. Any reader interested in reviewing a portion of the applicable literature should do so now before continuing on with the section.[8]

If you were going to build a single-equation linear model of SAT scores, what factors would you consider? First, you'd want to include some measures of a student's academic ability. Three such variables are cumulative high school grade point average (GPA) and participation in advanced placement math and English courses (APMATH and APENG). Advanced placement (AP) classes are academically rigorous courses that may help a student do well on the SAT. More important, students are invited to be in AP classes on the basis of academic potential, and students who choose to take AP classes are revealing their interest in academic subjects, both of which bode well for SAT scores. GPAs at Arcadia High School are weighted GPAs; each semester that a student takes an AP class adds one extra point to his or her total grade points. (For example, a semester grade of "A" in an AP math class counts for five grade points as opposed to the conventional four points.)

A second set of important considerations includes qualitative factors that may affect performance on the SAT. Available dummy variables in this category include measures of a student's gender (GEND), ethnicity (RACE), and native language (ESL). All of the students in the sample are either Asian or Caucasian, and RACE is assigned a value of one if a student is Asian. Asian students are a substantial proportion of the student body at Arcadia High. The ESL dummy is given a value of one if English is a student's second language. In addition, studying for the test may be relevant, so a dummy variable indicating whether or not a student has attended an SAT preparation class (PREP) is also included in the data.

To sum, the explanatory variables available for you to choose for your model are:

GPA_i = the weighted GPA of the ith student

$APMATH_i$ = a dummy variable equal to 1 if the ith student has taken AP math, 0 otherwise

$APENG_i$ = a dummy variable equal to 1 if the ith student has taken AP English, 0 otherwise

AP_i = a dummy variable equal to 1 if the ith student has taken AP math and/or AP English, 0 if the ith student has taken neither

ESL_i = a dummy variable equal to 1 if English is not the ith student's first language, 0 otherwise

---

8. See, for example, James Fallows, "The Tests and the 'Brightest': How Fair Are the College Boards?" *The Atlantic*, Vol. 245, No. 2, pp. 37–48. We are grateful to former Occidental student Bob Sego for his help in preparing this interactive exercise.

$RACE_i$ = a dummy variable equal to 1 if the ith student is Asian, 0 if the student is Caucasian

$GEND_i$ = a dummy variable equal to 1 if the ith student is male, 0 if the student is female

$PREP_i$ = a dummy variable equal to 1 if the ith student has attended a SAT preparation course, 0 otherwise

The data for these variables are presented in Table 8.2.

Table 8.2 Data for the SAT Interactive Learning Exercise

SAT	GPA	APMATH	APENG	AP	ESL	GEND	PREP	RACE
1060	3.74	0	1	1	0	0	0	0
740	2.71	0	0	0	0	0	1	0
1070	3.92	0	1	1	0	0	1	0
1070	3.43	0	1	1	0	0	1	0
1330	4.35	1	1	1	0	0	1	0
1220	3.02	0	1	1	0	1	1	0
1130	3.98	1	1	1	1	0	1	0
770	2.94	0	0	0	0	0	1	0
1050	3.49	0	1	1	0	0	1	0
1250	3.87	1	1	1	0	1	1	0
1000	3.49	0	0	0	0	0	1	0
1010	3.24	0	1	1	0	0	1	0
1320	4.22	1	1	1	1	1	0	1
1230	3.61	1	1	1	1	1	1	1
840	2.48	1	0	1	1	1	0	1
940	2.26	1	0	1	1	0	0	1
910	2.32	0	0	0	1	1	1	1
1240	3.89	1	1	1	0	1	1	0
1020	3.67	0	0	0	0	1	0	0
630	2.54	0	0	0	0	0	1	0
850	3.16	0	0	0	0	0	1	0
1300	4.16	1	1	1	1	1	1	0
950	2.94	0	0	0	0	1	1	0
1350	3.79	1	1	1	0	1	1	0
1070	2.56	0	0	0	0	1	0	0
1000	3.00	0	0	0	0	1	1	0
770	2.79	0	0	0	0	0	1	0
1280	3.70	1	0	1	1	0	1	1
590	3.23	0	0	0	1	0	1	1
1060	3.98	1	1	1	1	1	0	1
1050	2.64	1	0	1	0	0	0	0
1220	4.15	1	1	1	1	1	1	1

(continued)

Table 8.2   *(continued)*

SAT	GPA	APMATH	APENG	AP	ESL	GEND	PREP	RACE
930	2.73	0	0	0	0	1	1	0
940	3.10	1	1	1	1	0	0	1
980	2.70	0	0	0	1	1	1	1
1280	3.73	1	1	1	0	1	1	0
700	1.64	0	0	0	1	0	1	1
1040	4.03	1	1	1	1	0	1	1
1070	3.24	0	1	1	0	1	1	0
900	3.42	0	0	0	0	1	1	0
1430	4.29	1	1	1	0	1	0	0
1290	3.33	0	0	0	0	1	0	0
1070	3.61	1	0	1	1	0	1	1
1100	3.58	1	1	1	0	0	1	0
1030	3.52	0	1	1	0	0	1	0
1070	2.94	0	0	0	0	1	1	0
1170	3.98	1	1	1	1	1	1	0
1300	3.89	1	1	1	0	1	0	0
1410	4.34	1	1	1	1	0	1	1
1160	3.43	1	1	1	0	1	1	0
1170	3.56	1	1	1	0	0	0	0
1280	4.11	1	1	1	0	0	1	0
1060	3.58	1	1	1	1	0	1	0
1250	3.47	1	1	1	0	1	1	0
1020	2.92	1	0	1	1	1	1	1
1000	4.05	0	1	1	1	0	0	1
1090	3.24	1	1	1	1	1	1	1
1430	4.38	1	1	1	1	0	0	1
860	2.62	1	0	1	1	0	0	1
1050	2.37	0	0	0	0	1	0	0
920	2.77	0	0	0	0	0	1	0
1100	2.54	0	0	0	0	1	1	0
1160	3.55	1	0	1	1	1	1	1
1360	2.98	0	1	1	1	0	1	0
970	3.64	1	1	1	0	0	1	0

Datafile = SAT8

Now:

1. Hypothesize expected signs for the coefficients of each of these variables in an equation for the SAT score of the *i*th student. Examine each variable carefully; what is the theoretical content of your hypothesis?

2. Choose carefully the best set of explanatory variables. Start off by including GPA, APMATH, and APENG; what other variables do you think

should be specified? Don't simply include all the variables, intending to drop the insignificant ones. Instead, think through the problem carefully and find the best possible equation.

Once you've specified your equation, you're ready to move on. Keep following the instructions in the exercise until you have specified your equation completely. You may take some time to think over the questions or take a break, but when you return to the interactive exercise make sure to go back to the exact point from which you left rather than starting all over again. To the extent you can do it, try to avoid looking at the hints until after you've completed the entire project. The hints are there to help you if you get stuck, not to allow you to check every decision you make.

One final bit of advice: each regression result is accompanied by a series of questions. Take the time to answer all these questions, in writing if possible. Rushing through this interactive exercise will lessen its effectiveness.

The SAT Score Interactive Regression Exercise

To start, choose the specification you'd like to estimate, find the regression run number[9] of that specification in the following list, and then turn to that regression. Note that the simple correlation coefficient matrix for this data set is in Table 8.3 just before the results begin.

All the equations include SAT as the dependent variable and GPA, APMATH, and APENG as explanatory variables. Find the combination of explanatory variables (from ESL, GEND, PREP, and RACE) that you wish to include and go to the indicated regression:

None of them, go to regression run 8.1
ESL only, go to regression run 8.2
GEND only, go to regression run 8.3
PREP only, go to regression run 8.4
RACE only, go to regression run 8.5
ESL and GEND, go to regression run 8.6
ESL and PREP, go to regression run 8.7
ESL and RACE, go to regression run 8.8
GEND and PREP, go to regression run 8.9

---

9. All the regression results appear exactly as they are produced by the EViews regression package. Instructors who would prefer to use results produced by the Stata regression program can find these results in the Instructor's Manual on the book's website at www.pearsonhighered.com/studenmund.

GEND and RACE, go to regression run 8.10
PREP and RACE, go to regression run 8.11
ESL, GEND, and PREP, go to regression run 8.12
ESL, GEND, and RACE, go to regression run 8.13
ESL, PREP, and RACE, go to regression run 8.14
GEND, PREP, and RACE, go to regression run 8.15
All four, go to regression run 8.16

Table 8.3   Means, Standard Deviations, and Simple Correlation Coefficients for the SAT Interactive Regression Learning Exercise

Means, Standard Deviations, and Correlations
Sample Range: 1–65

Variable	Mean	Standard Deviation
SAT	1075.538	191.3605
GPA	3.362308	0.612739
APMATH	0.523077	0.503354
APENG	0.553846	0.500961
AP	0.676923	0.471291
ESL	0.400000	0.493710
GEND	0.492308	0.503831
PREP	0.738462	0.442893
RACE	0.323077	0.471291

	Correlation Coeff		Correlation Coeff
APMATH,GPA	0.497	GPA,SAT	0.678
APENG,SAT	0.608	APMATH,SAT	0.512
APENG,APMATH	0.444	APENG,GPA	0.709
AP,SAT	0.579	AP,GPA	0.585
AP,APMATH	0.723	AP,APENG	0.769
ESL,GPA	0.071	ESL,SAT	0.024
ESL,APENG	0.037	ESL,APMATH	0.402
GEND,GPA	−0.008	ESL,AP	0.295
GEND,APENG	−0.044	GEND,SAT	0.293
GEND,ESL	−0.050	GEND,APMATH	0.077
PREP,SAT	−0.100	GEND,AP	−0.109
PREP,APMATH	−0.147	PREP,GPA	0.001
PREP,AP	−0.111	PREP,APENG	0.029
PREP,GEND	−0.044	PREP,ESL	−0.085
RACE,SAT	−0.085	RACE,GPA	−0.025
RACE,APMATH	0.330	RACE,APENG	−0.107
RACE,AP	0.195	RACE,ESL	0.846
RACE,GEND	−0.022	RACE,PREP	−0.187

Regression Run 8.1

Dependent Variable: SAT				
Method: Least Squares				
Date: 02/29/00 Time: 15:05				
Sample: 1 65				
Included observations: 65				

Variable	Coefficient	Std. Error	t-Statistic	Prob.
C	545.2537	117.8141	4.628086	0.0000
GPA	131.8512	40.86212	3.226735	0.0020
APMATH	78.60445	39.13018	2.008793	0.0490
APENG	82.77424	48.40687	1.709969	0.0924

R-squared	0.524341	Mean dependent var	1075.538
Adjusted R-squared	0.500948	S.D. dependent var	191.3605
S.E. of regression	135.1840	Akaike info criterion	12.71071
Sum squared resid	1114757.	Schwarz criterion	12.84452
Log likelihood	-409.0982	F-statistic	22.41440
Durbin-Watson stat	1.998585	Prob(F-statistic)	0.000000

Answer each of the following questions for this regression run.

a. Evaluate this result with respect to its economic meaning, overall fit, and the signs and significance of the individual coefficients.

b. What econometric problems (out of omitted variables, irrelevant variables, or multicollinearity) does this regression have? Why? If you need feedback on your answer, see hint 2 in the material on this chapter in Appendix A.

c. Which of the following statements comes closest to your recommendation for further action to be taken in the estimation of this equation?

  i. No further specification changes are advisable (go to page 303).
  ii. I would like to add ESL to the equation (go to run 8.2).
  iii. I would like to add GEND to the equation (go to run 8.3).
  iv. I would like to add PREP to the equation (go to run 8.4).
  v. I would like to add RACE to the equation (go to run 8.5).

If you need feedback on your answer, see hint 6 in the material on this chapter in Appendix A.

Regression Run 8.2

```
Dependent Variable: SAT
Method: Least Squares
Date: 02/29/00   Time: 15:06
Sample: 1 65
Included observations: 65
```

Variable	Coefficient	Std. Error	t-Statistic	Prob.
C	566.7551	118.6016	4.778644	0.0000
GPA	128.3402	40.78800	3.146519	0.0026
APMATH	101.5886	43.19023	2.352121	0.0220
APENG	77.30713	48.40462	1.597102	0.1155
ESL	-46.72721	37.88203	-1.233493	0.2222

R-squared	0.536105	Mean dependent var	1075.538
Adjusted R-squared	0.505179	S.D. dependent var	191.3605
S.E. of regression	134.6098	Akaike info criterion	12.71644
Sum squared resid	1087187.	Schwarz criterion	12.88370
Log likelihood	-408.2843	F-statistic	17.33489
Durbin-Watson stat	2.027210	Prob(F-statistic)	0.000000

Answer each of the following questions for this regression run.

a. Evaluate this result with respect to its economic meaning, overall fit, and the signs and significance of the individual coefficients.

b. What econometric problems (out of omitted variables, irrelevant variables, or multicollinearity) does this regression have? Why? If you need feedback on your answer, see hint 3 in the material on this chapter in Appendix A.

c. Which of the following statements comes closest to your recommendation for further action to be taken in the estimation of this equation?

   i. No further specification changes are advisable (go to page 303).
   ii. I would like to drop ESL from the equation (go to run 8.1).
   iii. I would like to add GEND to the equation (go to run 8.6).
   iv. I would like to add RACE to the equation (go to run 8.8).
   v. I would like to add PREP to the equation (go to run 8.7).

If you need feedback on your answer, see hint 6 in the material on this chapter in Appendix A.

Regression Run 8.3

Dependent Variable: SAT Method: Least Squares Date: 02/29/00 Time: 15:07 Sample: 1 65 Included observations: 65				
Variable	Coefficient	Std. Error	t-Statistic	Prob.
C	491.8225	108.5429	4.531135	0.0000
GPA	131.5798	37.29970	3.527638	0.0008
APMATH	65.04046	35.91313	1.811049	0.0751
APENG	94.10841	44.29652	2.124510	0.0378
GEND	112.0465	30.82961	3.634379	0.0006
R-squared	0.610162	Mean dependent var		1075.538
Adjusted R-squared	0.584173	S.D. dependent var		191.3605
S.E. of regression	123.3982	Akaike info criterion		12.54251
Sum squared resid	913626.4	Schwarz criterion		12.70977
Log likelihood	-402.6317	F-statistic		23.47754
Durbin-Watson stat	2.104997	Prob(F-statistic)		0.000000

Answer each of the following questions for this regression run.

a. Evaluate this result with respect to its economic meaning, overall fit, and the signs and significance of the individual coefficients.

b. What econometric problems (out of omitted variables, irrelevant variables, or multicollinearity) does this regression have? Why? If you need feedback on your answer, see hint 5 in the material on this chapter in Appendix A.

c. Which of the following statements comes closest to your recommendation for further action to be taken in the estimation of this equation?

   i. No further specification changes are advisable (go to page 303).
   ii. I would like to add ESL to the equation (go to run 8.6).
   iii. I would like to add PREP to the equation (go to run 8.9).
   iv. I would like to add RACE to the equation (go to run 8.10).

If you need feedback on your answer, see hint 19 in the material on this chapter in Appendix A.

Regression Run 8.4

Dependent Variable: SAT
Method: Least Squares
Date: 02/29/00   Time: 15:07
Sample: 1 65
Included observations: 65

Variable	Coefficient	Std. Error	t-Statistic	Prob.
C	569.2532	121.1058	4.700463	0.0000
GPA	132.7666	40.94846	3.242287	0.0019
APMATH	72.29444	39.84456	1.814412	0.0746
APENG	85.68562	48.60529	1.762887	0.0830
PREP	-34.38129	38.88201	-0.884247	0.3801

R-squared	0.530460	Mean dependent var	1075.538
Adjusted R-squared	0.499157	S.D. dependent var	191.3605
S.E. of regression	135.4263	Akaike info criterion	12.72854
Sum squared resid	1100417.	Schwarz criterion	12.89580
Log likelihood	-408.6774	F-statistic	16.94616
Durbin-Watson stat	1.976378	Prob(F-statistic)	0.000000

Answer each of the following questions for this regression run.

a. Evaluate this result with respect to its economic meaning, overall fit, and the signs and significance of the individual coefficients.

b. What econometric problems (out of omitted variables, irrelevant variables, or multicollinearity) does this regression have? Why? If you need feedback on your answer, see hint 8 in the material on this chapter in Appendix A.

c. Which of the following statements comes closest to your recommendation for further action to be taken in the estimation of this equation?

    i. No further specification changes are advisable (go to page 303).

    ii. I would like to drop PREP from the equation (go to run 8.1).

    iii. I would like to add ESL to the equation (go to run 8.7).

    iv. I would like to add GEND to the equation (go to run 8.9).

    v. I would like to replace APMATH and APENG with AP, a linear combination of the two variables (go to run 8.17).

If you need feedback on your answer, see hint 12 in the material on this chapter in Appendix A.

Regression Run 8.5

Dependent Variable: SAT
Method: Least Squares
Date: 02/29/00   Time: 15:08
Sample: 1 65
Included observations: 65

Variable	Coefficient	Std. Error	t-Statistic	Prob.
C	570.8148	117.7382	4.848172	0.0000
GPA	128.2798	40.48924	3.168244	0.0024
APMATH	106.2137	42.71559	2.486533	0.0157
APENG	67.42362	48.92704	1.378044	0.1733
RACE	-60.33471	39.47330	-1.528494	0.1316

R-squared	0.542168	Mean dependent var	1075.538
Adjusted R-squared	0.511646	S.D. dependent var	191.3605
S.E. of regression	133.7271	Akaike info criterion	12.70328
Sum squared resid	1072977.	Schwarz criterion	12.87054
Log likelihood	-407.8567	F-statistic	17.76314
Durbin-Watson stat	2.033014	Prob(F-statistic)	0.000000

Answer each of the following questions for this regression run.

a. Evaluate this result with respect to its economic meaning, overall fit, and the signs and significance of the individual coefficients.

b. What econometric problems (out of omitted variables, irrelevant variables, or multicollinearity) does this regression have? Why? If you need feedback on your answer, see hint 3 in the material on this chapter in Appendix A.

c. Which of the following statements comes closest to your recommendation for further action to be taken in the estimation of this equation?

   i. No further specification changes are advisable (go to page 303).
   ii. I would like to drop RACE from the equation (go to run 8.1).
   iii. I would like to add ESL to the equation (go to run 8.8).
   iv. I would like to add GEND to the equation (go to run 8.10).
   v. I would like to add PREP to the equation (go to run 8.11).

If you need feedback on your answer, see hint 14 in the material on this chapter in Appendix A.

Regression Run 8.6

Dependent Variable: SAT				
Method: Least Squares				
Date: 02/29/00 Time: 15:08				
Sample: 1 65				
Included observations: 65				

Variable	Coefficient	Std. Error	t-Statistic	Prob.
C	508.8237	110.0355	4.624179	0.0000
GPA	129.0595	37.41416	3.449484	0.0010
APMATH	81.97538	40.00950	2.048898	0.0449
APENG	89.84960	44.54376	2.017109	0.0482
ESL	-33.64469	34.94751	-0.962721	0.3396
GEND	108.8598	31.02552	3.508717	0.0009

R-squared	0.616191	Mean dependent var	1075.538
Adjusted R-squared	0.583665	S.D. dependent var	191.3605
S.E. of regression	123.4735	Akaike info criterion	12.55770
Sum squared resid	899496.2	Schwarz criterion	12.75841
Log likelihood	-402.1251	F-statistic	18.94449
Durbin-Watson stat	2.142956	Prob(F-statistic)	0.000000

Answer each of the following questions for this regression run.

a. Evaluate this result with respect to its economic meaning, overall fit, and the signs and significance of the individual coefficients.

b. What econometric problems (out of omitted variables, irrelevant variables, or multicollinearity) does this regression have? Why? If you need feedback on your answer, see hint 7 in the material on this chapter in Appendix A.

c. Which of the following statements comes closest to your recommendation for further action to be taken in the estimation of this equation?

   i. No further specification changes are advisable (go to page 303).
   ii. I would like to drop ESL from the equation (go to run 8.3).
   iii. I would like to add PREP to the equation (go to run 8.12).
   iv. I would like to add RACE to the equation (go to run 8.13).

If you need feedback on your answer, see hint 4 in the material on this chapter in Appendix A.

Regression Run 8.7

Dependent Variable: SAT
Method: Least Squares
Date: 02/29/00   Time: 15:09
Sample: 1 65
Included observations: 65

Variable	Coefficient	Std. Error	t-Statistic	Prob.
C	591.2047	121.8609	4.851472	0.0000
GPA	129.2439	40.86539	3.162673	0.0025
APMATH	95.35163	43.81128	2.176417	0.0335
APENG	80.21916	48.58978	1.650947	0.1041
ESL	-47.03944	37.94402	-1.239706	0.2200
PREP	-34.82031	38.71083	-0.899498	0.3720

R-squared	0.542380	Mean dependent var	1075.538
Adjusted R-squared	0.503599	S.D. dependent var	191.3605
S.E. of regression	134.8244	Akaike info criterion	12.73359
Sum squared resid	1072480.	Schwarz criterion	12.93430
Log likelihood	-407.8417	F-statistic	13.98561
Durbin-Watson stat	2.008613	Prob(F-statistic)	0.000000

Answer each of the following questions for this regression run.

a. Evaluate this result with respect to its economic meaning, overall fit, and the signs and significance of the individual coefficients.

b. What econometric problems (out of omitted variables, irrelevant variables, or multicollinearity) does this regression have? Why? If you need feedback on your answer, see hint 8 in the material on this chapter in Appendix A.

c. Which of the following statements comes closest to your recommendation for further action to be taken in the estimation of this equation?

> i. No further specification changes are advisable (go to page 303).
> ii. I would like to drop ESL from the equation (go to run 8.4).
> iii. I would like to drop PREP from the equation (go to run 8.2).
> iv. I would like to add GEND to the equation (go to run 8.12).
> v. I would like to add RACE to the equation (go to run 8.14).

If you need feedback on your answer, see hint 18 in the material on this chapter in Appendix A.

Regression Run 8.8

Dependent Variable: SAT
Method: Least Squares
Date: 02/29/00   Time: 15:10
Sample: 1 65
Included observations: 65

Variable	Coefficient	Std. Error	t-Statistic	Prob.
C	570.6367	118.8985	4.799359	0.0000
GPA	128.3251	40.86223	3.140434	0.0026
APMATH	106.0310	43.55940	2.434170	0.0180
APENG	67.23015	49.81328	1.349643	0.1823
ESL	1.885689	66.79448	0.028231	0.9776
RACE	-61.96231	70.05962	-0.884423	0.3801

R-squared	0.542175	Mean dependent var	1075.538
Adjusted R-squared	0.503376	S.D. dependent var	191.3605
S.E. of regression	134.8548	Akaike info criterion	12.73404
Sum squared resid	1072962.	Schwarz criterion	12.93475
Log likelihood	-407.8563	F-statistic	13.97402
Durbin-Watson stat	2.032924	Prob(F-statistic)	0.000000

Answer each of the following questions for this regression run.

a. Evaluate this result with respect to its economic meaning, overall fit, and the signs and significance of the individual coefficients.

b. What econometric problems (out of omitted variables, irrelevant variables, or multicollinearity) does this regression have? Why? If you need feedback on your answer, see hint 9 in the material on this chapter in Appendix A.

c. Which of the following statements comes closest to your recommendation for further action to be taken in the estimation of this equation?

    i. No further specification changes are advisable (go to page 303).
    ii. I would like to drop ESL from the equation (go to run 8.5).
    iii. I would like to drop RACE from the equation (go to run 8.2).
    iv. I would like to add GEND to the equation (go to run 8.13).
    v. I would like to add PREP to the equation (go to run 8.14).

If you need feedback on your answer, see hint 15 in the material on this chapter in Appendix A.

Regression Run 8.9

Dependent Variable: SAT
Method: Least Squares
Date: 02/29/00   Time: 15:11
Sample: 1 65
Included observations: 65

Variable	Coefficient	Std. Error	t-Statistic	Prob.
C	513.9945	111.6115	4.605210	0.0000
GPA	132.4152	37.38088	3.542326	0.0008
APMATH	59.37168	36.54919	1.624432	0.1096
APENG	96.69438	44.47540	2.174109	0.0337
GEND	111.3943	30.89564	3.605501	0.0006
PREP	-31.31762	35.50451	-0.882074	0.3813

R-squared	0.615236	Mean dependent var	1075.538
Adjusted R-squared	0.582629	S.D. dependent var	191.3605
S.E. of regression	123.6270	Akaike info criterion	12.56018
Sum squared resid	901734.9	Schwarz criterion	12.76089
Log likelihood	-402.2059	F-statistic	18.86816
Durbin-Watson stat	2.065021	Prob(F-statistic)	0.000000

Answer each of the following questions for this regression run.

    a. Evaluate this result with respect to its economic meaning, overall fit, and the signs and significance of the individual coefficients.

    b. What econometric problems (out of omitted variables, irrelevant variables, or multicollinearity) does this regression have? Why? If you need feedback on your answer, see hint 8 in the material on this chapter in Appendix A.

    c. Which of the following statements comes closest to your recommendation for further action to be taken in the estimation of this equation?

        i. No further specification changes are advisable (go to page 303).
        ii. I would like to drop PREP from the equation (go to run 8.3).
        iii. I would like to add ESL to the equation (go to run 8.12).
        iv. I would like to add RACE to the equation (go to run 8.15).

If you need feedback on your answer, see hint 17 in the material on this chapter in Appendix A.

Regression Run 8.10

Dependent Variable: SAT
Method: Least Squares
Date: 02/29/00   Time: 15:11
Sample: 1 65
Included observations: 65

Variable	Coefficient	Std. Error	t-Statistic	Prob.
C	514.5822	109.0157	4.720259	0.0000
GPA	128.6381	37.08886	3.468376	0.0010
APMATH	88.26401	39.45591	2.237029	0.0291
APENG	81.07941	44.98391	1.802409	0.0766
GEND	108.5953	30.70716	3.536482	0.0008
RACE	-49.83756	36.27973	-1.373703	0.1747

R-squared	0.622244	Mean dependent var	1075.538
Adjusted R-squared	0.590231	S.D. dependent var	191.3605
S.E. of regression	122.4960	Akaike info criterion	12.54180
Sum squared resid	885310.6	Schwarz criterion	12.74251
Log likelihood	-401.6085	F-statistic	19.43712
Durbin-Watson stat	2.148211	Prob(F-statistic)	0.000000

Answer each of the following questions for this regression run.

a. Evaluate this result with respect to its economic meaning, overall fit, and the signs and significance of the individual coefficients.

b. What econometric problems (out of omitted variables, irrelevant variables, or multicollinearity) does this regression have? Why? If you need feedback on your answer, see hint 10 in the material on this chapter in Appendix A.

c. Which of the following statements comes closest to your recommendation for further action to be taken in the estimation of this equation?

  i. No further specification changes are advisable (go to page 303).
  ii. I would like to drop RACE from the equation (go to run 8.3).
  iii. I would like to add ESL to the equation (go to run 8.13).
  iv. I would like to add PREP to the equation (go to run 8.15).

If you need feedback on your answer, see hint 4 in the material on this chapter in Appendix A.

Regression Run 8.11

Dependent Variable: SAT				
Method: Least Squares				
Date: 02/29/00 Time: 15:12				
Sample: 1 65				
Included observations: 65				

Variable	Coefficient	Std. Error	t-Statistic	Prob.
C	602.4718	121.0769	4.975943	0.0000
GPA	129.0898	40.43172	3.192785	0.0023
APMATH	100.8919	42.92558	2.350391	0.0221
APENG	69.65070	48.89190	1.424586	0.1595
PREP	-42.14969	38.62038	-1.091385	0.2795
RACE	-65.60984	39.70586	-1.652397	0.1038

R-squared	0.551228	Mean dependent var	1075.538
Adjusted R-squared	0.513197	S.D. dependent var	191.3605
S.E. of regression	133.5147	Akaike info criterion	12.71407
Sum squared resid	1051744.	Schwarz criterion	12.91478
Log likelihood	-407.2071	F-statistic	14.49400
Durbin-Watson stat	2.020544	Prob(F-statistic)	0.000000

Answer each of the following questions for this regression run.

a. Evaluate this result with respect to its economic meaning, overall fit, and the signs and significance of the individual coefficients.

b. What econometric problems (out of omitted variables, irrelevant variables, or multicollinearity) does this regression have? Why? If you need feedback on your answer, see hint 8 in the material on this chapter in Appendix A.

c. Which of the following statements comes closest to your recommendation for further action to be taken in the estimation of this equation?

    i. No further specification changes are advisable (go to page 303).

    ii. I would like to drop PREP from the equation (go to run 8.5).

    iii. I would like to drop RACE from the equation (go to run 8.4).

    iv. I would like to add GEND to the equation (go to run 8.15).

    v. I would like to replace APMATH and APENG with AP, a linear combination of the two variables (go to run 8.18).

If you need feedback on your answer, see hint 18 in the material on this chapter in Appendix A.

Regression Run 8.12

Dependent Variable: SAT
Method: Least Squares
Date: 02/29/00 Time: 15:14
Sample: 1 65
Included observations: 65

Variable	Coefficient	Std. Error	t-Statistic	Prob.
C	531.4692	113.1041	4.698939	0.0000
GPA	129.8782	37.48974	3.464368	0.0010
APMATH	76.41832	40.55854	1.884149	0.0646
APENG	92.42253	44.71331	2.067002	0.0432
ESL	-34.01275	35.01006	-0.971513	0.3353
GEND	108.1642	31.08865	3.479219	0.0010
PREP	-31.72391	35.52388	-0.893030	0.3755

R-squared	0.621397	Mean dependent var	1075.538
Adjusted R-squared	0.582231	S.D. dependent var	191.3605
S.E. of regression	123.6859	Akaike info criterion	12.57481
Sum squared resid	887295.9	Schwarz criterion	12.80897
Log likelihood	-401.6813	F-statistic	15.86581
Durbin-Watson stat	2.106229	Prob(F-statistic)	0.000000

Answer each of the following questions for this regression run.

a. Evaluate this result with respect to its economic meaning, overall fit, and the signs and significance of the individual coefficients.

b. What econometric problems (out of omitted variables, irrelevant variables, or multicollinearity) does this regression have? Why? If you need feedback on your answer, see hint 8 in the material on this chapter in Appendix A.

c. Which of the following statements comes closest to your recommendation for further action to be taken in the estimation of this equation?

    i. No further specification changes are advisable (go to page 303).
    ii. I would like to drop ESL from the equation (go to run 8.9).
    iii. I would like to drop PREP from the equation (go to run 8.6).
    iv. I would like to add RACE to the equation (go to run 8.16).

If you need feedback on your answer, see hint 17 in the material on this chapter in Appendix A.

Regression Run 8.13

Dependent Variable: SAT
Method: Least Squares
Date: 02/29/00   Time: 15:14
Sample: 1 65
Included observations: 65

Variable	Coefficient	Std. Error	t-Statistic	Prob.
C	512.6796	110.0966	4.656635	0.0000
GPA	129.0460	37.41213	3.449311	0.0011
APMATH	86.52973	40.26408	2.149055	0.0358
APENG	79.42187	45.73811	1.736449	0.0878
ESL	16.88299	61.30223	0.275406	0.7840
GEND	109.1893	31.02557	3.519333	0.0008
RACE	-64.35243	64.14694	-1.003204	0.3199

R-squared	0.622738	Mean dependent var	1075.538
Adjusted R-squared	0.583711	S.D. dependent var	191.3605
S.E. of regression	123.4668	Akaike info criterion	12.57126
Sum squared resid	884154.4	Schwarz criterion	12.80543
Log likelihood	-401.5660	F-statistic	15.95653
Durbin-Watson stat	2.143234	Prob(F-statistic)	0.000000

Answer each of the following questions for this regression run.

a. Evaluate this result with respect to its economic meaning, overall fit, and the signs and significance of the individual coefficients.

b. What econometric problems (out of omitted variables, irrelevant variables, or multicollinearity) does this regression have? Why? If you need feedback on your answer, see hint 9 in the material on this chapter in Appendix A.

c. Which of the following statements comes closest to your recommendation for further action to be taken in the estimation of this equation?

i. No further specification changes are advisable (go to page 303).
ii. I would like to drop ESL from the equation (go to run 8.10).
iii. I would like to drop RACE from the equation (go to run 8.6).
iv. I would like to add PREP to the equation (go to run 8.16).

If you need feedback on your answer, see hint 15 in the material on this chapter in Appendix A.

Regression Run 8.14

```
Dependent Variable: SAT
Method: Least Squares
Date: 02/29/00   Time: 15:15
Sample: 1 65
Included observations: 65
```

Variable	Coefficient	Std. Error	t-Statistic	Prob.
C	602.1427	122.0822	4.932274	0.0000
GPA	129.4491	40.80133	3.172669	0.0024
APMATH	99.37976	43.89816	2.263871	0.0273
APENG	68.29405	49.73286	1.373218	0.1750
ESL	13.89708	67.55991	0.205700	0.8377
PREP	-43.45964	39.45502	-1.101498	0.2752
RACE	-77.76882	71.39042	-1.089345	0.2805

R-squared	0.551556	Mean dependent var	1075.538
Adjusted R-squared	0.505165	S.D. dependent var	191.3605
S.E. of regression	134.6116	Akaike info criterion	12.74411
Sum squared resid	1050977.	Schwarz criterion	12.97827
Log likelihood	-407.1834	F-statistic	11.88933
Durbin-Watson stat	2.020634	Prob(F-statistic)	0.000000

Answer each of the following questions for this regression run.

a. Evaluate this result with respect to its economic meaning, overall fit, and the signs and significance of the individual coefficients.

b. What econometric problems (out of omitted variables, irrelevant variables, or multicollinearity) does this regression have? Why? If you need feedback on your answer, see hint 9 in the material on this chapter in Appendix A.

c. Which of the following statements comes closest to your recommendation for further action to be taken in the estimation of this equation?

    i. No further specification changes are advisable (go to page 303).

    ii. I would like to drop ESL from the equation (go to run 8.11).

    iii. I would like to drop PREP from the equation (go to run 8.8).

    iv. I would like to add GEND to the equation (go to run 8.16).

    v. I would like to replace APMATH and APENG with AP, a linear combination of the two variables (go to run 8.19).

If you need feedback on your answer, see hint 15 in the material on this chapter in Appendix A.

Regression Run 8.15

Dependent Variable: SAT
Method: Least Squares
Date: 02/29/00   Time: 15:15
Sample: 1 65
Included observations: 65

Variable	Coefficient	Std. Error	t-Statistic	Prob.
C	543.6309	112.2128	4.844641	0.0000
GPA	129.3628	37.04936	3.491632	0.0009
APMATH	83.66463	39.64091	2.110563	0.0391
APENG	82.94048	44.96213	1.844674	0.0702
GEND	107.4700	30.68735	3.502094	0.0009
PREP	-37.90098	35.41026	-1.070339	0.2889
RACE	-54.68974	36.51752	-1.497630	0.1397

R-squared	0.629561	Mean dependent var	1075.538
Adjusted R-squared	0.591240	S.D. dependent var	191.3605
S.E. of regression	122.3451	Akaike info criterion	12.55301
Sum squared resid	868162.5	Schwarz criterion	12.78717
Log likelihood	-400.9728	F-statistic	16.42852
Durbin-Watson stat	2.114836	Prob(F-statistic)	0.000000

Answer each of the following questions for this regression run.

a. Evaluate this result with respect to its economic meaning, overall fit, and the signs and significance of the individual coefficients.

b. What econometric problems (out of omitted variables, irrelevant variables, or multicollinearity) does this regression have? Why? If you need feedback on your answer, see hint 8 in the material on this chapter in Appendix A.

c. Which of the following statements comes closest to your recommendation for further action to be taken in the estimation of this equation?

   i. No further specification changes are advisable (go to page 303).
   ii. I would like to drop PREP from the equation (go to run 8.10).
   iii. I would like to drop RACE from the equation (go to run 8.9).
   iv. I would like to add ESL to the equation (go to run 8.16).

If you need feedback on your answer, see hint 17 in the material on this chapter in Appendix A.

Regression Run 8.16

Dependent Variable: SAT
Method: Least Squares
Date: 02/29/00   Time: 15:16
Sample: 1 65
Included observations: 65

Variable	Coefficient	Std. Error	t-Statistic	Prob.
C	542.4723	113.0203	4.799777	0.0000
GPA	130.0882	37.34094	3.483794	0.0010
APMATH	80.47642	40.53608	1.985303	0.0519
APENG	80.32262	45.64401	1.759762	0.0838
ESL	27.96510	61.95989	0.451342	0.6535
GEND	108.3766	30.96543	3.499924	0.0009
PREP	-40.50116	36.11828	-1.121348	0.2668
RACE	-79.06514	65.33603	-1.210131	0.2312

R-squared	0.630880	Mean dependent var	1075.538
Adjusted R-squared	0.585550	S.D. dependent var	191.3605
S.E. of regression	123.1937	Akaike info criterion	12.58021
Sum squared resid	865070.9	Schwarz criterion	12.84783
Log likelihood	-400.8568	F-statistic	13.91736
Durbin-Watson stat	2.106524	Prob(F-statistic)	0.000000

Answer each of the following questions for this regression run.

a. Evaluate this result with respect to its economic meaning, overall fit, and the signs and significance of the individual coefficients.

b. What econometric problems (out of omitted variables, irrelevant variables, or multicollinearity) does this regression have? Why? If you need feedback on your answer, see hint 9 in the material on this chapter in Appendix A.

c. Which of the following statements comes closest to your recommendation for further action to be taken in the estimation of this equation?

   i. No further specification changes are advisable (go to page 303).
   ii. I would like to drop ESL from the equation (go to run 8.15).
   iii. I would like to drop PREP from the equation (go to run 8.13).
   iv. I would like to drop RACE from the equation (go to run 8.12).

If you need feedback on your answer, see hint 15 in the material on this chapter in Appendix A.

Regression Run 8.17

```
Dependent Variable: SAT
Method: Least Squares
Date: 02/29/00   Time: 15:17
Sample: 1 65
Included observations: 65
```

Variable	Coefficient	Std. Error	t-Statistic	Prob.
C	475.7963	104.7275	4.543185	0.0000
GPA	163.4716	34.41783	4.749619	0.0000
AP	107.7460	45.02942	2.392790	0.0198
PREP	-30.92277	38.84976	-0.795958	0.4291

R-squared	0.516299	Mean dependent var	1075.538
Adjusted R-squared	0.492511	S.D. dependent var	191.3605
S.E. of regression	136.3219	Akaike info criterion	12.72748
Sum squared resid	1133604.	Schwarz criterion	12.86129
Log likelihood	-409.6431	F-statistic	21.70368
Durbin-Watson stat	1.912398	Prob(F-statistic)	0.000000

Answer each of the following questions for this regression run.

a. Evaluate this result with respect to its economic meaning, overall fit, and the signs and significance of the individual coefficients.

b. What econometric problems (out of omitted variables, irrelevant variables, or multicollinearity) does this regression have? Why? If you need feedback on your answer, see hint 11 in the material on this chapter in Appendix A.

c. Which of the following statements comes closest to your recommendation for further action to be taken in the estimation of this equation?

   i. No further specification changes are advisable (go to page 303).
   ii. I would like to drop PREP from the equation (go to run 8.20).
   iii. I would like to add RACE to the equation (go to run 8.18).
   iv. I would like to replace the AP combination variable with APMATH and APENG (go to run 8.4).

If you need feedback on your answer, see hint 16 in the material on this chapter in Appendix A.

Regression Run 8.18

```
Dependent Variable: SAT
Method: Least Squares
Date: 02/29/00   Time: 15:17
Sample: 1 65
Included observations: 65
```

Variable	Coefficient	Std. Error	t-Statistic	Prob.
C	522.4920	107.1073	4.878210	0.0000
GPA	154.0768	34.42039	4.476323	0.0000
AP	125.9048	45.75812	2.751529	0.0078
PREP	-41.06153	38.80679	-1.058102	0.2943
RACE	-61.63421	37.41938	-1.647120	0.1048

R-squared	0.537225	Mean dependent var	1075.538
Adjusted R-squared	0.506373	S.D. dependent var	191.3605
S.E. of regression	134.4472	Akaike info criterion	12.71402
Sum squared resid	1084563.	Schwarz criterion	12.88128
Log likelihood	-408.2058	F-statistic	17.41313
Durbin-Watson stat	1.887634	Prob(F-statistic)	0.000000

Answer each of the following questions for this regression run.

a. Evaluate this result with respect to its economic meaning, overall fit, and the signs and significance of the individual coefficients.

b. What econometric problems (out of omitted variables, irrelevant variables, or multicollinearity) does this regression have? Why? If you need feedback on your answer, see hint 11 in the material on this chapter in Appendix A.

c. Which of the following statements comes closest to your recommendation for further action to be taken in the estimation of this equation?

   i. No further specification changes are advisable (go to page 303).
   ii. I would like to drop RACE from the equation (go to run 8.17).
   iii. I would like to add ESL to the equation (go to run 8.19).
   iv. I would like to replace the AP combination variable with APMATH and APENG (go to run 8.11).

If you need feedback on your answer, see hint 16 in the material on this chapter in Appendix A.

Regression Run 8.19

Dependent Variable: SAT				
Method: Least Squares				
Date: 02/29/00 Time: 15:18				
Sample: 1 65				
Included observations: 65				
Variable	Coefficient	Std. Error	t-Statistic	Prob.
C	524.8762	108.0514	4.857655	0.0000
GPA	153.7341	34.67841	4.433136	0.0000
AP	122.3201	47.01130	2.601930	0.0117
ESL	26.00898	67.33954	0.386236	0.7007
PREP	-43.55594	39.61488	-1.099484	0.2760
RACE	-84.43699	70.04203	-1.205519	0.2328
R-squared	0.538392	Mean dependent var		1075.538
Adjusted R-squared	0.499272	S.D. dependent var		191.3605
S.E. of regression	135.4107	Akaike info criterion		12.74227
Sum squared resid	1081828.	Schwarz criterion		12.94298
Log likelihood	-408.1237	F-statistic		13.76280
Durbin-Watson stat	1.894863	Prob(F-statistic)		0.000000

Answer each of the following questions for this regression run.

a. Evaluate this result with respect to its economic meaning, overall fit, and the signs and significance of the individual coefficients.

b. What econometric problems (out of omitted variables, irrelevant variables, or multicollinearity) does this regression have? Why? If you need feedback on your answer, see hint 11 in the material on this chapter in Appendix A.

c. Which of the following statements comes closest to your recommendation for further action to be taken in the estimation of this equation?

   i. No further specification changes are advisable (go to page 303).
   ii. I would like to drop ESL from the equation (go to run 8.18).
   iii. I would like to replace the AP combination variable with APMATH and APENG (go to run 8.14).

If you need feedback on your answer, see hint 16 in the material on this chapter in Appendix A.

Regression Run 8.20

Dependent Variable: SAT
Method: Least Squares
Date: 02/29/00   Time: 15:19
Sample: 1 65
Included observations: 65

Variable	Coefficient	Std. Error	t-Statistic	Prob.
C	457.2010	101.7863	4.491773	0.0000
GPA	161.2106	34.19889	4.713912	0.0000
AP	112.7129	44.46296	2.534985	0.0138

R-squared	0.511276	Mean dependent var	1075.538
Adjusted R-squared	0.495510	S.D. dependent var	191.3605
S.E. of regression	135.9185	Akaike info criterion	12.70704
Sum squared resid	1145378.	Schwarz criterion	12.80740
Log likelihood	-409.9789	F-statistic	32.43043
Durbin-Watson stat	1.917047	Prob(F-statistic)	0.000000

Answer each of the following questions for this regression run.

   a. Evaluate this result with respect to its economic meaning, overall fit, and the signs and significance of the individual coefficients.
   b. What econometric problems (out of omitted variables, irrelevant variables, or multicollinearity) does this regression have? Why? If you need feedback on your answer, see hint 13 in the material on this chapter in Appendix A.
   c. Which of the following statements comes closest to your recommendation for further action to be taken in the estimation of this equation?

   i. No further specification changes are advisable (go to page 303).
   ii. I would like to add PREP to the equation (go to run 8.17).
   iii. I would like to replace the AP combination variable with APMATH and APENG (go to run 8.1).

If you need feedback on your answer, see hint 13 in the material on this chapter in Appendix A.

Evaluating the Results from Your Interactive Exercise

Congratulations! If you've reached this section, you must have found a specification that met your theoretical and econometric goals. Which one did you pick? Our experience is that most beginning econometricians end up with either regression run 8.3, 8.6, or 8.10, but only after looking at three or more regression results (or a hint or two) before settling on that choice.

In contrast, we've found that most experienced econometricians gravitate to regression run 8.6, usually after inspecting, at most, one other specification. What lessons can we learn from this difference?

1. *Learn that a variable isn't irrelevant simply because its t-score is low.* In our opinion, ESL belongs in the equation for strong theoretical reasons, and a slightly insignificant *t*-score in the expected direction isn't enough evidence to get us to rethink the underlying theory.

2. *Learn to spot redundant (multicollinear) variables.* ESL and RACE wouldn't normally be redundant, but in this high school, with its particular ethnic diversity, they are. Once one is included in the equation, the other shouldn't even be considered.

3. *Learn to spot false variables.* At first glance, PREP is a tempting variable to include because prep courses almost surely improve the SAT scores of the students who choose to take them. The problem is that a student's decision to take a prep course isn't independent of his or her previous SAT scores (or expected scores). We trust the judgment of students who feel a need for a prep course, and we think that all the course will do is bring them up to the level of their peers who didn't feel they needed a course. As a result, we wouldn't expect a significant effect in either direction.

If you enjoyed and learned from this interactive regression learning exercise, you'll be interested to know that there is another in Chapter 11. Good luck!

9 Serial Correlation

- 9.1 Pure versus Impure Serial Correlation
- 9.2 The Consequences of Serial Correlation
- 9.3 The Durbin–Watson *d* Test
- 9.4 Remedies for Serial Correlation
- 9.5 Summary and Exercises

In the next two chapters we'll investigate the final component of the specification of a regression equation—choosing the correct form of the stochastic error term. Our first topic, serial correlation, is the violation of Classical Assumption IV that different observations of the error term are uncorrelated with each other. Serial correlation, also called autocorrelation, can exist in any research study in which the order of the observations has some meaning. It therefore occurs most frequently in time-series data sets. In essence, serial correlation implies that the value of the error term from one time period depends in some systematic way on the value of the error term in other time periods. Since time-series data are used in many applications of econometrics, it's important to understand serial correlation and its consequences for OLS estimators.

The approach of this chapter to the problem of serial correlation will be similar to that used in the previous chapter. We'll attempt to answer the same four questions:

1. What is the nature of the problem?
2. What are the consequences of the problem?
3. How is the problem diagnosed?
4. What remedies for the problem are available?

9.1 Pure versus Impure Serial Correlation

Pure Serial Correlation

Pure serial correlation occurs when Classical Assumption IV, which assumes uncorrelated observations of the error term, is violated in a *correctly specified* equation. Assumption IV implies that:

$$E(r_{\epsilon_i \epsilon_j}) = 0 \qquad (i \neq j)$$

If the expected value of the simple correlation coefficient between any two observations of the error term is not equal to zero, then the error term is said to be serially correlated. When econometricians use the term serial correlation without any modifier, they are referring to pure serial correlation.

The most commonly assumed kind of serial correlation is **first-order serial correlation**, in which the current value of the error term is a function of the previous value of the error term:

$$\epsilon_t = \rho\epsilon_{t-1} + u_t \qquad (9.1)$$

where: ϵ = the error term of the equation in question
ρ = the first-order autocorrelation coefficient
u = a classical (not serially correlated) error term

The functional form in Equation 9.1 is called a first-order Markov scheme. The new symbol, ρ (rho, pronounced "row"), called the **first-order auto-correlation coefficient**, measures the functional relationship between the value of an observation of the error term and the value of the previous observation of the error term.

The magnitude of ρ indicates the strength of the serial correlation in an equation. If ρ is zero, then there is no serial correlation (because ϵ would equal u, a classical error term). As ρ approaches one in absolute value, the value of the previous observation of the error term becomes more important in determining the current value of ϵ_t, and a high degree of serial correlation exists. For ρ to be greater than one in absolute value is unreasonable because it implies that the error term has a tendency to continually increase in absolute value over time ("explode"). As a result of this, we can state that:

$$-1 < \rho < +1 \qquad (9.2)$$

The sign of ρ indicates the nature of the serial correlation in an equation. A positive value for ρ implies that the error term tends to have the same sign from one time period to the next; this is called **positive serial correlation**. Such a tendency means that if ϵ_t happens by chance to take on a large value in one time period, subsequent observations would tend to retain a portion of this original large value and would have the same sign as the original. For example, in time-series models, a large external shock to an economy (like an earthquake) in one period may linger on for several time periods. The error term will tend to be positive for a number of observations, then negative for several more, and then back again.

Figure 9.1 shows two different examples of positive serial correlation. The error term observations plotted in Figure 9.1 are arranged in chronological order, with the first observation being the first period for which data are available, the second being the second, and so on. To see the difference between error terms with and without positive serial correlation, compare the patterns in Figure 9.1 with the depiction of no serial correlation ($\rho = 0$) in Figure 9.2.

A negative value of ρ implies that the error term has a tendency to switch signs from negative to positive and back again in consecutive observations; this is called **negative serial correlation**. It implies that there is some sort of cycle (like a pendulum) behind the drawing of stochastic disturbances. Figure 9.3 shows two different examples of negative serial correlation. For instance, negative serial correlation might exist in the error term of an equation that is in first differences because *changes* in a variable often follow a cyclical pattern. In most time-series applications, however, negative pure serial correlation is much less likely than positive pure serial correlation. As a result, most econometricians analyzing pure serial correlation concern themselves primarily with positive serial correlation.

Serial correlation can take on many forms other than first-order serial correlation. For example, in a quarterly model, the current quarter's error term observation may be functionally related to the observation of the error term from the same quarter in the previous year. This is called seasonally based serial correlation:

$$\epsilon_t = \rho \epsilon_{t-4} + u_t$$

Similarly, it is possible that the error term in an equation might be a function of more than one previous observation of the error term:

$$\epsilon_t = \rho_1 \epsilon_{t-1} + \rho_2 \epsilon_{t-2} + u_t$$

Such a formulation is called *second-order* serial correlation.

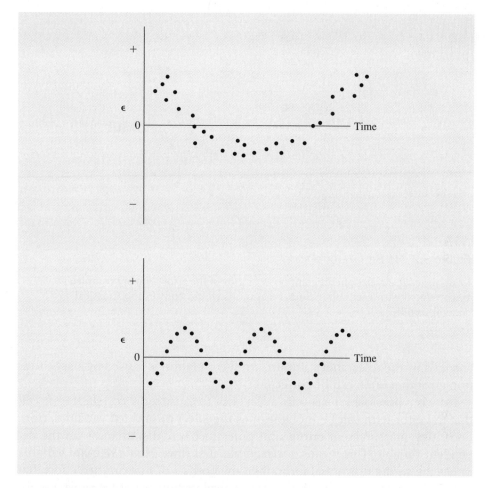

Figure 9.1 Positive Serial Correlation

With positive first-order serial correlation, the current observation of the error term tends to have the same sign as the previous observation of the error term. An example of positive serial correlation would be external shocks to an economy that take more than one time period to completely work through the system.

Impure Serial Correlation

By **impure serial correlation** we mean serial correlation that is caused by a specification error such as an omitted variable or an incorrect functional form. While pure serial correlation is caused by the underlying distribution of the error term of the true specification of an equation (which cannot be

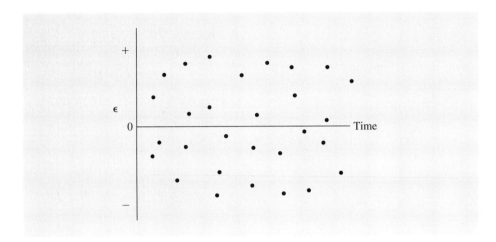

Figure 9.2 No Serial Correlation

With no serial correlation, different observations of the error term are completely uncorrelated with each other. Such error terms would conform to Classical Assumption IV.

changed by the researcher), impure serial correlation is caused by a specification error that often can be corrected.

How is it possible for a specification error to cause serial correlation? Recall that the error term can be thought of as the effect of omitted variables, non-linearities, measurement errors, and pure stochastic disturbances on the dependent variable. This means, for example, that if we omit a relevant variable or use the wrong functional form, then the portion of that omitted effect that cannot be represented by the included explanatory variables must be absorbed by the error term. The error term for an incorrectly specified equation thus includes a portion of the effect of any omitted variables and/or a portion of the effect of the difference between the proper functional form and the one chosen by the researcher. This new error term might be serially correlated even if the true one is not. If this is the case, the serial correlation has been caused by the researcher's choice of a specification and not by the pure error term associated with the correct specification.

As you'll see in Section 9.4, the proper remedy for serial correlation depends on whether the serial correlation is likely to be pure or impure. Not surprisingly, the best remedy for impure serial correlation is to attempt to find the omitted variable (or at least a good proxy) or the correct functional form for the equation. Both the bias and the impure serial correlation will disappear if the specification error is corrected. As a result, most econometricians

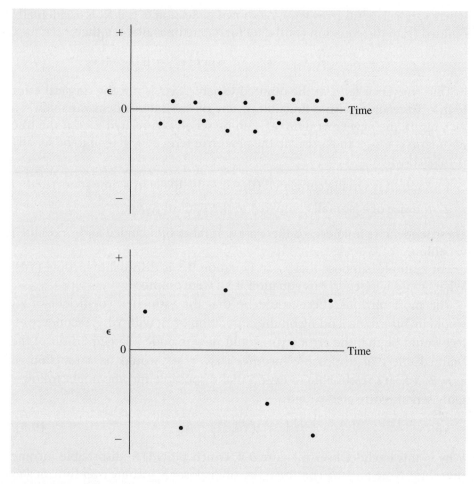

Figure 9.3 Negative Serial Correlation

With negative first-order serial correlation, the current observation of the error term tends to have the opposite sign from the previous observation of the error term. In most time-series applications, negative serial correlation is much less likely than positive serial correlation.

try to make sure they have the best specification possible before they spend too much time worrying about pure serial correlation.

To see how an omitted variable can cause the error term to be serially correlated, suppose that the true equation is:

$$Y_t = \beta_0 + \beta_1 X_{1t} + \beta_2 X_{2t} + \epsilon_t \qquad (9.3)$$

where ϵ_t is a classical error term. As shown in Section 6.1, if X_2 is accidentally omitted from the equation (or if data for X_2 are unavailable), then:

$$Y_t = \beta_0 + \beta_1 X_{1t} + \epsilon_t^* \qquad \text{where } \epsilon_t^* = \beta_2 X_{2t} + \epsilon_t \qquad (9.4)$$

Thus, the error term in the omitted variable case is not the classical error term ϵ. Instead, it's also a function of one of the independent variables, X_2. As a result, the new error term, ϵ^*, can be serially correlated even if the true error term ϵ, is not. In particular, the new error term ϵ^* will tend to be serially correlated when:

1. X_2 itself is serially correlated (this is quite likely in a time series) *and*

2. the size of ϵ is small compared to the size[1] of $\beta_2 \overline{X}_2$.

These tendencies hold even if there are a number of included and/or omitted variables.

For example, suppose that X_2 in Equation 9.3 is disposable income (Yd). What would happen to this equation if Yd were omitted?

The most obvious effect would be that the estimated coefficient of X_2 would be biased, depending on the correlation of X_2 with Yd. A secondary effect would be that the error term would now include a large portion of the omitted effect of disposable income. That is, ϵ_t^* would be a function of $\epsilon_t + \beta_2 Yd_t$. It's reasonable to expect that disposable income might follow a fairly serially correlated pattern:

$$Yd_t = f(Yd_{t-1}) + u_t \qquad (9.5)$$

Why is this likely? Observe Figure 9.4, which plots U.S. disposable income over time. Note that the continual rise of disposable income over time makes it act in a serially correlated or autoregressive manner. But if disposable income is serially correlated (and if its impact is not small relative to ϵ), then ϵ^* is likely to also be serially correlated, which can be expressed as:

$$\epsilon_t^* = \rho \epsilon_{t-1}^* + u_t \qquad (9.6)$$

---

1. If typical values of ϵ are significantly larger in absolute size than $\beta_2 \overline{X}_2$, then even a serially correlated omitted variable (X_2) will not change ϵ^* very much. In addition, recall that the omitted variable, X_2, will cause bias in the estimate of β_1, depending on the correlation between the two Xs. If $\hat{\beta}_1$ is biased because of the omission of X_2, then a portion of the $\beta_2 \overline{X}_2$ effect must have been absorbed by $\hat{\beta}_1$ and will not end up in the residuals. As a result, tests for serial correlation based on those residuals may give incorrect readings. Just as important, such residuals may leave misleading clues as to possible specification errors. This is only one of many reasons why an analysis of the residuals should not be the only procedure used to determine the nature of possible specification errors.

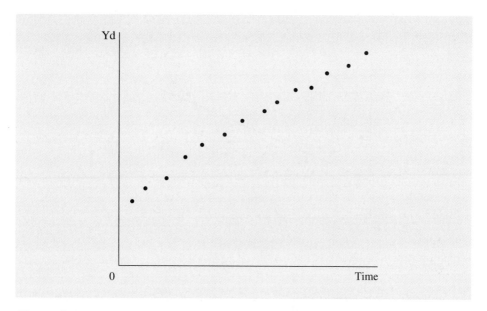

Figure 9.4 U.S. Disposable Income as a Function of Time

U.S. disposable income (and most other national aggregates) tends to increase steadily over time. As a result, such variables are serially correlated (or autocorrelated), and the omission of such a variable from an equation could potentially introduce impure serial correlation into the error term of that equation.

where ρ is the autocorrelation coefficient and u is a classical error term. This example has shown that it is indeed possible for an omitted variable to introduce "impure" serial correlation into an equation.

Another common kind of impure serial correlation is that caused by an incorrect functional form. Here, the choice of the wrong functional form can cause the error term to be serially correlated. Let's suppose that the true equation is polynomial in nature:

$$Y_t = \beta_0 + \beta X_{1t} + \beta_2 X_{1t}^2 + \epsilon_t \qquad (9.7)$$

but that instead a linear regression is run:

$$Y_t = \alpha_0 + \alpha_1 X_{1t} + \epsilon_t^* \qquad (9.8)$$

The new error term ϵ^* is now a function of the true error term ϵ and of the differences between the linear and the polynomial functional forms. As can be seen in Figure 9.5, these differences often follow fairly autoregressive patterns. That is, positive differences tend to be followed by positive differences, and negative differences tend to be followed by negative differences. As a result, using a linear functional form when a nonlinear one is appropriate will usually result in positive impure serial correlation.

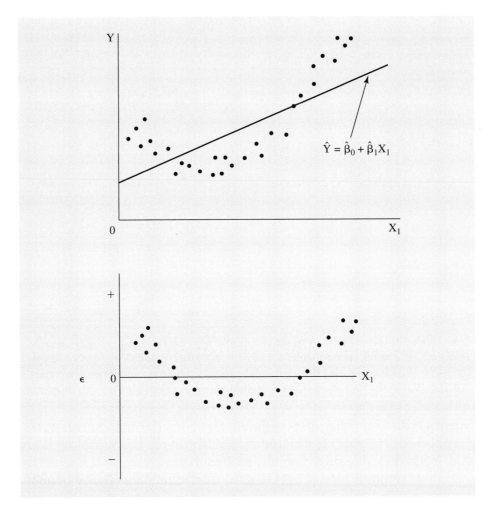

Figure 9.5 Incorrect Functional Form as a Source of Impure
Serial Correlation

The use of an incorrect functional form tends to group positive and negative residuals together, causing positive impure serial correlation.

9.2 The Consequences of Serial Correlation

The consequences of serial correlation are quite different in nature from the consequences of the problems discussed so far in this text. Omitted variables, irrelevant variables, and multicollinearity all have fairly recognizable external symptoms. Each problem changes the estimated coefficients and standard errors in a particular way, and an examination of these changes (and the underlying theory) often provides enough information for the problem to be detected. As we shall see, serial correlation is more likely to have internal symptoms; it affects the estimated equation in a way that is not easily observable from an examination of just the results themselves.

The existence of serial correlation in the error term of an equation violates Classical Assumption IV, and the estimation of the equation with OLS has at least three consequences:[2]

---

1. Pure serial correlation does not cause bias in the coefficient estimates.
2. Serial correlation causes OLS to no longer be the minimum variance estimator (of all the linear unbiased estimators).
3. Serial correlation causes the OLS estimates of the SE($\hat{\beta}$)s to be biased, leading to unreliable hypothesis testing.

---

1. *Pure serial correlation does not cause bias in the coefficient estimates.* If the error term is serially correlated, one of the assumptions of the Gauss–Markov Theorem is violated, but this violation does not cause the coefficient estimates to be biased. If the serial correlation is impure, however, bias may be introduced by the use of an incorrect specification.

   This lack of bias does not necessarily mean that the OLS estimates of the coefficients of a serially correlated equation will be close to the true coefficient values; the single estimate observed in practice can come from a wide range of possible values. In addition, the standard errors of these estimates will typically be increased by the serial correlation. This increase will raise the probability that a $\hat{\beta}$ will differ significantly from the true β value. What unbiased means in this case is that the distribution of the $\hat{\beta}$s is still centered around the true β.

2. *Serial correlation causes OLS to no longer be the minimum variance estimator (of all the linear unbiased estimators).* Although the violation of Classical Assumption IV causes no bias, it does affect the other main conclusion of the Gauss–Markov Theorem, that of minimum variance. In particular, we

---

2. If the regression includes a lagged dependent variable as an independent variable, then the problems worsen significantly. For more on this topic (called a dynamic model), see Chapter 12.

cannot prove that the distribution of the OLS $\hat{\beta}$s is minimum variance (among the linear unbiased estimators) when Assumption IV is violated.

The serially correlated error term causes the dependent variable to fluctuate in a way that the OLS estimation procedure sometimes attributes to the independent variables. Thus, OLS is more likely to misestimate the true β in the face of serial correlation. On balance, the $\hat{\beta}$s are still unbiased because overestimates are just as likely as underestimates, but these errors increase the variance of the distribution of the estimates, increasing the amount that any given estimate is likely to differ from the true β.

3. *Serial correlation causes the OLS estimates of the $SE(\hat{\beta})$s to be biased, leading to unreliable hypothesis testing.* With serial correlation, the OLS formula for the standard error produces biased estimates of the $SE(\hat{\beta})$s. Because the $SE(\hat{\beta})$ is a prime component in the *t*-statistic, these biased $SE(\hat{\beta})$s cause biased *t*-scores and unreliable hypothesis testing in general. In essence, serial correlation causes OLS to produce incorrect $SE(\hat{\beta})$s and *t*-scores! Not surprisingly, most econometricians therefore are very hesitant to put much faith in hypothesis tests that were conducted in the face of pure serial correlation.[3]

What sort of bias does serial correlation tend to cause? Typically, the bias in the estimate of $SE(\hat{\beta})$ is negative, meaning that OLS underestimates the size of the standard errors of the coefficients. This comes about because serial correlation usually results in a pattern of observations that allows a better fit than the actual (not serially correlated) observations would otherwise justify. This tendency of OLS to underestimate the $SE(\hat{\beta})$ means that OLS typically overestimates the *t*-scores of the estimated coefficients, since:

$$t = \frac{(\hat{\beta} - \beta_{H_0})}{SE(\hat{\beta})} \tag{9.9}$$

Thus the *t*-scores printed out by a typical software regression package in the face of serial correlation are likely to be too high.

What will happen to hypothesis testing if OLS underestimates the $SE(\hat{\beta})$s and therefore overestimates the *t*-scores? Well, the "too low" $SE(\hat{\beta})$

---

3. While our discussion here involves the *t*-test, the same conclusion of unreliability in the face of serial correlation applies to all other test statistics.

will cause a "too high" *t*-score for a particular coefficient, and this will make it more likely that we will reject a null hypothesis (for example H_0: $\beta \leq 0$) when it is in fact true. This increased chance of rejecting H_0 means that we're more likely to make a Type I Error, and we're more likely to make the mistake of keeping an irrelevant variable in an equation because its coefficient's *t*-score has been overestimated. In other words, hypothesis testing becomes both biased and unreliable when we have pure serial correlation.

(9.3) The Durbin–Watson *d* Test

How can we detect serial correlation? While the first step in detecting serial correlation often is observing a pattern in the residuals like that in Figure 9.1, the test for serial correlation that is most widely used is the Durbin–Watson *d* test.

The Durbin–Watson *d* Statistic

The **Durbin–Watson *d* statistic** is used to determine if there is first-order serial correlation in the error term of an equation by examining the *residuals* of a particular estimation of that equation.[4] It's important to use the Durbin–Watson *d* statistic only when the assumptions that underlie its derivation are met:

1. The regression model includes an intercept term.

2. The serial correlation is first-order in nature:

$$\epsilon_t = \rho \epsilon_{t-1} + u_t$$

where ρ is the autocorrelation coefficient and u is a classical (normally distributed) error term.

3. The regression model does not include a lagged dependent variable (discussed in Chapter 12) as an independent variable.[5]

---

4. J. Durbin and G. S. Watson, "Testing for Serial Correlation in Least-Squared Regression," *Biometrika*, 1951, pp. 159–177. The second most-used test, the Lagrange Multiplier test, is presented in Chapter 12.

5. In such a circumstance, the Durbin–Watson *d* is biased toward 2, but other tests can be used instead; see Section 12.2.

The equation for the *Durbin–Watson d statistic* for T observations is:

$$d = \sum_{2}^{T} (e_t - e_{t-1})^2 \Big/ \sum_{1}^{T} e_t^2 \qquad (9.10)$$

where the e_ts are the OLS residuals. Note that the numerator has one fewer observation than the denominator because an observation must be used to calculate e_{t-1}. The Durbin–Watson d statistic equals 0 if there is extreme positive serial correlation, 2 if there is no serial correlation, and 4 if there is extreme negative serial correlation. To see this, let's put appropriate residual values into Equation 9.10 for these three cases:

1. Extreme Positive Serial Correlation: d = 0
   In this case, $e_t = e_{t-1}$, so $(e_t - e_{t-1}) = 0$ and d = 0.
2. Extreme Negative Serial Correlation: d ≈ 4
   In this case, $e_t = -e_{t-1}$, and $(e_t - e_{t-1}) = (2e_t)$. Substituting into Equation 9.10, we obtain d = $\sum (2e_t)^2 / \sum (e_t)^2$ and d ≈ 4.
3. No Serial Correlation: d ≈ 2
   When there is no serial correlation, the mean of the distribution of d is equal to 2.[6] That is, if there is no serial correlation, d ≈ 2.

Using the Durbin–Watson *d* Test

The Durbin–Watson *d* test is unusual in two respects. First, econometricians almost never test the one-sided null hypothesis that there is negative serial correlation in the residuals because negative serial correlation, as mentioned previously, is quite difficult to explain theoretically in economic or business analysis. Its existence usually means that impure serial correlation has been caused by some error of specification.

Second, the Durbin–Watson test is sometimes inconclusive. Whereas previously explained decision rules always have had only "acceptance" regions and rejection regions, the Durbin–Watson test has a third possibility, called

---

6. To see this, multiply out the numerator of Equation 9.10, obtaining

$$d = \left[\sum_{2}^{T} e_t^2 - 2\sum_{2}^{T} (e_t e_{t-1}) + \sum_{2}^{T} e_{t-1}^2 \right] \Big/ \sum_{1}^{T} e_t^2 \approx \left[\sum_{2}^{T} e_t^2 + \sum_{2}^{T} e_{t-1}^2 \right] \Big/ \sum_{1}^{T} e_t^2 \approx 2 \qquad (9.11)$$

If there is no serial correlation, then e_t and e_{t-1} are not related, and, on average, $\sum (e_t e_{t-1}) = 0$.

the inconclusive region.[7] For reasons outlined in Section 9.4, we do not recommend the application of a remedy for serial correlation if the Durbin–Watson test is inconclusive.

With these exceptions, the use of the Durbin–Watson *d* test is quite similar to the use of the *t*-test. To test for positive serial correlation, the following steps are required:

1. Obtain the OLS residuals from the equation to be tested and calculate the d statistic by using Equation 9.10.

2. Determine the sample size and the number of explanatory variables and then consult Statistical Tables B-4, B-5, or B-6 in Appendix B to find the upper critical d value, d_U, and the lower critical d value, d_L, respectively. Instructions for the use of these tables are also in that appendix.

3. Given the null hypothesis of no positive serial correlation and a one-sided alternative hypothesis:

$$H_0: \rho \le 0 \quad \text{(no positive serial correlation)} \qquad (9.12)$$
$$H_A: \rho > 0 \quad \text{(positive serial correlation)}$$

the appropriate decision rule is:

$$
\begin{array}{ll}
\text{if } d < d_L & \text{Reject } H_0 \\
\text{if } d > d_U & \text{Do not reject } H_0 \\
\text{if } d_L \le d \le d_U & \text{Inconclusive}
\end{array}
$$

In rare circumstances, perhaps first differenced equations, a two-sided *d* test might be appropriate. In such a case, steps 1 and 2 are still used, but step 3 is now:

Given the null hypothesis of no serial correlation and a two-sided alternative hypothesis:

$$H_0: \rho = 0 \quad \text{(no serial correlation)} \qquad (9.13)$$
$$H_A: \rho \neq 0 \quad \text{(serial correlation)}$$

---

7. This inconclusive region is troubling, but the development of exact Durbin–Watson tests may eliminate this problem in the near future. Some computer programs allow the user the option of calculating an exact Durbin–Watson probability (of first-order serial correlation). Alternatively, it's worth noting that there is a growing trend toward the use of d_U as a sole critical value. This trend runs counter to our view that if the Durbin–Watson test is inconclusive, then no remedial action should be taken except to search for a possible cause of impure serial correlation.

the appropriate decision rule is:

$$
\begin{array}{ll}
\text{if } d < d_L & \text{Reject } H_0 \\
\text{if } d > 4 - d_L & \text{Reject } H_0 \\
\text{if } 4 - d_U > d > d_U & \text{Do not reject } H_0 \\
\text{otherwise} & \text{Inconclusive}
\end{array}
$$

Examples of the Use of the Durbin–Watson *d* Statistic

Let's work through some applications of the Durbin–Watson test. First, turn to Statistical Tables B-4, B-5, and B-6. Note that the upper and lower critical *d* values (d_U and d_L) depend on the number of explanatory variables (do not count the constant term), the sample size, and the level of significance of the test.

Now let's set up a one-sided 5-percent test for a regression with three explanatory variables and 25 observations. As can be seen from the 5-percent table (B-4), the critical d values are $d_L = 1.12$ and $d_U = 1.66$. As a result, if the hypotheses are:

$$
\begin{array}{lll}
H_0: \rho \leq 0 & \text{(no positive serial correlation)} & (9.14) \\
H_A: \rho > 0 & \text{(positive serial correlation)} &
\end{array}
$$

the appropriate decision rule is:

$$
\begin{array}{ll}
\text{if } d < 1.12 & \text{Reject } H_0 \\
\text{if } d > 1.66 & \text{Do not reject } H_0 \\
\text{if } 1.12 \leq d \leq 1.66 & \text{Inconclusive}
\end{array}
$$

A computed *d* statistic of 1.78, for example, would indicate that there is no evidence of positive serial correlation, a value of 1.28 would be inconclusive, and a value of 0.60 would imply positive serial correlation. Figure 9.6 provides a graph of the "acceptance," rejection, and inconclusive regions for this example.

For a more familiar example, we return to the chicken demand model of Equation 6.8. As can be confirmed with the data provided in Table 6.2, the Durbin–Watson statistic from Equation 6.8 is 0.99. Is that cause to be concerned about serial correlation? What would be the result of a one-sided 5-percent test of the null hypothesis of no positive serial correlation? Our first step would be to consult Statistical Table B-4. In that table, with K (the number of explanatory variables) equal to 3 and N (the number of observations) equal to 29, we would find the critical d values $d_L = 1.20$ and $d_U = 1.65$.

Figure 9.6 An Example of a One-Sided Durbin–Watson d Test

In a one-sided Durbin–Watson test for positive serial correlation, only values of d significantly below 2 cause the null hypothesis of no positive serial correlation to be rejected. In this example, a d of 1.78 would indicate no positive serial correlation, a d of 0.60 would indicate positive serial correlation, and a d of 1.28 would be inconclusive.

The decision rule would thus be:

$$\begin{array}{ll} \text{if } d < 1.20 & \text{Reject } H_0 \\ \text{if } d > 1.65 & \text{Do not reject } H_0 \\ \text{if } 1.20 \leq d \leq 1.65 & \text{Inconclusive} \end{array}$$

Since 0.99 is less than the critical lower limit of the d statistic, we would reject the null hypothesis of no positive serial correlation, and we would have to decide how to cope with that serial correlation.

9.4 Remedies for Serial Correlation

Suppose that the Durbin–Watson d statistic detects serial correlation in the residuals of your equation. Is there a remedy? Some students suggest reordering the observations of Y and the Xs to avoid serial correlation. They think that if this time's error term appears to be affected by last time's error term, why not reorder the data randomly to get rid of the problem? The answer is that the reordering of the data does not get rid of the serial correlation; it just makes the problem harder to detect. If $\epsilon_2 = f(\epsilon_1)$ and we reorder the data, then the error term observations are still related to each other, but they now no longer follow each other, and it becomes almost impossible to discover the serial correlation.

Interestingly, reordering the data changes the Durbin–Watson d statistic but does not change the estimates of the coefficients or their standard errors at all.[8]

> The place to start in correcting a serial correlation problem is to look carefully at the specification of the equation for possible errors that might be causing impure serial correlation. Is the functional form correct? Are you sure that there are no omitted variables? Only after the specification of the equation has been reviewed carefully should the possibility of an adjustment for pure serial correlation be considered.

It's worth noting that if an omitted variable increases or decreases over time, as is often the case, or if the data set is logically reordered (say, according to the magnitude of one of the variables), then the Durbin–Watson statistic can help detect impure serial correlation. A significant Durbin–Watson statistic can easily be caused by an omitted variable or an incorrect functional form. In such circumstances, the Durbin–Watson test does not distinguish between pure and impure serial correlation, but the detection of negative serial correlation is often a strong hint that the serial correlation is impure.

If you conclude that you have pure serial correlation, then the appropriate response is to consider the application of Generalized Least Squares or Newey–West standard errors, as described in the following sections.

Generalized Least Squares

Generalized least squares (GLS) is a method of ridding an equation of pure first-order serial correlation and in the process restoring the minimum variance property to its estimation. GLS starts with an equation that does not meet the Classical Assumptions (due in this case to the pure serial correlation in the error term) and transforms it into one (Equation 9.19) that does meet those assumptions.

At this point, you could skip directly to Equation 9.19, but it's easier to understand the GLS estimator if you examine the transformation from which it comes. Start with an equation that has first-order serial correlation:

$$Y_t = \beta_0 + \beta_1 X_{1t} + \epsilon_t \tag{9.15}$$

---

8. This can be proven mathematically, but it is usually more instructive to estimate a regression yourself, change the order of the observations, and then reestimate the regression. See Exercise 3 at the end of the chapter.

which, if $\epsilon_t = \rho\epsilon_{t-1} + u_t$ (due to pure serial correlation), also equals:

$$Y_t = \beta_0 + \beta_1 X_{1t} + \rho\epsilon_{t-1} + u_t \tag{9.16}$$

where ϵ is the serially correlated error term, ρ is the autocorrelation coefficient, and u is a classical (not serially correlated) error term.

If we could get the $\rho\epsilon_{t-1}$ term out of Equation 9.16, the serial correlation would be gone, because the remaining portion of the error term (u_t) has no serial correlation in it. To rid $\rho\epsilon_{t-1}$ from Equation 9.16, multiply Equation 9.15 by ρ and then lag the new equation by one time period, obtaining

$$\rho Y_{t-1} = \rho\beta_0 + \rho\beta_1 X_{1t-1} + \rho\epsilon_{t-1} \tag{9.17}$$

Notice that we now have an equation with a $\rho\epsilon_{t-1}$ term in it. If we now subtract Equation 9.17 from Equation 9.16, the equivalent equation that remains no longer contains the serially correlated component of the error term:

$$Y_t - \rho Y_{t-1} = \beta_0(1 - \rho) + \beta_1(X_{1t} - \rho X_{1t-1}) + u_t \tag{9.18}$$

Equation 9.18 can be rewritten as:

$$Y_t^* = \beta_0^* + \beta_1 X_{1t}^* + u_t \tag{9.19}$$

where: $Y_t^* = Y_t - \rho Y_{t-1}$ $\qquad\qquad\qquad\qquad$ (9.20)
$\qquad\quad X_{1t}^* = X_{1t} - \rho X_{1t-1}$
$\qquad\quad \beta_0^* = \beta_0 - \rho\beta_0$

Equation 9.19 is called a Generalized Least Squares (or "quasi-differenced") version of Equation 9.16. Notice that:

1. The error term is not serially correlated. As a result, OLS estimation of Equation 9.19 will be minimum variance. (This is true if we know ρ or if we accurately estimate ρ.)

2. The slope coefficient β_1 is the same as the slope coefficient of the original serially correlated equation, Equation 9.16. Thus coefficients estimated with GLS have the same meaning as those estimated with OLS.

3. The dependent variable has changed compared to that in Equation 9.16. This means that the GLS $\overline{R}^2$ is not directly comparable to the OLS $\overline{R}^2$.

4. To forecast with GLS, adjustments like those discussed in Section 15.2 are required.

Unfortunately we can't use OLS to estimate a Generalized Least Squares model because GLS equations are inherently nonlinear in the coefficients. To see why, take a look at Equation 9.18. We need to estimate values not only for β_0 and β_1 but also for ρ, and ρ is multiplied by β_0 and β_1 (which you can see if you multiply out the right-hand side of the equation). Since OLS requires that the equation be linear in the coefficients, we need a different estimation procedure.

Luckily, there are a number of techniques that can be used to estimate GLS equations. Perhaps the best known of these is the **Cochrane–Orcutt method**, a two-step iterative technique[9] that first produces an estimate of ρ and then estimates the GLS equation using that $\hat{\rho}$. The two steps are:

1. Estimate ρ by running a regression based on the residuals of the equation suspected of having serial correlation:

$$e_t = \rho e_{t-1} + u_t \tag{9.21}$$

    where the e_ts are the OLS residuals from the equation suspected of having pure serial correlation and u_t is a classical error term.

2. Use this $\hat{\rho}$ to estimate the GLS equation by substituting $\hat{\rho}$ into Equation 9.18 and using OLS to estimate Equation 9.18 with the adjusted data.

These two steps are repeated (iterated) until further iteration results in little change in $\hat{\rho}$. Once $\hat{\rho}$ has converged (usually in just a few iterations), the last estimate of step 2 is used as a final estimate of Equation 9.18.

As popular as Cochrane–Orcutt is, we suggest a different method, the AR(1) method, for GLS models. The **AR(1) method** estimates a GLS equation like Equation 9.18 by estimating β_0, β_1, and ρ simultaneously with iterative nonlinear regression techniques that are well beyond the scope of this chapter.[10] The AR(1) method tends to produce the same coefficient estimates as Cochrane–Orcutt but with superior estimates of the standard errors, so we recommend the AR(1) approach as long as your software can support such nonlinear regression.

Let's apply Generalized Least Squares, using the AR(1) estimation method, to the chicken demand example that was found to have positive serial correlation

---

9. D. Cochrane and G. H. Orcutt, "Application of Least Squares Regression to Relationships Containing Autocorrelated Error Terms," *Journal of the American Statistical Association*, 1949, pp. 32–61.

10. To run GLS with EViews, simply add "AR(1)" to the equation as if it were an independent variable. The resulting equation is a GLS estimate where $\hat{\rho}$ will appear as the estimated coefficient of the variable AR(1). To run GLS with Stata, click on "linear regression with AR(1) disturbance" in the appropriate drop-down window.

in the previous section. Recall that we estimated the per capita demand for chicken as a function of the price of chicken, the price of beef, and disposable income:

$$\hat{Y}_t = 27.7 - 0.11PC_t + 0.03PB_t + 0.23YD_t \qquad (6.8)$$
$$(0.03) \qquad (0.02) \qquad (0.01)$$
$$t = \qquad -3.38 \qquad + 1.86 \qquad + 15.7$$
$$\overline{R}^2 = .9904 \quad N = 29 \quad DW\, d = 0.99$$

Note that we have added the Durbin–Watson d statistic to the documentation with the notation DW. All future time-series results will include the DW statistic, but cross-sectional documentation of the DW is not required unless the observations are ordered in some meaningful manner (like smallest to largest or youngest to oldest).

If we reestimate Equation 6.8 with the AR(1) approach to GLS, we obtain:

$$\hat{Y}_t = 27.7 - 0.08PC_t + 0.02PB_t + 0.24YD_t \qquad (9.22)$$
$$(0.05) \qquad (0.02) \qquad (0.02)$$
$$t = \quad -1.70 \qquad + 0.76 \qquad + 12.06$$
$$\overline{R}^2 = .9921 \quad N = 28 \quad \hat{\rho} = 0.56$$

Let's compare Equations 6.8 and 9.22. Note that the $\hat{\rho}$ used in Equation 9.22 is 0.56. This means that Y was actually run as $Y^* = Y_t - 0.56Y_{t-1}$, PC as $PC^* = PC_t - 0.56PC_{t-1}$, etc. Second, $\hat{\rho}$ replaces DW in the documentation of GLS estimates in part because the DW of Equation 9.22 isn't strictly comparable to non-GLS DWs (it is biased toward 2). Finally, the sample size of the GLS regression is 28 because the first observation has to be used to create the lagged values for the calculation of the quasi-differenced variables in Equation 9.20.

Generalized Least Squares estimates, no matter how produced, have at least two problems. First, even though serial correlation causes no bias in the estimates of the $\hat{\beta}$s, the GLS estimates usually are different from the OLS ones. For example, note that all three slope coefficients change as we move from OLS in Equation 6.8 to GLS in Equation 9.22. This isn't surprising, since two different estimates can have different values even though their expected values are the same. The second problem is more important, however. It turns out that GLS works well if $\hat{\rho}$ is close to the actual ρ, but the GLS $\hat{\rho}$ is biased in small samples. If $\hat{\rho}$ is biased, then the biased $\hat{\rho}$ introduces bias into the GLS estimates of the $\hat{\beta}$s. Luckily, there is a remedy for serial correlation that avoids both of these problems: Newey–West standard errors.

Newey–West Standard Errors

Not all corrections for pure serial correlation involve Generalized Least Squares. **Newey–West standard errors** are SE($\hat{\beta}$)s that take account of serial correlation without changing the $\hat{\beta}$s themselves in any way.[11] The logic behind Newey–West standard errors is powerful. If serial correlation does not cause bias in the $\hat{\beta}$s but does impact the standard errors, then it makes sense to adjust the estimated equation in a way that changes the SE($\hat{\beta}$)s but not the $\hat{\beta}$s.

Thus Newey–West standard errors have been calculated specifically to avoid the consequences of pure first-order serial correlation. The Newey–West procedure yields an estimator of the standard errors that, while they are biased, is generally more accurate than uncorrected standard errors for large samples in the face of serial correlation. As a result, Newey–West standard errors can be used for t-tests and other hypothesis tests in most samples without the errors of inference potentially caused by serial correlation. Typically, Newey–West SE($\hat{\beta}$)s are larger than OLS SE($\hat{\beta}$)s, thus producing lower t-scores and decreasing the probability that a given estimated coefficient will be significantly different from zero.

To see how Newey–West standard errors work, let's apply them to the same serially correlated chicken demand equation to which we applied GLS in Equation 9.22. If we use Newey–West standard errors in the estimation of Equation 6.8, we get:

$$\hat{Y}_t = 27.7 - 0.11PC_t + 0.03PB_t + 0.23YD_t \qquad (9.23)$$
$$(0.03) \quad (0.02) \quad (0.01)$$
$$t = -3.51 \quad +1.92 \quad +19.4$$
$$\overline{R}^2 = .9904 \quad N = 29$$

Let's compare Equations 6.8 and 9.23. First of all, the $\hat{\beta}$s are identical in Equations 6.8 and 9.23. This is because Newey–West standard errors do not change the OLS $\hat{\beta}$s. Second, while we can't observe the change because of rounding, the Newey–West standard errors must be different from the OLS standard errors because the t-scores have changed even though the estimated coefficients are identical. However, the Newey-West SE($\hat{\beta}$)s are slightly lower than the OLS SE($\hat{\beta}$)s, which is a surprise even in a small sample like this one. Such a result indicates that there may well be an omitted variable or nonstationarity (to be discussed in Chapter 13) in this equation.

---

11. W. K. Newey and K. D. West, "A Simple, Positive Semi-Definite Heteroskedasticity and Autocorrelation Consistent Covariance Matrix," *Econometrica*, 1987, pp. 703–708. Newey–West standard errors are similar to HC standard errors (or White standard errors), discussed in Section 10.4.

9.5 Summary

1. Serial correlation, or autocorrelation, is the violation of Classical Assumption IV that the observations of the error term are uncorrelated with each other. Usually, econometricians focus on first-order serial correlation, in which the current observation of the error term is assumed to be a function of the previous observation of the error term and a not serially correlated error term (u):

$$\epsilon_t = \rho\epsilon_{t-1} + u_t \qquad -1 < \rho < 1$$

   where ρ is "rho," the autocorrelation coefficient.

2. Pure serial correlation is serial correlation that is a function of the error term of the correctly specified regression equation. Impure serial correlation is caused by specification errors such as an omitted variable or an incorrect functional form. While impure serial correlation can be positive ($0 < \rho < 1$) or negative ($-1 < \rho < 0$), pure serial correlation in economics or business situations is almost always positive.

3. The major consequence of serial correlation is bias in the OLS SE ($\hat{\beta}$)s, causing unreliable hypothesis testing. Pure serial correlation does not cause bias in the estimates of the βs.

4. The most commonly used method of detecting first-order serial correlation is the Durbin–Watson d test, which uses the residuals of an estimated regression to test the possibility of serial correlation in the error term. A d value of 0 indicates extreme positive serial correlation, a d value of 2 indicates no serial correlation, and a d value of 4 indicates extreme negative serial correlation.

5. The first step in ridding an equation of serial correlation is to check for possible specification errors. Only once the possibility of impure serial correlation has been reduced to a minimum should remedies for pure serial correlation be considered.

6. Generalized Least Squares (GLS) is a method of transforming an equation to rid it of pure first-order serial correlation. The use of GLS requires the estimation of ρ.

7. Newey–West standard errors are an alternative remedy for serial correlation that adjusts the OLS estimates of the SE($\hat{\beta}$)s to take account of the serial correlation without changing the $\hat{\beta}$s.

EXERCISES

(The answer to Exercise 2 is in Appendix A.)

1. Write the meaning of each of the following terms without referring to the book (or your notes), and compare your definition with the version in the text for each:

   a. impure serial correlation
   b. first-order serial correlation
   c. first-order autocorrelation coefficient
   d. Durbin–Watson *d* statistic
   e. Generalized Least Squares
   f. positive serial correlation
   g. Newey–West standard errors

2. Consider the following equation for U.S. per capita consumption of beef:

$$\hat{B}_t = -330.3 + 49.1\ln Y_t - 0.34PB_t + 0.33PRP_t - 15.4D_t \qquad (9.24)$$

$$\phantom{\hat{B}_t = -330.3 +} (7.4) \qquad (0.13) \qquad (0.12) \qquad (4.1)$$

$$\phantom{\hat{B}_t = -330.3 +} t = 6.6 \qquad -2.6 \qquad 2.7 \qquad -3.7$$

$$\phantom{\hat{B}_t = -330.3 +} \overline{R}^2 = .700 \qquad N = 28 \qquad DW = 0.94$$

where: B_t = the annual per capita pounds of beef consumed in the United States in year t

  $\ln Y_t$ = the log of real per capita disposable real income in the U.S. in year t

  PB_t = average annualized real wholesale price of beef in year t (in cents per pound)

  PRP_t = average annualized real wholesale price of pork in year t (in cents per pound)

  D_t = a dummy variable equal to 1 for years in which there was a "health scare" about the dangers of red meat, 0 otherwise

   a. Develop and test your own hypotheses with respect to the individual estimated slope coefficients.
   b. Test for serial correlation in Equation 9.24 using the Durbin–Watson *d* test at the 5-percent level.
   c. What econometric problem(s) (if any) does Equation 9.24 appear to have? What remedy would you suggest?

d. You take your own advice, and apply GLS to Equation 9.24, obtaining:

$$\hat{B}_t = -193.3 + 35.2\ln Y_t - 0.38PB_t + 0.10PP_t - 5.7D_t \qquad (9.25)$$

$$\begin{array}{cccc} (14.1) & (0.10) & (0.09) & (3.9) \\ t = 2.5 & -3.7 & 1.1 & -1.5 \end{array}$$

$$\overline{R}^2 = .857 \qquad N = 28 \qquad \hat{\rho} = 0.82$$

Compare Equations 9.24 and 9.25. Which do you prefer? Why?

3. Recall from Section 9.4 that switching the order of a data set will not change its coefficient estimates. A revised order will change the Durbin–Watson statistic, however. To see both these points, run regressions $(HS = \beta_0 + \beta_1 P + \epsilon)$ and compare the coefficient estimates and DW d statistics for this data set:

Year	Housing Starts	Population
1	9090	2200
2	8942	2222
3	9755	2244
4	10327	2289
5	10513	2290

in the following three orders (in terms of year):
a. 1, 2, 3, 4, 5
b. 5, 4, 3, 2, 1
c. 2, 4, 3, 5, 1

4. Use Statistical Tables B-4, B-5, and B-6 to test for serial correlation given the following Durbin–Watson d statistics for serial correlation.
a. $d = 0.81$, $K = 3$, $N = 21$,   5-percent, one-sided positive test
b. $d = 3.48$, $K = 2$, $N = 15$,   1-percent, one-sided positive test
c. $d = 1.56$, $K = 5$, $N = 30$,   2.5-percent, one-sided positive test
d. $d = 2.84$, $K = 4$, $N = 35$,   5-percent, two-sided test
e. $d = 1.75$, $K = 1$, $N = 45$,   5-percent, one-sided positive test
f. $d = 0.91$, $K = 2$, $N = 28$,   2-percent, two-sided test
g. $d = 1.03$, $K = 6$, $N = 26$,   5-percent, one-sided positive test

5. Carefully distinguish between the following concepts:
a. positive and negative serial correlation
b. pure and impure serial correlation

    c. serially correlated observations of the error term and serially corre-
      lated residuals

    d. the Cochrane–Orcutt method and the AR(1) method

    e. GLS and Newey–West standard errors

6. In Statistical Table B-4, column K = 5, d_U is greater than 2 for the five
   smallest sample sizes in the table. What does it mean if $d_U > 2$?

7. A study by M. Hutchinson and D. Pyle[12] found some evidence of a
   link between short-term interest rates and the budget deficit in a sample that pools annual time-series and cross-sectional data from six
   countries.
   a. Suppose you were told that the Durbin–Watson d from their best
      regression was 0.81. Test this DW for indications of serial correla-
      tion (N = 60, K = 4, 5-percent one-sided test for positive serial
      correlation).
   b. Based on this result, would you conclude that serial correlation ex-
      isted in their study? Why or why not? (*Hint:* The six countries were
      the United Kingdom, France, Japan, Canada, Italy, and the United
      States; assume that the order of the data was United Kingdom, fol-
      lowed by France, etc.)
   c. How would you use GLS to correct for serial correlation in this case?

8. Suppose that the data in a time-series study were entered in reverse
   chronological order. Would this change in any way the testing or adjusting for serial correlation? How? In particular:
   a. What happens to the Durbin–Watson statistic's ability to detect
      serial correlation if the order is reversed?
   b. What happens to the GLS method's ability to adjust for serial corre-
      lation if the order is reversed?
   c. What is the intuitive economic explanation of reverse serial correlation?

9. Suppose that a plotting of the residuals of a regression with respect to
   time indicates a significant outlier in the residuals. (Be careful here:
   this is not an outlier in the original data but is an outlier in the
   residuals of a regression.)
   a. How could such an outlier occur? What does it mean?
   b. Is the Durbin–Watson d statistic applicable in the presence of such
      an outlier? Why or why not?

---

12. M. M. Hutchinson and D. H. Pyle, "The Real Interest Rate/Budget Deficit Link: International
Evidence, 1973–82," *Federal Reserve Bank of San Francisco Economic Review,* Vol. 4, pp. 26–35.

10. After GLS has been run on an equation, the $\hat{\beta}$s are still good estimates of the original (nontransformed) equation except for the constant term:

   a. What must be done to the estimate of the constant term generated by GLS to compare it with the one estimated by OLS?

   b. Why is such an adjustment necessary?

   c. Return to Equation 9.22 and calculate the $\hat{\beta}_0$ that would be comparable to the one in Equation 6.8. (*Hint:* Take a look at Equation 9.20.)

   d. The two estimates are different. Why? Does such a difference concern you?

11. Your friend is just finishing a study of attendance at Los Angeles Laker regular-season home basketball games when she hears that you've read a chapter on serial correlation and asks your advice. Before running the equation on last season's data, she "reviewed the literature" by interviewing a number of basketball fans. She found out that fans like to watch winning teams. In addition, she learned that while some fans like to watch games throughout the season, others are most interested in games played late in the season. Her estimated equation (standard errors in parentheses) was:

$$\hat{A}_t = 14123 + 20L_t + 2600P_t + 900W_t$$
$$\phantom{\hat{A}_t = 14123 + } (500) \quad (1000) \quad (300)$$
$$DW = 0.85 \qquad N = 40 \qquad \overline{R}^2 = .46$$

   where: A_t = the attendance at game t
   L_t = the winning percentage (games won divided by games played) of the Lakers before game t
   P_t = the winning percentage before game t of the Lakers' opponent in that game
   W_t = a dummy variable equal to one if game t was on Friday, Saturday, or Sunday, 0 otherwise

   a. Test for serial correlation using the Durbin–Watson d test at the 5-percent level.

   b. Make and test appropriate hypotheses about the slope coefficients at the 1-percent level.

   c. Compare the size and significance of the estimated coefficient of L with that for P. Is this difference surprising? Is L an irrelevant variable? Explain your answer.

   d. If serial correlation exists, would you expect it to be pure or impure serial correlation? Why?

e. Your friend omitted the first game of the year from the sample because the first game is always a sellout and because neither team had a winning percentage yet. Was this a good decision?

12. About two thirds of the way through the 2008 season, the Los Angeles Dodgers baseball team traded for superstar Manny Ramirez, and the result was a divisional pennant and dramatically increased attendance. Suppose that you've been hired by Manny's agent to help prepare for his upcoming contract negotiations by determining how much money Manny generated for the Dodgers. You decide to build a model of the Dodgers' attendance, and, after learning as much as you can about such modeling, you collect data for 2008 (Table 9.1) and estimate the following equation:

$$\widehat{ATT_i} = 34857 + 4104MANNY_i + 2282PM_i + 5632WKND_i + 4029PROM_i + 8081TEAM_i$$
$$(1021) \qquad (1121) \quad (1096) \qquad (1068) \qquad (5819)$$
$$t = 4.02 \qquad\qquad 2.04 \qquad 5.14 \qquad\quad 3.77 \qquad\quad 1.39$$
$$N = 81 \qquad\quad \bar{R}^2 = .54 \qquad\quad DW = 1.30$$

where: ATT_i = the number of tickets sold for the ith Dodger home game

$MANNY_i$ = 1 after the trade for Manny Ramirez, 0 otherwise

PM_i = 1 if the ith game was a night game, 0 otherwise

$WKND_i$ = 1 if the ith game was on the weekend, 0 otherwise

$PROM_i$ = 1 if the ith game included a major promotion (for example, fireworks or a free bobble-head), 0 otherwise

$TEAM_i$ = the winning percentage of the Dodgers' opponent before the ith game (set equal to the 2007 percentage for the first three games of 2008)

a. You expect each coefficient to be positive. Test these expectations at the 5-percent level.

b. Test for serial correlation in this equation by running a Durbin–Watson test.

c. What potential econometric problems (out of omitted variables, irrelevant variables, incorrect functional form, multicollinearity, and serial correlation) do you see in this equation? Explain.

d. Assume that your answer to part c is that you're concerned with serial correlation. Use the data in Table 9.1 to estimate the equation with generalized least squares.

Table 9.1 Data for the Dodger Attendance Exercise

OBS	VS	ATT	PM	WKND	PROM	TEAM	MANNY	RIVAL
1	SF	56000	0	0	1	0.438	0	1
2	SF	44054	1	0	0	0.438	0	1
3	SF	43217	1	0	0	0.438	0	1
4	SD	54052	1	1	1	0.546	0	1
5	SD	54955	1	1	1	0.546	0	1
6	SD	47357	0	1	0	0.546	0	1
7	PIT	37334	1	0	0	0.420	0	0
8	PIT	37896	1	0	1	0.420	0	0
9	PIT	53629	1	0	1	0.420	0	0
10	ARI	42590	1	0	0	0.750	0	0
11	ARI	38350	1	0	0	0.714	0	0
12	COL	53205	1	1	1	0.455	0	0
13	COL	50469	1	1	0	0.435	0	0
14	COL	50670	0	1	1	0.417	0	0
15	NYM	44181	1	0	0	0.552	0	0
16	NYM	43927	1	0	0	0.533	0	0
17	NYM	40696	0	0	0	0.516	0	0
18	HOU	52658	1	1	1	0.514	0	0
19	HOU	45212	1	1	0	0.528	0	0
20	HOU	40217	0	1	1	0.541	0	0
21	CIN	34669	1	0	0	0.477	0	0
22	CIN	34306	1	0	0	0.467	0	0
23	CIN	33224	1	0	0	0.547	0	0
24	STL	52281	1	1	1	0.571	0	0
25	STL	44785	1	1	0	0.580	0	0
26	STL	46566	0	1	0	0.588	0	0
27	COL	39098	1	0	0	0.351	0	0
28	COL	38548	1	0	0	0.345	0	0
29	COL	36393	0	0	0	0.356	0	0
30	CHC	44998	1	0	1	0.633	0	0
31	CHC	52484	1	1	1	0.639	0	0
32	CHC	50020	0	1	0	0.629	0	0
33	CHC	49994	1	1	0	0.619	0	0
34	CLE	50667	1	1	1	0.452	0	0
35	CLE	45036	0	1	1	0.495	0	0
36	CLE	39993	0	1	0	0.467	0	0
37	CWS	43900	1	0	0	0.547	0	0
38	CWS	40162	1	0	0	0.553	0	0
39	CWS	37956	0	0	0	0.545	0	0
40	LAA	50419	1	1	0	0.608	0	1
41	LAA	55784	1	1	0	0.600	0	1
42	LAA	48155	0	1	0	0.593	0	1

(*continued*)

Table 9.1 (*continued*)

OBS	VS	ATT	PM	WKND	PROM	TEAM	MANNY	RIVAL
43	ATL	39896	1	0	0	0.472	0	0
44	ATL	39702	1	0	0	0.467	0	0
45	ATL	39815	1	0	0	0.473	0	0
46	FLA	40417	1	0	0	0.516	0	0
47	FLA	49545	1	1	0	0.522	0	0
48	FLA	55220	1	1	1	0.527	0	0
49	FLA	42213	0	1	1	0.532	0	0
50	WSH	47313	1	1	1	0.373	0	0
51	WSH	42122	1	1	0	0.369	0	0
52	WSH	38660	0	1	0	0.365	0	0
53	SF	37483	1	0	0	0.413	0	1
54	SF	40110	1	0	0	0.419	0	1
55	SF	41282	1	0	0	0.415	0	1
56	ARIZ	42440	1	0	0	0.514	0	0
57	ARIZ	55239	1	1	1	0.519	1	0
58	ARIZ	54544	1	1	0	0.523	1	0
59	ARIZ	52972	0	1	1	0.518	1	0
60	PHI	45547	1	0	0	0.547	1	0
61	PHI	47587	1	0	1	0.542	1	0
62	PHI	45786	1	0	0	0.538	1	0
63	PHI	51064	1	0	0	0.533	1	0
64	MIL	44546	1	1	1	0.574	1	0
65	MIL	52889	1	1	1	0.569	1	0
66	MIL	45267	0	1	0	0.573	1	0
67	COL	46687	1	0	0	0.452	1	0
68	COL	48183	1	0	0	0.457	1	0
69	COL	44885	0	0	0	0.461	1	0
70	SD	44085	1	0	1	0.390	1	1
71	SD	39330	1	0	0	0.387	1	1
72	SD	48822	1	0	1	0.384	1	1
73	ARIZ	52270	1	1	1	0.511	1	0
74	ARIZ	47543	0	1	0	0.507	1	0
75	ARIZ	54137	0	1	1	0.504	1	0
76	SF	55135	1	1	1	0.444	1	1
77	SF	55452	1	1	1	0.448	1	1
78	SF	54841	0	1	1	0.445	1	1
79	SD	48907	1	0	0	0.391	1	1
80	SD	46741	1	0	0	0.389	1	1
81	SD	51783	1	0	1	0.386	1	1

Datafile = DODGERS9

Source: www.dodgers.com

e. Assume that your answer to part c is that you are more concerned with an omitted variable than with serial correlation, especially because an omitted variable can cause impure serial correlation. Add $RIVAL_i$ (a dummy variable equal to 1 if the opponent in the ith game is an in-state rival of the Dodgers, 0 otherwise) to the equation and estimate your new specification using the data in Table 9.1.

f. Which do you prefer, using GLS or adding RIVAL? Explain.

g. Given your answer to part f, what's your conclusion? How many fans per game did Manny Ramirez attract to Dodger Stadium? Was this result fairly robust (stable as the specification was changed)?

13. You're hired by Farmer Vin, a famous producer of bacon and ham, to test the possibility that feeding pigs at night allows them to grow faster than feeding them during the day. You take 200 pigs (from newborn piglets to extremely old porkers) and randomly assign them to feeding only during the day or feeding only at night and, after six months, end up with the following (admittedly very hypothetical) equation:

$$\hat{W}_i = 12 + 3.5G_i + 7.0D_i - 0.25F_i$$
$$\phantom{\hat{W}_i = 12 + } (1.0) \quad (1.0) \quad (0.10)$$
$$\phantom{\hat{W}_i = 12 + } t = 3.5 \quad\ \ 7.0 \quad\ -2.5$$
$$\overline{R}^2 = .70 \quad\ \ N = 200 \quad\ \ DW = 0.50$$

where: W_i = the percentage weight gain of the ith pig
G_i = a dummy variable equal to 1 if the ith pig is a male, 0 otherwise
D_i = a dummy variable equal to 1 if the ith pig was fed only at night, 0 if only during the day
F_i = the amount of food (pounds) eaten per day by the ith pig

a. Test for serial correlation at the 5-percent level in this equation.

b. What econometric problems appear to exist in this equation? (*Hint:* Be sure to make and test appropriate hypotheses about the slope coefficients.)

c. The goal of your experiment is to determine whether feeding at night represents a significant improvement over feeding during the day. What can you conclude?

d. The observations are ordered from the youngest pig to the oldest pig. Does this information change any of your answers to the previous parts of this question? Is this ordering a mistake? Explain your answer.

14. In a 1988 article, Josef Brada and Ronald Graves built an interesting model of defense spending in the Soviet Union just before the breakup of that nation.[13] The authors felt sure that Soviet defense spending was a function of U.S. defense spending and Soviet GNP but were less sure about whether defense spending also was a function of the ratio of Soviet nuclear warheads to U.S. nuclear warheads. Using a double-log functional form, the authors estimated a number of alternative specifications, including (standard errors in parentheses):

$$\widehat{\ln SDH_t} = -1.99 + 0.056\ln USD_t + 0.969\ln SY_t + 0.057\ln SP_t \qquad (9.26)$$
$$(0.074) \qquad\quad (0.065) \qquad\quad (0.032)$$
$$t = 0.76 \qquad\qquad 14.98 \qquad\quad 1.80$$
$$N = 25 \text{ (annual 1960–1984)} \quad \overline{R}^2 = .979 \quad DW = 0.49$$

$$\widehat{\ln SDH_t} = -2.88 + 0.105\ln USD_t + 1.066\ln SY_t \qquad\qquad (9.27)$$
$$(0.073) \qquad\qquad (0.038)$$
$$t = 1.44 \qquad\qquad 28.09$$
$$N = 25 \text{ (annual 1960–1984)} \quad \overline{R}^2 = .977 \quad DW = 0.43$$

where: SDH_t = the CIA's "high" estimate of Soviet defense expenditures in year t (billions of 1970 rubles)

USD_t = U.S. defense expenditures in year t (billions of 1980 dollars)

SY_t = Soviet GNP in year t (billions of 1970 rubles)

SP_t = the ratio of the number of USSR nuclear warheads (NR_t) to the number of U.S. nuclear warheads (NU_t) in year t

---

13. Josef C. Brada and Ronald L. Graves, "The Slowdown in Soviet Defense Expenditures," *Southern Economic Journal*, Vol. 54, No. 4, pp. 969–984. In addition to the variables used in this exercise, Brada and Graves also provide data for SFP_t, the rate of Soviet factor productivity in year t, which we include in Table 9.2 because we suggest exercises using SFP in the instructor's manual.

Table 9.2   Data on Soviet Defense Spending

Year	SDH	SDL	USD	SY	SFP	NR	NU
1960	31	23	200.54	232.3	7.03	415	1734
1961	34	26	204.12	245.3	6.07	445	1846
1962	38	29	207.72	254.5	3.90	485	1942
1963	39	31	206.98	251.7	2.97	531	2070
1964	42	34	207.41	279.4	1.40	580	2910
1965	43	35	185.42	296.8	1.87	598	4110
1966	44	36	203.19	311.9	4.10	674	4198
1967	47	39	241.27	326.3	4.90	1058	4338
1968	50	42	260.91	346.0	4.07	1270	4134
1969	52	43	254.62	355.9	2.87	1662	4026
1970	53	44	228.19	383.3	4.43	2047	5074
1971	54	45	203.80	398.2	3.77	3199	6282
1972	56	46	189.41	405.7	2.87	2298	7100
1973	58	48	169.27	435.2	3.87	2430	8164
1974	62	51	156.81	452.2	4.30	2534	8522
1975	65	53	155.59	459.8	6.33	2614	9170
1976	69	56	169.91	481.8	0.63	3219	9518
1977	70	56	170.94	497.4	2.23	4345	9806
1978	72	57	154.12	514.2	1.03	5097	9950
1979	75	59	156.80	516.1	0.17	6336	9945
1980	79	62	160.67	524.7	0.27	7451	9668
1981	83	63	169.55	536.1	0.47	7793	9628
1982	84	64	185.31	547.0	0.07	8031	10124
1983	88	66	201.83	567.5	1.50	8730	10201
1984	90	67	211.35	578.9	1.63	9146	10630

Source: Josef C. Brada and Ronald L. Graves, "The Slowdown in Soviet Defense Expenditures," *Southern Economic Journal*, Vol. 54, No. 4, p. 974.

Datafile = DEFEND9

a. The authors expected positive signs for all the slope coefficients of both equations. Test these hypotheses at the 5-percent level.
b. Use our four specification criteria to determine whether SP is an irrelevant variable. Explain your reasoning.
c. Test both equations for positive first-order serial correlation. Does the high probability of serial correlation cause you to reconsider your answer to part b? Explain.
d. Someone might argue that because the DW statistic improved when lnSP was added, that the serial correlation was impure and

that GLS was not called for. Do you agree with this conclusion? Why or why not?

e. If we run a GLS version of Equation 9.26, we get Equation 9.28. Does this result cause you to reconsider your answer to part b? Explain:

$$\widehat{\ln SDH}_t = 3.55 + 0.108\ln USD_t + 0.137\ln SY_t - 0.0008\ln SP_t \qquad (9.28)$$
$$(0.067) \qquad\qquad (0.214) \qquad\quad (0.027)$$
$$t = 1.61 \qquad\qquad 0.64 \qquad\quad -0.03$$
$$N = 24 \text{ (annual 1960–1984)} \quad \overline{R}^2 = .994 \quad \hat{\rho} = 0.96$$

15. As an example of impure serial correlation caused by an incorrect functional form, let's return to the equation for the percentage of putts made (P_i) as a function of the length of the putt in feet (L_i) that we discussed originally in Exercise 6 in Chapter 1. The complete documentation of that equation is

$$\hat{P}_i = 83.6 - 4.1L_i \qquad (9.29)$$
$$(0.4)$$
$$t = -10.6$$
$$N = 19 \qquad \overline{R}^2 = .861 \qquad DW = 0.48$$

a. Test Equation 9.29 for serial correlation using the Durbin–Watson d test at the 1-percent level.

b. Why might the linear functional form be inappropriate for this study? Explain your answer.

c. If we now reestimate Equation 9.29 using a double-log functional form, we obtain:

$$\widehat{\ln P}_i = 5.50 - 0.92\ln L_i \qquad (9.30)$$
$$(0.07)$$
$$t = -13.0$$
$$N = 19 \qquad \overline{R}^2 = .903 \qquad DW = 1.22$$

Test Equation 9.30 for serial correlation using the Durbin–Watson d test at the 1-percent level.

d. Compare Equations 9.29 and 9.30. Which equation do you prefer? Why?

10 Heteroskedasticity

Heteroskedasticity is the violation of Classical Assumption V, which states that the observations of the error term are drawn from a distribution that has a constant variance.[1] The assumption of constant variances for different observations of the error term (homoskedasticity) is not always realistic. For example, in a model explaining heights, it's likely that error term observations associated with the height of a basketball player would come from distributions with larger variances than those associated with the height of a mouse. Heteroskedasticity is important because OLS, when applied to heteroskedastic models, is no longer the minimum variance estimator (it still is unbiased, however).

In general, heteroskedasticity is more likely to take place in cross-sectional models than in time-series models. This focus on cross-sectional models is not to say that heteroskedasticity in time-series models is impossible, though. In fact, heteroskedasticity has turned out to be an important factor in time-series studies of financial markets.

---

1. Various authors spell this "heteroscedasticity," but Huston McCulloch appears to settle this controversy in favor of "heteroskedasticity" because of the word's Greek origin. See J. Huston McCulloch, "On Heteros*edasticity," *Econometrica*, Vol. 53, No. 2, p. 483. Although heteroskedasticity is a difficult word to spell, at least it's an impressive comeback when parents ask, "What'd you learn for all that money?"

The structure of this chapter will be quite familiar. We'll attempt to answer the same four questions for heteroskedasticity that we answered for multi-collinearity and serial correlation in the previous two chapters:

1. What is the nature of the problem?
2. What are the consequences of the problem?
3. How is the problem diagnosed?
4. What remedies for the problem are available?

(10.1) Pure versus Impure Heteroskedasticity

Heteroskedasticity, like serial correlation, can be divided into pure and impure versions. Pure heteroskedasticity is caused by the error term of the correctly specified equation; impure heteroskedasticity is caused by a specification error such as an omitted variable.

Pure Heteroskedasticity

Pure heteroskedasticity refers to heteroskedasticity that is a function of the error term of a correctly specified regression equation. As with serial correlation, use of the word "heteroskedasticity" without any modifier (like pure or impure) implies *pure* heteroskedasticity.

Such **pure heteroskedasticity** occurs when Classical Assumption V, which assumes that the variance of the error term is constant, is violated in a correctly specified equation. Assumption V assumes that:

$$\text{VAR}(\epsilon_i) = \sigma^2 = \text{a constant} \qquad (i = 1, 2, \ldots, N) \qquad (10.1)$$

If this assumption is met, all the observations of the error term can be thought of as being drawn from the same distribution: a distribution with a mean of zero and a variance of σ^2. Since σ^2 does not change for different observations of the error term, this property is called homoskedasticity. A homoskedastic error term distribution is pictured in the top half of Figure 10.1; note that the variance of the distribution is constant (even though individual observations drawn from that sample will vary quite a bit).

With heteroskedasticity, this error term variance is not constant; instead, the variance of the distribution of the error term depends on exactly which observation is being discussed:

$$\text{VAR}(\epsilon_i) = \sigma_i^2 \qquad (i = 1, 2, \ldots, N) \qquad (10.2)$$

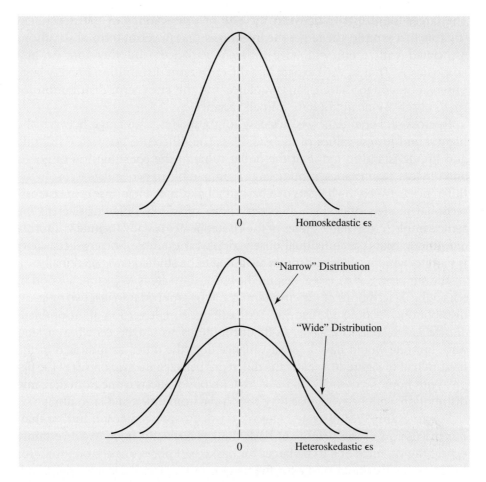

Figure 10.1 Homoskedasticity versus Discrete Heteroskedasticity

In homoskedasticity the distribution of the error term has a constant variance, so the observations are continually drawn from the same distribution (shown in the top panel). In the simplest heteroskedastic case, discrete heteroskedasticity, there would be two different error term variances and, therefore, two different distributions (one wider than the other, as in the bottom panel) from which the observations of the error term could be drawn.

Note that the only difference between Equations 10.1 and 10.2 is the subscript "i" attached to σ^2, which implies that instead of being constant over all the observations, a heteroskedastic error term's variance can change depending on the observation (hence the subscript).

Heteroskedasticity often occurs in data sets in which there is a wide disparity between the largest and smallest observed value of the dependent variable.

The larger the disparity between the size of observations of the dependent variable in a sample, the larger the likelihood that the error term observations associated with them will have different variances and therefore be heteroskedastic. That is, we'd expect that the error term distribution for very large observations might have a large variance, but the error term distribution for small observations might have a small variance.

In cross-sectional data sets, it's easy to get such a large range between the highest and lowest values of the variables. The difference between California and Rhode Island in terms of the dollar value of the consumption of goods and services, for instance, is quite large (comparable in percentage terms to the difference between the heights of a basketball player and a mouse). Since cross-sectional models often include observations of widely different sizes in the same sample (cross-state studies of the United States usually include California and Rhode Island as individual observations, for example), heteroskedasticity is hard to avoid if economic topics are going to be studied cross sectionally.

The simplest way to visualize pure heteroskedasticity is to picture a world in which the observations of the error term could be grouped into just two different distributions, "wide" and "narrow." We'll call this simple version of the problem *discrete heteroskedasticity*. Here, both distributions would be centered around zero, but one would have a larger variance than the other, as indicated in the bottom half of Figure 10.1. Note the difference between the two halves of the figure. With homoskedasticity, all the error term observations come from the same distribution; with heteroskedasticity, they come from different distributions.

For an example of discrete heteroskedasticity, we need go no further than our discussion of the heights of basketball players and mice. We'd certainly expect the variance of ϵ to be larger for basketball players as a group than for mice, so the distribution of ϵ for the heights of basketball players might look like the "wide" distribution in Figure 10.1, and the distribution of ϵ for mice would be even narrower than the "narrow" distribution in Figure 10.1.

Heteroskedasticity takes on many more complex forms. In fact, the number of different models of heteroskedasticity is virtually limitless, and an analysis of even a small percentage of these alternatives would be a huge task. Instead, we'd like to address the general principles of heteroskedasticity by focusing on the most frequently specified model of pure heteroskedasticity, just as we focused on pure, positive, first-order serial correlation in the previous chapter. However, don't let this focus mislead you into concluding that econometricians are concerned only with one kind of heteroskedasticity.

In this model of heteroskedasticity, the variance of the error term is related to an exogenous variable Z_i. For a typical regression equation:

$$Y_i = \beta_0 + \beta_1 X_{1i} + \beta_2 X_{2i} + \epsilon_i \tag{10.3}$$

the variance of the otherwise classical error term ϵ might be equal to:

$$\mathrm{VAR}(\epsilon_i) = \sigma^2 Z_i^2 \tag{10.4}$$

where Z may or may not be one of the Xs in the equation. The variable Z is called a **proportionality factor** because the variance of the error term changes proportionally to the square of Z_i. The higher the value of Z_i, the higher the variance of the distribution of the *i*th observation of the error term. There would be N different distributions, one for each observation, from which the observations of the error term could be drawn depending on the number of different values that Z takes. To see what homoskedastic and heteroskedastic distributions of the error term look like with respect to Z, compare Figures 10.2 and 10.3. Note that the heteroskedastic distribution gets wider as Z increases but that the homoskedastic distribution maintains the same width no matter what value Z takes.

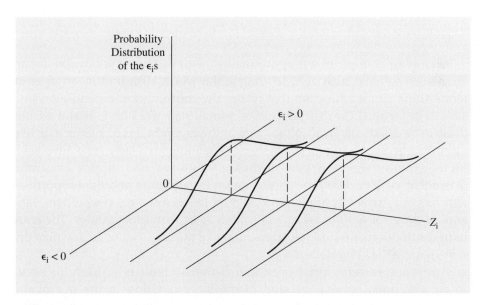

Figure 10.2 A Homoskedastic Error Term with Respect to Z_i

If an error term is homoskedastic with respect to Z_i, the variance of the distribution of the error term is the same (constant) no matter what the value of Z_i is: $\mathrm{VAR}(\epsilon_i) = \sigma^2$.

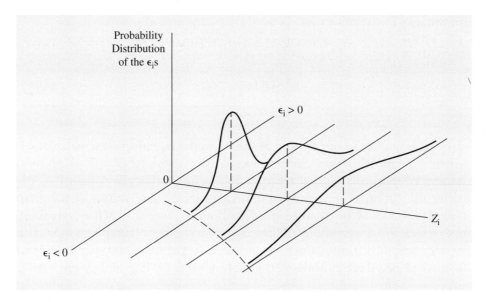

Figure 10.3 A Heteroskedastic Error Term with Respect to Z_i

If an error term is heteroskedastic with respect to Z_i, the variance of the distribution of the error term changes systematically as a function of Z_i. In this example, the variance is an increasing function of Z_i, as in $VAR(\epsilon_i) = \sigma^2 Z_i^2$.

What is an example of a proportionality factor Z? How is it possible for an exogenous variable such as Z to change the whole distribution of an error term? Think about a function that relates the consumption expenditures in a state to its income. The expenditures of a small state like Rhode Island are not likely to be as variable in absolute value as the expenditures of a large state like California because a 10-percent change in spending for a large state involves a lot more money than a 10-percent change for a small one. In such a case, the dependent variable would be consumption expenditures and the proportionality factor, Z, would be population. As population rose, so too would the variance of the error term of an equation built to explain expenditures. The error term distributions would look something like those in Figure 10.3, where the Z in Figure 10.3 is population.

This example helps emphasize that heteroskedasticity is likely to occur in cross-sectional models because of the large variation in the size of the dependent variable involved. An exogenous disturbance that might seem huge to a small state could seem miniscule to a large one, for instance.

Heteroskedasticity can occur in a time-series model with a significant amount of change in the dependent variable. If you were modeling sales of

DVD players from 1980 to 2009, it's quite possible that you would have a heteroskedastic error term. As the phenomenal growth of the industry took place, the variance of the error term probably increased as well. Such a possibility is unlikely in time series that have low rates of change, however.

Heteroskedasticity also can occur in any model, time series or cross sectional, where the quality of data collection changes dramatically within the sample. As data collection techniques get better, the variance of the error term should fall because measurement errors are included in the error term. As measurement errors decrease in size, so should the variance of the error term. For more on this topic (called "errors in the variables"), see Section 14.6.

Impure Heteroskedasticity

Heteroskedasticity that is caused by an error in specification, such as an omitted variable, is referred to as **impure heteroskedasticity**. Impure heteroskedasticity thus is similar to impure serial correlation.[2]

An omitted variable can cause a heteroskedastic error term because the portion of the omitted effect not represented by one of the included explanatory variables must be absorbed by the error term. If this effect has a heteroskedastic component, the error term of the misspecified equation might be heteroskedastic even if the error term of the true equation is not. This distinction is important because with impure heteroskedasticity the correct remedy is to find the omitted variable and include it in the regression. It's therefore important to be sure that your specification is correct before trying to detect or remedy pure heteroskedasticity.

(10.2) The Consequences of Heteroskedasticity

If the error term of your equation is known to be heteroskedastic, what does that mean for the estimation of your coefficients? If the error term of an equation is heteroskedastic, there are three major consequences:[3]

1. *Pure heteroskedasticity does not cause bias in the coefficient estimates.* Even if the error term of an equation is known to be purely heteroskedastic, that heteroskedasticity will not cause bias in the OLS estimates of the

---

2. Both can be caused by an omitted variable, but it is very unusual for impure heteroskedasticity to be caused by an improper functional form.

3. It turns out that the consequences of heteroskedasticity are almost identical in general framework to those of serial correlation, though the two problems are quite different.

coefficients. This is true because even though large positive errors are more likely, so too are large negative errors. The two tend to average each other out, leaving the OLS estimator still unbiased.

As a result, we can say that an otherwise correctly specified equation that has pure heteroskedasticity still has the property that:

$$E(\hat{\beta}) = \beta \qquad \text{for all } \beta\text{s}$$

Lack of bias does not guarantee "accurate" coefficient estimates, especially since heteroskedasticity increases the variance of the estimates, but the distribution of the estimates is still centered around the true β. Equations with impure heteroskedasticity caused by an omitted variable, of course, will have possible specification bias.

2. *Heteroskedasticity typically causes OLS to no longer be the minimum-variance estimator (of all the linear unbiased estimators).* Pure heteroskedasticity causes no bias in the estimates of the OLS coefficients, but it does affect the minimum-variance property. If the error term of an equation is heteroskedastic with respect to a proportionality factor Z:

$$VAR(\epsilon_i) = \sigma^2 Z_i^2 \qquad (10.5)$$

then the minimum-variance portion of the Gauss–Markov Theorem cannot be proven because there are other linear unbiased estimators that have smaller variances. This is because the heteroskedastic error term causes the dependent variable to fluctuate, and the OLS estimation procedure attributes this fluctuation to the independent variables. Thus, OLS is more likely to misestimate the true β in the face of heteroskedasticity. The $\hat{\beta}$s still are unbiased because overestimates are just as likely as underestimates.

3. *Heteroskedasticity causes the OLS estimates of the SE($\hat{\beta}$)s to be biased, leading to unreliable hypothesis testing.* With heteroskedasticity, the OLS formula for the standard error produces biased estimates of the SE($\hat{\beta}$)s. Because the SE($\hat{\beta}$) is a prime component in the t-statistic, these biased SE($\hat{\beta}$)s cause biased t-scores and unreliable hypothesis testing in general. In essence, heteroskedasticity causes OLS to produce incorrect SE($\hat{\beta}$)s and t-scores! Not surprisingly, most econometricians therefore are very hesitant to put much faith in hypothesis tests that were conducted in the face of pure heteroskedasticity.[4]

---

4. While our discussion here involves the t-test, the same conclusion of unreliability in the face of heteroskedasticity applies to all other test statistics.

What sort of bias does heteroskedasticity tend to cause? Typically, the bias in the estimate of $SE(\hat{\beta})$ is negative, meaning that OLS underestimates the size of the standard errors of the coefficients. This comes about because heteroskedasticity usually results in a pattern of observations that allows a better fit than the actual homoskedastic observations would otherwise justify. This tendency of OLS to underestimate the $SE(\hat{\beta})$ means that OLS typically overestimates the t-scores of the estimated coefficients. Thus the t-scores printed out by a typical software regression package in the face of heteroskedasticity are likely to be too high.

What'll happen to hypothesis testing if OLS underestimates the $SE(\hat{\beta})$s and therefore overestimates the t-scores? Well, the "too low" $SE(\hat{\beta})$ will cause a "too high" t-score for a particular coefficient, and this will make it more likely that we will reject a null hypothesis (for example, H_0: $\beta \leq 0$) when it is in fact true. This increased chance of rejecting the H_0 means that we're more likely to make a Type I Error, and we're more likely to make the mistake of keeping an irrelevant variable in an equation because its coefficient's t-score has been overestimated. In other words, hypothesis testing becomes both biased and unreliable when we have pure heteroskedasticity.

(10.3) Testing for Heteroskedasticity

Econometricians do not all use the same test for heteroskedasticity because heteroskedasticity takes a number of different forms, and its precise manifestation in a given equation is almost never known. The "Z_i proportionality factor" approach of this chapter, for example, is only one of many specifications of the form of heteroskedasticity. As a result, there is no universally agreed-upon method of testing for heteroskedasticity; econometrics textbooks list as many as eight different methods of such testing.

Because of this wide variety, we'll describe the use of two different tests for heteroskedasticity, the *Park test* and the *White test*. No test for heteroskedasticity can "prove" that heteroskedasticity exists in an equation, though, so the best we can do is to get a general indication of its likelihood.

There's no need to run a heteroskedasticity test for every specification estimated, however, so before using any test, it's a good idea to ask the following preliminary questions:

1. Are there any obvious specification errors? If the estimated equation is suspected of having an omitted variable, a test for heteroskedasticity should be delayed until the specification is as good as possible.

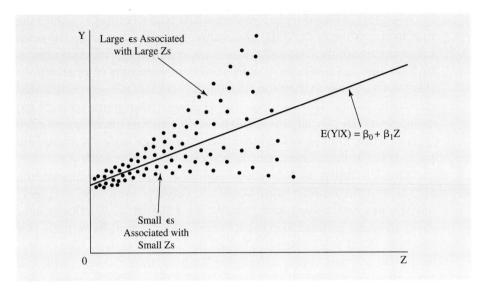

Figure 10.4 Eyeballing Residuals for Possible Heteroskedasticity

If you plot the residuals of an equation with respect to a potential Z proportionality factor, an expanding (or contracting) range of residuals is an indication of possible heteroskedasticity.

2. Is the subject of the research likely to be afflicted with heteroskedasticity? Not only are cross-sectional studies the most frequent source of heteroskedasticity, but cross-sectional studies with large variations in the size of the dependent variable are particularly susceptible to heteroskedasticity. For instance, a study of gasoline consumption by state is much more likely to encounter heteroskedasticity than is a study of the tax rate on gasoline because of the greater variation in the size of the dependent variable.

3. Does a graph of the residuals show any evidence of heteroskedasticity? It sometimes saves time to plot the residuals with respect to a potential Z proportionality factor. In such cases, the graph alone can often show that heteroskedasticity is or is not likely. Figure 10.4 shows an example of what to look for: an expanding (or contracting) *range* of the residuals.

The Park Test

How do we test for pure heteroskedasticity of the form that we assumed in the previous section? That form, as outlined in the previous section, is:

$$\text{VAR}(\epsilon_i) = \sigma^2 Z_i^2$$

where: ϵ = the error term of the equation being estimated
          σ^2 = the variance of the homoskedastic error term
          Z = the proportionality factor

The **Park test**[5] tests the residuals of an equation to see if there is heteroskedasticity in the error term of that equation. The Park test has three basic steps:

1. *Obtain the residuals of the estimated regression equation.* The first step is to estimate the equation with OLS and then find the residuals from their estimation:

$$e_i = Y_i - \hat{Y}_i = Y_i - (\hat{\beta}_0 + \hat{\beta}_1 X_{1i} + \hat{\beta}_2 X_{2i}) \qquad (10.6)$$

These residuals, which are printed out by most computer regression packages, are the same ones used to calculate the Durbin–Watson *d* statistic to test for serial correlation.

2. *Use these residuals to form the dependent variable in a second regression.* In particular, the Park test suggests that you run the following double-log regression:

$$\ln(e_i^2) = \alpha_0 + \alpha_1 \ln Z_i + u_i \qquad (10.7)$$

where: e_i = the residual from the *i*th observation from Equation 10.6
          Z_i = your best choice as to the possible proportionality
                 factor (Z)
          u_i = a classical (homoskedastic) error term[6]

3. *Test the significance of the coefficient of Z in Equation 10.7 with a t-test.* If the coefficient of Z is significantly different from zero, this is evidence of heteroskedastic patterns in the residuals with respect to Z; otherwise, heteroskedasticity related to this particular Z is not supported by the evidence in these residuals. However, it's impossible to prove that a particular equation's error terms are homoskedastic.

. A major problem with the Park Test is the identification of the proportionality factor Z. Although Z is often an explanatory variable in the original regression equation, there is no guarantee of that.

---

5. R. E. Park, "Estimation with Heteroskedastic Error Terms," *Econometrica*, Vol. 54, p. 888.

6. One criticism of the Park test is that this error term is not necessarily homoskedastic. See S. M. Goldfeld and R. E. Quandt, *Nonlinear Methods in Econometrics* (Amsterdam: North-Holland Publishing Company, 1972), pp. 93–94.

In most cross-sectional models, a good Z would be one that measured the size of the observation. In a time series regression a good Z might be t, the observation number. For more on this fairly thorny issue, see Exercise 6 at the end of the chapter.

An Example of the Use of the Park Test

Let's return to the Woody's Restaurants example of Section 3.2 and test for heteroskedasticity in the residuals of Equation 3.5. Recall that regression explained the number of customers, as measured by the check volume (Y) at a cross section of 33 different Woody's restaurants as a function of the number of nearby competitors (N), the nearby population (P), and the average household income of the local area (I):

$$\hat{Y}_i = 102,192 - 9075N_i + 0.355P_i + 1.288I_i \qquad (3.5)$$
$$(2053) \quad (0.073) \quad (0.543)$$
$$t = -4.42 \qquad 4.88 \qquad 2.37$$
$$N = 33 \qquad \overline{R}^2 = .579$$

Let's use the Park test to see if the residuals from Equation 3.5 give any indication of heteroskedasticity.

1. *Calculate the residuals.* In the Woody's example, these residuals have already been calculated. They're at the end of Section 3.2.

2. *Use these residuals as the dependent variable in a second regression.* Run a regression with the log of the squared residual as the dependent variable as a function of the log of the suspected proportionality factor Z as first outlined in Equation 10.7. Since larger error term variances might exist in more heavily populated areas, population (P) is a reasonable choice as a Z to try in our Park test. Any other variable related to the size of the market or of the particular restaurant would also be a reasonable possibility.[7]

---

7. Note that *this* Park test says nothing about *other* proportionality factors or other forms of heteroskedasticity. Although heteroskedasticity of any kind is unlikely in this example because of the nature of the dependent variable, it's possible to find homoskedasticity with respect to one proportionality factor (or form) but heteroskedasticity with respect to some other proportionality factor (or form). Careful thinking is necessary before a potential Z can be chosen. Running a Park test on every conceivable variable would do little but increase the chance of Type I Error (rejecting the null hypothesis of homoskedasticity when it's true).

If the logged and squared residuals from Equation 3.5 are regressed as a function of the log of P, we obtain:

$$\widehat{\ln(e_i^2)} = 21.05 - 0.2865\ln P_i \qquad (10.8)$$
$$(0.6263)$$
$$t = -0.457$$
$$N = 33 \qquad R^2 = .0067$$

3. *Test the significance of $\hat{\alpha}_1$ in Equation 10.7.* As can be seen from the calculated t-score, there is virtually no measurable relationship between the squared residuals of Equation 3.5 and population. The calculated t-score of -0.457 is quite a bit smaller in absolute value than 2.750, the critical t-value (from Statistical Table B-1) for a two-tailed, 1-percent test. As a result, we would not be able to reject the null hypothesis of homoskedasticity:[8]

$$H_0: \alpha_1 = 0$$
$$H_A: \alpha_1 \neq 0$$

For more practice in the use of the Park test, see Exercise 4 at the end of the chapter.

The White Test

Unfortunately, to use the Park test we must know Z_i, the variable suspected of being proportional to the possible heteroskedasticity. Quite often, however, we might not be able to decide which of a number of possible Z factors to test. In this situation, it's unadvisable to run a series of Park tests (one for each possible proportionality factor). Instead, it is appropriate to use the White test, one of a family of such tests.[9]

Like the Park test, the **White test**[10] approaches the detection of heteroskedasticity by running a regression with the squared residuals as the dependent variable. This time, though, the right-hand side of the secondary

---

8. Recall that not being able to reject the null hypothesis of homoskedasticity doesn't prove that the error term is homoskedastic.

9. These are a general group of tests based on the Lagrange Multiplier (LM). For more on LM tests, see Section 12.2.

10. Halbert White, "A Heteroskedasticity-Consistent Covariance Matrix Estimator and a Direct Test for Heteroskedasticity," *Econometrica*, Vol. 48, pp. 817–838.

equation includes all the original independent variables, the squares of all the original independent variables, and the cross products of all the original independent variables with each other. The White test thus has the distinct advantage of not assuming any particular form of heteroskedasticity. As a result, it's rapidly gaining support as the best[11] test yet devised to apply to all types of heteroskedasticity.

To run a White test:

1. *Obtain the residuals of the estimated regression equation.* This first step is identical to the first step in the Park test.

2. *Use these residuals (squared) as the dependent variable in a second equation that includes as explanatory variables each X from the original equation, the square of each X, and the product of each X times every other X.* For example, if the original equation's independent variables are X_1, X_2, and X_3, the appropriate White test equation is:

$$
\begin{aligned}
(e_i)^2 = \alpha_0 &+ \alpha_1 X_{1i} + \alpha_2 X_{2i} + \alpha_3 X_{3i} + \alpha_4 X_{1i}^2 \qquad (10.9)\\
&+ \alpha_5 X_{2i}^2 + \alpha_6 X_{3i}^2 + \alpha_7 X_{1i} X_{2i} + \alpha_8 X_{1i} X_{3i}\\
&+ \alpha_9 X_{2i} X_{3i} + u_i
\end{aligned}
$$

3. *Test the overall significance of Equation 10.9 with the chi-square test.* The appropriate test statistic here is NR^2, or the sample size (N) times the coefficient of determination (the unadjusted R^2) of Equation 10.9. This test statistic has a chi-square distribution with degrees of freedom equal to the number of slope coefficients in Equation 10.9. If NR^2 is larger than the critical chi-square value found in Statistical Table B-8, then we reject the null hypothesis and conclude that it's likely that we

---

11. For cross-sectional data, many econometricians prefer the Breusch–Pagan test, which involves running a linear regression with the squared residuals from your original equation as a function of all the independent variables in that equation. For more, see Jeffrey M. Wooldridge, *Introductory Econometrics* (Mason, OH: Southwestern, 2006), pp. 273–276. For time-series data, the best test is Engle's Autoregressive Conditional Heteroskedasticity (ARCH) test. An ARCH model considers the variance of the current observation of the error to be a function of (to be conditional on) the square of previous time periods' error term observations. Thus, testing for heteroskedasticity consists of measuring the fit of an equation that specifies e_t^2 as a function of e_{t-1}^2, e_{t-2}^2, e_{t-3}^2, etc. See Rob Engle, "Autoregressive Conditional Heteroskedasticity with Estimates of the Variance of United Kingdom Inflation," *Econometrica*, Vol. 50, pp. 987–1007.

have heteroskedasticity. If NR^2 is less than the critical chi-square value, then we cannot reject the null hypothesis of homoskedasticity.

The White test can be thought of as a generalized Park test, since the White test includes a variety of possible proportionality factors, but the Park test includes just one. In fact, if there is exactly one independent variable in the equation and if that variable is an appropriate proportionality factor, the White and Park tests are identical except that the Park test uses a double-log functional form.[12]

One problem with the White test is that, in some situations, the secondary equation cannot be estimated because it has negative degrees of freedom. This can happen when the original equation has a small sample size and/or so many variables that the secondary equation has more independent variables (including the squared and cross-product terms) than observations. Sometimes the difficulty can be avoided if there are dummy independent variables in the original equation because we must drop the squares of all dummies from Equation 10.9 (since $0^2 = 0$ and $1^2 = 1$, they're perfectly collinear). For practice in the use of the White test, see Exercises 7 and 8.

(10.4) Remedies for Heteroskedasticity

The first thing to do if the Park test or the White test indicates the possibility of heteroskedasticity is to examine the equation carefully for specification errors. Although you should never include an explanatory variable simply because a test indicates the possibility of heteroskedasticity, you ought to rigorously think through the specification of the equation. If this rethinking allows you to discover a variable that should have been in the regression from the beginning, then that variable should be added to the equation. However, if there are no obvious specification errors, the heteroskedasticity is probably pure in nature, and one of the remedies described in this section should be considered.

Heteroskedasticity-Corrected Standard Errors

The most popular remedy for heteroskedasticity is heteroskedasticity-corrected standard errors, which adjusts the estimation of the $SE(\hat{\beta})$s for heteroskedasticity while still using the OLS estimates of the slope coefficients.

---

12. Technically, the White test is a power series expansion that provides a nonparametric fit to any function of the independent variables. Many econometric software packages, including EViews and Stata, allow a researcher to run the White test at the click of a mouse, but this option is not available for the Park test because the researcher must choose a proportionality factor Z before a Park test can be run.

The logic behind this approach is powerful. Since heteroskedasticity causes problems with the SE($\hat{\beta}$)s but not with the $\hat{\beta}$s, it makes sense to improve the estimation of the SE($\hat{\beta}$)s in a way that doesn't alter the estimates of the slope coefficients. This approach is virtually identical to the use of Newey–West standard errors as a remedy for serial correlation.

Thus, **heteroskedasticity-corrected (HC) standard errors** are SE($\hat{\beta}$)s that have been calculated specifically to avoid the consequences of heteroskedasticity. The HC procedure yields an estimator of the standard errors that, while they are biased, are generally more accurate than uncorrected standard errors for large samples in the face of heteroskedasticity. As a result, the HC SE($\hat{\beta}$)s can be used in t-tests and other hypothesis tests in most samples without the errors of inference potentially caused by heteroskedasticity. Typically, the HC SE($\hat{\beta}$)s are larger than the OLS SE($\hat{\beta}$)s, thus producing lower t-scores and decreasing the probability that a given estimated coefficient will be significantly different from zero. The technique was suggested by Halbert White in the same article in which he proposed the White test for heteroskedasticity.[13]

There are a few problems with using heteroskedasticity-corrected standard errors. First, the technique works best in large samples. Second, details of the calculation of the HC SE($\hat{\beta}$)s are beyond the scope of this text and imply a model that is substantially more general than the basic theoretical construct, $VAR(\epsilon_i) = \sigma^2 Z_i^2$, of this chapter. In addition, not all computer regression software packages calculate heteroskedasticity-corrected standard errors.

Redefining the Variables

Another approach to ridding an equation of heteroskedasticity is to go back to the basic underlying theory of the equation and redefine the variables in a way that avoids heteroskedasticity. A redefinition of the variables often is useful in allowing the estimated equation to focus more on the behavioral aspects of the relationship. Such a rethinking is a difficult and discouraging process because it appears to dismiss all the work already done. However, once the theoretical work has been reviewed, the alternative approaches that are discovered are often exciting in that they offer possible ways to avoid problems that had previously seemed insurmountable. Be careful, however.

---

13. Note that Newey–West standard errors, introduced in Section 9.4, also can be used as HC standard errors. Indeed, some econometric software packages, including EViews, provide a choice between the White and Newey–West procedures. Unless otherwise noted, however, HC standard errors should be assumed to be of the White variety. Most authors refer to this method as HCCM, for heteroskedasticity-consistent covariance matrix.

Redefining your variables is a functional form specification change that can dramatically change your equation.

In some cases, the only redefinition that's needed to rid an equation of heteroskedasticity is to switch from a linear functional form to a double-log functional form. The double-log form has inherently less variation than the linear form, so it's less likely to encounter heteroskedasticity. In addition, there are many research topics for which the double-log form is just as theoretically logical as the linear form. This is especially true if the linear form was chosen by default, as is often the case.

In other situations, it might be necessary to completely rethink the research project in terms of its underlying theory. For example, consider a cross-sectional model of the total expenditures by the governments of different cities. Logical explanatory variables to consider in such an analysis are the aggregate income, the population, and the average wage in each city. The larger the total income of a city's residents and businesses, for example, the larger the city government's expenditures (see Figure 10.5). In this case, it's not very enlightening to

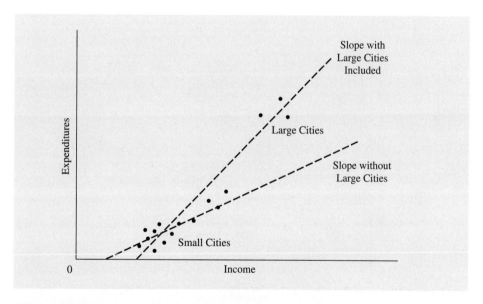

Figure 10.5 An Aggregate City Expenditures Function

If city expenditures are explained in an aggregate model, the larger cities play a major role in the determination of the coefficient values. Note how the slope would be somewhat lower without the heavy influence of the larger cities. In addition, heteroskedasticity is a potential problem in an aggregate model because the wide range of sizes of the dependent variable makes different error term variances more likely.

know that the larger cities have larger incomes and larger expenditures (in absolute magnitude) than the smaller ones.

Fitting a regression line to such data (see the line in Figure 10.5) also gives undue weight to the larger cities because they would otherwise give rise to large squared residuals. That is, since OLS minimizes the summed squared residuals, and since the residuals from the large cities are likely to be large due simply to the size of the city, the regression estimation will be especially sensitive to the residuals from the larger cities. This is often called "spurious correlation" due to size.

In addition, the residuals may indicate heteroskedasticity. It makes sense to consider reformulating the model in a way that will discount the scale factor (the size of the cities) and emphasize the underlying behavior. In this case, per capita expenditures would be a logical dependent variable. Such a transformation is shown in Figure 10.6. This form of the equation places New York and Los Angeles on the same scale as, say, Pasadena or New Brunswick and thus gives them the same weight in estimation. If an explanatory variable happened not to be a function of the size of the city, however, it would not need

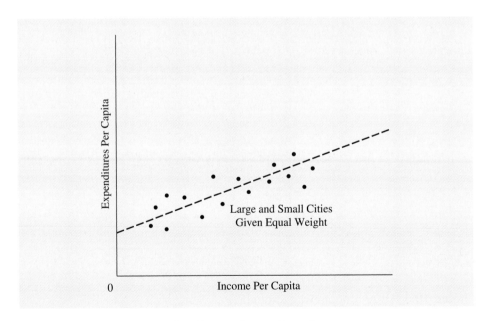

Figure 10.6 A Per Capita City Expenditures Function

If city expenditures are explained in a per capita model, then large and small cities have equal weights. In addition, heteroskedasticity is less likely, because the dependent variable does not vary over a wide range of sizes.

to be adjusted to per capita terms. If the equation included the average wage of city workers, for example, that wage would not be divided through by population in the transformed equation.

Suppose your original equation is:

$$EXP_i = \beta_0 + \beta_1 POP_i + \beta_2 INC_i + \beta_3 WAGE_i + \epsilon_i \qquad (10.10)$$

where EXP_i refers to expenditures, INC_i refers to income, $WAGE_i$ refers to the average wage, and POP_i refers to the population of the ith city.

The transformed equation[14] would be

$$EXP_i/POP_i = \alpha_0 + \alpha_1 INC_i/POP_i + \alpha_2 WAGE_i + u_i \qquad (10.12)$$

where u_i is a classical homoskedastic error term. While the directly transformed Equation 10.12 probably avoids heteroskedasticity, such a solution should be considered incidental to the benefits of rethinking the equation in a way that focuses on the basic behavior being examined.

Note that it's possible that the *reformulated* Equation 10.12 could have heteroskedasticity; the error variances might be larger for the observations having the larger per capita values for expenditures than they are for smaller per capita values. Thus, it is legitimate to suspect and test for heteroskedasticity even in this transformed model. Such heteroskedasticity in the transformed equation is unlikely, however, because there will be little of the variation in size normally associated with heteroskedasticity.

(10.5) A More Complete Example

Let's work through a more complete example involving heteroskedasticity, a cross-sectional model of petroleum consumption by state.

---

14. This transformed equation is very similar to the equation for Weighted Least Squares (WLS). *Weighted Least Squares* is a remedy for heteroskedasticity that consists of dividing the entire equation (including the constant and the heteroskedastic error term) by the proportionality factor Z and then re-estimating the equation with OLS. For the example in this section, the WLS equation would be:

$$EXP_i/POP_i = \beta_0/POP_i + \beta_1 + \beta_2 INC_i/POP_i + \beta_3 WAGE_i/POP_i + u_i \quad (10.11)$$

where the variables and βs in Equation 10.11 are identical to those in Equation 10.10. Dividing through by Z means that u is a homoskedastic error term as long as Z is the correct proportionality factor and as long as the functional form of the heteroskedasticity is that of Equation 10.4. These are not trivial problems, however, and other transformations and HCSEs are much easier to use than WLS is, so we no longer recommend the use of WLS.

Possible explanatory variables include functions of the size of the state (such as the number of miles of roadway, the number of motor vehicle registrations, or the population) and variables that are *not* functions of the size of the state (such as the price of gasoline or the speed limit). Since there is little to be gained by including more than one variable that measures the size of the state (because such an addition would be theoretically redundant and likely to cause needless multicollinearity), and since the speed limit was the same for all states (it would be a useful variable in a time-series model, however) a reasonable model to consider might be:

$$PCON_i \; = \; f(\overset{+}{REG}, \overset{-}{PRICE}) \; + \; \epsilon_i \; = \; \beta_0 \; + \; \beta_1 REG_i \; + \; \beta_2 PRICE_i \; + \; \epsilon_i \quad (10.13)$$

where: $PCON_i$ = petroleum consumption in the *i*th state (trillions of BTUs)
            REG_i = motor vehicle registrations in the *i*th state (thousands)
            $PRICE_i$ = the price of gasoline in the *i*th state (cents per gallon)
            ϵ_i = a classical error term

The more cars registered in a state, we would think, the more petroleum consumed, while a high gasoline price would decrease aggregate gasoline purchases in that state.[15] If we now collect data from 2005 for this example (see Table 10.1) we can estimate:

$$\widehat{PCON_i} = 4101 + 0.16REG_i - 1885PRICE_i \quad (10.14)$$
$$(0.01) \qquad\qquad (750)$$
$$t = \qquad\quad 12.4 \qquad\qquad -2.51$$
$$N = 50 \qquad \overline{R}^2 = .76$$

This equation seems to have no problems; the coefficients are significant in the hypothesized directions, and the overall equation is statistically significant. No Durbin–Watson *d* statistic is shown because there is no "natural" order of the observations to test for serial correlation (if you're curious, the DW for the order in Table 10.1 is 2.15).

Given the discussion in the previous sections, let's investigate the possibility of heteroskedasticity caused by variation in the size of the states. To test this

---

15. An alternative to using TAX as an independent variable in this equation is to use TAX*REG or TAX*POP (where POP_i is the population of the *i*th state). These are more sophisticated examples of the interaction terms we introduced in Section 7.5 in our discussion of slope dummy variables. A given tax rate would have a greater impact on petroleum usage in big states than in small ones, and multiplying TAX by a measure of the size of the state would allow the new variable (the interaction term) to better measure that effect.

Table 10.1 Data for the Petroleum Consumption Example

PCON	PRICE	REG	POP	STATE
580	2.11	4545	4548	Alabama
284	2.13	673	663	Alaska
537	2.23	3972	5953	Arizona
377	2.10	1940	2776	Arkansas
3837	2.47	32487	36154	California
463	2.19	1808	4663	Colorado
463	2.17	3059	3501	Connecticut
148	2.07	737	842	Delaware
1940	2.21	15691	17768	Florida
1058	2.09	8063	9133	Georgia
270	2.47	948	1273	Hawaii
139	2.14	1374	1429	Idaho
1313	2.22	9458	12765	Illinois
901	2.19	4955	6266	Indiana
393	2.13	3398	2966	Iowa
434	2.17	2368	2748	Kansas
664	2.14	3428	4173	Kentucky
1610	2.10	3819	4507	Louisiana
262	2.16	1075	1318	Maine
561	2.15	4322	5590	Maryland
734	2.08	5420	6433	Massachusetts
1010	2.24	8247	10101	Michigan
694	2.11	4647	5127	Minnesota
484	2.11	1978	2908	Mississippi
737	2.09	4589	5798	Missouri
161	2.17	1009	935	Montana
231	2.21	1703	1758	Nebraska
242	2.38	1349	2412	Nevada
198	2.08	1174	1307	New Hampshire
1233	1.99	6262	8703	New Jersey
250	2.19	1548	1926	New Mexico
1776	2.23	11863	19316	New York
947	2.14	6148	8672	North Carolina
121	2.19	695	635	North Dakota
1340	2.19	10634	11471	Ohio
545	2.08	3725	3543	Oklahoma
370	2.28	2897	3639	Oregon
1466	2.14	9864	12405	Pennsylvania
102	2.12	812	1074	Rhode Island
517	2.06	3339	4247	South Carolina
113	2.20	854	775	South Dakota

(continued)

Table 10.1 (*continued*)

PCON	PRICE	REG	POP	STATE
782	2.11	4980	5956	Tennessee
5628	2.07	17470	22929	Texas
276	2.12	2210	2490	Utah
86	2.13	508	622	Vermont
965	2.10	6591	7564	Virginia
793	2.28	5598	6292	Washington
255	2.20	1352	1814	West Virginia
597	2.26	4725	5528	Wisconsin
162	2.08	646	509	Wyoming

Source: *2008 Statistical Abstract* (U.S. Department of Commerce).

Datafile = GAS10

possibility, we obtain the residuals from Equation 10.14, and run Park and White tests on them.

Before we can run a Park test, we must decide what possible proportionality factor Z to investigate. Almost any variable related to market size would be appropriate, but motor vehicle registrations (REG) is certainly a reasonable choice. Note that to run a Park test with the gasoline tax rate (TAX) as the proportionality factor Z would be a mistake, since there is little evidence that the tax rate varies significantly with the size of the state.

If we run this Park test regression, we obtain:

$$\widehat{\ln(e_i^2)} = 3.66 + 0.73\ln REG_i \tag{10.15}$$
$$(0.35)$$
$$t = 2.09$$
$$\overline{R}^2 = .064 \qquad N = 50$$

Since 2.09 is greater than 2.01, the critical t-value[16] for a 5-percent two-tailed t-test in Statistical Table B-1, we can reject the null hypothesis of homoskedasticity, because the appropriate decision rule is:

Reject H_0: $\alpha_1 = 0$ (Homoskedasticity)   if $|t_{PARK}| > 2.01$

Do Not Reject H_0: (Heteroskedasticity)   if $|t_{PARK}| \leq 2.01$

---

16. Note that Table B-1 doesn't contain a value for 48 degrees of freedom (do you see why there are 48 degrees of freedom and not 47?), so we have to interpolate to get a critical value of 2.01.

To see whether the White test also will detect this heteroskedasticity, we'll need to modify Equation 10.9 to fit our example. The dependent variable will be the square of the residuals in Equation 10.14, and the independent variables will be REG, PRICE, their squares, and their cross-product:

$$(e_i)^2 = \alpha_0 + \alpha_1 REG_i + \alpha_2 PRICE_i + \alpha_3 REG_i^2 \qquad (10.16)$$
$$+ \alpha_4 PRICE_i^2 + \alpha_5 REG_i * PRICE_i + u_i$$

If we estimate[17] Equation 10.16 with the residuals from Equation 10.14 and the data from Table 10.1, we obtain an R^2 of .85. Now what?

Well, the White test requires us to multiply R^2 by N, resulting in $50*.85 = 42.5$. We then need to compare NR^2 with the critical value of the Chi-Square distribution for 5 degrees of freedom (the number of slope coefficients, in this case). As you can confirm by looking at Table B-8, the critical Chi-Square value at the 5-percent level for 5 degrees of freedom is 11.07. This means that our decision rule is:

Do not reject the null hypothesis of homoskedasticity if $NR^2 < 11.07$

Reject the null hypothesis of homoskedasticity if $NR^2 > 11.07$

Since $NR^2 = 42.5 > 11.07$, we can reject the null hypothesis of homoskedasticity. We have heteroskedasticity!

Since there appears to be heteroskedasticity in the residuals of Equation 10.14, what should we do? First, we should think through the specification of the equation in search of an omitted variable. While there are a number of possible omitted variables, it turns out that the heteroskedasticity in the equation very clearly is pure heteroskedasticity.

First, let's apply the most popular of our remedies, heteroskedasticity-corrected standard errors, to this example. If we start with Equation 10.14 and use White's suggested method for estimating $SE(\hat{\beta})$s that are minimum variance (for large samples) in the face of heteroskedasticity, we obtain:

$$\widehat{PCON_i} = 4101 + 0.16REG_i - 1885PRICE_i \qquad (10.17)$$
$$(0.03) \qquad (1360)$$
$$t = \qquad 4.85 \qquad -1.39$$
$$N = 50 \qquad \overline{R}^2 = .76$$

---

17. Most regression packages, including EViews and Stata, have "automatic" White test options to do this estimation, but we advise beginning econometricians to avoid these options until they have enough experience with the White test to fully understand how it works. Students interested in getting this experience should complete Exercise 8.

Compare Equation 10.14 with Equation 10.17. Note that the slope coefficients are identical, as you'd expect, since the HC approach uses OLS to estimate the coefficients. Also note that the HC $SE(\hat{\beta})$s are higher than the OLS $SE(\hat{\beta})$s, as is usually but not necessarily the case. While the resulting t-scores are lower, they are still reasonably large in the direction we expected, making Equation 10.17 very appealing indeed.

The second possible remedy for heteroskedasticity is to change to a double-log functional form. If we use the data in Table 10.1 to estimate a double-log equation, we get:

$$\widehat{\ln PCON_i} = -0.32 + 0.90\ln REG_i - 0.89\ln PRICE_i \qquad (10.18)$$
$$(0.04) \qquad\qquad (1.03)$$
$$t = \qquad 20.3 \qquad\qquad -0.87$$
$$N = 50 \qquad \overline{R}^2 = .89$$

As can be seen, switching to logs improves $\overline{R}^2$ and the significance of the coefficient of $\ln REG$, but the t-score for the coefficient of $\ln PRICE$ is below 1. We'd normally be concerned about such a low t-score, but the estimated coefficient is in the expected direction, and PRICE unambiguously belongs in the equation for theoretical reasons, so there's no reason to consider the possibility that PRICE might be irrelevant. As we'd hope, the White test indicates that the residuals of Equation 10.18 are indeed homoskedastic.

Finally, an alternative is to rethink the purpose of the regression and reformulate the variables of the equation to try to avoid heteroskedasticity resulting from spurious correlation due to size. If we were to rethink Equation 10.14, we might decide to attempt to explain per capita petroleum consumption, coming up with:

$$PCON_i/POP_i = \beta_0 + \beta_1 REG_i/POP_i + \beta_2 PRICE_i + \epsilon_i \quad (10.19)$$

where POP_i is the population of the ith state in thousands of people.

If we estimate Equation 10.19, we obtain:

$$\widehat{PCON_i/POP_i} = 0.23 + 0.15 REG_i/POP_i - 0.10 PRICE_i \qquad (10.20)$$
$$(0.06) \qquad\qquad (0.10)$$
$$t = \qquad 2.52 \qquad\qquad -1.00$$
$$N = 50 \qquad \overline{R}^2 = .12$$

If we compare Equation 10.20 with Equations 10.17 and 10.18, we see that this approach is quite different and not necessarily better. The statistical properties of Equation 10.20, though not directly comparable to the other equations, do not appear as strong as they might be, but this is not necessarily the deciding factor. One positive note is that the residuals of Equation 10.20 do indeed appear to be homoskedastic.

Which remedy is best: HC standard errors, the double-log functional form, or reformulating the equation? Most econometricians would prefer HC standard errors, though the sample size of 50 makes it unlikely that the large sample properties of HC estimators hold in this case. However, this answer could change depending on the underlying theory of your equation. If theory strongly supports either the double-log or the reformulated functional form, then that model clearly is best. In such a situation, however, it's worth asking why the theoretically superior functional form wasn't chosen in the first place. Finally, in the fairly unusual case that t-scores aren't used to test hypotheses or retain variables, then it's not at all clear that any sort of remedy for heteroskedasticity is required at all.

10.6 Summary

1. Heteroskedasticity is the violation of Classical Assumption V that the observations of the error term are drawn from a distribution with a constant variance. Homoskedastic error term observations are drawn from a distribution that has a constant variance for all observations, and heteroskedastic error term observations are drawn from distributions whose variances differ from different observations. Heteroskedasticity occurs most frequently in cross-sectional data sets.

2. The variance of a heteroskedastic error term is not equal to σ^2, a constant. Instead, it equals σ_i^2, where the subscript i indicates that the variance can change from observation to observation. Many different kinds of heteroskedasticity are possible, but a common model is one in which the variance changes systematically as a function of some other variable, a proportionality factor Z:

$$VAR(\epsilon_i) = \sigma^2 Z_i^2$$

    The proportionality factor Z is usually a variable related in some way to the size or accuracy of the dependent variable.

3. Pure heteroskedasticity is a function of the error term of the correctly specified regression equation. Impure heteroskedasticity is caused by a specification error such as an omitted variable.

4. The major consequence of heteroskedasticity is bias in the OLS $SE(\hat{\beta})$s, causing unreliable hypothesis testing. Pure heteroskedasticity does not cause bias in the estimates of the βs themselves.

5. Many tests use the residuals of an equation to test for the possibility of heteroskedasticity in the error term. The Park test uses a function of these residuals as the dependent variable of a second regression whose explanatory variable is the log of the suspected proportionality factor Z:

$$\ln(e_i^2) = \alpha_0 + \alpha_1 \ln Z_i + u_i$$

If $\hat{\alpha}_1$ is significantly different from zero, then we reject the null hypothesis of homoskedasticity.

6. The first step in correcting heteroskedasticity is to check for an omitted variable that might be causing impure heteroskedasticity. If the specification is as good as possible, then solutions such as HC standard errors or redefining the variables should be considered.

EXERCISES

(The answer to Exercise 2 is in Appendix A.)

1. Write the meaning of each of the following terms without referring to the book (or your notes), and compare your definition with the version in the text for each.
   a. impure heteroskedasticity
   b. pure heteroskedasticity
   c. proportionality factor Z
   d. the Park test
   e. the White test
   f. heteroskedasticity-corrected standard errors

2. Let's return to the analysis of the international pharmaceutical industry that we started in Exercise 14 of Chapter 5. That study was cross-sectional and included countries as large as the United States and as small as Luxembourg, so you'd certainly expect heteroskedasticity to be a potential problem. Luckily, the dependent variable in the original research was P_i, the pharmaceutical price level in the ith country divided by that of the United States, so the researchers didn't encounter the

wide variations in size typically associated with heteroskedasticity. (Do you see why?)

Suppose, however, that we use the same data set to build a model of pharmaceutical consumption:

$$\widehat{CV_i} = -15.9 + 0.18N_i + 0.22P_i + 14.3IPC_i \qquad (10.21)$$
$$\phantom{\widehat{CV_i} = -15.9 +} (0.05) \quad (0.09) \quad (6.39)$$
$$t = 3.32 \quad\;\; 2.53 \quad\;\; 2.24$$
$$N = 32 \quad \bar{R}^2 = .31$$

where: CV_i = the volume of consumption of pharmaceuticals in the ith country divided by that of the United States

N_i = the population of the ith country divided by that of the United States

IPC_i = a dummy variable equal to 1 if the ith country encouraged price competition, 0 otherwise

a. Does heteroskedasticity seem more likely when CV is the dependent variable than when P is the dependent variable? Explain your reasoning.

b. Use the data in Table 5.1 (datafile = DRUGS5) to test for heteroskedasticity in Equation 10.21 with both the Park test (using N as your proportionality factor) and the White test at the 5-percent level. (*Hint:* Remember to run Equation 10.21 first so that EViews, Stata, or your computer's regression program will have the correct residuals to analyze.)

c. If your answer to part b is heteroskedasticity, estimate HC standard errors for Equation 10.21.

d. Similarly, if you encountered heteroskedasticity, re-estimate Equation 10.21 using a double-log functional form.

e. Similarly, if you encountered heteroskedasticity, reformulate the variables in Equation 10.21 to avoid heteroskedasticity and estimate your reformulated equation.

f. Which of our three remedies for heteroskedasticity do you think is best in this case? Why?

g. In Chapter 5, we estimated an equation with P as a function of CVN (CV per capita), and now we've estimated an equation with CV as a function of P. Which Classical Assumption are you worried that we might have violated? Explain.

3. Of all the econometric problems we've encountered, heteroskedasticity is the one that seems the most difficult to understand. Close your

book and attempt to write an explanation of heteroskedasticity in your own words. Be sure to include a diagram in your description.

4. Use the Park test to test the null hypothesis of homoskedasticity in each of the following situations (1-percent level of significance):
   a. The calculated t-score of your suspected proportionality factor Z is 3.561 from a Park test regression with 25 degrees of freedom.
   b. The following residuals and values for the potential Z. (*Hint:* This requires running a regression.)

Observation	Residual	Proportionality Factor Z
1	3.147	120
2	9.394	240
3	−2.344	900
4	−1.034	50
5	5.678	600
6	2.113	20
7	−4.356	200

   c. How would your answer to Part b change if the seventh observation of Z was minus 200? How would you even take the log of Z?

5. A. Ando and F. Modigliani collected the following data on the income and consumption of non-self-employed homeowners:[18]

Income Bracket ($)	Average Income ($)	Average Consumption ($)
0–999	556	2760
1000–1999	1622	1930
2000–2999	2664	2740
3000–3999	3587	3515
4000–4999	4535	4350
5000–5999	5538	5320
6000–7499	6585	6250
7500–9999	8582	7460
10000–above	14033	11500

---

18. Albert Ando and Franco Modigliani, "The 'Permanent Income' and 'Life Cycle' Hypotheses of Saving Behavior: Comparisons and Tests," in I. Friend and R. Jones, eds. *Consumption and Saving*, Vol. II, 1960, p. 154.

a. Run a regression to explain average consumption as a function of average income.

b. Use the Park test to test the residuals from the equation you ran in part a for heteroskedasticity, using average income as the potential proportionality factor Z (5 percent).

c. Run a 5-percent White test on the same residuals.

d. If the tests run in Parts b or c show evidence of heteroskedasticity, then what, if anything, should be done about it?

6. In the Park test, one of the major difficulties is choosing a proportionality factor (Z). In each of the following equations, separate the listed explanatory variables into those that are likely or unlikely to be proportionality factors.

a. The number of economics majors in a cross section of various-sized colleges and universities as a function of the number of undergraduates attending a school, the number of required courses in that school's economics major, the average GPA in the major, and the number of economics professors there.

b. GDP in a cross section of various countries as a function of the aggregate gross investment in a nation, the percentage growth of its money supply, the maximum marginal tax rate on capital gains there, and its population.

c. The demand for carrots in a time-series model of the United States as a function of the real price of carrots, U.S. disposable income, U.S. per capita disposable income, population, the percentage error in carrot sales measurement, and the real price of celery.

7. Run a White test on the residuals from the Woody's example in Table 3.1 at the 5-percent level. Be sure to compare your answer with the Park test result in Section 10.3.

8. As further practice, estimate Equation 10.14 with the data in Table 10.1, and then run a 5-percent White test on the residuals from the state gasoline model.

9. What makes a college library great? While quality of holdings and ease of use are important, the simplest measure of the quality of a library is the number of books it holds. Suppose you've been hired by the Annual American Research on the Number of Books project (AARON) to build a model of the number of books in a cross section

of 60 U.S. university and college libraries. After researching the literature, you estimate (standard errors in parentheses):

$$\widehat{VOL}_i = -1842 + 0.038STU_i + 1.73FAC_i + 1.83SAT_i \quad (10.22)$$
$$\qquad\qquad (0.026) \qquad (0.44) \qquad (0.82)$$
$$\qquad\qquad t = 1.45 \qquad\quad 3.91 \qquad\quad 2.23$$
$$\qquad\qquad \overline{R}^2 = .81 \quad\; N = 60$$

where: VOL_i = thousands of books in the ith school's library
$\qquad\quad STU_i$ = the number of students in the ith school
$\qquad\quad FAC_i$ = the number of faculty members in the ith school
$\qquad\quad SAT_i$ = the average SATs of students in the ith school

a. The simple correlation coefficient between STU and FAC is 0.93, a Park test on the residuals of Equation 10.22 produces a t-score of 3.50, and the Durbin–Watson d for the equation is 1.91. Given this information, what econometric problems appear to exist in this equation? Explain. Which problem do you think you should attempt to correct first? Why?

b. You decide to create a linear combination of students and faculty $(TOT_i = 10FAC_i + STU_i)$ and to rerun Equation 10.22, obtaining Equation 10.23. Which equation do you prefer? Explain your reasoning.

$$\widehat{VOL}_i = -1704 + 0.087TOT_i + 1.69SAT_i \qquad\qquad (10.23)$$
$$\qquad\qquad (0.007) \qquad\; (0.84)$$
$$\qquad\qquad t = 12.87 \qquad\quad 2.02$$
$$\overline{R}^2 = .80 \quad\; N = 60 \qquad DW = 1.85$$

c. Use the data in Table 10.2 (datafile = BOOKS10) to test for heteroskedasticity in the residuals of Equation 10.23 using the Park test and/or the White test (depending on the test typically used in your class).

d. Start from the equation you prefer (between 10.22 and 10.23) and use the data in Table 10.2 to correct for heteroskedasticity. Use the method you think is most appropriate. Explain your choice.

Table 10.2 Data on College and University Library Holdings

Observation	VOL	FAC	STU	SAT
1	11.5	5	58	850
2	200.0	138	2454	954
3	70.0	44	573	874
4	100.0	98	2172	941
5	7000.0	1651	31123	1185
6	70.0	26	295	874
7	125.0	35	1131	902
8	2200.0	1278	22571	1048
9	400.0	365	6554	960
10	110.0	47	793	930
11	6000.0	1650	36330	1142
12	58.4	39	522	800
13	212.0	69	1041	1060
14	400.0	57	1059	1000
15	1888.0	896	16411	1150
16	486.0	125	1678	1170
17	439.0	135	2529	1100
18	1900.0	653	19082	1080
19	155.0	114	3523	1026
20	6.9	11	207	873
21	509.0	346	6781	1097
22	180.0	25	147	990
23	53.0	21	214	920
24	100.0	44	764	900
25	30.0	18	176	1176
26	157.0	99	3682	930
27	475.0	223	5665	1037
28	613.6	384	4411	960
29	483.6	141	3341	860
30	2500.0	2021	41528	1086
31	142.0	66	1251	1030
32	210.0	73	1036	1000
33	20.0	10	120	1070
34	150.0	94	2344	858
35	300.0	195	2400	1180
36	233.5	70	1416	910
37	235.0	165	4148	1001
38	460.7	316	9738	980
39	1632.0	355	5578	1060
40	93.0	30	505	930
41	263.0	185	3724	1124

(continued)

Table 10.2 (*continued*)

Observation	VOL	FAC	STU	SAT
42	144.5	101	2387	945
43	770.0	148	1900	1190
44	1700.0	960	16750	1057
45	1100.0	284	2833	1310
46	1900.0	905	15762	1090
47	60.0	55	875	848
48	1200.0	445	6603	1060
49	1600.0	623	14727	1120
50	1289.0	412	11179	1230
51	1666.0	1607	9251	883
52	15.0	26	608	800
53	160.0	48	656	1010
54	200.0	281	3892	980
55	263.0	195	2987	1070
56	487.0	275	5148	1060
57	3300.0	867	11240	1260
58	145.0	37	569	843
59	205.0	28	628	980
60	7377.0	2606	34055	1160

Datafile = BOOKS10

10. Consider the following double-log equation (standard errors in parentheses):[19]

$$\hat{Y}_i = 0.442X_{1i} + 0.092X_{2i} + 0.045X_{3i} + 0.259X_{4i}$$
$$\phantom{\hat{Y}_i = } (0.058) \qquad (0.042) \qquad (0.014) \qquad (0.034)$$
$$R^2 = .620 \qquad N = 430$$

where: Y_i = the log of the gross value of agricultural output (in drachmas) of the *i*th Greek farm in a given year
X_{1i} = the log of farmer workdays in a year on the *i*th farm
X_{2i} = the log of the amount of land on the *i*th farm (in stremmata, equal to a quarter of an acre)

---

19. Adapted from Pan A. Yotopoulos and Jeffrey B. Nugent, *Economics of Development* (New York: Harper & Row, 1976), p. 82. No estimate of the intercept was reported.

X_{3i} = the log of the value of the plant and equipment (plus operating expenses for plant and equipment) on the ith farm that year (in drachmas)

X_{4i} = the log of the value of livestock (including trees) plus operating expenses on livestock (in drachmas) in the ith farm that year

a. Create hypotheses about the signs of the various coefficients and then calculate the t-scores to test those hypotheses at the 5-percent level of significance.

b. Suppose you were now told that the Park test, using X_1 as a potential proportionality factor Z, indicated the likelihood of heteroskedasticity in the residuals of this equation. Is it likely that there actually is heteroskedasticity in such a double-log equation? Why or why not?

c. Is there a logical reformulation of the equation that might rid the model of heteroskedasticity?

11. Consider the following estimated regression equation for average annual hours worked (per capita) for young (16–21 years) black men in 94 standard metropolitan statistical areas (standard errors in parentheses):

$$\hat{B}_i = 300.0 + 0.50W_i - 7.5U_i - 18.3\ln P_i$$
$$\phantom{\hat{B}_i = 300.0 + } (0.05) \quad (7.5) \quad\quad (6.1)$$
$$DW = 2.00 \quad\quad N = 94 \quad\quad \overline{R}^2 = .64$$

where: B_i = average annual hours worked (per capita) by young (age 16 to 21) black men in the ith city

W_i = average annual hours worked (per capita) by young white men in the ith city

U_i = black unemployment rate in the ith city

$\ln P_i$ = natural log of the black population of the ith city

a. Develop and test (5-percent level) your own hypotheses with respect to the individual estimated slope coefficients.

b. How would you respond to the claim that an estimated coefficient of W that is far less than one is proof that racial discrimination exists in the labor markets in this country?

c. Since this is a cross-sectional model, is it reasonable to worry about heteroskedasticity? What variable would you choose as a possible Z? Explain your choice.

    d. Suppose you ran a Park test with respect to your chosen Z and found a t-score of 1.91. Does this support or refute your answer to part c? (*Hint:* Be sure to complete the Park test.)

    e. Suppose you were asked to make one change in the specification of this equation. What would you suggest? Explain your choice.

12. James Stock and Mark Watson suggest a quite different approach to heteroskedasticity. They state that "economic theory rarely gives any reason to believe that the errors are homoskedastic. It therefore is prudent to assume that the errors might be heteroskedastic unless you have compelling reasons to believe otherwise."[20] As a result, Stock and Watson automatically use HC standard errors without testing for heteroskedasticity. In fact, since they adjust every equation for heteroskedasticity, they don't even list homoskedasticity as a Classical Assumption.

    a. What do you think? Do you agree with Stock and Watson? Explain your reasoning.

    b. One key to the Stock and Watson's argument is that HC standard errors equal OLS standard errors if there is no heteroskedasticity. Does this fact change the opinion you stated in part a? Why or why not?

    c. If Stock and Watson are right, does this mean that we don't need to learn about heteroskedasticity in the first place? Did you waste your time reading this chapter?

13. R. Bucklin, R. Caves, and A. Lo estimated the following double-log model to explain the yearly circulation of metropolitan newspapers (standard errors in parentheses):[21]

$$\hat{C}_i = -8.2 - 0.56P_i + 0.90I_i + 0.76Q_i + 0.27A_i + 0.08S_i - 0.77T_i$$
$$\phantom{\hat{C}_i = -8.2}\ (0.58)\ \ (0.14)\ \ (0.21)\ \ \ (0.14)\ \ (0.05)\ \ (0.27)$$
$$N = 50$$

where: C_i = yearly circulation of the ith newspaper

          P_i = the weighted average single copy price of the ith newspaper

          I_i = the total disposable income of the metropolitan area of the ith newspaper

20. James Stock and Mark Watson, *Introduction to Econometrics* (Boston: Pearson, Addison-Wesley, 2007), p. 166.

21. R. E. Bucklin, R. E. Caves, and A. W. Lo, "Games of Survival in the U.S. Newspaper Industry," *Applied Economics*, Vol. 21, pp. 631–650. Note that the Park test results are hypothetical and that the equation was originally estimated with Two-Stage Least Squares (to be discussed in Chapter 14). These facts don't change the equation's usefulness as an exercise in this chapter.

Q_i = the number of personnel in editorial positions for the ith newspaper

A_i = the volume of retail advertising in the ith newspaper

S_i = amount of competition from suburban dailies in the ith newspaper's region

T_i = the number of television stations in the ith newspaper's region

(All variables are in logarithmic form.)

a. Hypothesize signs and run t-tests on each of the individual slope coefficients.

b. Does heteroskedasticity seem theoretically likely? Test for heteroskedasticity at the 1 percent level assuming that a Park test with I_i as Z produces a t-score of 3.13.

c. Given your responses to parts a and b, what econometric problems (out of omitted variables, irrelevant variables, incorrect functional form, multicollinearity, serial correlation, and heteroskedasticity) appear to exist in this equation?

d. If you could suggest just one change in the specification of this equation, what would that change be? Carefully explain your answer.

14. Think back to the Farmer Vin pig growing equation of Exercise 13 in Chapter 9:

$$\hat{W}_i = 12 + 3.5G_i + 7.0D_i - 0.25F_i \qquad (10.24)$$
$$\qquad\quad (1.0) \quad\ (1.0) \quad\ (0.10)$$
$$\qquad\ t = 3.5 \qquad 7.0 \qquad -2.5$$
$$\overline{R}^2 = .70 \qquad N = 200 \qquad DW = 0.50$$

where: W_i = the percentage weight gain of the ith pig during the six-month experiment

G_i = a dummy variable equal to 1 if the ith pig is a male, 0 otherwise

D_i = a dummy variable equal to 1 if the ith pig was fed only at night, 0 if the ith pig was fed only during the day

F_i = the amount of food (pounds) eaten per day by the ith pig

It turns out that this study was estimated originally with the dependent variable equal to "pounds gained by the ith pig," but a White test showed severe heteroskedasticity. (Recall that the sample pigs ranged all the way from pink piglets to ponderous porkers.) The dependent variable was converted to percentage terms in an effort to "rethink the equation" and eliminate the heteroskedasticity. Equation 10.24 was the result.

a. How theoretically likely is it that there is heteroskedasticity in the revised equation, Equation 10.24? Explain your answer.

b. Suppose that you run a Park test on the residuals of Equation 10.24 and find a t-score of −6.31 (using the weight of the ith pig as the potential proportionality factor). Do you have heteroskedasticity?

c. The t-score from your Park test in part b is negative, and yet we've never discussed "negative" or "positive" heteroskedasticity. What importance, if any, would you attach to the *sign* of the estimated slope coefficient in this Park test?

d. You appear to have heteroskedasticity in both the original and the revised versions of your equation. What should you do? Explain.

15. Let's investigate the possibility of heteroskedasticity in time-series data by looking at a model of the black market for U.S. dollars in Brazil that was studied by R. Dornbusch and C. Pechman.[22] In particular, the authors wanted to know if the Demsetz-Bagehot bid-ask theory, previously tested on cross-sectional data from the United States, could be extended to time-series data outside the United States.[23] They estimated the following model on monthly data from Brazil for March 1979 through December 1983:

$$S_t = f(\overset{+}{I_t}, \overset{+}{V_t}) + \epsilon_t = \beta_0 + \beta_1 I_t + \beta_2 \ln(1 + V_t) + \epsilon_t \quad (10.25)$$

where: S_t = the average daily spread between the bid and asking prices for the U.S. dollar on the Brazilian black market in month t

I_t = the average interest rate in month t

V_t = the variance of the daily premium between the black market rate and the official exchange rate for the dollar in month t

22. Rudiger Dornbusch and Clarice Pechman, "The Bid-Ask Spread in the Black Market for Dollars in Brazil," *Journal of Money, Credit and Banking,* Vol. 17, pp. 517–520. The data for this study were not published with the original article but are on the data diskette that accompanies William F. Lott and Subhash C. Ray, *Applied Econometrics: Problems with Data Sets* (Fort Worth: Dryden/Harcourt Brace, 1992). The analytical approach of this question also comes from Lott and Ray, pp. 169–173.

23. For a review of this literature at the time of Dornbusch and Pechman's research, see Kalman Cohen et al., "Market Makers and the Market Spread: A Review of Recent Literature," *Journal of Financial and Quantitative Studies,* Vol. 14, No. 4, pp. 813–835.

a. Use the authors' data in Table 10.3 (datafile = BID10) to estimate Equation 10.25 and test the residuals for positive first-order serial correlation.
b. If serial correlation appears to exist, reestimate Equation 10.25 using GLS. Do the coefficient estimates change? Which equation do you prefer? Why?

Table 10.3 Data on the Brazilian Black Market for Dollars

Month	S	I	V
1979:03	2.248	4.15	20.580
1979:04	2.849	4.04	12.450
1979:05	2.938	2.68	21.230
1979:06	2.418	2.81	26.300
1979:07	2.921	1.92	22.600
1979:08	2.587	2.37	18.750
1979:09	2.312	3.59	20.040
1979:10	2.658	2.03	31.110
1979:11	2.262	2.41	29.040
1979:12	4.056	4.09	20.590
1980:01	3.131	3.28	11.770
1980:02	3.404	2.89	7.900
1980:03	2.835	3.44	6.150
1980:04	3.309	2.43	6.780
1980:05	3.042	2.13	8.550
1980:06	3.417	2.94	13.380
1980:07	2.929	3.19	11.870
1980:08	3.821	3.26	15.560
1980:09	2.753	3.98	24.560
1980:10	2.633	3.69	21.110
1980:11	2.608	4.43	15.000
1980:12	2.168	5.86	7.480
1981:01	2.273	4.36	2.820
1981:02	1.892	5.66	1.540
1981:03	2.283	4.60	1.520
1981:04	2.597	4.42	4.930
1981:05	2.522	5.41	10.790
1981:06	2.865	4.63	17.160
1981:07	4.206	5.46	30.590
1981:08	2.708	5.88	23.900
1981:09	2.324	5.52	20.620
1981:10	2.736	6.07	18.900
1981:11	3.277	5.48	26.790
1981:12	3.194	6.79	29.640
1982:01	3.473	5.46	32.870

(*continued*)

Table 10.3 (*continued*)

Month	S	I	V
1982:02	2.798	6.20	30.660
1982:03	3.703	6.19	40.740
1982:04	3.574	6.06	48.040
1982:05	3.484	6.26	33.510
1982:06	2.726	6.27	23.650
1982:07	4.430	6.89	37.080
1982:08	4.158	7.55	51.260
1982:09	5.633	6.93	60.450
1982:10	5.103	8.14	83.980
1982:11	3.691	7.80	69.490
1982:12	3.952	9.61	68.030
1983:01	3.583	7.01	85.630
1983:02	4.459	7.94	77.060
1983:03	6.893	10.06	71.490
1983:04	5.129	11.82	51.520
1983:05	4.171	11.18	43.660
1983:06	5.047	10.92	59.500
1983:07	8.434	11.72	61.070
1983:08	5.143	9.54	75.380
1983:09	3.980	9.78	72.205
1983:10	4.340	9.91	59.258
1983:11	4.330	9.61	38.860
1983:12	4.350	10.09	33.380

Source: William F. Lott and Subhash C. Ray, *Applied Econometrics: Problems with Data Sets* (Fort Worth: Dryden/Harcourt Brace, 1992). (data diskette)

Datafile = BID10

c. The authors noted that S nearly doubled in size during their sample period. Does this make you concerned about the possibility of heteroskedasticity? Why or why not?

d. Test the residuals of Equation 10.25 for heteroskedasticity using the Park test or the White test. (*Hint:* A possible proportionality factor is a time-trend variable that equals 1 for March 1979 and that increases by one for each following month.)

e. Test the residuals of your GLS version of Equation 10.25 for heteroskedasticity using the Park test or the White test. Did running GLS change the possibility of heteroskedasticity?

f. What remedy would you suggest for any heteroskedasticity that might exist in such a time-series model? Be specific.

11 Running Your Own Regression Project

We believe that econometrics is best learned by doing, not by reading books, listening to lectures, or taking tests. To us, learning the art of econometrics has more in common with learning to fly a plane or learning to play golf than it does with learning about history or literature. In fact, we developed the interactive exercises of this chapter and Chapter 8 precisely because of our confidence in learning by doing.

Although interactive exercises are a good bridge between textbook examples and running your own regressions, they don't go far enough. You still need to "get your hands dirty." We think that you should run your own regression project before you finish reading this book even if you're not required to do so. We're not alone. Some professors substitute a research project for the final exam as their class's comprehensive learning experience.

Running your own regression project has three major components:

1. Choosing a topic
2. Applying the six steps in regression analysis to that topic
3. Writing your research report

The first and third of these components are the topics of Sections 11.1 and 11.5, respectively. The rest of the chapter focuses on helping you carry out the six steps in regression analysis.

11.1 Choosing Your Topic

The purpose of an econometric research project is to use regression analysis to build the best explanatory equation for a particular dependent variable for a particular sample. Often, though, the hardest part is getting started. How can you choose a good topic?

There are at least three keys to choosing a topic. First, try to pick a field that you find interesting and/or that you know something about. If you enjoy working on your project, the hours involved will seem to fly by. In addition, if you know something about your subject, you'll be more likely to make correct specification choices and/or to notice subtle indications of data errors or theoretical problems. A second key is to make sure that data are readily available with a reasonable sample (we suggest at least 25 observations). Nothing is more frustrating than searching through data source after data source in search of numbers for your dependent variable or one of your independent variables, so before you lock yourself into a topic, see if the data are there. The final key is to make sure that there is some substance to your topic. Try to avoid topics that are purely descriptive or virtually tautological in nature. Instead, look for topics that address an inherently interesting economic or behavioral question or choice.

Perhaps the best place to look for ideas for topics is to review your textbooks and notes from previous economics classes or to look over the examples and exercises of the first 10 chapters of this book. Often, you can take an idea from a previous study and update the data to see if the idea can be applied in a different context. Other times, reading an example will spark an idea about a similar or related study that you'd be interested in doing. Don't feel that your topic has to contain an original hypothesis or equation. On your first or second project, it's more important to get used to the econometrics than it is to create a publishable masterpiece.

Another way to find a topic is to read through issues of economics journals, looking for article topics that you find interesting and that might be possible to model. For example, Table 11.1 contains a list of the journals cited so far in this textbook (in order of the frequency of citation). These journals would be a great place to start if you want to try to replicate or update a previous research study. Although this is an excellent way to get ideas, it's also frustrating, because most current articles use econometric techniques that go beyond those that we've covered so far in this text. As a result, it's often difficult to compare your results to those in the article.

If you get stuck for a topic, go directly to the data sources themselves. That is, instead of thinking of a topic and then seeing if the data are available, look over what data are available and see if they help generate ideas for topics. Quite often, a reference will have data not only for a dependent variable but

Table 11.1 Sources of Potential Topic Ideas

American Economic Review
Econometrica
Journal of Applied Econometrics
Journal of Urban Economics
Southern Economic Journal
Economica
Economic Inquiry
Journal of the American Statistical Association
Journal of Econometrics
Journal of Economic Education
Journal of Money, Credit and Banking
Review of Economics and Statistics
World Development
Biometrica
The Annals of Statistics
American Psychologist
Annals of Mathematical Statistics
Applied Economics
Assessment and Evaluation of Higher Education
Journal of Business and Economic Statistics
Journal of Economic Literature
Journal of Economic Perspectives
Journal of Economic Surveys
Journal of Financial and Quantitative Studies
Journal of the Royal Statistical Society
National Tax Review
NBER (Working Papers)
Scandinavian Journal of Economics

also for most of the relevant independent variables all in one place, minimizing time spent collecting data.

Once you pick a topic, don't rush out and run your first regression. Remember, the more time you spend reviewing the literature and analyzing your expectations on a topic, the better the econometric analysis and, ultimately, your research report will be.

11.2 Collecting Your Data

Before any quantitative analysis can be done, the data must be collected, organized, and entered into a computer. Usually, this is a time-consuming and frustrating task because of the difficulty of finding data, the existence of definitional differences between theoretical variables and their empirical counterparts, and the high probability of data entry errors or data transmission errors. In general, though, time spent thinking about and collecting the data is well spent, since a researcher who knows the data sources and definitions is much less likely to make mistakes using or interpreting regressions run on that data.

What Data to Look For

Before you settle on a research topic, it's good advice to make sure that data for your dependent variable and all relevant independent variables are available. However, checking for data availability means deciding what specific variables you want to study. Half of the time that beginning researchers spend collecting data is wasted by looking for the wrong variables in the wrong places. A few minutes thinking about what data to look for will save hours of frustration later.

For example, if the dependent variable is the quantity of television sets demanded per year, then most independent variables should be measured annually as well. It would be inappropriate and possibly misleading to define the price of TVs as the price from a particular month. An average of prices over the year (usually weighted by the number of TVs sold per month) would be more meaningful. If the dependent variable includes all TV sets sold regardless of brand, then the price would appropriately be an aggregate based on prices of all brands. Calculating such aggregate variables, however, is not straightforward. Researchers typically make their best efforts to compute the respective aggregate variables and then acknowledge that problems still remain. For example, if the price data for all the various brands are not available, a researcher may be forced to compromise and use the price of one or a few of the major brands as a substitute for the proper aggregate price.

Another issue is suggested by the TV example. Over the years of the sample, it's likely that the market shares of particular kinds of TV sets have changed. For example, flat-screen HD TV sets might have made up a majority of the market in one decade, but black-and-white sets might have been the favorite 40 years before. In cases where the composition of the market share, the size, or the quality of the various brands have changed over time, it would make little sense to measure the dependent variable as the number of TV sets because a "TV set" from one year has little in common with a "TV set" from another. The approach usually taken to deal with this problem is to measure the variable in dollar terms, under the assumption that value encompasses size and quality. Thus, we would work with the dollar sales of TVs rather than the number of sets sold.

A third issue, whether to use nominal or real variables, usually depends on the underlying theory of the research topic. Nominal (or money) variables are measured in current dollars and thus include increases caused by inflation.

If theory implies that inflation should be filtered out, then it's best to state the variables in real (constant-dollar) terms by selecting an appropriate price deflator, such as the Consumer Price Index, and adjusting the money (or nominal) value by it.

As an example, the appropriate price index for Gross Domestic Product is called the GDP deflator. Real GDP is calculated by multiplying nominal GDP by the ratio of the GDP deflator from the base year to the GDP deflator from the current year:

Real GDP = nominal GDP × (base GDP deflator/current GDP deflator)

In 2007, U.S. nominal GDP was $13,807.5 billion and the GDP deflator was 119.82 (for a base year of 2000 = 100), so real GDP was:[1]

Real GDP = $13,807.5 (100/119.82) = $11,523.9 billion

That is, the goods and services produced in 2007 were worth $13,807.5 billion if 2007 dollars were used but were worth only $11,523.9 billion if 2000 prices were used.

Fourth, recall that all economic data are either time-series or cross-sectional in nature. Since time-series data are for the same economic entity from different time periods, whereas cross-sectional data are from the same time period but for different economic entities, the appropriate definitions of the variables depend on whether the sample is a time series or a cross-section.

To understand this, consider the TV set example once again. A time-series model might study the sales of TV sets in the United States from 1967 to 2005, and a cross-sectional model might study the sales of TV sets by state for 2005. The time-series data set would have 39 observations, each of which would refer to a particular year. In contrast, the cross-sectional model data set would have 50 observations, each of which would refer to a particular state. A variable that might be appropriate for the time-series model might be completely inappropriate for the cross-sectional model, and vice versa; at the very least, it would have to be measured differently. National advertising in a particular year would be appropriate for the time-series model, for example, while advertising in or near each particular state would make more sense for the cross-sectional one.

Finally, learn to be a critical reader of the descriptions of variables in econometric research. For instance, most readers breezed right through Equation 2.7 on the demand for beef without asking some vital questions. Are prices and

---

1. *2009 Economic Report of the President*, pp. 282–285.

income measured in nominal or real terms? Is the price of beef wholesale or retail? Where did the data originate? A careful reader would want to know the answers to these questions before analyzing the results of Equation 2.7. (For the record, Yd measures real income, P measures real wholesale prices, and the data come from various issues of *Agricultural Statistics,* published in Washington, D.C., by the U.S. Department of Agriculture.)

Where to Look for Economic Data

Although some researchers generate their own data through surveys or other techniques (and we'll address this possibility in Section 11.3), the vast majority of regressions are run on publicly available data. The best sources for such data are government publications and machine-readable data files. In fact, the U.S. government has been called the most thorough statistics-collecting agency in history.

Excellent government publications include the annual *Statistical Abstract of the U.S.,* the annual *Economic Report of the President,* the *Handbook of Labor Statistics,* and *Historical Statistics of the U.S.* (published in 1975). One of the best places to start with U.S. data is the annual *Census Catalog and Guide,* which provides overviews and abstracts of data sources and various statistical products as well as details on how to obtain each item.[2] Consistent international data are harder to come by, but the United Nations publishes a number of compilations of figures. The best of these are the *U.N. Statistical Yearbook* and the *U.N. Yearbook of National Account Statistics.*

Most researchers use on-line computer databases to find data instead of plowing through stacks of printed volumes. These on-line databases, available through most college and university libraries, contain complete series on literally thousands of possible variables. A huge variety of data is available directly on the Internet. The best guides to the data available in this rapidly changing world are "Resources for Economists on the Internet," Economagic, and WebEC.[3] Links to these sites and other good sources of data are on the text's Web site www.pearsonhighered.com/studenmund. Other good Internet resources are EconLit (www.econlit.org), which is an on-line summary of the *Journal of Economic Literature,* and "Dialog," which provides on-line access to a large number of data sets at a lower cost than many alternatives.

---

2. To obtain this guide, write the Superintendent of Documents, Government Printing Office, Washington, D.C.

3. On the Web, the Resources for Economists location is http://www.rfe.org. The Economagic location is www.economagic.com. The WebEC location is www.helsinki.fi/WebEc.

Missing Data

Suppose the data aren't there? What happens if you choose the perfect variable and look in all the right sources and can't find the data?

The answer to this question depends on how much data is missing. If a few observations have incomplete data in a cross-sectional study, you usually can afford to drop these observations from the sample. If the incomplete data are from a time series, you can sometimes estimate the missing value by interpolating (taking the mean of adjacent values). Similarly, if one variable is available only annually in an otherwise quarterly model, you may want to consider quarterly interpolations of that variable. In either case, interpolation can be justified only if the variable moves in a slow and smooth manner. Extreme caution should always be exercised when "creating" data in such a way (and full documentation is required).

If no data at all exist for a theoretically relevant variable, then the problem worsens significantly. Omitting a relevant variable runs the risk of biased coefficient estimates, as you learned in Chapter 6. After all, how can you hold a variable constant if it's not included in the equation? In such cases, most researchers resort to the use of proxy variables.

Proxy variables can sometimes substitute for theoretically desired variables for which data are missing. For example, the value of net investment is a variable that is not measured directly in a number of countries. As a result, a researcher might use the value of gross investment as a proxy, the assumption being that the value of gross investment is directly proportional to the value of net investment. This proportionality (which is similar to a change in units) is required because the regression analyzes the relationship between changes among variables, rather than the absolute levels of the variables.

In general, a proxy variable is a "good" proxy when its movements correspond relatively well to movements in the theoretically correct variable. Since the latter is unobservable whenever a proxy must be used, there is usually no easy way to examine a proxy's "goodness" directly. Instead, the researcher must document as well as possible why the proxy is likely to be a good or bad one. Poor proxies and variables with large measurement errors constitute "bad" data, but the degree to which the data are bad is a matter of judgment by the individual researcher.

(11.3) Advanced Data Sources

So far, all the data sets in this text have been cross-sectional or time-series in nature, and we have collected our data by observing the world around us, instead of by creating the data ourselves. It turns out, however, that time-series and cross-sectional data can be pooled to form *panel data*, and that data can be generated through *surveys*. The purpose of this short section is to introduce you to these more advanced data sources and to explain why it probably doesn't make sense to use these data sources on your first regression project.

Surveys

Surveys are everywhere in our society. Marketing firms use surveys to learn more about products and competition, political candidates use surveys to fine-tune their campaign advertising or strategies, and governments use surveys for all sorts of purposes, including keeping track of their citizens with instruments like the U.S. Census. As a result, many beginning researchers (particularly those who are having trouble obtaining data for their project) are tempted to run their own surveys in the hope that it'll be an easy way to generate the data they need.

However, running a survey is not as easy as it might seem. For example, the topics to be covered in the survey need to be thought through carefully, because once a survey has been run, it's virtually impossible to go back to the respondents and add another question. In addition, the questions themselves need to be worded precisely (and pretested) to avoid confusing the respondent or "leading" the respondent to a particular answer. Perhaps most importantly, it's crucial for the sample to be random and to avoid the selection, survivor, and nonresponse biases explained in Section 17.2. In fact, running a survey properly is so difficult that entire books and courses are devoted to the topic.

As a result, we don't encourage beginning researchers to run their own surveys, and we're cautious when we analyze the results of surveys run by others. As put by the American Statistical Association, "The quality of a survey is best judged not by its size, scope, or prominence, but by how much attention is given to preventing, measuring, and dealing with the many important problems that can arise."[4]

Panel Data

As mentioned previously, **panel data** are formed when cross-sectional and time-series data sets are pooled to create a single data set. Why would you want to use panel data? In some cases, researchers use panel data to increase

---

4. As quoted in "Best Practices for Survey and Public Opinion Research," on the web site of the American Association for Public Opinion Research: www.aapor.org/bestpractices. The best practices outlined on this web site are a good place to start if you decide to create your own survey.

their sample size, but the main reason for using panel data is to provide an insight into an analytical question that can't be obtained by using time-series or cross-sectional data alone.

What's an example of panel data? Suppose that we're interested in the relationship between budget deficits and interest rates but that we have only 10 years' worth of comparable annual data to study. Ten observations is too small a sample for a reasonable regression, so it might seem as if we're out of luck. However, if we can find time-series data on the same economic variables—interest rates and budget deficits—for the same ten years for six different countries, we'll end up with a sample of $10*6 = 60$ observations, which is more than enough to use. The result is a pooled cross-section time-series data set—a panel data set! (Interestingly, you may have already encountered this particular example—it was the subject of Exercise 7 in Chapter 9.)

Unfortunately, panel data can't be analyzed fully with the econometric techniques you've learned to date in this text, so we don't encourage beginning researchers to attempt to run regressions on panel data. Instead, we've devoted the majority of a chapter (Chapter 16) to panel data, and we urge you to read that chapter if you're interested. Chapter 16 also covers experimental methods in economics, since such experiments often generate panel data.

(11.4) Practical Advice for Your Project

> *"Econometrics is much easier without data."*[5]

The purpose of this section[6] is to give the reader some practical advice about actually doing applied econometric work. Such advice often is missing from econometrics textbooks and courses, but the advice is crucial because many of the skills of an applied econometrician are judgmental and subjective in nature. No single text or course can teach these skills, and that's not our goal. Instead, we want to alert you to some technical suggestions that a majority of experienced applied econometricians would be likely to support.

---

5. M. Verbeek, *A Guide to Modern Econometrics* (New York: Wiley, 2000), p. 1.

6. This section was inspired by and heavily draws upon Chapter 22, "Applied Econometrics," in Peter Kennedy's *A Guide to Econometrics* (Malden, MA: Blackwell, 2008), pp. 361–384. We are extremely grateful to Prof. Kennedy, the MIT Press, and Blackwell Publishing for their kind permission to reprint major portions of that chapter here.

We start off with Peter Kennedy's "10 commandments of applied econometrics," move on to discuss what to check if you get an unexpected sign, and finish up by bringing together a dozen practical tips from other sections of this text that are worth reiterating.

The 10 Commandments of Applied Econometrics

Rule 1: Use common sense and economic theory.

"Time and again I was thanked (and paid) for asking questions and suggesting perspectives that seemed to me to be little more than common sense. This common sense is an easily overlooked but extraordinarily valuable commodity."[7]

Common sense is not all that common. In fact, it sometimes seems as if not much thought (let alone good thought) has gone into empirical work. There are thousands of examples of common sense. For example, common sense should cause researchers to match per capita variables with per capita variables, to use real exchange rates to explain real imports or exports, to employ nominal interest rates to explain real money demand, and to never, never infer causation from correlation.

Rule 2: Ask the right questions.

"Far better an approximate answer to the right question, which is often vague, than an exact answer to the wrong question, which can always be made precise."[8]

Be sure that the question being asked is the relevant one. When a researcher encounters a regression problem, the solution to that problem often is quite simple. Asking simple questions about the context of the problem can bring to light serious misunderstandings. For example, it may be that it is the cumulative change in a variable that is relevant, not the most recent change, or it may be that the null hypothesis should be that a coefficient is equal to another coefficient, rather than equal to zero.

The main lesson here is a blunt one: Ask questions, especially seemingly foolish questions, to ensure that you have a full understanding of the goal of the research; it often turns out that the research question has not been formulated appropriately.

---

7. M. W. Trosset, Comment, *Statistical Science*, 1998, p. 23.

8. J. W. Tukey, "The Future of Data Analysis," *Annals of Mathematical Statistics*, Vol. 33, No. 1, pp. 13–14.

Rule 3: Know the context.

"Don't try to model without understanding the non-statistical aspects of the real-life system you are trying to subject to statistical analysis. Statistical analysis done in ignorance of the subject matter is just that —ignorant statistical analysis."[9]

It's crucial to become intimately familiar with the subject being investigated— its history, institutions, operating constraints, measurement peculiarities, cultural customs, and so on, going beyond a thorough literature review. Questions must be asked: Exactly how were the data gathered? Did government agencies impute the data using unknown formulas? What were the rules governing the auction? How were the interviewees selected? What instructions were given to the participants? What accounting conventions were followed? How were the variables defined? What is the precise wording of the questionnaire? How closely do measured variables match their theoretical counterparts? Another way of viewing this rule is to recognize that you, the researcher, know more than the computer—you know, for example, that water freezes at 0 degrees Celsius, that people tend to round their incomes to the nearest five thousand, and that some weekends are three-day weekends.

Rule 4: Inspect the data.

"Every number is guilty unless proved innocent."[10]

Even if a researcher knows the subject, he or she needs to become intimately familiar with the data. Economists are particularly prone to the complaint that researchers do not know their data very well, a phenomenon made worse by the computer revolution, which has allowed researchers to obtain and work with data electronically by pushing buttons.

Inspecting the data involves summary statistics, graphs, and data cleaning, to both check and "get a feel for" the data. Summary statistics tend to be very simple, such as means, standard errors, maximums, minimums, and correlation matrices, but they can help a researcher find data errors that otherwise would have gone undetected. If in doubt, graph your data. The advantage of graphing is that a picture can force us to notice what we never expected to

9. D. A. Belsley and R. E. Welch, "Modelling Energy Consumption—Using and Abusing Regression Diagnostics," *Journal of Business and Economic Statistics*, Vol. 6, p. 47.

10. C. R. Rao, *Statistics and Truth: Putting Chance to Work* (Singapore: World Scientific, 1997), p. 152.

see. Researchers should supplement their summary statistics with simple graphs: histograms, residual plots, scatterplots of residualized data, and graphs against time. Data cleaning looks for inconsistencies in the data—are any observations impossible, unrealistic, or suspicious? Do you know how missing data were coded? Are dummies all coded 0 or 1? Are all observations consistent with applicable minimum or maximum values? Do all observations obey the logical constraints that they must satisfy?

Rule 5: Keep it sensibly simple.

> *"Do not choose an analytic method to impress your readers or to deflect criticism. If the assumptions and strength of a simpler method are reasonable for your data and research problem, use it."*[11]

Progress in economics results from beginning with simple models, seeing how they work in applications, and then modifying them if necessary. Beginning with a simple model is referred to as a bottom-up (or specific-to-general) approach to developing an econometric specification. Its main drawback is that testing is biased if the simple model omits one or more relevant variables. The competing top-down (or general-to-specific) approach is unrealistic in that it requires the researcher to be able to think of the "right" general model from the start.

Over time, a compromise methodology has evolved. Practitioners begin with simple models which are expanded whenever they fail. When they fail, the general-to-specific approach is used to create a new simple model that is subjected to misspecification tests, and this process of discovery is repeated. In this way simplicity is combined with the general-to-specific methodology, producing a compromise process which, judging by its wide application, is viewed as an acceptable rule of behavior. Examples are the functional form specifications of some Nobel Laureates—Tinbergen's social welfare functions; Arrow's and Solow's work on the CES production function; Friedman's, Becker's, Tobin's, and Modigliani's consumer models; and Lucas's rational expectations model.

Rule 6: Look long and hard at your results.

> *"Apply the 'laugh' test—if the findings were explained to a layperson, could that person avoid laughing?"*[12]

---

11. Leland Wilkinson and the Task Force on Statistical Inference, "Statistical Methods in Psychology Journals," *American Psychologist*, Vol. 54, No. 8, p. 598.

12. Peter Kennedy, *A Guide to Econometrics* (Malden, MA: Blackwell, 2008), p. 393.

Part of this rule is to check whether the results make sense. Are the signs of coefficients as expected? Are important variables statistically significant? Are coefficient magnitudes reasonable? Are the implications of the results consistent with theory? Are there any anomalies? Are any obvious restrictions evident?

But another part of this rule is more subtle and subjective. By looking long and hard at reams of computer output, researchers should eventually recognize the message they are conveying and become comfortable with it. This subjective procedure should be viewed as separate from and complementary to formal statistical testing procedures.

Rule 7: Understand the costs and benefits of data mining.

"Any attempt to allow data to play a role in model specification . . . amounted to data mining, which was the greatest sin any researcher could commit."[13]

"Data mining is misunderstood, and once it is properly understood, it is seen to be no sin at all."[14]

As discussed in Chapter 6, there are two variants of "data mining": one classified as the greatest of the basement sins, but the other viewed as an important ingredient in data analysis. The undesirable version of data mining occurs when one tailors one's specification to the data, resulting in a specification that is misleading because it embodies the peculiarities of the particular data at hand. Furthermore, traditional testing procedures used to "sanctify" the specification are no longer legitimate, because these data, since they have been used to generate the specification, cannot be judged impartial if used to test that specification. The desirable version of "data mining" refers to experimenting with the data to discover empirical regularities that can inform economic theory and be tested on a second data set.

Data mining is inevitable; the art of the applied econometrician is to allow for data-driven theories while avoiding the considerable danger inherent in testing those data-driven theories on the same datasets that were used to create them.

---

13. C. Mukherjee, H. White, and M. Wuyts, *Econometrics and Data Analysis for Developing Countries* (London: Routledge, 1998), p. 30.

14. K. D. Hoover, "In Defense of Data Mining: Some Preliminary Thoughts," in K. D. Hoover and S. M. Sheffrin (eds.), *Monetarism and the Methodology of Economics: Essays in Honor of Thomas Mayer* (Aldershot: Edward Elgar, 1995), p. 243.

Rule 8: Be prepared to compromise.

"The three most important aspects of real data analysis are to compromise, compromise, compromise."[15]

In virtually every econometric analysis there is a gap—usually a vast gulf—between the problem at hand and the closest scenario to which standard econometric theory is applicable. Very seldom does one's problem even come close to satisfying the Classical Assumptions under which econometric theory delivers an optimal solution. A consequence of this is that practitioners are always forced to compromise and adopt suboptimal solutions, the characteristics of which are unknown.

The issue here is that in their econometric theory courses students are taught standard solutions to standard problems, but in practice there are no standard problems. Applied econometricians are continually faced with awkward compromises and must be willing to make ad hoc modifications to standard solutions.

Rule 9: Do not confuse statistical significance with meaningful magnitude.

"Few would deny that in the hands of the masters the methodologies perform impressively, but in the hands of their disciples it is all much less convincing."[16]

Very large sample sizes, such as those that have become common in cross-sectional data, can give rise to estimated coefficients with very small standard errors. A consequence of this is that coefficients of trivial magnitude may test significantly different from zero, creating a misleading impression of what is important. Because of this, researchers must always look at the magnitude of coefficient estimates as well as their significance.

An even more serious problem associated with significance testing is that there is a tendency to conclude that finding significant coefficients "sanctifies" a theory, with a resulting tendency for researchers to stop looking for further insights. Sanctification via significance testing should be replaced by continual searches for additional evidence, both corroborating evidence and, especially, disconfirming evidence. If your theory is correct, are there testable

15. Ed Leamer, "Revisiting Tobin's 1950 Study of Food Expenditure," *Journal of Applied Econometrics*, Vol. 12, No. 5, p. 552.

16. A. R. Pagan, "Three Econometric Methodologies: A Critical Appraisal," *Journal of Economic Surveys*, Vol. 1, p. 20.

implications? Can you explain a range of interconnected findings? Can you find a bundle of evidence consistent with your hypothesis but inconsistent with alternative hypotheses? Can your theory "encompass" its rivals in the sense that it can explain other models' results?

Rule 10: Report a sensitivity analysis.

> *"Sinners are not expected to avoid sins; they need only confess their errors openly."*[17]

It's important to check whether regression results are sensitive to the assumptions upon which the estimation has been based. This is the purpose of a sensitivity analysis, indicating to what extent the substantive results of the research are affected by adopting different specifications about which reasonable people might disagree. For example, are the results sensitive to the sample period, the functional form, the set of explanatory variables, or the choice of proxies? If they are, then this sensitivity casts doubt on the conclusions of the research.

There's a second dimension to sensitivity analyses. Published research papers are typically notoriously misleading accounts of how the research actually was conducted. Because of this, it's very difficult for readers of research papers to judge the extent to which data mining may have unduly influenced the results. Indeed, results tainted by subjective specification decisions undertaken during the heat of econometric battle should be considered the rule, rather than the exception. When reporting a sensitivity analysis, researchers should explain fully their specification search so that readers can judge for themselves how the results may have been affected.

What to Check If You Get an Unexpected Sign

An all-too-familiar problem for a beginning econometrician is to run a regression and find that the sign of one or more of the estimated coefficients is the opposite of what was expected. While an unexpected sign certainly is frustrating, it's not entirely bad news. Rather than considering this a disaster, a researcher should consider it a blessing—this result is a friendly message that some detective work needs to be done—there is undoubtedly some shortcoming in one's theory, data, specification, or estimation procedure. If the "correct" signs had been obtained, odds are that the analysis would not be double-checked. What should be checked?

---

17. Ed Leamer, *Specification Searches: Ad Hoc Inference with Nonexperimental Data* (New York: John Wiley, 1978), p. vi.

1. *Recheck the expected sign.* Every once in a while, a variable that is defined "upside down" will cause a researcher to expect the wrong sign. For example, in an equation for student SATs, the variable "high school rank in class" (where a rank of 1 means that the student was first in his or her class) can sometimes lure a beginning researcher into expecting a positive coefficient for rank.

2. *Check your data for input errors and/or outliers.* If you have data errors or oddball observations, the chances of getting an unexpected sign—even a significant unexpected sign—increase dramatically.

3. *Check for an omitted variable.* The most frequent source of a significant unexpected sign for the coefficient of a relevant independent variable is an omitted variable. Think hard about what might have been omitted, and, in particular, remember to use our equation for expected bias.

4. *Check for an irrelevant variable.* A frequent source of insignificant unexpected signs is that the variable doesn't actually belong in the equation in the first place. If the true coefficient for an irrelevant variable is zero, then you're likely to get an unexpected sign half the time.

5. *Check for multicollinearity.* Multicollinearity increases the variances and standard errors of the estimated coefficients, increasing the chance that a coefficient could have an unexpected sign. The sampling distributions will be widely spread and may straddle zero, implying that it is quite possible that a draw from this distribution will produce an unexpected sign. Indeed, one of the casual indicators of multicollinearity is the presence of unexpected signs.

6. *Check for sample selection bias.* An unexpected sign sometimes can be due to the fact that the observations included in the data were not obtained randomly.

7. *Check your sample size.* Multicollinearity isn't the only source of high variances; they could result from a small sample size or minimal variation in the explanatory variables. In some cases, all it takes to fix an unexpected sign is to increase the sample.

8. *Check your theory.* If you've exhausted every logical econometric explanation for your unexpected sign, there are only two likely remaining explanations. Either your theory is wrong, or you've got a bad data set. If your theory is wrong, then you of course have to change your expected sign, but remember to test this new expectation on a different

data set. However, be careful! It's amazing how economists can conjure up rationales for unexpected signs after the regression has been run! One theoretical source of bias, and therefore unexpected signs, is if the underlying model is simultaneous in nature (we'll cover simultaneous equations in Chapter 14).

A Dozen Practical Tips Worth Reiterating

Here are a number of practical tips for applied econometrics that we've made in previous chapters that are worth emphasizing. They work!

1. Don't attempt to maximize $\overline{R}^2$. (Chapter 2)

2. Always review the literature and hypothesize the signs of your coefficients before estimating a model. (Chapter 3)

3. Remember to inspect and clean your data before estimating a model. Know that outliers should not be automatically omitted; instead, they should be investigated to make sure that they belong in the sample. (Chapter 3)

4. Know the Classical Assumptions *cold*! (Chapter 4)

5. In general, use a one-sided *t*-test unless the expected sign of the coefficient actually is in doubt. (Chapter 5)

6. Don't automatically discard a variable with an insignificant *t*-score. In general, be willing to live with a variable with a *t*-score lower than the critical value in order to decrease the chance of omitting a relevant variable. (Chapter 6)

7. Know how to analyze the size and direction of the bias caused by an omitted variable. (Chapter 6)

8. Understand all the different functional form options and their common uses, and remember to choose your functional form primarily on the basis of theory, not fit. (Chapter 7)

9. Remember that multicollinearity doesn't create bias; the estimated variances are large, but the estimated coefficients themselves are unbiased. As a result, the most-used remedy for multicollinearity is to do nothing. (Chapter 8)

10. If you get a significant Durbin–Watson, Park, or White test, remember to consider the possibility that a specification error might be causing impure serial correlation or heteroskedasticity. Don't change your estimation technique from OLS to GLS or use adjusted standard errors until you have the best possible specification. (Chapters 9 and 10)

11. Remember that adjusted standard errors like Newey–West standard errors or HC standard errors use the OLS coefficient estimates. It's the standard errors of the estimated coefficients that change, not the estimated coefficients themselves. (Chapters 9 and 10)

12. Finally, and perhaps most importantly, if in doubt, rely on common sense and economic theory, not on statistical tests.

The Ethical Econometrician

One conclusion that a casual reader of this book might draw from the large number of specifications we include is that we encourage the estimation of numerous regression results as a way of ensuring the discovery of these best possible estimates.

Nothing could be further from the truth!

As every reader of this book should know by now, our opinion is that the best models are those on which much care has been spent to develop the theoretical underpinnings and only a short time is spent pursuing alternative estimations of that equation. Many econometricians, ourselves included, would hope to be able to estimate only *one* specification of an equation for each data set. Econometricians are fallible and our data are sometimes imperfect, however, so it is unusual for a first attempt at estimation to be totally problem free. As a result, two or even more regressions are often necessary to rid an estimation of fairly simple difficulties that perhaps could have been avoided in a world of perfect foresight.

Unfortunately, a beginning researcher usually has little motivation to stop running regressions until he or she likes the way the result looks. If running another regression provides a result with a better fit, why shouldn't one more specification be tested?

The reason is a compelling one. Every time an extra regression is run and a specification choice is made on the basis of fit or statistical significance, the chances of making a mistake of inference increase dramatically. This can happen in at least two ways:

1. If you consistently drop a variable when its coefficient is insignificant but keep it when it is significant, it can be shown, as discussed in Section 6.4, that you bias your estimates of the coefficients of the equation and of the *t*-scores.

2. If you choose to use a lag structure, or a functional form or an estimation procedure other than OLS, on the basis of fit rather than on the basis of previously theorized hypotheses, you run the risk that your

equation will work poorly when it's applied to data outside your sample. If you restructure your equation to work well on one data set, you might decrease the chance of it working well on another.

What might be thought of as ethical econometrics is also in reality good econometrics. That is, the real reason to avoid running too many different specifications is that the fewer regressions you run, the more reliable and more consistently trustworthy are your results. The instance in which professional ethics come into play is when a number of changes are made (different variables, lag structures, functional forms, estimation procedures, data sets, dropped outliers, and so on), but the regression results are presented to colleagues, clients, editors, or journals as if the final and best equation had been the first and only one estimated. Our recommendation is that all estimated equations be reported even if footnotes or an appendix have to be added to the documentation.

We think that there are two reasonable goals for econometricians when estimating models:

1. Run as few different specifications as possible while still attempting to avoid the major econometric problems. The only exception to our recommendation to run as few specifications as possible is sensitivity analysis, described in Section 6.4.

2. Report honestly the number and type of different specifications estimated so that readers of the research can evaluate how much weight to give to your results.

Therefore, the art of econometrics boils down to attempting to find the best possible equation in the fewest possible number of regression runs. Only careful thinking and reading before estimating first regression can bring this about. An ethical econometrician is honest and complete in reporting the different specifications and/or data sets used.

(11.5) Writing Your Research Report

Once you've finished your research, it's important to write a report on your results so that others can benefit from what you found out (or didn't find out) or so that you can get feedback on your econometric techniques from someone else. Most good research reports have a number of elements in common:

- A brief introduction that defines the dependent variable and states the goals of the research.
- A short review of relevant previous literature and research.

- An explanation of the specification of the equation (model). This should include explaining why particular independent variables and functional forms were chosen as well as stating the expected signs of (or other hypotheses about) the slope coefficients.
- A description of the data (including generated variables), data sources, and any irregularities with the data.
- A presentation of each estimated specification, using our standard documentation format. If you estimate more than one specification, be sure to explain which one is best (and why).
- A careful analysis of the regression results that includes a discussion of any econometric problems encountered and complete documentation of all equations estimated and all tests run. (Beginning researchers are well advised to test for every possible econometric problem; with experience, you'll learn to focus on the most likely difficulties.)
- A short summary/conclusion that includes any policy recommendations or suggestions for further research.
- A bibliography.
- An appendix that includes all data, all regression runs, and all relevant computer output. Do this carefully; readers appreciate a well-organized and labeled appendix.

We think that the easiest way to write such a research report is to keep a research journal as you go along. In this journal, you can keep track of *a priori* hypotheses, regression results, statistical tests, different specifications you considered, and theoretical analyses of what you thought was going on in your equation. You'll find that when it comes time to write your research report, this journal will almost write your paper for you! The alternative to keeping a journal is to wait until you've finished all your econometric work before starting to write your research report, but by doing this, you run the risk of forgetting the thought process that led you to make a particular decision (or some other important item).

11.6 A Regression User's Checklist and Guide

Table 11.2 contains a list of the items that a researcher checks when reviewing the output from a computer regression package. Not every item in the checklist will be produced by your computer package, and not every item in your computer output will be in the checklist, but the checklist can be a very useful reference. In most cases, a quick glance at the checklist will remind you of the text sections that deal with the item, but if this is not the case, the fairly minimal explanation in the checklist should *not* be relied on to cover everything needed for complete analysis and judgment. Instead, you should look up the item in the index. In addition, note that the actions in the right-hand column are merely suggestions. The circumstances of each individual research project are much more reliable guides than any dogmatic list of actions.

There are two ways to use the checklist. First, you can refer to it as a "glossary of packaged computer output terms" when you encounter something in your regression result that you don't understand. Second, you can work your way through the checklist in order, finding the items in your computer output and marking them. As with the Regression User's Guide (Table 11.3), the use of the Regression User's Checklist will be most helpful for beginning researchers, but we also find ourselves referring back to it once in a while even after years of experience.

Be careful. All simplified tables, like the two in this chapter, must trade completeness for ease of use. As a result, strict adherence to a set of rules is not recommended even if the rules come from one of our tables. Someone who understands the purpose of the research, the exact definitions of the variables, and the problems in the data is much more likely to make a correct judgment than is someone equipped with a set of rules created to apply to a wide variety of possible applications.

Table 11.3, the Regression User's Guide, contains a brief summary of the major econometric maladies discussed so far in this text. For each econometric problem, we list:

1. Its nature.
2. Its consequences for OLS estimation.
3. How to detect it.
4. How to attempt to get rid of it.

How might you use the guide? If an estimated equation has a particular problem, such as an insignificant coefficient estimate, a quick glance at the guide can give some idea of the econometric problems that might be causing the symptom. Both multicollinearity and irrelevant variables can cause regression coefficients to have insignificant *t*-scores, for example, and someone who remembered only one of these potential causes might take the wrong correction action. After some practice, the use of this guide will decrease until it eventually will seem fairly limiting and simplistic. Until then, however, our experience is that those about to undertake their first econometric research can benefit by referring to this guide.

Table 11.2 Regression User's Checklist

Symbol	Checkpoint	Reference	Decision
X, Y	Data observations	Check for errors, especially outliers, in the data. Spot-check transformations of variables. Check means, maximums, and minimums.	Correct any errors. If the quality of the data is poor, may want to avoid regression analysis or use just OLS.
df	Degrees of freedom	$N - K - 1 > 0$ N = number of observations K = number of explanatory variables	If $N - K - 1 \leq 0$, equation cannot be estimated, and if the degrees of freedom are low, precision is low. In such a case, try to include more observations.
$\hat{\beta}$	Estimated coefficient	Compare signs and magnitudes to expected values.	If they are unexpected, respecify model if appropriate or assess other statistics for possible correct procedures.
t	t-statistic $t_k = \dfrac{\hat{\beta}_k - \beta_{H_0}}{SE(\hat{\beta}_k)}$ or $t_k = \dfrac{\hat{\beta}_k}{SE(\hat{\beta}_k)}$ for computer-supplied t-scores or whenever $\beta_{H_0} = 0$	Two-sided test: $H_0: \beta_k = \beta_{H_0}$ $H_A: \beta_k \neq \beta_{H_0}$ One-sided test: $H_0: \beta_k \leq \beta_{H_0}$ $H_A: \beta_k > \beta_{H_0}$ β_{H_0}, the hypothesized β, is supplied by the researcher, and is often zero.	Reject H_0 if $|t_k| > t_c$ and if the estimate is of the expected sign. t_c is the critical value of α level of significance and $N - K - 1$ degrees of freedom.
R^2	Coefficient of determination	Measures the degree of overall fit of the model to the data.	A guide to the overall fit.
$\bar{R}^2$	R^2 adjusted for degrees of freedom	Same as R^2. Also attempts to show the contribution of an additional explanatory variable.	One indication that an explanatory variable is irrelevant is if the $\bar{R}^2$ falls when it is included.

Table 11.2 (continued)

Symbol	Checkpoint	Reference	Decision
F	F-statistic	To test $H_0: \beta_1 = \beta_2 = \ldots$ $= \beta_k = 0$ $H_A: H_0$ not true Calculate special F-statistic to test joint hypotheses.	Reject H_0 if $F \geq F_c$, the critical value for α level of significance and K numerator and $N - K - 1$ denominator d.f.
DW	Durbin–Watson d statistic	Tests: $H_0: p \leq 0$ $H_A: p > 0$ For positive serial correlation.	Reject H_0 if $DW < d_L$. Inconclusive if $d_L \leq DW \leq d_U$. (d_L and d_U are critical DW values.)
e_i	Residual	Check for transcription errors. Check for heteroskedasticity by examining the pattern of the residuals.	Correct the data. May take appropriate corrective action, but test first.
SEE	Standard error of the equation	An estimate of σ. Compare with $\overline{Y}$ for a measure of overall fit.	A guide to the overall fit.
TSS	Total sum of squares	$TSS = \sum_i (Y_i - \overline{Y})^2$	Used to compute F, R^2, and $\overline{R}^2$.
RSS	Residual sum of squares	$RSS = \sum_i (Y_i - \hat{Y}_i)^2$	Same as above. Also used in hypothesis testing.
$SE(\hat{\beta}_k)$	Standard error of $\hat{\beta}_k$	Used in t-statistic.	A guide to statistical significance.
$\hat{p}$	Estimated first-order autocorrelation coefficient	Usually provided by an autoregressive routine.	If negative, implies a specification error.
r_{12}	Simple correlation coefficient between X_1 and X_2	Used to detect multicollinearity.	Suspect severe multicollinearity if $r_{12} > .8$.
VIF	Variance inflation factor	Used to detect multicollinearity.	Suspect severe multicollinearity if $VIF > 5$.

Table 11.3 Regression User's Guide

What Can Go Wrong?	What Are the Consequences?	How Can It Be Detected?	How Can It Be Corrected?
Omitted Variable			
The omission of a relevant independent variable	Bias in the coefficient estimates (the $\hat{\beta}$s) of the included Xs.	Theory, significant unexpected signs, or surprisingly poor fits.	Include the omitted variable or a proxy.
Irrelevant Variable			
The inclusion of a variable that does not belong in the equation	Decreased precision in the form of higher standard errors and lower t-scores.	1. Theory 2. t-test on $\hat{\beta}$ 3. $\bar{R}^2$ 4. Impact on other coefficients if X is dropped.	Delete the variable if its inclusion is not required by the underlying theory.
Incorrect Functional Form			
The functional form is inappropriate	Biased estimates, poor fit, and difficult interpretation.	Examine the theory carefully; think about the relationship between X and Y.	Transform the variable or the equation to a different functional form.
Multicollinearity			
Some of the independent variables are (imperfectly) correlated	No biased $\hat{\beta}$s, but estimates of the separate effects of the Xs are not reliable, i.e., high SEs (and low t-scores).	No universally accepted rule or test is available. Use high r_{12}s or the VIF test.	Drop redundant variables, but to drop others might introduce bias. Often doing nothing is best.
Serial Correlation			
Observations of the error term are correlated, as in: $\epsilon_t = \rho\epsilon_{t-1} + u_t$	No biased $\hat{\beta}$s, but OLS no longer is minimum variance, and hypothesis testing is unreliable.	Use Durbin–Watson d test; if significantly less than 2, positive serial correlation exists.	If impure, add the omitted variable or change the functional form. Otherwise, consider Generalized Least Squares or Newey–West standard errors.
Heteroskedasticity			
The variance of the error term is not constant for all observations, as in: $VAR(\epsilon_i) = \sigma^2 Z_i^2$	Same as for serial correlation.	Use the Park or White tests.	If impure, add the omitted variable. Otherwise, use HC standard errors or reformulate the variables.

11.7 Summary

1. Running your own regression project involves choosing your dependent variable, applying the six steps in applied regression (of Chapter 3) to that dependent variable, and then writing a research report that summarizes your work.

2. A great research topic is one that you know something about, one that addresses an inherently interesting economic or behavioral question or choice, and one for which data are available not only for the dependent variable but also for the obvious independent variables.

3. Don't underestimate the difficulty and importance of collecting a complete and accurate data set. It's a lot of work, but it's worth it!

4. The art of econometrics boils down to finding the best possible equation in the fewest possible number of regression runs. The only way to do this is to spend quite a bit of time thinking through the underlying principles of your research project before you run your first regression.

5. Before you complete your research project, be sure to review the practical hints and regression user's guide and checklist in Sections 11.5 and 11.6.

11.8 Appendix: The Housing Price Interactive Exercise

This interactive regression learning exercise is somewhat different from the previous one in Section 8.7. Our goal is still to bridge the gap between textbook and computer, but we feel that if you completed the previous interactive exercise, you should be ready to do the computer work on your own.[18] As a result, this interactive exercise will provide you with a short literature review and the data, but you'll be asked to calculate your own estimates. Feedback on your specification choices will once again be found in the hints in Appendix A.

---

18. If you have not completed the interactive exercise in Section 8.7, we urge you to do so before beginning this one. Instructors interested in additional interactive exercises can find them in our instructor's manual on the text's web site, www.pearsonhighered.com/studenmund.

Since the only difference between this interactive exercise and the first one is that this one requires you to estimate your chosen specification(s) with the computer, our guidelines for interactive exercises still apply:

1. Take the time to look over a portion of the reading list before choosing a specification.

2. Try to estimate as few regression runs as possible.

3. Avoid looking at the hints until after you've reached what you think is your best specification.

We believe that the benefits you get from an interactive exercise are directly proportional to the effort you put into it. If you have to delay this exercise until you have the time and energy to do your best, that's probably a good idea.

Building a Hedonic Model of Housing Prices

In the next section, we're going to ask you to specify the independent variables and functional form for an equation whose dependent variable is the price of a house in Southern California. Before making these choices, it's vital to review the housing price literature and to think through the theory behind such models. Such a review is especially important in this case because the model we'll be building will be *hedonic* in nature.

What is a hedonic model? Recall that in Section 1.5 we estimated an equation for the price of a house as a function of the size of that house. Such a model is called **hedonic** because it uses measures of the quality of a product as independent variables instead of measures of the market for that product (like quantity demanded, income, etc.). Hedonic models are most useful when the product being analyzed is heterogeneous in nature because we need to analyze what causes products to be different and therefore to have different prices. With a homogeneous product, hedonic models are virtually useless.

Perhaps the most-cited early hedonic housing price study is that of G. Grether and P. Mieszkowski.[19] Grether and Mieszkowski collected a seven-year data set and built a number of linear models of housing price using

---

19. G. M. Grether and Peter Mieszkowski, "Determinants of Real Estate Values," *Journal of Urban Economics*, Vol. 1, pp. 127–146. Another classic article of the same era is J. Kain and J. Quigley, "Measuring the Value of Housing Quality," *Journal of American Statistical Association*, Vol. 45, pp. 532–548.

different combinations of variables. They included square feet of space, the number of bathrooms, and the number of rooms, although the number of rooms turned out to be insignificant. They also included lot size and the age of the house as variables, specifying a quadratic function for the age variable. Most innovatively, they used several slope dummies in order to capture the interaction effects of various combinations of variables (like a hardwood-floors dummy times the size of the house).

Peter Linneman[20] estimated a housing price model on data from Los Angeles, Chicago, and the entire United States. His goal was to create a model that worked for the two individual cities and then to apply it to the nation to test the hypothesis of a national housing market. Linneman did not include any lot characteristics, nor did he use any interaction variables. His only measures of the size of the living space were the number of bathrooms and the number of nonbathrooms. Except for an age variable, the rest of the independent variables were dummies describing quality characteristics of the house and neighborhood. Although many of the dummy variables were quite fickle, the coefficients of age, number of bathrooms, and the number of nonbathrooms were relatively stable and significant. Central air conditioning had a negative, insignificant coefficient for the Los Angeles regression.

K. Ihlanfeldt and J. Martinez-Vasquez[21] investigated sample bias in various methods of obtaining house price data and concluded that the house's sales price is the least biased of all measures. Unfortunately, they went on to estimate an equation by starting with a large number of variables and then dropping all those that had t-scores below 1, almost surely introducing bias into their equation.

Finally, Allen Goodman[22] added some innovative variables to an estimate on a national data set. He included measures of specific problems like rats, cracks in the plaster, holes in the floors, plumbing breakdowns, and the level of property taxes. Although the property tax variable showed the capitalization of

20. Peter Linneman, "Some Empirical Results on the Nature of the Hedonic Price Functions for the Urban Housing Market," *Journal of Urban Economics,* Vol. 8, No. 1, pp. 47–68.

21. Keith Ihlanfeldt and Jorge Martinez-Vasquez, "Alternate Value Estimates of Owner-Occupied Housing: Evidence on Sample Selection Bias and Systematic Errors," *Journal of Urban Economics,* Vol. 20, No. 3, pp. 356–369. Also see Eric Cassel and Robert Mendelsohn, "The Choice of Functional Forms for Hedonic Price Equations: Comment," *Journal of Urban Economics,* Vol. 18, No. 2, pp. 135–142.

22. Allen C. Goodman, "An Econometric Model of Housing Price, Permanent Income, Tenure Choice, and Housing Demand," *Journal of Urban Economics,* Vol. 23, pp. 327–353.

low property taxes, as would be expected, the rats coefficient was insignificant, and the cracks variable's coefficient asserted that cracks significantly increase the value of a house.

The Housing Price Interactive Exercise

Now that we've reviewed at least a portion of the literature, it's time to build your own model. Recall that in Section 1.5, we built a simple model of the price of a house as a function of the size of that house, Equation 1.23:

$$\hat{P}_i = 40.0 + 0.138S_i \tag{1.23}$$

where: P_i = the price (in thousands of dollars) of the ith house
S_i = the size (in square feet) of the ith house

Equation 1.23 was estimated on a sample of 43 houses that were purchased in the same Southern California town (Monrovia) within a few weeks of each other. It turns out that we have a number of additional independent variables for the data set we used to estimate Equation 1.23. Also available are:

N_i = the quality of the neighborhood of the ith house (1 = best, 4 = worst) as rated by two local real estate agents
A_i = the age of the ith house in years
BE_i = the number of bedrooms in the ith house
BA_i = the number of bathrooms in the ith house
CA_i = a dummy variable equal to 1 if the ith house has central air conditioning, 0 otherwise
SP_i = a dummy variable equal to 1 if the ith house has a pool, 0 otherwise
Y_i = the size of the yard around the ith house (in square feet)

Read through the list of variables again, developing your own analyses of the theory behind each variable. What are the expected signs of the coefficients? Which variables seem potentially redundant? Which variables *must* you include?

In addition, there are a number of functional form modifications that can be made. For example, you might consider a quadratic polynomial for age, as Grether and Mieszkowski did, or you might consider creating slope dummies such as SP·S or CA·S. Finally, you might consider interactive variables that involve the neighborhood proxy variable such as N·S or N·BA. What hypotheses would each of these imply?

Develop your specification carefully. Think through each variable and/or functional form decision, and take the time to write out your expectations for the sign and size of each coefficient. Don't take the attitude that you should include *every* possible variable and functional form modification and then drop the insignificant ones. Instead, try to design the best possible hedonic model of housing prices you can the first time around.

Once you've chosen a specification, estimate your equation, using the data in Table 11.4 and analyze the result.

Table 11.4 Data for the Housing Price Interactive Exercise

P	S	N	A	BE	BA	CA	SP	Y
107	736	4	39	2	1	0	0	3364
133	720	3	63	2	1	0	0	1780
141	768	2	66	2	1	0	0	6532
165	929	3	41	3	1	0	0	2747
170	1080	2	44	3	1	0	0	5520
173	942	2	65	2	1	0	0	6808
182	1000	2	40	3	1	0	0	6100
200	1472	1	66	3	2	0	0	5328
220	1200	1.5	69	3	1	0	0	5850
226	1302	2	49	3	2	0	0	5298
260	2109	2	37	3	2	1	0	3691
275	1528	1	41	2	2	0	0	5860
280	1421	1	41	3	2	0	1	6679
289	1753	1	1	3	2	1	0	2304
295	1528	1	32	3	2	0	0	6292
300	1643	1	29	3	2	0	1	7127
310	1675	1	63	3	2	0	0	9025
315	1714	1	38	3	2	1	0	6466
350	2150	2	75	4	2	0	0	14825
365	2206	1	28	4	2.5	1	0	8147
503	3269	1	5	4	2.5	1	0	10045
135	936	4	75	2	1	0	0	5054
147	728	3	40	2	1	0	0	1922
165	1014	3	26	2	1	0	0	6416
175	1661	3	27	3	2	1	0	4939
190	1248	2	42	3	1	0	0	7952
191	1834	3.5	40	3	2	0	1	6710
195	989	2	41	3	1	0	0	5911
205	1232	1	43	2	2	0	0	4618
210	1017	1	38	2	1	0	0	5083
215	1216	2	77	2	1	0	0	6834

(continued)

Table 11.4 (*continued*)

P	S	N	A	BE	BA	CA	SP	Y
228	1447	2	44	2	2	0	0	4143
242	1974	1.5	65	4	2	0	1	5499
250	1600	1.5	63	3	2	1	0	4050
250	1168	1.5	63	3	1	0	1	5182
255	1478	1	50	3	2	0	0	4122
255	1756	2	36	3	2	0	1	6420
265	1542	2	38	3	2	0	0	6833
265	1633	1	32	4	2	0	1	7117
275	1500	1	42	2	2	1	0	7406
285	1734	1	62	3	2	0	1	8583
365	1900	1	42	3	2	1	0	19580
397	2468	1	10	4	2.5	1	0	6086

Datafile = HOUSE11

1. Test your hypotheses for each coefficient with the *t*-test. Pay special attention to any functional form modifications.

2. Decide what econometric problems exist in the equation, testing, if appropriate, for multicollinearity, serial correlation, or heteroskedasticity.

3. Decide whether to accept your first specification as the best one or to make a modification in your equation and estimate again. Make sure you avoid the temptation to estimate an additional specification "just to see what it looks like."

Once you've decided to make no further changes, you're finished—congratulations! Now turn to the hints in Appendix A for feedback on your choices.

12 Time-Series Models

The purpose of this chapter is to provide an introduction to a number of interesting models that have been designed to cope with and take advantage of the special properties of time-series data. Working with time-series data often causes complications that simply can't happen with cross-sectional data. Most of these complications involve the order of the observations because order matters quite a bit in time-series data but doesn't matter much (if at all) in cross-sectional data.

The most important of the topics concerns a class of dynamic models in which a lagged value of the dependent variable appears on the right-hand side of the equation. As you will see, the presence of a lagged dependent variable on the right-hand side of the equation implies that the impact of the independent variables can be spread out over a number of time periods.

Why would you want to distribute the impact of an independent variable over a number of time periods? To see why, consider the impact of advertising on sales. Most analysts believe that people remember advertising for more than one time period, so advertising affects sales in the future as well as in the current time period. As a result, models of sales should include current *and lagged* values of advertising, thus distributing the impact of advertising over a number of different lags.

While this chapter focuses on such dynamic models, you'll also learn about models in which different numbers of lags appear and we'll investigate how the presence of these lags affects our estimators. The chapter concludes with a brief introduction to a topic called nonstationarity. If variables have significant changes in basic properties (like their mean or variance) over time, they are said to be nonstationary, and it turns out that nonstationary variables have the potential to inflate *t*-scores and measures of overall fit in an equation.

(12.1) Dynamic Models

Distributed Lag Models

As described in Section 7.3, lagged independent variables can be used whenever you expect X to affect Y after a period of time. For example, if the underlying theory suggests that X_1 affects Y with a one-time-period lag (but X_2 has an instantaneous impact on Y), we use equations like:

$$Y_t = \beta_0 + \beta_1 X_{1t-1} + \beta_2 X_{2t} + \epsilon_t \qquad (12.1)$$

Such lags are called simple lags, and the estimation of β_1 with OLS is no more difficult than the estimation of the coefficients of nonlagged equations, except for possible impure serial correlation if the lag is misspecified. Remember, however, that the coefficients of such equations should be interpreted carefully. For example, β_2 in Equation 12.1 measures the effect of a one-unit increase in this time's X_2 on this time's Y holding *last time's* X_1 constant.

A case that's more complicated than this simple lag model occurs when the impact of an independent variable is expected to be spread out over a number of time periods. For example, suppose we're interested in studying the impact of a change in the money supply on GDP. Theoretical and empirical studies have provided evidence that because of rigidities in the marketplace, it takes time for the economy to react completely to a change in the money supply. Some of the effect on GDP will take place in the first quarter, some more in the second quarter, and so on. In such a case, the appropriate econometric model would be a distributed lag model:

$$Y_t = \alpha_0 + \beta_0 X_t + \beta_1 X_{t-1} + \beta_2 X_{t-2} + \cdots + \beta_p X_{t-p} + \epsilon_t \qquad (12.2)$$

A **distributed lag model** explains the current value of Y as a function of current and past values of X, thus "distributing" the impact of X over a number of time periods. Take a careful look at Equation 12.2. The coefficients β_0, β_1, and β_2 through β_p measure the effects of the various lagged values of X on the current value of Y. In most economic applications, including our money supply example, we'd expect the impact of X on Y to decrease as the length of the lag (indicated by the subscript of the β) increases. That is, although β_0 might be larger or smaller than β_1, we certainly would expect either β_0 or β_1 to be larger in absolute value than β_6 or β_7.

Unfortunately, the estimation of Equation 12.2 with OLS causes a number of problems:

1. The various lagged values of X are likely to be severely multicollinear, making coefficient estimates imprecise.

2. In large part because of this multicollinearity, there is no guarantee that the estimated βs will follow the smoothly declining pattern that economic theory would suggest. Instead, it's quite typical for the estimated coefficients of Equation 12.2 to follow a fairly irregular pattern, for example:

$$\hat{\beta}_0 = 0.26 \quad \hat{\beta}_1 = 0.07 \quad \hat{\beta}_2 = 0.17 \quad \hat{\beta}_3 = -0.03 \quad \hat{\beta}_4 = 0.08$$

3. The degrees of freedom tend to decrease, sometimes substantially, for two reasons. First, we have to estimate a coefficient for each lagged X, thus increasing K and lowering the degrees of freedom $(N - K - 1)$. Second, unless data for lagged Xs outside the sample are available, we have to decrease the sample size by one for each lagged X we calculate, thus lowering the number of observations, N, and therefore the degrees of freedom.

As a result of these problems with OLS estimation of functions like Equation 12.2, called *ad hoc* distributed lag equations, it's standard practice to use a simplifying assumption in such situations. The most commonly used simplification is to replace all the lagged independent variables with a lagged value of the dependent variable, and we'll call that kind of equation a *dynamic model*.

What Is a Dynamic Model?

The simplest dynamic model is:

$$Y_t = \alpha_0 + \beta_0 X_t + \lambda Y_{t-1} + u_t \tag{12.3}$$

Note that Y is on both sides of the equation! Luckily, the subscripts are different in that the Y on the left-hand side is Y_t, and the Y on the right-hand side is Y_{t-1}. It's this difference in time period that makes the equation dynamic. Thus, the simplest **dynamic model** is an equation in which the current value of the dependent variable Y is a function of the current value of X and a lagged value of Y itself. Such a model with a lagged dependent variable is often called an *autoregressive* equation.

Let's take a look at Equation 12.3 to try to see why it can be used to represent a distributed lag model or any model in which the impact of X on Y is distributed over a number of lags. Suppose that we lag Equation 12.3 one time period:

$$Y_{t-1} = \alpha_0 + \beta_0 X_{t-1} + \lambda Y_{t-2} + u_{t-1} \tag{12.4}$$

If we now substitute Equation 12.4 into Equation 12.3, we get:

$$Y_t = \alpha_0 + \beta_0 X_t + \lambda(\alpha_0 + \beta_0 X_{t-1} + \lambda Y_{t-2} + u_{t-1}) + u_t \tag{12.5}$$

or

$$Y_t = (\alpha_0 + \lambda \alpha_0) + \beta_0 X_t + \lambda \beta_0 X_{t-1} + \lambda^2 Y_{t-2} + (\lambda u_{t-1} + u_t) \tag{12.6}$$

If we do this one more time (that is, if we lag Equation 12.3 two time periods, substitute it into Equation 12.5 and rearrange), we get:

$$Y_t = \alpha_0^* + \beta_0 X_t + \lambda \beta_0 X_{t-1} + \lambda^2 \beta_0 X_{t-2} + \lambda^3 Y_{t-3} + u_t^* \tag{12.7}$$

where α_0^* is the new (combined) intercept and u_t^* is the new (combined) error term. In other words, $Y_t = f(X_t, X_{t-1}, X_{t-2})$. We've shown that a dynamic model can indeed be used to represent a distributed lag model!

In addition, note that the coefficients of the lagged Xs follow a clear pattern. To see this, let's go back to Equation 12.2:

$$Y_t = \alpha_0 + \beta_0 X_t + \beta_1 X_{t-1} + \beta_2 X_{t-2} + \cdots + \beta_p X_{t-p} + \epsilon_t \tag{12.2}$$

and compare the coefficients in Equation 12.2 to those in Equation 12.7, we get:

$$\begin{aligned} \beta_1 &= \lambda \beta_0 \\ \beta_2 &= \lambda^2 \beta_0 \\ \beta_3 &= \lambda^3 \beta_0 \\ &\vdots \\ \beta_p &= \lambda^p \beta_0 \end{aligned} \tag{12.8}$$

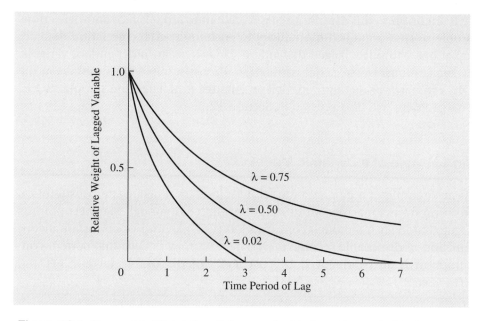

Figure 12.1 Geometric Weighting Schemes for Various Dynamic Models

As long as λ is between 0 and 1, a dynamic model has the impact of the independent variable declining as the length of the lag increases.

As long as λ is between 0 and 1, these coefficients will indeed smoothly decline,[1] as shown in Figure 12.1.

Dynamic models like Equation 12.3 avoid the three major problems with ad hoc distributed lag equations that we outlined in the previous section. The degrees of freedom have increased dramatically, and the multicollinearity problem has disappeared. If u_t is well behaved, OLS estimation of Equation 12.3 can be shown to have desirable properties for large samples. How large is "large enough"? Our recommendation, based more on experience than proof, is to aim for a sample of at least 50 observations. The smaller the sample, the more likely you are to encounter bias. Samples below 25 in size should be avoided entirely, in part because of the bias and in part because hypothesis testing becomes untrustworthy.

1. This model sometimes is referred to as a Koyck distributed lag model because it was originally developed by L. M. Koyck in *Distributed Lags and Investment Analysis* (Amsterdam: North-Holland Publishing, 1954).

In addition to this sample size issue, dynamic models face another serious problem. They are much more likely to encounter serial correlation than are equations without a lagged dependent variable as an independent variable. To make things worse, serial correlation almost surely will cause bias in the OLS estimates of dynamic models no matter how large the sample size is. This problem will be discussed in Section 12.2.

An Example of a Dynamic Model

As an example of a dynamic model, let's look at an aggregate consumption function from a macroeconomic equilibrium GDP model. Many economists argue that in such a model, consumption (CO_t) is not just an instantaneous function of disposable income (YD_t). Instead, they believe that current consumption is also influenced by past levels of disposable income (YD_{t-1}, YD_{t-2}, etc.):

$$CO_t = f(\overset{+}{YD_t}, \overset{+}{YD_{t-1}}, \overset{+}{YD_{t-2}}, \text{etc.}) + \epsilon_t \qquad (12.9)$$

Such an equation fits well with simple models of consumption, but it makes sense only if the weights given past levels of income decrease as the length of the lag increases. That is, the impact of lagged income on current consumption should decrease as the lag gets bigger. Thus we'd expect the coefficient of YD_{t-2} to be less than the coefficient of YD_{t-1}, and so on.

As a result, most econometricians would model Equation 12.9 with a dynamic model:

$$CO_t = \alpha_0 + \beta_0 YD_t + \lambda CO_{t-1} + u_t \qquad (12.10)$$

To estimate Equation 12.10, we use data from Section 14.3, where we will build a small macromodel of the U.S. economy from 1976 through 2007. The OLS estimates of Equation 12.10 for this data set are (standard errors in parentheses):

$$\widehat{CO}_t = -266.6 + 0.46YD_t + 0.56CO_{t-1} \qquad (12.11)$$
$$(0.10) \qquad (0.10)$$
$$4.70 \qquad 5.66$$
$$\overline{R}^2 = .999 \qquad N = 32 \qquad \text{(annual 1976–2007)}$$

If we substitute $\hat{\beta}_0 = 0.46$ and $\hat{\lambda} = 0.56$ into Equation 12.3 for i = 1, we obtain $\hat{\beta}_1 = \hat{\beta}_0\hat{\lambda}^1 = (0.46)(0.56)^1 = 0.26$. If we continue this process, it turns out that Equation 12.11 is equivalent to:[2]

$$\widehat{CO}_t = -605.91 + 0.46YD_t + 0.26YD_{t-1} + 0.14YD_{t-2} \qquad (12.12)$$
$$+ 0.08YD_{t-3} + \cdots$$

As can be seen, the coefficients of YD in Equation 12.12 do indeed decline as we'd expect in a dynamic model.

To compare this estimate with an OLS estimate of the same equation without the dynamic model format, we'd need to estimate an ad hoc distributed lag equation with the same number of lagged variables.

$$CO_t = \alpha_0 + \beta_0YD_t + \beta_1YD_{t-1} + \beta_2YD_{t-2} + \beta_3YD_{t-3} + \epsilon_t \qquad (12.13)$$

If we estimate Equation 12.13 using the same data set, we get:

$$\widehat{CO}_t = -695.89 + 0.73YD_t + 0.38YD_{t-1} + 0.006YD_{t-2} - 0.08YD_{t-3}$$

$$(12.14)$$

How do the coefficients of Equation 12.14 look? As the lag increases, the coefficients of YD decrease sharply, actually going negative for t−3. Neither economic theory nor common sense leads us to expect this pattern. Such a poor result is due to the severe multicollinearity between the lagged Xs. Most econometricians therefore estimate consumption functions with a lagged dependent variable simplification scheme like the dynamic model in Equation 12.10.

An interesting interpretation of the results in Equation 12.11 concerns the long-run multiplier implied by the model. The long-run multiplier measures the total impact of a change in income on consumption after all the lagged effects have been felt. One way to get this estimate would be to add up all the $\hat{\beta}$s, but an easier alternative is to calculate $\hat{\beta}_0[1/(1-\hat{\lambda})]$, which in this case equals $0.46[1/(1-0.56)]$ or 1.05. A sample of this size is likely to encounter small sample bias, however, so we shouldn't overanalyze the results. For more on this data set and the other equations in the model, see Section 14.3. For more on testing and adjusting dynamic equations like Equation 12.11 for serial correlation, let's move on to the next section.

---

2. Note that the constant term equals $\alpha_0/(1 - \lambda)$.

(12.2) Serial Correlation and Dynamic Models

The consequences of serial correlation depend crucially on the type of model we're talking about. For an *ad hoc* distributed lag model such as Equation 12.2, serial correlation has the effects outlined in Section 9.2: Serial correlation causes OLS to no longer be the minimum variance unbiased estimator, serial correlation causes the $SE(\hat{\beta})$s to be biased, and serial correlation causes no bias in the OLS $\hat{\beta}$s themselves.

For dynamic models such as Equation 12.3, however, all this changes, and serial correlation does indeed cause bias in the $\hat{\beta}$s produced by OLS. Compounding this is the fact that the consequences, detection, and remedies for serial correlation that we discussed in Chapter 9 are all either incorrect or need to be modified in the presence of a lagged dependent variable.

Serial Correlation Causes Bias in Dynamic Models

If an equation with a lagged dependent variable as an independent variable has a serially correlated error term, then OLS estimates of the coefficients of that equation will be biased, even in large samples. To see where this bias comes from, let's look at a dynamic model like Equation 12.3 (ignore the arrows for a bit):

$$Y_t = \alpha_0 + \beta_0 X_t + \lambda \overset{\uparrow}{Y}_{t-1} + \overset{\uparrow}{u}_t \qquad (12.3)$$

and assume that the error term u_t is serially correlated: $u_t = \rho u_{t-1} + \epsilon_t$ where ϵ_t is a classical error term. If we substitute this serially correlated error term into Equation 12.3, we get:

$$Y_t = \alpha_0 + \beta_0 X_t + \lambda \overset{\uparrow}{Y}_{t-1} + \rho \overset{\uparrow}{u}_{t-1} + \epsilon_t \qquad (12.15)$$

Let's also look at Equation 12.3 lagged one time period:

$$\overset{\uparrow}{Y}_{t-1} = \alpha_0 + \beta_0 X_{t-1} + \lambda Y_{t-2} + \overset{\uparrow}{u}_{t-1} \qquad (12.16)$$

What happens when the previous time period's error term (u_{t-1}) is positive? In Equation 12.16, the positive u_{t-1} causes Y_{t-1} to be larger than it would have been otherwise (these changes are marked by upward-pointing arrows for u_{t-1} in Equation 12.16 and for Y_{t-1} in Equations 12.3, 12.15, and 12.16). In addition, the positive u_{t-1} is quite likely to cause u_t to be positive in Equation 12.3 because $u_t = \rho u_{t-1} + \epsilon_t$ and ρ usually is positive (these changes are marked by upward-pointing arrows in Equation 12.15 and Equation 12.3).

Take a look at the arrows in Equation 12.3. Y_{t-1} and u_t are correlated! Such a correlation violates Classical Assumption III, which assumes that the error term is not correlated with any of the explanatory variables.

The consequences of this correlation include biased estimates, in particular of the coefficient λ, because OLS attributes to Y_{t-1} some of the change in Y_t actually caused by u_t. In essence, the uncorrected serial correlation acts like an omitted variable (u_{t-1}). Since an omitted variable causes bias whenever it is correlated with one of the included independent variables, and since u_{t-1} is correlated with Y_{t-1}, the combination of a lagged dependent variable and serial correlation causes bias in the coefficient estimates.[3]

Serial correlation in a dynamic model also causes estimates of the standard errors of the estimated coefficients and the residuals to be biased. The former bias means that hypothesis testing is invalid, even for large samples. The latter bias means that tests based on the residuals, like the Durbin–Watson d test, are potentially invalid.

Testing for Serial Correlation in Dynamic Models

Until now, we've relied on the Durbin–Watson d test of Section 9.3 to test for serial correlation, but, as mentioned above, the Durbin–Watson d statistic is potentially invalid for an equation that contains a lagged dependent variable as an independent variable. This is because the biased residuals described in the previous paragraph cause the DW d statistic to be biased toward 2. This bias toward 2 means that the Durbin–Watson test sometimes fails to detect the presence of serial correlation in a dynamic model.[4]

The widely used alternative is to use a special case of a general testing procedure called the **Lagrange Multiplier Serial Correlation (LMSC) Test**, which is a method that can be used to test for serial correlation by analyzing how well the lagged residuals explain the residuals of the original equation (in an equation that includes all the explanatory variables of the original model).

---

3. The reason that pure serial correlation doesn't cause bias in the coefficient estimates of equations that don't include a lagged dependent variable is that the "omitted variable" u_{t-1} isn't correlated with any of the included independent variables.

4. The opposite is not a problem. A Durbin–Watson d test that indicates serial correlation in the presence of a lagged dependent variable, despite the bias toward 2, is an even stronger affirmation of serial correlation.

If the lagged residuals are significant in explaining this time's residuals (as shown by the chi-square test), then we can reject the null hypothesis of no serial correlation. Interestingly, although we suggest using the LMSC test for dynamic models, it also could have been used instead of the Durbin–Watson test in Chapter 9 to test for serial correlation in equations without a lagged dependent variable. Other applications of the general Lagrange Multiplier test approach are as a specification test and as a test for heteroskedasticity and other econometric problems.[5]

Using the Lagrange Multiplier to test for serial correlation for a typical dynamic model involves three steps:

1. Obtain the residuals from the estimated equation:

$$e_t = Y_t - \hat{Y}_t = Y_t - \hat{\alpha}_0 - \hat{\beta}_0 X_{1t} - \hat{\lambda} Y_{t-1} \qquad (12.17)$$

2. Use these residuals as the dependent variable in an auxiliary equation that includes as independent variables all those on the right-hand side of the original equation as well as the lagged residuals:

$$e_t = a_0 + a_1 X_t + a_2 Y_{t-1} + a_3 e_{t-1} + u_t \qquad (12.18)$$

3. Estimate Equation 12.18 using OLS and then test the null hypothesis that $a_3 = 0$ with the following test statistic:

$$LM = N^* R^2 \qquad (12.19)$$

where N is the sample size and R^2 is the unadjusted coefficient of determination, both of the auxiliary equation, Equation 12.18. For large samples, LM has a chi-square distribution with degrees of freedom equal to the number of restrictions in the null hypothesis (in this case, one). If LM is greater than the critical chi-square value from Statistical Table B-8, then we reject the null hypothesis that $a_3 = 0$ and conclude that there is indeed serial correlation in the original equation.

To run an LMSC test for second-order or higher-order serial correlation, add lagged residuals (e_{t-2} for second order, e_{t-2} and e_{t-3} for third order) to the auxiliary equation, Equation 12.18. This latter change makes the null hypothesis $a_3 = a_4 = a_5 = 0$. Such a null hypothesis raises the degrees of

---

5. For example, some readers may remember that the White test of Section 10.3 is a Lagrange Multiplier test. For a survey of the various uses to which Lagrange Multiplier tests can be put and a discussion of the LM test's relationship to the Wald and Likelihood Ratio tests, see Rob Engle, "Wald, Likelihood Ratio, and Lagrange Multiplier Tests in Econometrics," in Z. Griliches and M. D. Intriligator (eds.), *Handbook of Econometrics*, Volume II (Amsterdam: Elsevier Science Publishers, 1984).

freedom in the chi-square test to three because we have imposed three restrictions on the equation (three coefficients are jointly set equal to zero). To run an LMSC test with more than one lagged dependent variable, add the lagged variables (Y_{t-2}, Y_{t-3}, etc.) to the original equation. For practice with the LM test, see Exercise 6; for practice with testing for higher-order serial correlation, see Exercise 7.

Correcting for Serial Correlation in Dynamic Models

There are three strategies for attempting to rid a dynamic model of serial correlation: improving the specification, instrumental variables, and modified GLS.

The first strategy is to consider the possibility that the serial correlation could be impure, caused by either omitting a relevant variable or by failing to capture the actual distributed lag pattern accurately. Unfortunately, finding an omitted variable or an improved lag structure is easier said than done, as seen in previous chapters. Because of the dangers of sequential specification searches, this option should be considered only if an alternative specification exists that has a theoretically sound justification.

The second strategy, called instrumental variables, consists of substituting an "instrument" (a variable that is highly correlated with Y_{t-1} but is uncorrelated with u_t) for Y_{t-1} in the original equation, thus eliminating the correlation between Y_{t-1} and u_t. Although using an instrument is a reasonable option that is straightforward in principle, it's not always easy to find a proxy that retains the distributed lag nature of the original equation. For a more complete discussion of instrumental variables, see Section 14.3.

The final solution to serial correlation in dynamic models (or in models with lagged dependent variables and similar error term structures) is to use an iterative maximum likelihood technique to estimate the components of the serial correlation and then to transform the original equation so that the serial correlation has been eliminated. This technique, which is similar to the GLS procedure outlined in Section 9.4, is not without its complications. In particular, the sample needs to be large, the standard errors of the estimated coefficients potentially need to be adjusted, and the estimation techniques are flawed under some circumstances.[6]

---

6. For more on these complications, see R. Betancourt and H. Kelejian, "Lagged Endogenous Variables and Cochrane-Orcutt Procedure," *Econometrica*, Vol. 49, No. 4, pp. 1073–1078.

In essence, serial correlation causes bias in dynamic models, but ridding the equation of that serial correlation is not an easy task.

12.3 Granger Causality

One application of ad hoc distributed lag models is to provide evidence about the direction of causality in economic relationships. Such a test is useful when we know that two variables are related but we don't know which variable causes the other to move. For example, most economists believe that increases in the money supply stimulate GDP, but others feel that increases in GDP eventually lead the monetary authorities to increase the money supply. Who's right?

One approach to such a question of indeterminate causality is to theorize that the two variables are determined simultaneously. We'll address the estimation of simultaneous equation models in Chapter 14. A second approach to the problem is to test for what is called "Granger causality."

How can we claim to be able to test for causality? After all, didn't we say in Chapter 1 that even though most economic relationships are causal in nature, regression analysis can't prove such causality? The answer is that we don't actually test for theoretical causality; instead, we test for Granger causality.

Granger causality, or precedence, is a circumstance in which one time-series variable consistently and predictably changes before another variable.[7] Granger causality is important because it allows us to analyze which variable precedes or "leads" the other, and, as we shall see, such leading variables are extremely useful for forecasting purposes.

Despite the value of Granger causality, however, we shouldn't let ourselves be lured into thinking that it allows us to prove economic causality in any rigorous way. If one variable precedes ("Granger causes") another, we can't be sure that the first variable "causes" the other to change.[8]

---

7. See C. W. J. Granger, "Investigating Causal Relations by Econometric Models and Cross-Spectral Methods," *Econometrica*, Vol. 37, No. 3, pp. 424−438.

8. In the fifth edition, we ended this paragraph by saying, "For example, Christmas cards typically arrive before Christmas, but it's clear that Christmas wasn't caused by the arrival of the cards." However, this isn't a true example of Granger causality, because the date of Christmas is fixed and therefore isn't a "time-series variable." See Erdal Atukeren, "Christmas cards, Easter bunnies, and Granger-causality," *Quality & Quantity*, Vol. 42, No. 6, Dec. 2008, pp. 835−844. For an in-depth discussion of causality, see Kevin Hoover, *Causality in Macroeconomics* (Cambridge: Cambridge University Press, 2001).

As a result, even if we're able to show that event A always happens before event B, we have not shown that event A "causes" event B.

There are a number of different tests for Granger causality, and all the various methods involve distributed lag models in one way or another.[9] Our preference is to use an expanded version of a test originally developed by Granger. Granger suggested that to see if A Granger-caused Y, we should run:

$$Y_t = \beta_0 + \beta_1 Y_{t-1} + \cdots + \beta_p Y_{t-p} + \alpha_1 A_{t-1} + \cdots + \alpha_p A_{t-p} + \epsilon_t$$

$$(12.20)$$

and test the null hypothesis that the coefficients of the lagged As (the αs) jointly equal zero.[10] If we can reject this null hypothesis using the F-test, then we have evidence that A Granger-causes Y. Note that if $p = 1$, Equation 12.20 is similar to the dynamic model, Equation 12.3.

Applications of this test involve running two Granger tests, one in each direction. That is, run Equation 12.20 and also run:

$$A_t = \beta_0 + \beta_1 A_{t-1} + \cdots + \beta_p A_{t-p} + \alpha_1 Y_{t-1} + \cdots + \alpha_p Y_{t-p} + \epsilon_t$$

$$(12.21)$$

testing for Granger causality in both directions by testing the null hypothesis that the coefficients of the lagged Ys (again, the αs) jointly equal zero. If the F-test is significant for Equation 12.20 but not for Equation 12.21, then we can conclude that A Granger-causes Y. For practice with this dual version of the Granger test, see Exercise 8.

(12.4) Spurious Correlation and Nonstationarity

One problem with time-series data is that independent variables can appear to be more significant than they actually are if they have the same underlying trend as the dependent variable. In a country with rampant inflation, for example, almost any nominal variable will appear to be highly correlated with

9. See John Geweke, R. Meese, and W. Dent, "Comparing Alternative Tests of Causality in Temporal Systems," *Journal of Econometrics*, Vol. 21, pp. 161–194, and Rodney Jacobs, Edward Leamer, and Michael Ward, "Difficulties with Testing for Causation," *Economic Inquiry*, Vol. 17, No. 3, pp. 401–413.

10. Such a joint test requires the use of the F-test of Appendix 5.6.

all other nominal variables. Why? Nominal variables are unadjusted for inflation, so every nominal variable will have a powerful inflationary component. This inflationary component will usually outweigh any real causal relationship, making nominal variables appear to be correlated even if they aren't.

Such a problem is an example of **spurious correlation**, a strong relationship between two or more variables that is not caused by a real underlying causal relationship. If you run a regression in which the dependent variable and one or more independent variables are spuriously correlated, the result is a *spurious regression*, and the *t*-scores and overall fit of such spurious regressions are likely to be overstated and untrustworthy.

There are many causes of spurious correlation. In a cross-sectional data set, for example, spurious correlation can be caused by dividing both the dependent variable and one independent variable by a third variable that varies considerably more than do the first two. The focus of this section, however, will be on time-series data and in particular on spurious correlation caused by *nonstationary time series*.

Stationary and Nonstationary Time Series

A stationary series is one whose basic properties, for example its mean and its variance, do not change over time. In contrast, a nonstationary series has one or more basic properties that *do* change over time. For instance, the real per capita output of an economy typically increases over time, so it's nonstationary. By contrast, the growth *rate* of real per capita output often does not increase over time, so this variable is stationary even though the variable it's based on, real per capita output, is nonstationary. A time series can be nonstationary even with a constant mean if another property, such as the variance, changes over time.

More formally, a time-series variable, X_t, is **stationary** if:

1. the mean of X_t is constant over time,
2. the variance of X_t is constant over time, and
3. the simple correlation coefficient between X_t and X_{t-k} depends on the length of the lag (k) but on no other variable (for all k).[11]

If one or more of these properties is not met, then X_t is **nonstationary**. If a series is nonstationary, that problem is often referred to as **nonstationarity**.

---

11. There are two different definitions of stationarity. The particular definition we use here is a simplification of the most frequently cited definition, referred to by various authors as weak, wide-sense, or covariance stationarity.

Although our definition of a stationary series focuses on stationary and nonstationary *variables*, it's important to note that *error terms* (and, therefore, residuals) also can be nonstationary. In fact, we've already had experience with a nonstationary error term. Many cases of heteroskedasticity in time-series data involve an error term with a variance that tends to increase with time. That kind of heteroskedastic error term is also nonstationary!

The major consequence of nonstationarity for regression analysis is spurious correlation that inflates R^2 and the *t*-scores of the nonstationary independent variables, which in turn leads to incorrect model specification. This occurs because the regression estimation procedure attributes to the nonstationary X_t changes in Y_t that were actually caused by some factor (trend, for example) that also affects X_t. Thus, the variables move together because of the nonstationarity, increasing R^2 and the relevant *t*-scores. This is especially important in macroeconometrics, and the macroeconomic literature is dominated by articles that examine various series for signs of nonstationarity.[12]

Some variables are nonstationary mainly because they increase rapidly over time. Spurious regression results involving these kinds of variables often can be avoided by the addition of a simple time trend (t = 1, 2, 3, . . . , T) to the equation as an independent variable.

Unfortunately, many economic time-series variables are nonstationary even after the removal of a time trend. This nonstationarity typically takes the form of the variable behaving as though it were a "random walk." A **random walk** is a time-series variable where next period's value equals this period's value plus a stochastic error term. A random-walk variable is nonstationary because it can wander up and down without an inherent equilibrium and without approaching a long-term mean of any sort.

To get a better understanding of the relationship between nonstationarity and a random walk, let's suppose that Y_t is generated by an equation that includes only past values of itself (an *autoregressive* equation):

$$Y_t = \gamma Y_{t-1} + v_t \tag{12.22}$$

where v_t is a classical error term.

Take a look at Equation 12.22. Can you see that if $|\gamma| < 1$, then the expected value of Y_t will eventually approach 0 (and therefore be stationary) as the sample size gets bigger and bigger? (Remember, since v_t is a classical error term, its

12. See, for example, C. R. Nelson and C. I. Plosser, "Trends and Random Walks in Macroeconomics Time Series: Some Evidence and Implication," *Journal of Monetary Economics*, Vol. 10, pp. 169–182, and J. Campbell and N. G. Mankiw, "Permanent and Transitory Components in Macroeconomic Fluctuations," *American Economic Review*, Vol. 77, No. 2, pp. 111–117.

expected value $= 0$.) Similarly, can you see that if $|\gamma| > 1$, then the expected value of Y_t will continuously increase, making Y_t nonstationary? This is nonstationarity due to a trend, but it still can cause spurious regression results.

Most importantly, what about if $|\gamma| = 1$? In this case,

$$Y_t = Y_{t-1} + v_t \qquad (12.23)$$

It's a random walk! The expected value of Y_t does not converge on any value, meaning that it is nonstationary. This circumstance, where $\gamma = 1$ in Equation 12.23 (or similar equations), is called a **unit root**. If a variable has a unit root, then Equation 12.23 holds, and the variable follows a random walk and is nonstationary. The relationship between unit roots and nonstationarity is so strong that most econometricians use the words interchangeably, even though they recognize that both trends and unit roots can cause nonstationarity.

Spurious Regression

As noted at the beginning of Section 12.4, if the dependent variable and at least one independent variable in an equation are nonstationary, it's possible for the results of an OLS regression to be spurious.[13]

Consider the linear regression model

$$Y_t = \alpha_0 + \beta_0 X_t + u_t \qquad (12.24)$$

If both X and Y are nonstationary, then they can be highly correlated for non-causal reasons, and our standard regression inference measures will almost surely be very misleading in that they'll overstate $\overline{R}^2$ and the t-score for $\hat{\beta}_0$.

For example, take a look at the following estimated equation:

$$\widehat{PRICE}_t = -27.8 + 0.070 TUITION_t \qquad (12.25)$$
$$(0.006)$$
$$t = \qquad 11.4$$
$$\overline{R}^2 = .94 \qquad T = 10 \text{ (annual)}$$

The R^2 of this equation and the t-score for the coefficient of TUITION are clearly significant, but what are the definitions of the variables? Well, PRICE is the price of a gallon of gasoline in Portland, Oregon, and TUITION is the tuition for a semester of study at Occidental College (Oxy) in Los Angeles (both measured in nominal dollars). Is it possible that an increase in the tuition at

---

13. See C. W. J. Granger and P. Newbold, "Spurious Regression in Econometrics," *Journal of Econometrics*, Volume 2, pp. 111–120.

Oxy caused gas prices in Portland to go up? Not unless every Oxy student was the child of a Portland gas station owner! What's going on? Well, the 1970s were a decade of inflation, so any nominally measured variables are likely to result in an equation that fits as well as Equation 12.25. Both variables are nonstationary, and this particular regression result clearly is spurious.

To avoid spurious regression results, it's crucial to be sure that time-series variables are stationary before running regressions.

The Dickey–Fuller Test

To ensure that the equations we estimate are not spurious, it's important to test for nonstationarity. If we can be reasonably sure that all the variables are stationary, then we need not worry about spurious regressions. How can you tell if a time series is nonstationary? The first step is to visually examine the data. For many time series, a quick glance at the data (or a diagram of the data) will tell you that the mean of a variable is increasing dramatically over time and that the series is nonstationary.

After this trend has been removed, the standard method of testing for non-stationarity is the **Dickey–Fuller test**,[14] which examines the hypothesis that the variable in question has a unit root[15] and, as a result, is likely to benefit from being expressed in first-difference form.

To best understand how the Dickey–Fuller test works, let's return to the discussion of the role that unit roots play in the distinction between stationarity and nonstationarity. Recall that we looked at the value of γ in Equation 12.22 to help us determine if Y was stationary or nonstationary:

$$Y_t = \gamma\, Y_{t-1} + v_t \qquad (12.22)$$

We decided that if $|\gamma| < 1$ then Y is stationary, and that if $|\gamma| > 1$, then Y_t is nonstationary. However, if $|\gamma| = 1$, then Y_t is nonstationary due to a unit root. Thus we concluded that the autoregressive model is stationary if $|\gamma| < 1$ and nonstationary otherwise.

---

14. D. A. Dickey and W. A. Fuller, "Distribution of the Estimators for Autoregressive Time-Series with a Unit Root," *Journal of the American Statistical Association*, Vol. 74, pp. 427–431. The Dickey–Fuller test comes in a variety of forms, including an augmented test to use in cases of a serially correlated error term.

15. For more on unit roots, see John Y. Campbell and Pierre Peron, "Pitfalls and Opportunities: What Macroeconomists Should Know About Unit Roots," *NBER Macroeconomics Annual* (Cambridge, MA: MIT Press, 1991), pp. 141–219.

From this discussion of stationarity and unit roots, it makes sense to estimate Equation 12.22 and determine if $|\gamma| < 1$ to see if Y is stationary, and that's almost exactly how the Dickey–Fuller test works. First, we subtract Y_{t-1} from both sides of Equation 12.22, yielding:

$$(Y_t - Y_{t-1}) = (\gamma - 1) Y_{t-1} + v_t \qquad (12.26)$$

If we define $\Delta Y_t = Y_t - Y_{t-1}$ then we have the simplest form of the Dickey–Fuller test:

$$\Delta Y_t = \beta_1 Y_{t-1} + v_t \qquad (12.27)$$

where $\beta_1 = \gamma - 1$. The null hypothesis is that Y_t contains a unit root and the alternative hypothesis is that Y_t is stationary. If Y_t contains a unit root, $\gamma = 1$ and $\beta_1 = 0$. If Y_t is stationary, $|\gamma| < 1$ and $\beta_1 < 0$. Hence we construct a one-sided t-test on the hypothesis that $\beta_1 = 0$:

$$H_0: \beta_1 = 0$$
$$H_A: \beta_1 < 0$$

Interestingly, the Dickey–Fuller test actually comes in three versions:

1. Equation 12.27,
2. Equation 12.27 with a constant term added (Equation 12.28), and
3. Equation 12.27 with a constant term and a trend term added (Equation 12.29).

The form of the Dickey–Fuller test in Equation 12.27 is correct if Y_t follows Equation 12.22, but the test must be changed if Y_t doesn't follow Equation 12.22. For example, if we believe that Equation 12.22 includes a constant, then the appropriate Dickey–Fuller test equation is:

$$\Delta Y_t = \beta_0 + \beta_1 Y_{t-1} + v_t \qquad (12.28)$$

In a similar fashion, if we believe Y_t contains a trend "t" (t = 1, 2, 3, . . . , T) then we'd add "t" to the equation as a *variable* with a coefficient, and the appropriate Dickey–Fuller test equation is:

$$\Delta Y_t = \beta_0 + \beta_1 Y_{t-1} + \beta_2 t + v_t \qquad (12.29)$$

No matter what form of the Dickey–Fuller test we use, the decision rule is based on the estimate of β_1. If $\hat{\beta}_1$ is significantly less than 0, then we can

Table 12.1 Large-Sample Critical Values for the Dickey–Fuller Test

One-Sided Significance Level:	.01	.025	.05	.10
t_c	3.43	3.12	2.86	2.57

reject the null hypothesis of nonstationarity. If $\hat{\beta}_1$ is not significantly less than 0, then we cannot reject the null hypothesis of nonstationarity. (Recall from Chapter 5 that if we're not able to reject the null hypothesis, we still have not "proven" that Y is nonstationary.)

Be careful, however. The standard t-table does not apply to Dickey–Fuller tests. The critical values depend on the version of the Dickey–Fuller test that is applicable. For the case of no constant and no trend (Equation 12.27) the large-sample values for t_c are listed in Table 12.1.[16] Although not displayed in Table 12.1, the critical t-values for smaller samples are about 60 percent larger in magnitude than those in Statistical Table B-1. For example, a 2.5 percent one-sided t-test of β_1 from Equation 12.27 with 50 degrees of freedom has a critical t-value of 3.22, compared to 2.01 for a standard t-test. For practice in running Dickey–Fuller tests, see Exercises 10 and 11.

Note that the equation for the Dickey–Fuller test and the critical values for each of the specifications are derived under the assumption that the error term is serially uncorrelated. If the error term is serially correlated, then the regression specification must be modified to take this serial correlation into account. This adjustment takes the form of adding in several lagged first differences as independent variables in the equation for the Dickey–Fuller test. There are several good methods for choosing the number of lags to add, but there currently is no universal agreement as to which of these methods is optimal.

Cointegration

If the Dickey–Fuller test reveals nonstationarity, what should we do?

---

16. Most sources list negative critical values for the Dickey–Fuller test, because the unit root test is one sided with a negative expected value. However, the t-test decision rule of this text is based on the absolute value of the t-score, so negative critical values would cause every null hypothesis to be rejected. As a result, the critical values in Table 12.1 are positive. For adjusted critical t-values for the Dickey–Fuller test, including those in Table 12.1, see J. G. MacKinnon, "Critical Values of Cointegration Tests," in Rob Engle and C. W. J. Granger, eds., *Long-Run Economic Relationships: Readings in Cointegration* (New York: Oxford University Press, 1991), Chapter 13. Most software packages provide these critical values with the output from a Dickey–Fuller test.

The traditional approach has been to take the first differences ($\Delta Y = Y_t - Y_{t-1}$ and $\Delta X = X_t - X_{t-1}$) and use them in place of Y_t and X_t in the equation. With economic data, taking a first difference usually is enough to convert a nonstationary series into a stationary one. Unfortunately, using first differences to correct for nonstationarity throws away information that economic theory can provide in the form of equilibrium relationships between the variables when they are expressed in their original units (X_t and Y_t). As a result, first differences should not be used without carefully weighing the costs and benefits of that shift, and in particular first differences should not be used until the residuals have been tested for *cointegration.*

Cointegration consists of matching the degree of nonstationarity of the variables in an equation in a way that makes the error term (and residuals) of the equation stationary and rids the equation of any spurious regression results. Even though individual variables might be nonstationary, it's possible for linear combinations of nonstationary variables to be stationary, or *cointegrated.* If a long-run equilbrium relationship exists between a set of variables, those variables are said to be cointegrated. If the variables are cointegrated, then you can avoid spurious regressions even though the dependent variable and at least one independent variable are nonstationary.

To see how this works, let's return to Equation 12.24:

$$Y_t = \alpha_0 + \beta_0 X_t + u_t \tag{12.24}$$

As we saw in the previous section, if X_t and Y_t are nonstationary, it's likely that we'll get spurious regression results. To understand how it's possible to get sensible results from Equation 12.24 if the nonstationary variables are cointegrated, let's focus on the case in which both X_t and Y_t contain one unit root. The key to cointegration is the behavior of u_t.

If we solve Equation 12.24 for u_t, we get:

$$u_t = Y_t - \alpha_0 - \beta_0 X_t \tag{12.30}$$

In Equation 12.30, u_t is a function of two nonstationary variables, so you'd certainly expect u_t also to be nonstationary, but that's not necessarily the case. In particular, suppose that X_t and Y_t are related? More specifically, if economic theory supports Equation 12.24 as an equilibrium, then departures from that equilibrium should not be arbitrarily large.

Hence, if Y_t and X_t are related, then the error term u_t may well be stationary even though X_t and Y_t are nonstationary. If u_t is stationary, then the unit roots in Y_t and X_t have "cancelled out" and Y_t and X_t are said to be cointegrated.[17]

We thus see that if X_t and Y_t are cointegrated then OLS estimation of the coefficients in Equation 12.24 can avoid spurious results. To determine if X_t and Y_t are cointegrated, we begin with OLS estimation of Equation 12.24 and calculate the OLS residuals:

$$e_t = Y_t - \hat{\alpha}_0 - \hat{\beta}_0 X_t \qquad (12.31)$$

We then perform a Dickey–Fuller test on the residuals. Once again, the standard t-values do not apply to this application, so adjusted critical t-values should be used.[18] However, these adjusted critical values are only slightly higher than standard critical t-values, so the numbers in Statistical Table B-1 can be used as rough estimates of the more accurate figures. If we are able to reject the null hypothesis of a unit root in the residuals, we can conclude that Y_t and X_t are cointegrated and our OLS estimates are not spurious.

To sum, if the Dickey–Fuller test reveals that our variables have unit roots, the first step is to test for cointegration in the residuals. If the nonstationary variables are not cointegrated, then the equation should be estimated using first differences (ΔY and ΔX). However, if the nonstationary variables are cointegrated, then the equation can be estimated in its original units.[19]

---

17. For more on cointegration, see Peter Kennedy, *A Guide to Econometrics* (Malden, MA: Blackwell, 2008), pp. 309–313 and 327–330, and B. Bhaskara Rau, ed., *Cointegration for the Applied Economist* (New York: St. Martin's Press, 1994).

18. See J. G. MacKinnon, "Critical Values of Cointegration Tests," in Rob Engle and C. W. J. Granger, eds., *Long-Run Economic Relationships: Readings in Cointegration* (New York: Oxford University Press, 1991), Chapter 13, and Rob Engle and C. W. J. Granger, "Co-integration and Error Correction: Representation, Estimation and Testing," *Econometrica*, Vol. 55, No. 2.

19. In this case, it's common practice to use a version of the original equation called the Error Correction Model (ECM). While the equation for the ECM is fairly complex, the model itself is a logical extension of the cointegration concept. If two variables are cointegrated, then there is an equilibrium relationship connecting them. A regression on these variables therefore is an estimate of this equilibrium relationship along with a residual, which is a measure of the extent to which these variables are out of equilibrium. When formulating a dynamic relationship between the variables, economic theory suggests that the current change in the dependent variable should be affected not only by the current change in the independent variable but also by the extent to which these variables were out of equilibrium in the preceding period (the residual from the cointegrating process). The resulting equation is the ECM. For more on the ECM, see Peter Kennedy, *A Guide to Econometrics* (Malden, MA: Blackwell, 2008), pp. 299–301 and 322–323.

A Standard Sequence of Steps for Dealing with Nonstationary Time Series

This material is fairly complex, at least compared to previous chapters, so let's pause for a moment to summarize the various steps suggested in Section 12.4. To deal with the possibility that nonstationary time series might be causing regression results to be spurious, most empirical work in time series follows a standard sequence of steps:

1. Specify the model. This model might be a time-series equation with no lagged variables, it might be a dynamic model in its simplest form (Equation 12.3), or it might be a dynamic model that includes lags in both the dependent and the independent variables.

2. Test all variables for nonstationarity (technically unit roots) using the appropriate version of the Dickey–Fuller test.

3. If the variables don't have unit roots, estimate the equation in its original units (Y and X).

4. If the variables have unit roots, test the residuals of the equation for cointegration using the Dickey–Fuller test.

5. If the variables have unit roots but are not cointegrated, then change the functional form of the model to first differences (ΔY and ΔX) and estimate the equation.

6. If the variables have unit roots and also are cointegrated, then estimate the equation in its original units

12.5 Summary

1. A distributed lag explains the current value of Y as a function of current and past values of X, thus "distributing" the impact of X over a number of lagged time periods. OLS estimation of distributed lag equations without any constraints (ad hoc distributed lags) encounters problems with multicollinearity, degrees of freedom, and a non-continuous pattern of coefficients over time.

2. A dynamic model avoids these problems by assuming that the coefficients of the lagged independent variables decrease in a geometric

fashion the longer the lag. Given this, the dynamic model is:

$$Y_t = \alpha_0 + \beta_0 X_t + \lambda Y_{t-1} + u_t$$

where Y_{t-1} is a lagged dependent variable and $0 < \lambda < 1$.

3. In small samples, OLS estimates of a dynamic model are biased and have unreliable hypothesis testing properties. Even in large samples, OLS will produce biased estimates of the coefficients of a dynamic model if the error term is serially correlated.

4. In a dynamic model, the Durbin–Watson d test sometimes can fail to detect the presence of serial correlation because d is biased toward 2. The most-used alternative is the Lagrange Multiplier test.

5. Granger causality, or precedence, is a circumstance in which one time-series variable consistently and predictably changes before another variable does. If one variable precedes (Granger-causes) another, we still can't be sure that the first variable "causes" the other to change.

6. A nonstationary series is one that exhibits significant changes (for example, in its mean and variance) over time. If the dependent variable and at least one independent variable are nonstationary, a regression may encounter spurious correlation that inflates $\overline{R}^2$ and the t-scores of the nonstationary independent variable(s).

7. Nonstationarity can be detected using the Dickey–Fuller test. If the variables are nonstationary (have unit roots) then the residuals of the equation should be tested for cointegration using the Dickey–Fuller test. If the variables are nonstationary but are not cointegrated, then the equation should be estimated with first differences. If the variables are nonstationary and also are cointegrated, then the equation can be estimated in its original units.

EXERCISES

(The answer to Exercise 2 is in Appendix A.)

1. Write the meaning of each of the following terms without referring to the book (or your notes), and then compare your definition with the version in the text for each:
   a. dynamic model
   b. ad hoc distributed lag model

  c. Lagrange Multiplier Serial Correlation test
  d. Granger causality
  e. nonstationary series
  f. Dickey–Fuller test
  g. unit root
  h. random walk
  i. cointegration

2. Consider the following equation aimed at estimating the demand for real cash balances in Mexico (standard errors in parentheses):

$$\widehat{\ln M_t} = 2.00 - 0.10\ln R_t + 0.70\ln Y_t + 0.60\ln M_{t-1}$$
$$(0.10) \qquad (0.35) \qquad (0.10)$$
$$\overline{R}^2 = .90 \qquad DW = 1.80 \qquad N = 26$$

where: M_t = the money stock in year t (millions of pesos)
     R_t = the long-term interest rate in year t (percent)
     Y_t = the real GNP in year t (millions of pesos)

  a. What economic relationship between Y and M is implied by the equation?
  b. How are Y and R similar in terms of their relationship to M?
  c. Does this equation seem likely to have serial correlation? Explain.

3. Calculate and graph the pattern of the impact of a lagged X on Y as the lag increases for each of the following estimated dynamic models:
  a. $Y_t = 13.0 + 12.0X_t + 0.04Y_{t-1}$
  b. $Y_t = 13.0 + 12.0X_t + 0.08Y_{t-1}$
  c. $Y_t = 13.0 + 12.0X_t + 2.0Y_{t-1}$
  d. $Y_t = 13.0 + 12.0X_t - 0.4Y_{t-1}$
  e. Look over your graphs for parts c and d. What λ restriction do they combine to show the wisdom of?

4. Consider the following equation for the determination of wages in the United Kingdom (standard error in parentheses):

$$\widehat{W_t} = 8.562 + 0.364P_t + 0.004P_{t-1} - 2.56U_t$$
$$(0.080) \qquad (0.072) \qquad (0.658)$$
$$\overline{R}^2 = .87 \qquad N = 19$$

where: W_t = wages and salaries per employee in year t
     P_t = the price level in year t
     U_t = the percent unemployment in year t

    a. Develop and test your own hypotheses with respect to the individual slope coefficients at the 10-percent level.

    b. Discuss the theoretical validity of P_{t-1} and how your opinion of that validity has been changed by its statistical significance. Should P_{t-1} be dropped from the equation? Why or why not?

    c. If P_{t-1} is dropped from the equation, the general functional form of the equation changes radically. Why?

5. You've been hired to determine the impact of advertising on gross sales revenue for "Four Musketeers" candy bars. Four Musketeers has the same price and more or less the same ingredients as competing candy bars, so it seems likely that only advertising affects sales. You decide to build a distributed lag model of sales as a function of advertising, but you're not sure whether an ad hoc or a dynamic model is more appropriate.

    Using data on Four Musketeers candy bars from Table 12.2, estimate both of the following distributed lag equations from 1985–2009 and compare the lag structures implied by the estimated coefficients. (*Hint:* Be careful to use the correct sample.)

    a. an ad hoc distributed lag model (4 lags)

    b. a dynamic model

6. Test for serial correlation in the estimated dynamic model you got as your answer to Exercise 5b.

7. Suppose you're building a dynamic model and are concerned with the possibility that serial correlation, instead of being first order, is second order: $u_t = f(u_{t-1}, u_{t-2})$.

    a. What is the theoretical meaning of such second-order serial correlation?

    b. Carefully write out the formula for the Lagrange Multiplier Serial Correlation (LMSC) test auxiliary equation (similar to Equation 12.18) that you would have to estimate to test such a possibility. How many degrees of freedom would there be in such an LMSC test?

    c. Test for second-order serial correlation in the estimated dynamic model you got as your answer to Exercise 5b.

8. Most economists consider investment and output to be jointly (simultaneously) determined. One test of this simultaneity would be to see whether one of the variables could be shown to Granger-cause the other. Take the data set from the small macroeconomic model in Table 14.1 and test the possibility that investment (I) Granger-causes

Table 12.2 Data for the Four Musketeers Exercise

Year	Sales	Advertising
1981	*	30
1982	*	35
1983	*	36
1984	320	39
1985	360	40
1986	390	45
1987	400	50
1988	410	50
1989	400	50
1990	450	53
1991	470	55
1992	500	60
1993	500	60
1994	490	60
1995	580	65
1996	600	70
1997	700	70
1998	790	60
1999	730	60
2000	720	60
2001	800	70
2002	820	80
2003	830	80
2004	890	80
2005	900	80
2006	850	75
2007	840	75
2008	850	75
2009	850	75

Datafile = MOUSE12

GDP (Y) (or vice versa) with a two-sided Granger test with four lagged Xs.

9. Some farmers were interested in predicting inches of growth of corn as a function of rainfall on a monthly basis, so they collected data from the growing season and estimated an equation of the following form:

$$G_t = \beta_0 + \beta_1 R_t + \beta_2 G_{t-1} + \epsilon_t$$

where: G_t = inches of growth of corn in month t
R_t = inches of rain in month t
ϵ_t = a normally distributed classical error term

The farmers expected a negative sign for β_2 (they felt that since corn can only grow so much, if it grows a lot in one month, it won't grow much in the next month), but they got a positive estimate instead. What suggestions would you have for this problem?

10. Run 2.5 percent Dickey–Fuller tests (of the form in Equation 12.27) for the following variables using the data in Table 6.2 from the chicken demand equation and determine which variables, if any, you think are nonstationary. (*Hint:* Use 3.12 as your critical *t*-value.)
    a. Y_t
    b. PC_t
    c. PB_t
    d. YD_t

11. Run 2.5 percent Dickey–Fuller tests (of the form in Equation 12.27) for the following variables using the data from the small macroeconomic model in Table 14.1 and determine which variables, if any, you think are nonstationary. (*Hint:* Use 3.12 as your critical *t*-value.)
    a. Y   (GDP)
    b. r   (the interest rate)
    c. CO   (consumption)
    d. I   (investment)

12. In 2001, Heo and Tan published an article[20] in which they used the Granger causality model to test the relationship between economic growth and democracy. For years, political scientists have noted a strong positive relationship between economic growth and democracy, but the authors of previous studies (which included Granger causality studies) disagreed about the causality involved. Heo and Tan studied 32 developing countries and found that economic growth "Granger-caused" democracy in 11 countries, while democracy "Granger-caused" economic growth in 10 others.

---

20. Uk Heo and Alexander Tan, "Democracy and Economic Growth: a Causal Analysis," *Comparative Politics*, Vol. 33, No. 4 (July 2001), pp. 463–473.

a. How is it possible to get significant Granger causality results in two different directions in the same study? Is this evidence that the study was done incorrectly? Is this evidence that Granger causality tests cannot be applied to this topic?

b. Based on the evidence presented, what's your conclusion about the relationship between economic growth and democracy? Explain.

c. If this were your research project, what would your next step be? (*Hint:* In particular, is there anything to be gained by learning more about the countries in the two different Granger causality groups?[21])

---

21. For the record, the 11 countries in which growth Granger caused democracy were Costa Rica, Egypt, Guatemala, India, Israel, South Korea, Mexico, Nicaragua, Thailand, Uruguay, and Venezuela, and the 10 countries in which democracy Granger caused growth were Bolivia, Burma, Colombia, Ecuador, El Salvador, Indonesia, Iran, Paraguay, the Philippines, and South Africa.

13 Dummy Dependent Variable Techniques

Until now, our discussion of dummy variables has been restricted to dummy independent variables. However, there are many important research topics for which the *dependent* variable is appropriately treated as a dummy, equal only to 0 or 1.

In particular, researchers analyzing consumer choice often must cope with dummy dependent variables (also called qualitative dependent variables). For example, how do high school students decide whether to go to college? What distinguishes Pepsi drinkers from Coke drinkers? How can we convince people to use public transportation instead of driving? For an econometric study of these topics, or of any topic that involves a *discrete* choice of some sort, the dependent variable is typically a dummy variable.

In the first two sections of this chapter, we'll present two frequently used ways to estimate equations that have dummy dependent variables: the linear probability model and the binomial logit model. In the last section, we'll briefly discuss two other useful dummy dependent variable techniques: the binomial probit model and the multinomial logit model.

13.1 The Linear Probability Model

What Is a Linear Probability Model?

The most obvious way to estimate a model with a dummy dependent variable is to run OLS on a typical linear econometric equation. A **linear probability**

---

model is just that, a linear-in-the-coefficients equation used to explain a dummy dependent variable:

$$D_i = \beta_0 + \beta_1 X_{1i} + \beta_2 X_{2i} + \epsilon_i \qquad (13.1)$$

where D_i is a dummy variable and the Xs, βs, and ϵ are typical independent variables, regression coefficients, and an error term, respectively.

For example, suppose you're interested in understanding why some states have female governors and others don't. In such a model, the appropriate dependent variable would be a dummy, for example D_i equal to one if the ith state has a female governor and equal to zero otherwise. If we hypothesize that states with a high percentage of females and a low percentage of social conservatives would be likely to have a female governor, then a linear probability model would be:

$$D_i = \beta_0 + \beta_1 F_i + \beta_2 R_i + \epsilon_i \qquad (13.2)$$

where: D_i = 1 if the ith state has a female governor, 0 otherwise
          F_i = females as a percent of the ith state's population
          R_i = conservatives as a percent of the ith state's registered voters

The term *linear probability model* comes from the fact that the right side of the equation is linear while the expected value of the left side measures the probability that $D_i = 1$. To understand this second statement, let's assume that we estimate Equation 13.2 and get a $\hat{D}_i$ of 0.10 for a particular state. What does that mean? Well, since $D = 1$ if the governor is female and $D = 0$ if the governor is male, a state with a $\hat{D}_i$ of 0.10 can perhaps best be thought of as a state in which there is a 10-percent chance that the governor will be female, based on the state's values for the independent variables. Thus $\hat{D}_i$ measures the probability that $D_i = 1$ for the ith observation, and:

$$\hat{D}_i = Pr(D_i = 1) = \hat{\beta}_0 + \hat{\beta}_1 F_i + \hat{\beta}_2 R_i \qquad (13.3)$$

where $Pr(D_i = 1)$ indicates the probability that $D_i = 1$ for the ith observation.

How should we interpret the coefficients of Equation 13.3? Since $\hat{D}_i$ measures the probability that $D_i = 1$, then a coefficient in a linear probability model tells us the percentage point change in the probability that $D_i = 1$

caused by a one-unit increase in the independent variable in question, holding constant the other independent variables in the equation.

We can never observe the actual probability, however, because it reflects the situation before a discrete decision is made. After the choice is made, we can observe only the outcome of that choice, and so the dependent variable D_i can take on the values of only 0 or 1. Thus, even though the expected value can be anywhere from 0 to 1, we can only observe the two extremes (0 and 1) in our dependent variable (D_i).

Problems with the Linear Probability Model

Unfortunately, the use of OLS to estimate the coefficients of an equation with a dummy dependent variable encounters two major problems:[1]

1. $\overline{R}^2$ *is not an accurate measure of overall fit.* For models with a dummy dependent variable, $\overline{R}^2$ tells us very little about how well the model explains the choices of the decision makers. To see why, take a look at Figure 13.1. D_i can equal only 1 or 0, but $\hat{D}_i$ must move in a continuous fashion from one extreme to the other. This means that $\hat{D}_i$ is likely to be quite different from D_i for some range of X_i. Thus, $\overline{R}^2$ is likely to be much lower than 1 even if the model actually does an exceptional job of explaining the choices involved. As a result, $\overline{R}^2$ (or R^2) should not be relied on as a measure of the overall fit of a model with a dummy dependent variable.

2. $\hat{D}_i$ *is not bounded by 0 and 1.* Since D_i is a dummy variable, we'd expect $\hat{D}_i$ to be limited to a range of 0 to 1. After all, the prediction that a probability equals 2.6 (or -2.6, for that matter) is almost meaningless. However, take another look at Equation 13.3. Depending on the values of the Xs and the $\hat{\beta}$s, the right-hand side might well be outside the meaningful range. For instance, if all the Xs and $\hat{\beta}$s in Equation 13.3 equal 1.0, then $\hat{D}_i$ equals 3.0, substantially greater than 1.0.

The first of these two major problems isn't impossible to deal with, because there are a variety of alternatives to $\overline{R}^2$ for equations with dummy-dependent

---

1. In addition, the error term of a linear probability model is neither homoskedastic nor normally distributed, mainly because D takes on just two values (0 and 1). In practice, however, the impact of these problems on OLS estimation is minor, and many researchers ignore potential heteroskedasticity and nonnormality and apply OLS directly to the linear probability model. See R. G. McGillvray, "Estimating the Linear Probability Function," *Econometrica*, Vol. 38, pp. 775–776.

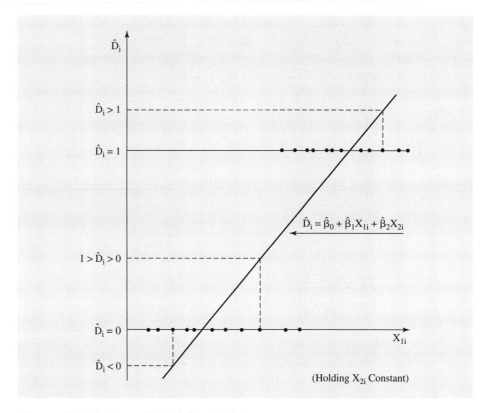

Figure 13.1 A Linear Probability Model

In a linear probability model, all the observed D_is equal either 0 or 1 but $\hat{D}_i$ moves linearly from one extreme to the other. As a result, $\overline{R}^2$ is often quite low even if the model does an excellent job of explaining the decision maker's choice. In addition, exceptionally large or small values of X_{1i} (holding X_{2i} constant), can produce values of $\hat{D}_i$ outside the meaningful range of 0 to 1.

variables.[2] Our preference is to create a measure based on the percentage of the observations in the sample that a particular estimated equation explains correctly. To use this approach, consider a $\hat{D}_i > .5$ to predict that $D_i = 1$ and a $\hat{D}_i < .5$ to predict that $D_i = 0$. If we then compare these

2. See M. R. Veal and K. F. Zimmerman, "Pseudo-R^2 Measures for Some Common Limited Dependent Variables Models," *Journal of Economic Surveys*, Vol. 10, No. 3, pp. 241–259 and C. S. McIntosh and J. J. Dorfman, "Qualitative Forecast Evaluation: A Comparison of Two Performance Measures," *American Journal of Agricultural Economics*, Vol. 74, pp. 209–214.

predictions[3] with the actual D_i, we can calculate the percentage of observations explained correctly.

Unfortunately, using the percentage explained correctly as a substitute for $\overline{R}^2$ for the entire sample has a flaw. Suppose that 85 percent of your observations are ones and 15 percent are zeroes. Explaining 85 percent of the sample correctly sounds good, but your results are no better than naively guessing that every observation is a one! A better way might be to calculate the percentage of ones explained correctly, calculate the percentage of zeroes explained correctly, and then report the average of these two percentages. As a shorthand, we'll call this average $\overline{R}_p^2$. That is, we'll define $\overline{\mathbf{R}_p^2}$ to be the average of the percentage of ones explained correctly and the percentage of zeroes explained correctly. Since $\overline{R}_p^2$ is a new statistic, we'll calculate and discuss both $\overline{R}_p^2$ and $\overline{R}^2$ throughout this chapter.

For most researchers, therefore, the major difficulty with the linear probability model is the unboundedness of the predicted D_is. Take another look at Figure 13.1 for a graphical interpretation of the situation. Because of the linear relationship between the X_is and $\hat{D}_i$, $\hat{D}_i$ can fall well outside the relevant range of 0 to 1. Using the linear probability model, despite this unboundedness problem, may not cause insurmountable difficulties. In particular, the signs and general significance levels of the estimated coefficients of the linear probability model are often similar to those of the alternatives we will discuss later in this chapter.

One simplistic way to get around the unboundedness problem is to assign $\hat{D}_i = 1.0$ to all values of $\hat{D}_i$ above 1 and $\hat{D}_i = 0.0$ to all negative values. This approach copes with the problem by ignoring it, since an observation for which the linear probability model predicts a probability of 2.0 has been judged to be more likely to be equal to 1.0 than an observation for which the model predicts a 1.0, and yet they are lumped together. Even $\hat{D}_i = 1$ isn't very useful, because it implies that events will happen with certainty, surely a foolish prediction to make. What is needed is a systematic method of forcing the $\hat{D}_i$s to range from 0 to 1 in a smooth and meaningful fashion. We'll present such a method, the binomial logit, in Section 13.2.

---

3. Although it's standard to use $\hat{D}_i = .5$ as the value that distinguishes a prediction of $D_i = 1$ from a prediction of $D_i = 0$, there's no rule that requires that .5 be used. This is because it's possible to imagine circumstances in which .5 is too high or too low. For example, if the payoff when you're right if you classify $D_i = 1$ is much lower than the payoff when you're right if you classify $D_i = 0$, then a value lower than .5 might make sense. We're grateful to Peter Kennedy for this observation.

An Example of a Linear Probability Model

Before moving on to investigate the logit, however, let's take a look at an example of a linear probability model: a disaggregate study of the labor force participation of women.

A person is defined as being in the labor force if she either has a job or is actively looking for a job. Thus, a disaggregate (cross-sectional by person) study of women's labor force participation is appropriately modeled with a dummy dependent variable:

$$D_i = 1 \text{ if the } i\text{th woman has or is looking for a job,}$$
$$0 \text{ otherwise (not in the labor force)}$$

A review of the literature reveals that there are many potentially relevant independent variables. Two of the most important are the marital status and the number of years of schooling of the woman. The expected signs for the coefficients of these variables are fairly straightforward, since a woman who is unmarried and well educated is much more likely to be in the labor force than her opposite:

$$D_i = f(\overset{-}{M_i}, \overset{+}{S_i}) + \epsilon_i \tag{13.4}$$

where: $M_i = 1$ if the ith woman is married and 0 otherwise
         S_i = the number of years of schooling of the ith woman

The data are presented in Table 13.1. The sample size is limited to 30 in order to make it easier for readers to enter the dataset on their own. Unfortunately, such a small sample will make hypothesis testing fairly unreliable. Table 13.1 also includes the age of the ith woman for use in Exercises 8 and 9. Another typically used variable, O_i = other income available to the ith woman, is not available for this sample, introducing possible omitted variable bias.

If we choose a linear functional form for both independent variables, we've got a linear probability model:

$$D_i = \beta_0 + \beta_1 M_i + \beta_2 S_i + \epsilon_i \tag{13.5}$$

If we now estimate Equation 13.5 with the data on the labor force participation of women from Table 13.1, we obtain (standard errors in parentheses):

$$\hat{D}_i = -0.28 - 0.38M_i + 0.09S_i \tag{13.6}$$
$$(0.15) \quad (0.03)$$
$$N = 30 \quad \overline{R}^2 = .32 \quad \overline{R}_p^2 = .81$$

Table 13.1 Data on the Labor Force Participation of Women

Observation #	D_i	M_i	A_i	S_i	$\hat{D}_i$
1	1.0	0.0	31.0	16.0	1.20
2	1.0	1.0	34.0	14.0	0.63
3	1.0	1.0	41.0	16.0	0.82
4	0.0	0.0	67.0	9.0	0.55
5	1.0	0.0	25.0	12.0	0.83
6	0.0	1.0	58.0	12.0	0.45
7	1.0	0.0	45.0	14.0	1.01
8	1.0	0.0	55.0	10.0	0.64
9	0.0	0.0	43.0	12.0	0.83
10	1.0	0.0	55.0	8.0	0.45
11	1.0	0.0	25.0	11.0	0.73
12	1.0	0.0	41.0	14.0	1.01
13	0.0	1.0	62.0	12.0	0.45
14	1.0	1.0	51.0	13.0	0.54
15	0.0	1.0	39.0	9.0	0.17
16	1.0	0.0	35.0	10.0	0.64
17	1.0	1.0	40.0	14.0	0.63
18	0.0	1.0	43.0	10.0	0.26
19	0.0	1.0	37.0	12.0	0.45
20	1.0	0.0	27.0	13.0	0.92
21	1.0	0.0	28.0	14.0	1.01
22	1.0	1.0	48.0	12.0	0.45
23	0.0	1.0	66.0	7.0	−0.01
24	0.0	1.0	44.0	11.0	0.35
25	0.0	1.0	21.0	12.0	0.45
26	1.0	1.0	40.0	10.0	0.26
27	1.0	0.0	41.0	15.0	1.11
28	0.0	1.0	23.0	10.0	0.26
29	0.0	1.0	31.0	11.0	0.35
30	1.0	1.0	44.0	12.0	0.45

Datafile = WOMEN13

How do these results look? Despite the small sample and the possible bias due to omitting O_i, both independent variables have estimated coefficients that are significant in the expected direction. In addition, the $\overline{R}^2$ of .32 is fairly high for a linear probability model (since D_i equals only 0 or 1, it's almost impossible to get an $\overline{R}^2$ much higher than .70). Further evidence of good fit is the fairly high $\overline{R}_p^2$ of .81, meaning that an average of 81 percent of the choices were explained "correctly" by Equation 13.6.

We need to be careful when we interpret the estimated coefficients in Equation 13.6, however. Remember that the slope coefficient in a linear probability model represents the change in the probability that D_i equals one caused by a one-unit increase in the independent variable (holding the other independent variables constant). Viewed in this context, do the estimated coefficients make economic sense? The answer is yes: the probability of a woman participating in the labor force falls by 38 percent if she is married (holding constant schooling). Each year of schooling increases the probability of labor force participation by 9 percent (holding constant marital status).

The values for $\hat{D}_i$ have been included in Table 13.1. Note that $\hat{D}_i$ is indeed often outside the meaningful range of 0 and 1, causing most of the problems cited earlier. To attack this problem of the unboundedness of $\hat{D}_i$, however, we need a new estimation technique, so let's take a look at one.

13.2 The Binomial Logit Model

What Is the Binomial Logit?

The **binomial logit** is an estimation technique for equations with dummy dependent variables that avoids the unboundedness problem of the linear probability model by using a variant of the cumulative logistic function:

$$D_i = \frac{1}{1 + e^{-[\beta_0 + \beta_1 X_{1i} + \beta_2 X_{2i} + \epsilon_i]}} \tag{13.7}$$

Are the $\hat{D}_i$s produced by a logit now limited by 0 and 1? The answer is yes, but to see why we need to take a close look at Equation 13.7. What is the largest that $\hat{D}_i$ can be? Well, if $\hat{\beta}_0 + \hat{\beta}_1 X_{1i} + \hat{\beta}_2 X_{2i}$ equals infinity, then:

$$\hat{D}_i = \frac{1}{1 + e^{-\infty}} = \frac{1}{1} = 1 \tag{13.8}$$

because e to the minus infinity equals zero. What's the smallest that $\hat{D}_i$ can be? If $\hat{\beta}_0 + \hat{\beta}_1 X_{1i} + \hat{\beta}_2 X_{2i}$ equals minus infinity, then:

$$\hat{D}_i = \frac{1}{1 + e^{\infty}} = \frac{1}{\infty} = 0 \tag{13.9}$$

Thus, $\hat{D}_i$ is bounded by 1 and 0. As can be seen in Figure 13.2, $\hat{D}_i$ approaches 1 and 0 very slowly (asymptotically). The binomial logit model therefore

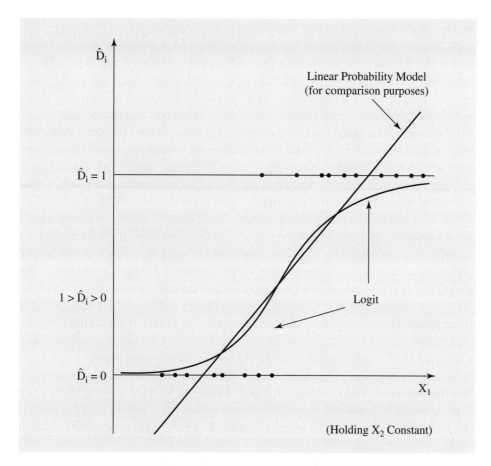

Figure 13.2 $\hat{D}_i$ Is Bounded by 0 and 1 in a Binomial Logit Model

In a binomial logit model, $\hat{D}_i$ is nonlinearly related to X_1, so even exceptionally large or small values of X_{1i}, holding X_{2i} constant, will not produce values of $\hat{D}_i$ outside the meaningful range of 0 to 1.

avoids the major problem that the linear probability model encounters in dealing with dummy dependent variables. In addition, the logit is quite satisfying to most researchers because it turns out that real-world data often are described well by S-shape patterns like that in Figure 13.2.

Logits cannot be estimated using OLS. Instead, we use **maximum likelihood (ML)**, an iterative estimation technique that is especially useful for equations that are nonlinear in the coefficients. ML estimation is inherently different from least squares in that it chooses coefficient estimates that *maximize the likelihood* of the sample data set being observed.[4] Interestingly, OLS and ML estimates are not necessarily different; for a linear equation that meets the Classical Assumptions (including the normality assumption), ML estimates are identical to the OLS ones.

One of the reasons that maximum likelihood is used is that ML has a number of desirable large sample properties; ML is consistent and asymptotically efficient (unbiased and minimum variance for large samples). With very large samples, ML has the added advantage of producing normally distributed coefficient estimates, allowing the use of typical hypothesis testing techniques. As a result, sample sizes for logits should be substantially larger than for linear regressions. Some researchers aim for samples of 500 or more.

It's also important to make sure that a logit sample contains a reasonable representation of both alternative choices. For instance, if 98 percent of a sample chooses alternative A and 2 percent chooses B, a random sample of 500 would have only 10 observations that choose B. In such a situation, our estimated coefficients would be overly reliant on the characteristics of those 10 observations. A better technique would be to disproportionately sample from those who choose B. It turns out that using different sampling rates for subgroups within the sample does not cause bias in the slope coefficients of a logit model,[5] even though it might do so in a linear regression.

When we estimate a logit, we apply the ML technique to Equation 13.7, but that equation's functional form is complex, so let's try to simplify it a bit. First, a few mathematical steps can allow us to rewrite Equation 13.7 so that the right side of the equation looks identical to the linear probability model:

$$\ln\left(\frac{D_i}{[1 - D_i]}\right) = \beta_0 + \beta_1 X_{1i} + \beta_2 X_{2i} + \epsilon_i \qquad (13.10)$$

where D_i is the dummy variable. If you're interested in the math behind this transformation, see Exercise 4.

---

4. Actually, the ML program chooses coefficient estimates that maximize the log of the probability (or likelihood) of observing the particular set of values of the dependent variable in the sample ($Y_1, Y_2, \ldots, Y_N$) for a given set of Xs. For more on maximum likelihood, see Robert S. Pindyck and Daniel L. Rubinfeld, *Economic Models and Economic Forecasts* (New York: McGraw-Hill, 1998), pp. 51–53 and 329–330.

5. The constant term, however, needs to be adjusted. Multiply $\hat{\beta}_0$ by $[\ln(p_1) - \ln(p_2)]$, where p_1 is the proportion of the observations chosen if $D_i = 1$ and p_2 is the proportion of the observations chosen if $D_i = 0$. See G. S. Maddala, *Limited-Dependent and Qualitative Variables in Econometrics* (Cambridge: Cambridge University Press, 1983), pp. 90–91.

Even Equation 13.10 is a bit cumbersome, however, since the left side of the equation contains the log of the ratio of D_i to $(1 - D_i)$, sometimes called the "log of the odds." To make things simpler still, let's adopt a shorthand for the logit functional form on the left side of Equation 13.10. Let's define:

$$L{:}Pr(D_i = 1) = \ln\left(\frac{D_i}{[1 - D_i]}\right) \qquad (13.11)$$

The L indicates that the equation is a logit of the functional form in Equation 13.10 (derived from Equation 13.7), and the "$Pr(D_i = 1)$" is a reminder that the dependent variable is a dummy and that a $\hat{D}_i$ produced by an estimated logit equation is an estimate of the probability that $D_i = 1$. If we now substitute Equation 13.11 into Equation 13.10, we get:

$$L{:}Pr(D_i = 1) = \beta_0 + \beta_1 X_{1i} + \beta_2 X_{2i} + \epsilon_i \qquad (13.12)$$

Equation 13.12 will be our standard documentation format for estimated logit equations.

Interpreting Estimated Logit Coefficients

Once you've estimated a binomial logit, then hypothesis testing and the analysis of potential econometric problems can be undertaken using the techniques discussed in previous chapters. The signs of the coefficients have the same meaning as they do in a linear probability model, and the *t*-test can be used for tests of hypotheses about logit coefficients.

When it comes to the economic interpretation of the estimated logit coefficients, however, all this changes. In particular, the absolute sizes of estimated logit coefficients tend to be quite different from the absolute sizes of estimated linear probability model coefficients for the same specification and the same data. What's going on?

There are two powerful reasons for these differences. First, as you can see by comparing Equations 13.1 and 13.10, the dependent variable in a logit equation isn't the same as the dependent variable in a linear probability model. Since the dependent variable is different, it makes complete sense that the coefficients are different. The second reason that logit coefficients are different is even more dynamic. Take a look at Figure 13.2. The slope of the graph of the logit changes as $\hat{D}_i$ moves from 0 to 1! Thus the change in the probability that $\hat{D}_i = 1$ caused by a one-unit increase in an independent variable (holding the other independent variables constant) will vary as we move from $\hat{D}_i = 0$ to $\hat{D}_i = 1$.

Given all this, how can we interpret estimated logit coefficients? How can we use them to measure the impact of an independent variable on the probability that $\hat{D}_i = 1$? It turns out that there are three reasonable ways of answering this question:

1. *Change an average observation.* Create an "average" observation by plugging the means of all the independent variables into the estimated logit equation and then calculating an "average" $\hat{D}_i$. Then increase the independent variable of interest by one unit and recalculate the $\hat{D}_i$. The difference between the two $\hat{D}_i$s tells you the impact of a one-unit increase in that independent variable on the probability that $\hat{D}_i = 1$ (holding constant the other independent variables) for an average observation. This approach has the weakness of not being very meaningful when one or more of the independent variables is a dummy variable (after all, what is an average gender?), but it's possible to work around this weakness if you estimate the impact for an "average female" and an "average male" by setting the dummy independent variable equal first to zero and then to one.

2. *Use a partial derivative.* It turns out that if you take a derivative[6] of the logit, you'll find that the change in the expected value of $\hat{D}_i$ caused by a one unit increase in X_{1i} holding constant the other independent variables in the equation equals $\hat{\beta}_1 \hat{D}_i (1 - \hat{D}_i)$. To use this formula, plug in your estimates of β_1 and D_i. As you can see, the marginal impact of X does indeed depend on the value of $\hat{D}_i$.

3. *Use a rough estimate of 0.25.* The previous two methods are reasonably accurate, but they're hardly very handy. However, if you plug $\hat{D}_i = 0.5$ into the previous equation, you get the much more useful result that if you multiply a logit coefficient by 0.25, you'll get an equivalent linear probability model coefficient.[7]

On balance, which approach do we recommend? For all situations except those requiring precise accuracy, we find ourselves gravitating toward the third approach. To get a rough approximation of the economic meaning of a logit coefficient, multiply by 0.25 (or, equivalently, divide by 4). Remember, however, that the dependent variable in question still is the probability that $\hat{D}_i = 1$.

---

6. Ramu Ramanathan, *Introductory Econometrics* (Fort Worth: Harcourt Brace, 1998), p. 607.

7. See, for example, Jeff Wooldridge, *Introductory Econometrics* (Mason, OH: Southwestern, 2009), p. 584. Wooldridge also suggests a multiple of 0.40 for converting a probit coefficient into a linear probability coefficient. We'll briefly cover probits in Section 13.3.

Measuring the overall fit also is not straightforward. Recall from Section 7.6 that since the functional form of the dependent variable has been changed, $\overline{R}^2$ should not be used to compare the fit of a logit with an otherwise comparable linear probability model. In addition, don't forget the general faults inherent in using $\overline{R}^2$ with equations with dummy dependent variables. Our suggestion is to use the mean percentage of correct predictions, $\overline{R}_p^2$, from Section 13.1.

To get some practice interpreting logit estimates, let's estimate a logit on the same women's labor force participation data that we used in the previous section. The OLS linear probability model estimate of that model, Equation 13.6, was:

$$\hat{D}_i = -0.28 - 0.38M_i + 0.09S_i \tag{13.6}$$
$$(0.15) \quad (0.03)$$
$$N = 30 \quad \overline{R}^2 = .32 \quad \overline{R}_p^2 = .81$$

where: D_i = 1 if the ith woman is in the labor force, 0 otherwise
M_i = 1 if the ith woman is married, 0 otherwise
S_i = the number of years of schooling of the ith woman

If we estimate a logit on the same data (from Table 13.1) and the same independent variables, we obtain:

$$L{:}Pr\,(D_i = 1) = -5.89 - 2.59M_i + 0.69S_i \tag{13.13}$$
$$(1.18) \quad (0.31)$$
$$t = -2.19 \quad 2.19$$
$$N = 30 \quad \overline{R}_p^2 = .81 \quad \text{iterations} = 5$$

Let's compare Equations 13.6 and 13.13. As expected, the signs and general significance of the slope coefficients are the same. Even if we divide the logit coefficients by 4, as suggested earlier, they still are larger than the linear probability model coefficients. Despite these differences, the overall fits are roughly comparable, especially after taking account of the different dependent variables and estimation techniques. In this example, then, the two estimation procedures differ mainly in that the logit does not produce $\hat{D}_i$s outside the range of 0 and 1.

However, if the size of the sample in this example is too small for a linear probability model, it certainly is too small for a logit, making any in-depth analysis of Equation 13.13 problematic. Instead, we're better off finding an example with a much larger sample.

A More Complete Example of the Use of the Binomial Logit

For a more complete example of the binomial logit, let's look at a model of the probability of passing the California State Department of Motor Vehicles drivers' license test. To obtain a license, each driver must pass a written and a behind-the-wheel test. Even though the tests are scored from 0 to 100, all that matters is that you pass and get your license.

Since the test requires some boning up on traffic and safety laws, driving students have to decide how much time to spend studying. If they don't study enough, they waste time because they have to retake the test. If they study too much, however, they also waste time, because there's no bonus for scoring above the minimum, especially since there is no evidence that doing well on the test has much to do with driving well after the test (this, of course, might be worth its own econometric study).

Recently, two students decided to collect data on test takers in order to build an equation explaining whether someone passed the Department of Motor Vehicles test. They hoped that the model, and in particular the estimated coefficient of study time, would help them decide how much time to spend studying for the test. (Of course, it took more time to collect the data and run the model than it would have taken to memorize the entire traffic code, but that's another story.)

After reviewing the literature, choosing variables, and hypothesizing signs, the students realized that the appropriate functional form was a binomial logit because their dependent variable was a dummy variable:

$$D_i = \begin{cases} 1 \text{ if the } i\text{th test taker passed the test on the first try} \\ 0 \text{ if the } i\text{th test taker failed the test on the first try} \end{cases}$$

Their hypothesized equation was:

$$D_i = f(\overset{+}{A_i}, \overset{+}{H_i}, \overset{+}{E_i}, \overset{+}{C_i}) + \epsilon_i \qquad (13.14)$$

where: A_i = the age of the ith test taker
H_i = the number of hours the ith test taker studied (usually less than one hour!)
E_i = a dummy variable equal to 1 if the ith test taker's primary language was English, 0 otherwise
C_i = a dummy variable equal to 1 if the ith test taker had any college experience, 0 otherwise

After collecting data from 480 test takers, the students estimated the following equation:

$$\widehat{L:Pr(D_i = 1)} = -1.18 + 0.011A_i + 2.70H_i + 1.62E_i + 3.97C_i \qquad (13.15)$$

$$\begin{array}{ccccc} & (0.009) & (0.54) & (0.34) & (0.99) \\ t = & 1.23 & 4.97 & 4.65 & 4.00 \end{array}$$

$$N = 480 \qquad \overline{R}_p^2 = .74 \qquad \text{iterations} = 5$$

Note how similar these results look to a typical linear regression result. All the estimated coefficients have the expected signs, and all but one are significantly different from zero. Remember that the logit coefficients need to be divided by 4 to get meaningful estimates of the impact of the independent variables on the probability of passing the test. If we divide $\hat{\beta}_H$ by 4, for example, the impact of an hour's studying turns out to be huge: according to our estimates, the probability of passing the test would go up by 67.5 percent, holding constant the other three independent variables. Note that $\overline{R}_p^2$ is .74, indicating that the equation correctly explained almost three quarters of the sample based on nothing but the four variables in Equation 13.15.

And what about the two students? Did the equation help them? How much did they end up deciding to study? They found that given their ages, their college experience, and their English-speaking backgrounds, the expected value of $\hat{D}_i$ for each of them was quite high, even if H_i was set equal to zero. So what did they actually do? They studied for a half hour "just to be on the safe side" and passed with flying colors, having devoted more time to passing the test than anyone else in the history of the state.

(13.3) Other Dummy Dependent Variable Techniques

Although the binomial logit is the most frequently used estimation technique for equations with dummy dependent variables, it's by no means the only one. In this section, we'll mention two alternatives, the binomial probit and the multinomial logit, that are useful in particular circumstances. Our main goal is to briefly describe these estimation techniques, not to cover them in any detail.[8]

---

8. For more, see G. S. Maddala, *Limited Dependent Variables and Qualitative Variables in Econometrics* (Cambridge: Cambridge University Press, 1983) and T. Amemiya, "Qualitative Response Models: A Survey," *Journal of Economic Literature*, Vol. 19, pp. 1483–1536. These surveys also cover additional techniques, like the Tobit model, that are useful with bounded dependent variables or other special situations.

The Binomial Probit Model

The **binomial probit model** is an estimation technique for equations with dummy dependent variables that avoids the unboundedness problem of the linear probability model by using a variant of the cumulative normal distribution.

$$P_i = \frac{1}{\sqrt{2\pi}} \int_{-\infty}^{Z_i} e^{-s^2/2} \, ds \tag{13.16}$$

where: P_i = the probability that the dummy variable $D_i = 1$
$Z_i = \beta_0 + \beta_1 X_{1i} + \beta_2 X_{2i}$
s = a standardized normal variable

As different as this probit looks from the logit that we examined in the previous section, it can be rewritten to look quite familiar:

$$Z_i = \Phi^{-1}(P_i) = \beta_0 + \beta_1 X_{1i} + \beta_2 X_{2i} \tag{13.17}$$

where Φ^{-1} is the inverse of the normal cumulative distribution function. Probit models typically are estimated by applying maximum likelihood techniques to the model in the form of Equation 13.16, but the results often are presented in the format of Equation 13.17.

The fact that both the logit and the probit are cumulative distributive functions means that the two have similar properties. For example, a graph of the probit looks almost exactly like the logit in Figure 13.2. In addition, the probit has the same requirement of a fairly large sample before hypothesis testing becomes meaningful. Finally, $\overline{R}^2$ continues to be of questionable value as a measure of overall fit.

From a researcher's point of view, the probit is theoretically appealing because many economic variables are normally distributed. With extremely large samples, this advantage falls away, since maximum likelihood procedures can be shown to be asymptotically normal under fairly general conditions.

For an example of a probit, let's estimate one on the same women's labor force participation data we used in the previous logit and linear probability examples (standard errors in parentheses):

$$\hat{Z}_i = \widehat{\Phi^{-1}(P_i)} = -3.44 - 1.44 M_i + 0.40 S_i \tag{13.18}$$
$$(0.62) \quad (0.17)$$
$$N = 30 \qquad \overline{R}_p^2 = .81 \qquad \text{iterations} = 5$$

Compare this result with Equation 13.13 from the previous section. Note that except for a slight difference in the scale of the coefficients, the logit and probit models provide virtually identical results in this example.

The Multinomial Logit Model

In many cases, there are more than two qualitative choices available. In some cities, for instance, a commuter has a choice of car, bus, or subway for the trip to work. How could we build and estimate a model of choosing from more than two different alternatives?

One answer is to hypothesize that choices are made sequentially and to model a multichoice decision as a series of binary decisions. For example, we might hypothesize that the commuter would first decide whether to drive to work, and we could build a binary model of car versus public transportation. For those commuters who choose public transportation, the next step would be to choose whether to take the bus or the subway, and we could build a second binary model of that choice. This method, called a **sequential binary logit**, is cumbersome and at times unrealistic, but it does allow a researcher to use a binary technique to model an inherently multichoice decision.

If a decision between multiple alternatives is truly made simultaneously, a better approach is to build a multinomial logit model of the decision. A **multinomial logit model** is an extension of the binomial logit technique that allows several discrete alternatives to be considered at the same time. If there are N different alternatives, we need N − 1 dummy variables to describe the choice, with each dummy equalling 1 only when that particular alternative is chosen. For example, D_{1i} would equal 1 if the ith person chose alternative number 1 and would equal 0 otherwise. As before, the probability that D_{1i} is equal to 1, P_{1i}, cannot be observed.

In a multinomial logit, one alternative is selected as the "base" alternative, and then each other possible choice is compared to this base alternative with a logit equation. A key distinction is that the dependent variable of these equations is the log of the odds of the ith alternative being chosen *compared to the base alternative:*

$$\ln\left(\frac{P_{1i}}{P_{bi}}\right) \tag{13.19}$$

where: P_{1i} = the probability of the ith person choosing the first alternative
P_{bi} = the probability of the ith person choosing the base alternative

If there are N alternatives, there should be N − 1 different logit equations in the multinomial logit model system, because the coefficients of the last equation can be calculated from the coefficients of the first N − 1 equations. (If you know that A/C = 6 and B/C = 2, then you can calculate that A/B = 3.)

For example, if $N = 3$, as in the commuter-work-trip example cited previously, and the base alternative is taking the bus, then a multinomial logit model would have a system of two equations:

$$\ln\left(\frac{P_{si}}{P_{bi}}\right) = \alpha_0 + \alpha_1 X_{1i} + \alpha_2 X_{2i} \tag{13.20}$$

$$\ln\left(\frac{P_{ci}}{P_{bi}}\right) = \beta_0 + \beta_1 X_{1i} + \beta_2 X_{3i} \tag{13.21}$$

where $s =$ subway, $c =$ car, and $b =$ bus.

13.4 Summary

1. A linear probability model is a linear-in-the-coefficients equation used to explain a dummy dependent variable (D_i). The expected value of D_i is the probability that D_i equals 1.

2. The estimation of a linear probability model with OLS encounters two major problems:
   a. $\overline{R}^2$ is not an accurate measure of overall fit.
   b. The expected value of D_i is not limited by 0 and 1.

3. When measuring the overall fit of equations with dummy dependent variables, an alternative to $\overline{R}^2$ is $\overline{R}_p^2$, the average percentage of the observations in the sample that a particular estimated equation would have explained correctly.

4. The binomial logit is an estimation technique for equations with dummy dependent variables that avoids the unboundedness problem of the linear probability model by using a variant of the cumulative logistic function:

$$L:\Pr(D_i = 1) = \ln\left(\frac{D_i}{[1 - D_i]}\right) = \beta_0 + \beta_1 X_{1i} + \beta_2 X_{2i} + \epsilon_i$$

5. The binomial logit is best estimated using the maximum likelihood technique and a large sample. A slope coefficient from a logit measures the impact of a one-unit increase of the independent variable in question (holding the other explanatory variables constant) on the log of the odds of a given choice.

6. The binomial probit model is an estimation technique for equations with dummy dependent variables that uses the cumulative normal distribution function. The binomial probit has properties quite similar to the binomial logit.

7. The multinomial logit model is an extension of the binomial logit that allows more than two discrete alternatives to be considered simultaneously.

EXERCISES

(The answer to Exercise 2 is in Appendix A.)

1. Write the meaning of each of the following terms without referring to the book (or your notes), and compare your definition with the version in the text for each:
   a. linear probability model
   b. $\overline{R}^2_p$
   c. binomial logit model
   d. The interpretation of an estimated logit coefficient
   e. binomial probit model
   f. sequential binary model
   g. multinomial logit model

2. R. Amatya[9] estimated the following logit model of birth control for 1,145 continuously married women aged 35 to 44 in Nepal:

$$\widehat{L:Pr(D_i = 1)} = -4.47 + 2.03WN_i + 1.45ME_i$$
$$(0.36) \qquad (0.14)$$
$$t = 5.64 \qquad 10.36$$

where: D_i = 1 if the *i*th woman has ever used a recognized form of birth control, 0 otherwise

WN_i = 1 if the *i*th woman wants no more children, 0 otherwise

ME_i = number of methods of birth control known to the *i*th woman

---

9. Ramesh Amatya, "Supply-Demand Analysis of Differences in Contraceptive Use in Seven Asian Nations" (paper presented at the Annual Meetings of the Western Economic Association, 1988, Los Angeles).

a. Explain the theoretical meaning of the coefficients for WN and ME. How would your answer differ if this were a linear probability model?
b. Do the signs, sizes, and significance of the estimated slope coefficients meet your expectations? Why or why not?
c. What is the theoretical significance of the constant term in this equation?
d. If you could make one change in the specification of this equation, what would it be? Explain your reasoning.

3. Bond ratings are letter ratings (Aaa = best) assigned to firms that issue debt. These ratings measure the quality of the firm from the point of view of the likelihood of repayment of the bond. Suppose you've been hired by an arbitrage house that wants to predict *Moody's Bond Ratings* before they're published in order to buy bonds whose ratings are going to improve. In particular, suppose your firm wants to distinguish between A-rated bonds (high quality) and B-rated bonds (medium quality) and has collected a data set of 200 bonds with which to estimate a model. As you arrive on the job, your boss is about to buy bonds based on the results of the following model (standard errors in parentheses):

$$\hat{Y}_i = 0.70 + 0.05P_i + 0.05PV_i - 0.020D_i$$
$$\qquad\quad (0.05)\quad (0.02)\qquad (0.002)$$
$$\overline{R}^2 = .69 \qquad DW = 0.50 \qquad N = 200$$

where: Y_i = 1 if the rating of the *i*th bond = A, 0 otherwise
P_i = the profit rate of the firm that issued the *i*th bond
PV_i = the standard deviation of P_i over the last five years
D_i = the ratio of debt to total capitalization of the firm that issued the *i*th bond

a. What econometric problems, if any, exist in this equation?
b. What suggestions would you have for a rerun of this equation with a different specification?
c. Suppose that your boss rejects your suggestions, saying, "This is the real world, and I'm sure that my model will forecast bond ratings just as well as yours will." How would you respond? (*Hint:* Saying "Okay, boss, you win," is sure to keep your job for you, but it won't get much credit on this question.)

4. Show that the logistic function, $D = 1/(1 + e^{-Z})$, is indeed equivalent to the binomial logit model, $\ln[D/(1 - D)] = Z$, where $Z = \beta_0 + \beta_1X_1 + \beta_2X_2 + \epsilon$.

5. On graph paper, plot each of the following models. For what range of X_i is $1 < \hat{D}_i$? How about $\hat{D}_i < 0$?

   a. $\hat{D}_i = 0.3 + 0.1X_i$

   b. $\hat{D}_i = 3.0 - 0.2X_i$

   c. $\hat{D}_i = -1.0 + 0.3X_i$

   d. $\ln[D_i/(1 - D_i)] = 0.3 + 0.1X_i$

   e. $\ln[D_i/(1 - D_i)] = 3.0 - 0.2X_i$

   f. $\ln[D_i/(1 - D_i)] = -1.0 + 0.3X_i$

6. Because their college had just upgraded its residence halls, two seniors decided to build a model of the decision to live on campus. They collected data from 533 upper-class students (first-year students were required to live on campus) and estimated the following equation:

$$L{:}\Pr(D_i = 1) = 3.26 + 0.03UNIT_i - 0.13ALCO_i - 0.99YEAR_i - 0.39GREK_i$$
$$(0.04) \qquad (0.08) \qquad (0.12) \qquad (0.21)$$
$$t = \quad +0.84 \qquad -1.55 \qquad -8.25 \qquad -1.38$$
$$N = 533 \qquad R_p^2 = .668 \qquad \text{iterations} = 4$$

   where: D_i = 1 if the ith student lived on campus, 0 otherwise

   $UNIT_i$ = the number of academic units the ith student was taking

   $ALCO_i$ = the nights per week that the ith student consumed alcohol

   $YEAR_i$ = 2 if the ith student was a sophomore, 3 if a junior, and 4 if a senior

   $GREK_i$ = 1 if the ith student was a member of a fraternity/sorority, 0 otherwise

   a. The two seniors expected UNIT to have a positive coefficient and the other variables to have negative coefficients. Test these hypotheses at the 10-percent level.

   b. What problem do you see with the definition of the YEAR variable? What constraint does this definition place on the estimated coefficients?

   c. Carefully state the meaning of the coefficient of ALCO and analyze the size of the coefficient. (*Hint:* Be sure to discuss how the size of the coefficient compares with your expectations.)

   d. If you could add one variable to this equation, what would it be? Explain.

7. What happens if we define a dummy dependent variable over a range other than 0 to 1? For example, suppose that in the research cited in

Exercise 2, Amatya had defined D_i as being equal to 2 if the ith woman had ever used birth control, 0 otherwise.

a. What would happen to the size and theoretical meaning of the estimated logit coefficients? Would they stay the same? Would they change? (If so, how?)

b. How would your answers to part a change if Amatya had estimated a linear probability model instead of a binomial logit?

8. Return to our data on women's labor force participation and consider the possibility of adding A_i, the age of the ith woman, to the equation. Be careful when you develop your expected sign and functional form because the expected impact of age on labor force participation is difficult to pin down. For instance, some women drop out of the labor force when they get married, but others continue working even while they're raising their children. Still others work until they get married, stay at home to have children, and then return to the workforce once the children reach school age. Malcolm Cohen et al., for example, found the age of a woman to be relatively unimportant in determining labor force participation, except for women who were 65 and older and were likely to have retired.[10] The net result for our model is that age appears to be a theoretically irrelevant variable. A possible exception, however, is a dummy variable equal to 1 if the ith woman is 65 or over, 0 otherwise.

a. Look over the data set in Table 13.1. What problems do you see with adding an independent variable equal to 1 if the ith woman is 65 or older and 0 otherwise?

b. If you go ahead and add the dummy implied to Equation 13.13 and reestimate the model, you obtain Equation 13.22. Which equation do you prefer, Equation 13.13 or Equation 13.22? Explain your answer.

$$\widehat{L{:}Pr(D_i = 1)} = -5.89 - 2.59M_i + 0.69S_i - 0.03AD_i \quad (13.22)$$
$$(1.18) \quad (0.31) \quad (0.30)$$
$$t = -2.19 \quad 2.19 \quad -0.01$$
$$N = 30 \qquad \overline{R}_p^2 = .82 \qquad \text{iterations} = 5$$

where: $AD_i = 1$ if the age of the ith woman is >65, 0 otherwise

9. To get practice in actually estimating your own linear probability, logit, and probit equations, test the possibility that age (A_i) is actually

---

10. Malcolm Cohen, Samuel A. Rea, Jr., and Robert I. Lerman, *A Micro Model of Labor Supply* (Washington, D.C.: U.S. Bureau of Labor Statistics, 1970), p. 212.

a relevant variable in our women's labor force participation model. That is, take the data from Table 13.1 and estimate each of the following equations. Then use our specification criteria to compare your equation with the parallel version in the text (without A_i). Explain why you do or do not think that age is a relevant variable. (*Hint:* Be sure to calculate $\overline{R}_p^2$.)

a. the linear probability model $D = f(M,A,S)$
b. the logit $D = f(M,A,S)$
c. the probit $D = f(M,A,S)$

10. An article published in a book edited by A. Kouskoulaf and B. Lytle[11] presents coefficients from an estimated logit model of the choice between the car and public transportation for the trip to work in Boston. All three public transportation modes in Boston (bus, subway, and train, of which train is the most preferred) were lumped together as a single alternative to the car in a binomial logit model. The dependent variable was the log of the odds of taking public transportation for the trip to work, so the first coefficient implies that as income rises, the log of the odds of taking public transportation falls, and so on.

Independent Variable	Coefficient
Family income (9 categories with 1 = low and 9 = high)	−0.12
Number employed in the family	−1.09
Out-of-pocket costs (cents)	−3.16
Wait time (tenths of minutes)	0.18
Walk time (tenths of minutes)	−0.03
In-vehicle travel time (tenths of minutes)	−0.01

The last four variables are defined as the difference between the value of the variable for taking public transportation and its value for taking the car.

a. Do the signs of the estimated coefficients agree with your prior expectations? Which one(s) differ?

b. The transportation literature hypothesizes that people would rather spend time traveling in a vehicle than waiting for or walking to that vehicle. Do the sizes of the estimated coefficients of time support this hypothesis?

---

11. "The Use of the Multinomial Logit in Transportation Analysis," in A. Kouskoulaf and B. Lytle, eds. *Urban Housing and Transportation* (Detroit: Wayne State University, 1975), pp. 87–90.

   c. Since trains run relatively infrequently, the researchers set wait time for train riders fairly high. Most trains run on known schedules, however, so the average commuter learns that schedule and attempts to hold down wait time. Does this fact explain any of the unusual results indicated in your answers to parts a and b?

11. Suppose that you want to build a multinomial logit model of how students choose which college to attend. For the sake of simplicity, let's assume that there are only four colleges to choose from: your college (c), the state university (u), the local junior college (j), and the nearby private liberal arts college (a). Further assume that everyone agrees that the important variables in such a model are the family income (Y) of each student, the average SAT scores of each college (SAT), and the tuition (T) of each college.

   a. How many equations should there be in such a multinomial logit system?

   b. If your college is the base, write out the definition of the dependent variable for each equation.

12. In 2008, Goldman and Romley[12] studied hospital demand by analyzing how 8,721 Medicare-covered pneumonia patients chose from among 117 hospitals in the greater Los Angeles area. The authors concluded that clinical quality (as measured by a low pneumonia mortality rate) played a smaller role in hospital choice than did a variety of other factors.

   Let's focus on a subset of the Goldman–Romley sample: the 499 patients who chose either the UCLA Medical Center or the nearby Cedars Sinai Medical Center. Typically, economists would expect price to have a major influence on such a choice, but Medicare patients pay roughly the same price no matter what hospital they choose. Instead, factors like the distance the patient lives from the hospital and the age and income of the patient become potentially important factors:

$$\widehat{L{:}Pr(D_i = 1)} = 4.41 - 0.38DISTANCE_i - 0.072INCOME_i - 0.29OLD_i \qquad (13.23)$$

$$\phantom{\widehat{L{:}Pr(D_i = 1)} = 4.41 -} (0.05) \qquad\qquad (0.036) \qquad\qquad (0.31)$$

$$t = -8.12 \qquad\qquad -2.00 \qquad\qquad -0.94$$

$$N = 499 \qquad\qquad R_p^2 = .66 \qquad\qquad \text{iterations} = 8$$

12. Dana Goldman and John Romley, "Hospitals as Hotels: The Role of Patient Amenities in Hospital Demand," *NBER Working Paper* 14619, December 2008. We appreciate the permission of the authors to use a portion of their data set.

where: D_i = 1 if the ith patient chose Cedars Sinai, 0 if they chose UCLA

$DISTANCE_i$ = the distance from the ith patient's (according to zip code) to Cedars Sinai *minus* the distance from that point to the UCLA Medical Center (in miles)

$INCOME_i$ = the income of the ith patient (as measured by the average income of their zip code in thousands of dollars)

OLD_i = 1 if the ith patient was older than 75, 0 otherwise

a. Create and test appropriate hypotheses about the coefficient of DISTANCE at the 5-percent level.

b. Carefully state the meaning of the estimated coefficient of DISTANCE in terms of the "per mile" impact on the probability of choosing Cedars Sinai Medical Center.

c. Think about the definition of DISTANCE. Why do you think we defined DISTANCE as the difference between the distances as opposed to entering the distance to Cedars and the distance to UCLA as two different independent variables?

d. This data set is available on our Web site (www.pearsonhighered. com/studenmund) and data disc as datafile = HOSPITAL13. Load the data into your computer and use EViews, Stata, or your computer's regression program to estimate the linear probability model and probit versions of this equation. What is the coefficient of DISTANCE in your two estimates? Which model do you prefer? Explain. (*Hint:* It also makes sense to estimate a logit, just to make sure that you're using the same sample.)

e. (optional) Now create a slope dummy by adding OLD*DISTANCE to Equation 13.23 and estimating a new logit equation. Why do you think we're suggesting this particular slope dummy? Create and test the appropriate hypotheses about the slope dummy at the 5-percent level. Which equation do you prefer, Equation 13.23 or the new slope dummy logit? Explain.

14 Simultaneous Equations

14.1 Structural and Reduced-Form Equations

14.2 The Bias of Ordinary Least Squares (OLS)

14.3 Two-Stage Least Squares (2SLS)

14.4 The Identification Problem

14.5 Summary and Exercises

14.6 Appendix: Errors in the Variables

The most important models in economics and business are simultaneous in nature. Supply and demand, for example, is obviously simultaneous. To study the demand for chicken without also looking at the supply of chicken is to take a chance on missing important linkages and thus making significant mistakes. Virtually all the major approaches to macroeconomics, from Keynesian aggregate demand models to rational expectations schemes, are inherently simultaneous. Even models that appear to be inherently single-equation in nature often turn out to be much more simultaneous than you might think. The price of housing, for instance, is dramatically affected by the level of economic activity, the prevailing rate of interest in alternative assets, and a number of other simultaneously determined variables.

All this wouldn't mean much to econometricians if it weren't for the fact that the estimation of simultaneous equations systems with OLS causes a number of difficulties that aren't encountered with single equations. Most important, Classical Assumption III, which states that all explanatory variables should be uncorrelated with the error term, is violated in simultaneous models. Mainly because of this, OLS coefficient estimates are biased in simultaneous models. As a result, an alternative estimation procedure called Two-Stage Least Squares usually is employed in such models instead of OLS.

You're probably wondering why we've waited until now to discuss simultaneous equations if they're so important in economics and if OLS encounters bias when estimating them. The answer is that the simultaneous estimation of an equation changes every time the specification of any equation in the entire system is changed, so a researcher must be well equipped to deal with specification problems like those of previous chapters. As a result, it does not make sense to learn how to estimate a simultaneous system until you are fairly adept at estimating a single equation.

14.1 Structural and Reduced-Form Equations

Before we can study the problems encountered in the estimation of simultaneous equations, we need to introduce a few concepts.

The Nature of Simultaneous Equations Systems

Which came first, the chicken or the egg? This question is impossible to answer satisfactorily because chickens and eggs are **jointly determined**; there is a two-way causal relationship between the variables. The more eggs you have, the more chickens you'll get, but the more chickens you have, the more eggs you'll get.[1] More realistically, the economic world is full of the kind of *feedback effects and dual causality* that require the application of simultaneous equations. Besides the supply and demand and simple macroeconomic model examples mentioned previously, we could talk about the dual causality of population size and food supply, the joint determination of wages and prices, or the interaction between foreign exchange rates and international trade and capital flows. In a typical econometric equation:

$$Y_t = \beta_0 + \beta_1 X_{1t} + \beta_2 X_{2t} + \epsilon_t \tag{14.1}$$

a simultaneous system is one in which Y clearly has an effect on at least one of the Xs in addition to the effect that the Xs have on Y.

Such topics are usually modeled by distinguishing between variables that are simultaneously determined (the Ys, called **endogenous variables**) and those that are not (the Xs, called **exogenous variables**):

$$Y_{1t} = \alpha_0 + \alpha_1 Y_{2t} + \alpha_2 X_{1t} + \alpha_3 X_{2t} + \epsilon_{1t} \tag{14.2}$$

$$Y_{2t} = \beta_0 + \beta_1 Y_{1t} + \beta_2 X_{3t} + \beta_3 X_{2t} + \epsilon_{2t} \tag{14.3}$$

---

1. This also depends on how hungry you are, which is a function of how hard you're working, which depends on how many chickens you have to take care of. (Although this chicken/egg example is simultaneous in an annual model, it would not be truly simultaneous in a quarterly or monthly model because of the time lags involved.)

For example, Y_1 and Y_2 might be the quantity and price of chicken (respectively), X_1 the income of the consumers, X_2 the price of beef (beef is a substitute for chicken in both consumption and production), and X_3 the price of chicken feed. With these definitions, Equation 14.2 would characterize the behavior of consumers of chickens and Equation 14.3 the behavior of suppliers of chickens. These behavioral equations are also called *structural equations*. **Structural equations** characterize the underlying economic theory behind each endogenous variable by expressing it in terms of both endogenous and exogenous variables. Researchers must view them as an entire system in order to see all the feedback loops involved. For example, the Ys are jointly determined, so a change in Y_1 will cause a change in Y_2, which will in turn cause Y_1 to change *again*. Contrast this feedback with a change in X_1, which will not eventually loop back and cause X_1 to change again. The αs and the βs in the equation are *structural coefficients,* and hypotheses should be made about their signs just as we did with the regression coefficients of single equations.

Note that a variable is endogenous because it is jointly determined, not just because it appears in both equations. That is, X_2, which is the price of beef but could be another factor beyond our control, is in both equations but is still exogenous in nature because it is not simultaneously determined within the chicken market. In a large general equilibrium model of the entire economy, however, such a price variable would also likely be endogenous. How do you decide whether a particular variable should be endogenous or exogenous? Some variables are almost always exogenous (the weather, for example), but most others can be considered either endogenous or exogenous, depending on the number and characteristics of the other equations in the system. Thus, the distinction between endogenous and exogenous variables usually depends on how the researcher defines the scope of the research project.

Sometimes, lagged endogenous variables appear in simultaneous systems, usually when the equations involved are distributed lag equations (described in Chapter 12). Be careful! Such lagged endogenous variables are not simultaneously determined in the current time period. They thus have more in common with exogenous variables than with nonlagged endogenous variables. To avoid problems, we'll define the term **predetermined variable** to include all exogenous variables and lagged endogenous variables. "Predetermined" implies that exogenous and lagged endogenous variables are determined outside the system of specified equations or prior to the current period. Endogenous variables that are not lagged are not predetermined, because they are jointly determined by the system in the current time period. Therefore, econometricians tend to speak in terms of endogenous and predetermined variables when discussing simultaneous equations systems.

Let's look at the specification of a simple supply and demand model, say for the "cola" soft-drink industry:

$$Q_{Dt} = \alpha_0 + \alpha_1 P_t + \alpha_2 X_{1t} + \alpha_3 X_{2t} + \epsilon_{Dt} \qquad (14.4)$$

$$Q_{St} = \beta_0 + \beta_1 P_t + \beta_2 X_{3t} + \epsilon_{St} \qquad (14.5)$$

$$Q_{St} = Q_{Dt} \quad \text{(equilibrium condition)}$$

where: Q_{Dt} = the quantity of cola demanded in time period t
Q_{St} = the quantity of cola supplied in time period t
P_t = the price of cola in time period t
X_{1t} = dollars of advertising for cola in time period t
X_{2t} = another "demand-side" exogenous variable (e.g., income or the prices or advertising of other drinks)
X_{3t} = a "supply-side" exogenous variable (e.g., the price of artificial flavors or other factors of production)
ϵ_t = classical error terms (each equation has its own error term, subscripted "D" and "S" for demand and supply)

In this case, price and quantity are simultaneously determined, but price, one of the endogenous variables, is not on the left side of any of the equations. It's incorrect to assume automatically that the endogenous variables are those that appear on the left side of at least one equation; in this case, we could have just as easily written Equation 14.5 with price on the left side and quantity supplied on the right side, as we did in the chicken example in Equations 14.2 and 14.3. Although the estimated coefficients would be different, the underlying relations would not. Note also that there must be as many equations as there are endogenous variables. In this case, the three endogenous variables are Q_D, Q_S, and P.

What would be the expected signs for the coefficients of the price variables in Equations 14.4 and 14.5? We'd expect price to enter negatively in the demand equation but to enter positively in the supply equation. The higher the price, after all, the less quantity will be demanded, but the more quantity will be supplied. These signs would result in the typical supply and demand diagram (Figure 14.1) that we're all used to. Look at Equations 14.4 and 14.5 again, however, and note that they would be identical but for the different predetermined variables. What would happen if we accidentally

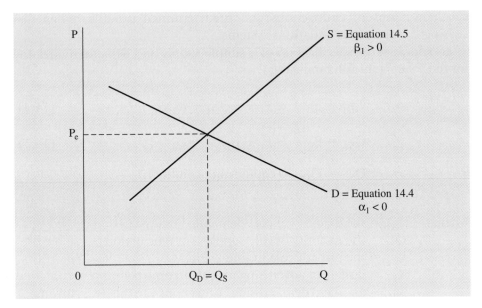

Figure 14.1 Supply and Demand Simultaneous Equations

An example of simultaneous equations that jointly determine two endogenous variables is the supply and demand for a product. In this case, Equation 14.4, the downward-sloping demand function, and Equation 14.5, the upward-sloping supply function, intersect at the equilibrium price and quantity for this market.

put a supply-side predetermined variable in the demand equation or vice versa? We'd have a very difficult time identifying which equation was which, and the expected signs for the coefficients of the endogenous variable P would become ambiguous. As a result, we must take care when specifying the structural equations in a system.

Simultaneous Systems Violate Classical Assumption III

Recall from Chapter 4 that Classical Assumption III states that the error term and each explanatory variable must be uncorrelated with each other. If there is such a correlation, then the OLS regression estimation program is likely to attribute to the particular explanatory variable variations in the dependent variable that are actually being caused by variations in the error term. The result will be biased estimates.

To see why simultaneous equations violate the assumption of independence between the error term and the explanatory variables, look again at a simultaneous system, Equations 14.2 and 14.3 (repeated with directional errors):

$$\overset{\uparrow}{Y_{1t}} = \alpha_0 + \alpha_1 \overset{\uparrow}{Y_{2t}} + \alpha_2 X_{1t} + \alpha_3 \overset{\uparrow}{X_{2t}} + \epsilon_{1t} \qquad (14.2)$$

$$\overset{\uparrow}{Y_{2t}} = \beta_0 + \beta_1 \overset{\uparrow}{Y_{1t}} + \beta_2 X_{3t} + \beta_3 X_{2t} + \epsilon_{2t} \qquad (14.3)$$

Let's work through the system and see what happens when one of the error terms increases, holding everything else in the equations constant:

1. If ϵ_1 increases in a particular time period, Y_1 will also increase due to Equation 14.2.

2. If Y_1 increases, Y_2 will also rise[2] due to Equation 14.3.

3. But if Y_2 increases in Equation 14.3, it also increases in Equation 14.2 where it is an explanatory variable.

Thus, an increase in the error term of an equation causes an increase in an explanatory variable in the same equation: If ϵ_1 increases, Y_1 increases, and then Y_2 increases, violating the assumption of independence between the error term and the explanatory variables.

This is not an isolated result that depends on the particular equations involved. Indeed, as you'll find in Exercise 3, this result works for other error terms, equations, and simultaneous systems. All that is required for the violation of Classical Assumption III is that there be endogenous variables that are jointly determined in a system of simultaneous equations.

Reduced-Form Equations

An alternative way of expressing a simultaneous equations system is through the use of **reduced-form equations**, equations that express a particular endogenous variable solely in terms of an error term and all the predetermined (exogenous plus lagged endogenous) variables in the simultaneous system.

---

2. This assumes that β_1 is positive. If β_1 is negative, Y_2 will decrease and there will be a negative correlation between ϵ_1 and Y_2, but this negative correlation will still violate Classical Assumption III. Also note that both Equations 14.2 and 14.3 could have Y_{1t} on the left side; if two variables are jointly determined, it doesn't matter which variable is considered dependent and which explanatory, because they are actually mutually dependent. We used this kind of simultaneous system in the cola model portrayed in Equations 14.4 and 14.5.

The reduced-form equations for the structural Equations 14.2 and 14.3 would thus be:

$$Y_{1t} = \pi_0 + \pi_1 X_{1t} + \pi_2 X_{2t} + \pi_3 X_{3t} + v_{1t} \tag{14.6}$$

$$Y_{2t} = \pi_4 + \pi_5 X_{1t} + \pi_6 X_{2t} + \pi_7 X_{3t} + v_{2t} \tag{14.7}$$

where the vs are stochastic error terms and the πs are called **reduced-form coefficients** because they are the coefficients of the predetermined variables in the reduced-form equations. Note that each equation includes only one endogenous variable, the dependent variable, and that each equation has exactly the same set of predetermined variables. The reduced-form coefficients, such as π_1 and π_5, are known as **impact multipliers** because they measure the impact on the endogenous variable of a one-unit increase in the value of the predetermined variable, after allowing for the feedback effects from the entire simultaneous system.

There are at least three reasons for using reduced-form equations:

1. Since the reduced-form equations have no inherent simultaneity, they do not violate Classical Assumption III. Therefore, they can be estimated with OLS without encountering the problems discussed in this chapter.

2. The interpretation of the reduced-form coefficients as impact multipliers means that they have economic meaning and useful applications of their own. For example, if you wanted to compare a government spending increase with a tax cut in terms of the per-dollar impact in the first year, estimates of the impact multipliers (reduced-form coefficients or πs) would allow such a comparison.

3. Perhaps most importantly, reduced-form equations play a crucial role in the estimation technique most frequently used for simultaneous equations. This technique, Two-Stage Least Squares, will be explained in Section 14.3.

To conclude, let's return to the cola supply and demand model and specify the reduced-form equations for that model. (To test yourself, flip back to Equations 14.4 and 14.5 and see if you can get the right answer before going on.) Since the equilibrium condition forces Q_D to be equal to Q_S, we need only two reduced-form equations:

$$Q_t = \pi_0 + \pi_1 X_{1t} + \pi_2 X_{2t} + \pi_3 X_{3t} + v_{1t} \tag{14.8}$$

$$P_t = \pi_4 + \pi_5 X_{1t} + \pi_6 X_{2t} + \pi_7 X_{3t} + v_{2t} \tag{14.9}$$

Even though P never appears on the left side of a structural equation, it's an endogenous variable and should be treated as such.

14.2 The Bias of Ordinary Least Squares (OLS)

All the Classical Assumptions must be met for OLS estimates to be BLUE; when an assumption is violated, we must determine which of the properties no longer holds. It turns out that applying OLS directly to the structural equations of a simultaneous system produces biased estimates of the coefficients. Such bias is called simultaneous equations bias or simultaneity bias.

Understanding Simultaneity Bias

Simultaneity bias refers to the fact that in a simultaneous system, the expected values of the OLS-estimated structural coefficients ($\hat{\beta}$s) are not equal to the true βs. We are therefore faced with the problem that in a simultaneous system:

$$E(\hat{\beta}) \neq \beta \qquad (14.10)$$

Why does this simultaneity bias exist? Recall from Section 14.1 that in simultaneous equations systems, the error terms (the ϵs) tend to be correlated with the endogenous variables (the Ys) whenever the Ys appear as explanatory variables. Let's follow through what this correlation means (assuming positive coefficients for simplicity) in typical structural equations like 14.11 and 14.12:

$$Y_{1t} = \beta_0 + \beta_1 Y_{2t} + \beta_2 X_t + \epsilon_{1t} \qquad (14.11)$$

$$Y_{2t} = \alpha_0 + \alpha_1 Y_{1t} + \alpha_2 Z_t + \epsilon_{2t} \qquad (14.12)$$

Since we cannot observe the error term (ϵ_1) and don't know when ϵ_{1t} is above average, it will appear as if every time Y_1 is above average, so too is Y_2. As a result, the OLS estimation program will tend to attribute increases in Y_1 caused by the error term ϵ_1 to Y_2, thus typically overestimating β_1. This overestimation is simultaneity bias. If the error term is abnormally negative, Y_{1t} is less than it would have been otherwise, causing Y_{2t} to be less than it would have been otherwise, and the computer program will attribute the decrease in Y_1 to Y_2, once again causing us to overestimate β_1 (that is, induce upward bias).

Recall that the causation between Y_1 and Y_2 runs in both directions because the two variables are interdependent. As a result, β_1, when estimated by OLS, can no longer be interpreted as the impact of Y_2 on Y_1, holding X constant. Instead, $\hat{\beta}_1$ now measures some mix of the effects of the two endogenous variables on each other! In addition, consider β_2. It's supposed to be the effect of X on Y_1 holding Y_2 constant, but how can we expect Y_2 to be held constant when a change in Y_1 takes place? As a result, there is potential bias in all the estimated coefficients in a simultaneous system.

What does this bias look like? It's possible to derive an equation for the expected value of the regression coefficients in a simultaneous system that is estimated by OLS. This equation shows that as long as the error term and any of the explanatory variables in the equation are correlated, then the coefficient estimates will be biased. In addition, it also shows that the bias will have the same sign as the correlation between the error term and the endogenous variable that appears as an explanatory variable in that error term's equation. Since that correlation is usually positive in economic and business examples, the bias usually will be positive, although the direction of the bias in any given situation will depend on the specific details of the structural equations and the model's underlying theory.

This does not mean that every coefficient from a simultaneous system estimated with OLS will be a bad approximation of the true population coefficient. However, it's vital to consider an alternative to OLS whenever simultaneous equations systems are being estimated. Before we investigate the alternative estimation technique most frequently used (Two-Stage Least Squares), let's look at an example of simultaneity bias.

An Example of Simultaneity Bias

To show how the application of OLS to simultaneous equations estimation causes bias, we used a Monte Carlo experiment[3] to generate an example of such biased estimates. Since it's impossible to know whether any bias exists unless you also know the true βs, we arbitrarily picked a set of

---

3. *Monte Carlo* experiments are computer-generated simulations that typically follow seven steps: 1. Assume a "true" model with specific coefficient values and an error term distribution. 2. Select values for the independent variables. 3. Select an estimating technique (usually OLS). 4. Create various samples of the dependent variable, using the assumed model, by randomly generating error terms from the assumed distribution; often, the number of samples created runs into the thousands. 5. Compute the estimates of the βs from the various samples using the estimating technique. 6. Summarize and evaluate the results. 7. Consider sensitivity analyses using different values, distributions, or estimating techniques.

coefficients to be considered "true." We then stochastically generated data sets based on these "true" coefficients, and obtained repeated OLS estimates of these coefficients from the generated data sets. The expected value of these estimates turned out to be quite different from the true coefficient values, thus exemplifying the bias in OLS estimates of coefficients in simultaneous systems.

We used a supply and demand model as the basis for our example:

$$Q_t = \beta_0 + \beta_1 P_t + \beta_2 X_t + \epsilon_{Dt} \tag{14.13}$$

$$Q_t = \alpha_0 + \alpha_1 P_t + \alpha_2 Z_t + \epsilon_{St} \tag{14.14}$$

where: Q_t = the quantity demanded and supplied in time period t
P_t = the price in time period t
X_t = a "demand-side" exogenous variable, such as income
Z_t = a "supply-side" exogenous variable, such as weather
ϵ_t = classical error terms (different for each equation)

The first step was to choose a set of true coefficient values that corresponded to our expectations for this model:

$$\beta_1 = -1 \qquad \beta_2 = +1 \qquad \alpha_1 = +1 \qquad \alpha_2 = +1$$

In other words, we have a negative relationship between price and quantity demanded, a positive relationship between price and quantity supplied, and positive relationships between the exogenous variables and their respective dependent variables.

The next step was to randomly generate a number of data sets based on the true values. This also meant specifying some other characteristics of the data[4] before generating the different data sets (5,000 in this case).

The final step was to apply OLS to the generated data sets and to calculate the estimated coefficients of the demand equation (14.13). (Similar results were obtained for the supply equation.) The arithmetic means of the results for the 5,000 regressions were:

$$\hat{Q}_{Dt} = \hat{\beta}_0 - 0.37 P_t + 1.84 X_t \tag{14.15}$$

---

4. Other assumptions included a normal distribution for the error term, $\beta_0 = 0$, $\alpha_0 = 0$, $\sigma_S^2 = 3$, $\sigma_D^2 = 2$, $r_{xz}^2 = 0.4$, and $N = 20$. In addition, we assumed that the error terms of the two equations were not correlated.

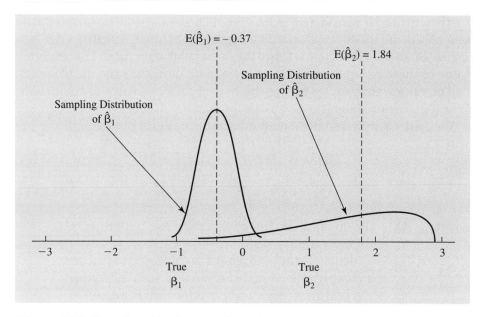

Figure 14.2 Sampling Distributions Showing Simultaneity Bias of OLS Estimates

In the experiment in Section 14.2, simultaneity bias is evident in the distribution of the estimates of β_1, which had a mean value of -0.37 compared with a true value of -1.00, and in the estimates of β_2, which had a mean value of 1.84 compared with a true value of 1.00.

In other words, the expected value of $\hat{\beta}_1$ should have been -1.00, but instead it was -0.37; the expected value of $\hat{\beta}_2$ should have been $+1.00$, but instead it was 1.84:

$$E(\hat{\beta}_1) = -0.37 \neq -1.00$$

$$E(\hat{\beta}_2) = 1.84 \neq 1.00$$

This is simultaneity bias! As the diagram of the sampling distributions of the $\hat{\beta}$s in Figure 14.2 shows, the OLS estimates of β_1 were almost never very close to -1.00, and the OLS estimates of β_2 were distributed over a wide range of values.

14.3 Two-Stage Least Squares (2SLS)

How can we get rid of (or at least reduce) simultaneity bias? There are a number of estimation techniques that help mitigate simultaneity bias, but the most frequently used alternative to OLS is called Two-Stage Least Squares (2SLS).

What Is Two-Stage Least Squares?

OLS encounters bias in the estimation of simultaneous equations mainly because such equations violate Classical Assumption III, so one solution to the problem is to explore ways to avoid violating that assumption. We could do this if we could find a variable that is:

1. a good proxy for the endogenous variable, and
2. uncorrelated with the error term.

If we then substitute this new variable for the endogenous variable where it appears as an explanatory variable, our new explanatory variable will be uncorrelated with the error term, and Classical Assumption III will be met.

That is, consider Equation 14.16 in the following system:

$$Y_{1t} = \beta_0 + \beta_1 Y_{2t} + \beta_2 X_{1t} + \epsilon_{1t} \tag{14.16}$$

$$Y_{2t} = \alpha_0 + \alpha_1 Y_{1t} + \alpha_2 X_{2t} + \epsilon_{2t} \tag{14.17}$$

If we could find a variable that was highly correlated with Y_2 but that was uncorrelated with ϵ_1, then we could substitute this new variable for Y_2 on the right side of Equation 14.16, and we'd conform to Classical Assumption III. This new variable is called an *instrumental variable*. An **instrumental variable** replaces an endogenous variable (when it is an explanatory variable); it is a good substitute for the endogenous variable and is independent of the error term.

Since there is no joint causality between the instrumental variable and any endogenous variable, the use of the instrumental variable avoids the violation of Classical Assumption III. The job of finding such a variable is another story, though. How do we go about finding variables with these qualifications? For simultaneous equations systems, it turns out that finding instrumental variables is straightforward. We use 2SLS.

Two-Stage Least Squares (2SLS) is a method of systematically creating instrumental variables to replace the endogenous variables where they appear as explanatory variables in simultaneous equations systems. 2SLS does this by running a regression on the reduced form of the right-side endogenous variables in need of replacement and then using the $\hat{Y}$s (or fitted values) from those reduced-form regressions as the instrumental variables. Why do we do this? Every predetermined variable in the simultaneous system is a candidate to be an instrumental variable for every endogenous variable, but if we choose only one, we're throwing away information. To avoid this, we use a linear combination of all the predetermined variables. We form this linear combination by running a regression for a given endogenous variable as a function of all the predetermined variables—the predicted value of the endogenous variable is the instrument we want. Thus, the 2SLS two-step procedure is:

> **STAGE ONE:** *Run OLS on the reduced-form equations for each of the endogenous variables that appear as explanatory variables in the structural equations in the system.*

Since the predetermined (exogenous plus lagged endogenous) variables are uncorrelated with the reduced-form error term, the OLS estimates of the reduced-form coefficients (the $\hat{\pi}$s) are unbiased. These $\hat{\pi}$s can then be used to calculate estimates of the endogenous variables:

$$\hat{Y}_{1t} = \hat{\pi}_0 + \hat{\pi}_1 X_{1t} + \hat{\pi}_2 X_{2t} \qquad (14.18)$$

$$\hat{Y}_{2t} = \hat{\pi}_3 + \hat{\pi}_4 X_{1t} + \hat{\pi}_5 X_{2t} \qquad (14.19)$$

These $\hat{Y}$s then are used as instruments in the structural equations.

> **STAGE TWO:** *Substitute the reduced form $\hat{Y}$s for the Ys that appear on the right side (only) of the structural equations, and then estimate these revised structural equations with OLS.*

That is, stage two consists of estimating the following equations with OLS:

$$Y_{1t} = \beta_0 + \beta_1 \hat{Y}_{2t} + \beta_2 X_{1t} + u_{1t} \qquad (14.20)$$

$$Y_{2t} = \alpha_0 + \alpha_1 \hat{Y}_{1t} + \alpha_2 X_{2t} + u_{2t} \qquad (14.21)$$

Note that the dependent variables are still the original endogenous variables and that the substitutions are only for the endogenous variables where they appear on the right-hand side of the structural equations. This procedure produces consistent (for large samples), but biased (for small samples), estimates of the coefficients of the structural equations.

If second-stage equations such as Equations 14.20 and 14.21 are estimated with OLS, the $SE(\hat{\beta})$s will be incorrect, so be sure to use your computer's 2SLS estimation procedure.[5]

This description of 2SLS can be generalized to m different simultaneous structural equations. Each reduced-form equation has as explanatory variables every predetermined variable in the entire system of equations. The OLS estimates of the reduced-form equations are used to compute the estimated values of all the endogenous variables that appear as explanatory variables in the m structural equations. After substituting these fitted values for the original values of the endogenous independent variables, OLS is applied to each stochastic equation in the set of structural equations.

The Properties of Two-Stage Least Squares

1. *2SLS estimates are still biased in small samples.* For small samples, the expected value of a $\hat{\beta}$ produced by 2SLS is still not equal to the true β,[6] but as the sample size gets larger, the expected value of the $\hat{\beta}$ approaches the true β. As the sample size gets bigger, the variances of both the OLS and the 2SLS estimates decrease. OLS estimates become very precise estimates of the wrong number, and 2SLS estimates become very precise estimates of the correct number. As a result, the larger the sample size, the better a technique 2SLS is.

   To illustrate, let's look again at the example of Section 14.2. The 2SLS estimate of β_1 was -1.25. This estimate is biased, but it's much closer to the truth ($\beta_1 = -1.00$) than is the OLS estimate of -0.37. We then returned to that example and expanded the data set from 5,000 different samples of size 20 each to 5,000 different samples of 50 observations each. As expected, the average $\hat{\beta}_1$ for 2SLS moved from -1.25 to -1.06 compared to the true value of -1.00. By contrast, the OLS average estimate went from -0.37 to -0.44. Such results are typical; large sample

---

5. Most econometric software packages, including EViews and Stata, offer such a 2SLS option. For more on this issue, see Exercise 9 and footnote 9 of this chapter.

6. This bias is caused by remaining correlation between the $\hat{Y}$s produced by the first-stage reduced-form regressions and the ϵs. The effect of the correlation tends to decrease as the sample size increases. Even for small samples, though, it's worth noting that the expected bias due to 2SLS usually is smaller than the expected bias due to OLS.

sizes will allow 2SLS to produce unbiased estimates, but OLS still will produce biased estimates.

2. *The bias in 2SLS for small samples typically is of the opposite sign of the bias in OLS.* Recall that the bias in OLS typically was positive, indicating that a $\hat{\beta}$ produced by OLS for a simultaneous system is likely to be greater than the true β. For 2SLS, the expected bias is negative, and thus a $\hat{\beta}$ produced by 2SLS is likely to be less than the true β. For any given set of data, the 2SLS estimate can be larger than the OLS estimate, but it can be shown that the majority of 2SLS estimates are likely to be less than the corresponding OLS estimates. For large samples, there is little bias in 2SLS.

    Return to the example of Section 14.2. Compared to the true value of -1.00 for β_1, the small sample 2SLS average estimate was -1.25, as mentioned earlier. This means that the 2SLS estimates showed negative bias. The OLS estimates, on the other hand, averaged -0.37; since -0.37 is more positive than -1.00, the OLS estimates exhibited positive bias. Thus, the observed bias due to OLS was opposite the observed bias due to 2SLS, as is generally the case.

3. *If the fit of the reduced-form equation is quite poor, then 2SLS will not rid the equation of bias even in a large sample.* Recall that the instrumental variable is supposed to be a good substitute for the endogenous variable. To the extent that the fit (as measured by $\overline{R}^2$) of the reduced-form equation is poor, then the instrumental variable isn't highly correlated with the original endogenous variable, and there is no reason to expect 2SLS to be effective. As the $\overline{R}^2$ of the reduced-form equation increases, the usefulness of 2SLS will increase.

4. *2SLS estimates have increased variances and $SE(\hat{\beta})s$.* While 2SLS does an excellent job of reducing the amount of bias in the $\hat{\beta}s$, there's a price to pay for this reduced bias. This price is that 2SLS estimates tend to have higher variances and $SE(\hat{\beta})s$ than do OLS estimates of the same equations.

On balance, then, 2SLS will almost always be a better estimator of the coefficients of a simultaneous system than OLS will be. The major exception to this general rule is when the fit of the reduced-form equation in question is quite poor for a small sample.

An Example of Two-Stage Least Squares

Let's work through an example of 2SLS, a naive linear Keynesian macroeconomic model of the U.S. economy. We'll specify the following system:

$$Y_t = CO_t + I_t + G_t + NX_t \tag{14.22}$$

$$CO_t = \beta_0 + \beta_1 YD_t + \beta_2 CO_{t-1} + \epsilon_{1t} \tag{14.23}$$

$$YD_t = Y_t - T_t \tag{14.24}$$

$$I_t = \beta_3 + \beta_4 Y_t + \beta_5 r_{t-1} + \epsilon_{2t} \tag{14.25}$$

where: Y_t = Gross Domestic Product (GDP) in year t
CO_t = total personal consumption in year t
I_t = total gross private domestic investment in year t
G_t = government purchases of goods and services in year t
NX_t = net exports of goods and services (exports minus imports) in year t
T_t = taxes (actually equal to taxes, depreciation, corporate profits, government transfers, and other adjustments necessary to convert GDP to disposable income) in year t
r_t = the interest rate in year t
YD_t = disposable income in year t

All variables are in real terms (measured in billions of 2000 dollars) except the interest rate variable, which is measured in nominal percent. The data for this example are from 1976 through 2007 and are presented in Table 14.1.

Equations 14.22 through 14.25 are the structural equations of the system, but only Equations 14.23 and 14.25 are stochastic (behavioral) and need to be estimated. The other two are identities, as can be determined by the lack of coefficients.

Stop for a second and look at the system; which variables are endogenous? Which are predetermined? The endogenous variables are those that are jointly determined by the system, namely, Y_t, CO_t, YD_t, and I_t. To see why these four variables are simultaneously determined, note that if you change one of them and follow this change through the system, the change will get back to the original causal variable. For instance, if I_t goes up for some reason, that will cause Y_t to go up, which will feed right back into I_t again. They're simultaneously determined.

Table 14.1 Data for the Small Macromodel

YEAR	Y	CO	I	G	YD	r
1975	NA	2876.9	NA	NA	NA	8.83
1976	4540.9	3035.5	544.7	1031.9	3432.2	8.43
1977	4750.5	3164.1	627.0	1043.3	3552.9	8.02
1978	5015.0	3303.1	702.6	1074.0	3718.8	8.73
1979	5173.4	3383.4	725.0	1094.1	3811.2	9.63
1980	5161.7	3374.1	645.3	1115.4	3857.7	11.94
1981	5291.7	3422.2	704.9	1125.6	3960.0	14.17
1982	5189.3	3470.3	606.0	1145.4	4044.9	13.79
1983	5423.8	3668.6	662.5	1187.3	4177.7	12.04
1984	5813.6	3863.3	857.7	1227.0	4494.1	12.71
1985	6053.7	4064.0	849.7	1312.5	4645.2	11.37
1986	6263.6	4228.9	843.9	1392.5	4791.0	9.02
1987	6475.1	4369.8	870.0	1426.7	4874.5	9.38
1988	6742.7	4546.9	890.5	1445.1	5082.6	9.71
1989	6981.4	4675.0	926.2	1482.5	5224.8	9.26
1990	7112.5	4770.3	895.1	1530.0	5324.2	9.32
1991	7100.5	4778.4	822.2	1547.2	5351.7	8.77
1992	7336.6	4934.8	889.0	1555.3	5536.3	8.14
1993	7532.7	5099.8	968.3	1541.1	5594.2	7.22
1994	7835.5	5290.7	1099.6	1541.3	5746.4	7.96
1995	8031.7	5433.5	1134.0	1549.7	5905.7	7.59
1996	8328.9	5619.4	1234.3	1564.9	6080.9	7.37
1997	8703.5	5831.8	1387.7	1594.0	6295.8	7.26
1998	9066.9	6125.8	1524.1	1624.4	6663.9	6.53
1999	9470.3	6438.6	1642.6	1686.9	6861.3	7.04
2000	9817.0	6739.4	1735.5	1721.6	7194.0	7.62
2001	9890.7	6910.4	1598.4	1780.3	7333.3	7.08
2002	10048.8	7099.3	1557.1	1858.8	7562.2	6.49
2003	10301.0	7295.3	1613.1	1904.8	7729.9	5.67
2004	10675.8	7561.4	1770.2	1931.8	8008.9	5.63
2005	10989.5	7791.7	1873.5	1939.0	8121.4	5.24
2006	11294.8	8029.0	1912.5	1971.2	8407.0	5.59
2007	11523.9	8252.8	1809.7	2012.1	8644.0	5.56

Source: *The Economic Report of the President, 2009.* Note that T and NX can be calculated using Equations 14.22 and 14.24.

Datafile = MACRO14

What about interest rates? Is r_t an endogenous variable? The surprising answer is that, strictly speaking, r_t is *not* endogenous in this system because r_{t-1} (not r_t) appears in the investment equation. Thus, there is no simultaneous feedback through the interest rate in this simple model.[7]

Given this answer, which are the predetermined variables? The predetermined variables are G_t, NX_t, T_t, CO_{t-1}, and r_{t-1}. To sum, the simultaneous system has four structural equations, four endogenous variables, and five predetermined variables.

What is the economic content of the stochastic structural equations? The consumption function, Equation 14.23, is a dynamic model distributed lag consumption function of the kind we discussed in Chapter 12. We discussed this exact equation in Section 12.1, going so far as to estimate Equation 14.23 with OLS on data from Table 14.1, and the reader is encouraged to reread that analysis.

The investment function, Equation 14.25, includes simplified multiplier and cost of capital components. The multiplier term β_4 measures the stimulus to investment that is generated by an increase in GDP. In a Keynesian model, β_4 thus would be expected to be positive. On the other hand, the higher the cost of capital, the less investment we'd expect to be undertaken (holding multiplier effects constant), mainly because the expected rate of return on marginal capital investments is no longer sufficient to cover the higher cost of capital. Thus β_5 is expected to be negative. It takes time to plan and start up investment projects, though, so the interest rate is lagged one year.[8]

Stage One: Even though there are four endogenous variables, only two of them appear on the right-hand side of stochastic equations, so only two reduced-form equations need to be estimated to apply 2SLS. These reduced-form

---

7. Although this sentence is technically correct, it overstates the case. In particular, there are a couple of circumstances in which an econometrician might want to consider r_{t-1} to be part of the simultaneous system for theoretical reasons. For our naive Keynesian model with a lagged interest rate effect, however, the equation is not in the simultaneous system.

8. This investment equation is a simplified mix of the accelerator and the neoclassical theories of the investment function. The former emphasizes that changes in the level of output are the key determinant of investment, and the latter emphasizes that user cost of capital (the opportunity cost that the firm incurs as a consequence of owning an asset) is the key. For an introduction to the determinants of consumption and investment, see any intermediate macroeconomics textbook.

equations are estimated automatically by all 2SLS computer estimation programs, but it's instructive to take a look at one anyway:

$$\widehat{YD}_t = -288.55 + 0.78G_t - 0.37NX_t + 0.52T_t + 0.67CO_{t-1} + 37.63r_{t-1}$$
$$(0.22) \quad (0.16) \quad (0.14) \quad (0.09) \quad (9.14)$$
$$t = \quad 3.49 \quad -2.30 \quad 3.68 \quad 7.60 \quad 4.12$$
$$N = 32 \quad \bar{R}^2 = .998 \quad DW = 2.21 \qquad (14.26)$$

This reduced form has an excellent overall fit but is almost surely suffering from severe multicollinearity. Note that we don't test any hypotheses on reduced forms, nor do we consider dropping a variable that is statistically and theoretically irrelevant. The whole purpose of stage one of 2SLS is not to generate meaningful reduced-form estimated equations but rather to generate useful instruments ($\hat{Y}$s) to use as substitutes for endogenous variables in the second stage. To do that, we calculate the $\hat{Y}_t$s and $\widehat{YD}_t$s for all 32 observations by plugging the actual values of all 5 predetermined variables into reduced-form equations like Equation 14.26.

Stage Two: We then substitute these $\hat{Y}_t$s, and $\widehat{YD}_t$s, for the endogenous variables where they appear on the right sides of Equations 14.23 and 14.25. For example, the $\widehat{YD}_t$ from Equation 14.26 would be substituted into Equation 14.23, resulting in:

$$CO_t = \beta_0 + \beta_1\widehat{YD}_t + \beta_2CO_{t-1} + \epsilon_{1t} \qquad (14.27)$$

If we estimate Equation 14.27 and the other second-stage equation given the data in Table 14.1, we obtain the following 2SLS[9] results:

$$\widehat{CO}_t = -209.06 + 0.37\widehat{YD}_t + 0.66CO_{t-1} \qquad (14.28)$$
$$(0.13) \quad (0.14)$$
$$2.73 \quad 4.84$$
$$N = 32 \quad \bar{R}^2 = .999 \quad DW = 0.83$$

---

9. A few notes about 2SLS estimation and this model are in order. The 2SLS estimates in Equations 14.28 and 14.29 are correct, but if you were to estimate those equations with OLS (using as instruments $\hat{Y}$s and $\widehat{YD}$s generated as in Equation 14.26) you would obtain the same coefficient estimates but a different set of estimates of the standard errors (and *t*-scores). This difference comes about because running OLS on the second stage alone ignores the fact that the first stage was run at all. To get accurate estimated standard errors and *t*-scores, the estimation should be done with a 2SLS program.

$$\hat{I}_t = -261.48 + 0.19\hat{Y}_t - 9.55r_{t-1} \qquad (14.29)$$
$$(0.01) \quad (11.20)$$
$$15.82 \quad -0.85$$
$$N = 32 \qquad \overline{R}^2 = .956 \qquad DW = 0.47$$

If we had estimated these equations with OLS alone instead of with 2SLS, we would have obtained:

$$\widehat{CO}_t = -266.65 + 0.46YD_t + 0.56CO_{t-1} \qquad (14.30)$$
$$(0.10) \qquad (0.10)$$
$$4.70 \qquad 5.66$$
$$N = 32 \text{ (annual 1976–2007)} \qquad \overline{R}^2 = .999 \qquad DW = 0.77$$

$$\hat{I}_t = -267.16 + 0.19Y_t - 9.26r_{t-1} \qquad (14.31)$$
$$(0.01) \quad (11.19)$$
$$15.87 \quad -0.83$$
$$N = 32 \qquad \overline{R}^2 = .956 \qquad DW = 0.47$$

Let's compare the OLS and 2SLS results. First, there doesn't seem to be much difference between them. If OLS is biased, how could this occur? When the fit of the stage-one reduced-form equations is excellent, as in Equation 14.26, then Y and $\hat{Y}$ are virtually identical, and the second stage of 2SLS is quite similar to the OLS estimate. Second, we'd expect positive bias in the OLS estimation and smaller negative bias in the 2SLS estimation, but the differences between OLS and 2SLS appear to be in the expected direction only about half the time. This might have been caused by the extreme multicollinearity in the 2SLS estimations as well as by the superb fit of the reduced forms mentioned previously.

Also, take a look at the Durbin–Watson statistics. DW is well below the d_L of 1.31 (one-sided 5-percent significance, N = 32, K = 2) in all the equations despite DW's bias toward 2 in the consumption equation (because it's a dynamic model). Consequently, positive serial correlation is likely to exist in the residuals of both equations. Applying GLS to the two 2SLS-estimated equations is tricky, however, especially because, as mentioned in Section 12.2, serial correlation causes bias in an equation with a lagged dependent variable, as in the consumption function. One solution to this problem, running GLS *and* 2SLS, is discussed in Exercise 12.

Finally, what about nonstationarity? We learned in Chapter 12 that time-series models like these have the potential to be spurious in the face of nonstationarity. Are any of these regressions spurious? Well, as you can guess from looking at the data (or as you know if you did Exercise 11 in Chapter 12), quite a few of the series in this model are, indeed, nonstationary. Luckily, the interest rate is stationary. In addition, it turns out that the consumption function is reasonably cointegrated (see Exercise 15 of this chapter), so Equations 14.28 and 14.30 probably can stand as estimated. Unfortunately, the investment equation suffers from nonstationarity that almost surely results in an inflated t-score for GDP and a low t-score for r_{t-1} (because r_{t-1} is stationary when all the other variables in the equation are nonstationary). In fact, most macromodels encounter similar problems with the significance (and sometimes the sign) of the interest rate variable in investment equations, at least partially because of the nonstationarity of the other variables in the equation. Given the tools covered so far in this text, however, there is little we can do to improve the situation.

These caveats aside, this model has provided us with a complete example of the use of 2SLS to estimate a simultaneous system. However, the application of 2SLS requires that the equation being estimated be "identified," so before we can conclude our study of simultaneous equations, we need to address the problem of identification.

(14.4) The Identification Problem

Two-Stage Least Squares cannot be applied to an equation unless that equation is *identified*. Before estimating any equation in a simultaneous system, you therefore must address the identification problem. Once an equation is found to be identified, then it can be estimated with 2SLS, but if an equation is not identified (*underidentified*), then 2SLS cannot be used no matter how large the sample. Such underidentified equations can be estimated with OLS, but OLS estimates of underidentified equations are difficult to interpret because the estimates don't necessarily match the coefficients we want to estimate. It's important to point out that an equation being identified (and therefore capable of being estimated with 2SLS) does not ensure that the resulting 2SLS estimates will be good ones. The question being asked is not how good the 2SLS estimates will be but whether the 2SLS estimates can be obtained at all.

What Is the Identification Problem?

Identification is a precondition for the application of 2SLS to equations in simultaneous systems; a structural equation is identified only when enough of the system's predetermined variables are omitted from the equation in question to allow that equation to be distinguished from all the others in the system. Note that one equation in a simultaneous system might be identified and another might not.

How could we have equations that we could not identify? To see how, let's consider a supply and demand simultaneous system in which only price and quantity are specified:

$$Q_{Dt} = \alpha_0 + \alpha_1 P_t + \epsilon_{Dt} \quad \text{(demand)} \quad (14.32)$$

$$Q_{St} = \beta_0 + \beta_1 P_t + \epsilon_{St} \quad \text{(supply)} \quad (14.33)$$

where: $\qquad Q_{Dt} = Q_{St}$

Although we've labeled one equation as the demand equation and the other as the supply equation, the computer will not be able to identify them from the data because the right-side and the left-side variables are exactly the same in both equations; without some predetermined variables included to distinguish between these two equations, it would be impossible to distinguish supply from demand.

What if we added a predetermined variable like weather (W) to the supply equation for an agricultural product? Then, Equation 14.33 would become:

$$Q_{St} = \beta_0 + \beta_1 P_t + \beta_2 W_t + \epsilon_{St} \quad (14.34)$$

In such a circumstance, every time W changed, the supply curve would shift, but the demand curve would not, so that eventually we would be able to collect a good picture of what the demand curve looked like.

Figure 14.3 demonstrates this. Given four different values of W, we get four different supply curves, each of which intersects with the constant demand curve at a different equilibrium price and quantity (intersections 1–4). These equilibria are the data that we would be able to observe in the real world and are all that we could feed into the computer. As a result, we would be able to identify the demand curve because we left out at least one predetermined variable; when this predetermined variable changed, but the demand curve didn't, the supply curve shifted so that quantity demanded moved along the demand curve and we gathered enough information to estimate the coefficients of the demand curve. The supply curve, on the other hand, remains as much a mystery as ever because its shifts give us no clue whatsoever about its shape. In essence, the demand curve was identified by the predetermined variable that was included in the system but excluded from the demand equation. The supply curve is not identified because there is no such excluded predetermined variable for it.

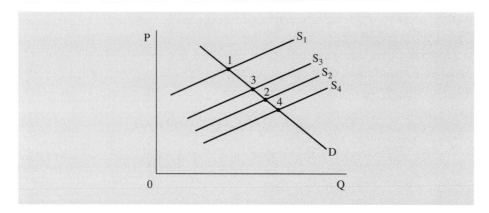

Figure 14.3 A Shifting Supply Curve Allows the Identification of the Demand Curve

If the supply curve shifts but the demand curve does not, then we move along the demand curve, allowing us to identify and estimate the demand curve (but not the supply curve).

Even if we added W to the demand curve as well, that would not identify the supply curve. In fact, if we had W in both equations, the two would be identical again, and although both would shift when W changed, those shifts would give us no information about either curve! As illustrated in Figure 14.4, the observed equilibrium prices and quantities would be almost random intersections describing neither the demand nor the supply curve. That is, the shifts in the supply curve are the same as before, but now the demand curve also shifts with W. In this case, it's not possible to identify either the demand curve or the supply curve.[10]

The way to identify both curves is to have at least one predetermined variable in each equation that is not in the other, as in:

$$Q_{Dt} = \alpha_0 + \alpha_1 P_t + \alpha_2 X_t + \epsilon_{Dt} \tag{14.35}$$

$$Q_{St} = \beta_0 + \beta_1 P_t + \beta_2 W_t + \epsilon_{St} \tag{14.36}$$

Now when W changes, the supply curve shifts, and we can identify the demand curves from the data on equilibrium prices and quantities. When X changes, the demand curve shifts, and we can identify the supply curve from the data.

To sum, identification is a precondition for the application of 2SLS to equations in simultaneous systems. A structural equation is identified only

---

10. An exception would be if you knew the relative magnitudes of the true coefficients of W in the two equations, but such knowledge is unlikely.

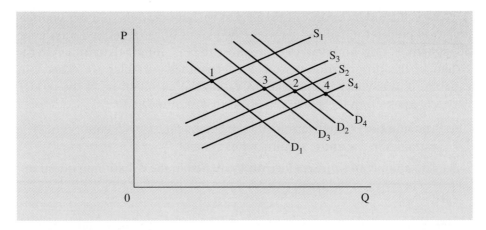

Figure 14.4 If Both the Supply Curve and the Demand Curve Shift, Neither Curve Is Identified

If both the supply curve and the demand curve shift in response to the same variable, then we move from one equilibrium to another, and the resulting data points identify neither curve. To allow such an identification, at least one exogenous factor must cause one curve to shift while allowing the other to remain constant.

when the predetermined variables are arranged within the system so as to allow us to use the observed equilibrium points to distinguish the shape of the equation in question. Most systems are quite a bit more complicated than the previous ones, however, so econometricians need a general method by which to determine whether equations are identified. The method typically used is the *order condition* of identification.

The Order Condition of Identification

The **order condition** is a systematic method of determining whether a particular equation in a simultaneous system has the potential to be identified. If an equation can meet the order condition, then it is identified in all but a very small number of cases. We thus say that the order condition is a necessary but not sufficient condition of identification.[11]

---

11. A sufficient condition for an equation to be identified is called the *rank condition,* but most researchers examine just the order condition before estimating an equation with 2SLS. These researchers let the computer estimation procedure tell them whether the rank condition has been met (by its ability to apply 2SLS to the equation). Those interested in the rank condition are encouraged to consult an advanced econometrics text.

What is the order condition? Recall that we have used the phrases endogenous and predetermined to refer to the two kinds of variables in a simultaneous system. Endogenous variables are those that are jointly determined in the system in the current time period. Predetermined variables are exogenous variables plus any lagged endogenous variables that might be in the model. For each equation in the system, we need to determine:

1. The number of predetermined (exogenous plus lagged endogenous) variables in the entire simultaneous system.
2. The number of slope coefficients estimated in the equation in question.

> **THE ORDER CONDITION:** *A necessary condition for an equation to be identified is that the number of predetermined (exogenous plus lagged endogenous) variables in the system be greater than or equal to the number of slope coefficients in the equation of interest.*

In equation form, a structural equation meets the order condition if:

The number of predetermined variables ≥ The number of slope coefficients
(in the simultaneous system)   (in the equation)

Two Examples of the Application of the Order Condition

Let's apply the order condition to some of the simultaneous equations systems encountered in this chapter. For example, consider once again the cola supply and demand model of Section 14.1:

$$Q_{Dt} = \alpha_0 + \alpha_1 P_t + \alpha_2 X_{1t} + \alpha_3 X_{2t} + \epsilon_{Dt} \qquad (14.37)$$

$$Q_{St} = \beta_0 + \beta_1 P_t + \beta_2 X_{3t} + \epsilon_{St} \qquad (14.38)$$

$$Q_{St} = Q_{Dt} \qquad (14.39)$$

Equation 14.37 is identified by the order condition because the number of predetermined variables in the system (three, X_1, X_2, and X_3) is equal to the number of slope coefficients in the equation (three: α_1, α_2, and α_3). This particular result (equality) implies that Equation 14.37 is *exactly identified* by the order condition. Equation 14.38 is also identified by the order condition because there still are three predetermined variables in the system, but there are only two slope coefficients in the equation; this condition implies that Equation 14.38 is *overidentified*. 2SLS can be applied to equations that are identified (which includes exactly identified and overidentified), but not to equations that are underidentified.

A more complicated example is the small macroeconomic model of Section 14.3:

$$Y_t = CO_t + I_t + G_t + NX_t \tag{14.22}$$

$$CO_t = \beta_0 + \beta_1 YD_t + \beta_2 CO_{t-1} + \epsilon_{1t} \tag{14.23}$$

$$YD_t = Y_t - T_t \tag{14.24}$$

$$I_t = \beta_3 + \beta_4 Y_t + \beta_5 r_{t-1} + \epsilon_{2t} \tag{14.25}$$

As we've noted, there are five predetermined variables (exogenous plus lagged endogenous) in this system (G_t, NX_t, T_t, CO_{t-1}, and r_{t-1}). Equation 14.23 has two slope coefficients (β_1 and β_2), so this equation is overidentified ($5 > 2$) and meets the order condition of identification. As the reader can verify, Equation 14.25 also turns out to be overidentified. Since the 2SLS computer program did indeed come up with estimates of the βs in the model, we knew this already. Note that Equations 14.22 and 14.24 are identities and are not estimated, so we're not concerned with their identification properties.

14.5 Summary

1. Most economic and business models are inherently simultaneous because of the dual causality, feedback loops, or joint determination of particular variables. These simultaneously determined variables are called endogenous, and nonsimultaneously determined variables are called exogenous.

2. A structural equation characterizes the theory underlying a particular variable and is the kind of equation we have used to date in this text. A reduced-form equation expresses a particular endogenous variable solely in terms of an error term and all the predetermined (exogenous and lagged endogenous) variables in the simultaneous system.

3. Simultaneous equations models violate the Classical Assumption of independence between the error term and the explanatory variables because of the feedback effects of the endogenous variables. For example, an unusually high observation of an equation's error term works

through the simultaneous system and eventually causes a high value for the endogenous variables that appear as explanatory variables in the equation in question, thus violating the assumption of no correlation (Classical Assumption III).

4. If OLS is applied to the coefficients of a simultaneous system, the resulting estimates are biased and inconsistent. This occurs mainly because of the violation of Classical Assumption III; the OLS regression package attributes to explanatory variables changes in the dependent variable actually caused by the error term (with which the explanatory variables are correlated).

5. Two-Stage Least Squares is a method of decreasing the amount of bias in the estimation of simultaneous equations systems. It works by systematically using the reduced-form equations of the system to create substitutes for the endogenous variables that are independent of the error terms (called instrumental variables). It then runs OLS on the structural equations of the system with the instrumental variables replacing the endogenous variables where they appear as explanatory variables.

6. Two-Stage Least Squares estimates are biased (with a sign opposite that of the OLS bias) but consistent (becoming more unbiased with closer to zero variance as the sample size gets larger). If the fit of the reduced-form equations is poor, then 2SLS will not work very well. The larger the sample size, the better it is to use 2SLS.

7. 2SLS cannot be applied to an equation that's not identified. A necessary (but not sufficient) requirement for identification is the order condition, which requires that the number of predetermined variables in the system be greater than or equal to the number of slope coefficients in the equation of interest. Sufficiency is usually determined by the ability of 2SLS to estimate the coefficients.

EXERCISES

(The answer to Exercise 2 is in Appendix A.)

1. Write the meaning of each of the following terms without referring to the book (or your notes), and compare your definition with the version in the text for each:
   a. endogenous variable
   b. predetermined variable

   c. structural equation
   d. reduced-form equation
   e. simultaneity bias
   f. Two-Stage Least Squares
   g. identification
   h. order condition for identification

2. Damodar Gujarati[12] estimated the following two money supply equations on U.S. annual data. The first was estimated with OLS, and the second was estimated with 2SLS (with Investment and Government Expenditure as predetermined variables in the reduced form equation).

   OLS: $\widehat{M2}_t = 115.0 + 0.561GDP_t$
                           (0.013)
                   $t = 40.97$ $\overline{R}^2 = .986$

   2SLS: $\widehat{M2}_t = 146.8 + 0.551\widehat{GDP}_t$
                           (0.013)
                   $t = 41.24$ $\overline{R}^2 = .987$

   where: $M2_t$ = the M2 money stock in year t, in billions of dollars
            GDP_t = Gross Domestic Product in year t, in billions of dollars

   a. What, exactly, does the caret (hat) over $\widehat{GDP}$ in the 2SLS equation mean?
   b. Which equation makes more sense on theoretical grounds? Explain.
   c. Which equation is more likely to have biased coefficients? Explain.
   d. If you had to choose one equation, which would you prefer? Why? (*Hint:* Assume that the residuals are cointegrated.)
   e. If your friend claims that "it doesn't matter which equation you use because they're virtually identical," how would you respond?

3. Section 14.1 works through Equations 14.2 and 14.3 to show the violation of Classical Assumption III by an unexpected increase in ϵ_1.

---

12. Damodar Gujarati, *Essentials of Econometrics* (Boston: Irwin McGraw-Hill, 1999), p. 492, with special thanks to Bill Wood.

Show the violation of Classical Assumption III by working through the following examples:

a. a decrease in ϵ_2 in Equation 14.3

b. an increase in ϵ_D in Equation 14.4

c. an increase in ϵ_1 in Equation 14.23

4. The word *recursive* is used to describe an equation that has an impact on a simultaneous system without any feedback from the system to the equation. Which of the equations in the following systems are simultaneous, and which are recursive? Be sure to specify which variables are endogenous and which are predetermined:

a. $Y_{1t} = f(Y_{2t}, X_{1t}, X_{2t-1})$

 $Y_{2t} = f(Y_{3t}, Y_{1t}, X_{4t})$

 $Y_{3t} = f(X_{2t}, X_{1t-1}, X_{4t-1})$

b. $Z_t = g(X_t, Y_t, H_t)$

 $X_t = g(Z_t, P_{t-1})$

 $H_t = g(Z_t, B_t, CS_t, D_t)$

c. $Y_t = f(Y_{2t}, X_{1t}, X_{2t})$

 $Y_{2t} = f(Y_{3t}, X_{5t})$

5. Section 14.2 makes the statement that the correlation between the ϵs and the Ys (where they appear as explanatory variables) usually is positive in economics. To see if this is true, investigate the sign of the error term/explanatory variable correlation in the following cases:

a. the three examples in Exercise 3

b. the more general case of all the equations in a typical supply and demand model (for instance, the model for cola in Section 14.1)

c. the more general case of all the equations in a simple macroeconomic model (for instance, the small macroeconomic model in Section 14.3)

6. Determine the identification properties of the following equations. In particular, be sure to note the number of predetermined variables in the system, the number of slope coefficients in the equation, and whether the equation is underidentified, overidentified, or exactly identified.

a. Equations 14.2–14.3

b. Equations 14.13–14.14

c. part a of Exercise 4 (assume all equations are stochastic)

d. part b of Exercise 4 (assume all equations are stochastic)

7. Determine the identification properties of the following equations. In particular, be sure to note the number of predetermined variables in the system, the number of slope coefficients in the equation, and whether the equation is underidentified, overidentified, or exactly identified. (Assume that all equations are stochastic unless specified otherwise.)

   a. $A_t = f(B_t, C_t, D_t)$

   $B_t = f(A_t, C_t)$

   b. $Y_{1t} = f(Y_{2t}, X_{1t}, X_{2t}, X_{3t})$

   $Y_{2t} = f(X_{2t})$

   $X_{2t} = f(Y_{1t}, X_{4t}, X_{3t})$

   c. $C_t = f(Y_t)$

   $I_t = f(Y_t, R_t, E_t, D_t)$

   $R_t = f(M_t, R_{t-1}, Y_t - Y_{t-1})$

   $Y_t = C_t + I_t + G_t$ (nonstochastic)

8. Return to the supply and demand example for cola in Section 14.1 and explain exactly how 2SLS would estimate the αs and βs of Equations 14.4 and 14.5. Write out the equations to be estimated in both stages, and indicate precisely what, if any, substitutions would be made in the second stage.

9. As an exercise to gain familiarity with the 2SLS program on your computer, take the data provided for the simple Keynesian model in Section 14.3, and:

   a. Estimate the investment function with OLS.

   b. Estimate the reduced form for Y with OLS.

   c. Substitute the $\hat{Y}$ from your reduced form into the investment function and run the second stage yourself with OLS.

   d. Estimate the investment function with your computer's 2SLS program (if there is one) and compare the results with those obtained in part c.

10. Suppose that one of your friends recently estimated a simultaneous equation research project and found the OLS results to be virtually identical to the 2SLS results. How would you respond if he or she said "What a waste of time! I shouldn't have bothered with 2SLS in the first place! Besides, this proves that there wasn't any bias in my model anyway."

    a. What is the value of 2SLS in such a case?

    b. Does the similarity between the 2SLS and OLS estimates indicate a lack of bias?

11. Think over the problem of building a model for the supply of and demand for labor (measured in hours worked) as a function of the wage and other variables.
   a. Completely specify labor supply and labor demand equations and hypothesize the expected signs of the coefficients of your variables.
   b. Is this system simultaneous? That is, is there likely to be feedback between the wage and hours demanded and supplied? Why or why not?
   c. Is your system likely to encounter biased estimates? Why?
   d. What sort of estimation procedure would you use to obtain your coefficient estimates? (*Hint:* Be sure to determine the identification properties of your equations.)

12. Let's analyze the problem of serial correlation in simultaneous models. For instance, recall that in our small macroeconomic model, the 2SLS version of the consumption function, Equation 14.28, was:

$$\widehat{CO}_t = -209.06 + 0.37\widehat{YD}_t + 0.66CO_{t-1} \qquad (14.28)$$
$$(0.13) \qquad (0.14)$$
$$2.73 \qquad 4.84$$
$$N = 32 \qquad \overline{R}^2 = .999 \qquad DW = 0.83$$

where CO is consumption and YD is disposable income.
   a. Test Equation 14.28 to confirm that we do indeed have a serial correlation problem. (*Hint:* This should seem familiar.)
   b. Equation 14.28 will encounter both simultaneity bias and bias due to serial correlation with a lagged endogenous variable. If you could solve only one of these two problems, which would you choose? Why? (*Hint:* Compare Equation 14.28 with the OLS version of the consumption function, Equation 14.30.)
   c. Suppose you wanted to solve both problems? Can you think of a way to adjust for both serial correlation and simultaneity bias at the same time? Would it make more sense to run GLS first and then 2SLS, or would you rather run 2SLS first and then GLS? Could they be run simultaneously?

13. Suppose that a fad for oats (resulting from the announcement of the health benefits of oat bran) has made you toy with the idea of becoming a broker in the oat market. Before spending your money, you decide to build a simple model of supply and demand (identical to those in Sections 14.1 and 14.2) of the market for oats:

$$Q_{Dt} = \beta_0 + \beta_1 P_t + \beta_2 YD_t + \epsilon_{Dt}$$
$$Q_{St} = \alpha_0 + \alpha_1 P_t + \alpha_2 W_t + \epsilon_{St}$$
$$Q_{Dt} = Q_{St}$$

where: Q_{Dt} = the quantity of oats demanded in time period t
Q_{St} = the quantity of oats supplied in time period t
P_t = the price of oats in time period t
W_t = average oat-farmer wages in time period t
YD_t = disposable income in time period t

a. You notice that no left-hand-side variable appears on the right side of either of your stochastic simultaneous equations. Does this mean that OLS estimation will encounter no simultaneity bias? Why or why not?

b. You expect that when P_t goes up, Q_{Dt} will fall. Does this mean that if you encounter simultaneity bias in the demand equation, it will be negative instead of the positive bias we typically associate with OLS estimation of simultaneous equations? Explain your answer.

c. Carefully outline how you would apply 2SLS to this system. How many equations (including reduced forms) would you have to estimate? Specify precisely which variables would be in each equation.

d. Given the following hypothetical data,[13] estimate OLS and 2SLS versions of your oat supply and demand equations.

e. Compare your OLS and 2SLS estimates. How do they compare with your prior expectations? Which equation do you prefer? Why?

Year	Q	P	W	YD
1	50	10	100	15
2	54	12	102	12
3	65	9	105	11
4	84	15	107	17
5	75	14	110	19
6	85	15	111	30
7	90	16	111	28
8	60	14	113	25
9	40	17	117	23
10	70	19	120	35

Datafile = OATS14

---

13. These data are from the excellent course materials that Professors Bruce Gensemer and James Keeler prepared to supplement the use of this text at Kenyon College.

14. Simultaneous equations make sense in cross-sectional as well as time-series applications. For example, James Ragan[14] examined the effects of unemployment insurance (hereafter UI) eligibility standards on unemployment rates and the rate at which workers quit their jobs. Ragan used a pooled data set that contained observations from a number of different states from four different years (requirements for UI eligibility differ by state). His results are as follows (t-scores in parentheses):

$$\widehat{QU}_i = 7.00 + 0.089UR_i - 0.063UN_i - 2.83RE_i - 0.032MX_i$$
$$(0.10) \quad (-0.63) \quad (-1.98) \quad (-0.73)$$

$$+ 0.003IL_i - 0.25QM_i + \cdots$$
$$(0.01) \quad (-0.52)$$

$$\widehat{UR}_i = -0.54 + 0.44QU_i + 0.13UN_i + 0.049MX_i$$
$$(1.01) \quad (3.29) \quad (1.71)$$

$$+ 0.56IL_i + 0.63QM_i + \cdots$$
$$(2.03) \quad (2.05)$$

where: QU_i = the quit rate (quits per 100 employees) in the ith state

UR_i = the unemployment rate in the ith state

UN_i = union membership as a percentage of nonagricultural employment in the ith state

RE_i = average hourly earnings in the ith state relative to the average hourly earnings for the United States

IL_i = dummy variable equal to 1 if workers in the ith state are eligible for UI if they are forced to quit a job because of illness, 0 otherwise

QM_i = dummy variable equal to 1 if the ith state maintains full UI benefits for the quitter (rather than lowering benefits), 0 otherwise

MX_i = maximum weekly UI benefits relative to average hourly earnings in the ith state

a. Hypothesize the expected signs for the coefficients of each of the explanatory variables in the system. Use economic theory to justify

14. James F. Ragan, Jr., "The Voluntary Leaver Provisions of Unemployment Insurance and Their Effect on Quit and Unemployment Rates," *Southern Economic Journal*, Vol. 15, No. 1, pp. 135–146.

your answers. Which estimated coefficients are different from your expectations?

b. Ragan felt that these two equations would encounter simultaneity bias if they were estimated with OLS. Do you agree? Explain your answer. (*Hint:* Start by deciding which variables are endogenous and why.)

c. The actual equations included a number of variables not documented earlier, but the only predetermined variable in the system that was included in the QU equation but not the UR equation was RE. What does this information tell you about the identification properties of the QU equation? The UR equation?

d. What are the implications of the lack of significance of the endogenous variables where they appear on the right-hand side of the equations?

e. What, if any, policy recommendations do these results suggest?

15. Return to the consumption function of the small macromodel of Section 14.3 and consider again the issue of cointegration as a possible solution to the problem of nonstationarity.

a. Which of the variables in the equation are nonstationary? (*Hint:* See Exercises 10 and 11 in Chapter 12.)

b. Test the possibility that Equation 14.30 is cointegrated. That is, test the hypothesis that the residuals of Equation 14.30 are stationary. (*Hint:* Use the Dickey–Fuller test.)

c. Equation 14.30 is a dynamic model distributed lag equation. Do you think that this makes it more or less likely that the equation is cointegrated?

d. Equation 14.30 is the OLS estimate of the consumption function. Would your approach be any different if you were going to test the 2SLS estimate for cointegration? How? Why?

(14.6) Appendix: Errors in the Variables

Until now, we have implicitly assumed that our data were measured accurately. That is, although the stochastic error term was defined as including measurement error, we never explicitly discussed what the existence of such measurement error did to the coefficient estimates. Unfortunately, in the real world, errors of measurement are common. Mismeasurement might result from the data being based on a sample, as are almost all national aggregate statistics, or simply because the data were reported incorrectly. Whatever the cause, these **errors in the variables** are mistakes in the measurement of the dependent and/or one or more of the independent variables that are large enough to have potential impacts on the estimation of the coefficients. Such errors in the variables might be better called "measurement errors in the data." We will tackle this subject by first examining errors in the dependent variable and then moving on to look at the more serious problem of errors in an independent variable. We assume a single equation model. The reason we have included this topic here is that errors in explanatory variables give rise to biased OLS estimates very similar to simultaneity bias.

Measurement Errors in the Data for the Dependent Variable

Suppose that the true regression model is

$$Y_i = \beta_0 + \beta_1 X_i + \epsilon_i \tag{14.40}$$

and further suppose that the dependent variable, Y_i, is measured incorrectly, so that Y_i^* is observed instead of Y_i, where

$$Y_i^* = Y_i + v_i \tag{14.41}$$

and where v_i is an error of measurement that has all the properties of a classical error term. What does this mismeasurement do to the estimation of Equation 14.40?

To see what happens when $Y_i^* = Y_i + v_i$, let's add v_i to both sides of Equation 14.40, obtaining

$$Y_i + v_i = \beta_0 + \beta_1 X_i + \epsilon_i + v_i \tag{14.42}$$

which is the same as

$$Y_i^* = \beta_0 + \beta_1 X_i + \epsilon_i^* \tag{14.43}$$

where $\epsilon_i^* = (\epsilon_i + v_i)$. That is, we estimate Equation 14.43 when in reality we want to estimate Equation 14.40. Take another look at Equation 14.43. When v_i changes, both the dependent variable and the error term ϵ_i^* move together. This is no cause for alarm, however, since the dependent variable is always correlated with the error term. Although the extra movement will increase the variability of Y and therefore be likely to decrease the overall statistical fit of the equation, an error of measurement in the dependent variable does not cause any bias in the estimates of the βs.

Measurement Errors in the Data for an Independent Variable

This is not the case when the mismeasurement is in the data for one or more of the independent variables. Unfortunately, such errors in the independent variables cause bias that is quite similar in nature (and in remedy) to simultaneity bias. To see this, once again suppose that the true regression model is Equation 14.40:

$$Y_i = \beta_0 + \beta_1 X_i + \epsilon_i \qquad (14.40)$$

But now suppose that the independent variable, X_i, is measured incorrectly, so that X_i^* is observed instead of X_i, where

$$X_i^* = X_i + u_i \qquad (14.44)$$

but where u_i is an error of measurement like v_i in Equation 14.41. To see what this mismeasurement does to the estimation of Equation 14.40, let's add the term $0 = (\beta_1 u_i - \beta_1 u_i)$ to Equation 14.40, obtaining

$$Y_i = \beta_0 + \beta_1 X_i + \epsilon_i + (\beta_1 u_i - \beta_1 u_i) \qquad (14.45)$$

which can be rewritten as

$$Y_i = \beta_0 + \beta_1 (X_i + u_i) + (\epsilon_i - \beta_1 u_i) \qquad (14.46)$$

or

$$Y_i = \beta_0 + \beta_1 X_i^* + \epsilon_i^{**} \qquad (14.47)$$

where $\epsilon_i^{**} = (\epsilon_i - \beta_1 u_i)$. In this case, we estimate Equation 14.47 when we should be trying to estimate Equation 14.40. Notice what happens to Equation 14.47 when u_i changes, however. When u_i changes, the stochastic error term ϵ_i^{**} and the independent variable X_i^* move in opposite directions; they are correlated! Such a correlation is a direct violation of Classical Assumption III in a way that is remarkably similar to the violation (described in Section 14.1) of the same assumption in simultaneous equations. Not surprisingly, this violation causes the same problem, bias, for errors-in-the-variables models that it causes for simultaneous equations. That is, because of the measurement error in the independent variable, the OLS estimates of the coefficients of Equation 14.47 are *biased*.

A frequently used technique to rid an equation of the bias caused by measurement errors in the data for one or more of the independent variables is to use an *instrumental variable,* the same technique used to alleviate simultaneity bias. A substitute for X is chosen that is highly correlated with X but is uncorrelated with ϵ. Recall that 2SLS is an instrumental variables technique. Such techniques are applied only rarely to errors in the variables problems, however, because although we may suspect that there are errors in the variables, it's unusual to know positively that they exist, and it's difficult to find an instrumental variable that satisfies both conditions. As a result, X* is about as good a proxy for X as we usually can find, and no action is taken. If the mismeasurement in X were known to be large, however, some remedy would be required.

To sum, an error of measurement in one or more of the independent variables will cause the error term of Equation 14.47 to be correlated with the independent variable, causing bias analogous to simultaneity bias.[15]

---

15. If errors exist in the data for the dependent variable and one or more of the independent variables, then both decreased overall statistical fit and bias in the estimated coefficients will result. Indeed, a famous econometrician, Zvi Griliches, warned that errors in the data coming from their measurement, usually computed from samples or estimates, imply that the fancier estimating techniques should be avoided because they are more sensitive to data errors than is OLS. See Zvi Griliches, "Data and Econometricians—the Uneasy Alliance," *American Economic Review,* Vol. 75, No. 2, p. 199. See also, B. D. McCullough and H. D. Vinod, "The Numerical Reliability of Econometric Software," *Journal of Economic Literature,* Vol. 37, pp. 633–665.

15 Forecasting

15.1 What Is Forecasting?

15.2 More Complex Forecasting Problems

15.3 ARIMA Models

15.4 Summary and Exercises

Of the uses of econometrics outlined in Chapter 1, we have discussed forecasting the least. Accurate forecasting is vital to successful planning, so it's the primary goal of many business and governmental uses of econometrics. For example, manufacturing firms need sales forecasts, banks need interest rate forecasts, and governments need unemployment and inflation rate forecasts.

To many business and government leaders, the words *econometrics* and *forecasting* mean the same thing. Such a simplification gives econometrics a bad name because many econometricians overestimate their ability to produce accurate forecasts, resulting in unrealistic claims and unhappy clients. Some of their clients would probably applaud the nineteenth century New York law (luckily unenforced but apparently also unrepealed) that provides that persons "pretending to forecast the future" shall be liable to a $250 fine and/or six months in prison.[1] Although many econometricians might wish that such consultants would call themselves "futurists" or "soothsayers," it's impossible to ignore the importance of econometrics in forecasting in today's world.

The ways in which the prediction of future events is accomplished are quite varied. At one extreme, some forecasters use models with hundreds of equations.[2] At the other extreme, quite accurate forecasts can be created with nothing more than a good imagination and a healthy dose of self-confidence.

---

1. Section 899 of the N.Y. State Criminal Code: the law does not apply to "ecclesiastical bodies acting in good faith and without personal fees."

2. For an interesting comparison of such models, see Ray C. Fair and Robert J. Shiller, "Comparing Information in Forecasts from Econometric Models," *American Economic Review,* Vol. 80, No. 3, pp. 375–389.

Unfortunately, it's unrealistic to think we can cover even a small portion of the topic of forecasting in one short chapter. Indeed, there are a number of excellent books and journals on this subject alone.[3] Instead, this chapter is meant to be a brief introduction to the use of econometrics in forecasting. We will begin by using simple linear equations and then move on to investigate a few more complex forecasting situations. The chapter concludes with an introduction to a technique, called ARIMA, that calculates forecasts entirely from past movements of the dependent variable without the use of any independent variables at all. ARIMA is almost universally used as a benchmark forecast, so it's important to understand even though it's not based on economic theory.

15.1 What Is Forecasting?

In general, forecasting is the act of predicting the future; in econometrics, **forecasting** is the estimation of the expected value of a dependent variable for observations that are not part of the same data set. In most forecasts, the values being predicted are for time periods in the future, but cross-sectional predictions of values for countries or people not in the sample are also common. To simplify terminology, the words prediction and forecast will be used interchangeably in this chapter. (Some authors limit the use of the word forecast to out-of-sample prediction for a time series.)

We've already encountered an example of a forecasting equation. Think back to the weight/height example of Section 1.4 and recall that the purpose of that model was to guess the weight of a male customer based on his height. In that example, the first step in building a forecast was to estimate Equation 1.21:

$$\text{Estimated weight}_i = 103.4 + 6.38 \cdot \text{Height}_i \text{ (inches over five feet)} \qquad (1.21)$$

That is, we estimated that a customer's weight on average equaled a base of 103.4 pounds plus 6.38 pounds for each inch over 5 feet. To actually make the prediction, all we had to do was to substitute the height of the individual whose weight we were trying to predict into the estimated equation. For a male who is 6'1" tall, for example, we'd calculate:

$$\text{Predicted weight} = 103.4 + 6.38 \cdot (13 \text{ inches over five feet}) \qquad (15.1)$$

---

3. See, for example, G. Elliott, C. W. J. Granger, and A. G. Timmermann, *Handbook of Economic Forecasting* (Oxford, UK: North-Holland Elsevier, 2006), and N. Carnot, V. Koen, and B. Tissot, *Economic Forecasting* (Basingstoke, UK: Palgrave MacMillan, 2005).

or

$$103.4 \ + \ 82.9 \ = \ 186.3 \text{ pounds}$$

The weight-guessing equation is a specific example of using a single linear equation to predict or forecast. Our use of such an equation to make a forecast can be summarized into two steps:

1. *Specify and estimate an equation that has as its dependent variable the item that we wish to forecast.* We obtain a forecasting equation by specifying and estimating an equation for the variable we want to predict:

$$\hat{Y}_t = \hat{\beta}_0 + \hat{\beta}_1 X_{1t} + \hat{\beta}_2 X_{2t} \qquad (t = 1, 2, \ldots, T) \qquad (15.2)$$

Such specification and estimation have been the topics of the first 14 chapters of this book. The use of $(t = 1, 2, \ldots, T)$ to denote the sample size is fairly standard for time-series forecasts (t stands for "time").

2. *Obtain values for each of the independent variables for the observations for which we want a forecast and substitute them into our forecasting equation.* To calculate a forecast with Equation 15.2, this would mean finding values for period $T + 1$ for X_1 and X_2 and substituting them into the equation:

$$\hat{Y}_{T+1} = \hat{\beta}_0 + \hat{\beta}_1 X_{1T+1} + \hat{\beta}_2 X_{2T+1} \qquad (15.3)$$

What is the meaning of this $\hat{Y}_{T+1}$? It is a prediction of the value that Y will take in observation $T + 1$ (outside the sample) based upon our values of X_{1T+1} and X_{2T+1} and based upon the particular specification and estimation that produced Equation 15.2.

To understand these steps more clearly, let's look at two applications of this forecasting approach:

Forecasting Chicken Consumption: Let's return to the chicken demand model, Equation 6.8 of Section 6.1, to see how well that equation forecasts aggregate per capita chicken consumption:

$$\hat{Y}_t = 27.7 - 0.11 PC_t + 0.03 PB_t + 0.23 YD_t \qquad (6.8)$$
$$\phantom{\hat{Y}_t = 27.7 -} (0.03) \qquad (0.02) \qquad (0.01)$$
$$\phantom{\hat{Y}_t = 27.7} t = -3.38 \qquad + 1.86 \qquad + 15.7$$
$$\overline{R}^2 = .9904 \qquad N = 29 \text{ (annual 1974−2002)} \qquad DW \ d = 0.99$$

where: Y = pounds of chicken consumption per capita
        PC and PB = the prices of chicken and beef, respectively, per pound
        YD = per capita U.S. disposable income

To make these forecasts as realistic as possible, we held out the last three available years from the data set used to estimate Equation 6.8. We'll thus be able to compare the equation's forecasts with what actually happened. To forecast with the model, we first obtain values for the three independent variables and then substitute them into Equation 6.8. For 2003, PC = 34.1, PB = 374.6, and YD = 280.2 giving us:

$$\hat{Y}_{2003} = 27.7 - 0.11(34.1) + 0.03(374.6) + 0.23(280.2) = 99.63 \qquad (15.4)$$

Continuing on through 2005, we end up with[4]:

Year	Forecast	Actual	Percent Error
2003	99.63	95.63	4.2
2004	105.06	98.58	6.6
2005	107.44	100.60	6.8

How does the model do? Well, forecasting accuracy, like beauty, is in the eye of the beholder, and there are many ways to answer the question.[5] The simplest method is to take the mean of the percentage errors (in absolute value), an approach called, not surprisingly, the **mean absolute percentage error (MAPE)** method. The MAPE for our forecast is 6.2 percent.

The most popular alternative method of evaluating forecast accuracy is the **root mean square error criterion (RMSE)**, which is calculated by squaring the forecasting error for each time period, averaging these squared amounts, and then taking the square root of this average. One advantage of the RMSE is that it penalizes large errors because the errors are squared before they're added together. For the chicken demand forecasts, the RMSE of our forecast is 5.97 pounds (or 6 percent).

---

4. The rest of the actual values are PC: 2004 = 24.8, 2005 = 26.8; PB: 2004 = 406.5, 2005 = 409.1; YD: 2004 = 295.17, 2005 = 306.16. Many software packages, including EViews and Stata, have forecasting modules that will allow you to calculate forecasts using equations like Equation 15.4 automatically. If you use that module, you'll note that the forecasts differ slightly because we rounded the coefficient estimates.

5. For a summary of seven different methods of measuring forecasting accuracy, see Peter Kennedy, *A Guide to Econometrics* (Malden, MA: Blackwell, 2008), pp. 334–335.

As you can see in Figure 15.1, it really doesn't matter which method you use, because the unconditional forecasts generated by Equation 6.8 track quite well with reality. We missed by around 6 percent.

Forecasting Stock Prices: Some students react to the previous example by wanting to build a model to forecast stock prices and make a killing on the stock market. "If we could predict the price of a stock three years from now to

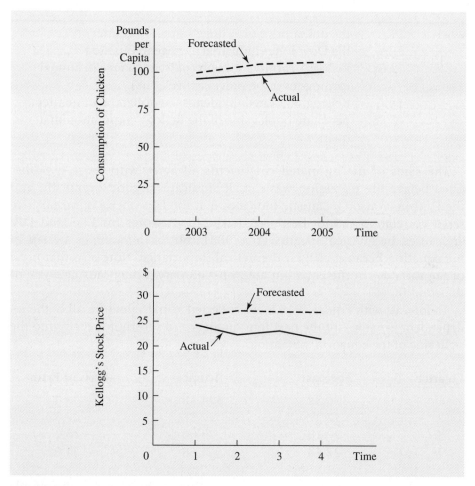

Figure 15.1 Forecasting Examples

In the chicken consumption example, the equation's forecast errors averaged around 6 percent. For the stock price model, even actual values for the independent variables and an excellent fit within the sample could not produce an accurate forecast.

within six percent," they reason, "we'd know which stocks to buy." To see how such a forecast might work, let's look at a simplified model of the quarterly price of a particular individual stock, that of the Kellogg Company (maker of breakfast cereals and other products):

$$\widehat{PK_t} = -7.80 + 0.0096DJA_t + 2.68KEG_t + 16.18DIV_t + 4.84BVPS_t$$

$$\phantom{\widehat{PK_t} = -7.80 + }(0.0024) \qquad (2.83) \qquad (22.70) \qquad (1.47)$$

$$\phantom{\widehat{PK_t} = -7.80 + }t = 3.91 \qquad\quad 0.95 \qquad\quad 0.71 \qquad\quad 3.29$$

$$\phantom{\widehat{PK_t} = -7.80 + }\overline{R}^2 = .95 \qquad N = 35 \qquad DW = 1.88 \qquad\qquad (15.5)$$

where:
- PK_t = the dollar price of Kellogg's stock in quarter t
- DJA_t = the Dow-Jones industrial average in quarter t
- KEG_t = Kellogg's earnings growth (percent change in annual earnings over the previous five years)
- DIV_t = Kellogg's declared dividends (in dollars) that quarter
- $BVPS_t$ = per-share book value of the Kellogg corporation that quarter

The signs of the estimated coefficients all agree with those hypothesized before the regression was run, $\overline{R}^2$ indicates a good overall fit, and the Durbin–Watson d statistic indicates that the hypothesis of no positive serial correlation cannot be rejected. The low t-scores for KEG and DIV are caused by multicollinearity ($r = .985$), but both variables are left in the equation because of their theoretical importance. Note also that most of the variables in the equation are nonstationary, surely causing some of the good fit.

To forecast with Equation 15.5, we collected actual values for all of the independent variables for the next four quarters and substituted them into the right side of the equation, obtaining:

Quarter	Forecast	Actual	Percent Error
1	$26.32	$24.38	8.0
2	27.37	22.38	22.3
3	27.19	23.00	18.2
4	27.13	21.88	24.0

How did our forecasting model do? Even though the $\overline{R}^2$ within the sample was .95, even though we used actual values for the independent variables, and even though we forecasted only four quarters beyond our sample, the model was something like 20 percent off. If we had decided to buy Kellogg's stock based on our forecast, we'd have *lost* money! Since other attempts to forecast stock prices have also encountered difficulties, this doesn't seem like a reasonable use for econometric forecasting. Individual stock prices (and many other items) are simply too variable and depend on too many nonquantifiable items to consistently forecast accurately, even if the forecasting equation has an excellent fit! The reason for this apparent contradiction is that equations that worked well in the past may or may not work well in the future.

15.2 More Complex Forecasting Problems

The forecasts generated in the previous section are quite simple, however, and most actual forecasting involves one or more additional questions. For example:

1. *Unknown Xs:* It's unrealistic to expect to know the values for the independent variables outside the sample. For instance, we'll almost never know what the Dow-Jones industrial average will be in the future when we are making forecasts of the price of a given stock, and yet we assumed that knowledge when making our Kellogg price forecasts. What happens when we don't know the values of the independent variables for the forecast period?

2. *Serial Correlation:* If there is serial correlation involved, the forecasting equation may be estimated with GLS. How should predictions be adjusted when forecasting equations are estimated with GLS?

3. *Confidence Intervals:* All the previous forecasts were single values, but such single values are almost never exactly right. Wouldn't it be more helpful if we forecasted an interval within which we were confident that the actual value would fall a certain percentage of the time? How can we develop these confidence intervals?

4. *Simultaneous Equations Models:* As you saw in Chapter 14, many economic and business equations are part of simultaneous models. How can we use an independent variable to forecast a dependent variable when we know that a change in value of the dependent variable will change, in turn, the value of the independent variable that we used to make the forecast?

Even a few questions like these should be enough to convince you that forecasting is more complex than is implied by Section 15.1.

Conditional Forecasting (Unknown X Values for the Forecast Period)

A forecast in which all values of the independent variables are known with certainty can be called an **unconditional forecast**, but, as mentioned previously, the situations in which one can make such unconditional forecasts are rare. More likely, we will have to make a **conditional forecast**, for which actual values of one or more of the independent variables are *not* known. We are forced to obtain forecasts for the independent variables before we can use our equation to forecast the dependent variable, making our forecast of Y conditional on our forecast of the Xs.

One key to an accurate conditional forecast is accurate forecasting of the independent variables. If the forecasts of the independent variables are unbiased, using a conditional forecast will not introduce bias into the forecast of the dependent variable. Anything but a perfect forecast of the independent variables will contain some amount of forecast error, however, and so the expected error variance associated with conditional forecasting will be larger than that associated with unconditional forecasting. Thus, one should try to find unbiased, minimum variance forecasts of the independent variables when using conditional forecasting.

To get good forecasts of the independent variables, take the forecastability of potential independent variables into consideration when making specification choices. For instance, when you choose which of two redundant variables to include in an equation to be used for forecasting, you should choose the one that is easier to forecast accurately. When you can, you should choose an independent variable that is regularly forecasted by someone else (an econometric forecasting firm, for example) so that you don't have to forecast X yourself.

The careful selection of independent variables can sometimes help you avoid the need for conditional forecasting in the first place. This opportunity can arise when the dependent variable can be expressed as a function of leading indicators. A **leading indicator** is an independent variable the movements of which anticipate movements in the dependent variable. The best known leading indicator, the Index of Leading Economic Indicators, is produced each month.

For instance, the impact of interest rates on investment typically is not felt until two or three quarters after interest rates have changed. To see this, let's look at the investment function of the small macroeconomic model of Section 14.3:

$$I_t = \beta_0 + \beta_1 Y_t + \beta_2 r_{t-1} + \epsilon_t \qquad (15.6)$$

where I equals gross investment, Y equals GDP, and r equals the interest rate. In this equation, actual values of r can be used to help forecast I_{T+1}. Note, however, that to predict I_{T+2}, we need to forecast r_{T+1}. Thus, leading indicators like r help avoid conditional forecasting for only a time period or two. For long-range predictions, a conditional forecast is usually necessary.

Forecasting with Serially Correlated Error Terms

Recall from Chapter 9 that pure first-order serial correlation implies that the current observation of the error term ϵ_t is affected by the previous error term and an autocorrelation coefficient, ρ:

$$\epsilon_t = \rho\epsilon_{t-1} + u_t$$

where u_t is a non–serially correlated error term. Also recall that when serial correlation is severe, one remedy is to run Generalized Least Squares (GLS) as noted in Equation 9.18:

$$Y_t - \rho Y_{t-1} = \beta_0(1 - \rho) + \beta_1(X_t - \rho X_{t-1}) + u_t \qquad (9.18)$$

Unfortunately, whenever the use of GLS is required to rid an equation of pure first-order serial correlation, the procedures used to forecast with that equation become a bit more complex. To see why this is necessary, note that if Equation 9.18 is estimated, the dependent variable will be:

$$Y_t^* = Y_t - \hat{\rho}Y_{t-1} \qquad (15.7)$$

Thus, if a GLS equation is used for forecasting, it will produce predictions of Y_{T+1}^* rather than of Y_{T+1}. Such predictions thus will be of the wrong variable.

If forecasts are to be made with a GLS equation, Equation 9.18 should first be solved for Y_t before forecasting is attempted:

$$Y_t = \rho Y_{t-1} + \beta_0(1 - \rho) + \beta_1(X_t - \rho X_{t-1}) + u_t \qquad (15.8)$$

We now can forecast with Equation 15.8 as we would with any other. If we substitute $T + 1$ for t (to forecast time period $T + 1$) and insert estimates for the coefficients, ρs and Xs into the right side of the equation, we obtain:

$$\hat{Y}_{T+1} = \hat{\rho}Y_T + \hat{\beta}_0(1 - \hat{\rho}) + \hat{\beta}_1(\hat{X}_{T+1} - \hat{\rho}X_T) \qquad (15.9)$$

Equation 15.9 thus should be used for forecasting when an equation has been estimated with GLS to correct for serial correlation.[6]

We now turn to an example of such forecasting with serially correlated error terms. In particular, recall from Chapter 9 that the Durbin–Watson statistic of the chicken demand equation used as an example in Section 15.1 was 0.99, indicating significant positive first-order serial correlation. As a result, we estimated the chicken demand equation with GLS, obtaining Equation 9.22:

$$\hat{Y}_t = 27.7 - 0.08PC_t + 0.02PB_t + 0.24YD_t \qquad (9.22)$$
$$(0.05) \quad (0.02) \quad (0.02)$$
$$t = -1.70 \quad + 0.76 \quad + 12.06$$
$$\overline{R}^2 = .9921 \quad N = 28 \quad \hat{\rho} = 0.56$$

Since Equation 9.22 was estimated with GLS, Y is actually Y_t^*, which equals $(Y_t - \hat{\rho}Y_{t-1})$, PC_t is actually PC_t^*, which equals $PC_t - \hat{\rho}PC_{t-1}$, and so on. Thus, to forecast with Equation 9.22, we have to convert it to the form of Equation 15.9, or:

$$\hat{Y}_{T+1} = 0.56Y_T + 27.70(1 - 0.56) - 0.08(PC_{T+1} - 0.56PC_T) \qquad (15.10)$$
$$+ 0.02(PB_{T+1} - 0.56PB_T) + 0.23(YD_{T+1} - 0.56YD_T)$$

Substituting the actual values for the independent variables into Equation 15.10, we obtain:

Year	Forecast	Actual	Percent Error
2003	97.54	95.63	2.0
2004	101.02	98.58	2.5
2005	102.38	100.60	1.8

The MAPE of the GLS forecasts is 2.1 percent, far better than that of the OLS forecasts. In general, GLS usually will provide superior forecasting performance to OLS in the presence of serial correlation.

Forecasting Confidence Intervals

Until now, the emphasis in this text has been on obtaining point (or single-value) estimates. This has been true whether we have been estimating coefficient

---

6. If $\hat{\rho}$ is less than 0.3, many researchers prefer to use the OLS forecast plus $\hat{\rho}$ times the lagged residual as their forecast instead of the GLS forecast from Equation 15.9.

values or estimating forecasts. Recall, though, that a point estimate is only one of a whole range of such estimates that could have been obtained from different samples (for coefficient estimates) or different independent variable values or coefficients (for forecasts). The usefulness of such point estimates is improved if we can also generate some idea of the variability of our forecasts. The measure of variability typically used is the *confidence interval*, which was defined in Section 5.2 as the range of values that contains the actual value of the item being estimated a specified percentage of the time (called the level of confidence). This is the easiest way to warn forecast users that a sampling distribution exists.

Suppose you are trying to decide how many hot dogs to order for your city's Fourth of July fireworks show and that the best point forecast is that you'll sell 24,000 hot dogs. How many hot dogs should you order? If you order 24,000, you're likely to run out about half the time! This is because a point forecast is usually an estimate of the mean of the distribution of possible sales figures; you will sell more than 24,000 about as frequently as less than 24,000. It would be easier to decide how many dogs to order if you also had a confidence interval that told you the range within which hot dog sales would fall 95 percent of the time. This is because the usefulness of the 24,000 hot dog forecast changes dramatically depending on the confidence interval; an interval of 22,000 to 26,000 would pin down the likely sales, but an interval of 4,000 to 44,000 would leave you virtually in the dark about what to do.

The decision as to how many hot dogs to order would also depend on the costs of having the wrong number. These may not be the same per hot dog for overestimates as they are for underestimates. For example, if you don't order enough, then you lose the entire retail price of the hot dog minus the wholesale price of the dog (and bun) because your other costs, like hiring employees and building hot dog stands, are essentially fixed. On the other hand, if you order too many, you lose the wholesale cost of the dog and bun minus whatever salvage price you might be able to get for day-old buns, etc. As a result, the right number to order would depend on your profit margin and the importance of nonreturnable inputs in your total cost picture.

The same techniques we use to test hypotheses can also be adapted to create confidence intervals. Given a point forecast, $\hat{Y}_{T+1}$, all we need to generate a confidence interval around that forecast are t_c, the critical t-value (for the desired level of confidence), and S_F, the estimated standard error of the forecast:

$$\text{Confidence interval} = \hat{Y}_{T+1} \pm S_F t_c \qquad (15.11)$$

or, equivalently,

$$\hat{Y}_{T+1} - S_F t_c \leq Y_{T+1} \leq \hat{Y}_{T+1} + S_F t_c \qquad (15.12)$$

The critical t-value, t_c, can be found in Statistical Table B-1 (for a two-tailed test with $T - K - 1$ degrees of freedom). The standard error of the forecast, S_F, for an equation with just one independent variable, equals the square root of the forecast error variance:

$$S_F = \sqrt{s^2 \left[1 + 1/T + (\hat{X}_{T+1} - \overline{X})^2 \middle/ \sum_{t=1}^{T} (X_t - \overline{X})^2 \right]} \qquad (15.13)$$

where s^2 = the estimated variance of the error term
           T = the number of observations in the sample
           $\hat{X}_{T+1}$ = the forecasted value of the single independent variable
           $\overline{X}$ = the arithmetic mean of the observed Xs in the sample[7]

Note that Equation 15.13 implies that the forecast error variance decreases the larger the sample, the more X varies within the sample, and the closer $\hat{X}$ is to its within-sample mean. An important implication is that the farther the X used to forecast Y is from the within-sample mean of the Xs, the wider the confidence interval around the $\hat{Y}$ is going to be. This can be seen in Figure 15.2, in which the confidence interval actually gets wider as $\hat{X}_{T+1}$ is farther from $\overline{X}$. Since forecasting outside the sample range is common, researchers should be aware of this phenomenon. Also note that Equation 15.13 is for unconditional forecasting. If there is any forecast error in $\hat{X}_{T+1}$, then the confidence interval is larger and more complicated to calculate.

As mentioned, Equation 15.13 assumes that there is only one independent variable; the equation to be used with more than one variable is similar but more complicated.

Let's look at an example of building a forecast confidence interval by returning to the weight/height example. In particular, let's create a 95 percent confidence interval around the forecast for a 6'1" male calculated in Equation 15.1 (repeated for convenience):

$$\text{Predicted weight} = 103.4 + 6.38 \cdot (13 \text{ inches over five feet}) \qquad (15.1)$$

---

7. Equation 15.13 is valid whether Y_t is in the sample period or outside the sample period, but it applies only to point forecasts of individual Y_ts. If a confidence interval for the expected value of Y, $E(Y_t)$, is desired, then the correct equation to use is:

$$S_F = \sqrt{s^2 [1/T + (\hat{X}_{T+1} - \overline{X})^2 / \sum (X_t - \overline{X})^2]}$$

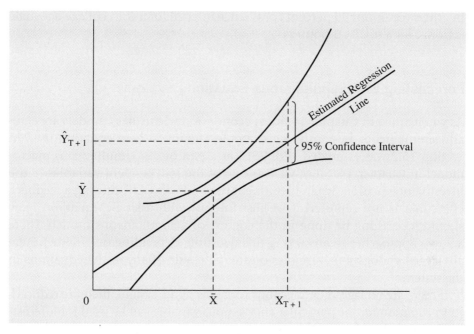

Figure 15.2 A Confidence Interval for $\hat{Y}_{T+1}$

A 95 percent confidence interval for $\hat{Y}_{T+1}$ includes the range of values within which the actual Y_{T+1} will fall 95 percent of the time. Note that the confidence interval widens as X_{T+1} differs more from its within-sample mean, $\overline{X}$.

for a predicted weight of 103.4 + 82.9 or 186.3 pounds. To calculate a 95 percent confidence interval around this prediction, we substitute Equation 15.13 into Equation 15.11, obtaining a confidence interval of:

$$186.3 \pm \left(\sqrt{ s^2 \left[1 + 1/T + (\hat{X}_{T+1} - \overline{X})^2 / \sum_{t=1}^{T} (X_t - \overline{X})^2 \right] } \right) t_c \qquad (15.14)$$

We then substitute the actual figures into Equation 15.14. From the data set for the example, we find that T = 20, the mean X = 10.35, the summed square deviations of X around its mean is 92.50, and s^2 = 65.05. From Statistical Table B-1, we obtain the 5-percent, two-tailed critical t-value for 18 degrees of freedom of 2.101. If we now combine this with the information that our $\hat{X}$ is 13, we obtain:

$$186.3 \pm \left(\sqrt{ 65.05[1 + 1/20 + (13.0 - 10.35)^2/92.50] } \right) t_c \qquad (15.15)$$

$$186.3 \pm 8.558(2.101) = 186.3 \pm 18.0 \qquad (15.16)$$

In other words, our 95 percent confidence interval for a 6'1" college-age male is from 168.3 to 204.3 pounds.

Forecasting with Simultaneous Equations Systems

As you learned in Chapter 14, most economic and business models are actually simultaneous in nature; for example, the investment equation used in Section 15.2 was estimated with 2SLS as a part of our simultaneous macromodel in Chapter 14. Since GDP is one of the independent variables in the investment equation, when investment rises, so will GDP, causing a feedback effect that is not captured if we just forecast with a single equation. How should forecasting be done in the context of a simultaneous model? There are two approaches to answering this question, depending on whether there are lagged endogenous variables on the right side of any of the equations in the system.

If there are no lagged endogenous variables in the system, then the reduced-form equation for the particular endogenous variable can be used for forecasting because it represents the simultaneous solution of the system for the endogenous variable being forecasted. Since the reduced-form equation is the endogenous variable expressed entirely in terms of the predetermined variables in the system, it allows the forecasting of the endogenous variable without any feedback or simultaneity impacts. This result explains why some researchers forecast potentially simultaneous dependent variables with single equations that appear to combine supply-side and demand-side predetermined variables; they are actually using modified reduced-form equations to make their forecasts.

If there are lagged endogenous variables in the system, then the approach must be altered to take into account the dynamic interaction caused by the lagged endogenous variables. For simple models, this sometimes can be done by substituting for the lagged endogenous variables where they appear in the reduced-form equations. If such a manipulation is difficult, however, then a technique called simulation analysis can be used. *Simulation* involves forecasting for the first postsample period by using the reduced-form equations to forecast all endogenous variables where they appear in the reduced-form equations. The forecast for the second postsample period, however, uses the endogenous variable *forecasts* from the last period as lagged values for any endogenous variables that have one-period lags while continuing to use sample values for endogenous variables that have lags of two or more periods. This process continues until all forecasting is done with reduced-form equations that use as data for lagged endogenous variables the forecasts from previous time periods. Although such dynamic analyses are beyond the scope of this chapter, they're important to remember when considering forecasting with a simultaneous system.[8]

(15.3) ARIMA Models

The forecasting techniques of the previous two sections are applications of familiar regression models. We use linear regression equations to forecast the dependent variable by plugging likely values of the independent variables into the estimated equations and calculating a predicted value of Y; this bases the prediction of the dependent variable on the independent variables (and on their estimated coefficients).

ARIMA (the name will be explained shortly) is an increasingly popular forecasting technique that completely ignores independent variables in making forecasts. **ARIMA** is a highly refined curve-fitting device that uses current and past values of the dependent variable to produce often accurate short-term forecasts of that variable. Examples of such forecasts are stock market price predictions created by brokerage analysts (called "chartists" or "technicians") based entirely on past patterns of movement of the stock prices.

Any forecasting technique that ignores independent variables also essentially ignores all potential underlying theories except those that hypothesize repeating patterns in the variable under study. Since we have emphasized the advantages of developing the theoretical underpinnings of particular equations before estimating them, why would we advocate using ARIMA? The answer is that the use of ARIMA is appropriate when little or nothing is known about the dependent variable being forecasted, when the independent variables known to be important really cannot be forecasted effectively, or when all that is needed is a one or two-period forecast. In these cases, ARIMA has the potential to provide short-term forecasts that are superior to more theoretically satisfying regression models. In addition, ARIMA can sometimes produce better explanations of the residuals from an existing regression equation (in particular, one with known omitted variables or other problems). In other circumstances, the use of ARIMA is not recommended. This introduction to ARIMA is intentionally brief; a more complete coverage of the topic can be obtained from a number of other sources.[9]

The ARIMA approach combines two different specifications (called *processes*) into one equation. The first specification is an *autoregressive* process (hence

---

8. For more on this topic, see Chapters 12–14 in Robert S. Pindyck and Daniel L. Rubinfeld, *Econometric Models and Economic Forecasts* (New York: McGraw-Hill, 1998).

9. See, for example, Chapters 15–19 in Robert S. Pindyck and Daniel L. Rubinfeld, *Econometric Models and Economic Forecasts* (New York: McGraw-Hill, 1998).

the AR in ARIMA), and the second specification is a *moving average* (hence the MA).

An **autoregressive process** expresses a dependent variable Y_t as a function of past values of the dependent variable. This is similar to the serial correlation error term function of Chapter 9 and to the dynamic model of Chapter 12. If we have p different lagged values of Y, the equation is often referred to as a "pth-order" autoregressive process.

A **moving-average process** expresses a dependent variable Y_t as a function of past values of the error term. Such a function is a moving average of past error term observations that can be added to the mean of Y to obtain a moving average of past values of Y. If we used q past values of ϵ, we'd call it a qth-order moving-average process.

To create an ARIMA model, we begin with an econometric equation with no independent variables ($Y_t = \beta_0 + \epsilon_t$) and add to it both the autoregressive and moving-average processes:

autoregressive process

$$Y_t = \beta_0 + \overbrace{\theta_1 Y_{t-1} + \theta_2 Y_{t-2} + \cdots + \theta_p Y_{t-p}} + \epsilon_t$$
$$\underbrace{+ \phi_1 \epsilon_{t-1} + \phi_2 \epsilon_{t-2} + \cdots + \phi_q \epsilon_{t-q}} \qquad (15.17)$$

moving-average process

where the θs and the ϕs are the coefficients of the autoregressive and moving-average processes, respectively, and p and q are the number of past values used of Y and ϵ, respectively.

Before this equation can be applied to a time series, however, it must be ensured that the time series is *stationary*, as defined in Section 12.4. If a series is nonstationary, then steps must be taken to convert the series into a stationary one before the ARIMA technique can be applied. For example, a nonstationary series can often be converted into a stationary one by taking the first difference of the variable in question:

$$Y_t^* = \Delta Y_t = Y_t - Y_{t-1} \qquad (15.18)$$

If the first differences do not produce a stationary series, then first differences of this first-differenced series can be taken.[10] The resulting series is a second-difference transformation:

$$Y_t^{**} = (\Delta Y_t^*) = Y_t^* - Y_{t-1}^* = \Delta Y_t - \Delta Y_{t-1} \qquad (15.19)$$

---

10. For variables that are growing in percentage terms rather than absolute amounts, it often makes sense to take logs before taking first differences.

In general, successive differences are taken until the series is stationary. The number of differences required to be taken before a series becomes stationary is denoted with the letter d. For example, suppose that GDP is increasing by a fairly consistent amount each year. A plot of GDP with respect to time would depict a nonstationary series, but a plot of the first differences of GDP might depict a fairly stationary series. In such a case, d would be equal to one because one first difference was necessary to convert the nonstationary series into a stationary one.

The dependent variable in Equation 15.17 must be stationary, so the Y in that equation may be Y, Y*, or even Y**, depending on the variable in question.[11] If a forecast of Y* or Y** is made, then it must be converted back into Y terms before its use; for example, if $d = 1$, then

$$\hat{Y}_{T+1} = Y_T + \hat{Y}^*_{T+1} \tag{15.20}$$

This conversion process is similar to integration in mathematics, so the "I" in ARIMA stands for "integrated." ARIMA thus stands for *AutoRegressive Integrated Moving Average*. (If the original series is stationary and d therefore equals 0, this is sometimes shortened to ARMA.)

As a shorthand, an ARIMA model with p, d, and q specified is usually denoted as ARIMA (p,d,q) with the specific integers chosen inserted for p, d, and q, as in ARIMA (2,1,1). ARIMA (2,1,1) would indicate a model with two autoregressive terms, one first difference, and one moving-average term:

$$\text{ARIMA}(2,1,1)\colon Y^*_t = \beta_0 + \theta_1 Y^*_{t-1} + \theta_2 Y^*_{t-2} + \epsilon_t + \phi_1 \epsilon_{t-1} \tag{15.21}$$

where $Y^*_t = Y_t - Y_{t-1}$.

It's remarkable how very small values of p and q can model extremely rich dynamics.

15.4 Summary

1. Forecasting is the estimation of the expected value of a dependent variable for observations that are not part of the sample data set. Forecasts are generated (via regressions) by estimating an equation for the

---

11. If Y in Equation 15.17 is Y*, then β_0 represents the coefficient of the linear trend in the original series, and if Y is Y**, then β_0 represents the coefficient of the second-difference trend in the original series. In such cases—for example, Equation 15.21–it's not always necessary that β_0 be in the model.

dependent variable to be forecasted, and substituting values for each of the independent variables (for the observations to be forecasted) into the equation.

2. An excellent fit within the sample period for a forecasting equation does not guarantee that the equation will forecast well outside the sample period.

3. A forecast in which all the values of the independent variables are known with certainty is called an unconditional forecast, but if one or more of the independent variables have to be forecasted, it is a conditional forecast. Conditional forecasting introduces no bias into the prediction of Y (as long as the X forecasts are unbiased), but increased forecast error variance is unavoidable with conditional forecasting.

4. If the coefficients of an equation have been estimated with GLS (to correct for pure first-order serial correlation), then the forecasting equation is:

$$\hat{Y}_{T+1} = \hat{\rho}Y_T + \hat{\beta}_0(1 - \hat{\rho}) + \hat{\beta}_1(\hat{X}_{T+1} - \hat{\rho}X_T)$$

where ρ is the autocorrelation coefficient rho.

5. Forecasts are often more useful if they are accompanied by a confidence interval, which is a range within which the actual value of the dependent variable should fall a given percentage of the time (the level of confidence). This is:

$$\hat{Y}_{T+1} \pm S_F t_c$$

where S_F is the estimated standard error of the forecast and t_c is the critical two-tailed t-value for the desired level of confidence.

6. ARIMA is a highly refined curve-fitting technique that uses current and past values of the dependent variable (and only the dependent variable) to produce often accurate short-term forecasts of that variable. The first step in using ARIMA is to make the dependent variable series stationary by taking d first differences until the resulting transformed variable has a constant mean and variance. The ARIMA(p,d,q) approach then combines an autoregressive process (with $\theta_1 Y_{t-1}$ terms) of order p with a moving-average process (with $\phi_1 \epsilon_{t-1}$ terms) of order q to explain the dth differenced dependent variable.

EXERCISES

(The answer to Exercise 2 is in Appendix A.)

1. Write the meaning of each of the following terms without referring to the book (or your notes), and compare your definition with the version in the text for each:
   a. conditional forecast
   b. leading indicator
   c. confidence interval
   d. MAPE
   e. RMSE
   f. autoregressive process
   g. moving-average process
   h. ARIMA(p,d,q)

2. Calculate the following unconditional forecasts:
   a. the median price of a new single-family house in 2008, given the simplified equation in Exercise 10 in Chapter 1 and the fact that the U.S. GDP in 2008 was $14,288.6 billion.
   b. the expected level of check volume at three possible future sites for new Woody's restaurants, given Equation 3.5 and the following data. If you could only build one new eatery, in which of these three sites would you build (all else equal)?

Site	Competition	Population	Income
Richburgh	6	58,000	38,000
Nowheresville	1	14,000	27,000
Slick City	9	190,000	15,000

   c. Per capita consumption of fish in the United States for 1971–1974 given Equation 8.23 and the following data:

Year	PF	PB	Yd
1971	130.2	116.7	2679
1972	141.9	129.2	2767
1973	162.8	161.1	2934
1974	187.7	164.1	2871

   (Hint: Reread Exercise 13 in Chapter 8 before attempting this forecast.)

3. To understand the difficulty of conditional forecasting, use Equation 1.21 to forecast the weights of the next three males you see, using your *estimates* of their heights. (Ask for actual values after finishing.)

4. Calculate 95 percent confidence interval forecasts for the following:
   a. the weight of a male who is 5'9" tall. (*Hint:* Modify Equation 15.15.)
   b. next month's sales of ice cream cones at the Campus Cooler given an expected price of 60 cents per cone and:

$$\hat{C}_t = 2{,}000 - 20.0P_t \qquad \overline{R}^2 = .80$$
$$(5.0) \qquad T = 30$$
$$t = -4.0 \qquad \overline{P} = 50$$

   where: C_t = the number of ice cream cones sold in month t
   P_t = the price of the Cooler's ice cream cones (in cents) in month t
   $s^2 = 25{,}000$ and $\sum(P_t - \overline{P})^2 = 1000$

5. Some of the most interesting applications of econometric forecasting are in the political arena. Examples of regression analysis in politics range from part-time marketing consultants who help local candidates decide how best to use their advertising dollars to a fairly rich professional literature on U.S. presidential elections.[12]

   In 2008, Haynes and Stone[13] added to this literature with an article that specified (among others) the following equation:

$$\text{VOTE}_i = \beta_0 + \beta_1 P_i + \beta_2(\text{DUR*P})_i + \beta_3(\text{DOW*P})_i + \beta_4(\text{GROWTH*P})_i$$
$$+ \beta_5(\text{INFLATION*P})_i + \beta_6(\text{ARMY*P})_i + \beta_7(\text{SPEND*P})_i + \varepsilon_i \qquad (15.22)$$

   where: VOTE_i = the Democratic share of the popular two-party presidential vote
   P_i = 1 if the incumbent is a Democrat and -1 if the incumbent is a Republican

---

12. See, particularly, the work of Ray Fair: "The Effect of Economic Events on Votes for President," *Review of Economics and Statistics*, Vol. 60, pp. 159–173, and "Econometrics and Presidential Elections," *Journal of Economic Perspectives*, Vol. 10, pp. 89–102.

13. Stephen Haynes and Joe Stone, "A Disaggregate Approach to Economic Models of Voting in U.S. Presidential Elections: Forecasts of the 2008 Election," *Economics Bulletin*, Vol. 4, No. 28 (2008), pp. 1–11.

$$DUR_i \quad = \text{the number of consecutive terms the incumbent party has held the presidency}$$

$$DOW_i \quad = \text{the annual rate of change in the Dow Jones Industrial Average between January and October of the election year}$$

$$GROWTH_i \quad = \text{the annual percent growth of real per capita GDP in the second and third quarters of the election year}$$

$$INFLATION_i = \text{the absolute value of the annualized inflation rate in the two-year period prior to the election}$$

$$ARMY_i \quad = \text{the annualized percent change of the proportion of the population in the armed forces in the two-year period prior to the election}$$

$$SPEND_i \quad = \text{the annualized percentage change in the proportion of government spending devoted to national security in the two-year period prior to the election}$$

a. What kind of variable is P? Is it a dummy variable? If not, what is it?
b. The authors specified their equation as a series of interaction variables between P and the other variables of interest. Look at the equation carefully. Why do you think that these interaction variables were required?
c. Using the data[14] in Table 15.1 (datafile = ELECTION15) estimate Equation 15.22 for the years 1916–1996.
d. Create and test appropriate hypotheses on the coefficients of your estimated equation at the 5-percent level. Do any of the coefficients have unexpected signs? Which ones?
e. Create unconditional forecasts for the years 2000 and 2004 and compare your forecasts with the actual figures in Table 15.1. How did you do?
f. The authors wrote their article before the 2008 election. Create an unconditional forecast for that election using the data in Table 15.1. Who did the model predict would win?

---

14. These data are from Haynes and Stone, ibid., p. 10, but similar tables are available from a variety of sources, including: fairmodel.econ.yale.edu/vote2008/pres.txt.

Table 15.1 Data for the Presidential Election Exercise

YEAR	VOTE	P	DUR	DOW	GROWTH	INFLATION	ARMY	SPEND
1916	51.682	1	1	12.00	6.38	7.73	2.33	4.04
1920	36.119	1	2	-23.50	-6.14	8.01	-107.60	11.24
1924	41.756	-1	1	6.00	-2.16	0.62	-3.38	-23.05
1928	41.240	-1	2	31.30	-0.63	0.81	-0.48	10.15
1932	59.140	-1	3	-25.00	-13.98	10.01	-2.97	-37.56
1936	62.458	1	1	24.90	13.41	1.36	7.60	28.86
1940	54.999	1	2	-12.90	6.97	0.53	16.79	8.33
1944	53.774	1	3	9.00	6.88	1.98	53.10	17.16
1948	52.370	1	4	6.30	3.77	10.39	-38.82	-86.56
1952	44.595	1	5	-1.80	-0.34	2.66	43.89	71.59
1956	42.240	-1	1	2.40	-0.69	3.59	-9.93	-14.34
1960	50.090	-1	2	-13.90	-1.92	2.16	-4.10	-8.44
1964	61.344	1	1	15.80	2.38	1.73	-3.68	-5.88
1968	49.596	1	2	10.00	4.00	3.94	0.06	6.28
1972	38.210	-1	1	5.40	5.05	5.17	-11.91	-19.71
1976	51.050	-1	2	3.00	0.78	7.64	-2.56	-20.15
1980	44.697	1	1	12.40	-5.69	8.99	-1.37	-0.44
1984	40.830	-1	1	-6.90	2.69	3.68	-0.22	7.38
1988	46.070	-1	2	12.60	2.43	3.30	-1.58	-1.09
1992	53.455	-1	3	-0.90	1.34	3.15	-7.33	-10.11
1996	54.736	1	1	24.54	3.08	1.95	-5.62	-12.67
2000	50.265	1	2	-5.02	2.95	1.80	-2.00	1.83
2004	48.586	-1	1	-8.01	3.49	2.50	-0.51	14.91
2008	?	-1	2	30.70	2.10	3.70	-0.87	0.41

Source: Stephen Haynes and Joe Stone, "A Disaggregate Approach to Economic Models of Voting in U.S. Presidential Elections: Forecasts of the 2008 Election," *Economics Bulletin*, Vol. 4, No. 8 (2008), p. 10.

Datafile = ELECTION15

6. For each of the following series, calculate and plot Y_t, $Y_t^* = \Delta Y_t$, and $Y_t^{**} = \Delta Y_t^*$, describe the stationarity properties of the series, and choose an appropriate value for d.

a. 2, 3, 4, 5, 6, 7, 8, 9, 10, 11, 12, 13
b. 2, 2, 3, 4, 5, 6, 8, 10, 12, 15, 19, 24
c. 2, 3, 6, 3, 4, 2, 3, 5, 1, 4, 4, 6

7. Take the three Y_t^* series you calculated as part of your answer to Exercise 6 and check to see whether they are correct by calculating backward from one of the endpoints and seeing if you can derive the original three Y_t series from your three Y_t^* series. (*Hint:* Equation 15.20 can be adapted for this "integration" purpose.)

8. Suppose you have been given two different ARIMA(1,0,0) fitted time-series models of the variable Y_t:

$$\text{Model A: } Y_t = 15.0 + 0.5Y_{t-1} + \epsilon_t$$
$$\text{Model T: } Y_t = 45.0 - 0.5Y_{t-1} + \epsilon_t$$

where ϵ_t is a normally distributed error term with mean zero and standard deviation equal to one.

a. The final observation in the sample (time period 06) is $Y_{06} = 31$. Determine forecasts for periods 07, 08, and 09 for both models.

b. Suppose you now find out that the actual Y_{07} was equal to 33. Revise your forecasts for periods 08 and 09 to take the new information into account.

c. Based on the fitted time series and your two forecasts, which model (model A or model T) do you expect to exhibit smoother behavior? Explain your reasoning.

9. Suppose you have been given an ARIMA(1,0,1) fitted time-series model:

$$Y_t = 0.0 + 1.0Y_{t-1} + \epsilon_t - 0.5\epsilon_{t-1}$$

where ϵ_t is a normally distributed error term with mean zero and standard deviation equal to one and where $T = 09$, $Y_{09} = 27$, and where $\hat{Y}_{09} = 27.5$.

a. Calculate e_{09}.

b. Calculate forecasts for Y_{10}, Y_{11}, and Y_{12}. (*Hint:* Use your answer to part a.)

10. You've been hired to forecast *Sports Illustrated* subscriptions (S) using the following function of GDP (Y) and a classical error term (ϵ):

$$S_t = \beta_0 + \beta_1 Y_t + \beta_2 S_{t-1} + \epsilon_t$$

Explain how you would forecast (out two time periods) with this equation in the following cases:

a. If future values of Y are known. (*Hint:* Be sure to comment on the functional form of this relationship.)

b. If future values of Y are unknown and *Sports Illustrated* subscriptions are small in comparison to GDP.

c. If *Sports Illustrated* subscriptions are about half of GDP (obviously a sports-lover's heaven!) and all other components of GDP are known to be stochastic functions of time.

16 Experimental and Panel Data

16.1 **Experimental Methods in Economics**

16.2 **Panel Data**

16.3 **Fixed versus Random Effects**

16.4 **Summary and Exercises**

This chapter is a brief introduction to experimental data and panel data.[1] The first section is devoted to experimental methods in economics.[2] The experimental approach is important because it provides a possible way for regression analysis to provide evidence of causality. If one group is exposed to a particular policy (like an increased tax or a decreased price) and a control group isn't, then any meaningful difference between the behavior of the two groups is evidence that the policy caused that difference. Such experiments already are standard procedure in some areas of research, for example the testing of the safety and effectiveness of new medicines by the US Food and Drug Administration.

The remainder of the chapter focuses on panel data. As mentioned in Chapter 11, panel data are formed when cross-sectional and time-series data sets are combined to create a single data set. Although some researchers use panel data to increase their sample size, the main reason for working with panel data is to provide an insight into analytical questions that can't be answered by using time-series or cross-sectional data alone.

---

1. The first draft of this chapter was written by Prof. Susan Averett of Lafayette College.

2. We use this awkward phrase to avoid confusion with the already existing field of experimental economics. Experimental economists run actual laboratory experiments on human subjects. By offering real-world incentives (usually money), experimental economists can reproduce supply and demand equilibria, test economic theories, and study market phenomena that otherwise are difficult to observe. For more on experimental economics, see Daniel Friedman and Allesandra Cassar, *An Introduction to Experimental Economics* (London: Routledge, 2004). For more on experimental methods in economics, see James Stock and Mark Watson, *Introductory Econometrics* (Boston: Addison-Wesley, 2007) pp. 468–521.

16.1 Experimental Methods in Economics

Any good statistician knows that correlation doesn't prove causality, but understanding causality is important if we're going to assess the effectiveness of economic policies, the profitability of business practices, or the value of not-for-profit programs. To try to solve this problem, some econometricians have imported experimental techniques from medicine and psychology. Can experimental methods provide evidence of causality in economics?

Random Assignment Experiments

When medical researchers want to examine the effect of a new drug, they use an experimental design called *random assignment*. You're probably familiar with random assignment experiments because medical research studies are in the news virtually every week. The experiment generally proceeds as follows. First, a sample of subjects is chosen or recruited, and then they are randomly assigned to one of two groups—the *control group* or the *treatment group*. The treatment group receives the medicine that is being tested, and the control group receives a harmless ineffective placebo. Similar experiments are possible in economics. To test whether a job training program has an impact on earnings, for example, the treatment group would receive the training and the control group wouldn't. If the treatment and control groups are chosen randomly, then such experiments are called **random assignment experiments**.

It's not hard to see why some researchers refer to random assignment as the gold standard in terms of establishing causality. Randomization helps ensure that any difference in the outcome between the control and the treatment group is causal and that the difference in outcome was caused by the treatment and not merely correlated with the treatment. The subjects' random assignment to the groups should be enough to guarantee that the only *systematic* reason for observed differences between the treatment and control groups is the treatment. Any other differences are the chance consequence of the random assignment. For example, the random assignment may result in more males in one group than in the other, or one of the subjects may die for a reason that is unrelated to the disease or treatment being studied. With reasonably sized samples, such random fluctuations will most likely balance out so that, on average, the two groups are similar except that one group receives the treatment and the other doesn't. The larger the sample, the more likely it is that random fluctuations will balance out.

Factors other than the treatment that may affect the outcome are put in the error term, and the resulting equation is:

$$OUTCOME_i = \beta_0 + \beta_1 TREATMENT_i + \epsilon_i \qquad (16.1)$$

where: $OUTCOME_i$ = a measure of the desired outcome in the ith individual

$TREATMENT_i$ = a dummy variable equal to 1 for individuals in the treatment group and 0 for individuals in the control group

β_1 is often called the *differences estimator* because it measures the difference between the average outcome for the treatment group and the average outcome for the control group. If the estimated value of β_1 is substantially different from zero in the direction predicted by theory, then we have evidence that the treatment did indeed cause the outcome to move in the expected direction.

However, random assignment can't always control for all possible other factors, and we may be able to identify some of these factors and add them to our equation. In our job training example, suppose that random assignment, by chance, results in one group having more males and being slightly older than the other group. If gender and age matter in determining earnings, then we can control for the different composition of the two groups by including gender and age in our regression equation:

$$OUTCOME_i = \beta_0 + \beta_1 TREATMENT_i + \beta_2 X_{1i} + \beta_3 X_{2i} + \epsilon_i \qquad (16.2)$$

where X_1 is a dummy variable for the individual's gender and X_2 is the individual's age.

Our recommendation is to use Equation 16.2 rather than Equation 16.1 if important additional factors are observable. After all, if the estimates of β_1 in the two equations are quite similar, then the choice doesn't matter. However, if the estimates differ, then we have evidence that random assignment did not control for other factors by evenly distributing these factors between the treatment and control groups. If that's the case, then including these other factors (as in Equation 16.2) is likely to provide a better estimate of the difference caused by the treatment.

Unfortunately, random assignment experiments are not common in economics because they're subject to problems that typically do not plague medical experiments. For example:

1. *Non-Random Samples.* In medical experiments the researcher controls the assignment of subjects to treatment and control groups, but most

subjects in economic experiments are volunteers, and samples of volunteers often aren't random. Not everyone is willing to volunteer, some potential subjects are willing to participate if they're in the treatment group but not if they're in the control group, and some volunteers change their mind and drop out during the experiment. Unsurprisingly, the characteristics of a volunteer sample are not necessarily representative of the population. Suppose, for example, that our research question is whether financial incentives for student achievement actually increase test scores. The professors and students who are willing to participate in this experiment may not be representative of the overall population and, as a result, our conclusions may not apply to everyone.

2. *Unobservable Heterogeneity.* In Equation 16.2, we added observable factors to the equation to avoid omitted variable bias, but not all omitted factors in economics are observable. This "unobservable omitted variable" problem is called *unobserved heterogeneity.*

3. *The Hawthorne Effect.* Human subjects typically know that they're being studied, and they usually know whether they're in the treatment group or the control group. The fact that human subjects know that they're being observed sometimes can change their behavior, and this change in behavior could clearly change the results of the experiment. For example, workers at the Western Electric Company's Hawthorne Works plant were once put in a special room where researchers could study their productivity under controlled conditions. In one study, the lights were dimmed and the workers seemed to work harder, mainly because they knew that the researchers were watching to see if they worked harder! The fact that people behave differently when they know they are being watched is now called the *Hawthorne Effect.*

4. *Impossible Experiments.* It's often impossible (or unethical) to run a random assignment experiment in economics. Think about how difficult it would be to use a random assignment experiment to study the impact of marriage on earnings. On average, married men earn more than single men even after accounting for observable differences in factors such as education and work experience. Unfortunately, there are a number of potential sources of unobservable heterogeneity, such as the possibility that women are more likely to marry men who they judge to have high future earnings. A random assignment experiment might be able to sort these issues out, but imagine what such an experiment would entail. You'd have to randomly assign some men to marry and others to stay single! As you can see, this experiment, just like many other random assignment experiments in economics, simply isn't feasible.

Natural Experiments

If random assignment experiments aren't always feasible in economics, what's a good alternative? One approach is to use data from *natural experiments* to try to get at issues of causality. **Natural experiments** (or *quasi-experiments*) are similar to random assignment experiments except that observations fall into treatment and control groups "naturally" (because of an exogenous event) instead of being randomly assigned by the researcher. This approach requires finding natural events or policy changes that can be analyzed as if they were treatments in a random assignment experiment. As long as the natural event is exogenous (for example not under the control of either of the groups), it turns out that a natural experiment can come very close to mimicking a random assignment experiment. The key thus is to find naturally occurring events that mimic a random assignment experiment.

For instance, in 1992 New Jersey increased its minimum wage substantially while Pennsylvania kept its minimum wage constant. This led some economists to expect a decrease in employment at New Jersey fast-food restaurants (and other businesses that paid workers the minimum wage). In a famous study, Card and Krueger compared fast-food restaurants in New Jersey (the "treatment group") with similar restaurants in nearby parts of Pennsylvania (the "control group") and found no indication that the rise in the minimum wage reduced employment.[3] Their study was a natural experiment!

A strict approach to natural experiments would seem to require that one find equivalents of "treatment" and "control" groups that have no systematic differences except for the treatment variable and other factors that can be observed and added to the equation. However, in economics, the treatment and control groups seem quite likely to have started off with different levels of the outcome measure. In addition, unobserved heterogeneity or nonrandom samples could result in the groups having different outcome measures. If the outcomes don't start off equal, then comparing outcomes after the treatment won't give us a true measure of the impact of the treatment. To understand why this is a problem, suppose that you were studying the impact of job training on income, and further suppose that your treatment group was earning an average of $30,000 per year while the control group was earning an average of $29,000 before the treatment. If the treatment group ended up earning $1,000 more than the control group after the

---

3. David Card and Alan Krueger, "Minimum Wages and Employment: A Case Study of the Fast-Food Industry in New Jersey and Pennsylvania," *American Economic Review*, Vol. 84, No. 4, pp. 772–793.

treatment, would this be convincing evidence that the treatment had a positive causal effect on income? Of course not!

To get around this problem, economists who run natural experiments don't compare outcomes between the treatment and control groups. Instead, they compare the changes in the outcomes. Using this approach, we compare the change in the treatment group caused by the treatment with any change in the control group. The resulting "difference in differences" measures the impact of the treatment on the outcome in the natural experiment.

In a regression equation, the appropriate dependent variable in such a natural experiment thus is the difference in the outcome measure, not the outcome level we used in Equation 16.2. If we make this adjustment in Equation 16.2, we get:

$$\Delta OUTCOME_i \; = \; \beta_0 + \; \beta_1 TREATMENT_i \; + \; \beta_2 X_{1i} \; + \; \beta_3 X_{2i} \; + \; \epsilon_i \quad (16.3)$$

where $\Delta OUTCOME_i$ is defined as the outcome after the treatment minus the outcome before the treatment for the ith observation. β_1 is called the **difference-in-differences estimator**, and it measures the difference between the change in the treatment group and the change in the control group, holding constant X_1 and X_2. If the estimate of β_1 is substantively different from zero in the expected direction, then we have evidence that the treatment caused this change.

In essence, the difference-in-differences estimator uses the change in the control group as a measure of what would have happened to the treatment group if there hadn't been a treatment. The validity of this approach thus depends on the assumption that the changes in the outcome would have been the same in both the treatment and control group had there been no treatment.

Be careful, however. Because the dependent variable has changed in Equation 16.3 from what it was in Equation 16.2, we also should change our interpretation of the independent variables and their coefficients. β_2 now measures the impact of a one-unit increase in X_1 on the *change* in the outcome (holding constant the other independent variables), not the level of the outcome. In addition, we should choose independent variables for Equation 16.3 keeping in mind that the dependent variable now is a difference.

One final note. It's important to think through the appropriate "before" and "after" time frames when you're collecting data for a natural experiment. Data on the control and treatment groups should come from a time period far enough in advance of the policy change (treatment) that you are not picking up any anticipatory effects of the intended policy change. For example, if the post office announces that it's going to increase the price of stamps in the future, many people will mail things a day or two before the price increase takes effect in order to save money. As a result, data collected just before the price increase will overstate the true "before" quantity. Similarly, "after" data need to be collected a reasonable amount of time after the policy change in order to allow individuals and firms to adjust to the change.

An Example of a Natural Experiment

Let's take a look at an example of a natural experiment. In 1997, ARCO, one of the largest petroleum refiners and gasoline retailers in the world, acquired the Thrifty Oil Company, by far the biggest independent chain of gas stations in Southern California.[4] Economists and consumers were concerned that the acquisition would reduce competition and therefore allow ARCO to increase prices.

This topic has the potential to be a good natural experiment, as the gas stations can be split into a treatment group (gas stations that competed with each other before the merger) and a control group (gas stations that didn't compete with each other before the merger). To measure the impact of the merger on gasoline prices, a researcher would compare the difference in prices between the treatment and control groups before the acquisition with the price difference after the acquisition.

The treatment group consisted of ARCO gas stations that had a competing Thrifty station within a one-mile radius, and the control group was made up of ARCO gas stations that didn't compete directly with a Thrifty station. Data were collected on a station-by-station basis, and gasoline prices before the acquisition were compared to those afterward.

Before the acquisition, prices in the treatment group were, on average, two to three cents lower than in the control group, which makes sense because the ARCO gas stations had to compete with the nearby Thrifty gas stations. After the acquisition, however, the treatment group prices were two to three cents *higher* than those in the control group!

Take a look at Figure 16.1, which illustrates these results for Los Angeles. As can be seen, prices in the treatment group were lower than the control group before the acquisition and were higher afterward. In essence, prices at ARCO gas stations that competed with Thrifty gas stations rose dramatically after ARCO acquired Thrifty.

Does this constitute evidence that the acquisition reduced gasoline price competition in Southern California? Take another look at Figure 16.1 and compare the slopes of the two lines. The price trends in the treatment and control groups are virtually parallel in other time periods, suggesting that

---

4. This example is drawn from Justine Hastings, "Vertical Relationships and Competition in Retail Gasoline Markets: Empirical Evidence from Contract Changes in Southern California," *American Economic Review*, March 2004, pp. 317–328.

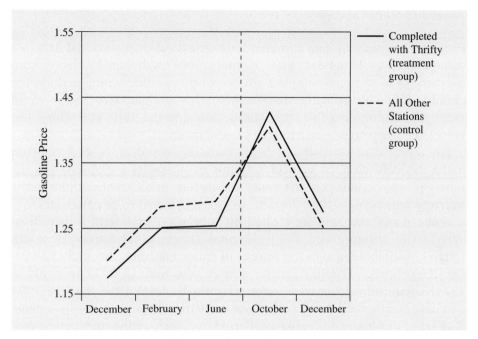

Figure 16.1 Treatment and Control Groups for Los Angeles

Gasoline prices in the treatment group were lower than the control group before the acquisition and higher afterward.

these results do indeed provide preliminary evidence that the elimination of an independent competitor raised market prices by 4 to 6 cents.[5]

16.2 Panel Data

Let's think for a second about the data in the ARCO gasoline price example of the previous section. Is it a time-series data set? Is it a cross-sectional data set? Well, the data set includes gasoline prices from five different months, so it clearly has a time-series component. However, the data set also includes prices for hundreds of individual gas stations for each month, so it clearly has a cross-sectional component. Because it has both time-series and cross-sectional dimensions, it's neither time-series nor cross-sectional; it's a *panel data set*!

5. Ibid., p. 323. Because Prof. Hastings had data from five time periods instead of just two, she didn't estimate her equation using the difference-in-differences model of this section. Instead, she used the fixed-effects estimation technique to be described in Section 16.2.

What Are Panel Data?

Panel (or *longitudinal*) data combine time-series and cross-sectional data in a very specific way. **Panel data** include observations on the same variables from the same cross sectional sample from two or more *different* time periods. For example, if you surveyed 200 students when they graduated from your school and then administered the same questionnaire to the same individuals five years later, you would have created a panel data set.

Not every data set that combines time-series and cross-sectional data meets this definition. In particular, if different variables are observed in the different time periods or if the data are drawn from different samples in the different time periods, then the data are not considered to be panel data.[6]

Some panel data sets are created by large-scale, long-term longitudinal surveys, for instance the 1979 National Longitudinal Survey of Youth (NLSY). Available through the Bureau of Labor Statistics, the NLSY has followed a cohort of 12,686 men and women who were 14 to 22 years old in 1979. These individuals were surveyed annually from 1979 through 1994 and have been surveyed every other year since then.[7] Quite obviously, a panel data set of this many individuals collected over such a long time period provides an extremely rich source of labor force data. Other well-known longitudinal surveys include the U.S. Panel Survey of Income Dynamics (PSID), the British Household Panel Data Survey, and the Canadian National Public Health Survey.

Why use panel data? As mentioned earlier, panel data certainly will increase sample sizes, but a second advantage of panel data is to provide insight into analytical questions that can't be answered by using time-series or cross-sectional data alone.[8] For example, panel data can help policymakers design programs aimed at reducing unemployment by allowing researchers to determine whether the same people are unemployed year after year or whether different

---

6. Instead, we refer to these data sets as "pooled cross sections across time." An example of pooled cross sections across time would be if you administered a survey to 200 graduating seniors from the class of 2009 and combined the results of this survey with the results of a survey of 200 graduating seniors from the class of 2004. The combined data set is not a panel data set because the sample changed as the time period changed. Equations can be estimated with pooled cross sections across time data by using a variant of the difference-in-differences estimator of the previous section. For more, see Jeff Wooldridge, *Introductory Econometrics* (Mason, OH: South-Western, 2009), pp. 445–455.

7. http://www.bls.gov/nls/nlsy79.htm.

8. For a more detailed analysis of the benefits of panel data, see Badi H. Baltagi, *Econometric Analysis of Panel Data* (Chichester, UK: John Wiley & Sons, 2008), pp. 6–11.

individuals are unemployed in different years.[9] A final advantage of panel data is that panel data often allow researchers to avoid omitted variable problems that otherwise would cause bias in cross-sectional studies. We'll come back to this topic soon.

There are four different kinds of variables that we encounter when we use panel data. First we have variables that can differ between individuals but don't change over time, such as gender, ethnicity, and race. Second, we have variables that change over time but are the same for all individuals in a given time period, such as the retail price index and the national unemployment rate. Third, we have variables that vary both over time and between individuals, such as income and marital status. Fourth, we have trend variables that vary in predictable ways such as an individual's age.

To estimate an equation using panel data, it's crucial to ensure that the data are in the right order. Regression packages like EViews and Stata need to be able to identify which observations belong to which time periods and which cross-sectional entities, and they rely on the order of the data to do so. Typically, panel data are grouped by starting with the first cross-section for all time periods, followed by the second cross-section for all time periods, and so on. This format is usually called the "long form" because it results in a fairly narrow but long data file. Not all programs use the long form, however, so it's important to check to make sure that the order of your data matches that required by your regression program.

For instance, let's look at how the long form would require that we order a panel data set that includes 50 states and two time periods. The first line of data would be for the first state and the first year, and the second line of data would be for the first state and the second year. So far, so good! However, the third line of data would be for the second state and the *first* year, the fourth line of data would be for the second state and the *second* year, and so on. For a complete example of state level panel data in the long form, see Table 16.1.

Finally, the use of panel data requires a slight expansion of our notation. In the past we've used the subscript i to indicate the observation number in a cross-sectional data set, so Y_i indicated Y for the ith cross-sectional observation. Similarly, we've used the subscript t to indicate the observation number in a time-series data set, so Y_t indicated Y for the tth time-series observation. In a panel data set, however, variables will have both a cross-sectional and time-series component, so we'll use *both* subscripts. As a result, Y_{it} indicates Y for the ith cross-sectional and tth time series observation. This notation expansion also applies to independent variables and error terms.

---

9. Peter Kennedy, *A Guide to Econometrics* (Malden, MA: Blackwell, 2008), p. 282.

The Fixed Effects Model

How can we estimate panel data equations? There are several alternative estimation procedures,[10] but most researchers use the *fixed effects model*. The **fixed effects model** is a method of estimating panel data equations that works by allowing each cross-sectional unit to have a different intercept:

$$Y_{it} = \beta_0 + \beta_1 X_{it} + \beta_2 D2_i + \cdots + \beta_N DN_i + v_{it} \qquad (16.4)$$

where D2 is an intercept dummy equal to 1 for the second cross-sectional entity and 0 otherwise and DN is an intercept dummy equal to 1 for the Nth cross-sectional entity and 0 otherwise. As you'd expect with a panel data set, Y, X, and v have two subscripts. Although there is only one X in Equation 16.4, the model can be easily generalized to any number of independent variables.

What we're doing is allowing each cross-section's intercept to differ. Because the βs are constant across units, in essence we have N parallel regression lines. Observations across time in each unit vary around a baseline level specific to that unit.

One major advantage of the fixed effects model is that it avoids bias due to omitted variables that don't change over time (like race or gender). Such time-invariant omitted variables often are referred to as unobserved heterogeneity or a fixed effect. To understand how the fixed effects model does this, let's take a look at what Equation 16.4 would look like with only two years worth of data:

$$Y_{it} = \beta_0 + \beta_1 X_{it} + \beta_2 D2_i + v_{it} \qquad (16.5)$$

Now let's think about the error term v_{it} for a second. If there are time-invariant omitted variables in Equation 16.5, then the unobserved effect of those omitted variables will be pushed into the error term, and v_{it} can be thought of as having two components, a classical error term (ϵ_{it}) and the unobserved impact of the time-invariant omitted variables (a_i).

$$v_{it} = \epsilon_{it} + a_i \qquad (16.6)$$

Although v and ε have two subscripts (as most panel data variables and error terms do), a_i has only the cross-sectional subscript because it's a function of omitted variables that don't change over time (such as race or gender). If we substitute Equation 16.6 into Equation 16.5, we get:

$$Y_{it} = \beta_0 + \beta_1 X_{it} + \beta_2 D2_i + \epsilon_{it} + a_i \qquad (16.7)$$

How does the fixed effects model get the a_i out of Equation 16.7? The key is to think about how much each observation of a variable differs from the

---

10. One of these alternatives, the *random effects model*, is described very briefly in Section 16.3, another, the *differencing model*, is the subject of Exercise 7.

average for that variable. We'll start by averaging Equation 16.7 over time for each observation i, producing:

$$\overline{Y}_i = \beta_0 + \beta_1\overline{X}_i + \beta_2 D2_i + \overline{\epsilon}_i + a_i \qquad (16.8)$$

where the bar over a variable indicates the mean of that variable with respect to time. Note that a_i, $\beta_2 D2_i$, and β_0 don't have bars over them because they're constant with respect to time.

If we now subtract Equation 16.8 from Equation 16.7, we get:

$$Y_{it} - \overline{Y}_i = \beta_1(X_{it} - \overline{X}_i) + \epsilon_{it} - \overline{\epsilon}_i \qquad (16.9)$$

Take another look at Equation 16.9. Note that a_i, $\beta_2 D2_i$, and β_0 are subtracted out because they're in both equations. We've therefore shown that estimating panel data with the fixed effects model does indeed drop the a_i out of the equation, and therefore the fixed effects model will not experience bias due to time-invariant omitted variables!

If we use the symbol θ to indicate a "demeaned variable" (a variable that has had its mean subtracted from it) and if we add β_0 to Equation 16.9 to avoid violating Classical Assumption II, we obtain:[11]

$$\theta Y_{it} = \beta_0 + \beta_1 \theta X_{it} + \theta \epsilon_{it} \qquad (16.10)$$

where: θY_{it} = the demeaned Y = $Y_{it} - \overline{Y}_i$
θX_{it} = the demeaned X = $X_{it} - \overline{X}_i$
$\theta \epsilon_{it}$ = the demeaned ϵ = $\epsilon_{it} - \overline{\epsilon}_i$

Though fixed effects models can be estimated by applying OLS to Equation 16.10, in actual practice many researchers use Equation 16.4. This shortcut method circumvents having to demean the data before running the regression. The two approaches produce mathematically identical results. Researchers who use Equation 16.4 to estimate panel data equations tend not to report estimates of all the intercept dummies (the fixed effects) in their research reports.

The fixed effects model has some drawbacks. Degrees of freedom for the fixed-effects model tend to be low because we lose one degree of freedom for cross-sectional observation because of the time-demeaning. In addition, any substantive explanatory variables that do not vary across time in each unit will be perfectly collinear with the fixed effects, so we can't include them in the model or estimate their coefficients. These drawbacks are minor when compared to the advantages of the fixed effects model, however, so our

---

11. Not all statistical packages will automatically add in β_0 when estimating fixed effects models, but Stata and EViews do. Researchers who use other software packages should check to make sure that a constant term is added in.

recommendation is that readers of this text should tend to use the fixed effects model whenever they estimate panel data.

An Example of Fixed Effects Estimation

Let's take a look at a simple application of the fixed effects model. Suppose that you're interested in the relationship between the death penalty and the murder rate, and you collect data on the murder rate in the 50 states.

If you were to estimate a cross-sectional model (Table 16.2) of the annual murder rate as a function of, say, the number of convicted murderers who were executed in the previous three years, you'd end up with:

$$\widehat{MURDER_i} = 6.20 + 0.90EXECUTIONS_i \qquad (16.11)$$
$$(.22)$$
$$t = 4.09$$
$$N = 50 \text{ (states in 1990)} \qquad \bar{R}^2 = .24$$

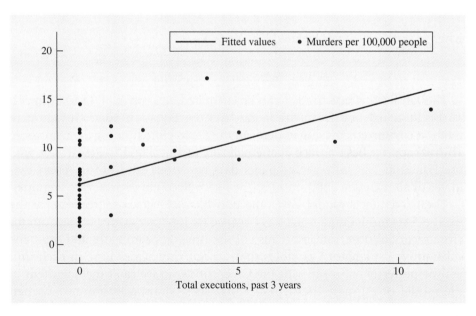

Figure 16.2 In a Single-Year Cross-Sectional Model, the Murder Rate Appears to Increase with Executions

In a cross-sectional model for 1990, the murder rate appears to increase with the number of executions, quite probably because of omitted variable bias.

where: MURDER$_i$ = the number of murders per 100,000 people
                        in the ith state in 1990
         EXECUTIONS$_i$ = the number of executions in the ith state in
                        1987–89

In a cross-sectional model for 1990, the murder rate appears to increase with
the number of executions, quite probably because of omitted variable bias.
This result implies that the more executions there are, the more murders there
are! Such a result is completely counter to our expectations. To make things
worse, it's not a fluke. If we collect data from another year, 1993, and estimate a
single-time-period regression on the 1993 data set, we also get a positive slope.

However, if we combine the two cross-sectional data sets to create the
panel data set in Table 16.1, we can estimate a fixed effects model, using the
"demeaned" format of Equation 16.10.

$$\widehat{\theta MURDER}_{it} = 7.15 + 0.35D93 - 0.10\theta EXECUTIONS_{it} \qquad (16.12)$$
$$ (0.16) \quad\ \ (0.04)$$
$$ t = 2.23 \quad\ -2.38$$
$$N = 50 \text{ (states in 1990)} \quad R^2 = .15$$

where: θMURDER$_{it}$ = the "demeaned" murder rate for the ith state
                        in the tth year
         θEXECUTIONS$_{it}$ = the "demeaned" number of executions in the
                        ith state in the three years before the tth year

As can be seen in Equation 16.12 and Figure 16.3, a fixed effects model
estimated on panel data from 1990 and 1993 results in a significant negative
estimated slope for the relationship between the murder rate and the number
of executions.[12] This example illustrates how the omitted variable bias aris-
ing from unobserved heterogeneity can be mitigated with panel data and the
fixed effects model.

Note that we included D93, a year fixed effect variable, in Equation
16.12. A year fixed effect captures any impact that altered the level of executions, across the country for a given year. For example, if the Supreme
Court declared a moratorium on a type of execution in that year, we would
see a decline in executions across states that used that type of execution

---

12. This example was kept simple to show the value of panel data and how to apply the fixed
effects model to panel data, so no inferences about the death penalty should be drawn from it.
The correct specification surely includes a number of other variables. In addition, the state of
Texas plays too large a role in determining the coefficients in this sample, in part because many
states didn't allow capital punishment between 1987 and 1993.

Table 16.1 Data for the Murder Example

OBS	STATE	YEAR	MRDRTE	EXEC	D93
1	AL	90	11.6	5	0
2	AL	93	11.6	2	1
3	AK	90	7.5	0	0
4	AK	93	9	0	1
5	AZ	90	7.7	0	0
6	AZ	93	8.6	3	1
7	AR	90	10.3	2	0
8	AR	93	10.2	2	1
9	CA	90	11.9	0	0
10	CA	93	13.1	2	1
11	CO	90	4.2	0	0
12	CO	93	5.8	0	1
13	CT	90	5.1	0	0
14	CT	93	6.3	0	1
15	DE	90	5	0	0
16	DE	93	5	0	1
17	DC	90	77.8	0	0
18	DC	93	78.5	0	1
19	FL	90	10.7	8	0
20	FL	93	8.9	7	1
21	GA	90	11.8	2	0
22	GA	93	11.4	3	1
23	HI	90	4	0	0
24	HI	93	3.8	0	1
25	ID	90	2.7	0	0
26	ID	93	2.9	0	1
27	IL	90	10.3	0	0
28	IL	93	11.4	0	1
29	IN	90	6.2	0	0
30	IN	93	7.5	0	1
31	IA	90	1.9	0	0
32	IA	93	2.3	0	1
33	KS	90	4	0	0
34	KS	93	6.4	0	1
35	KY	90	7.2	0	0
36	KY	93	6.6	0	1
37	LA	90	17.2	4	0
38	LA	93	20.3	2	1
39	ME	90	2.4	0	0
40	ME	93	1.6	0	1
41	MD	90	11.5	0	0
42	MD	93	12.7	0	1
43	MA	90	4	0	0
44	MA	93	3.9	0	1

(continued)

Table 16.1 (*continued*)

OBS	STATE	YEAR	MRDRTE	EXEC	D93
45	MI	90	10.4	0	0
46	MI	93	9.8	0	1
47	MN	90	2.7	0	0
48	MN	93	3.4	0	1
49	MS	90	12.2	1	0
50	MS	93	13.5	0	1
51	MO	90	8.8	5	0
52	MO	93	11.3	6	1
53	MT	90	4.9	0	0
54	MT	93	3	0	1
55	NE	90	2.7	0	0
56	NE	93	3.9	0	1
57	NV	90	9.7	3	0
58	NV	93	10.4	0	1
59	NH	90	1.9	0	0
60	NH	93	2	0	1
61	NJ	90	5.6	0	0
62	NJ	93	5.3	0	1
63	NM	90	9.2	0	0
64	NM	93	8	0	1
65	NY	90	14.5	0	0
66	NY	93	13.3	0	1
67	NC	90	10.7	0	0
68	NC	93	11.3	2	1
69	ND	90	0.8	0	0
70	ND	93	1.7	0	1
71	OH	90	6.1	0	0
72	OH	93	6	0	1
73	OK	90	8	1	0
74	OK	93	8.4	2	1
75	OR	90	3.8	0	0
76	OR	93	4.6	0	1
77	PA	90	6.7	0	0
78	PA	93	6.8	0	1
79	RI	90	4.8	0	0
80	RI	93	3.9	0	1
81	SC	90	11.2	1	0
82	SC	93	10.3	1	1
83	SD	90	2	0	0
84	SD	93	3.4	0	1
85	TN	90	10.5	0	0
86	TN	93	10.2	0	1
87	TX	90	14.1	11	0
88	TX	93	11.9	34	1

(*continued*)

Table 16.1 (*continued*)

OBS	STATE	YEAR	MRDRTE	EXEC	D93
89	UT	90	3	1	0
90	UT	93	3.1	1	1
91	VT	90	2.3	0	0
92	VT	93	3.6	0	1
93	VA	90	8.8	3	0
94	VA	93	8.3	11	1
95	WA	90	4.9	0	0
96	WA	93	5.2	1	1
97	WV	90	5.7	0	0
98	WV	93	6.9	0	1
99	WI	90	4.6	0	0
100	WI	93	4.4	0	1
101	WY	90	4.9	0	0
102	WY	93	3.4	1	1

Source: U.S. Department of Justice, FBI *Annual*, www.deathpenaltyinfo.org/execution

Datafile = MURDER16

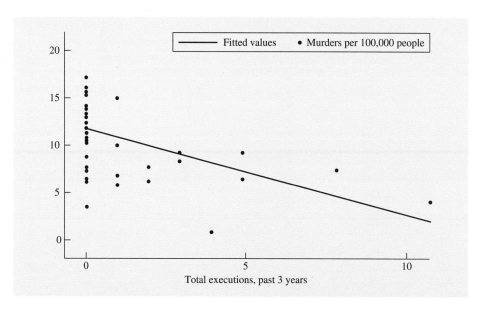

Figure 16.3 In a Panel Data Model, the Murder Rate Decreases with Executions

If we use the fixed effects model to estimate panel data from 1990 and 1993, the murder rate decreases with the number of executions, as you'd expect.

during the year for reasons unrelated to the relation between murders and executions with each state.[13]

In our example, we used only two time periods, but the fixed effects model can be extended to many more time periods. Fixed effects estimation is a standard statistical routine in most econometric software packages making it particularly accessible for researchers. Notice that we report an intercept. Depending upon which software program you use to estimate the fixed effects model, you may or may not be provided with an intercept estimate.

(16.3) Fixed versus Random Effects

The fixed effects model does a good job of estimating panel data equations, and it also helps avoid omitted variable bias due to unobservable heterogeneity. As a result, the fixed effects model is the panel data estimation procedure that we recommend to most readers of this text.

However, if you read the panel data literature, you'll find that many experienced researchers use an advanced panel data method called the *random effects model*. Although we don't suggest that beginning researchers use the random effects model, we think that it's important to have a general understanding of that model.

The Random Effects Model

An alternative to the fixed effects model is called the random effects model. While the fixed effects model is based on the assumption that each cross-sectional unit has its own intercept, the **random effects model** is based on the assumption that the intercept for each cross-sectional unit is drawn from a distribution that is centered around a mean intercept. Thus each intercept is a random draw from an "intercept distribution" and therefore is independent of the error term for any particular observation.

The random effects model has several clear advantages over the fixed effects model. In particular, a random effects model will have quite a few more degrees of freedom than a fixed effects model, because rather than estimating an intercept for virtually every cross-sectional unit, all we need to do is to estimate the parameters that describe the distribution of the intercepts. Another nice property is that you can estimate coefficients for explanatory variables that are constant over time (like race or gender). However, the random effects estimator has

---

13. With thanks to Doug Steigerwald.

a major disadvantage in that it requires us to assume that a_i is uncorrelated with the independent variables, the Xs, if we're going to avoid omitted variable bias.

Choosing Between Fixed and Random Effects

How do researchers decide whether to use the fixed effects model or the random effects model? One key is the nature of the relationship between a_i and the Xs. If they're likely to be correlated, then it makes sense to use the fixed effects model, as that sweeps away the a_i and the potential omitted variable bias.[14]

Many researchers use the *Hausman test*, which is well beyond the scope of this text, to see whether there is correlation between a_i and X. Essentially, this procedure tests to see whether the regression coefficients under the fixed effects and random effects models are statistically different from each other.[15] If they are different, then the fixed effects model is preferred even though it uses up many more degrees of freedom. If the coefficients aren't different, then researchers either use the random effects model (in order to conserve degrees of freedom) or provide estimates of both the fixed effects and random effects models.

(16.4) Summary

1. Random assignment experiments are considered the gold standard when it comes to establishing a causal effect from treatment to outcome. A randomly chosen treatment group is exposed to a treatment while a control group isn't, and we test to see if the outcome is significantly different between the two groups. Unfortunately, such experiments aren't feasible in many areas of economics.

2. Natural experiments can be used to provide evidence of causality in economics if a naturally occurring event (or a policy change) can be found that mimics a random assignment treatment. If the event causes the mean of the outcome for the treatment group to change substantially more than the mean of the outcome for the control group does, then we have evidence that the treatment was a causal factor in the outcome.

3. Equations involving data from natural experiments can be estimated with a difference-in-differences model, which compares the difference

---

14. For an excellent explanation of the choice between fixed and random effects, see Peter Kennedy, *A Guide to Econometrics* (Malden, MA: Blackwell, 2008), pp. 284–292.

15. For an illustration of the Hausman test, see E. DiCioccio and P. Wunnava, "Working and Educated Women: Culprits of a European Kinder-Crisis," *Eastern Economic Journal*, April 2008, pp. 213–222.

between the change in the treatment group and the change in the control group

4. Panel data (also called longitudinal data) combine time-series and cross-sectional data by including observations on the same variables from the same cross-sectional sample from two or more time periods. Panel data often are produced by large, multi-year survey projects and provide a rich source of material for econometric analysis.

5. Equations involving panel data can be estimated using the fixed effects model and a more advanced technique, the random effects model.

EXERCISES

(The answer to Exercise 2 is in Appendix A.)

1. Write the meaning of each of the following terms without referring to the book (or your notes), and then compare your definition with the version in the text for each.
   a. treatment group
   b. control group
   c. differences estimator
   d. difference in differences
   e. unobserved heterogeneity
   f. the Hawthorne effect
   g. panel data
   h. the fixed effects model
   i. the random effects model

2. Ten years ago, the town of Easton decided to increase its annual spending on education so that its high school graduates would be able to earn higher wages. Now Easton has asked you to evaluate the effectiveness of the spending increase. Their data show that before the spending increase, the average annual salary of recent high school graduates was $25,000 and that now that average salary has risen to $28,500. Fortunately for your analysis, a neighboring community (Allentown) did not change its annual spending on education. Ten years ago, recent Allentown high school graduates earned an average of $22,500, and now that average is $23,750.
   a. Use a difference-in-differences estimator to determine whether Easton's spending increase caused the wages of their high school graduates to increase.

b. What underlying assumption do you have to make in order for your estimate to be valid? What might cause your underlying assumption to be invalid?

c. This data set contains only two observations. Even if the underlying assumption in part b is met, how much confidence can you have in conclusions based on two observations?

3. The discussion of random assignment experiments in Section 16.1 includes models both with (Equation 16.2) and without (Equation 16.1) two additional observable factors (X_1 and X_2). In contrast, the discussion of natural experiments in Section 16.1 jumped immediately to Equation 16.3 below (which includes these factors) without discussing an equation similar to Equation 16.1.

$$\Delta \text{OUTCOME}_i = \beta_0 + \beta_1 \text{TREATMENT}_i + \beta_2 X_{1i} + \beta_3 X_{2i} + \epsilon_i \quad (16.3)$$

Was this a mistake? What reasons are there for thinking that a natural experiment is more likely to benefit from the inclusion of additional observable factors than is a random assignment experiment? Explain.

4. In 2003, ten states increased the taxes they placed on cigarettes. Because taxes increase the price of cigarettes, we'd expect that a tax increase would reduce the consumption of cigarettes. In Table 16.2, we present cross-sections of state level data on cigarette consumption for the years 2000 and 2006. Forty-five states plus the District of Columbia are listed here with those states that did not have a tax increase in 2003 listed first.

a. Would you consider this to be a random assignment experiment data set, a natural experiment data set, or a panel data set? Explain.

b. Depending on your answer to part a, use the appropriate estimation technique to determine the impact of the cigarette tax increase on the consumption of cigarettes.

c. Do these results conform with your expectations? If they don't, what problems do you see with this research design?

5. Let's take another look at Equation 16.6:

$$v_{it} = \epsilon_{it} + a_i \quad (16.6)$$

a. What is the real-world meaning of a_i?

b. Why does a have one subscript while v and ϵ have two?

c. Why do we need to remove a_i? (*Hint:* What assumption are we violating if we don't?)

Table 16.2 Cigarette Consumption by State

State	Tax	2000	2006
Alabama	0	25.3	23.2
Arizona	0	18.6	18.2
Alaska	0	25	24
Arkansas	0	25.2	23.7
Colorado	0	20.1	17.9
Connecticut	0	20	17
Delaware	0	23	21.7
Hawaii	0	19.7	17.5
Illinois	0	22.3	20.5
Indiana	0	27	24.1
Iowa	0	23.3	21.4
Kentucky	0	30.5	28.5
Louisiana	0	24.1	23.4
Maine	0	23.8	20.9
Maryland	0	20.6	17.7
Massachusetts	0	20	17.8
Michigan	0	24.2	22.4
Minnesota	0	19.8	18.3
Montana	0	18.9	18.9
Nebraska	0	21.4	18.7
New Hampshire	0	25.4	18.7
New Jersey	0	21	18
New York	0	21.6	18.2
North Carolina	0	26.1	22.1
Ohio	0	26.3	22.4
Oklahoma	0	23.3	25.1
Oregon	0	20.8	18.5
Pennsylvania	0	24.3	21.5
Rhode Island	0	23.5	19.2
Tennessee	0	25.7	22.6
Texas	0	22	17.9
Utah	0	12.9	9.8
Virginia	0	21.5	19.3
Washington	0	20.7	17.1
Wisconsin	0	24.1	20.8
Washington, DC	1	20.9	17.9
Georgia	1	23.6	19.9
Idaho	1	22.4	16.8
Kansas	1	21.1	20
Nevada	1	29.1	22.2
New Mexico	1	23.6	20.1
South Dakota	1	22	20.3
Vermont	1	21.5	18
West Virginia	1	26.1	25.7
Wyoming	1	23.8	21.6

6. Suppose that you're interested in the effect of price on the demand for a "salon" haircut and that you collect the following data for four U.S. cities for 2003:

Location	Year	Average Price	Per Capita Quantity
New York	2003	$75	2
Boston	2003	$50	1
Washington, DC	2003	$60	1.5
Philadelphia	2003	$55	.8

and for 2008:

Location	Year	Average Price	Per Capita Quantity
New York	2008	$85	1.8
Boston	2008	$48	1.1
Washington, DC	2008	$65	1.4
Philadelphia	2008	$60	.7

a. Estimate a cross-sectional OLS regression of per capita quantity as a function of average price for 2003. Is the slope positive or negative? Does that meet your expectations?

b. Now estimate a cross-sectional regression on the data for 2008. How is the result different?

c. Now estimate a fixed effects model on the combined data and compare your results with parts a and b.

d. What's your conclusion? Which model offers the best approach to answering your question?

7. A simple alternative to the fixed effects model is called the **differencing model**, in which all the variables and the error term are expressed as differences. For a panel data set with two time periods, the estimating equation would be:

$$\Delta Y_i = \beta_0 + \beta_1 \Delta X_i + \Delta \epsilon_i$$

where: $\Delta Y_i = Y_{2i} - Y_{1i}$, $\Delta X_i = X_{2i} - X_{1i}$, and $\Delta \epsilon_i = \epsilon_{2i} - \epsilon_{1i}$.

a. Using the data in Exercise 6, estimate a differencing model for the price of salon haircuts.

b. Now compare your answer in part a to your answer for part c of Exercise 6. What do you notice? What does this tell you about the relationship between the differencing model and the fixed effects model when there are exactly two time periods?

c. Think about the error term in the differencing model. Which of the Classical Assumptions does $\Delta \epsilon_i$ seem likely to violate? How might you deal with this problem?

17 Statistical Principles

This chapter[*] reviews the basic statistical principles that underlie the specification and estimation of econometric models. The first two sections discuss how our interpretation of data should recognize that data are usually samples and that different samples will yield somewhat different data. The third section explains how a sample can be used to draw inferences about the population that it came from.

To make the discussion very concrete, we will focus on the data shown in Table 17.1 (page 555) on the 2004 market prices and square footage of 22 homes in Diamond Bar, California, a suburb of Los Angeles. What can we infer from these data about the average price of Diamond Bar homes and the relationship (if any) between price and size? Is the average price of all Diamond Bar homes about $400,000? This chapter will answer those questions.

17.1 Probability Distributions

In order to draw valid statistical inferences from a data set, we need to think about where the data come from—the sample of households used in a study of consumer borrowing, the sample of businesses used in a study of investment spending, the sample of stocks used in a study of the stock market, and the sample of houses used in a study of a housing market. In this section, we

---

[*] Written by Gary Smith of Pomona College. Gary is also the author of *Introduction to Statistical Reasoning* (New York, McGraw-Hill, 1998).

will see how probabilities can be used to quantify uncertainty and to help us explain and interpret empirical data by considering the probability of obtaining samples with various characteristics.

Probability

When we say that a flipped coin has a 0.5 probability of landing with its heads side up, we mean that if this coin were to be flipped an interminable number of times (the "long run"), we anticipate that it will come up heads about half the time. More generally, if an event has a probability P of occurring, then the fraction of the times that it occurs in the long run will be very close to P. Obviously, a probability cannot be negative or larger than one.

A **random variable** X is a variable whose numerical value is determined by chance, the outcome of a random phenomenon.[1] A *discrete random variable* has a countable number of possible values, such as 0, 1, and 2; in the next section, we will consider *continuous random variables*, such as time and distance, which can take on any value in an interval. All of the discrete random variables that we will examine have a finite number of outcomes, though there are other discrete variables that have an infinite number of countable values. For example, if X is equal to the number of times that a coin will be flipped before heads is obtained, there is no upper limit on the value of X; nonetheless, X is a discrete variable because its values are obtained by counting. Measures of time and distance, in contrast, are continuous variables; between any two possible values, such as 4.7 and 4.8, there are other possible values, such as 4.75 and 4.76.

A **probability distribution** $P[X_i]$ for a discrete random variable X assigns probabilities to the possible values X_1, X_2, and so on. For example, when a fair six-sided die is rolled, there are six equally likely outcomes, each with a 1/6 probability of occurring. Figure 17.1 shows this probability distribution. Probability distributions are scaled so that the total area inside the rectangles is equal to 1.

For housing data, the random variable might be market price and the probability distribution would state the probability that we select a house with a specified market price. For example, if there are 100,000 houses in

---

1. To be mathematically precise, statisticians often use uppercase and lowercase notation to distinguish between a random variable, which can take on different values, and the actual values that happen to occur. Uppercase notation is used throughout this book for simplicity and convenience.

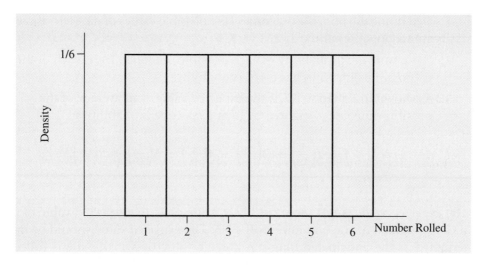

Figure 17.1 Probability Distribution for a Six-Sided Die

the geographic area that we are studying and 2,000 of these houses have market prices of \$400,000, then there is a 0.02 probability of picking a \$400,000 house: P[\$400,000] = 2,000/100,000 = 0.02.

Mean, Variance, and Standard Deviation

Sometimes, a few simple numbers can summarize effectively the important characteristics of a probability distribution. The **expected value** (or **mean**) of a discrete random variable X is a weighted average of all possible values of X, using the probability of each X value as weights:

$$\mu = E[X] = \sum_i X_i P[X_i] \qquad (17.1)$$

The Greek symbol μ (pronounced "mew") and the notation E[X] denote the expected value of the random variable X. The Greek letter Σ (uppercase "sigma") indicates that the values of X_i should be added up. In this case, that means that we multiply each possible value of the random variable by its associated probability and then add up these products: $X_i P[X_i]$.

Suppose, for example, that X is equal to the number obtained when a single six-sided die is rolled and we want to find the expected value of X.

1. Determine the possible outcomes (the possible values of X). Here, there are six possible values: 1, 2, 3, 4, 5, 6.

2. Determine the probability of each possible outcome. Here, each of the six possible outcomes has a 1/6 probability.

3. As shown in Equation 17.1, the expected value is an average of the possible outcomes weighted by their respective probabilities:

$$\mu = 1\left(\frac{1}{6}\right) + 2\left(\frac{1}{6}\right) + 3\left(\frac{1}{6}\right) + 4\left(\frac{1}{6}\right) + 5\left(\frac{1}{6}\right) + 6\left(\frac{1}{6}\right)$$
$$= 3.5$$

The expected value is not the most likely value of X: the expected value of a dice roll is 3.5, but you will never roll a 3.5. The expected value should be interpreted as the anticipated long-run average value of X if this die is rolled over and over and over. If, in accord with their probabilities, the six sides come up equally often, the average value of X will be 3.5.

Pascal and other early probability theorists used probabilities to calculate the expected value of various games of chance and determine which were the most profitable. They assumed that a rational person would choose the course of action with the highest expected value. This expected-value criterion is appealing for gambles that are repeated over and over. It makes good sense to look at the long-run average when there is a long run to average over. Casinos, state lotteries, and insurance companies are very interested in the expected values on the repetitive gambles they offer, because anything with a negative expected value will almost certainly be unprofitable in the long run.

However, an expected-value criterion is often inappropriate. State lotteries have a positive expected value for the state and, because their gain is our loss, a negative expected value for people who buy lottery tickets. Those who buy lottery tickets are not maximizing expected value. Insurance policies give insurance companies a positive expected value and insurance buyers a negative expected value. People who buy insurance are not maximizing expected value either. Diversified investments provide yet another example. An expected-value maximizer should invest everything in the single asset with the highest expected value. Individuals and financial institutions that hold dozens or thousands of assets must not be maximizing expected value.

The primary inadequacy of expected-value maximization is that it neglects risk—how certain or uncertain a situation is. An expected value maximizer considers a sure $1 million and a 1-percent chance at $100 million equally attractive because each has an expected value of $1 million. If these alternatives were offered over and over, there would be little difference in the long run because the payoffs from each would almost certainly average close to

$1 million per play. But if you get only one chance at this game, the outcome may differ considerably from its expected value, a difference ignored by an expected-value calculation. Much of the uncertainty we face is unique, not repetitive, and the possible divergence between the actual outcome and its expected value is properly described as risk.

To measure the extent to which the outcomes may differ from the expected value, we can use the **variance** of a discrete random variable X, which is a weighted average, for all possible values of X, of the squared difference between X and its expected value, using the probability of each X value as weights:

$$\sigma^2 = E[(X - \mu)^2] = \sum_i (X_i - \mu)^2 P[X_i] \qquad (17.2)$$

The **standard deviation** σ is the square root of the variance.

The interpretation of the variance is best understood by dissecting Equation 17.2. The variance is the expected value of $(X - \mu)^2$, that is, the anticipated long-run average value of the squared deviations of the possible values of X from its expected value μ.

The variance and standard deviation are probability-weighted measures of the dispersion of the possible outcomes about their expected value. The standard deviation is usually easier to interpret than the variance because it has the same units (for example, dollars) as X and μ, while the units for the variance are squared (for example, dollars squared). A compact probability distribution has a low standard deviation; a spread-out probability distribution has a high standard deviation.

Consider again a random variable X equal to the number obtained when a six-sided die is rolled:

1. Determine the expected value μ, here 3.5.
2. For each possible value of X, determine the size of the squared deviation from the expected value μ:

Die Outcome X_i	Deviation $X_i - \mu$	Squared Deviation $(X_i - \mu)^2$
1	−2.5	6.25
2	−1.5	2.25
3	−0.5	0.25
4	0.5	0.25
5	1.5	2.25
6	2.5	6.25

3. As shown in Equation 17.2, the variance is equal to the sum of the squared deviations of X_i from μ, multiplied by their respective probabilities:

$$\sigma^2 = 6.25\left(\frac{1}{6}\right) + 2.25\left(\frac{1}{6}\right) + \cdots + 6.25\left(\frac{1}{6}\right)$$
$$= 2.9167$$

4. The standard deviation is equal to the square root of the variance; here,

$$\sigma = \sqrt{2.9167} = 1.71$$

Continuous Random Variables

Our examples to this point have involved discrete random variables, for which we can count the number of possible outcomes. The coin can be heads or tails; the die can be 1, 2, 3, 4, 5, or 6. Other random variables can take on a continuum of values. For these *continuous* random variables, the outcome can be any value in a given interval.

For example, Figure 17.2 shows a spinner for randomly selecting a point on a circle. We can imagine that this is a clean, well-balanced device in which each point on the circle is equally likely to be picked. How many possible outcomes are there? How many points are there on the circle? In theory, there are an uncountable infinity of points in that between any two points on the circle, there are still more points.

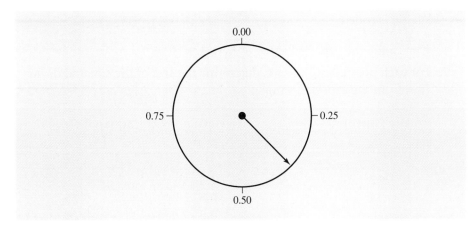

Figure 17.2 Pick a Number, Any Number

Weight, height, and time are other examples of continuous variables. Many variables are essentially continuous even though they might in practice be measured only in whole units, such as dollars, miles, or years. Even though we might say that Sarah Cunningham is 19 years old, a person's age can, in theory, be specified with infinite precision. Instead of saying that she is 19 or 20, we could say that she is 19 and a half, or 19 years and 7 months, or 19 years, 220 days, and 10 hours. With continuous variables, we can specify finer and finer gradations within any interval. Many economic variables (such as GDP, interest rates, and prices) are continuous, but some (such as the number of bedrooms in a house, number of people in a family, and number of stocks in a portfolio) are discrete.

How can we specify probabilities when there are an uncountable number of possible outcomes? In Figure 17.2, each point on the circle is equally likely and a point surely will be selected, but if we give each point a positive probability, the sum of this uncountable number of probabilities will be infinity, not one. Mathematicians handle this vexing situation of an uncountable number of possible outcomes by assigning probabilities to *intervals* of outcomes, rather than to individual outcomes. For example, the probability that the spinner will stop between 0.25 and 0.50 is 1/4.

We can display these interval probabilities by using a continuous **probability density curve**, as in Figure 17.3, in which the probability that the

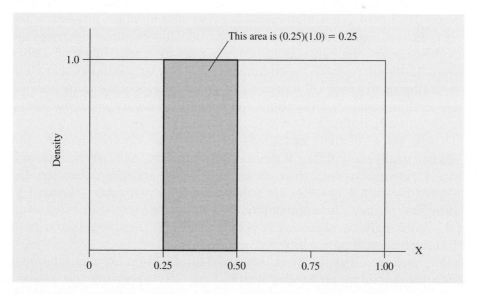

Figure 17.3 A Continuous Probability Distribution for the Spinner

outcome is in a specified interval is given by the corresponding area under the curve. The shaded area shows the probability that the spinner will stop between 0.25 and 0.50. This rectangular area is (base)(height) = (0.25)(1.0) = 1/4. What is the probability that the spinner will stop between 0 and 1? This probability is the entire area under the curve: (base)(height) = (1)(1.0) = 1. In fact, the height of the probability density curve, 1.0, was derived from the requirement that the total probability must be 1. If the numbers on our spinner went from 0 to 12, like a clock, the height of the probability density curve would have to be 1/12 for the total area to be 1: (base)(height) = (12)(1/12) = 1.

The density curve for a continuous random variable is analogous to the probability distribution for a discrete random variable, and the population mean and the standard deviation have the same interpretation. The population mean is the anticipated long-run average value of the outcomes if the experiment is repeated a great many times; the standard deviation measures the extent to which the outcomes are likely to differ from the mean. With a symmetrical density function, the mean is in the center—at 0.50 in Figure 17.3, for example. More generally, however, the formulas for the mean and standard deviation of a continuous random variable involve integrals and can be difficult to calculate.

Standardized Variables

Many random variables are the cumulative result of a sequence of random events. For instance, a random variable giving the sum of the numbers when eight dice are rolled can be viewed as the cumulative result of eight separate random events—the eight dice rolls. The percentage change in a stock's price over a 12-month period is the cumulative result of a large number of random events during that interval. A person's height at 11 years of age is the cumulative result of a great many random events, some hereditary and some having to do with diet, health, and exercise.

These three different examples—dice rolls, stock price changes, and height—involve very different units of measurement: number, percent, and inches. However, in the eighteenth and nineteenth centuries, researchers discovered that when variables are *standardized*, in a particular way that will soon be explained, their probability distributions are often virtually identical! This remarkable similarity is perhaps the most important discovery in the long history of probability and statistics.

We have seen that the mean and standard deviation are two important tools for describing probability distributions. One appealing way to standardize variables is to transform them so that they have the same mean and the same standard deviation. This reshaping is easily done in the statistical beauty parlor. To standardize a random variable X, we subtract its mean μ and then divide by its standard deviation σ:

$$Z = \frac{X - \mu}{\sigma} \qquad\qquad (17.3)$$

No matter what the initial units of X, the **standardized random variable Z** has a mean of 0 and a standard deviation of 1.

The standardized variable Z measures how many standard deviations X is above or below its mean. If X is equal to its mean, Z is equal to 0. If X is one standard deviation above its mean, Z is equal to 1. If X is two standard deviations below its mean, Z is equal to -2.

For example, if we look at the height of a randomly selected U.S. woman between the ages of 25 and 34, we can consider this height to be a random variable X drawn from a population with a mean of 66 inches and a standard deviation of 2.5 inches. Here are the standardized Z-values corresponding to five different values of X:

X (inches)	Z = (X − 66)/2.5 (standard deviations)
61.0	−2
63.5	−1
66.0	0
68.5	+1
71.0	+2

Instead of saying that a woman is 71 inches tall (which is useful for some purposes, such as clothing sizes), we can say that her height is two standard deviations above the mean (which is useful for other purposes, such as comparing her height with the heights of other women).

Another reason for standardizing variables is that it is difficult to compare the shapes of distributions when they have different means and/or standard deviations. Figure 17.1 showed the probability distribution for a single six-sided die. Now suppose that we want to compare the three probability distributions for random variables equal to the sum of the numbers obtained when rolling 2, 10, and 100 standard six-sided dice. If we work with the nonstandardized variable X, each probability distribution has a different mean and standard deviation. With one dice roll, the mean is 3.5 and the standard deviation is 1.7; with 100 dice rolls, the mean is 350 and the standard deviation is 17. By converting these variables to standardized Z values that have the same mean (0) and the same standard deviation (1), we

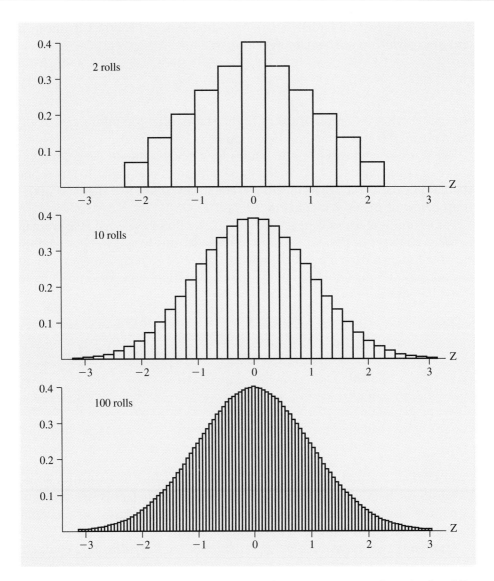

Figure 17.4 Probability Distribution for Six-Sided Dice, Using Standardized Z

can focus our attention on the shapes of these probability distributions without being distracted by their location and spread. The results of this standardization are given in Figure 17.4, which shows that as the number of dice increases, the probability distribution becomes increasingly shaped like a bell.

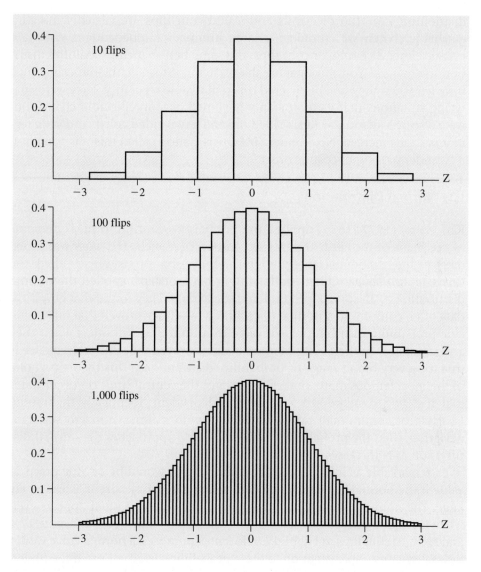

Figure 17.5 Probability Distribution for Fair Coin Flips, Using Standardized Z

Figure 17.5 shows the same pattern with 10, 100, and 1,000 coin flips: the probability distribution becomes increasingly bell-shaped as the number of coins increases. (Because the number of equally likely outcomes is larger with a die than with a coin, fewer trials are needed for dice rolls to become bell-shaped.) Comparing Figures 17.4 and 17.5, the standardized probability distributions for 100 dice rolls and 1,000 coin flips are virtually indistinguishable. When we cumulate a large number of independent uncertain events, either dice rolls or coin flips, the same bell-shaped probability distribution emerges! You can imagine the excitement that mathematicians must have felt when they first discovered this remarkable regularity. They were analyzing situations that were not only governed by unpredictable chance but were also very dissimilar (a six-sided die and a two-sided coin), and yet a regular pattern emerged. No wonder Sir Francis Galton called this phenomenon a "wonderful form of cosmic order."

The Normal Distribution

Karl Gauss (1777–1855) applied the normal distribution to measurements of the shape of the earth and the movements of planets. His work was so extensive and influential that the normal distribution is often called the *Gaussian distribution*. Others, following in his footsteps, applied the normal distribution to all sorts of physical and social data. They found that empirical data often conform to a normal distribution, and they proved that many specific probability distributions converge to a normal distribution when they are cumulated. In the 1930s, mathematicians proved that this convergence is true for a very broad range of probability distributions. This theorem is one of the most famous mathematical theorems: the **central limit theorem** states that if Z is a standardized sum of N independent, identically distributed (discrete or continuous) random variables with a finite, nonzero standard deviation, then the probability distribution of Z approaches the normal distribution as N increases.

As remarkable as it is, the central limit theorem would be of little practical value if the normal curve emerged only when the sample size N is extremely large. The normal distribution is important because it so often appears even when N is quite small. Look again at the case of N = 2 dice rolls in Figure 17.4 and N = 10 coin flips in Figure 17.5; for most purposes, a normal curve would be a satisfactory approximation to these probability distributions. If the underlying distribution is reasonably smooth and symmetrical (as with dice rolls and coin flips) the approach to a normal curve is very rapid and values of N larger than 20 or 30 are sufficient for the normal distribution to provide an acceptable approximation. A very asymmetrical distribution, such as a 0.99 probability of success and 0.01 probability of failure, requires a much larger number of trials.

The central limit theorem is remarkably robust in that even if its assumptions aren't exactly true, the normal distribution is still a pretty good approximation. A normal distribution appears when we examine the weights of humans, dogs, and tomatoes. The lengths of thumbs, widths of shoulders, and breadths of skulls are all normally distributed. Scores on IQ, SAT, and GRE tests are normally distributed. So are the number of kernels on ears of corn, ridges on scallop shells, hairs on cats, and leaves on trees. If some phenomenon is the cumulative result of a great many separate influences, then the normal distribution may be a very useful approximation.

This is why the normal distribution is so popular and the central limit theorem so celebrated. However, don't be lulled into thinking that probabilities always follow the normal curve. These examples are approximately, but not perfectly, normal and there are many phenomena whose probability distributions are not normal at all. Our purpose is not to persuade you that there is only one probability distribution, but to explain why many phenomena are well described by the normal distribution.

The density curve for the normal distribution is graphed in Figure 17.6. The probability that the value of Z will be in a specified interval is given by the corresponding area under this curve. However, there is no simple formula for computing areas under a normal curve. These areas can be determined from complex numerical procedures, but nobody wants to do these computations every time a normal probability is needed. Instead, they consult statistical software or a table, such as Table B-7 in Appendix B, that shows the normal probabilities for hundreds of values of Z.

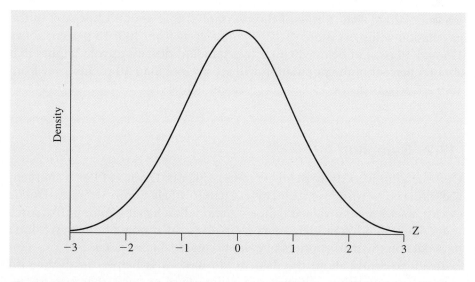

Figure 17.6 The Normal Distribution

The following three rules of thumb can help us estimate probabilities for normally distributed random variables without consulting Table B-7:

$$P[-1 < Z < 1] = 0.6826$$
$$P[-2 < Z < 2] = 0.9544$$
$$P[-3 < Z < 3] = 0.9973$$

A normally distributed random variable has about a 68 percent (roughly two-thirds) chance of being within one standard deviation of its mean, a 95 percent chance of being within two standard deviations of its mean, and better than a 99.7 percent chance of being within three standard deviations. Turning these around, a normally distributed random variable has less than a 0.3 percent chance of being more than three standard deviations from its mean, roughly a 5 percent chance of being more than two standard deviations from its mean, and a 32 percent chance of being more than one standard deviation from its mean.

For example, there are a number of tests designed to measure a person's IQ (intelligence quotient), reflecting an accurate memory and the ability to reason logically and clearly. Because an individual's score on an IQ test depends on a very large number of hereditary and environmental factors, the central limit theorem explains why IQ scores are approximately normally distributed. One of the most widely used tests today is the Wechsler Adult Intelligence Scale, which has a mean IQ of 100 and a standard deviation of 15. About half the people tested score above 100; half score below 100. Our one-standard-deviation rule of thumb implies that about 32 percent of the population will score more than 15 points away from 100; 16 percent above 115 and 16 percent below 85. Our two-standard-deviations rule implies that about 5 percent of the population will score more than 30 points away from 100: 2.5 percent above 130 and 2.5 percent below 70.

17.2 Sampling

Our intention is to study the real estate market in Diamond Bar, a southern California city with approximately 20,000 single-family homes. Unlike stocks, houses are not valued daily on national exchanges. And, unlike some states, the California property tax system does not appraise houses. We don't have data on the market prices of every home in Diamond Bar.

To think clearly about the data we do have, it is helpful to distinguish between a **population**, which is the entire group of items that interests us, and a **sample**, which is the part of this population that we actually observe.

Statistical inference involves using the sample to draw conclusions about the characteristics of the population from which the sample came. In a medical experiment, for example, the population consists of all persons who might use this medication; the sample is the group of people used to test the medication; a possible statistical inference is that people who take the medication tend, on average, to live longer than people who don't. In our housing study, the population is all single-family homes in Diamond Bar; the sample is the 22 houses in Table 17.1; a possible statistical inference is that housing prices depend on the size of the house.

We use samples to draw inferences about a population because it is often impractical to scrutinize the entire population. If we burn every lightbulb that a manufacturer produces to see how long each bulb lasts, all we will have is a large electricity bill and a lot of burned-out lightbulbs. Many tests

Table 17.1 A Sample of 22 Single-Family Homes in Diamond Bar, California, Summer 2004

Price ($)	Square Feet
425,000	1349
451,500	1807
508,560	1651
448,050	1293
500,580	1745
524,160	1900
500,580	1759
399,330	1740
442,020	1950
537,660	1771
515,100	2078
589,000	2268
696,000	2400
540,750	2050
659,200	2267
492,450	1986
567,047	2950
684,950	2712
668,470	2799
733,360	2933
775,590	3203
788,888	2988

Datafile = STATS17

are not this destructive, but are simply too expensive to apply to the entire population. Instead, we sample. A lightbulb manufacturer tests a sample of its bulbs. Housing studies examine a sample of houses because it is too expensive to collect data on every house.

Selection Bias

Any sample that differs systematically from the population that it is intended to represent is called a *biased sample*. Because a biased sample is unrepresentative of the population, it gives a distorted picture of the population and may lead to unwarranted conclusions. One of the most common causes of biased samples is **selection bias**, which occurs when the selection of the sample systematically excludes or underrepresents certain groups. Selection bias often happens when we use a convenience sample consisting of data that are readily available.

If we are trying to estimate how often people get colds and have a friend who can give us medical records from an elementary school, this is a convenience sample with selection bias. If our intended population is people of all ages, we should not use samples that systematically exclude certain ages. Similarly, the medical records from a prison, military base, or nursing home are convenience samples with selection bias. Military personnel are in better physical health than those living in nursing homes, and both differ systematically from the population as a whole.

Self-selection bias can occur when we examine data for a group of people who have chosen to be in that group. For example, the accident records of people who buy collision insurance may be unrepresentative of the population as a whole; they might buy insurance because they know that they are accident-prone. The physical fitness of joggers may provide biased estimates of the benefits of jogging; most of those who choose to run regularly may be more physically fit than the general population, even before they began running.

In a study of housing prices, a convenience sample of houses that were sold recently might be unrepresentative of all the houses in the area. Perhaps a new housing development was just completed and most sales involved these new homes, which differ systematically in size and amenities from other houses in the area, which may have been built many years ago. Suppose, for example, that we are estimating the profit that homeowners have made from their houses and our data are dominated by the prices of new homes. Thus we are interested in comparing the 1980 and 2000 prices of homes purchased in 1980, but our data would primarily compare the 1980 prices of homes built in 1980 with the 2000 prices of homes built in 2000.

Survivor Bias

Retrospective studies look at past data for a contemporaneously selected sample; for example, an examination of the lifetime medical records of 65-year-olds. A *prospective* study, in contrast, selects a sample and then tracks the members over time. Retrospective studies are notoriously unreliable, and not just because of faulty memories and lost data. When we choose a sample from a current population in order to draw inferences about a past population, we necessarily exclude members of the past population who are no longer around—an exclusion that causes **survivor bias**, in that we look only at the survivors. If we examine the medical records of 65-year-olds in order to identify the causes of health problems, we overlook those who died before reaching 65 years of age and consequently omit data on some fatal health problems. Survivor bias is a form of selection bias in that the use of retrospective data excludes part of the relevant population.

Here is another example. Stock market studies sometimes examine historical data for companies that have been selected randomly from the New York Stock Exchange (NYSE). If we restrict our analysis to companies currently listed on the NYSE, our data will be subject to survivor bias, because we will ignore companies that were listed in the past but have subsequently gone bankrupt. If we want to estimate the average return for an investment in NYSE stocks over the past 50 years, and do not consider the stock of any company that went bankrupt, we will overestimate the average return.

Nonresponse Bias

The systematic refusal of some groups to participate in an experiment or to respond to a poll is called **nonresponse bias**. A study is naturally more suspect the fewer the people who bother to respond. In the 1940s, the makers of Ipana Tooth Paste boasted that a national survey had found that "Twice as many dentists personally use Ipana Tooth Paste as any other dentifrice preparation. In a recent nationwide survey, more dentists said they recommended Ipana for their patients' daily use than the next two dentifrices combined."[2] The Federal Trade Commission banned this ad after it learned that less than 1 percent of the dentists surveyed had named the brand of toothpaste they used and that even fewer had named a brand recommended for their patients.[3]

---

2. Earl W. Kintner, *A Primer on the Law of Deceptive Practices* (New York: Macmillan, 1971), p. 153.

3. Ibid.

The Power of Random Selection

If we want to put together a representative sample of Diamond Bar houses, it might seem logical to wander around the city and carefully select houses that appear to be "typical." If we did, however, we'd probably slight the very largest and the very smallest houses and end up with a sample that has far less variation than does the population. Our sample probably would be biased, because the houses we exclude for being "above average" and those we exclude for being "below average" are extremely unlikely to balance each other out perfectly. Worst of all, these biases would depend, in unknowable ways, on our undoubtedly mistaken perception of the "typical" house. We might also be influenced by the results we hope to obtain. If we intend to show that houses in Diamond Bar are, on average, more expensive than the houses in another town, this intention may well influence our choice of houses.

To avoid being influenced by subjective biases, statisticians advise that, paradoxically, the researcher should not hand-pick the sample! A fair hand in a card game is not one in which the dealer turns the deck face up and carefully selects representative cards. A fair hand is whatever results from a blind deal from a well-shuffled deck. What card players call a fair deal, statisticians call a random sample. In a simple random sample of size N from a given population, each member of the population is equally likely to be included in the sample, and every possible sample of size N from this population has an equal chance of being selected. For a random sample of five cards, each of the 52 cards in the deck is equally likely to be included in the sample and every possible five-card hand is equally likely to be dealt.

How do we actually make random selections? Returning to our housing study, we would like a procedure that is equivalent to the following: put each house's address on a slip of paper, drop these slips into a box, mix thoroughly, and pick houses out randomly, just as cards are dealt from a well-shuffled deck. Each house, whether expensive, inexpensive, or somewhere in between, has an equal chance of inclusion in our sample. In practice, instead of putting pieces of paper into a box, random sampling is usually done through some sort of numerical identification combined with a computerized random selection of numbers.

In our housing study, we would ideally select a random sample of Diamond Bar houses and pay a professional appraiser to estimate the market value of the houses in our sample. However, we don't want to spend thousands of dollars on this study and, in any case, many homeowners wouldn't welcome the appraiser into their homes to obtain the information needed to make an informed estimate of market value. So, for pedagogic purposes, we will assume the houses in Table 17.1 are a random sample. This assumption is probably

OK because there aren't any new houses in our data and there doesn't seem to be any compelling reason why the houses that went on the market in the summer of 2004 differed systematically from the houses that didn't.

(17.3) Estimation

Sampling provides an economical way to estimate the characteristics of a large population. Samples are used to estimate the amount of cholesterol in a person's body, the average acidity of a farmer's soil, and the number of fish in a lake. Production samples are used to estimate the fraction of a company's products that is defective and marketing samples to estimate how many people will buy a new product. The federal government uses samples to estimate the unemployment rate and the rate of inflation. Public opinion polls are used to predict the winners of elections and to estimate the fraction of the population that agrees with certain positions.

In each case, sample data are used to estimate a population value. But exactly how should the data be used to make these estimates? And how much confidence can we have in estimates that are based on a small sample from a large population? In this section we will answer these questions. First, some terminology. A characteristic of the population whose value is unknown, but can be estimated, is called a *parameter*. A sample statistic that will be used to estimate the value of the population parameter is called an *estimator*. The specific value of the estimator that is obtained in one particular sample is an *estimate*. Here, the average price of all single-family homes in Diamond Bar is a parameter; the average price of the homes in a random sample is an estimator; and the average price of the 22 homes in Table 17.1 is an estimate.

How seriously can we take an estimate of the average price of 20,000 Diamond Bar homes when our estimate is based on just 22 houses? We know that if we were to take another random sample, we would almost certainly not select the same 22 houses. Because samples are chosen randomly, *sampling variation* will cause the sample average to vary from sample to sample, sometimes being larger than the population mean and sometimes lower. How much faith can we place in the average of one small sample? Let's find out.

Sampling Distributions

It is said that the three most important factors in real estate are location, location, location. The three most important concepts in statistics are sampling distributions, sampling distributions, sampling distributions. Consider, for example, the average price of the houses in our sample. The sample average (also called the sample mean) is the simple arithmetic average of N observations $X_1, X_2, \ldots, X_N$:

$$\text{Sample average} = \frac{X_1 + X_2 + \cdots + X_N}{N} = \overline{X} \qquad (17.4)$$

The sample average is often written as $\overline{X}$, or X with a bar over it (which can be pronounced "X-bar"), and we can use the shorthand notation

$$\overline{X} = \frac{\sum X_i}{N}$$

For the 22 homes in Table 17.1, we add up the 22 prices and divide by 22:

$$X = \frac{\$425,000 + \$451,500 + \cdots + \$788,888}{22}$$
$$= \$565,829$$

It is tempting to regard a sample average as definitive. That temptation should be resisted. Our particular sample is just one of many samples that might have been selected; other samples would yield somewhat different sample averages. We cannot say whether a particular sample average is above or below the population mean because we don't know the value of the population mean. But we can use probabilities to deduce how likely it is that a sample will be selected whose mean is close to the population mean.

The **sampling distribution** of a statistic, such as $\overline{X}$, is the probability distribution or density curve that describes the population of all possible values of this statistic. It can be shown mathematically that if the individual observations are drawn from a normal distribution, then the sampling distribution for $\overline{X}$ is also normal. Even if the population does not have a normal distribution, the sampling distribution of $\overline{X}$ will approach a normal distribution as the sample size increases. Here's why. Each observation in a random sample is an independent random variable drawn from the same population. The sample average is the sum of these N outcomes, divided by N. Except for the unimportant division by N, these are the same assumptions in the central limit theorem! Therefore the sampling distribution for the mean of a random sample from any population approaches a normal distribution as N increases.

Thus the sampling distribution for the mean of a reasonably sized random sample is bell-shaped. The only caution is that the sample be large enough for the central limit theorem to work its magic. With data that are themselves approximately normally distributed, a sample of 10 observations is large enough. If the underlying distribution is not normal, but roughly symmetrical, a sample of size 20 or 30 is generally sufficient for the normal distribution to be appropriate.

In addition to its general shape, we need to know the mean and standard deviation of the sampling distribution. It can be shown mathematically that the sampling distribution of $\overline{X}$ has a mean equal to μ and a standard deviation equal to σ divided by the square root of the sample size N:

$$\text{Mean of } \overline{X} = \mu \qquad (17.5)$$
$$\text{Standard deviation of } \overline{X} = \frac{\sigma}{\sqrt{N}}$$

The Mean of the Sampling Distribution

Thus the sampling distribution of $\overline{X}$, which describes the probability of obtaining various values for $\overline{X}$, is approximately normally distributed with a mean equal to μ. Although we can never know with certainty exactly how close a particular sample average $\overline{X}$ is to the unknown population mean μ, we can use the mean and standard deviation of the sampling distribution to gauge the reliability of $\overline{X}$ as an estimator of μ.

A sample statistic is an **unbiased estimator** of a population parameter if the mean of the sampling distribution of this statistic is equal to the value of the population parameter. Because the mean of the sampling distribution of $\overline{X}$ is μ, $\overline{X}$ is an unbiased estimator of μ.

Unbiased estimators have considerable appeal. It would be discomforting to use an estimator that one knows to be systematically too high or too low. A statistician who uses unbiased estimators can anticipate estimation errors that, over a lifetime, average close to zero. Of course, average performance is not the only thing that counts. A British Lord Justice once summarized his career by saying that "When I was a young man practicing at the bar, I lost a great many cases I should have won. As I got along, I won a great many cases I ought to have lost; so on the whole justice was done." The conscientious statistician should be concerned not only with the average value of the estimates, but also with how accurate they are in individual cases. Estimates that are almost always within 1 percent of the correct answer are better than estimates that are usually off by 10 percent or more.

The Standard Deviation of the Sampling Distribution

One way of gauging the accuracy of an estimator is with its standard deviation. If an estimator has a large standard deviation, there is a substantial probability that an estimate will be far from its mean. If an estimator has a small standard deviation, there is a high probability that an estimate will be close to its mean.

Equation 17.5 states that the standard deviation of the sampling distribution for $\overline{X}$ is equal to σ divided by the square root of the sample size, N. As the number of observations increases, the standard deviation of the sampling distribution declines. To understand this phenomenon, remember that the standard deviation is a measure of the uncertainty of the outcome. With a large sample, it is extremely unlikely that all of the observations will be far above μ, and equally improbable that all of the observations will be far below μ. Instead, it is almost certain that some of the observations will be above μ and some below, and that the average will be close to μ.

The *t*-Distribution

The standard deviation of the sampling distribution depends on the value of population standard deviation σ, a parameter that is unknown but can be estimated. The most natural estimator of σ, the standard deviation of the population is s, the standard deviation of the sample data. The *sample variance* of N observations $X_1, X_2, \ldots, X_N$ is the average squared deviation of these observations about the sample average $\overline{X}$:

$$\text{Sample variance} = \frac{(X_1 - \overline{X})^2 + (X_2 - \overline{X})^2 + \cdots + (X_N - \overline{X})^2}{N - 1} \qquad (17.6)$$

The sample **standard deviation** s is the square root of the variance, $s = \sqrt{\text{sample variance}}$.

Notice that the variance of a set of data is calculated by dividing the sum of the squared deviations by $N - 1$, rather than N. It can be shown mathematically that if the variance in a random sample is used to estimate the variance of the population from which these data came, this estimate will, on average, be too low if we divide by N, but will, on average, be correct if we divide by $N - 1$.

When the standard deviation of an estimator, such as $\overline{X}$, is itself estimated from the data, this estimated standard deviation is called the estimator's *standard error*. The standard error of $\overline{X}$ is calculated by replacing the unknown parameter σ with its estimate s:

$$\text{Standard error of } \overline{X} = \frac{s}{\sqrt{N}}$$

The need to estimate the standard deviation creates another source of uncertainty in gauging the reliability of $\overline{X}$ as an estimator of the population mean.

In 1908, W. S. Gosset figured out how to handle this increased uncertainty. Gosset was a statistician employed by the Irish brewery Guinness, which encouraged statistical research but not publication. Because of the importance of his findings, he was able to persuade Guinness to allow his work to be published under the pseudonym "Student" and his calculations became known as the **Student's _t_-distribution**. When the mean of a sample from a normal distribution is standardized by subtracting the mean μ of its sampling distribution and dividing by the standard deviation $\sigma/\sqrt{N}$ of its sampling distribution, the resulting Z variable

$$Z = \frac{\overline{X} - \mu}{\sigma/\sqrt{N}}$$

has a normal distribution. Gosset determined the sampling distribution of the variable that is created when the mean of a sample from a normal distribution is standardized by subtracting μ and dividing by its standard error:

$$t = \frac{\overline{X} - \mu}{s/\sqrt{N}} \tag{17.7}$$

The exact distribution of t depends on the sample size, because as the sample size increases, we are increasingly confident of the accuracy of the estimated standard deviation. For an infinite sample, the estimate s will equal the actual value σ, and the distributions of t and Z coincide. With a small sample, s may be either larger or smaller than s and the distribution of t is consequently more dispersed than the distribution of Z.

Table B-1 at the end of this book shows some probabilities for various _t_-distributions that are identified by the number of **degrees of freedom**:

$$\begin{matrix} \text{degrees of} \\ \text{freedom} \end{matrix} = \begin{matrix} \text{number of} \\ \text{observations} \end{matrix} - \begin{matrix} \text{number of parameters that} \\ \text{must be estimated} \end{matrix}$$

Here, we calculate s by using N observations and one estimated parameter ($\overline{X}$); therefore, there are $N - 1$ degrees of freedom.

There is another way to think about degrees of freedom that is more closely related to the name itself. We calculate s from N squared deviations about $\overline{X}$. However, the sum of the deviations about the sample average is always zero. Thus if we know the values of $N - 1$ of these deviations, we know the value of the last deviation, too. Only $N - 1$ deviations are freely determined by the sample.

Confidence Intervals

Now we are ready to use the t-distribution and the standard error of $\overline{X}$ to measure the reliability of our estimate of the population mean price of homes in Diamond Bar. If we specify a probability, such as $\alpha = 0.05$, we can use Table B-1 to find the t-value t^* such that there is a probability $\alpha/2$ that the value of t will exceed t^*, a probability $\alpha/2$ that the value of t will be less than $-t^*$, and a probability $1 - \alpha$ that the value of t will be in the interval $-t^*$ to t^*:

$$1 - \alpha = P[-t^* < t < t^*]$$

Using Equation 17.7 and rearranging,

$$1 - \alpha = P\left[\mu - t^*\frac{s}{\sqrt{N}} < \overline{X} < \mu + t^*\frac{s}{\sqrt{N}}\right]$$

We can rephrase this probability computation to show the confidence that we have in using the sample average to estimate the population mean. If there is a $1 - \alpha$ probability that $\overline{X}$ will turn out to be within t^* standard errors of the population mean μ, then there is a $1 - \alpha$ probability that the interval from

$$\overline{X} - t^*\frac{s}{\sqrt{N}} \text{ to } \overline{X} + t^*\frac{s}{\sqrt{N}}$$

will include the value of μ. Such an interval is called a **confidence interval** and the $1 - \alpha$ probability is the interval's **confidence level**. The shorthand formula for a $1 - \alpha$ percent confidence interval for the population mean μ is

$$1 - \alpha \text{ confidence interval for } \mu: \overline{X} \pm t^*\frac{s}{\sqrt{N}} \qquad (17.8)$$

There is a 0.95 probability that the sample average $\overline{X}$ will be between $\mu - t^*$(standard error of $\overline{X}$) and $\mu + t^*$ (standard error of $\overline{X}$), in which case the interval $\overline{X} - t^*$ (standard error of $\overline{X}$) to $\overline{X} + t^*$ (standard error of $\overline{X}$) will encompass μ. There is a 0.05 probability that the sample average will, by the luck of the draw, turn out to be more than t^* (standard error of $\overline{X}$) from the population mean μ, and that the confidence interval will consequently not include μ.

Gosset derived the t-distribution by assuming that the sample data are taken from a normal distribution. Subsequent research has shown that because of the power of the central limit theorem, confidence intervals based on the t-distribution are remarkably accurate even if the underlying data are not normally distributed, as long as we have at least 15 observations from a roughly symmetrical distribution or at least 30 observations from a clearly asymmetrical distribution.[4] A histogram can be used for a rough symmetry check. Ninety-five percent confidence levels are standard, but there is no compelling reason why we can't use others.

Let's use the housing prices in Table 17.1 to construct a 95 percent confidence interval and a 99 percent confidence interval for the average price of all single-family homes in Diamond Bar. The sample average is $565,829 and the standard deviation is $116,596. The sample size is 22 and we've estimated one parameter, so consequently there are $22 - 1 = 21$ degrees of freedom. Table B-1 shows that there is a 0.05 probability that the absolute value of t will exceed $t^* = 2.080$ and a 0.01 probability that it will exceed $t^* = 2.831$. Thus,

95 percent confidence interval for μ:

$$\$565{,}829 \pm 2.080\left(\frac{\$116{,}596}{\sqrt{22}}\right) = \$565{,}829 \pm \$51{,}697$$

99 percent confidence interval for μ:

$$\$565{,}829 \pm 2.831\left(\frac{\$116{,}596}{\sqrt{22}}\right) = \$565{,}829 \pm \$70{,}366$$

Notice that it is the sample average $\overline{X}$ that varies from sample to sample, not the population mean μ. A 95 percent confidence interval for μ is interpreted as follows: "There is a 0.95 probability that the sample average will turn out to be sufficiently close to μ so that my confidence interval includes μ. There is a 0.05 probability that the sample average will happen to be so far from μ that my confidence interval does not include μ." The 0.95 probability refers to the chances that random sampling will result in an interval that encompasses the fixed parameter μ, not the probability that random sampling will give a value of μ that is inside a fixed confidence interval.

The general procedure for determining a confidence interval for a population mean is summarized here:

1. Calculate the sample average $\overline{X}$.
2. Calculate the standard error of $\overline{X}$ by dividing the sample standard deviation s by the square root of the sample size N.

---

4. E. S. Pearson and N. W. Please, "Relation Between the Shape of Population Distribution and the Robustness of Four Simple Tests Statistics," *Biometrika*, 1975, 62, pp. 223–241; Harry O. Poston, "The Robustness of the One-Sample t-test Over the Pearson System," *Journal of Statistical Computation and Simulation*, Vol. 9, pp. 133–149.

3. Select a confidence level (such as 95 percent) and look in Table B-1 with N − 1 degrees of freedom to determine the *t*-value t* that corresponds to this probability.

4. A confidence interval for the population mean is equal to the sample average $\overline{X}$ plus or minus t* standard errors of $\overline{X}$:

$$\text{confidence interval for } \mu: \overline{X} \pm t^*(\text{standard error of } \overline{X}) = \overline{X} \pm t^*\frac{s}{\sqrt{N}}$$

Sampling from Finite Populations

A very interesting characteristic of a confidence interval is that it does not depend on the size of the population. At first glance, this conclusion may seem surprising. If we are trying to estimate a characteristic of a large population, then there is a natural tendency to believe that a large sample is needed. If there are 25 million items in the population, a sample of 25 includes only one out of every million. How can we possibly obtain a reliable estimate with a sample that looks at only one out of every million items?

A moment's reflection reveals why a confidence interval doesn't depend on whether the population consists of one thousand or one billion items. The chances that the luck of the draw will yield a sample whose mean differs substantially from the population mean depends on the size of the sample and the chances of selecting items that are far from the population mean, not on how many items there are in the population.

(17.4) Summary

1. The probability that the value of a continuous random variable will be in a specified interval is shown by the area under a probability density curve. The expected value of a random variable is the anticipated long-run average value of the outcomes. The standard deviation measures the extent to which the outcomes may differ from the expected value; a large standard deviation indicates a great deal of uncertainty, as the outcomes are likely to be far from the expected value.

2. A (discrete or continuous) random variable X is standardized by subtracting its mean μ and then dividing by the standard deviation σ:

$$Z = \frac{X - \mu}{\sigma}$$

which has a mean of 0 and a standard deviation of 1. The central limit theorem explains why so many random variables are approximately normally distributed.

3. A population is the entire group of items that interests us; a sample is the part of the population that we actually observe and use to make inferences about the population from which the sample came. Deliberate attempts to construct representative samples are unwise; instead, statisticians recommend that observational data be based on a random sample. A selection bias occurs when some members of the population are systematically excluded or underrepresented in the group from which the sample is taken.

4. If a random variable X is normally distributed with a mean μ and standard deviation σ, then the sampling distribution for the average $\overline{X}$ of a random sample is a normal distribution with a mean μ and a standard deviation equal to σ divided by the square root of the sample size N. Even if the underlying distribution is not normal, a sufficiently large sample will ensure that the sampling distribution of $\overline{X}$ is approximately normal.

5. The sample average $\overline{X}$ is an unbiased estimator of μ, and a confidence interval can be used to gauge the reliability of our estimate:

$$\text{Confidence interval for } \mu = \overline{X} \pm t^* (\text{standard error of } \overline{X})$$
$$= \overline{X} \pm t^* \frac{s}{\sqrt{N}}$$

where s is the sample standard deviation, N is the sample size, and t^* is given by a *t*-distribution with N $-$ 1 degrees of freedom.

EXERCISES

(The answer to Exercise 2 is in Appendix A.)

1. Write the meaning of each of the following terms without referring to the book (or your notes), and compare your definition with the version in the text for each.
    a. probability distribution
    b. random variable
    c. standardized random variable
    d. sample
    e. sampling distribution
    f. population mean

g. sample average
h. population standard deviation
i. sample standard deviation
j. degrees of freedom
k. confidence interval

2. The heights of U.S. females between the age of 25 and 34 are approximately normally distributed with a mean of 66 inches and a standard deviation of 2.5 inches. What fraction of the U.S. female population in this age bracket is taller than 70 inches, the height of the average adult U.S. male of this age?

3. A stock's price-earnings (P/E) ratio is the per-share price of its stock divided by the company's annual profit per share. The P/E ratio for the stock market as a whole is used by some analysts as a measure of whether stocks are cheap or expensive, in comparison with other historical periods. Here are some annual P/E ratios for the S&P 500:

Year	P/E
1980	7.90
1981	8.36
1982	8.62
1983	12.45
1984	9.98
1985	12.32
1986	16.42
1987	18.25
1988	12.48
1989	13.48
1990	15.46
1991	20.88
1992	23.70
1993	22.42
1994	17.15
1995	16.42
1996	19.08
1997	21.88
1998	28.90
1999	31.55

Calculate the mean and standard deviation. Was the 1999 price-earnings ratio of 31.55 more than one standard deviation above the mean P/E for 1980–1999? Was it more than two standard deviations above the mean?

4. Which has a higher mean and which has a higher standard deviation: a standard six-sided die or a four-sided die with the numbers 1 through 4 printed on the sides? Explain your reasoning, without doing any calculations.

5. A nationwide test has a mean of 75 and a standard deviation of 10. Convert the following raw scores to standardized Z values: X = 94, 75, and 67. What raw score corresponds to Z = 1.5?

6. A woman wrote to Dear Abby, saying that she had been pregnant for 310 days before giving birth.[5] Completed pregnancies are normally distributed with a mean of 266 days and a standard deviation of 16 days. Use Table B-7 to determine the probability that a completed pregnancy lasts at least 310 days.

7. Calculate the mean and standard deviation of this probability distribution for housing prices:

Price X (dollars)	Number of Houses	Probability P[X]
400,000	15,000	0.30
500,000	20,000	0.40
600,000	15,000	0.30

8. Explain why you think that high-school seniors who take the Scholastic Aptitude Test (SAT) are not a random sample of all high-school seniors. If we were to compare the 50 states, do you think that a state's average SAT score tends to increase or decrease as the fraction of the state's seniors who take the SAT increases?

9. American Express and the French tourist office sponsored a survey that found that most visitors to France do not consider the French to be especially unfriendly.[6] The sample consisted of "1,000 Americans who have visited France more than once for pleasure over the past two years." Why is this survey biased?

---

5. Harold Jacobs, *Mathematics: A Human Endeavor* (San Francisco: W. H. Freeman), 1982, p. 570.

6. Cynthia Cross, "Studies Galore Support Products and Positions, But Are They Reliable?," *The Wall Street Journal*, November 14, 1991.

10. The first American to win the Nobel prize in physics was Albert Michelson (1852–1931), who was given the award in 1907 for developing and using optical precision instruments. His October 12–November 14, 1882 measurements of the speed of light in air (in kilometers per second) were as follows:[7]

299,883 299,796 299,611 299,781 299,774 299,696 299,748 299,809

299,816 299,682 299,599 299,578 299,820 299,573 299,797 299,723

299,778 299,711 300,051 299,796 299,772 299,748 299,851

Assuming that these measurements were a random sample from a normal distribution, does a 99 percent confidence interval include the value 299,710.5 that is now accepted as the speed of light?

11. A *Wall Street Journal* (July 6, 1987) poll asked 35 economic forecasters to predict the interest rate on three-month Treasury bills in June 1988. These 35 forecasts had a mean of 6.19 and a variance of 0.47. Assuming these to be a random sample, give a 95 percent confidence interval for the mean prediction of all economic forecasters and then explain why each of these interpretations is or is not correct:
    a. There is a 0.95 probability that the actual Treasury bill rate on June 1988 will be in this interval.
    b. Approximately 95 percent of the predictions of all economic forecasters are in this interval.

12. The earlobe test was introduced in a letter to the prestigious *New England Journal of Medicine*, in which Dr. Sanders Frank reported that 20 of his male patients with creases in their earlobes had many of the risk factors (such as high cholesterol levels, high blood pressure, and heavy cigarette usage) associated with heart disease. For instance, the average cholesterol level for his patients with noticeable earlobe creases was 257 (mg per 100 ml), compared to an average of 215 with a standard deviation of 10 for healthy middle-aged men. If these 20 patients were a random sample from a population with a mean of 215 and a standard deviation of 10, what is the probability their average cholesterol level would be 257 or higher? Explain why these 20 patients may, in fact, not be a random sample.

---

7. S. M. Stigler, "Do Robust Estimators Work with Real Data?," *Annals of Statistics*, Vol. 5, No. 6, pp. 1055–1078.

A Answers

Chapter 1, Exercise 2

Using EViews:

    a. Install and launch the software.

    b. Open the datafile. All datafiles can be found in EViews format at www.pearsonhighered.com/studenmund. Alternatively, on your EViews disc, you can click through File > Open > Workfile. Then browse to the CD-ROM, select the folder "Studenmund," and double-click on "HTWT1" followed by "OK."

    c. Run the regression. Type "LS Y C X" on the top line, making sure to leave spaces between the variable names. (LS stands for Least Squares and C stands for constant.) Press Enter, and the regression results will appear on your screen.

Using Stata:

    a. Install and launch the regression software.

    b. Open the datafile. All datafiles can be found in Stata format at www.pearsonhighered.com/studenmund. This particular datafile is "HTWT1."

    c. Run the regression. Click through Statistics > Linear Models and Related > Linear Regression. Select Y as your dependent variable and X as your independent variable. Then click "OK," and the regression results will appear on your screen.

Chapter 2, Exercise 2

    a. $\hat{\beta}_1 = -0.5477$, $\hat{\beta}_0 = 12.289$

    b. $R^2 = .465$, $\overline{R}^2 = .398$

    c. Income $= 12.289 - 0.5477 (8) = 7.907$

Chapter 3, Exercise 2

   a. D = 1 if graduate student and D = 0 if undergraduate (or D = 1 if undergraduate and D = 0 if graduate).
   b. Yes; for example, E = how many exercises the student did.
   c. If D is defined as in answer a, then its coefficient's sign would be expected to be positive. If D is defined as 0 if graduate student, 1 if undergraduate, then the expected sign would be negative.
   d. A coefficient with value of 0.5 indicates that holding constant the other independent variables in the equation, a graduate student would be expected to earn half a grade point higher than an undergraduate. If there were only graduate students or only undergraduates in class, the coefficient of D could not be estimated.

Chapter 4, Exercise 2

   a. An additional pound of fertilizer per acre will cause corn yield to increase by 0.10 bushels per acre, holding rainfall constant. An additional inch of rain will increase corn yield by 5.33 bushels per acre, holding fertilizer per acre constant.
   b. No, for a couple of reasons. First, it's hard to imagine *zero* inches of rain falling in an entire year, so this particular intercept has no real-world meaning. More generally, recall that the OLS estimate of the intercept includes the nonzero mean of the error term in order to meet Classical Assumption II, so even if rainfall were zero, it wouldn't make sense to attempt to analyze the OLS estimate of the intercept.
   c. No. An unbiased estimator will produce a distribution of estimates that is centered around the true β, but individual estimates can vary widely from that true value. 0.10 is the estimated coefficient for this sample, not for the entire population, so it could be an unbiased estimate.
   d. Not necessarily: 5.33 still could be close to or even equal to the true value. More generally, an estimated coefficient produced by an estimator that is not BLUE still could be accurate. For example, the amount of the bias could be very small, or the variation due to sampling could offset the bias.

Chapter 5, Exercise 2

For all three parts:

	X_1	X_2	X_3
H_0:	$\beta_1 \leqslant 0$	$\beta_2 \geqslant 0$	$\beta_3 \geqslant 0$
H_A:	$\beta_1 > 0$	$\beta_2 < 0$	$\beta_3 < 0$
	$t_1 = 2.1$	$t_2 = 5.6$	$t_3 = -0.1$

a. $t_c = 1.363$. For β_1, we reject H_0, because $|t_1| > 1.363$ and the sign of t_1 is that implied by H_A. For β_2, we cannot reject H_0, even though $|t_2| > 1.363$, because the sign of t_2 does not agree with H_A. For β_3, we cannot reject H_0, even though the sign of t_3 agrees with H_A, because $|t_3| < 1.363$.

b. $t_c = 1.318$. The decisions are identical to those in part a, except that $t_c = 1.318$.

c. $t_c = 3.143$. For β_1, we cannot reject H_0, even though the sign of t_1 is that implied by H_A, because $|t_1| < 3.143$. For β_2 and β_3, the decisions are identical to those in parts a and b, except that $t_c = 3.143$.

Chapter 6, Exercise 2

a.

	W_i	T_i	C_i	L_i
H_0	$\beta_1 \leqslant 0$	$\beta_2 \leqslant 0$	$\beta_3 \leqslant 0$	$\beta_4 \leqslant 0$
H_A	$\beta_1 > 0$	$\beta_2 > 0$	$\beta_3 > 0$	$\beta_4 > 0$
	$t_W = 4$	$t_T = 3$	$t_C = 2$	$t_L = 0.95$
	$t_c = 1.697$	$t_c = 1.697$	$t_c = 1.697$	$t_c = 1.697$

For the first three coefficients, we can reject the null hypothesis, because the absolute value of t_k is greater than t_c and the sign of t_k is that specified in H_A. For L, however, we cannot reject the null hypothesis, even though the sign is as expected, because the absolute value of t_L is less than 1.697.

b. Almost any equation potentially could have an omitted variable, and this one is no exception. In addition, L_i might be an irrelevant variable. Finally, the coefficient of C seems far too large, suggesting at least one omitted variable. C appears to be acting as a proxy for other luxury options or the general quality of the car.

c. *Theory:* Bigger engines cost more, so the variable's place in the equation seems theoretically sound. However, sedans with large engines tend to weigh more, so perhaps the two variables are measuring more or less the same thing.

t-Test: The variable's estimated coefficient is insignificant in the expected direction.

$\bar{R}^2$: The overall fit of the equation (adjusted for degrees of freedom) improves when the variable is dropped from the equation.

Bias: When the variable is dropped from the equation, the estimated coefficients remain virtually unchanged.

The last three criteria are evidence in favor of dropping L_i and the theoretical argument for keeping it isn't overwhelming, so we prefer Model T. However, a researcher who firmly believed in the theoretical importance of engine size would pick Model A.

Chapter 7, Exercise 2

a. Semilog right [where $Y = f(\ln X)$]; as income increases, the sales of shoes will increase, but at a declining rate.
b. Linear (intercept dummy); there is little justification for any other form.
c. Semilog right [where $Y = f(\ln X)$] or linear are both justifiable.
d. Inverse function [where $Y = f(1/X)$]; as the interest rate gets higher, the quantity of money demanded will decrease, but even at very high interest rates, there still will be some money held to allow for transactions.
e. Quadratic function [where $Y = f(X, X^2)$]; as output levels are increased, we will encounter diminishing returns to scale.

Chapter 8, Exercise 2

a.

	EMP_i	UNITS	$LANG_i$	EXP_i
H_0	$\beta_1 \leq 0$	$\beta_2 \leq 0$	$\beta_3 \leq 0$	$\beta_4 \leq 0$
H_A	$\beta_1 > 0$	$\beta_2 > 0$	$\beta_3 > 0$	$\beta_4 > 0$
	$t_{EM} = -.098$	$t_U = 2.39$	$t_L = 2.08$	$t_{EX} = 4.97$
	$t_c = 1.725$	$t_c = 1.725$	$t_c = 1.725$	$t_c = 1.725$

For the first last three coefficients, we can reject H_0, because the absolute value of t_k is greater than t_c and the sign of t_k is that specified in H_A. For EMP, however, we cannot reject H_0, because the sign of the coefficient is unexpected and because the absolute value of t_{EM} is less than 1.725.

b. The functional form is semilog left (or semilog lnY). Semilog left is an appropriate functional form for an equation with salary as the dependent variable, because salaries often increase in percentage terms when an independent variable (like experience) increases by one unit.

c. There's a chance that an omitted variable is pulling down the coefficient of EMP, but it's more likely that EMP and EXP are redundant (because in essence they measure the same thing) and are causing multicollinearity.

d. This lends support to our opinion that EMP_i and EXP_i are redundant.

e. If we knew that this particular school district didn't give credit for teaching experience elsewhere, then it would make sense to drop EXP. Without that specific knowledge, however, we'd drop EMP because EXP includes EMP.

f. *Theory:* EMP clearly has a theoretically strong impact on salary, but EMP and EXP are redundant, so we should keep only one.
t-Test: The variable's estimated coefficient is insignificant in the unexpected direction.
$\overline{R}^2$: The overall fit of the equation (adjusted for degrees of freedom) improves when the variable is dropped from the equation.
Bias: The exercise gives t-scores only, but if you work backward, you can calculate the $SE(\hat{\beta})$s. If you do this, you'll find that the coefficient of EXP does indeed change by more than a standard error when EMP is dropped from the equation. This is exactly what you'd expect to happen when a redundant variable is dropped from an equation; the coefficient of the remaining redundant variable will adjust to pick up the effect of both variables.

Thus even though it might appear that two of the specification criteria support keeping EMP in the equation, in actuality all four support the conclusion that they're redundant and that EMP should be removed. As a result, we have a strong preference for Equation 8.22 over Equation 8.21.

Chapter 8

Hints for the SAT Interactive Regression Learning Exercise

1. Severe multicollinearity between APMATH and APENG is the only possible problem in this regression. You should switch to the AP linear combination immediately.
2. An omitted variable is a distinct possibility, but be sure to choose the one to add on the basis of theory.
3. Either an omitted or irrelevant variable is a possibility. In this case, theory seems more important than any mild statistical insignificance.
4. On balance, this is a reasonable regression. We see no reason to worry about theoretically sound variables that have slightly in-significant coefficients with expected signs. We're concerned that the coefficient of GEND seems larger in absolute size than those reported in the literature, but none of the specification alterna-tives seems remotely likely to remedy this problem.
5. An omitted variable is a possibility, but there are no signs of bias and this is a fairly reasonable equation already.
6. We'd prefer not to add PREP (since many students take prep courses because they did poorly on their first shots at the SAT) or RACE (because of its redundancy with ESL and the lack of real di-versity at Arcadia High). If you make a specification change, be sure to evaluate the change with our four specification criteria.
7. Either an omitted or irrelevant variable is a possibility, although GEND seems theoretically and statistically strong.
8. The unexpected sign makes us concerned with the possibility that an omitted variable is causing bias or that PREP is irrelevant. If PREP is relevant, what omission could have caused this result? How strong is the theory behind PREP?
9. This is a case of imperfect multicollinearity. Even though the VIFs are only between 3.8 and 4.0, the definitions of ESL and RACE (and the high simple correlation coefficient between them) make them seem like redundant variables. Remember to use theory (and not statistical fit) to decide which one to drop.
10. An omitted variable or irrelevant variable is a possibility, but there are no signs of bias and this is a fairly reasonable equation already.
11. Despite the switch to the AP linear combination, we still have an unexpected sign, so we're still concerned with the possibility that

an omitted variable is causing bias or that PREP is irrelevant. If PREP is relevant, what omission could have caused this result? How strong is the theory behind PREP?

12. All of the choices would improve this equation except switching to the AP linear combination. If you make a specification change, be sure to evaluate the change with our four specification criteria.

13. To get to this result, you had to have made at least three suspect specification decisions, and you're running the risk of bias due to a sequential specification search. Our advice is to stop, take a break, review Chapters 6–8, and then try this interactive exercise again.

14. We'd prefer not to add PREP (since many students take prep courses because they did poorly on their first shots at the SAT) or ESL (because of its redundancy with RACE and the lack of real diversity at Arcadia High). If you make a specification change, be sure to evaluate the change with our four specification criteria.

15. Unless you drop one of the redundant variables, you're going to continue to have severe multicollinearity.

16. From theory and from the results, it seems as if the decision to switch to the AP linear combination was a waste of a regression run. Even if there were severe collinearity between APMATH and APENG (which there isn't), the original coefficients are significant enough in the expected direction to suggest taking no action to offset any multicollinearity.

17. On reflection, PREP probably should not have been chosen in the first place. Many students take prep courses only because they did poorly on their first shots at the SAT or because they anticipate doing poorly. Thus, even if the PREP courses improve SAT scores, which they probably do, the students who think they need to take them were otherwise going to score worse than their colleagues (holding the other variables in the equation constant). The two effects seem likely to offset each other, making PREP an irrelevant variable. If you make a specification change, be sure to evaluate the change with our four specification criteria.

18. Either adding GEND or dropping PREP would be a good choice, and it's hard to choose between the two. If you make a specification change, be sure to evaluate the change with our four specification criteria.

19. On balance, this is a reasonable regression. We'd prefer not to add PREP (since many students take prep courses because they did poorly on their first shots at the SAT), but the theoretical case for ESL (or RACE) seems strong. We're concerned that the coefficient of

GEND seems larger in absolute size than those reported in the literature, but none of the specification alternatives seems remotely likely to remedy this problem. If you make a specification change, be sure to evaluate the change with our four specification criteria.

Chapter 9, Exercise 2

a.

	Y_t	PB_t	PRP_t	D_t
H_0	$\beta_1 \leq 0$	$\beta_2 \geq 0$	$\beta_3 \leq 0$	$\beta_4 \geq 0$
H_A	$\beta_1 > 0$	$\beta_2 < 0$	$\beta_3 > 0$	$\beta_4 < 0$
	$t_Y = 6.6$	$t_{PB} = -2.6$	$t_{PRP} = 2.7$	$t_D = -3.17$
	$t_c = 1.714$	$t_c = 1.714$	$t_c = 1.714$	$t_c = 1.714$

We can reject the null hypothesis for all four coefficients because the t-scores all are in the expected direction with absolute values greater than 1.714 (the 5-percent one-sided critical t-value for 23 degrees of freedom).

b. With a 5-percent, one-sided test and $N = 28$, $K = 4$, the critical values are $d_L = 1.10$ and $d_u = 1.75$. Since $d = 0.94 < 1.10$, we can reject the null hypothesis of no positive serial correlation.

c. The probable positive serial correlation suggests GLS.

d. We prefer the GLS equation, because we've rid the equation of much of the serial correlation while retaining estimated coefficients that make economic sense. Note that the dependent variables in the two equations are different, so an improved fit is not evidence of a better equation.

Chapter 10, Exercise 2

a. Yes, heteroskedasticity is much more likely when CV is the dependent variable than it is when P is the dependent variable, because the aggregate consumption of pharmaceuticals will vary much more widely by country than will the prices of those pharmaceuticals.

b. *Park Test:* $t_{PARK} = 2.14 > t_c = 2.042$, so we can reject the null hypothesis of homoskedasticity.

White Test: $NR^2 = 28.62$, > the critical chi-square value of 16.92, so we can reject the null hypothesis of homoskedasticity. 16.92 is the critical value because there are nine degrees of freedom—one each for N, P, IPC, their squares, and their cross- products.

c. The HC standard error for N is 0.107; for P it is 0.127; and for IPC it is 10.61.

d. $\widehat{\ln CV_i} = -8.21 + 1.11\ln N_i + 1.46\ln P_i + 0.88 IPC_i$

$$
\begin{array}{ccccc}
 & & (0.14) & (0.44) & (0.48) \\
t & = & 7.94 & 3.30 & 1.82 \\
 & & N = 32 & \overline{R}^2 = .71 &
\end{array}
$$

e. $\widehat{CVN_i} = 10.89 + 1.17 GDPN_i - 0.36 P_i - 1.95 IPC_i$

$$
\begin{array}{ccccc}
 & & (0.13) & (0.11) & (5.52) \\
t & = & 9.22 & -3.23 & -0.35 \\
 & & N = 32 & \overline{R}^2 = .80 &
\end{array}
$$

where CVN = CV/N and GDPN = GDP/N.

f. Most experienced econometricians use HC standard errors to deal with heteroskedasticity, so the most obvious answer is to choose that approach. It's worth noting, however, that the reformulated approach allows the price variable's coefficient to switch from being significant in the unexpected direction to being significant in the expected direction. (That comes at the cost, admittedly, of the insignificance of the coefficient of IPC.)

g. Although Classical Assumption V is the focus of this chapter, we also have to worry about violating Classical Assumption III in this situation. If P is a function of CV and if CV is a function of P, then we have a simultaneous system, and the error term is no longer independent of the explanatory variables. For more on this, see Chapter 14.

Chapter 11

Hints for the Housing Price Interactive Exercise

The biggest problem most students have with this interactive exercise is that they run far too many different specifications "just to see" what the results look like. In our opinion, all but one or two of the specification decisions involved in this exercise should be made before the first regression is estimated, so one measure of the quality of your work is the number of different equations you estimated. Typically, the fewer the better.

As to which specification to run, most of the decisions involved are matters of personal choice and experience. Our favorite model on theoretical grounds is:

$$P = f(\overset{+}{S}, \overset{-}{N}, \overset{-}{A}, \overset{+}{A^2}, \overset{+}{Y}, \overset{+}{CA})$$

We think that BE and BA are redundant with S. In addition, we can justify both positive and negative coefficients for SP, giving it an ambiguous expected sign, so we'd avoid including it. We would not quibble with someone who preferred a linear functional form for A to our quadratic. In addition, we recognize that CA is quite insignificant for this sample, but we'd retain it, at least in part because it gets quite hot in Monrovia in the summer.

As to interactive variables, the only one we can justify is between S and N. Note, however, that the proper variable is not $S \cdot N$ but instead is $S \cdot (5 - N)$, or something similar, to account for the different expected signs. This variable turns out to improve the fit while being quite collinear (redundant) with N and S.

In none of our specifications did we find evidence of serial correlation or heteroskedasticity, although the latter is certainly a possibility in such cross-sectional data.

Chapter 12, Exercise 2

a. The double-log functional form doesn't change the fact that this is a dynamic model. As a result, Y and M almost surely are related by a distributed lag.

b. In their relationship to M, both Y and R have the same distributed lag pattern over time, since the lambda of 0.60 applies to both. (The equation is in double-log form, so technically the relationships are between the logs of those variables.)

c. Serial correlation is always a concern in a dynamic model. Many students will look at the Durbin–Watson statistic of 1.80 and conclude that there is no evidence of positive serial correlation in this equation, but the d-statistic is biased toward 2 in the presence of a lagged dependent variable. Ideally, we would use the Lagrange Multiplier Serial Correlation Test, but we don't have the data to do so. Durbin's h test, which is beyond the scope of this text, provides evidence that there is indeed serial correlation in the equation. For more, see Robert Raynor, "Testing for Serial Correlation in the Presence of Lagged Dependent Variables," *The Review of Economics and Statistics*, Vol. 75, No. 4, pp. 716–721.

Chapter 13, Exercise 2

a. *WN:* The log of the odds that a woman has used a recognized form of birth control is 2.03 higher if she doesn't want any more children than it is if she wants more children, holding ME constant.

ME: A one-unit increase in the number of methods of birth control known to a woman increases the log of the odds that she has used a form of birth control by 1.45, holding WN constant.

LPM: If the model were a linear probability model, then each individual slope coefficient would represent the impact of a one-unit increase in the independent variable on the probability that the ith woman had ever used a recognized form of birth control, holding the other independent variable constant.

b. Yes, but we didn't expect $\hat{\beta}_{ME}$ to be more significant than $\hat{\beta}_{WN}$.

c. As we've said before, β_0 has virtually no theoretical significance. See Section 7.1.

d. We'd add one of a number of potentially relevant variables; for instance, the educational level of the ith woman, whether the ith woman lives in a rural area, and so on.

Chapter 14, Exercise 2

a. The caret over GDP is an indication that two-stage least squares was used. A reduced-form equation was run with GDP as a function of investment and government expenditure. The estimated GDPs from the reduced form were then substituted for GDP where it appears on the right-hand side of the money supply equation in order to act as a proxy (an instrumental variable) for GDP.

b. The 2SLS equation makes significantly more sense from a theoretical point of view. Most economists agree that GDP has an impact on the money supply and that the money supply also has an impact on GDP, leading to a simultaneous model being the model of choice.

c. The OLS equation is more likely to have biased coefficients, but the 2SLS model also will face potential bias in small samples. The bias in the OLS model is likely to be positive, while the bias in the 2SLS model is likely be negative (and smaller in absolute value).

d. We prefer the 2SLS model by a wide margin, because it is theoretically more compelling, and because it has less expected bias.

e. It's true that in this case the 2SLS and OLS estimates are virtually identical, but that doesn't change the fact that 2SLS is preferable from both a theoretical and econometric point of view.

Chapter 15, Exercise 2

a. $256,977.28

b. 117,276; 132,863; 107,287; Nowheresville

c. 15.13; 15.56; 16.35; 17.11

Chapter 16, Exercise 2

a. $\Delta OUTCOME_{Easton} = 28,500 - 25,000 = 3,500$
$\Delta OUTCOME_{Allentown} = 23,750 - 22,500 = 1,250$

b. We must assume that the changes in the outcome would have been the same in both the treatment and control group (had there been no treatment) in order for this estimation to be valid. However, there was a $2,500 disparity between the average incomes prior to the treatment, so there most likely are several differences between the two groups.

c. Even if the underlying assumption in part b is met, we should be cautious when interpreting our conclusions. A data set with only two observations is absurdly small and is unlikely to provide accurate results except by chance.

Chapter 17, Exercise 2

$Z = (70-66)2.5 = 1.60.$ $P[Z > 1.60] = 0.0548.$

B Statistical Tables

The following tables present the critical values of various statistics used primarily for hypothesis testing. The primary applications of each statistic are explained and illustrated. The tables are:

Table B-1: The *t*-Distribution

The *t*-distribution is used in regression analysis to test whether an estimated slope coefficient (say, $\hat{\beta}_k$) is significantly different from a hypothesized value (such as β_{H_0}). The *t*-statistic is computed as:

$$t_k = (\hat{\beta}_k - \beta_{H_0})/SE(\hat{\beta}_k)$$

where $\hat{\beta}_k$ is the estimated slope coefficient and $SE(\hat{\beta}_k)$ is the estimated standard error of $\hat{\beta}_k$. To test the one-sided hypothesis:

$$H_0: \beta_k \leq \beta_{H_0}$$
$$H_A: \beta_k > \beta_{H_0}$$

the computed *t*-value is compared with a critical *t*-value t_c, found in the *t*-table on the opposite page in the column with the desired level of significance for a one-sided test (usually 5 percent) and the row with $N - K - 1$ degrees of freedom, where N is the number of observations and K is the number of explanatory variables. If $|t_k| > t_c$ and if t_k has the sign implied by the alternative hypothesis, then reject H_0; otherwise, do not reject H_0. In most econometric applications, β_{H_0} is zero and most computer regression programs will calculate t_k for $\beta_{H_0} = 0$. For example, for a 5-percent one-sided test with 15 degrees of freedom, $t_c = 1.753$, so any positive t_k larger than 1.753 would lead us to reject H_0 and declare that $\hat{\beta}_k$ is statistically significant in the hypothesized direction at the 5-percent level.

For a two-sided test, $H_0: \beta_k = \beta_{H_0}$ and $H_A: \beta_k \neq \beta_{H_0}$, the procedure is identical except that the column corresponding to the two-sided level of significance is used. For example, for a 5-percent two-sided test with 15 degrees of freedom, $t_c = 2.131$, so any t_k larger in absolute value than 2.131 would lead us to reject H_0 and declare that $\hat{\beta}_k$ is significantly different from β_{H_0} at the 5-percent level of significance. For more on the *t*-test, see Chapter 5.

Table B-1 Critical Values of the *t*-Distribution

Degrees of Freedom	One-Sided: 10% Two-Sided: 20%	5% 10%	2.5% 5%	1% 2%	0.5% 1%
		Level of Significance			
1	3.078	6.314	12.706	31.821	63.657
2	1.886	2.920	4.303	6.965	9.925
3	1.638	2.353	3.182	4.541	5.841
4	1.533	2.132	2.776	3.747	4.604
5	1.476	2.015	2.571	3.365	4.032
6	1.440	1.943	2.447	3.143	3.707
7	1.415	1.895	2.365	2.998	3.499
8	1.397	1.860	2.306	2.896	3.355
9	1.383	1.833	2.262	2.821	3.250
10	1.372	1.812	2.228	2.764	3.169
11	1.363	1.796	2.201	2.718	3.106
12	1.356	1.782	2.179	2.681	3.055
13	1.350	1.771	2.160	2.650	3.012
14	1.345	1.761	2.145	2.624	2.977
15	1.341	1.753	2.131	2.602	2.947
16	1.337	1.746	2.120	2.583	2.921
17	1.333	1.740	2.110	2.567	2.898
18	1.330	1.734	2.101	2.552	2.878
19	1.328	1.729	2.093	2.539	2.861
20	1.325	1.725	2.086	2.528	2.845
21	1.323	1.721	2.080	2.518	2.831
22	1.321	1.717	2.074	2.508	2.819
23	1.319	1.714	2.069	2.500	2.807
24	1.318	1.711	2.064	2.492	2.797
25	1.316	1.708	2.060	2.485	2.787
26	1.315	1.706	2.056	2.479	2.779
27	1.314	1.703	2.052	2.473	2.771
28	1.313	1.701	2.048	2.467	2.763
29	1.311	1.699	2.045	2.462	2.756
30	1.310	1.697	2.042	2.457	2.750
40	1.303	1.684	2.021	2.423	2.704
60	1.296	1.671	2.000	2.390	2.660
120	1.289	1.658	1.980	2.358	2.617
(Normal)					
∞	1.282	1.645	1.960	2.326	2.576

Source: Reprinted from Table IV in Sir Ronald A. Fisher, *Statistical Methods for Research Workers,* 14th ed. (copyright © 1970, University of Adelaide) with permission of Hafner, a division of the Macmillan Publishing Company, Inc.

Table B-2: The *F*-Distribution

The *F*-distribution is used in regression analysis to deal with a null hypothesis that contains multiple hypotheses or a single hypothesis about a group of coefficients. To test the most typical joint hypothesis (a test of the overall significance of the regression):

$$H_0: \beta_1 = \beta_2 = \cdots = \beta_K = 0$$
$$H_A: H_0 \text{ is not true}$$

the computed *F*-value is compared with a critical *F*-value, found in one of the two tables that follow. The *F*-statistic has two types of degrees of freedom, one for the numerator (columns) and one for the denominator (rows). For the null and alternative hypotheses above, there are K numerator (the number of restrictions implied by the null hypothesis) and $N - K - 1$ denominator degrees of freedom, where N is the number of observations and K is the number of explanatory variables in the equation. This particular *F*-statistic is printed out by most computer regression programs. For example, if K = 5 and N = 30, there are 5 numerator and 24 denominator degrees of freedom, and the critical *F*-value for a 5-percent level of significance (Table B-2) is 2.62. A computed *F*-value greater than 2.62 would lead us to reject the null hypothesis and declare that the equation is statistically significant at the 5-percent level. For more on the *F*-test, see Section 5.6.

Table B-2 Critical Values of the *F*-Statistic: 5-Percent Level of Significance

		v_1 = Degrees of Freedom for Numerator										
	1	**2**	**3**	**4**	**5**	**6**	**7**	**8**	**10**	**12**	**20**	**∞**
1	161	200	216	225	230	234	237	239	242	244	248	254
2	18.5	19.0	19.2	19.2	19.3	19.3	19.4	19.4	19.4	19.4	19.4	19.5
3	10.1	9.55	9.28	9.12	9.01	8.94	8.89	8.85	8.79	8.74	8.66	8.53
4	7.71	6.94	6.59	6.39	6.26	6.16	6.09	6.04	5.96	5.91	5.80	5.63
5	6.61	5.79	5.41	5.19	5.05	4.95	4.88	4.82	4.74	4.68	4.56	4.36
6	5.99	5.14	4.76	4.53	4.39	4.28	4.21	4.15	4.06	4.00	3.87	3.67
7	5.59	4.74	4.35	4.12	3.97	3.87	3.79	3.73	3.64	3.57	3.44	3.23
8	5.32	4.46	4.07	3.84	3.69	3.58	3.50	3.44	3.35	3.28	3.15	2.93
9	5.12	4.26	3.86	3.63	3.48	3.37	3.29	3.23	3.14	3.07	2.94	2.71
10	4.96	4.10	3.71	3.48	3.33	3.22	3.14	3.07	2.98	2.91	2.77	2.54
11	4.84	3.98	3.59	3.36	3.20	3.09	3.01	2.95	2.85	2.79	2.65	2.40
12	4.75	3.89	3.49	3.26	3.11	3.00	2.91	2.85	2.75	2.69	2.54	2.30
13	4.67	3.81	3.41	3.18	3.03	2.92	2.83	2.77	2.67	2.60	2.46	2.21
14	4.60	3.74	3.34	3.11	2.96	2.85	2.76	2.70	2.60	2.53	2.39	2.13
15	4.54	3.68	3.29	3.06	2.90	2.79	2.71	2.64	2.54	2.48	2.33	2.07
16	4.49	3.63	3.24	3.01	2.85	2.74	2.66	2.59	2.49	2.42	2.28	2.01
17	4.45	3.59	3.20	2.96	2.81	2.70	2.61	2.55	2.45	2.38	2.23	1.96
18	4.41	3.55	3.16	2.93	2.77	2.66	2.58	2.51	2.41	2.34	2.19	1.92
19	4.38	3.52	3.13	2.90	2.74	2.63	2.54	2.48	2.38	2.31	2.16	1.88
20	4.35	3.49	3.10	2.87	2.71	2.60	2.51	2.45	2.35	2.28	2.12	1.84
21	4.32	3.47	3.07	2.84	2.68	2.57	2.49	2.42	2.32	2.25	2.10	1.81
22	4.30	3.44	3.05	2.82	2.66	2.55	2.46	2.40	2.30	2.23	2.07	1.78
23	4.28	3.42	3.03	2.80	2.64	2.53	2.44	2.37	2.27	2.20	2.05	1.76
24	4.26	3.40	3.01	2.78	2.62	2.51	2.42	2.36	2.25	2.18	2.03	1.73
25	4.24	3.39	2.99	2.76	2.60	2.49	2.40	2.34	2.24	2.16	2.01	1.71
30	4.17	3.32	2.92	2.69	2.53	2.42	2.33	2.27	2.16	2.09	1.93	1.62
40	4.08	3.23	2.84	2.61	2.45	2.34	2.25	2.18	2.08	2.00	1.84	1.51
60	4.00	3.15	2.76	2.53	2.37	2.25	2.17	2.10	1.99	1.92	1.75	1.39
120	3.92	3.07	2.68	2.45	2.29	2.18	2.09	2.02	1.91	1.83	1.66	1.25
∞	3.84	3.00	2.60	2.37	2.21	2.10	2.01	1.94	1.83	1.75	1.57	1.00

v_2 = Degrees of Freedom for Denominator (row labels)

Source: Abridged from M. Merrington and C. M. Thompson, "Tables of percentage points of the inverted beta (*F*) distribution," *Biometrika,* Vol. 33, 1943, p. 73, by permission of the *Biometrika* trustees.

Table B-3: The *F*-Distribution

The *F*-distribution is used in regression analysis to deal with a null hypothesis that contains multiple hypotheses or a single hypothesis about a group of coefficients. To test the most typical joint hypothesis (a test of the overall significance of the regression):

$$H_0: \beta_1 = \beta_2 = \cdots = \beta_K = 0$$
$$H_A: H_0 \text{ is not true}$$

the computed *F*-value is compared with a critical *F*-value, found in Tables B-2 and B-3. The *F*-statistic has two types of degrees of freedom, one for the numerator (columns) and one for the denominator (rows). For the null and alternative hypotheses above, there are K numerator (the number of restrictions implied by the null hypothesis) and $N - K - 1$ denominator degrees of freedom, where N is the number of observations and K is the number of explanatory variables in the equation. This particular *F*-statistic is printed out by most computer regression programs. For example, if K = 5 and N = 30, there are 5 numerator and 24 denominator degrees of freedom, and the critical *F*-value for a 1-percent level of significance (Table B-3) is 3.90. A computed *F*-value greater than 3.90 would lead us to reject the null hypothesis and declare that the equation is statistically significant at the 1-percent level. For more on the *F*-test, see Section 5.6.

Table B-3 Critical Values of the *F*-Statistic: 1-Percent Level of Significance

	v_1 = Degrees of Freedom for Numerator											
	1	2	3	4	5	6	7	8	10	12	20	∞
1	4052	5000	5403	5625	5764	5859	5928	5982	6056	6106	6209	6366
2	98.5	99.0	99.2	99.2	99.3	99.3	99.4	99.4	99.4	99.4	99.4	99.5
3	34.1	30.8	29.5	28.7	28.2	27.9	27.7	27.5	27.2	27.1	26.7	26.1
4	21.2	18.0	16.7	16.0	15.5	15.2	15.0	14.8	14.5	14.4	14.0	13.5
5	16.3	13.3	12.1	11.4	11.0	10.7	10.5	10.3	10.1	9.89	9.55	9.02
6	13.7	10.9	9.78	9.15	8.75	8.47	8.26	8.10	7.87	7.72	7.40	6.88
7	12.2	9.55	8.45	7.85	7.46	7.19	6.99	6.84	6.62	6.47	6.16	5.65
8	11.3	8.65	7.59	7.01	6.63	6.37	6.18	6.03	5.81	5.67	5.36	4.86
9	10.6	8.02	6.99	6.42	6.06	5.80	5.61	5.47	5.26	5.11	4.81	4.31
10	10.0	7.56	6.55	5.99	5.64	5.39	5.20	5.06	4.85	4.71	4.41	3.91
11	9.65	7.21	6.22	5.67	5.32	5.07	4.89	4.74	4.54	4.40	4.10	3.60
12	9.33	6.93	5.95	5.41	5.06	4.82	4.64	4.50	4.30	4.16	3.86	3.36
13	9.07	6.70	5.74	5.21	4.86	4.62	4.44	4.30	4.10	3.96	3.66	3.17
14	8.86	6.51	5.56	5.04	4.70	4.46	4.28	4.14	3.94	3.80	3.51	3.00
15	8.68	6.36	5.42	4.89	4.56	4.32	4.14	4.00	3.80	3.67	3.37	2.87
16	8.53	6.23	5.29	4.77	4.44	4.20	4.03	3.89	3.69	3.55	3.26	2.75
17	8.40	6.11	5.19	4.67	4.34	4.10	3.93	3.79	3.59	3.46	3.16	2.65
18	8.29	6.01	5.09	4.58	4.25	4.01	3.84	3.71	3.51	3.37	3.08	2.57
19	8.19	5.93	5.01	4.50	4.17	3.94	3.77	3.63	3.43	3.30	3.00	2.49
20	8.10	5.85	4.94	4.43	4.10	3.87	3.70	3.56	3.37	3.23	2.94	2.42
21	8.02	5.78	4.87	4.37	4.04	3.81	3.64	3.51	3.31	3.17	2.88	2.36
22	7.95	5.72	4.82	4.31	3.99	3.76	3.59	3.45	3.26	3.12	2.83	2.31
23	7.88	5.66	4.76	4.26	3.94	3.71	3.54	3.41	3.21	3.07	2.78	2.26
24	7.82	5.61	4.72	4.22	3.90	3.67	3.50	3.36	3.17	3.03	2.74	2.21
25	7.77	5.57	4.68	4.18	3.86	3.63	3.46	3.32	3.13	2.99	2.70	2.17
30	7.56	5.39	4.51	4.02	3.70	3.47	3.30	3.17	2.98	2.84	2.55	2.01
40	7.31	5.18	4.31	3.83	3.51	3.29	3.12	2.99	2.80	2.66	2.37	1.80
60	7.08	4.98	4.13	3.65	3.34	3.12	2.95	2.82	2.63	2.50	2.20	1.60
120	6.85	4.79	3.95	3.48	3.17	2.96	2.79	2.66	2.47	2.34	2.03	1.38
∞	6.63	4.61	3.78	3.32	3.02	2.80	2.64	2.51	2.32	2.18	1.88	1.00

v_2 = Degrees of Freedom for Denominator

Tables B-4, B-5, and B-6: The Durbin–Watson d Statistic

The Durbin–Watson d statistic is used to test for first-order serial correlation in the residuals. First-order serial correlation is characterized by $\epsilon_t = \rho\epsilon_{t-1} + u_t$, where ϵ_t, is the error term found in the regression equation and u_t is a classical (not serially correlated) error term. Since $\rho = 0$ implies no serial correlation, and since most economic and business models imply positive serial correlation if any pure serial correlation exists, the typical hypotheses are:

$$H_0: \rho \leq 0$$
$$H_A: \rho > 0$$

To test the null hypothesis of no positive serial correlation, the Durbin–Watson d statistic must be compared to two different critical d-values, d_L and d_U found in Tables B-4, B-5, and B-6, depending on the level of significance, the number of explanatory variables (K) and the number of observations (N). For example, with 2 explanatory variables and 30 observations, the 1-percent one-tailed critical values are $d_L = 1.07$ and $d_U = 1.34$, so any computed Durbin–Watson statistic less than 1.07 would lead to the rejection of the null hypothesis. For computed DW d-values between 1.07 and 1.34, the test is inconclusive, and for values greater than 1.34, we can say that there is no evidence of positive serial correlation at the 1-percent level. These ranges are illustrated in the following diagram:

Two-sided tests are done similarly, with $4 - d_U$ and $4 - d_L$ being the critical DW d-values between 2 and 4. Tables B-5 and B-6 (for 2.5- and 1-percent levels of significance in a one-sided test) go only up to five explanatory variables, so extrapolation for more variables (and interpolation for observations between listed points) is often in order.

Table B-4 Critical Values of the Durbin–Watson Test Statistics d_L and d_U:
5-Percent One-Sided Level of Significance
(10-Percent Two-Sided Level of Significance)

N	K = 1		K = 2		K = 3		K = 4		K = 5		K = 6		K = 7	
	d_L	d_U	d_L	d_U	d_L	d_U	d_L	d_U	d_L	d_U	d_L	d_U	d_L	d_U
15	1.08	1.36	0.95	1.54	0.81	1.75	0.69	1.97	0.56	2.21	0.45	2.47	0.34	2.73
16	1.11	1.37	0.98	1.54	0.86	1.73	0.73	1.93	0.62	2.15	0.50	2.39	0.40	2.62
17	1.13	1.38	1.02	1.54	0.90	1.71	0.78	1.90	0.66	2.10	0.55	2.32	0.45	2.54
18	1.16	1.39	1.05	1.53	0.93	1.69	0.82	1.87	0.71	2.06	0.60	2.26	0.50	2.46
19	1.18	1.40	1.07	1.53	0.97	1.68	0.86	1.85	0.75	2.02	0.65	2.21	0.55	2.40
20	1.20	1.41	1.10	1.54	1.00	1.68	0.89	1.83	0.79	1.99	0.69	2.16	0.60	2.34
21	1.22	1.42	1.13	1.54	1.03	1.67	0.93	1.81	0.83	1.96	0.73	2.12	0.64	2.29
22	1.24	1.43	1.15	1.54	1.05	1.66	0.96	1.80	0.86	1.94	0.77	2.09	0.68	2.25
23	1.26	1.44	1.17	1.54	1.08	1.66	0.99	1.79	0.90	1.92	0.80	2.06	0.72	2.21
24	1.27	1.45	1.19	1.55	1.10	1.66	1.01	1.78	0.93	1.90	0.84	2.04	0.75	2.17
25	1.29	1.45	1.21	1.55	1.12	1.66	1.04	1.77	0.95	1.89	0.87	2.01	0.78	2.14
26	1.30	1.46	1.22	1.55	1.14	1.65	1.06	1.76	0.98	1.88	0.90	1.99	0.82	2.12
27	1.32	1.47	1.24	1.56	1.16	1.65	1.08	1.76	1.00	1.86	0.93	1.97	0.85	2.09
28	1.33	1.48	1.26	1.56	1.18	1.65	1.10	1.75	1.03	1.85	0.95	1.96	0.87	2.07
29	1.34	1.48	1.27	1.56	1.20	1.65	1.12	1.74	1.05	1.84	0.98	1.94	0.90	2.05
30	1.35	1.49	1.28	1.57	1.21	1.65	1.14	1.74	1.07	1.83	1.00	1.93	0.93	2.03
31	1.36	1.50	1.30	1.57	1.23	1.65	1.16	1.74	1.09	1.83	1.02	1.92	0.95	2.02
32	1.37	1.50	1.31	1.57	1.24	1.65	1.18	1.73	1.11	1.82	1.04	1.91	0.97	2.00
33	1.38	1.51	1.32	1.58	1.26	1.65	1.19	1.73	1.13	1.81	1.06	1.90	0.99	1.99
34	1.39	1.51	1.33	1.58	1.27	1.65	1.21	1.73	1.14	1.81	1.08	1.89	1.02	1.98
35	1.40	1.52	1.34	1.58	1.28	1.65	1.22	1.73	1.16	1.80	1.10	1.88	1.03	1.97
36	1.41	1.52	1.35	1.59	1.30	1.65	1.24	1.73	1.18	1.80	1.11	1.88	1.05	1.96
37	1.42	1.53	1.36	1.59	1.31	1.66	1.25	1.72	1.19	1.80	1.13	1.87	1.07	1.95
38	1.43	1.54	1.37	1.59	1.32	1.66	1.26	1.72	1.20	1.79	1.15	1.86	1.09	1.94
39	1.43	1.54	1.38	1.60	1.33	1.66	1.27	1.72	1.22	1.79	1.16	1.86	1.10	1.93
40	1.44	1.54	1.39	1.60	1.34	1.66	1.29	1.72	1.23	1.79	1.18	1.85	1.12	1.93
45	1.48	1.57	1.43	1.62	1.38	1.67	1.34	1.72	1.29	1.78	1.24	1.84	1.19	1.90
50	1.50	1.59	1.46	1.63	1.42	1.67	1.38	1.72	1.34	1.77	1.29	1.82	1.25	1.88
55	1.53	1.60	1.49	1.64	1.45	1.68	1.41	1.72	1.37	1.77	1.33	1.81	1.29	1.86
60	1.55	1.62	1.51	1.65	1.48	1.69	1.44	1.73	1.41	1.77	1.37	1.81	1.34	1.85
65	1.57	1.63	1.54	1.66	1.50	1.70	1.47	1.73	1.44	1.77	1.40	1.81	1.37	1.84
70	1.58	1.64	1.55	1.67	1.53	1.70	1.49	1.74	1.46	1.77	1.43	1.80	1.40	1.84
75	1.60	1.65	1.57	1.68	1.54	1.71	1.52	1.74	1.49	1.77	1.46	1.80	1.43	1.83
80	1.61	1.66	1.59	1.69	1.56	1.72	1.53	1.74	1.51	1.77	1.48	1.80	1.45	1.83
85	1.62	1.67	1.60	1.70	1.58	1.72	1.55	1.75	1.53	1.77	1.50	1.80	1.47	1.83
90	1.63	1.68	1.61	1.70	1.59	1.73	1.57	1.75	1.54	1.78	1.52	1.80	1.49	1.83
95	1.64	1.69	1.62	1.71	1.60	1.73	1.58	1.75	1.56	1.78	1.54	1.80	1.51	1.83
100	1.65	1.69	1.63	1.72	1.61	1.74	1.59	1.76	1.57	1.78	1.55	1.80	1.53	1.83

Source: N. E. Savin and Kenneth J. White, "The Durbin–Watson Test for Serial Correlation with Extreme Sample Sizes or Many Regressors," *Econometrica*, November 1977, p. 1994. Reprinted with permission.

Note: N = number of observations, K = number of explanatory variables excluding the constant term. We assume that the equation contains a constant term and no lagged dependent variables.

Table B-5 Critical Values of the Durbin–Watson Test Statistics of d_L and d_U: 2.5-Percent One-Sided Level of Significance (5-Percent Two-Sided Level of Significance)

N	K = 1 d_L	K = 1 d_U	K = 2 d_L	K = 2 d_U	K = 3 d_L	K = 3 d_U	K = 4 d_L	K = 4 d_U	K = 5 d_L	K = 5 d_U
15	0.95	1.23	0.83	1.40	0.71	1.61	0.59	1.84	0.48	2.09
16	0.98	1.24	0.86	1.40	0.75	1.59	0.64	1.80	0.53	2.03
17	1.01	1.25	0.90	1.40	0.79	1.58	0.68	1.77	0.57	1.98
18	1.03	1.26	0.93	1.40	0.82	1.56	0.72	1.74	0.62	1.93
19	1.06	1.28	0.96	1.41	0.86	1.55	0.76	1.72	0.66	1.90
20	1.08	1.28	0.99	1.41	0.89	1.55	0.79	1.70	0.70	1.87
21	1.10	1.30	1.01	1.41	0.92	1.54	0.83	1.69	0.73	1.84
22	1.12	1.31	1.04	1.42	0.95	1.54	0.86	1.68	0.77	1.82
23	1.14	1.32	1.06	1.42	0.97	1.54	0.89	1.67	0.80	1.80
24	1.16	1.33	1.08	1.43	1.00	1.54	0.91	1.66	0.83	1.79
25	1.18	1.34	1.10	1.43	1.02	1.54	0.94	1.65	0.86	1.77
26	1.19	1.35	1.12	1.44	1.04	1.54	0.96	1.65	0.88	1.76
27	1.21	1.36	1.13	1.44	1.06	1.54	0.99	1.64	0.91	1.75
28	1.22	1.37	1.15	1.45	1.08	1.54	1.01	1.64	0.93	1.74
29	1.24	1.38	1.17	1.45	1.10	1.54	1.03	1.63	0.96	1.73
30	1.25	1.38	1.18	1.46	1.12	1.54	1.05	1.63	0.98	1.73
31	1.26	1.39	1.20	1.47	1.13	1.55	1.07	1.63	1.00	1.72
32	1.27	1.40	1.21	1.47	1.15	1.55	1.08	1.63	1.02	1.71
33	1.28	1.41	1.22	1.48	1.16	1.55	1.10	1.63	1.04	1.71
34	1.29	1.41	1.24	1.48	1.17	1.55	1.12	1.63	1.06	1.70
35	1.30	1.42	1.25	1.48	1.19	1.55	1.13	1.63	1.07	1.70
36	1.31	1.43	1.26	1.49	1.20	1.56	1.15	1.63	1.09	1.70
37	1.32	1.43	1.27	1.49	1.21	1.56	1.16	1.62	1.10	1.70
38	1.33	1.44	1.28	1.50	1.23	1.56	1.17	1.62	1.12	1.70
39	1.34	1.44	1.29	1.50	1.24	1.56	1.19	1.63	1.13	1.69
40	1.35	1.45	1.30	1.51	1.25	1.57	1.20	1.63	1.15	1.69
45	1.39	1.48	1.34	1.53	1.30	1.58	1.25	1.63	1.21	1.69
50	1.42	1.50	1.38	1.54	1.34	1.59	1.30	1.64	1.26	1.69
55	1.45	1.52	1.41	1.56	1.37	1.60	1.33	1.64	1.30	1.69
60	1.47	1.54	1.44	1.57	1.40	1.61	1.37	1.65	1.33	1.69
65	1.49	1.55	1.46	1.59	1.43	1.62	1.40	1.66	1.36	1.69
70	1.51	1.57	1.48	1.60	1.45	1.63	1.42	1.66	1.39	1.70
75	1.53	1.58	1.50	1.61	1.47	1.64	1.45	1.67	1.42	1.70
80	1.54	1.59	1.52	1.62	1.49	1.65	1.47	1.67	1.44	1.70
85	1.56	1.60	1.53	1.63	1.51	1.65	1.49	1.68	1.46	1.71
90	1.57	1.61	1.55	1.64	1.53	1.66	1.50	1.69	1.48	1.71
95	1.58	1.62	1.56	1.65	1.54	1.67	1.52	1.69	1.50	1.71
100	1.59	1.63	1.57	1.65	1.55	1.67	1.53	1.70	1.51	1.72

Source: J. Durbin and G. S. Watson, "Testing for Serial Correlation in Least Squares Regression," *Biometrika,* Vol. 38, 1951, pp. 159–171. Reprinted with permission of the *Biometrika* trustees.

Note: N = number of observations, K = number of explanatory variables excluding the constant term. It is assumed that the equation contains a constant term and no lagged dependent variables.

Table B-6 Critical Values of the Durbin–Watson Test Statistics d_L and d_U:
1-Percent One-Sided Level of Significance
(2-Percent Two-Sided Level of Significance)

N	K = 1		K = 2		K = 3		K = 4		K = 5	
	d_L	d_U	d_L	d_U	d_L	d_U	d_L	d_U	d_L	d_U
15	0.81	1.07	0.70	1.25	0.59	1.46	0.49	1.70	0.39	1.96
16	0.84	1.09	0.74	1.25	0.63	1.44	0.53	1.66	0.44	1.90
17	0.87	1.10	0.77	1.25	0.67	1.43	0.57	1.63	0.48	1.85
18	0.90	1.12	0.80	1.26	0.71	1.42	0.61	1.60	0.52	1.80
19	0.93	1.13	0.83	1.26	0.74	1.41	0.65	1.58	0.56	1.77
20	0.95	1.15	0.86	1.27	0.77	1.41	0.68	1.57	0.60	1.74
21	0.97	1.16	0.89	1.27	0.80	1.41	0.72	1.55	0.63	1.71
22	1.00	1.17	0.91	1.28	0.83	1.40	0.75	1.54	0.66	1.69
23	1.02	1.19	0.94	1.29	0.86	1.40	0.77	1.53	0.70	1.67
24	1.04	1.20	0.96	1.30	0.88	1.41	0.80	1.53	0.72	1.66
25	1.05	1.21	0.98	1.30	0.90	1.41	0.83	1.52	0.75	1.65
26	1.07	1.22	1.00	1.31	0.93	1.41	0.85	1.52	0.78	1.64
27	1.09	1.23	1.02	1.32	0.95	1.41	0.88	1.51	0.81	1.63
28	1.10	1.24	1.04	1.32	0.97	1.41	0.90	1.51	0.83	1.62
29	1.12	1.25	1.05	1.33	0.99	1.42	0.92	1.51	0.85	1.61
30	1.13	1.26	1.07	1.34	1.01	1.42	0.94	1.51	0.88	1.61
31	1.15	1.27	1.08	1.34	1.02	1.42	0.96	1.51	0.90	1.60
32	1.16	1.28	1.10	1.35	1.04	1.43	0.98	1.51	0.92	1.60
33	1.17	1.29	1.11	1.36	1.05	1.43	1.00	1.51	0.94	1.59
34	1.18	1.30	1.13	1.36	1.07	1.43	1.01	1.51	0.95	1.59
35	1.19	1.31	1.14	1.37	1.08	1.44	1.03	1.51	0.97	1.59
36	1.21	1.32	1.15	1.38	1.10	1.44	1.04	1.51	0.99	1.59
37	1.22	1.32	1.16	1.38	1.11	1.45	1.06	1.51	1.00	1.59
38	1.23	1.33	1.18	1.39	1.12	1.45	1.07	1.52	1.02	1.58
39	1.24	1.34	1.19	1.39	1.14	1.45	1.09	1.52	1.03	1.58
40	1.25	1.34	1.20	1.40	1.15	1.46	1.10	1.52	1.05	1.58
45	1.29	1.38	1.24	1.42	1.20	1.48	1.16	1.53	1.11	1.58
50	1.32	1.40	1.28	1.45	1.24	1.49	1.20	1.54	1.16	1.59
55	1.36	1.43	1.32	1.47	1.28	1.51	1.25	1.55	1.21	1.59
60	1.38	1.45	1.35	1.48	1.32	1.52	1.28	1.56	1.25	1.60
65	1.41	1.47	1.38	1.50	1.35	1.53	1.31	1.57	1.28	1.61
70	1.43	1.49	1.40	1.52	1.37	1.55	1.34	1.58	1.31	1.61
75	1.45	1.50	1.42	1.53	1.39	1.56	1.37	1.59	1.34	1.62
80	1.47	1.52	1.44	1.54	1.42	1.57	1.39	1.60	1.36	1.62
85	1.48	1.53	1.46	1.55	1.43	1.58	1.41	1.60	1.39	1.63
90	1.50	1.54	1.47	1.56	1.45	1.59	1.43	1.61	1.41	1.64
95	1.51	1.55	1.49	1.57	1.47	1.60	1.45	1.62	1.42	1.64
100	1.52	1.56	1.50	1.58	1.48	1.60	1.46	1.63	1.44	1.65

Source: J. Durbin and G. S. Watson, "Testing for Serial Correlation in Least Squares Regression," *Biometrika,* Vol. 38, 1951, pp. 159–171. Reprinted with permission of the *Biometrika* trustees.

Note: N = number of observations, K = number of explanatory variables excluding the constant term. It is assumed that the equation contains a constant term and no lagged dependent variables.

Table B-7: The Normal Distribution

The normal distribution is usually assumed for the error term in a regression equation. Table B-7 indicates the probability that a randomly drawn number from the standardized normal distribution (mean = 0 and variance = 1) will be greater than or equal to the number identified in the side tabs, called Z. For a normally distributed variable ϵ with mean μ and variance σ^2, $Z = (\epsilon - \mu)/\sigma$. The row tab gives Z to the first decimal place, and the column tab adds the second decimal place of Z.

Table B-7 The Normal Distribution

z	.00	.01	.02	.03	.04	.05	.06	.07	.08	.09
0.0	.5000	.4960	.4920	.4880	.4840	.4801	.4761	.4721	.4681	.4641
0.1	.4602	.4562	.4522	.4483	.4443	.4404	.4364	.4325	.4286	.4247
0.2	.4207	.4168	.4129	.4090	.4052	.4013	.3974	.3936	.3897	.3859
0.3	.3821	.3873	.3745	.3707	.3669	.3632	.3594	.3557	.3520	.3483
0.4	.3446	.3409	.3372	.3336	.3300	.3264	.3228	.3192	.3156	.3121
0.5	.3085	.3050	.3015	.2981	.2946	.2912	.2877	.2843	.2810	.2776
0.6	.2743	.2709	.2676	.2643	.2611	.2578	.2546	.2514	.2483	.2451
0.7	.2420	.2389	.2358	.2327	.2296	.2266	.2236	.2206	.2217	.2148
0.8	.2119	.2090	.2061	.2033	.2005	.1977	.1949	.1922	.1894	.1867
0.9	.1841	.1814	.1788	.1762	.1736	.1711	.1685	.1660	.1635	.1611
1.0	.1587	.1562	.1539	.1515	.1492	.1469	.1446	.1423	.1401	.1379
1.1	.1357	.1335	.1314	.1292	.1271	.1251	.1230	.1210	.1190	.1170
1.2	.1151	.1131	.1112	.1093	.1075	.1056	.1038	.1020	.1003	.0985
1.3	.0968	.0951	.0934	.0918	.0901	.0885	.0869	.0853	.0838	.0823
1.4	.0808	.0793	.0778	.0764	.0749	.0735	.0721	.0708	.0694	.0681
1.5	.0668	.0655	.0643	.0630	.0618	.0606	.0594	.0582	.0571	.0559
1.6	.0548	.0537	.0526	.0516	.0505	.0495	.0485	.0475	.0465	.0455
1.7	.0446	.0436	.0427	.0418	.0409	.0401	.0392	.0384	.0375	.0367
1.8	.0359	.0351	.0344	.0366	.0329	.0322	.0314	.0307	.0301	.0294
1.9	.0287	.0281	.0274	.0268	.0262	.0256	.0250	.0244	.0239	.0233
2.0	.0228	.0222	.0217	.0212	.0207	.0202	.0197	.0192	.0188	.0183
2.1	.0179	.0174	.0170	.0166	.0162	.0158	.0154	.0150	.0146	.0143
2.2	.0139	.0136	.0132	.0129	.0125	.0122	.0119	.0116	.0113	.0110
2.3	.0107	.0104	.0102	.0099	.0096	.0094	.0091	.0089	.0087	.0084
2.4	.0082	.0080	.0078	.0075	.0073	.0071	.0069	.0068	.0066	.0064
2.5	.0062	.0060	.0059	.0057	.0055	.0054	.0052	.0051	.0049	.0048
2.6	.0047	.0045	.0044	.0043	.0041	.0040	.0039	.0038	.0037	.0036
2.7	.0035	.0034	.0033	.0032	.0031	.0030	.0029	.0028	.0027	.0026
2.8	.0026	.0025	.0024	.0023	.0023	.0022	.0021	.0020	.0020	.0019
2.9	.0019	.0018	.0018	.0017	.0016	.0016	.0015	.0015	.0014	.0014
3.0	.0013	.0013	.0013	.0012	.0012	.0011	.0011	.0011	.0011	.0010

Source: Based on *Biometrika Tables for Statisticians,* Vol. 1, 3rd ed., 1966, with the permission of the *Biometrika* trustees.

Note: The table plots the cumulative probability $Z > z$.

Table B-8: The Chi-Square Distribution

The chi-square distribution describes the distribution of the estimate of the variance of the error term. It is useful in a number of tests, including the White test of Section 10.3 and the Lagrange Multiplier Serial Correlation Test of Section 12.2. The rows represent degrees of freedom, and the columns denote the probability that a number drawn randomly from the chi-square distribution will be greater than or equal to the number shown in the body of the table. For example, the probability is 10 percent that a number drawn randomly from any chi-square distribution will be greater than or equal to 22.3 for 15 degrees of freedom.

To run a White test for heteroskedasticity, calculate NR^2, where N is the sample size and R^2 is the coefficient of determination (unadjusted R^2) from Equation 10.9. (This equation has as its dependent variable the squared residual of the equation to be tested and has as its independent variables the independent variables of the equation to be tested plus the squares and cross-products of these independent variables.)

The test statistic NR^2 has a chi-square distribution with degrees of freedom equal to the number of slope coefficients in Equation 10.9. If NR^2 is larger than the critical chi-square value found in Statistical Table B-8, then we reject the null hypothesis and conclude that it's likely that we have heteroskedasticity. If NR^2 is less than the critical chi-square value, then we cannot reject the null hypothesis of homoskedasticity.

Table B-8 The Chi-Square Distribution

Degrees of Freedom	Level of Significance (Probability of a Value of at Least as Large as the Table Entry)			
	10%	5%	2.5%	1%
1	2.71	3.84	5.02	6.63
2	4.61	5.99	7.38	9.21
3	6.25	7.81	9.35	11.34
4	7.78	9.49	11.14	13.28
5	9.24	11.07	12.83	15.09
6	10.64	12.59	14.45	16.81
7	12.02	14.07	16.01	18.48
8	13.36	15.51	17.53	20.1
9	14.68	16.92	19.02	21.7
10	15.99	18.31	20.5	23.2
11	17.28	19.68	21.9	24.7
12	18.55	21.0	23.3	26.2
13	19.81	22.4	24.7	27.7
14	21.1	23.7	26.1	29.1
15	22.3	25.0	27.5	30.6
16	23.5	26.3	28.8	32.0
17	24.8	27.6	30.2	33.4
18	26.0	28.9	31.5	34.8
19	27.2	30.1	32.9	36.2
20	28.4	31.4	34.2	37.6

Source: Based on *Biometrika Tables for Statisticians,* Vol. 1, 3rd ed., 1966, with the permission of the *Biometrika* trustees.

Note: The table plots the cumulative probability Z > z.

INDEX

NOTE to readers: Page numbers in *italics* refer to figures; page numbers including *n* refer to footnotes.